A Radical History of the World

Also available

A Radical History of the World

Neil Faulkner

PLUTO PRESS

A Radical History of the World draws on text originally published in
A Marxist History of the World (Pluto Press, 2013).

This edition first published 2018 by Pluto Press
345 Archway Road, London N6 5AA

www.plutobooks.com

The Left Book Club pays homage to the original Left Book Club
founded by Victor Gollancz in 1936.

British Library Cataloguing in Publication Data
A catalogue record for this book is available from the British Library

ISBN   978 0 7453 3805 7   Hardback
ISBN   978 0 7453 3804 0   Paperback
ISBN   978 1 7868 0327 6   PDF eBook
ISBN   978 1 7868 0329 0   Kindle eBook
ISBN   978 1 7868 0328 3   EPUB eBook

Typeset by Stanford DTP Services, Northampton, England
Printed in the United Kingdom

Contents

Series Preface

The first Left Book Club (1936–48) had 57,000 members, had distributed two million books, and had formed 1,200 workplace and local groups by the time it peaked in 1939. LBC members were active throughout the labour and radical movement at the time, and the Club became an educational mass movement, remodelling British public opinion and contributing substantially to the Labour landslide of 1945 and the construction of the welfare state.

Publisher Victor Gollancz, the driving force, saw the LBC as a movement against poverty, fascism, and the growing threat of war. He aimed to resist the tide of austerity and appeasement, and to present radical ideas for progressive social change in the interests of working people. The Club was about enlightenment, empowerment, and collective organisation.

The world today faces a crisis on the scale of the 1930s. Capitalism is trapped in a long-term crisis. Financialisation and austerity are shrinking demand, deepening the depression, and widening social inequalities. The social fabric is being torn apart. International relations are increasingly tense and militarised. War threatens on several fronts, while fascist and racist organisations are gaining ground across much of Europe. Global warming threatens the planet and the whole of humanity with climate catastrophe. Workplace organisation has been weakened, and social democratic parties have been hollowed out by acceptance of pro-market dogma. Society has become more atomised, and mainstream politics suffers an acute democratic deficit.

Yet the last decade has seen historically unprecedented levels of participation in street protest, implying a mass audience for progressive alternatives. But socialist ideas are no longer, as in the immediate post-war period, 'in the tea'. One of neoliberalism's achievements has been to undermine ideas of solidarity, collective provision, and public service.

The Left Book Club aspires to meet this ideological challenge. Our aim is to offer high-quality books at affordable prices that are carefully selected to address the central issues of the day and to be accessible to a wide general audience. Our list represents the full range of progressive traditions, perspectives, and ideas. We hope the books will be used as the basis of reading circles, discussion groups, and other educational and cultural activities relevant to developing, sharing, and disseminating ideas for change in the interests of the common people at home and abroad.

Introduction

History is contested. How we understand the past affects how we think and act in the present. Partly because of this, history is a battleground of rival interpretations. All knowledge of the present – of its crises, wars, and revolutions – is necessarily historical. We can no more make sense of our own world without reference to the past than we could manufacture a computer without reference to the accumulated technical knowledge of many decades.

But elites with wealth and power to defend – and conservative historians who reflect the worldview of elites past and present – tend to promote a sanitised view of history. They emphasise continuity and tradition, obedience and conformity, nationalism and empire. They usually downplay the exploitation and violence of the rich, and often ignore the lives of the poor and their struggles for change. In doing so – in having a lopsided view of the past – they frequently miss the motor forces of history.

This version of history has become more dominant over the last 40 years. Past empires – like the Roman and the British – have been held up as models of civilisation by supporters of Western military intervention in today's world. Medieval Europe has been reinterpreted as an exemplar of the 'neoclassical' economics favoured by millionaire bankers. Great revolutions have been reinterpreted as mere coups or faction-fights by 'revisionists' keen to write social conflict out of history. Attempts to *explain* the past – so that we can *understand* the present, and act to *change* the future – have been rubbished by 'postmodern' theories that argue history has no structure, pattern, or meaning.

Sometimes these theories are dressed up as 'new research'. Historians research the archives to collect new data all the time. This may change some of our interpretations. It is rare, however, for new data to overturn an old paradigm wholesale. Scholars trying to build an academic career or advance a political theory sometimes claim too much for new data. Revisionist historians may be better informed, but none the wiser.

Much modern research, inserted into a postmodern framework, merely leaves us with disconnected fragments of information. History is left without pattern or trajectory. It becomes, as the automobile mogul Henry Ford once said, just 'one damn thing after another'.

The basic job of the historian, on the other hand, is to divine the general amid the particular, the pattern amid the detail, the direction of travel amid the chaos of events, history's arrows of development amid its cycles of reproduction. For, as the great German philosopher Georg Hegel taught us, the truth is the whole.

This is the tradition in which this book stands. It rejects the view of Henry Ford, with its implication that human beings are just flotsam and jetsam on the tide of events. This, incidentally, was also the view of Soviet dictator Joseph Stalin, where history was seen as a succession of predetermined 'stages' through which human society was bound to advance (and it was seen as 'advance', or 'progress').

This study takes a diametrically opposite view, arguing that history is continually created and recreated by conscious, collective human action. It argues that the struggles of the common people – slaves and serfs, handloom weavers and mine workers, women fighting oppression, black people fighting racism, colonised people fighting imperialism – these struggles, occasionally fusing into mass revolutionary upsurges, drive the historical process.

So this is an approach to history that emphasises agency, contingency, and the existence of alternatives; an approach that rejects the view that war and empire are inevitable, that there is no alternative to the market, and that greed, bullying, and violence are universal. Quite the reverse, argued the revolutionary thinker and activist Karl Marx, who wrote in a political pamphlet published in 1852: 'Men [and women] make their own history, but not of their own free will, and not under circumstances of their own choosing.'

In other words, the course of history is not predetermined; its outcome is not inevitable; it can go in different directions according to what human beings do.

This book began life as a series of online articles on a left-wing website between 2010 and 2012. Six years on, the text is being published in a much expanded form in this book. I have done this for three reasons. First, because I had become aware of major omissions and wanted to plug the gaps. Second, because I had received much constructive critical comment and wanted to act on this and make appropriate amendments. Third, because major changes in global politics over the last six years seemed to demand an expanded and updated final chapter dealing with the world crisis.

A Radical History of the World can be read in different ways. It can be read cover-to-cover as a single study, or it can be treated as a collection of short analytical essays and dipped into for information and ideas about specific events – an approach facilitated by the fact that it retains the structure of the web series, being divided into both chapters and sections. Partly with this in mind, material is occasionally repeated where I felt it might be helpful to readers. I have also sometimes used modern place-names – like Iraq and Pakistan – in reference to earlier periods, believing it might help readers to place events geographically. By the same token, the timeline at the back is there to help readers get their chronological bearings. Scattered through the narrative are a handful of theoretical 'excursuses', where I step out of the frame, as it were, to set out some general ideas about the historical process as a whole; these are clearly marked as such.

Because this is a work of extreme compression – a one-volume world history: the ultimate grand narrative – I have dispensed with the conventional academic apparatus of references and notes. Instead, there is an extended discussion of sources and an annotated bibliography at the back so that readers can check up on my sources and find guidance on further reading.

A common criticism of the web version was that I had neglected certain places and periods; that the text suffered in particular from 'Euro-centrism', even 'Anglo-centrism'. This criticism was justified. I have done my best to correct it. There are, for example, fresh sections on Spanish and Latin American history. But I cannot claim that this is a truly 'global history'. The reason is simple and obvious: I am a British-based archaeologist and historian with uneven expertise. Like all generalists, I can never wholly escape the constraints of my training, experience, and reading. I must therefore seek the indulgence and forbearance of readers who are neither British nor European.

Even over the ground I have covered, I suspect I leave a trail of errors and misunderstandings – inviting denunciation by sundry cohorts of specialists. This, too, is the inevitable fate of the generalist. There is only one defence. Would correcting the errors and misunderstandings invalidate the main arguments? If so, the project fails. If not – if the Marxist approach has provided a convincing explanation of the main events and developments of human history *irrespective* of misconstrued details – then the project succeeds.

Hopefully, though, it will achieve something more. For it is first and foremost a book for activists, and it will have served its purpose in so far as it persuades people that, since humans make their own history, the future is open and will be determined by what each of us does.

I am not, as one reviewer suggested I should be, 'a disinterested historian'. Because I share with Marx the view that 'the history of all hitherto existing society is the history of class struggles', I share with him also the view that whereas 'the philosophers have only interpreted the world, the point is to change it'.

Acknowledgements

The following people took time and trouble to read the original text, in whole or in part, and offer invaluable critical comment: William Alderson, Dominic Alexander, David Castle, Fran Exxon-Smith, Lindsey German, Elaine Graham-Leigh, Jackie Mulhallen, John Rees, Alex Snowdon, Alastair Stephens, and Vernon Trafford. Needless to say, I sometimes proved stubborn and refused their advice, so the final result is entirely my own fault.

Among the reviewers of the original work, a number made constructive criticisms which I have acted upon in this new text. They include: Keith Flett, John Green, Sean Ledwith, Michael Seltzer, and Andrew Stone. I am grateful to them for taking the book seriously and suggesting ways of improving it. I must also make special mention of my friend and colleague Nadia Durrani, who rewrote the whole of the first section on human evolution, where I was woefully out of date.

1

Hunters and Farmers

c. 7 million–3000 BP

The White Lady of Aouanrhet. Rock painting, Tassili, Central Sahara, *c.* 3000 BC. She appears to be a goddess or priestess of fertility. Note the field and shower of grain above her head.

The Agricultural Revolution of the Neolithic (or New Stone Age) transformed the whole of human social experience. Only the Industrial Revolution has had a comparable impact.

Our story begins with a rapid survey of a vast span of time from about seven million years ago to about 5,000 years ago. During this period, as a product of biological, environmental, cultural, and social evolution, a succession of radical transformations took place. First, around 7–6 million years ago, in Chad or Kenya, we have the appearance of the first potential hominins, that is, creatures on our evolutionary tree after our split from the ancestors of the chimpanzees.

Second, around 3.3 million years ago, in Kenya, we have the first evidence of tool-making, representing a fundamental change in hominin behaviour. This and subsequent early technologies (such as the more famous Oldowan tools) are very basic. But then, around 1.9 million years ago, in East and South Africa, certain hominins evolved into creatures with larger brains, greater capacity for tool-making, and higher levels of social organisation and environmental adaptability. This creature had a fairly modern body-shape and is known as *Homo ergaster* ('Working Human'). This species was very similar to *Homo erectus* ('Upright Human'), a fossil type not really known in Africa, but widely distributed across Asia.

Third, after *c.* 350,000 years ago, we have the first evidence for ourselves: *Homo sapiens* ('Thinking Human'). These, our direct ancestors, seem to have originated in Morocco. The early fossils, however, display a mix of archaic and modern characteristics, and our species only became fully anatomically (and presumably cerebrally) modern by about 120,000 years ago.

Fourth, about 10,000 years ago, under the impact of climate change and food shortages, some communities made the transition from hunting and gathering to farming.

Fifth, about 6,000 years ago, new techniques of land reclamation and intensive farming allowed some communities in favoured locations to increase their output substantially by moving from hoe-based cultivation to plough-based agriculture.

The Hominin Transformations

We have evidence for creatures considered to be hominins reaching back to seven million years BP (before the present; the usual term when discussing hominin evolution). On the human tree roll-call the earliest is *Sahelanthropus tchadensis*, found in Chad (7–6 BP), whose status as a hominin is rather insecure, but it may have partially walked on two feet (bipedalism being one of the main characteristics of hominins). Then comes *Orrorin tugensis* from Kenya (6.2–5.6 BP), who may also hold the title of earliest bipedal hominin.

These two creatures (and there were probably many more: we just have not found them) were followed by other hominins such as *Ardipithecus ramidus* (4.5–4.3 BP) from Ethiopia and *Kenyanthropus platyops* from Kenya (3.5–3.3 BP).

But perhaps the best-known early hominin was the australopithecine, who emerged around 4.2 BP in East Africa. One of these, *Australopithecus afarensis* ('Southern Ape of Afar'), roamed throughout parts of East Africa (including Laetoli, where a small family left footsteps in the mud) around 3.7–3 million BP. We have found the fragmented remains of several hundred such creatures, and they reveal evidence for both a bipedal and a tree-based (arboreal) lifestyle. The best-known specimen of *Australopithecus afarensis* is the 40 per cent complete skeleton of 'Lucy' found in 1974 (though she may have been male).

Lucy stood just 1.1 m tall, weighed around 29 kg, and was probably about 20 years old when she died. With short legs, long arms, and a small brain case, Lucy would have looked rather like a modern chimpanzee. But there was a crucial difference: like all (certain) hominins, she was able to walk upright (though she could also climb and would have spent some of her time in trees). The shape of her pelvis and legs, and the knee joint of another member of the species found a short distance away, proved this beyond reasonable doubt.

Lucy was probably one of a small foraging group that moved around gathering fruit, nuts, seeds, eggs, and other foodstuffs. As climate change reduced the forests and created savannah, natural selection had favoured a species able to range over greater distances in search of food. But Lucy's bipedalism had revolutionary implications. It freed the hands and arms for tool-making and other forms of labour. This in turn encouraged natural selection in favour of larger brain capacity. A powerful dynamic of evolutionary change was set in motion: hand and brain, labour and intellect, skill and thought began an explosive interaction – one which culminated in modern humans.

We do not know whether Lucy made tools. None were found in association with her remains. But very early and very crude stone tools have recently been discovered dating to 3.3 million BP in Kenya – and may be associated with other forms of local australopithecines.

And certainly, by 2.5 million BP, *Homo habilis* ('Handy Human') – Lucy's potential descendant – certainly did. Choppers made from crudely chipped pebbles represent the archaeological imprint of a new family of species defined by tool-making behaviour: the genus *Homo* ('Human'). Tools embody conceptual thought, forward planning, and manual dexterity. They reveal the use of intellect and skill to modify nature in order to exploit its resources more efficiently.

The genus *Homo*, like the australopithecines before them, evolved in Africa, and for about 1.5 million BP that is where they largely remained. After around 1.8 million BP, however, we start finding evidence for *Homo erectus* in the Far East (China, Java, Indonesia) and also in Georgia near the Black Sea (though some define this creature as *Homo georgicus*).

Homo erectus seems to have been very closely related to an African form, *Homo ergaster*, an upright creature who emerged around 1.9 BP and is known from East and South Africa. *Homo ergaster* would have looked much like us in terms of body form, but she had a smaller brain. Her close relative, *Homo erectus*, persisted in parts of the Far East down the millennia, with the latest examples possibly dating to as recently as 30,000 years ago.

Meantime, back in Europe and Western Asia, other hominin forms were appearing, such as *Homo antecessor* and *Homo heidelbergensis*. The latter was probably the last common ancestor of the Neanderthals in Europe and modern humans in Africa.

The Ice Age epoch which began 2.5 million years ago had a great impact on human evolution. Ice Age climate is dynamic, shifting between cold glacials and relatively warm interglacials. We are currently in an interglacial, but 20,000 years ago much of Northern Europe and North America was in the middle of a glacial and covered by ice-sheets up to 4 km thick, with winters lasting nine months, and temperatures below −20°C for weeks on end.

The early hominins were not adapted to the cold, so they migrated north in warm periods and moved south again when the glaciers advanced. They first arrived in Britain, for example, at least 800,000 years ago, but then retreated and returned at least eight times. Britain was probably occupied for only about 20 per cent of its Old Stone Age (*c.* 800,000–10,000 years ago).

Homo antecessor ('Pioneer Human') – who was probably the first human in Britain, shortly followed by the closely related *Homo heidelbergensis* ('Heidelberger Human') – seems to have inhabited coastal or estuarine regions, where animal resources were rich and varied. The standard tool was either an 'Acheulian' handaxe – essentially a chopper – or a 'Clactonian' flake – a cutter. These general-purpose tools were mass-produced as needed. Excavations at Boxgrove in England recovered 300 handaxes and much associated flint-knapping debris dating to around 500,000 years ago. They had been used to butcher horse, deer, and rhinoceros on what was then a savannah-like coastal plain.

During the last glaciation, however, there was no wholesale retreat. *Homo neanderthalensis* was a cold-adapted hominin that we think evolved out of *Homo heidelbergensis* in Europe and Western Asia about 350,000 years ago. Neanderthal adaptation was a matter of both biological evolution and new technology. With large heads, big noses, prominent brows, low foreheads, little chin development, and short, squat, powerfully built bodies, the Neanderthal was designed to survive winters with average temperatures as low as −10°C. But culture was more important, and this was linked to brain power.

Hominin brains had been getting bigger. Selection for this characteristic was a serious matter. Brain tissue is more expensive than other kinds: the brain accounts for only about 2 per cent of our body weight but no less than 20 per cent of food-energy consumption. It is also high-risk. Humans are adapted for walking upright, which requires a narrow pelvis, yet have a large brain-case, which imposes a strain on the woman's pelvis in childbirth; the result is slow, painful, and sometimes dangerous birth trauma. But the advantages are considerable. Large brains enable modern humans to create and sustain complex social relationships with, typically, about 150 others. Humans are not just social animals, but social animals to an extreme degree, with brains especially enlarged and sophisticated for this purpose.

Sociability confers enormous evolutionary benefits. Hominin hunter-gatherer bands were probably very small – perhaps 30 or 40 people. But they would have had links with other groups, perhaps half a dozen of similar size, with whom they shared mates, resources, labour, information, and ideas. Sociability, cooperation, and culture are closely related, and achieving them requires high levels of intelligence: in biological terms, brain tissue.

The Neanderthals were certainly clever. The 'Mousterian' tool-kit of the classic Neanderthals contained a range of specialised points, knives, and scrapers – as many as 63 different types according to one famous study of archaeological finds from south-western France. Intelligent, networked, and well equipped, the Neanderthals were superbly adapted to Ice Age extremes, building shelters, making clothes, and organising themselves for large-scale hunting on the frozen plains. Lynford in England is a hunting site dating from 60,000 years ago. Here, archaeologists found Neanderthal tools associated with the bones, tusks, and teeth of mammoths.

But natural organisms are conservative in relation to their evolutionary perfection. The Neanderthals, in adapting so well to the cold, had entered a biological cul-de-sac. Meanwhile, in Africa, the crucible of species, a new type of super-hominin had evolved out of an ancient African line, probably representing an evolutionary transition from African *Homo heidelbergensis*. Such was its creativity, collective organisation, and cultural adaptability that, migrating from Africa 85,000 years ago, it spread rapidly across the world and eventually colonised its remotest corners. This new species was *Homo sapiens* – modern humans – and though other hominins still existed while we roamed the earth (notably the Neanderthals in the West and *Homo erectus* in the East), for whatever reason, these other hominins were not able to adapt sufficiently. Perhaps we even had a hand in their demise. Whatever the case, in the end, only we remain after some seven million years of hominin evolution.

The Hominin Transformations, which began around six or seven million years ago, had culminated in a species whose further progress would be determined not by biological evolution, but by intelligence, culture, social organisation, and planned collective labour.

The Hunting (or Upper Palaeolithic) Revolution

Somewhere in Africa, 200,000 years ago, lived a woman who is the common ancestor of every human being on earth today. She is the primeval progenitor of the entire species *Homo sapiens* – modern humans. We know her as 'African Eve'. It is DNA analysis that has revealed this, confirming and refining the conclusions reached by other scientists based on the evidence of fossilised bone.

DNA is the chemical coding within cells which provides the blueprint for organic life. Similarities and differences can be studied to see how closely various life forms are related. Mutations occur and accumulate at fairly steady rates. This allows geneticists not only to measure biological diversity within and between species, but also to estimate how much time has passed since two groups separated and ceased interbreeding. Mutations in our DNA therefore constitute 'fossil' evidence of our past inside living tissue.

The DNA date for African Eve matches the date of the earliest known fossils of *Homo sapiens*. Two skulls and a partial skeleton found at Omo in Ethiopia in 1967 have been dated to *c.* 195,000 BP.

The new species looked different. Early humans had long, low skulls, sloping foreheads, projecting brow ridges, and heavy jaws. Modern humans have large, dome-shaped skulls, much flatter faces, and smaller jaws. The change was mainly due to increased brain size: *Homo sapiens* was highly intelligent. Big brains make it possible to store information, think imaginatively, and communicate in complex ways. Language is the key to all this. The world is classified, analysed, and discussed through speech. African Eve was a non-stop talker. Because of this, in evolutionary terms, she was adaptable and dynamic.

Homo sapiens had this unique characteristic: unlike all other animals, including other hominins, she was not restricted by biology to a limited range of environments. Thinking it through, talking it over, working together, *Homo sapiens* could adapt to life almost anywhere. Biological evolution was therefore superseded by cultural evolution. And the pace of change accelerated. Handaxe-wielding *Homo erectus* had remained in Africa for 1.5 million years. In a fraction of that time, the descendants of African Eve were on the move. Or some of them were. The genetic evidence appears to show that the whole of Asia, Europe, Australia, and the Americas were populated by the descendants of a single group of hunter-gatherers who left Africa about 3,000 generations ago – around 85,000 BP. South Asia and Australia were colonised by 50,000 BP, Northern Asia and Europe by 40,000 BP, and the Americas by 15,000 BP.

Why did people move? Almost certainly, as hunter-gatherers, they went in search of food, responding to resource depletion, population pressure, and climate change. They were adapted for this – adapted to adapt. Designed for endurance walking and running, they were capable of long-distance movement. Their manual dexterity made them excellent tool-makers. Their large brains rendered them capable of abstract thought, detailed planning, linguistic communication, and social organisation.

They formed small, tight-knit, cooperative groups. These groups were linked in loose but extensive networks based on kinship, exchange, and mutual support. They were, in the sense in which archaeologists use the term, 'cultured': their ways of getting food, living together, sharing tasks, making tools, ornamenting themselves, burying the dead, and much else were agreed within the groups and followed set rules.

This implies something more: they were making conscious, collective choices. You talk things through and then you decide. The challenges of the endless search for food often posed alternatives. Some groups will have made a more conservative choice: stay where you are, carry on as before, hope for the best. Others will have been more enterprising, perhaps moving into unknown territory, trying new hunting techniques, or linking up with other groups to pool knowledge, resources, and labour.

A dominant characteristic of *Homo sapiens*, therefore, was an unrivalled ability to meet the demands of diverse and changeable environments. Initially, they would have migrated along resource-rich coastlines and river systems. But they seem soon to have spread into the hinterland; and wherever they went, they adapted and fitted in. In the Arctic, they hunted reindeer; on the frozen plains, mammoth; on the grasslands, wild deer and horses; in the tropics, pigs, monkeys, and lizards.

Toolkits varied with the challenges. Instead of simple handaxes and flakes, they manufactured a range of 'blades' – sharp-edged stone tools longer than they were wide which were struck from specially prepared prismatic cores. They also made clothes and shelters as conditions demanded. They used fire for heating, cooking, and protection. And they produced art – paintings and sculptures of the animals they hunted. Above all, they experimented and innovated. Successes were shared and copied. Culture was not static, but changeable and cumulative. *Homo sapien*s met environmental challenges with new ways of doing things, and the lessons learned became part of a growing store of knowledge and know-how.

Instead of modern humans either evolving biologically or dying out when environmental conditions changed, they found solutions in better shelters, warmer clothes, and sharper tools. Nature and culture interacted, and through this interaction, humans became progressively better at making a living.

In some places, for a while, *Homo sapiens* coexisted with early humans. Between *c.* 40,000 and 30,000 BP, Europe was inhabited by both moderns and Neanderthals. There is DNA evidence for some interbreeding – and, by implication, social interaction – but the main story seems to be the slow replacement of one species by the other. The Neanderthals eventually died out because they could neither adapt nor compete as the climate changed, as *Homo sapiens* populations grew, and as the big game on which all hominins depended were over-hunted.

Stone-tool technology seems to shadow this species displacement. Neanderthal fossils are associated with Mousterian flakes. Cro-Magnon fossils (as *Homo sapiens* remains are known in European archaeology) are associated with a range of sophisticated Aurignacian blades. The terms reflect two tool-making traditions recognised in the archaeological record. But that is not all. The new culture was diverse and dynamic, producing, in the course of time, spear-throwers, the harpoon, and the bow, and domesticating the dog for use in the hunt. The Neanderthals had been at the top of the food chain, but the new arrivals engaged them in a 'cultural arms race' they could not win.

Gough's Cave in Cheddar Gorge in England is a classic *Homo sapiens* site. It has yielded human remains, animal bones, thousands of stone tools, and artefacts made of bone and antler. These date to around 14,000 BP and belonged to a community of horse hunters. The cave offered shelter and a vantage point overlooking a gorge through which herds of wild horses and deer regularly passed. Here was a community of *Homo sapiens* adapted to a very specific ecological niche: a natural funnel on the migration routes of wild animals during the latter part of the last great glaciation.

The period from 2.5 million years ago, when tool-making began, to 10,000 BP is known as the Old Stone Age or Palaeolithic. Its last phase, the Upper Palaeolithic, is the period of *Homo sapiens*. It represents a revolutionary break with earlier phases. The Upper Palaeolithic Revolution was both biological and cultural. A new species of super-hominin emerged from Africa and spread across the world. In this first globalisation, the species adapted to diverse environments and opportunities by creating numerous distinctive 'cultures' – repertoires of tools, work methods, social customs, and ritual practices.

But by 10,000 BP there was a problem. The big game were dying out because hominins had been too successful: mammoths, giant deer, and wild horses had been hunted to extinction. At the same time, the earth was warming and the open plains were disappearing, overtaken by regenerated forest. The Upper Palaeolithic world had reached an impasse. The existing way of making a living could no longer ensure survival. *Homo sapiens* faced a supreme test of evolutionary fitness.

The Agricultural (or Early Neolithic) Revolution

Around 20,000 years ago the ice of the last glaciation began to melt. By *c.* 8000 BC global temperatures had stabilised at levels similar to today's. By *c.* 5000 BC the world had assumed its current form. Europe, for example, took shape as rising sea levels broke through land bridges and flooded the Baltic, North Sea, and Black Sea. The result was a slowly evolving ecological crisis for the peoples of the world. In the North the open tundra gave way to dense forest, reducing the biomass of animals available to hunters by about 75 per cent. In Central and Western Asia the crisis was more serious: there climate change turned large areas into desert, and life retreated towards damp uplands, river valleys, and oases.

It was not the first time. During the 2.5 million years of the Ice Age, the glaciers had advanced and retreated many times. The difference now was the identity of the hominins faced with the challenge of a warming world. *Homo sapiens* was far better equipped than her predecessors, both intellectually and culturally, to cope with ecological crisis.

In the forested lands of the North, most humans settled by rivers, lakes, deltas, estuaries, and seashores, where food was both abundant and varied. Around 7500 BC, Star Carr in Yorkshire was the site of a seasonal camp used in late spring and summer each year. The Mesolithic (Middle Stone Age) people who used it hunted wild cattle, elk, red deer, roe deer, and wild pig, and also smaller animals like pine marten, red fox, and beaver. Stalking and close-range ambush was their chosen method. As well as scrapers, borers, and other stone implements, their toolkit included barbed spearheads made from antler.

The people of Star Carr had a fairly easy life. Refined techniques of hunting and gathering enabled them to exploit the new food resources of a wet and wooded landscape. But in the arid regions of Asia something more radical was necessary: not new variants of food gathering, but food *production*.

Hunters had long existed in a symbiotic relationship with their prey. They created clearings, channelled movement, provided food, warded off predators, and spared the young. For maintaining plentiful game close by was in their interests. The transition from hunting to pastoralism (the rearing of domesticated animals on pasture) could be gradual and seamless.

That plants grow from seeds is a matter of observation. That people might sow seeds in order to harvest plants was therefore not a giant leap. But it involved a choice – and not necessarily a welcome one. Farming is hard work: it requires long, repetitive, back-breaking toil – clearing land, breaking up the soil, hoeing the ground, scattering seed, weeding, warding off vermin, irrigating or draining the fields, harvesting the crop; and doing so with the ever-present danger of drought, flood, or blight. Then the same again, year after year after year. Farming is rarely an ideal option. Hunting and fishing, gathering and scavenging are much easier.

The Agricultural Revolution is therefore an example of human beings making their own history, but not in circumstances of their own choosing. They were driven to the hard labour of cultivation and animal husbandry by necessity in an increasingly desiccated landscape depleted of natural food supplies. El-Beidha near Petra in modern Jordan, for example, was home to a community of Early Neolithic (New Stone Age) farmers in *c.* 6500 BC. They lived in communal houses made of stone, timber, and mud, ground grain to make flour on saddle querns (grinding stones in the shape of a horse's saddle), and manufactured many and varied flint-flake tools, including arrowheads, knives, and scrapers.

Geography and climate interacted with human ingenuity to produce different economies in different places. Farming developed in Western and Central Asia partly because it was drier and the pressure on food resources greater, and partly because wild varieties of key species were available for domestication – barley and emmer wheat, and cattle, sheep, goats, and pigs. But climate change was global and farming was invented independently at different times in widely separate places. In Highland Papua New Guinea, for instance, a Neolithic economy developed in *c.* 7000 BC based on sugar cane, bananas, nuts, taro, grasses, roots, and green vegetables. It remained essentially unchanged into the twentieth century.

The first European farmers were Asian pioneers who crossed the Aegean into eastern Greece in 7500–6500 BC. They brought the 'Neolithic package' with them – cultivated crops and domesticated animals; permanent settlements and square houses; spinning and weaving; hoes, sickles, and polished axes; pottery and quern-stones; and ceramic 'Venus' or 'fat lady' figurines representing fertility deities. It all appears suddenly in the archaeological record alongside the burials of people with a distinctive 'Asian' DNA.

The spread of farming took thousands of years, and even now is still not universal. Since *c.* 7500 BC, hunting-gathering, pastoralism, and cultivation have coexisted. Many Early Neolithic communities operated a mixed economy with elements of all three. Others resisted farming altogether. Not before *c.* 5500 BC did it spread from the Balkans, across the Hungarian Plain, to Northern and Western Europe. There it halted again. For a thousand years the Mesolithic hunters of the Baltic, the North Sea coasts, the Atlantic fringes, and the British Isles held out. Then, between 4300 and 3800 BC, they too went Neolithic. Others again, like the Australian Aborigines or the Kalahari Bushmen, retained a hunting-gathering economy into recent times.

Farming may always have been a reluctant choice, but once begun there was no going back. Because farming exploited the landscape more intensively, it could support much larger populations than hunting-gathering. This meant that if farmers were to abandon their work, their community would starve, for there were now too many people simply to live off what the wilderness naturally provided. Humanity was trapped in toil by its own success.

By *c.* 5000 BC Neolithic farmers (known to archaeologists as the *Linearbandkeramik* culture) had settled across much of Europe. They lived in villages of two or three dozen timber longhouses, up to 30–40 m long and 5 m wide. Building them would have required collective effort. Each one would have accommodated an extended family group. Neither houses nor burials give any indication of social inequality; one assumes that everyone contributed and everyone consumed on an equal basis according to their ability. So Early Neolithic society had neither class divisions nor nuclear families. There is nothing 'natural' about either. Like hunter-gatherers, the first farmers were what Karl Marx and Frederick Engels called 'primitive communists'.

But this was a communism of scarcity. Early agriculture was wasteful: land was cleared, cultivated, exhausted, and then abandoned. Fallowing and manuring to keep the land 'in good heart' were not yet common practice. And as the population expanded, so accessible and workable land began to run out. These contradictions of the Early Neolithic economy eventually exploded into warfare.

The Origins of War and Religion

The bodies of 34 people, half of them children, had been dumped in a 3 m-wide pit. Two of the adults had been shot in the head with arrows. Twenty others, including children, had been clubbed. The archaeologists were in no doubt that it was a massacre site. The Talheim death pit in south-west Germany revealed a gruesome truth about the Early Neolithic world of 5000 BC: humans had begun to engage in warfare.

In the beginning, there had been no war. For 2.5 million years, throughout the Old Stone Age, small bands of hominins had roamed the land in search of food by hunting, gathering, and scavenging. Meetings were few; clashes of any kind scarcer still. Only later, as the numbers of people increased, were there occasional conflicts over resources. Cave art shows hunters with bows shooting not only animals but sometimes each other. But this was not war as such. War is large-scale, sustained, organised violence between opposing groups. There is no evidence for this before the Agricultural Revolution which began around 7500 BC.

Farming was a much more efficient way of getting food than hunting, so the population increased enormously in the New Stone Age. Palaeolithic fossils number in the hundreds, Neolithic skeletons in the tens of thousands. But herein lay the problem. Technique was primitive, productivity low, surpluses small. People lived close to the edge, susceptible to natural disasters like crop blight, animal disease, and extreme weather. Early Neolithic farming communities were haunted by the spectres of famine, hunger, and death.

The problem was rooted in the very success of the Early Neolithic economy, for the population kept growing, but the land was finite. As the nutrients were taken from the soil and not replenished, new fields had to be hacked from the wilderness. As populations grew, existing villages could not feed everyone, and groups of pioneers headed off to found new settlements. As the last tracts of wilderness close to the earliest settlements were cleared, the wasteful Early Neolithic economy reached its limits. Land hunger and food hunger could then drive neighbouring groups into conflict.

Early farmers had communal property – fields, animals, store houses, permanent homes – to defend in hard times. This combination of poverty and property, scarcity and surplus, was the root cause of the first wars. The starving might eat by seizing the grain and sheep of their neighbours. The Talheim death pit seems to bear witness to just such a primeval struggle.

But if you want to wage war, you need warriors, allies, and defence works. Groups with more of these will defeat those with fewer. Groups that invest surplus in warfare will dominate those that do not. Archaeologists now see the decades around 3500 BC as the time of the first wars in Britain, for example, just a few centuries after the start of the Neolithic Revolution there. Great hilltop causewayed camps were built. Windmill Hill in Wiltshire, enclosed by three concentric rings of bank and ditch, is the size of 15 football pitches. It was probably used for political meetings, religious rituals, and defence. It symbolised a new order – one that united people from distant villages in a single tribal polity. At the same time, people were buried in communal tombs of monumental stone slabs and mounds of earth. West Kennet long barrow in Wiltshire is 100 m long and 20 m wide. Built to impress, it was an assertion of territorial control. That it was necessary shows that control was contested.

Causewayed camps like Windmill Hill were places of worship; long barrows like West Kennet were mausoleums. The larger polities of the Early Neolithic were being cemented together by collective belief and ritual. Magic and religion were taking on new functions, becoming mechanisms for creating stronger social groups, better able to compete with other groups for control of territory and scarce resources.

Magic (an attempt to get what you want by mimicry) and religion (an attempt to do so by supplicating higher powers) have long histories. Upper Palaeolithic hunters had painted game beasts on the walls in the dark depths of their caves. In the prehistoric mind, the symbol, the painted image, seems to have conjured the reality, the future kill. Not only in art, but through dance, music, and personal ornament, magic was performed. Choreographic movement, rhythmic noise, and costume embodied collective desires and hopes. Psychically charged by ritual, hunters then resumed the quest for food with renewed confidence.

The human group – its cohesion, fertility, and survival – was also a matter of cult. Totemism is a primeval amalgam of magic and religion: it equates the human group with an animal and then venerates that animal to secure the well-being of the group. Ancestor worship is equally ancient: it conceives dead kinsmen as benevolent spirits hovering protectively over living progeny. But full-fledged religion involves the worship of deities – the sun, the moon, the earth-mother. Alienation – lack of control over nature – then acquires its most elaborate expression. Humans seek to protect themselves from forces they cannot control through entreaties (prayers) and bribes (sacrifices and offerings) to those they imagine can.

Early forms of religion – totemism, ancestor worship, cults of the sun, the moon, and the earth – survive 'fossilised' in later cults. Much of what we know derives from this. Artemis, Greek goddess of wild nature, was worshipped in Ancient Athens by dancing girls dressed as she-bears. Lupercus, an Italian god of the countryside, was worshipped in Ancient Rome by young noblemen who feasted in a cave and then raced around the city wearing the skins of slaughtered goats.

Religion took on new significance as Early Neolithic villages were welded into tribal polities. Competition and war over territory forced small groups to seek security in larger units. Common worship of totems, ancestors, and deities created new social identities. Shared beliefs and rituals fostered solidarity. But the result could be murderous clashes between rival groups. The Early Neolithic causewayed camp at Crickley Hill in Gloucestershire was attacked and burned. Over 400 flint arrowheads were found around the perimeter. Many of the dead found in Early Neolithic long barrows were killed by arrowshot or by clubs, picks, axes, or stones.

A combination of radiocarbon determinations (based on the decay of carbon-14 in organic remains) and Bayesian statistics has produced new dates for these events. The construction of causewayed camps and long barrows and the advent of mass killing were broadly simultaneous. Between c. 3700 and 3400 BC, a new order, one based on territorial control, tribal groups, large-scale ritual, and warfare, was established in Britain. This order empowered a new social layer of war chiefs and high priests. From them, in the course of time, a ruling class would evolve.

The Late Neolithic Revolution

The Early Neolithic economy, riddled with intractable contradictions, was doomed. Technique was primitive and wasteful. Society lacked reserves to see it through natural disasters and hard times. Virgin land ran out as old fields became exhausted and populations grew.

War was an expression of these contradictions. It offered some groups a way out of poverty by seizing the property of others. But it was not a solution, for it did nothing to increase productivity; it merely redistributed existing reserves of wealth in land, animals, and grain stores.

A defining characteristic of *Homo sapiens* is inventiveness. Modern humans respond to challenges by developing new tools and techniques. They are adapted to adapt. They flourish through cultural innovation. The economic impasse of the Early Neolithic was broken by revolutionary advances in agriculture, transport, and tool-making.

Plough-based 'agriculture' (the tillage of fields) replaced hoe-based 'horticulture' (the working of garden plots). An ox-drawn plough allows farmers to work large fields, to break up the soil, and to tap reserves of nutrients. Traction animals also produce manure to fertilise the soil.

Irrigation schemes brought water to arid land. When communities of farmers organised themselves to dig, maintain, and operate networks of dams, channels, and sluices, this compensated for the risk of irregular rainfall and brought fertile land into permanent cultivation. Drainage schemes, on the other hand, turned swamps into fields, bringing nutrient-rich land into cultivation where none previously had existed. Again, communal labour was necessary, both to dig the channels and to keep them clear.

Land transport was transformed by the invention of the wheel and the breeding and rearing of pack animals (oxen, asses, horses, and camels). Loads were no longer limited to what a human could carry or haul. Water transport was transformed by the sail. In this case, wind power was harnessed to replace (or supplement) the muscle power of the rower.

Tools made of stone, bone, and wood are limited. They can be fashioned only by hacking bits off. Once broken, they have to be discarded. Metals seemed magical by comparison. They could be melted, mixed, and moulded into countless different forms. On cooling, they became solid, hard, and durable. And there was no waste: scrap metal could be endlessly recycled.

Copper was the first metal to be worked. Later, it was mixed with others to make harder alloys. By 3000 BC it was being mixed with tin to make bronze. For the next two millennia, this was to be the preferred material for making weapons, ornaments, and prestige items.

Metalworking technology was altogether new. Ceramic technology was already established, but it now developed apace with the introduction of the potter's wheel. A serviceable vessel – and, if desired, one of finer quality and decoration – could be formed on a wheel in a fraction of the time taken to mould one by hand from coils or slabs of clay.

In sum, between c. 4000 and 3000 BC, a series of innovations transformed the work of farmers in Western Asia. Land was reclaimed by irrigation and drainage, was more easily worked with the plough, and was improved by regular manuring. Metalworkers added to the range of artefacts, and potters used wheels to manufacture more and better containers. Pack animals, wheeled vehicles, and sailing vessels allowed heavy loads to be moved and goods to be traded.

Though many of the new ideas originated in Western Asia, some were imported from elsewhere. The steppe nomads of Central Asia may have been the first to domesticate the horse and construct carts. The metalworkers of Europe were in the forefront of their craft.

Good ideas soon catch on. The improved farming methods of the Late Neolithic spread quickly from Western Asia to Europe. In more far-flung regions there was independent development at a later date. The Chinese, for example, invented the wheelbarrow, terraced hillsides, and pioneered the laborious cultivation and transplanting of rice seedlings.

The new techniques brought social change. The low-tech economy of the Early Neolithic did not require specialised labour: everyone participated. The high-tech world of the Late Neolithic, the Chalcolithic (Copper Age), and the Bronze Age depended on a range of specialists. Skilled carpenters were needed to make ploughs, carts, and boats. Potters mass-produced wheel-thrown vessels in exchange for a share of farm produce. Metalworkers served long apprenticeships to learn the mysteries of smelting and smithing.

Specialisation separated labour from the homestead. Traders travelled long distances with valuable loads of copper, obsidian, lava, ornamental shells, and semi-precious stones. Many prehistoric craft workers, like their historical descendants, were itinerants, selling their skills from village to village. As a result, ties of family, clan, and tribe weakened. In addition to social relationships based on kinship, there were now new relationships based on patronage and commerce.

A second agricultural revolution – what might be called 'the Late Neolithic Revolution' (though more accurately it was a slow accumulation of radical innovations) – had transformed the economy and subverted the social order. The hoe and the temporary garden plot had been replaced by the plough and the irrigated and manured field. Because of this, matriarchal, family-based, and egalitarian communities were being transformed by new notions of authority, hierarchy, and patriarchy.

The implications for the female half of the human race were so serious that we must consider this aspect of the Late Neolithic Revolution in more detail.

The Oppression of Women

'The overthrow of mother-right was the world-historical defeat of the female sex.' That is how Frederick Engels described the establishment of patriarchy during the Neolithic. He considered it nothing less than a 'revolution' – 'one of the most decisive ever experienced by humanity'.

His book on the subject, *The Origin of the Family, Private Property, and the State* (1884), drew heavily on new anthropological studies, especially those by Johann Bachofen (on mother-right) and Lewis Morgan (on the Iroquois people of North America).

Two insights were critical. First, the evidence, both archaeological and anthropological, was unequivocal that patriarchy had not always existed: it had emerged at a certain stage in human social development and displaced earlier, more matriarchal forms of organisation. Second, the rise of patriarchy seemed to be rooted in wider economic, social, and political developments. As Engels implied in his title, the family, private property, and the state came as a package.

From earliest times, if human groups were to survive and prosper, they required a steady supply of adolescents and young adults for economic labour. To provide this, because of high mortality rates, young women had to spend much of their lives either pregnant or suckling. However, Palaeolithic gathering and Early Neolithic hoeing could be combined with the carrying and feeding of children. In hunter-gatherer and early farming communities, therefore, though women performed somewhat different roles to men, they enjoyed equal status. There had been a sexual division of labour, but no oppression of women. Men hunted, women gathered, and everyone discussed when to move camp or open up a new area for cultivation.

The nuclear family did not exist in its modern form. Early Neolithic long-houses accommodated extended families. Group marriage appears to have been common. Matrilocal residence (men and children living with the mother's family) and matrilineal descent (tracing family membership through the female line) were normal.

This is what Bachofen meant by 'mother-right'. The maternity of offspring is always known, and it is the mother who gives birth and produces milk. Paternity is more problematic, even in societies with strict rules about marriage, monogamy, and extra-marital sex designed to make the identity of the father certain. Relations between men and women have to be carefully engineered and regulated to enforce 'father-right'.

In early human societies – under what Marx and Engels called 'primitive communism' – paternity had little importance. Though social organisation varied greatly, a fairly general pattern was for people to be organised into large, loose, geographically dispersed 'tribes' and subdivided into smaller, tighter, more concentrated 'clans'. People were typically expected to marry within the tribe ('endogamy'), but outside the clan ('exogamy'). Originally, it seems, the men of one clan would marry the women of another. When this happened, the men would move to the women's village. Everything – place of residence, control of resources, organisation of labour, rearing of children – would be mother-centred.

In the Early Neolithic, the economic process underpinning this kinship system was based on the self-sufficient subsistence village. Here is archaeologist Gordon Childe's description of its likely character in gender terms:

> The women would till the plots, grind and cook the grain, spin, weave and manufacture clothes, build and bake pots, and prepare some ornaments and magic articles. Men, on the other hand, may have cleared the plots, built the huts, tended the livestock, hunted, and manufactured needful tools and weapons.

Thus, the clan structure, mother-right, and gender equality were wholly compatible with simple hoe-based cultivation. What eventually destabilised this system was pastoralism and the plough.

The tending and movement of herds of animals – sheep, goats, cattle, horses, camels – was difficult for women to manage when they were heavily pregnant or suckling infants. Just as men in hunter-gatherer society tended to hunt because they were free to roam, so men in pastoralist society tended to have control over the herds. Equally, ploughing large fields – as opposed to hoeing small garden-plots – involved heavier, more sustained labour, often at a greater distance from the village; it also drew upon the traction power of cattle, and relied upon the craft skills of specialists, both male domains.

This more advanced technology of production – an achievement of the Late Neolithic – yielded a surplus. Since men controlled the technology, they also controlled the surplus. The new economic system found itself in contradiction to the old social order. Male control of surplus was incompatible with mother-right. The male herder or ploughman was reluctant to see the fruits of his labour appropriated by his wife's brothers. His reluctance was reinforced by accumulation – by the fact that private appropriation of surplus led to private amassing of wealth. Patriarchy and private property therefore asserted themselves against kinship and communal production.

The herd, the plough, and the workshop created the preconditions for patriarchy. Secondary activities – all still rooted in surplus production – then reinforced male power. The rising surplus created demand for trade-goods and craft-production. These tended to require full-time application, investment in equipment or cargo, and long-distance movement. Women could not usually undertake such work, for the burden of child-bearing and child-rearing restricted them to forms of labour that were low-tech, close to home, and part-time. So again, they were denied access to, and therefore control over, the productive processes and economic surpluses of a more advanced agricultural society.

The surplus also underpinned warfare – it provided both the resources and the incentive to wage it – and the warrior was almost invariably male. Successful warfare, moreover, meant plunder and enslavement, further augmenting male control over society's resources. And here, of course, was the embryo of the state – men organised as a military force – which we can define in this context as not only a repressive apparatus to be used against foreign enemies and subject classes, but also as an instrument of patriarchal domination.

Patriarchy, which arose in the context of private property, social class, and state violence, was also the basis of the nuclear family. Once communal control over resources had been replaced by private appropriation of wealth, the matriarchal kinship system was bound to break down. Private ownership of land, cattle, grain-stores, metalwork, and precious objects required that the father knew his own son.

The implication was strict control over the sexuality of women in the context of monogamous or polygamous marriage. Men remained free to have sex with slaves, prostitutes, and others outside the framework of marriage. Women did not: their role henceforward was to produce legitimate offspring for male property-owners.

Thus was 'the overthrow of mother-right the world-historical defeat of the female sex'. Women became, in Engels' words, 'the slaves of slaves' – for most men, as we shall see in the next chapter, were themselves exploited. Women would henceforward bear a double burden – that of labour in the fields and drudgery in the home.

2
The First Class Societies
c. 3000–1000 BC

The Pharaoh Menkaura with two goddesses
in attendance. Greywacke stone sculpture,
Egypt, *c.* 2500 BC.

The world's first class societies were ruled by autocrats who
combined the roles of god, priest, judge, and war-leader.

In certain parts of the world, from around 3000 BC, especially in the fertile river valleys of Mesopotamia, Egypt, Pakistan, and China, the first fully formed class societies emerged. Priests, war leaders, and civil officials used their positions to monopolise control over surpluses, impose their authority on the rest of society, and begin to exploit the labour of others in their own interest.

In this period, known to archaeologists as the Bronze Age, metals were used to fashion weapons, ornaments, and trinkets, but the main tools of everyday labour continued to be made of stone, wood, and bone. Because of this, productivity remained low and surpluses small, the spread of civilisation was limited, and, while empires rose and fell, most of humanity continued to live beyond their reach.

Owing to the conservatism of the Bronze Age elites, technical innovation occurred on the periphery of the world system rather than at its core, and, by *c.* 1000 BC, one such innovation was helping to topple the old empires and start an economic revolution: iron-working.

The First Ruling Class

Prehistoric Sumer, a tract of land in the Tigris–Euphrates delta of southern Iraq, was made up of swamp and desert. But here, by *c.* 3000 BC, Neolithic pioneers had created a real-life version of the mythic Garden of Eden.

They drained the swamps and irrigated the sandbanks between them. In doing so, they created fields of exceptional fertility. By 2500 BC, the average yield on a field of barley was 86 times the sowing. We know this from written records inscribed on baked-clay tablets. The Sumerians had invented writing because the complex, urban, class-based society they created required them to maintain detailed records – especially records of tax and other dues.

Ancient Sumer was roughly the size of modern Denmark. Once its rich soils were under cultivation, it could produce massive agricultural surpluses. These made possible a qualitative shift from living in villages to living in towns. Sumer accomplished what the great interwar archaeologist Gordon Childe called the 'Urban Revolution'.

The main archaeological markers of this revolution are the 'tells' of Sumer (and other parts of the Middle East) – flat-topped artificial mounds formed by thousands of years of settlement. Layers of soil representing levelled, mud-brick buildings tell the story of successive generations of inhabitants. They show Copper Age villages expanding into Bronze Age cities between the fourth and third millennium BC.

Excavations have revealed cities dominated by large temples and artificial mounds known as ziggurats. At Erech, a ziggurat of Early Dynastic date (c. 2900–2300 BC) was 10 m high, built of sun-dried bricks, faced with thousands of pottery goblets, and topped by an asphalt platform. The city as a whole, with its residential and industrial districts, covered 5 square km.

The temples, and the estates in the surrounding countryside that supported them, belonged to the gods. The territory of Lagash was divided among some 20 deities. The goddess Baü owned 44 square km. Some of this was allocated to individual families, and some was worked as Baü's personal estate by wage-labourers, tenant-farmers, or 'clansmen' doing customary labour service.

In the absence of Baü herself, the property was managed on her behalf by temple priests. Many of Baü's people held only 0.32–1 ha of land. But one high temple official is known to have held 14.4 ha. So the priests formed a social elite, with both collective control over the wealth of temple estates and private wealth from their own estates.

Wealth made them powerful, and their power was used to accumulate more wealth. A decree aimed to restore the old order of Lagash 'as it had existed from the beginning'; it records that priests were stealing from the poor, practising various kinds of extortion, and treating temple land, cattle, equipment, and servants as their private property or slaves.

From the ranks of the priests came city governors (later styled kings). At Lagash, the city governor was both high priest of the chief god and commander-in-chief of the citizen army. He enjoyed the use of 246 ha of Baü's estate. The city governor of Lagash was one of many rulers, for Sumer was divided into separate city-states. These were often at war. The Standard of Ur – a highly decorated box from a royal tomb dating to around 2600 BC – depicts four-wheeled chariots trampling enemies, spearmen wearing helmets and metal-studded cloaks, and naked prisoners in front of the King.

Each polity lived in fear of its neighbours. Each had land, flocks, granaries, treasure, and a workforce to protect. Military power was imperative for defence. But military power, once acquired, could be used proactively. Pre-emptive aggression might be the best guarantee of future security. Predatory aggression might enhance the wealth and power of a ruler.

Military power also had an internal function. The state – the ruler, the priests, a bureaucracy of officials and clerks, and the armed bodies of men they commanded – was a mechanism for maintaining the new social order of the city. Bureaucracy was itself an instrument of class power. The complexity of urban society demanded writing for record-keeping, standardised weights and measures for trade, and geometry and arithmetic for land measurement. In an increasingly complex and class-dominated society, who owed what to whom needed to be measured, written down, and enforced.

New sorts of specialists were trained in these arts. Their education was esoteric and exclusive. The state hierarchy imbued them with authority and status. Older categories of specialists – traders and artisans – were also embedded in the new class structure. There was no free market. The economy of the ancient city was rooted in the political order. Rulers controlled what was traded, where it was sold, and by whom. In particular, they maintained a monopoly of metals, especially bronze and gold.

Early Dynastic Sumer, in short, was the world's first fully developed class society. At the bottom were slaves. Above them were commoners of subordinate status. Above these were free citizens. One baked-clay tablet refers to 205 slave girls and children, probably employed in a centralised weaving establishment. Another describes the occupational hierarchy at the temple of Baü in Lagash. At the top were clerks, officials, and priests. At the bottom were bakers, brewers, and textile workers, many of them women, many of them slaves.

The houses excavated at Eshnunna reveal clear class differences. The larger houses on the main roads occupied 200 square metres or more. But smaller houses, often only 50 square metres and lining narrow alleys, were far more numerous.

Class inequality was resented and resisted. Sumerian tablets allude to the tensions. The new social order was not based on consensus. It had to be imposed and maintained by force.

How had a minority acquired the power to elevate itself above the majority? What enabled the few to accumulate wealth at the expense of the many?

Class is both a social relationship between rich and poor, and an economic process of exploitation and surplus accumulation. It has to be continually reproduced. And because it is contested, it involves class struggle. The rulers' drive for wealth and power gained traction from the combination of poverty and property – a combination that holds all pre-industrial class societies in a vice-like grip.

Poverty is a general condition. Traditional agricultural economies do not produce enough to provide abundance for all. Sometimes they do not produce enough to provide even the necessities. Property is a privileged, *a priori* claim to scarce resources. It allocates wealth to certain individuals, families, landowners, temples, tribes, or city-states. Property can be private or collective, but is never universal.

This contradictory pairing – poverty and property – gave rise to class inequality, state power, and warfare. The religious and military specialists of prehistoric Sumer had been granted control over the surplus so that they could carry out their functions on behalf of society as a whole. At first, their position had depended on public sanction. But control over surplus made them powerful, and as they consolidated their authority, they found that they could use it to enrich themselves further and maintain their position *without* public sanction. In this way, the high priests, war chiefs, city governors, and petty kings of urban Sumer evolved into an exploitative ruling class accumulating and consuming surplus in its own interest: a power *over* society, no longer a power *of* society.

The Spread of Civilisation

Something similar occurred at around the same time or somewhat later in several other places. Civilisation did not spread outwards from a single centre: it arose independently where circumstances made it possible.

In Sumer, priests formed the core of the ruling class, temple estates provided their wealth, and temple ziggurats their most imposing monuments. City governors and war leaders were recruited from the theocracy. In Egypt, the reverse was true. Menes, chief of the Falcon clan and legendary first pharaoh, united the Nile Delta (Lower Egypt) and the Nile Valley (Upper Egypt) by military conquest. Having created a centralised state, he proclaimed himself a god-king (pharaoh). Priests, officials, merchants, artisans, and peasants were all subordinate to the pharaoh. The ruling class – priests and officials – owed their estates and position to royal patronage. The pyramids, iconic monuments of Old Kingdom Egypt (2700–2250 BC), were not temples, but royal tombs.

Like the Sumerian priests and city governors, the pharaohs fostered the cultural prerequisites of the Urban Revolution: irrigation works, long-distance trade (especially in metals, timber, and stone), literacy and record-keeping, numerical notation and geometry, standard weights and measures, the calendar and timekeeping, and the science of astronomy.

This urban package reflected the needs of the state and the elite. Control of the waters of the Nile ensured abundant harvests, large surpluses, and a healthy workforce. Official trade missions secured the raw materials needed for arms manufacture, monumental architecture, and luxury consumption. A literate and numerate bureaucracy managed the tribute and labour services on which state power depended.

Independent urban revolutions occurred in several other places. This shows that all humans are capable of the highest achievements. There are no 'superior races' or 'nations' that give the lead to the rest. It is culture and circumstance – not biology – that determine historical differences.

Around 2600 BC, urban civilisation emerged in the Indus Valley in modern Pakistan. The great monuments and residential suburbs of Mohenjo-daro cover 2.6 square km. The walled perimeter of Harappa is 4 km long. Inscribed seal stamps and standard weights and measures indicate complex administration.

Ancient Anyang in the Yellow River region of northern China was an unwalled complex measuring almost 10 km in length by 4 km in width. It was probably the capital of the Shang Dynasty in the thirteenth century BC. Excavations have revealed rich royal tombs, great caches of decorated bronzes, and tens of thousands of cracked and inscribed 'oracle bones'.

If we glance forward in time, we see the same pattern elsewhere. Teotihuacan in Mexico, at its peak between AD 450 and 650, was a city of 20 square km and around 150,000 people. At its centre was a monumental complex dominated by giant pyramids. The Pyramid of the Sun is 210 square metres at the base and 64 m high.

Great Zimbabwe (AD 1100–1500) in the heart of Africa was a city of 20,000 people. Its wealth was based on cattle, crop cultivation, and trade in gold, copper, ivory, and slaves. Its territory extended over 100,000 square km between the Rivers Zambezi and Limpopo.

It was once believed that civilisation was exported from a single centre. Scholars wrote of 'light from the Ancient East'. This fitted with nineteenth-century notions of the 'White Man's Burden' – the 'civilising mission' of European imperialists. Archaeology has demonstrated something different: civilisation developed independently at different places at different times. The message is that all people share a common humanity and similar creative potential.

But the major centres of civilisation did have an impact on surrounding societies. There was interaction between 'core' – more advanced metropolitan areas – and 'periphery' – less-developed areas economically dependent on them.

The Egyptian pharaoh obtained wood from Lebanon, copper from Cyprus, and gold from Sudan. Sometimes this was a matter of peaceful exchange. The city of Byblos in Lebanon grew rich on the timber trade. Local merchants employed clerks who could read Egyptian. There was cultural interaction. But it could also be a matter of conquest. Northern Sudan was annexed and forced to pay tribute in gold. The interaction between core and periphery was therefore multifaceted – it had economic, political, military, and cultural dimensions.

The demands of trade encouraged merchants, sea captains, and shipbuilders. Longboats powered by rowers were used in the Aegean from c. 3000 BC onwards. The citadel of Troy in 2700 BC (known as Troy II) was built to guard a harbour at the entrance to the Dardanelles in north-western Turkey. The Thalassocracy (sea power) of Minos rose to dominance in c. 1950–1450 BC on the basis of Crete's central location in the Eastern Mediterranean and the islanders' revolutionary design of deep-hulled, high-capacity, sail-powered cargo ships. The rulers of Minoan Crete lived in sprawling stone palaces decorated with frescos, and had storerooms packed with giant ceramic containers.

The Greek poet Homer, describing Odysseus' travel-worn appearance, says he was like 'some captain of a merchant crew, who spends his life on a hulking tramp, worrying about his outward freight, or keeping a sharp eye on the cargo when he comes home with extortionate profits'. Seafarers and merchants were familiar figures in many Bronze Age societies.

Trade drove change on the periphery of the great empires. So, too, did the threat of war. Sargon of Akkad united the cities of Mesopotamia some time after 2330 BC, forging an empire that eventually extended from the Persian Gulf to the Mediterranean. The Old Kingdom pharaohs conquered Sinai for its copper. Threatened by superpower militarism, the minor states and tribes of the periphery therefore organised for war. Warriors, weapons, and war fleets dominated the Bronze Age world. An arms race gathered pace through the centuries. Frescos depict merchant ships loaded with goods, but also warships filled with armed men.

Through trade and war, and by the movement of goods, people, and ideas, the societies of core and periphery influenced one another. The sharing and spreading of culture is what archaeologists call diffusion. It is one of the primary mechanisms by which knowledge and productivity advance. Progress is impeded by barriers and facilitated by bridges.

But a world of competing elites and rival armies also harboured the potential for waste and regression. As we shall see, the contradictions of Bronze Age civilisation repeatedly plunged humanity into crisis and barbarism.

Crisis in the Bronze Age

Bronze Age empires rose and fell. The 140-year Akkadian Empire, based in Iraq, collapsed suddenly around 2190 BC. Equally sudden had been the overthrow of the Old Kingdom pharaohs in Egypt a short time before, around 2250 BC.

Why did Early Bronze Age civilisation fail? Detail is lacking, but Egyptian sources record famine, a fragmentation of the state, and incursions by Libyan raiders from the west and Nubians from the south. What is not clear is why these events should have happened. Why was the once-strong centralised state of the pyramid builders no longer able to feed the people, enforce its authority, and defend its borders?

This pattern of rise and fall repeated itself. New empires emerged from the chaos of the Early Bronze Age crisis. Between 1600 and 1200 BC, the eastern Mediterranean was again divided among rival empires – New Kingdom Egypt, the Hittites of Anatolia (Turkey), the Mitanni of northern Mesopotamia (Iraq), and the Mycenaean Greeks. But this Late Bronze Age geopolitical system also collapsed amid storm and strife during the twelfth century BC. The embattled New Kingdom pharaohs record coordinated attacks by Libyans and 'northerners coming from all lands'. The latter were the more dangerous. The multi-ethnic Sea Peoples amassed great pirate fleets. 'All at once,' declared Ramesses III, 'these peoples were on the move … No country could stand up to them.'

Pre-eminent as seafarers and warriors, Greeks were among these Sea Peoples. Homer's *Iliad* and *Odyssey* are probably based on an oral record of real events that took place around 1190 BC. His epics have transformed them into tales of derring-do by legendary heroes. The kernel of truth about the Trojan War appears to be that it was a massive seaborne raid by Greek pirates out for plunder.

So the Late Bronze Age empires collapsed as the Early Bronze Age empires had done. And when we look beyond the Mediterranean, to places where civilisation developed at different times, we see the same pattern of rise and fall.

The Indus civilisation of Mohenjo-daro and Harappa in Pakistan collapsed around 1900 BC. Excavators found numerous unburied remains of people suddenly and violently killed in the uppermost levels of the great city of Mohenjo-daro.

Chinese history, from the Shang of the second millennium BC to the Manchu of AD 1644–1911, records the rise and fall of a long succession of imperial dynasties, with occasional periods, sometimes lasting centuries, of division and civil war. Throughout this epoch, despite impressive technical achievements and huge increases in output and population, Chinese civilisation remained essentially conservative. The socio-economic order simply replicated itself, from generation to generation, from dynasty to dynasty. China provides an extreme example of the cyclical trajectory of ancient civilisation.

So we have two historical problems. Why did ancient empires rise and fall? And why did this contradictory social form replicate itself over such long periods of time?

The ancient world was characterised by stagnation of technique. On several occasions, humans had escaped the contradictions of an existing 'mode of production' (an economic and social system) by transforming it. Climate change had destroyed the habitats of the big game on which Upper Palaeolithic hunters depended. The response – the Agricultural or Early Neolithic Revolution – had achieved massive increases in productivity, output, and population through the adoption of crop cultivation and stock raising. Soil exhaustion and population pressure had later created a crisis for this Early Neolithic mode of production. In the Late Neolithic and Urban Revolutions, the contradictions were resolved with a second leap forward, based on land reclamation, irrigation schemes, and ploughing. But the Urban Revolution also erected an impediment to further progress: the existence of a ruling class. We have charted its emergence. We have noted its roots in specialised religious, military, and political functions, and in the shortages and insecurities inherent in a primitive economic system: the first rulers were those whose social roles gave them control over scarce resources.

Why should the ruling class have been a barrier to new ideas? Surely it was in their interest to improve techniques in order to increase surplus? Yes and no: as with all things in social life, there were contradictory pressures.

The new ruling classes sat uneasy on their thrones. They were divided among themselves, family against family, city against city, tribe against tribe, empire against empire. To overcome domestic rivals, top families had retinues of loyalists and bodyguards. Against foreign enemies, they needed armies and fortresses. The rulers were also divided from the mass of the people, who, because they were exploited, were potentially rebellious and had to be cowed by a judicious combination of force and fraud.

Force meant the threat posed by aristocratic retinues and state forces. Fraud meant the ideological claim that the rulers played an essential role and acted in the public interest. Both were embodied in the great monuments that dominate the archaeological record. Take the pyramids of Old Kingdom Egypt. They were the royal tombs of god-kings who were expected to live for eternity: monuments to a false ideology by which the ruler was elevated into a figure of awesome and intimidating power. The pyramids were designed to teach people their place. They were ideological weapons in a class war.

So the Bronze Age elites did not invest the surplus they controlled in improved technique and higher productivity. Instead they squandered resources on military competition, prestige monuments, and, of course, luxury lifestyles. Power, propaganda, and privilege – not productivity – consumed the surpluses created by the labour of Bronze Age peasants.

Innovation, indeed, was more likely to be perceived as a threat than an opportunity. The ruling class itself did not get its hands dirty; productive labour was performed by the common people. For this reason, new inventions, in so far as they appeared at all, were likely to come from below, empowering ordinary people, disrupting established economic arrangements, and perhaps destabilising the social order. They were therefore viewed with suspicion.

Bronze Age rulers were rarely interested in new technology unless it had military applications. Their focus was on accumulating power in a competitive geopolitical system. That is why the greed of the rich was never sated. The grandeur of past monuments set a standard to be surpassed by those who followed. Rulers competed in the luxury of their palaces, the splendour of their tombs, the art and architecture of their great cities. But above all, they competed militarily as rival polities expanded and clashed. A slow-motion arms race can be detected in the Late Bronze Age world. There seem to be more soldiers, better armed, defending stronger fortresses in 1200 BC than there had been in 1600 BC. The world was becoming ever more militarised.

Technique was stagnant, therefore, but surplus consumption was rising. War, monuments, and luxury meant higher levels of exploitation were necessary, and over-accumulation at the top was mirrored by the degradation of society's agricultural base. The proud warrior-lords of the Late Bronze Age were a parasitic social elite whose economic cost was increasingly unsustainable. That is the fundamental reason for the implosion of their world in the twelfth century BC.

But this was a problem without an internal solution. Stagnant technique meant socio-economic conservatism. There were no new forces developing inside the old society. The choice, therefore, was between the barbarism of invading hordes and a reincarnation of the old (failed) imperial civilisation. Humanity was again at an impasse. Only this time, the existence of classes and states had raised formidable barriers to human creativity and progress.

Excursus 1: How History Works

The Bronze Age impasse provides a useful occasion to pause and take stock. All the elements of a complex society are now in place, so it is convenient to ask: how does history work?

Three engines drive the historical process. First, there is the development of technique. Progress can be defined as the accumulation of knowledge that makes possible better control over nature, increases in labour productivity, and a bigger store of economic resources available for the satisfaction of human need.

Progress in this sense is not inevitable. Entire generations of peasants in, say, Shang China, Mycenaean Greece, or Norman England might live out their entire lives without experiencing a significant innovation in either agricultural or domestic equipment. Only in modern capitalist society is the development of technique inherent in the mode of production. In making this point, Marx explicitly states: 'Conservation of old modes of production in unaltered form was … the first condition of existence of all earlier industrial classes.'

Progress in pre-capitalist society was haphazard, not intrinsic to the dynamic of the socio-economic system. In pre-class society, for example, ecological crisis threatening the survival of human groups was probably of critical significance. The Early Neolithic Revolution seems to have been a response to climate change and a sharp decline in game. In early class society, on the other hand, the development of technique was subject to a wider variety of influences, some of them catalysts of innovation, others barriers to progress. To understand this, we need to review the other two engines of the historical process.

The second engine is competition among rulers for wealth and power. This takes the form of conflict *within* ruling classes – among rival aristocratic factions, for example – and conflict *between* ruling classes, as in wars between rival states and empires.

In modern capitalist society, such competition has both economic and politico-military dimensions. The two world wars were essentially wars between rival national-capitalist blocs.

In pre-capitalist class societies, by contrast, competition between rulers was essentially political and took the form of competitive military accumulation. The world was divided into rival factions and polities. Political insecurity was a permanent condition. The result was military competition – a relentless drive to amass soldiers, fortifications, and armaments faster than one's rivals.

The third engine of the historical process is the struggle between classes. In the ancient world, competitive military accumulation required the ruling class to increase the rate of exploitation and extract more surplus from the peasantry. But there were two limits to this process. First, the peasantry and the economic system had to be able to reproduce themselves: over-taxation would – and sometimes did – destroy the material foundations of the social order. The second was the peasants' resistance to exploitation.

We know very little about the class struggle in the Bronze Age. One exception is provided by documents of the second millennium BC from Thebes (modern Luxor) in Egypt. They concern a community of skilled quarrymen, stonemasons, and carpenters who made the temples and tombs of the elite. These documents record class tension. Though the craftsmen were relatively well paid and worked moderate hours, bullying managers sometimes tried to tighten the screws. On one occasion, those deemed 'surplus' to requirements were made to undertake forced labour. But the exploited sometimes fought back. One of the documents records that, in 1170 BC, backed by their wives, the craftsmen went on strike – the first recorded strike in history – when their rations were delayed and their families faced hunger.

So we see three engines of history at work: the development of technique, competition among rival rulers, and a struggle between classes. Each engine is very different. Each operates in a different register, at varying speed, and with intermittent effect. Because of this, the historical process is immensely complex. Not only is each engine itself a nexus of contradictions, but all three engines operate simultaneously, pulling sometimes in the same direction, sometimes in opposite directions. For this reason, each historical situation is unique. Each one is a distinctive conjuncture of economic problems, social tensions, political antagonisms, cultural differences, and personal influences. The conjuncture provides the context in which historical action takes place. But the context does not determine the outcome. It is the clash of social forces – of organised human groups – that decides history's future direction.

Let us return to the successive crises of Bronze Age civilisation. Waste expenditure drained resources from productive technique and effectively choked off experiment and innovation. More than that: the advance of knowledge was blocked by magic, religion, and other forms of mystification, and by the ruling class's innate suspicion of things they did not understand and feared might prove subversive.

Progress is contingent on 'true consciousness' – knowledge of the world which, because it corresponds with external reality, is an effective guide to human action. 'False consciousness' – belief in

god-kings, divine inspiration, or the efficacy of ritual, for example –
has the opposite effect: it is a barrier to knowledge, to practical work,
and therefore to social progress. Instead of theory and practice inter-
acting in the real world to improve technique and productivity, the
two – mind and matter, literacy and labour – became separated in
the imperial civilisations. Egyptian priests studied the stars, not the
soil, and wrote manuals on mummification, not natural science. The
wealth produced by Egyptian peasants was wasted on monuments to
mysticism. The skills of Egyptian artisans were despised precisely for
being manual.

So progress was blocked in the old civilisations. No new forces
capable of breaking through the impasse were fostered. History's
energy was wasted turning the wheel of imperial rise and fall.

But if the core of the world system in c. 1200 BC can be seen as a
froth of geopolitical turmoil above stagnant depths of socio-economic
conservatism, the periphery was more dynamic. Here, relatively free of
the control of kings, priests, and bureaucrats, the nomads, farmers, and
artisans of the wider Bronze Age world were pushing at the limits of
knowledge and skill.

Many were the innovations, but one was to be of supreme
importance. Bronze was expensive, aristocratic, and too soft to make
strong tools and weapons. A metal that was cheap, hard, and available
to all would conquer the world.

Into the storm and strife of the Late Bronze Age crisis came new
invaders from the North: men of iron.

Men of Iron

Many revolutions occur on the periphery rather than at the core of
global systems. Life on the periphery is less secure, less entrenched,
and therefore less conservative.

Manual labour was both exploited and despised in the old
imperial civilisations of the Bronze Age. Vast surpluses were extorted
and wasted on war, monuments, and luxury. There was little left for
investment in new technology and little incentive to use it for that
purpose. Innovation involved thought, questioning, imagining new
possibilities. So human creativity was not only denied the material
resources on which to work; it was also mesmerised by the spells and
mysticism of priests.

The occasional spark of ingenuity stands out against a backcloth of
stagnation. The Egyptians invented glass-working, the Babylonians

accounting, the Phoenicians the alphabet. The exceptions to the rule are revealing: a luxury commodity, a way of measuring wealth, and a script for recording it. Such inventions are of little use to farmers or artisans. They concern the consumption and control of wealth, not its production. They reflect a society in which the world of learning was divorced from the world of labour.

Not so on the periphery. Here, around 1300 BC, an industrial revolution had begun that was to transform the world. Where exactly it took place we do not know; but it was, for sure, beyond the reach of over-mighty rulers.

The archaeological record is unequivocal: from this time onwards, the quantity, range, and sophistication of metal objects exploded. Mining technology advanced to provide an ever greater supply of copper, tin, and gold. Smelting technique improved. And metalsmiths began to use multiple moulds and the lost-wax technique to produce objects of unprecedented complexity.

There are bronze figurines of warriors from Sardinia, bronze trumpets from Danish bogs, bronze breastplates moulded to look like pectoral muscles, bronze shields, swords, scabbards, spearheads, axes, horse harnesses, knives, and much more. Sometimes it is found in massive hoards. Thousands of Late Bronze Age hoards are known to archaeologists. One at Isleham in Cambridgeshire contained 6,500 pieces of metal.

Soon something even more momentous occurred: metalworkers started experimenting with ways of extracting iron from its stubbornly intractable ores.

Iron was not new. For centuries, crude implements of wrought iron had occasionally been used. But no technique had been developed for the mass production of quality ironwork at an economical cost. This may have been the achievement of a barbarian tribe living in the Caucasus mountains in remote antiquity. The new technology seems to have spread from there to the Hittite Empire of Anatolia (Turkey). Its further spread was then delayed by the determination of the Hittite imperial ruling class to monopolise iron weaponry.

Iron artefacts did not become widespread until after 1200 BC, when ironworking took off amid the collapse of the Bronze Age empires. As it did so, the greatest advances in technique, productivity, and output were registered on the periphery of, and in the interstices between, the great powers.

Ironworking launched a chain of economic, social, and political changes. Bronze was expensive and relatively soft, which is why most Bronze Age farmers continued to work with tools of wood and stone. Iron is abundant, cheap, and hard, but the barrier to its use until then had been its high melting-point.

Smelting required specialised bloomeries – furnaces in which bellows were used to force air through iron ore and charcoal to achieve very high temperatures. Once the technique had been invented, ordinary farmers could build their own bloomeries and equip themselves with metal tools.

Anyone who doubts the increase in productivity made possible by iron should try digging clay with a wooden spade or chopping wood with a stone axe. Three thousand years ago, iron revolutionised agriculture, industry, and war. Its impact was as transformative as that of steam power in the nineteenth century.

It also threatened to turn the social world upside down. Bronze was the prerogative of the aristocracy. The Bronze Age world was dominated by chariot-mounted warlords equipped with expensive arms and armour. They were supported by peasant masses bound to ceaseless toil with primitive tools.

Iron was the supreme chopper and cutter. Men with iron axes could clear thick forests and jungles to create new farms. Then, with iron ploughs, they could till heavy clay soils. Iron technology unleashed a new wave of agricultural pioneers and free peasants.

Iron was also democratic. The bronzesmiths worked for the palaces, the blacksmiths for the villages. Iron gave the common man a spear, even a sword. If he stood shoulder-to-shoulder with other men – if he formed a phalanx – he could stop a chariot charge. And if he could do that, he could kill the landlord. The ironworkers of 1000 BC, had they but known it, were smelting revolution.

Moving from settlement to settlement in zones ruled by petty chieftains, trading his wares and his skills, the metalsmith of the Early Iron Age was the unwitting agent of a new world order. Rival chieftains competed for his services, which raised his economic value, his social standing, and his own valuation of himself and his craft. This, in turn, gave him the rewards, independence, and self-confidence to be an innovator.

Homer captures something of this. The *Iliad* and the *Odyssey* span four centuries. They purport to describe events in the twelfth century BC, but they took on their final (written) form only in the eighth. Sometimes Homer describes the Late Bronze Age, sometimes his own Archaic Age. When he says that 'a soothsayer, a doctor, a singer, and a craftsman are sure of a welcome everywhere', he tells us how things were in a post-imperial age, in the 'Dark Age' of the eighth century BC, in a world of petty chieftains and itinerant ironsmiths. The new class of free artisans that first emerged in the barbarian north had, by Homer's time, been long established in the eastern Mediterranean.

In the twelfth century BC, the Late Bronze Age empires had collapsed, exhausted by military struggle against one another, broken by resistance from within and attack from without. The geopolitical system that replaced them was a mosaic of smaller polities – shrunken imperial states like Egypt, mercantile city-states like Ugarit, and barbarian settlements like Palestine. Ironworking flourished in this new, more open, less top-down world. Cyprus, a centre of maritime commerce, pioneered the iron-based industrial revolution of the twelfth and eleventh centuries BC in the eastern Mediterranean. The old cycle of rise and fall, the recurrent rhythm of Bronze Age civilisation, was broken. A new technology was creating a new economy, new social relationships, and new political forms. History was carving out fresh channels.

3

Ancient Empires
c. 1000–30 BC

Greek sprinter. Black-figure vase painting,
Athens, late sixth century BC.

The Greek Democratic Revolution placed political power in the
hands of common citizens and created the basis for the ancient
world's greatest cultural achievements.

Iron was the basis of humanity's third great technological leap. It made possible a steep increase in labour productivity comparable with those achieved by the transition from hunting-gathering to farming around 10,000 years earlier, and then that from shifting hoe-based cultivation to intensive plough-based agriculture around 6,000 years earlier. One consequence of each of these technological leaps was that the scale of human social organisation was transformed.

The Bronze Age empires had been small and discrete. They were based on the great alluvial floodplains of the Nile in Egypt, the Tigris and Euphrates in Iraq, the Indus in Pakistan, and the Yellow in northern China. Vast tracts of desert, steppe land, and mountain had divided these early centres of civilisation. With tools made of wood and stone, productivity was low and surpluses small. Using Bronze Age technology, only the extraordinary fertility of the great river valleys had yielded sufficient wealth to build cities, sustain armies, and create empires.

This changed in the centuries after 1000 BC: the scale of civilisation and empire increased exponentially. Iron Age farmers hacked fields out of the wilderness and ploughed the heavy soils they exposed. Productivity and population soared, and the surpluses available to Iron Age empire-builders dwarfed those of their Bronze Age predecessors.

In this chapter, we analyse the great Iron Age civilisations and empires of the first millennium BC – Persian, Indian, Chinese, Greek, and Roman.

Persia: The Achaemenid Empire

In the mid to late sixth century BC, three great Persian conquerors, Cyrus, Cambyses, and Darius (the Achaemenid dynasty), built an empire that extended from Thrace (Bulgaria) in the west to the Indus (Pakistan) in the east, and from the Caucasus Mountains in the north to the Nubian desert of Sudan in the south.

The Persians were settled farmers of the rugged mountain valleys in south-western Iran. The Medes were nomadic horsemen of the great steppes in north-eastern Iran. In 550 BC, Persia and Media were united by conquest. Within two generations, Iraq, Egypt, Turkey, Pakistan, and Afghanistan (to use the modern names for these regions) had been added to the empire. The Persian Empire of the sixth century BC therefore encompassed three of the four original centres of civilisation – the Nile, the Tigris-Euphrates, and the Indus river valleys. These, and the territories between, were integrated into a single imperial polity and ruled as a patchwork of tribute-bearing provinces. There was no attempt to weld the provinces of the empire into a unified cultural whole. The Persian emperor was styled the 'Great King' or 'the King of Kings' and ruled over distinct subject-peoples who retained their own ethnic and religious identities, their own economic and social organisation, their own political structures.

Stone relief-sculptures decorate the ceremonial stairway leading to the principal audience hall of the imperial palace at Persepolis. They depict delegations from 23 subject-peoples bringing gifts or tribute to the Great King, including clothing, metal vessels, gold, elephant tusks, horses and camels, and such exotic animals as antelope, lions, and okapi. Building inscriptions at Persepolis list the principal peoples of the empire, while thousands of inscribed clay tablets record disbursements of food or silver to royalty, officials, and workmen.

How was the collection of tribute from such a vast area enforced? The empire was divided into large provinces ruled by satraps (viceroys). A network of roads and an official postal system linked the satraps with the imperial capital. The Royal Road, for example, ran from the provincial capital at Sardis in western Turkey to the imperial administrative capital at Susa in western Iran. Satraps controlled large armies and fleets. But in the event of a major rebellion or foreign expedition, a grand army would be formed under the leadership of the Great King. Its composition would reflect the polyglot character of the empire: each separate ethnic component would fight in its own manner.

The wealth of the Great King is evident from the size of the royal palaces at Persepolis, Susa, Hamadan, Pasargadae, and Babylon. Persepolis was a vast complex of audience halls, reception rooms, royal residences, store-rooms for tribute, barracks for imperial guards, a walled hunting park, a huge ornamental lake, and a sprawling town of artisans, traders, and labourers. When Alexander the Great captured Persepolis in 331 BC, it contained treasure equal in value to the annual income of Athens, the richest of the Greek city-states, for 300 years.

Despite its wealth, the Persian Empire was relatively unstable and short-lived. Cyrus had created a powerful instrument of conquest when he united the Persians and the Medes. The Persians fought as infantry with spears and bows; the Medes were first-class light cavalry. This combination of mobility, firepower, and shock action produced a maelstrom of conquest. But military supremacy does not equate to political hegemony or social transformation. The Persians merely incorporated existing ruling classes and appropriated part of their surplus. Their empire lacked all cohesion save that imposed by force.

The sheer size and diversity of the empire weakened the centre. Native kings and provincial satraps wielded immense power. Rebellion was endemic, especially on the more remote frontiers. The Persian Empire was an attempt to cement together geopolitically separate and culturally alien entities – Turkey, Egypt, Iraq, Iran, Afghanistan, and Pakistan. Because of this, its tendency was to disintegrate rather than cohere.

It was an external force, however, that shattered the fragile carapace. As it reached its fullest extent in the late sixth century BC, the Persian Empire collided with another civilisation on its furthest north-western fringes. This collision pitted the wealth of the greatest empire the world had ever seen against small communities of peasant-farmers. It tested to the limit two entirely different social and political orders. Both were products of the Iron Age. But while one was simply a replication of ancient imperialism on a global scale, the other was a new social order created in the storm and strife of revolution. It was in the tiny city-states of Ancient Greece that the Iron Age transformation achieved its most advanced social form. Before turning to it, however, we must chart the course of civilisation in India and China.

India: The Mauryan Empire

In the late fourth century BC, the Mauryan warlord Chandragupta founded the first Indian empire. Reaching its peak a century later, it eventually encompassed much of the Indus Valley, the whole of the Northern Plain, and also the Ganges Valley, Nepal, and a large part of the Deccan. This Iron Age empire of the late first millennium BC was about ten times the size of the Indian subcontinent's Bronze Age civilisation of the late third millennium. Let us consider what had changed.

Farming began in India around 7000 BC in the Kacchi Plain west of the Indus Valley. Here, the wild progenitors of wheat, barley, cattle, sheep, and goats were available for domestication. These natural resources offered a way out of the ecological crisis represented by climate change and over-hunting.

The people of the Indus Valley, however, remained largely immune to the influence of the agriculturalists for three millennia. Until about 4000 BC, the continuing natural abundance of the alluvial floodplain made the toil of farming unnecessary. Thereafter, the spread of farming was rapid. During the fourth millennium BC, the Indus Valley filled with agricultural villages. In the middle of the third, the huge surpluses generated by river-valley cultivation sustained an urban revolution. The Indus became one of only four places where independent civilisations existed in the Early Bronze Age.

Around 1900 BC, after only half a millennium of existence, Mohenjo-daro, Harappa, and the other Indus cities were abandoned. Early Bronze Age civilisation in the Indian subcontinent collapsed under its own weight. Over-accumulation of surpluses by urban-based elites probably crippled the reproductive capacity of an agricultural economy based on wooden spades and stone sickles.

To the north, a very different culture developed among the nomadic pastoralists of the Central Asian steppes. This vast territory comprised grassland hundreds of miles deep, extending from the Carpathians in the west to Manchuria in the east: ideal for stock-raising. A combination of low rainfall, bitterly cold winters, and scorching summers impeded the spread of cultivation in this region.

The steppe nomads domesticated the horse, invented the horse-drawn cart, developed the composite bow (made from horn, wood, and sinew laminated together), and produced stunning artefacts of copper, bronze, silver, and gold. Formidable natural warriors, they were the world's finest horse-archers.

Life on the steppes was precarious. The numbers of people, the size of herds, and the adequacy of pasture were in fine balance. If a hot summer burnt out the grasslands, war, displacement, and mass migration might follow. Then, the steppe peoples might impact on the wider world with devastating force. Periodically – but unpredictably – they poured out of Central Asia, heading west, south, and east, from desiccated grasslands to abundant plough-lands, in search of food and fodder, plunder and riches, and new territory on which to settle. Such were the Mongols of the thirteenth century AD, the Huns of the fifth century AD, and the Xiongnu against whom the Chinese built the Great Wall in the third century BC.

Long before, in the years around 1500 BC, a people we know as the Aryans left the steppes, crossed the mountain passes of the Hindu Kush, and entered the Indus Valley of Pakistan. They came first as nomadic pastoralist invaders, relatively few in number, and their lifestyle and culture seem to have continued as before. Over the centuries, however, they spread across the Northern Plain into the Ganges Valley, and later again, southwards into the Deccan.

By then, they had iron, which reached India around 800 BC, enabling the Indo-Aryans (a thoroughly mixed population by now) to hack down forests and jungles and settle northern and central India with farms.

The Aryans introduced horses, chariots, and the warrior culture of conquerors. As they imposed themselves, they created the rudiments of both a new social structure – the caste system – and a new ideological framework – Hinduism. By defining themselves as warriors (*kshatriyas*), priests (*brahmans*), or landowners (*vaishyas*), they formalised the social exclusion and domination implicit in conquest. Mixed-race peasants formed a fourth group – the *shudras* – and others were integrated into the social order as members of a growing mass of sub-castes, or, in the case of those deemed wholly outside the Aryan tribal system, as 'outcasts'.

The beliefs that eventually coalesced into Hinduism – a religion notable for its conservatism, elaborate ritual, and fearsome power-deities – legitimised the caste system. The social order was natural, divinely approved, and advancement was an individual matter. The virtuous were those who conformed; they would be reincarnated in a higher caste. Dissidents, on the other hand, could expect relegation in the next life.

Iron technology filled the Ganges Valley with productive farms, powerful monarchies, and large armies. For some three centuries, rival states battled for supremacy. By 321 BC, when Chandragupta Maurya usurped its throne, Magadha had emerged as the strongest of these states. One Greek writer estimated its army's strength to be 200,000 infantry, 20,000 cavalry, 3,000 elephants, and 2,000 chariots; an exaggeration, no doubt, but an indication of how impressed he was. Between 321 and 303 BC, Chandragupta conquered the Ganges

Valley, the Northern Plain, and the Indus Valley. His immediate successors waged further wars of conquest in southern India, and by 260 BC the Mauryan Empire encompassed almost the whole of what is today India, Pakistan, and Bangladesh.

Mauryan conquest was violent. The Kalingans were the last to hold out, but the Mauryan emperor Ashoka crushed them totally: '150,000 people were deported, 100,000 were killed, and many times that number perished…'.

Exploitation of conquered territory was systematic. Slaves – usually war captives – were employed in mining, construction, industry, and household service. Peasants toiled on the land. The government maintained dams, reservoirs, and canals. Individual peasants paid rents on their plots and taxes on their produce. Merchants and artisans also paid taxes and tolls.

The Mauryan Empire was a military superstructure resting on a base of tribute-paying peasants and petty-traders. This is clear from the *Arthashastra*, a treatise on government and economics written in the reign of Chandragupta. All land was owned by the emperor and all peasants owed him tribute. The only intermediaries were state-appointed officials. The empire was divided into provinces. These in turn were subdivided into districts, these into groups of villages, and the smallest unit was the village. Each village had a headman. Each group of villages had an accountant and a tax-collector. And so on up the hierarchy, with subordinates accountable to those above them, not those below.

A network of informers reported dissidents to the authorities. Ashoka (269–232 BC), the emperor who completed the Mauryan conquest and then refined the imperial administration, attempted to achieve an overarching ideological hegemony by promoting the concept of *Dhamma*. A social ethic that stressed toleration and the suppression of differences in the interests of harmony, it was an attempt to fossilise the contradictions of Mauryan society.

It did not work. In the 50 years after Ashoka's death, the Mauryan Empire disintegrated. There were tensions between Hindu and Buddhist sections of the ruling class, subjugated states rebelled, and external enemies seized fragments of territory.

The military superstructure had become ever more swollen: one Roman writer quotes figures of 600,000 infantry, 30,000 cavalry, and 9,000 elephants. But the Mauryan state remained a hastily assembled amalgam of smaller polities onto which an imperial apparatus had been imposed. The essential glue of a broad-based ruling class united by common culture, good communications, and effective mechanisms for social integration and political cohesion was lacking.

The Persian Empire was destroyed by foreign conquest. The Mauryan Empire imploded for lack of internal coherence. The Chinese Empire, by contrast, was destined to last for 2,000 years. It is to China that we now turn.

China: The Qin Empire

At the end of the third century BC, China was united by the Qin warlord Shi Huangdi. He ruled a territory five times larger than that of the Shang Dynasty of the Late Bronze Age. How had this been achieved?

China's Agricultural Revolution had begun around 6000 BC. The first farming villages were in the Yellow River valley of northern China. Pigs were domesticated and millet (later wheat) was cultivated on irrigated hillside terraces. Farming spread southwards from here across the vast Central Plain over the succeeding millennia. Much later, starting around 2000 BC, China's urban revolution produced a Bronze Age civilisation centred on ancient cities like Anyang. It culminated in the Shang Dynasty, which ruled north-eastern China for 400 years (1523–1027 BC).

Shang power rested on control of grain surpluses to pay for horses, chariots, and bronze. But it followed the trajectory of other Bronze Age civilisations: the dynamic of geopolitical competition caused Shang China to become over-militarised and overextended. Thus weakened, the Shang were overthrown by Zhou invaders from the west during the eleventh century BC.

Zhou China (1027–221 BC) was never effectively centralised; it remained divided into rival polities. In each state, the King appointed his own kinsmen, retainers, and officials to key territorial commands. These regional lords ruled from walled cities, extracting surplus from peasant cultivators in the surrounding countryside.

Civilisation advanced. Under the Zhou, rice was cultivated and buffalo herded in the Yangtze River Valley on the southern edge of the Central Plain. A network of canals was constructed for long-distance transport of surpluses and luxuries. The boundaries of agriculture extended into the mountains to the north, the west, and the south. But with only wooden and stone tools, surpluses were small. And with an infrastructure of walled cities and regional armies to support, the proportion creamed off by the Zhou elite was high. A peasant folk-song from Ancient China records the endless toil and political alienation of civilisation's human 'beasts of burden':

> Work, work from the rising sun,
> till sunset comes and the day is done.
> I plough the sod, and harrow the clod,
> and meat and drink both come to me,
> so what care I for the powers that be?

In the fourth and third centuries BC, regional violence reached a peak in 'the Age of Warring States'. But as the Zhou states of the east fought one another, a new power was rising in the west.

From around 500 BC the Chinese began iron-casting on a large scale. Huge quantities of cast-iron tools – axes, ploughs, hoes, spades, sickles, chisels, and knives – appear in the archaeological record. Iron also facilitated a military revolution engendered by the intensification of warfare. By increasing productivity, iron tools guaranteed the surpluses needed to support armies; and iron weapons increased the killing power of those armies.

The chariot was the shock weapon of Ancient China. These could now be greatly increased in number. But the chariot was also the weapon of a narrow warrior elite. Iron, on the other hand, put powerful weapons in the hands of infantry. An iron-tipped bolt fired from a crossbow could pierce the armour of a great lord. The iron sword, with its hard, razor-sharp edges, could slice through harness and horses and send him crashing from his chariot.

As well as more chariots, and more and better armed infantry, there were also advances in fortification, war machines, and siege warfare. Finally, as important as any of these, there was the introduction of cavalry, making a Chinese army a truly combined-arms force.

For many centuries, along the northern frontier of Zhou China, the Xiongnu horse nomads of the steppes, ancestors of the Huns and the Mongols, had waged campaigns of raid and plunder. The Xiongnu taught the Chinese the value of light horse-archers, who represented an unprecedented combination of mobility and firepower. The lesson was learned best in the semi-barbarous north-western state of Qin. Other Chinese rulers regarded this mountainous frontier kingdom, ruled by warrior-kings, as beyond the pale of civilisation. Qin stood in the front-line against the Xiongnu. Military effectiveness was the sole priority. Tradition and conservatism could not be allowed to stand in the way. The Qin were innovators by necessity.

Local lordship was weak in the far north-west. Taxes, labour services, and military conscription were imposed directly on independent peasant-farmers. The tribute-levying parasitism of the walled cities was much less burdensome than elsewhere.

So it was in wild Qin, on the outermost fringe of Zhou China, that the Iron Age revolution in agriculture and war achieved critical mass. The architect of the new order was the King of Qin. In the bloody climax of the Warring States period, Qin chariots, crossbowmen, and horse-archers defeated their Zhou rivals one after another.

The cost in human life was colossal. After one victory, 100,000 prisoners were beheaded. And after the final victory, 120,000 of the 'rich and powerful' were deported. The King of Qin now adopted the title Shi Huangdi – 'Divine Emperor'.

The victory created a centralised empire controlled by a military-bureaucratic elite. That it was five times larger than its Shang predecessor was due to the enlarged surpluses made possible by China's new iron-based farming technology. The road system was longer than that of the Roman Empire. The canal system was unparalleled. Weights and measures, road and wagon gauges, even the forms of agricultural tools were standardised.

The Great Wall of China, the greatest construction project in human history, was built by the First Emperor as a barrier against the Xiongnu. Some 3,600 km long, the original wall was 7.3 m high and wide enough for eight men to march abreast along the rampart. Set at varying intervals along the length were around 25,000 projecting towers. The wall took just 12 years to build. Its construction required the conscription of hundreds of thousands of forced labourers and consumed the grain surpluses of millions of peasants.

Created by conquest and terror, the short-lived Qin Empire was characterised by extreme centralisation, military-style exploitation, and murderous repression. Shi Huangdi, the First Emperor, has been portrayed as a warlord and tyrant of exceptional brutality, paranoia, and derangement. Perhaps he was; certainly his enemies considered him so. The regime attempted to destroy the intellectual underpinnings of dissent by ordering all books to be burnt. Scholars who had hidden books were either beheaded or worked to death on the Great Wall. The regime's political insecurity found expression in an attempt to erase all previous history and start again from a new 'year zero'.

The First Emperor's mausoleum, guarded by the now celebrated Terracotta Army, represents waste on a scale that dwarfs even the Great Pyramid and the Tomb of Tutankhamen. (The mausoleum itself is known from ancient descriptions; it has not yet been excavated.)

The Qin Dynasty collapsed after Shi Huangdi's death in 210 BC. A power struggle within the palace coincided with a series of aristocratic and peasant revolts across China. The eventual victor was a peasant revolutionary, Liu Pang, who became the first emperor of the new Han Dynasty (206 BC–AD 220).

The Han succession represented the consolidation of the Qin revolution. The centralised imperial superstructure was retained, but its ruling class of bureaucrats, officers, and scholars was no longer threatened by the arbitrary murderousness of an unstable dictator, and the exploitation of the masses was reduced sufficiently to quell popular discontent. The question was whether this new imperial order, the culmination of China's Iron Age transformation, would facilitate or hinder subsequent social development. Was the Chinese Empire a starting-gate or a barrier?

The Greek Democratic Revolution

Iron technology made possible huge increases in the productivity of human labour and the size of the surplus. Appropriation of the new wealth by centralised ruling classes allowed them to construct the Persian, Indian, and Chinese Empires. But iron technology also made possible an alternative. Because the raw material was abundant and the production process simple, iron tools and weapons were available to all. While bronze empowered only the aristocracy, iron had the potential to empower the masses.

Whether or not this happened depended on the outcome of the class struggle. In one small corner of the world, it was the masses who triumphed. The landed aristocracy was defeated by revolution from below, a radical experiment in participatory democracy was launched, and the conditions were created for one of the greatest explosions of cultural achievement in human history. The epicentre of the democratic revolution was the Greek city-state of Athens. Between 510 and 506 BC, revolutionary class struggles inside the city brought about a transition from dictatorship to democracy.

The movement passed through three distinct stages. First, a 30-year-old dictatorship was overthrown and replaced by an interim aristocratic government. Second, attempts by conservative aristocrats to block reform provoked a popular uprising and installed a government of democrats. Third, a Spartan military intervention in support of aristocratic counter-revolution was defeated by a second popular uprising.

The Athenian democracy was to last for almost two centuries. It was copied in other city-states across the Greek world, so that by the mid-fifth century BC virtually every city-state in the Aegean was a democracy.

Athenian democracy empowered the small farmers who made up the bulk of the citizen-body. During the sixth century BC, big landowners had attempted to expand their estates through debt-bondage. This mechanism was so central to the class struggle in the ancient world that it requires explanation.

Small farmers in a traditional society have no protection against hard times. Sometimes, in order to survive, they must borrow from the rich. Their only security for a loan is their land and their labour. The big landowners' main incentive to lend is the prospect of acquiring more land. If debts can be repaid, so be it. If they cannot, so much the better. Small farms can then be taken over, and small farmers may become debt-bondsmen, forced to work for the big landowner as serfs.

The Athenian masses broke this chain of debt and debt-bondage through struggle. They emerged at the end of the sixth century BC secure in possession of their property and their freedom. The basic building-blocks of Athenian society were not great estates but peasant *oikoi* (singular, *oikos*): patriarchal households based on ownership of a small farm or workshop.

The small citizen-farmers formed a city-state militia. The rich peasants, perhaps a third of the total, fought as heavy infantry (hoplites). The poorer peasants fought as light infantry or as rowers in warships (triremes: essentially rams powered by three banks of oarsmen).

War between the city-states was rife. Greece was divided into a thousand or more miniature polities, each competing for land, resources, and mercantile advantage. Democracy united citizens *within* each city, only to turn them into a military force *against* other cities. Democracy was the political expression of a *specific* citizen-body, not that of a *universal* social class. Athens, for example, the premier city-state democracy, was at war three years out of every four during the fifth and fourth centuries BC.

Success in land warfare depended on the size and resilience of the city's hoplite phalanx (a tight formation of spearmen). Success at sea depended on the number, speed, and manoeuvrability of the trireme fleet. Landownership and militia service made the small citizen-farmers of Athens into a revolutionary force. The democratic revolution of 510–506 BC was, on the one hand, a revolution of farmers, artisans, and petty-traders, and on the other, a revolution of citizen-soldiers and citizen-rowers.

Ancient Athenian democracy was both more limited and more profound than our own. Women, foreigners, and slaves had no political rights; only adult male citizens could vote. But a majority of the latter were working people, and the power they wielded was very real. The ten leading city officials (*strategoi*) stood for election every year. The Council of Four Hundred (*boule*), the main deliberative body, was selected by lot. The Popular Assembly (*ekklesia*), a mass, open-air meeting of all citizens, was the sovereign decision-making body of the state. Justice was administered by jury courts of up to 2,500 ordinary citizens. Ostracism was an election in reverse: anyone who secured 6,000 negative votes was expelled from the city for ten years.

The democratic constitution meant that small property was secure – only the rich paid taxes, and any decision to go to war was made by those who would have to fight. Anyone who has any doubts about the reality of Ancient Greek democracy should read the vitriolic opinions of its aristocratic enemies. The Greek world was bitterly divided between oligarchs and democrats – those who favoured the rule of 'the few' (*oligoi*) as against those who favoured the rule of 'the citizen-body' (*demos*). Hatred of democracy inspired much of Greek philosophy, history, and the arts. The work of intellectuals like Socrates, Plato, and Aristotle can be interpreted as in large part anti-democratic polemic.

In most ancient societies, education and culture were restricted to a tiny minority preoccupied with defending wealth and power. In Ancient Athens, 30,000 men shared political power. This created a huge mass base for education and culture. The result was an explosion of creativity. Much of the content of this was right-wing – a reaction *against* democracy more often than a celebration *of* it – but that does not alter the fact that it was democracy that made this possible and necessary. There were great architectural monuments like the Parthenon, and superb naturalistic representations of the human form in sculpture and painting. There was the history of Thucydides, the philosophy of Socrates, and the tragic drama of Aeschylus, Sophocles, and Euripides. Not least, there was a working-out in theory and practice of democratic politics. This is how Pericles, the greatest of Athens' democratic leaders, described the government of the city:

> Our constitution is called a democracy, because power is in the hands not of a minority, but of the whole people ... everyone is equal before the law ... what counts is not membership of a particular class, but the actual ability which the man possesses ... No one ... is kept in political obscurity because of poverty ... We give our allegiance to those whom we put in positions of authority ...

Equally impressive were the democracy's military achievements. Twice, the mighty Persian Empire attempted to subjugate Greece. Twice, the Athenians led the Greek resistance, first on land at Marathon in 490 BC, then at sea at Salamis in 480 BC. Though heavily outnumbered, though farmer-amateurs fighting military professionals, on each occasion the Athenians were victorious. In the Persian Wars, an army of free men, representing the most advanced political order the world had ever seen, triumphed over the crude militarism of a traditional empire. Yet, as we shall see, Greek democracy proved to be a historical cul-de-sac.

The Macedonian Empire

As well as being the foremost democracy in Greece, the city-state of Athens was also the richest. Its wealth came from silver mines in southern Attica, from maritime trade, and from its leadership of an anti-Persian alliance of Aegean city-states which gradually mutated into an empire.

The democratic form of Greek society contradicted the division of the Greek world into rival city-states. The former promoted the empowerment and cultural development of the working population. The latter meant military competition, war, and imperialism.

To the more conservative city-states of mainland Greece, Athens was a double threat. Athenian democracy made oligarchs elsewhere fearful of revolution from below; and the growing wealth of the Athenian Empire threatened the delicate balance of power between the rival city-states.

By the middle of the fifth century BC, democratic-imperialist Athens appeared poised to achieve hegemony over Greece. The Peloponnesian War of 431–404 BC pitted a conservative alliance led by Sparta against a democratic confederation led by Athens. When Athens was finally defeated, her empire was dissolved, and the democratic cause overshadowed by a new Spartan supremacy. The war was, in effect, the first phase of a protracted counter-revolution by which Greek aristocrats, Macedonian kings, and Roman viceroys destroyed the democratic experiment which had begun with the Athenian Revolution of 510–506 BC.

The second phase centred on the Battle of Chaeronea in 338 BC, when the Macedonian army of King Philip II defeated the combined army of the Greek city-states. Thereafter, the Greek city-states came under foreign rule. Formal democracy continued in Athens and some other cities for a while, but real power henceforward lay elsewhere. When, in 336 BC, the city-state of Thebes defied Alexander the Great, it was attacked, captured, and razed to the ground.

The Kingdom of Macedonia was a hybrid state. The royal court was a centre of Hellenism (Greek culture), and Philip II (360–336 BC) had forged an army modelled in part on the heavy infantry phalanx of the Greek city-states. But Macedonia was also a confederation of feudal landowners and tribal chieftains loosely strapped together by a would-be autocratic monarch. This makeshift state was plagued by internal revolt. The central preoccupation of the Macedonian King was to keep his throne and prevent the state from falling apart.

Instability spawned imperialism. The King's power rested on his ability to reward his barons for loyalty and service. The easiest way to fund royal patronage was through war and booty. Under Philip, the kingdom swelled into an empire in control of the whole of the southern Balkans. Conquest yielded booty and tribute, and these paid for soldiers. The Macedonian army expanded and became a fully professional force. Philip's distinctive contribution was to mix three separate elements to create a combined-arms force.

The hill tribes on the frontiers of the kingdom supplied light infantry. The aristocratic retinues of Macedonian lords formed a feudal-type heavy cavalry. And the free peasantry provided a Greek-style phalanx. The royal state combined the traditional martial qualities of its human raw material with the methods and principles of Greek warfare. The result was a military machine of unprecedented power.

In 338 BC, the Macedonian army had destroyed the independence of the Greek city-states at the Battle of Chaeronea in central Greece. Seven years later, at the Battle of Gaugamela in northern Iraq, it destroyed the Persian Empire. The Athenians had defeated the Persians in 490 and again in 480 BC, and then liberated the Greek cities of western Turkey. But they later succumbed to the relatively backward Kingdom of Macedonia. And it was then the Macedonians, under Philip's successor, Alexander the Great, not the Athenians, who conquered Western Asia. Why was this?

Only 15 per cent of Greece can be cultivated. The many, small, scattered agricultural plains are separated by mountain ranges. This was the basis for the independence of each city-state. In total, there were about a thousand city-states in the fifth century BC. Democracy was cocooned inside these tiny rival polities. Athens, the largest and richest, contained only about 30,000 adult male citizens. The total population – including women, children, foreigners, and slaves – was probably around 200,000. Greek democracy rested on a narrow and fragmented social base.

Geopolitical division meant endless local wars, and the struggle between the major states and their respective allies escalated into occasional full-scale wars. Greek society, always highly militarised, became more so as its surpluses increased and geopolitical rivalries intensified. The Peloponnesian War was the supreme expression of this tendency.

No state was ever strong enough to establish a lasting hegemony. Athens was defeated by Sparta in 404 BC. Sparta was in turn defeated by Thebes in 371 BC. The Greek city-states remained divided among themselves while Philip II, 'the Lion of the North', built the empire that would eventually subjugate them all.

At the same time, city-state democracy was eroded at home by growing militarisation. Long, distant, hard-fought campaigns saw the emergence of professional commanders, mercenary bands, and military specialists. Power in Greece was projected by hoplite spears. When these were wielded by citizen-farmers, democracy was strong. When wielded by professional mercenaries, it was undermined.

Ancient Greek civilisation was of unprecedented sophistication and dynamism, but it existed in sharp contradiction to the geopolitical and sociological framework within which it was set. Democracy was generalised neither within the city-state nor across city-states. The division of the Greek world into rival polities meant that, in the long run, military professionals gained ground at the expense of democratic assemblies. Macedonia, on the other hand, appropriated the advances of Greek civilisation and used them to create a military system capable of transforming a medium-sized royal state into a Balkan empire. Technique mattered, but so did size: only the King of Macedon controlled the territory and surpluses necessary to wage major wars of conquest and then to unite the Greek world.

Because Greece was united by force from above rather than by revolution from below, democracy was doomed. Greece became the logistical base for the conquest of Western Asia. Later, after the disintegration of Alexander's empire, it became a mere province within a wider Macedonian 'successor' state. The appropriation of the territory and surpluses of the Persian Empire – representing wealth hundreds of times greater than that of Greece – enabled the transformation of Greek civilisation from a network of city-states into a global imperial system.

Meanwhile, further west, a yet more dynamic form of military imperialism was rising. The ancient city-state of Rome was also being transformed into a global empire. In time, it would bring down even the mighty Macedonian kingdoms of the new world order in the East.

Roman Military Imperialism

Rome was a fusion of Greek-style citizenship with Macedonian-style militarism. The result was the most dynamic imperialist state in the ancient world.

Rome evolved from an Iron Age village in the ninth century BC into a Latin chieftain's hill-fort during the eighth century BC. It was then re-founded as a small town by Etruscan invaders in the mid to late seventh century BC, and thereafter ruled by a dynasty of Etruscan kings until about 510 BC. The last of these kings was overthrown in an aristocratic revolution, and the next two centuries were characterised by both internal class struggle and external imperial expansion. These two processes were closely linked.

The internal struggle – 'the Struggle of the Orders' – pitted patricians against plebeians. The former constituted a hereditary landowning aristocracy who enjoyed exclusive control over the state apparatus. Only patricians were admitted to the Senate, the ruling aristocratic assembly, and only patricians could hold senior magistracies, the top government posts.

Most plebeians were ordinary citizen-farmers. As in the Greek city-states, small farmers, with no margin against hard times, frequently got into debt. The rights of creditors were protected by laws enacted by patrician senators and enforced by patrician magistrates. Debt was the primary mechanism by which big estates were enlarged at the expense of small farms.

A minority of plebeians were better-off. Some were very wealthy. But they were still excluded from political power. The plebeian movement was therefore a class alliance between plebeian nobles and plebeian masses. Its principal weapon was secession – a military mass strike. Like the citizen-farmers of Greek city-states, the Roman plebs formed the city militia – the *legio* ('levy') – and their periodic refusals to fight were used to press social and political demands.

The Greek masses had taken revolutionary action and won full-blooded democracy. The Roman masses never succeeded in overthrowing the Senate. But they did make huge gains, the cumulative effect of which was a radical redistribution of power within Roman society. Rich plebeians were admitted to the Senate and senior magistracies. The mass of plebeians won effective veto powers. New laws had to be approved by the Assembly of the Plebs (a civic body), and any decision to go to war by the Assembly of the Centuries (a military body). Unpopular proposals could be blocked by new magistrates, the Tribunes of the Plebs.

The Struggle of the Orders ended with a class compromise and a mixed constitution. The ruling class was not overthrown, but its ranks were opened to newcomers, its political power was constrained, and its decisions became contingent on popular consent. This meant that the property of small farmers was protected against tax and debt. The ability of big landowners to enrich themselves at the expense of their fellow citizens was reined in. Instead, Roman aristocrats' ambition was redirected against foreign enemies.

The Roman aristocracy was highly competitive. Top families competed for senior state posts, and the rewards were power, prestige, and rich pickings. Wealth was the means rather than the end: aristocrats required wealth in order to accumulate political power. Rival factions built up retinues of dependants and clients through patronage. They amassed supporters and consolidated voting blocs through bribery. Families that failed to accumulate power declined. Membership of the aristocratic classes – senators and equestrians – depended increasingly on wealth. Patronage, public office, and the political power struggle were essential to maintaining class status.

Plebeian resistance to exploitation determined the form of intra-aristocratic competition. On the one hand, plebeian support became essential to factional power. On the other, plebeian landownership limited opportunities to amass wealth by enlarging existing estates.

War and conquest offered an alternative. Victory over foreign enemies meant booty (especially bullion), captives (who became slaves), and land (to create new farms and estates). Some was shared with ordinary citizen-legionaries, who thus acquired an interest in voting for war and fighting effectively. But the lion's share went to the state and its senator-generals.

Thus Rome became a predatory imperial system of robbery with violence. Instead of accumulating surplus by raising the rate of exploitation at home, the Roman ruling class seized by force the surplus, labour, and means of production controlled by foreign ruling classes.

During the fifth and fourth centuries BC, the Romans conquered peninsular Italy. During the third, they fought two major wars against the Carthaginian Empire for control of the Western Mediterranean. During the second, they fought two major wars against the Kingdom of Macedonia for control of Greece. The process of military accumulation was self-feeding. The surpluses seized in one war provided the resources to launch the next. Defeated ruling classes were 'Romanised': granted Roman citizenship, they were encouraged to adopt Roman elite culture and offered a share in future Roman conquests. This ensured a steady supply of new recruits for the expanding legions.

With the Struggle of the Orders resolved, Rome was stable at home but relentlessly aggressive abroad throughout the third and second centuries BC. The one depended on the other: social peace was funded by imperial surpluses. Thus Rome grew from a small Latin city-state in the late seventh century BC into the most powerful empire of antiquity by the late second century.

Iron Age technology had generated the massive surpluses necessary to construct the imperial polities of the first millennium BC – Achaemenid Persia, Mauryan India, Qin China, the Macedonian successor kingdoms, and the Roman Empire. But Roman imperialism had an exceptional dynamism and durability.

At the Battle of Gaugamela in 331 BC, the culmination of a four-year lightning campaign, Alexander the Great destroyed the Persian Empire. At the Battle of Cannae in 216 BC, Hannibal of Carthage inflicted an equally shattering defeat on the Roman Republic. But Rome refused to surrender and eventually triumphed. The critical difference was the social base of Roman imperialism. Achaemenid Persia levied tribute on subject peasants to pay professional soldiers. The army of the Roman Republic was a militia of free citizens. The Roman peasantry was not only numerous, but, unlike the Persian peasantry, it had a stake in the system. The Romans lost 80,000 men at Cannae. But their reserves are estimated to have been 700,000 infantry and 70,000 cavalry; and both aristocracy and peasantry had an interest in continuing the struggle.

The superiority of the Roman imperial polity was to be tested again in the great crisis of the Late Republic (133–30 BC).

The Roman Revolution

In 133 BC, Tiberius Gracchus was elected Tribune of the Plebs on a radical platform of land reform. Because of aristocratic opposition, he bypassed the Senate and passed his land bill into law by taking it direct to the Assembly of the Plebs. The following year, he was assassinated by a right-wing mob.

A new period of crisis had opened in Roman politics. It would last a century, passing through several phases of civil war, and at times threatening the survival of the empire. It eventually brought about a radical restructuring of the ruling class, a bureaucratic recasting of the state, and the military dictatorship of the emperors.

The crisis arose from the inability of the city-state form inherited from the past to accommodate the new social forces created by world empire. The patrician–plebeian nobility that controlled the Senate had ossified into an exclusive aristocratic caste hostile to 'new men'. The senatorial elite's monopoly of high office was resented by other sections of the aristocracy – minor senatorial families, second division 'equestrian' families, and many Italian provincial families now involved in the government and commerce of empire.

Inherited privilege was in contradiction with new social realities. After the mid-second century BC, the ruling class could not continue to rule in the old way. A minority favoured reform. Another minority were diehard reactionaries. The majority vacillated, but, preoccupied with the defence of property and privilege, usually favoured the reactionaries in a crisis. Because of this, the reformers looked to wider forces to defeat senatorial opposition.

Fighting wars of conquest on distant frontiers was ruinous for small farmers in Italy. The Third Spanish War (154–133 BC) required tens of thousands of soldiers. In a typical year, more than one in eight Roman citizens would be serving in the army. Many of those shipped to Spain remained there for years.

Farms were left uncultivated. Often they were bought up by big landowners. Roman citizens were then replaced by foreign slaves. The rich, explained one contemporary historian,

> ... used persuasion or force to buy or seize property that adjoined their own, or any other smallholdings belonging to poor men, and came to operate great ranches instead of single farms. They employed slave-hands and shepherds on these estates to avoid having free men dragged off the land to serve in the army.

The result was a double-edged social crisis. The decline of the Italian peasantry was draining the manpower pool on which the military vitality of the Republic depended. And a countryside populated with slaves posed a major security problem.

The new slave economy was centred in Sicily and southern Italy. Hundreds of thousands of captives were sold as slaves and sent to work on aristocratic estates. On three occasions slave revolts exploded across the region – in Sicily in 136–134 BC and again in 103–101 BC, and finally in mainland Italy in 73–71 BC. It is no accident that the crisis of the Late Republic began during the First Sicilian Slave War. The immediate concerns of Tiberius Gracchus and the reformist wing of the ruling class were army recruitment and internal security. The debates took place against a backdrop of burning Sicilian villas.

Many demobilised soldiers and ruined small farmers ended up in Rome. The fast-growing imperial city – fuelled by war booty, public works projects, and aristocratic patronage and consumption – sucked in impoverished 'surplus' citizens. The Roman mob became a factor in politics.

The growth of empire had also changed the relationship between Romans and non-Romans in Italy. At least half the legionaries were not Roman citizens, but 'Latin' or 'Allied' citizens. Increasingly, those who did an equal share of the fighting demanded an equal share in the spoils. The franchise became an explosive issue. The Social War of 91–88 BC was a full-scale civil war between Romans and Italians fought on the issue of equal political rights.

Italy was filled with combustible material: decayed senators, equestrian officials, and provincial gentry; small farmers ruined by debt; demobilised conscripts living in poverty after years fighting at the front; the swelling mass of the urban poor; and the many non-Romans who served the state but were excluded from its politics.

But the Roman Revolution – for revolution it became – had this peculiarity. No single class among the discontented was able to dominate the movement. None was able to establish leadership over the others by offering a coherent vision of a world transformed and a strategy for achieving it. None was able to provide a revolutionary alternative. The aristocratic opposition feared the popular masses and threats to their property. Small farmers feared the landless poor. Free citizens feared the competition of slaves. Romans feared the dilution of citizen privileges with the mass enfranchisement of Italians.

The popular movement, therefore, was a multi-class alliance riddled with contradictions. It was this that made the Roman Revolution a complex, convoluted, century-long process.

Reform through the Senate was blocked. The Populists (*populares*: those who favoured the rule of 'the People') remained a minority of the ruling class, unable to bring about a revolution from above against the entrenched opposition of the Optimates (*optimates* or 'best men': those who favoured the rule of the Senate). But without a revolutionary class able to break the impasse, only military force could decide the matter. The Roman Revolution became, therefore, a struggle of warlords.

Ambitious politicians sought prestigious and lucrative military commands. Booty and veterans became high-value counters in the game of Roman politics. The revolution was transformed into civil war between Populist and Optimate generals, Marius against Sulla, then Caesar against Pompey.

The decisive figure was Julius Caesar. A top-ranking aristocrat, single-minded careerist, and murderous imperialist, he was also a brilliant commander, politician, and reformer. Caesar embodied the contradictions of the Roman Revolution whose principal protagonist he was.

Caesar was victorious in the Civil War of 49–45 BC, but, being the leader of a popular movement rather than a revolutionary class, he was forced to seek an accommodation with the old order. In the short run, this proved impossible. The ruling class was too divided and embittered. Caesar attempted to straddle the contradictions through personal dictatorship – something that culminated in his assassination and a renewal of civil war.

The senatorial opposition led by Brutus and Cassius was quickly defeated by the leaders of Caesar's faction, Antony and Octavian. But these two then divided the empire between them and set about building rival power bases. The final struggle of the Roman Revolution was therefore a factional civil war between Antony and Octavian.

Octavian became Caesar Augustus, the first Roman emperor. He founded a military dictatorship based on 'new men', moderate reform, and imperialist war. His regime represented the final transformation of an Italian city-state into a bureaucratically administered global empire. But even this, the most successful of the ancient empires, contained the seeds of its own decay and eventual disintegration.

4
The End of Antiquity
c. 30 BC–AD 650

St Augustine preaches Christianity to King Ethelbert of Kent,
c. AD 597. Nineteenth-century book illustration.

The early medieval world inherited rich cultural traditions from the ancient
empires. German and Arab warlords dressed up as Roman, Byzantine, and
Persian emperors.

The decline and fall of the Roman Empire, which had embodied the greatest achievements of the Iron Age civilisations of the first millennium BC, was of global significance. From the disintegration of the imperial superpower emerged the new social forces and geopolitical order that would form the basis of medieval Europe.

The Iron Age empires, though writ large across the map, shared many of the weaknesses of their Bronze Age predecessors. Political unity was a function of military power, not of economic, social, or cultural homogeneity. Imperial rulers ratcheted up exploitation to accumulate surplus and waste it on war. Society was organised in rigid, top-down rankings of status groups. Creativity and innovation were suppressed, and the common people became mere hewers of wood and drawers of water. Technology stagnated, poverty festered, and alienation spread. The Iron Age empires eventually proved as conservative as the Bronze Age empires had been.

Because of this, though the collapse of the Roman Empire represented the passing of an entire social order, this process did not give rise to new forces capable of raising humanity to a higher cultural level. It merely resulted in what Marx called 'the common ruin of the contending classes'.

In this chapter, we analyse the internal contradictions which doomed the Roman Empire, the character of the ruling classes (mainly Germanic, Gothic, and Arab) which displaced it, and the creation, in the context of Rome's crisis, of the three great monotheistic religions, Judaism, Christianity, and Islam.

The Crisis of Late Antiquity

The Roman Empire represented a powerful fusion of citizenship and imperialism. Citizenship provided an expanding social base of stakeholders and soldiers. Conquered elites were slowly assimilated and acculturated: they were allowed to become 'Roman' and share the benefits of imperial rule. Imperialism, at the same time, provided a continual flow of booty, slaves, and land. This strengthened the state, enriched the ruling class, secured the allegiance of subject elites, and funded the patronage which bound client groups to the system.

But it came at a heavy price. Empire and civilisation are expensive. While some benefit, others lose. Roman rule safeguarded property and power. But the wealth of the army, the towns, and the villas depended on a system of exploitation in which taxes, rents, interest payments, and labour services were extracted from the rural population.

The majority of the inhabitants of the Roman Empire worked on the land as peasants, labourers, serfs, or slaves. They were the beasts of burden on whose backs empire and civilisation were built. At first, the burden – the rate of exploitation – was relatively moderate and sustainable. Much was taken, but enough was left to enable peasant families to feed themselves, sow their fields, restock their pastures, and obtain the essentials of Iron Age rural life in local markets. This was possible because others paid a much heavier price. The empire was subsidised by wars of conquest. The defeated were robbed to enrich the victors. The victims paid the bulk of the cost of supporting the state, the army, and the rich. As long as the empire continued to expand, robbery at home was moderated by robbery abroad.

The system was inherently expansionist. It was fed by the military appropriation of foreign surpluses. Its vitality therefore depended on the continuing availability of such surpluses. After each imperial leap, another became necessary if the system was not to face stagnation and crisis. But foreign surpluses were a finite resource. By the first century AD, Roman military imperialism was running up against barriers to further expansion.

The limits of Graeco-Roman imperial civilisation corresponded with the limits of Iron Age agriculture. Iron Age technology had created an extensive plough-based agriculture stretching from southern Britain to Syria, from the Rhine and the Danube in Europe to the Atlas Mountains of North Africa. This was an opulent land, full of cultivated fields, villages, and hard-working peasants. Surpluses were large. Those who organised themselves to seize these surpluses could build armies and cities. But beyond the plough-lands lay wilderness: the hills of northern Britain, the forests of Germany, the deserts of Arabia and North Africa. And when imperial armies marched into the wilderness, they became mired in unwinnable guerrilla wars against scattered and elusive opponents who were too impoverished to yield a profit even if they could be subjugated.

In 53 BC, a Roman army of 30,000 had been destroyed by Parthian horse-archers at the Battle of Carrhae in Syria. In AD 9, another Roman army of 30,000 was annihilated by German tribesmen at the Battle of the Teutoburg Forest. In AD 208–11, the final Roman attempt to conquer northern Britain was defeated by guerrilla resistance. 'Let no one escape utter destruction at our hands', was the chilling injunction of the Roman emperor Septimus Severus to his men. 'Let not the infant still carried in its mother's womb, if it be male, escape its fate.' But they did escape. Severus died at York, and Scotland was never conquered. In the bogs and glens of the British North, the imperial leviathan, lashing out in the mist and drizzle, was reduced to despair by bands of blue-painted skirmishers.

The Roman Empire, then, had limits. Its foundation stone was Iron Age agriculture. It depended on cultivated land and abundant labour to yield the large surpluses necessary to support the army, the ruling class, and the essential infrastructure of roads, forts, and towns. War was profitable where the plough ran. But it was waste where it did not, and the empire became overextended when armies entered the wilderness.

Expansion peaked in the second and first centuries BC, slowed sharply after the early first century AD, and then ceased almost entirely after the early second century AD. The flow of war booty was cut off. External subsidy ceased. The Roman Empire became entirely dependent on internally generated resources.

Yet the cost of empire and civilisation did not diminish. A strong army and extensive fortifications were required to defend thousands of miles of open frontier. The cohesion of the imperial elite and the loyalty of its client groups, above all the army's rank and file, depended on luxury consumption and state largesse.

From the first century AD onwards, and with increasing intensity, especially from the late second century, the imperial state faced chronic financial crises. Its response – increased agrarian surplus extraction to maintain its politico-military infrastructure – led inexorably to a slow spiral of economic decline. Increases in taxation, forced labour, and military requisitioning ruined marginal peasant-farmers. This shrank the tax base – such that in the next round taxes had to be raised even further, pushing another tranche of farms over the edge. And so it went on. The Late Roman imperial state, increasingly militarised and totalitarian, ended up consuming its own socio-economic capital in its effort to maintain essential expenditure. The military predator had turned cannibal.

These pressures had three main political effects. First, the ruling class repeatedly fragmented along regional lines, each group attempting to retain control of its own surpluses and soldiers. Civil wars, usually between army factions led by rival emperors in different parts of the empire, became endemic.

Second, foreign invasions became more frequent and increasingly menacing. On the European frontiers they involved large barbarian tribal confederations, and in the East the dynamic Sassanian Empire, based in Iran and Iraq. Rome's military decline is symbolised by two battles. At Adrianople in Thrace (Bulgaria) in AD 378, the entire field army of the Eastern Roman Empire was destroyed by the Goths. Sixteen years later, at the River Frigidus in the Julian Alps on Italy's north-east frontier, the bulk of the reconstituted army of the Eastern Roman Empire was formed of Gothic mercenaries. Such was the internal crisis of finance and manpower that the Roman Empire had become dependent on 'barbarian' soldiers.

The third consequence of the empire's financial crisis was a resurgence of class struggle. The local peasantry, squeezed by the demands of the military-bureaucratic state, reduced to serf status and subject to ever-harsher exploitation, found ways to fight back. Many farms were abandoned. Social bandits stalked much of the countryside. Resistance to tax-collectors, press-gangs, and bailiffs was widespread. And sometimes, discontent spilled over into peasant insurrection and the creation of rural communes.

Ancient aristocratic writers tell of mysterious rural rebels called *bagaudae*, under whose rule people lived by popular laws, peasants made speeches, death sentences were pronounced under an oak tree and recorded on pieces of bone, and 'anything goes'. Apparently, under the *bagaudae*, 'the Bretons were slaves of their own domestics'. Here, it seems, dimly understood and darkly described, we have a world turned upside down, a world without landlords and tax-collectors.

Fragmentation, invasion, and internal revolt: these symptoms of imperial decline reflected the rottenness of the system. Consequently, between AD 410 and 476 the Western Roman Empire disintegrated, with successive chunks of territory taken over by barbarian war-bands until eventually nothing was left.

By the end of the fifth century, Europe had been divided into a patchwork of independent proto-states. A new world order had been forged in the firestorms of Late Antiquity. The primary agents of this transformation were tribal confederations from Central and Eastern Europe and from Central Asia.

The Germans, the Goths, and the Huns

The Eurasian steppe is a belt of land several hundred miles wide which extends from the Hungarian Plain to the Pacific Ocean. A grassland of climatic extremes, devoid of trees, it was, from earliest prehistory until medieval times, populated mainly by nomadic pastoralists.

The history of Europe, Turkey, Persia, India, and China is punctuated by military crises brought on by incursions of steppe nomads from their homeland. But it was the Huns who, between the 370s and 450s AD, precipitated the collapse of the Western Roman Empire.

The Huns combined hunting and gathering with the herding of horses, cattle, sheep, and goats. The barrenness of the steppe and the primitiveness of their way of life meant that numbers were few and scattered, social organisation loose and non-hierarchical. Specialisation was extreme. The Huns were first-class horsemen. They fought tribal wars as light cavalry armed with composite bow, lasso, and sword. The bow and the lasso were the equipment of the steppe; the sword was a prized trade good.

It is impossible to be sure why the Huns began to move west in the mid-fourth century AD. But their poverty meant that they had no margin of safety: drought meant death on the steppe. So probably they were set in motion by an ecological crisis. Violence, subjugation, and westward expansion were an escape route from an exhausted, overpopulated homeland.

When they reached the Ukraine, they overran the Ostrogoths (Eastern Goths). As they pressed further west, they drove the Visigoths (Western Goths) to seek refuge inside the Eastern Roman Empire. The tensions between Goths and Romans then exploded into war, and the army of the Eastern Roman Empire, based in Constantinople, was annihilated at the Battle of Adrianople in AD 378. The steppe nomads, indirectly, were beginning to remake the old world.

As they did so, they were themselves transformed. The Goths, like the German tribes further west on the Roman Empire's Rhine and Upper Danube frontiers, were prosperous peasant-farmers. When conquered by the Huns, they were forced to pay tribute to their new masters. The steppe nomads were therefore enriched by agricultural surpluses, and they used these surpluses to increase their military retinues and thus their ability to make further conquests.

Yet greater prizes awaited them within the Roman Empire itself. And, as the Goths had proved at Adrianople, the empire was militarily much weakened. The Roman provincial peasantry had been turned into serfs. Exploitation and alienation had depleted the traditional manpower base of Roman military imperialism. Increasingly, instead of citizen-legionaries, Roman emperors relied on bribes and barbarian mercenaries to defend their frontiers. At times the Huns were hired as Roman allies. Sometimes they might be bought off. Either way, Roman treasure was added to Gothic tribute to complete the transformation of the Huns from tribal nomads into continent-straddling militarists: a transformation marked by the accession of Attila as King of the Huns in AD 434.

At its height, Attila's empire extended from the Baltic to the Alps, from the Rhine to the Caspian. Into the Hunnic capital – half-permanent village, half-nomadic encampment – flowed tribute from within the empire and subsidies and bribes from beyond. Half a century earlier, the Huns had fought as tribal forces of a few hundred under elected war-chiefs. Now, war was a permanent condition, the militarisation of their social world complete, the power of their supreme commander absolute.

The Hunnic war-state fed off the decay of the Roman Empire, devouring the surpluses made possible by the Iron Age revolution in technique. In the heyday of Roman military imperialism, the Roman surplus had supported armies of free peasant citizen-soldiers. In its decline, a mercenary military imperialism evolved in which the surplus fed a monstrous nomad empire centred on the Hungarian Plain.

As a war leader, Attila controlled the military surpluses, and as war was now permanent, so too was his authority. The King was able to sever the anchor-chain of tribal obligations and social constraints that had once limited the power of any single individual. But the vast network of patronage that bound Attila's client-kings, subject-chiefs, and leading retainers depended on an unbroken flow of tribute and subsidies, plunder and prestige goods. So Attila was a robber-baron, a warmonger, a restless conqueror pushing ever onwards. Dynamism was inherent in the Hunnic state.

Attila was the 'Scourge of God' to the Late Roman ruling classes. Many of the poor saw him differently. Huns and Gallic *bagaudae* sometimes formed alliances against the Romano-Gallic landlords in the 440s AD. But the kingdom of the Huns was too crude, predatory, and unstable to become a force for progressive social change. When Attila attacked Gaul (France and Belgium) in AD 451, his lunge westwards lacked diplomatic finesse. The *bagaudae* had been alienated and did not move, and Romano-Gallic landlords and Visigothic free peasants had joined forces. So the West, briefly united, inflicted a decisive defeat on Attila at the Battle of Châlons. He was forced to withdraw to his Central European heartland. Two years later he was dead, and his empire disintegrated, destroyed by territorial struggles between his successors and revolts from below among the subject-peoples.

The intervention of the steppe nomads had been sudden and catastrophic, but they made no positive contribution to history. The Western Roman Empire fragmented into myriad barbarian kingdoms ruled by Germans or Goths. The Eastern Roman Empire ossified, becoming bureaucratic, conservative, and inert. But the Hunnic Empire simply vanished from the face of the earth.

Why was its collapse so sudden and total? In the space of a generation, the Huns had been transformed from nomadic pastoralists into military predators. They ceased to have any productive forces of their own, depending entirely on their ability to extort from others the tribute, subsidy, and plunder essential to sustain their polity.

They were few in number, but their domains were vast, so theirs was an overextended empire subject to extreme manpower shortage. Fear and force enabled them to sustain the system as long as it appeared powerful. But an end to expansion would have cut off the flow of extorted surplus necessary to sustain the state infrastructure of chieftains, retainers, and warriors. Thus was over-extension inherent in a dynamic system of robbery with violence which lacked its own productive base. There was no ballast, only an engine hurtling through history to its own destruction. Yet the violence of that engine's motion had propelled the Germans and the Goths into the Western Roman Empire, ensuring the eventual collapse of the imperial state apparatus and its replacement by a patchwork of new states ruled by barbarian kings.

The change, however, was less than might appear. Much of ancient civilisation was embraced by the barbarian kings, so that Rome contributed richly to the making of the medieval world. The principal vehicle of cultural transmission was the Christian Church. To grasp the significance of this, we must backtrack to analyse the growth of monotheistic religion within the womb of an ancient pagan culture rooted in the prehistoric past.

Mother-Goddesses and Power-Deities

Myth, ritual, and religion are multifaceted. Their deepest root lies amid the insecurities of primeval hunter-gatherer existence. Anxiety about the food-quest was soothed by magical representations of the beasts of the hunt in art, dance, music, and personal ornament.

Early farmers, equally prey to the vicissitudes of nature, conceived of the earth as a mother-goddess, a fount of fertility and food, who could be petitioned and bribed into delivering her bounty. The fertility deities of early farmers were invariably female. The woman – menstruating, giving birth, lactating – was the obvious symbol of natural fecundity. But there was another reason she was female: women were powerful in pre-class societies. Descent was often matrilineal (through the female line), residence matrilocal (in the wife's village, not the husband's), and authority matriarchal (where women's voices were predominant).

Why was this? Because women were the fixed points in simple societies based on cooperative labour and collective ownership. Their child-bearing and child-feeding functions made them less mobile, both geographically and socially, and the absence of private property and the privileges to which private property gives rise precluded alternative sources of social power. Women were society's centres of gravity. Men orbited around them. The great earth-mother goddess of early farmers was the mirror image of a social reality.

Private property, class division, and state power came into being simultaneously, the one dependent on the others. Sharing and a rough equality were intrinsic to communal property. But the division of land into private farms, or of cattle into separate herds, allowed some to grow rich at the expense of others. The resulting tensions called for some sort of control if society was not to fragment. The state – armed bodies of men – evolved to defend the new property-based status quo. And now it was men who had power. For it was men, not women, who herded the stock and ploughed the fields. When stock and fields were held in common, everyone benefitted. When they were in private hands, they enriched and empowered only those who worked them.

What Frederick Engels called 'the world historic defeat of the female sex' was represented in myth and ritual. The old mother-goddesses were cast from their thrones, replaced by a new generation of male power-deities. The Greek heaven was ruled by Zeus, the Roman by Jupiter, the Jewish by Yahweh, the Arab by Dushara, and so on, across the world. And just as the old earth-mothers symbolised the forces of nature, the new power-deities symbolised the forces of tribes, city-states, and empires.

At Olympus, the holiest site in ancient Greece, the oldest cults were those of the mother-goddesses, Gaia, Rhea, Hera, and Demeter. But by the Classical Age, the fifth and fourth centuries BC, they had long since been displaced, and it was Zeus who was honoured with the richest offerings, the grandest temple, and the famous games. In the 'War of the Giants' myth, Zeus leads the new gods to victory over the Titans – his father Kronos and the other old gods. Zeus represents order, patriarchy, and civilisation. Kronos is the embodiment of barbarism: his is a world of chaos and matriarchy. Matriarchy became myth-code for a world of disorder. When the Greek hero Agamemnon returns home from the Trojan War, he is slain by his own wife, Clytemnestra, who has taken another man as her lover and king. The world is turned upside down and the moral order collapses. Then Agamemnon's son Orestes slays Clytemnestra to avenge his father. Murder begets murder. A cycle of slaughter is the price of woman-power.

Misogynist myth sanctified Greek civilisation's patriarchal order. The male-run *oikos* (a property-owning household) was the basic building-block of the social structure. The city-state was run by assemblies of citizen-men, of *oikos* patriarchs, of small property-owners. Not the least of the contradictions that doomed Greek democracy was the political exclusion, social segregation, and domestic oppression of women.

Other social tensions also found expression in the myth-worlds of ancient peoples. Myths are good to think with. They provide ways of describing, narrating, and analysing social contradictions. They represent and project social norms, but they also debate them when they are contested. Who are we? Where have we come from? Who are our friends, who our enemies? In a divided world, what is it that defines and unites us? Cultural identities are forged in struggle, and it was myth, ritual, and religion that give them form and expression in the ancient world.

Rome was a class-ridden, militaristic, imperial state. Little wonder that its supreme deity was a war-god. Jupiter *Optimus Maximus* – Best and Greatest – was the patron deity of the city-state of Rome. As such, in the totemic form of an eagle, he was carried into battle on the standard of every Roman legion. As such, he was worshipped at special altars in every army camp in the empire. And as such, he was the recipient of sacrifice and honour at the climax of every Roman triumph, when victorious troops and enslaved captives paraded through the city, and defeated enemy leaders were ritually strangled in the Forum.

But if the violence and exploitation of empire had their religious expression, so did the resistance of the oppressed. Myth could both legitimate the social order and inspire resistance to it. One ancient faith stands out in this respect. Over centuries of struggle it was fashioned into a cudgel of counter-cultural resistance – resilient, ineradicable, deep-rooted in the hearts and minds of the common people of Palestine. Later, it would produce two offspring, also weapons of ideological struggle, and between them, these three religious faiths would eventually conquer half the world. They are Judaism, Christianity, and Islam. Though capable of endless recasting as deeply conservative ideologies, the three great monotheistic religions produced by the contradictions of the ancient world owe their extraordinary power to their origins in the myths and rituals of the oppressed.

Judaism, Christianity, and Islam

In 537 BC, Cyrus the Great, the Persian ruler of Babylonia (modern Iraq), granted the descendants of a group of Jewish aristocratic exiles permission to 'return' to their homeland. Cyrus wanted loyalists in control of newly conquered imperial territory. The Jewish exiles aspired to become a new ruling class.

The return from Babylonian captivity is one of the central events in Judaeo-Christian historical tradition. The reality was that the Jewish elite was planted in Palestine as the quisling administration of an imperial superpower. But they brought with them an ideological powder-keg. Forged in decades of disunity, defeat, and dispersal, the Jewish cult of a supreme power-deity, Yahweh, had been transformed into an intolerant monotheism that denied the existence of all other gods.

In the past, the Jewish prophets had railed in vain against false idols. Now, the frustrated nationalism of an exiled leadership found expression in Yahweh's claim to worldwide dominion. Political impotence had its religious counterpoint in divine megalomania. If, instead of a pantheon of warring deities, there was one all-powerful god, then history moved to a single divine purpose, and those chosen for God's special favour were bound to win out in the end – just so long as they remained loyal and obedient.

The myths of Abraham and Moses and the legends of Saul, David, and Solomon were largely constructs of the sixth century BC: a rewriting of Jewish history and the proclamation of a new set of religious 'truths' designed to legitimise the tenuous grip on power of a newly installed Jewish elite that claimed descent from these heroic founders. This was the belligerent myth-history of an embattled elite fighting for its place in the world.

Thus, the one and only god was Yahweh, the Jews were his Chosen People, and Palestine was their Promised Land. This, though, was the view of a marginal sect, a small exile group whose restorationist ambition took the form of religious fantasy. Alone, they could have done nothing but hope and pray. It was Persian imperialism that lifted them out of historical oblivion and placed them on a global stage. It was Cyrus the Great who planted the New Judaism in Palestine and allowed it to flourish.

It proved to be a complex hybrid. The Jews were overshadowed by greater peoples – the Persians, the Greeks, and the Romans. Palestine was a small country, occasionally capable of precarious independence, more usually subordinate to a foreign empire. The Jewish aristocracy was therefore torn between fighting for independence and collaborating with imperialism. The risks of fighting were high. Defeat could mean losing everything – but so could victory if mass mobilisation to fight for independence conjured a popular revolutionary movement from below. The Jewish peasantry was also torn – between fear of authority, a sense of powerlessness, and a deep-rooted hatred of the exploiter. So Judaism splintered into rival sects, some aristocratic and collaborationist, others popular, radical, and calling openly for resistance.

Religion welded the Jewish masses into a powerful revolutionary force on at least four occasions. When a Seleucid Greek king attempted to replace the worship of Yahweh with that of Zeus, he provoked nationwide resistance, and the Maccabaean Revolt of 167–142 BC eventually secured an independent Jewish state.

As Roman rule tightened, the Jews rose in revolt three more times, in AD 66–73, 115–17, and 132–6. Each time, the fighting was long, hard, and bloody. Each time, tens of thousands were killed, hundreds of thousands displaced. The final revolt was suppressed with such genocidal ferocity that the Jewish population was reduced to a rump. Thereafter, the ten million Jews of the ancient world were almost entirely a people of the diaspora, living mainly in towns across the eastern Mediterranean.

Among those involved in the Jewish anti-imperialist movement was a preacher from Nazareth called Jesus. A charismatic radical, he attracted a growing following among the village poor, so he was arrested, tried, and executed. The group he had founded survived as a small sect, but it soon split into two distinct tendencies. One remained committed to the Jewish national-revolutionary movement. This group was destroyed in the defeat of the First Jewish Revolt of AD 66–73. The other, led by Paul of Tarsus, a Greek-educated Jewish merchant, adopted a conservative ideology of spiritual – not material – redemption. And this, the Pauline Christians argued, was a message not just for Jews, but for all of humanity.

The New Testament, which records the mission of Jesus and the early history of the Church, is a work of revisionism, written by Pauline Christians of the Jewish diaspora in the aftermath of the defeat of the First Revolt. Jesus, it turned out, was both a man *and* a god, his kingdom was not of this earth but of heaven, and his message was universal and spiritual rather than revolutionary. The Gospel writers created a depoliticised and de-nationalised Jesus capable of surviving the 'war on terror' which swept the Roman Empire in the wake of the Revolt.

Yet something of the original remained. In a way that the awesome power-deities of the pagan pantheon could not, the all-powerful and supremely benevolent Christian god offered what Marx called 'a heart in a heartless world' – a message with a strong appeal to the oppressed of the Roman Empire.

Pauline Christianity was a potent synthesis. It represented a fusion of Jewish prophecy and popular preaching with an essentially Greek tradition of salvation cult. Jesus the Jewish prophet was transformed into Jesus the universal saviour-god. To this were added two distinctively Christian elements, both derived from the religion's roots in the Jewish revolutionary movement: in contrast to the rigid class hierarchies of Roman society, the idealisation of an egalitarian and democratic community; and, in place of the greed and violence legitimised by mainstream paganism, an emphasis on compassion and cooperation.

The exploitation and oppression of the Roman Empire inflicted misery on millions, but the violence of the state usually prevented effective resistance. This was the contradiction that allowed the Christian Church to grow and grow. Recruiting among slaves, women, and the poor, the Church was viewed with deep suspicion and was repeatedly battered by repression. It did not work. The men and women burnt, eaten by animals, or nailed to wooden crosses provided the Early Church with a roll call of martyrs as impressive as any in history.

By the early fourth century AD, the Church had become the most powerful ideological apparatus in the Mediterranean world, with an underground network of priests, congregations, and meeting places extending across the empire. Many army officers, government officials, and wealthy landowners eventually converted, and in AD 312 the Emperor Constantine the Great decided to adopt Christianity himself, to legalise the religion, and to make the state the protector and patron of the Church. Before the century was out, his successor, Theodosius the Great, would make paganism illegal and hand over the temple estates to the Church.

Judaeo-Christian monotheism was now recast as an ideology of state power, empire, and war. The Roman emperor became at once a defender of civilisation against barbarism, a crusader for the Church against paganism, and a champion of Christian orthodoxy against heresy. In consequence, Christianity became as fragmented as Judaism by the social contradictions it encompassed. Competition between rival factions and states, and tensions between antagonistic classes, destroyed the ideal of a single, universal Church.

The growing political division between an Eastern Roman Empire based on Constantinople and a Western Roman Empire based on Rome – a division which became complete and permanent after AD 395 – was mirrored in the separation of the eastern Orthodox and western Catholic traditions. The class struggle between landlords and peasants similarly found expression in the split between the more conservative Catholic and more radical Donatist Churches in North Africa. Every group, pursuing different and sometimes conflicting aims, claimed the one all-powerful god as its ally. At its most extreme, the ideological ferment could produce entirely new offspring, just as Judaism had brought forth Christianity. One such development was destined to produce another great world religion.

Out of the cultural crucible of two Arabian caravan-cities, where ancient pagan traditions from the desert mingled with versions of the Jewish and Christian faiths, emerged a new synthesis of monotheism: Islam. This faith would bind together the traders and tribal nomads of the Arabian Desert and turn them into a revolutionary force capable of bringing down the ancient empires of the Eastern Romans and the Persians in a whirlwind military campaign of a few short years. These conquerors would then build a new civilisation which fused the language and religion of Arabia with the cities, techniques, learning, and arts inherited from antiquity.

The Arab-Islamic Conquests

Turmoil is intellectually fertile. It created each of the great religions. Judaism was forged in the struggle of an embattled ruling class to establish itself in Palestine in the sixth century BC. Christianity has its origins in the bitterness of the oppressed under Roman imperial rule during the first century AD. Islam was a third branch from the same stem. Its early growth, in the 620s AD, took place beneath the gaze of history, a matter of minor squabbles in two remote desert towns in the Hijaz region of western-central Arabia. But its violent eruption would change the world forever.

The Huns had been nomads without any leavening of towns, merchants, and urban culture. Cut adrift from the lifeways of the steppe, they were weightless. Because of this, their military onslaught streaked across dying antiquity and, equally suddenly, was extinguished without a trace. Not so the Arabs. The desert nomads, herders of sheep and goats, breeders of camels and horses, were much like the Huns. But the camel, first domesticated in about 1000 BC, could cross great expanses of desert carrying heavy burdens, and many of the camel breeders had become merchants. Luxury goods arriving at the coastal ports of the Gulf, southern Arabia, and the Red Sea were then carried overland to the Levant and the Mediterranean by Arab traders. Mecca, Medina, and other Arabian towns grew rich on this trade. The towns, along with the oasis villages on the desert routeways, were also home to communities of artisans and cultivators.

In Arabia, in short, in contrast to the Central Asian steppe, there were complex settlements, social classes, and urban culture. In particular, coexisting with the tribal customs, oral traditions, and polytheistic beliefs of the desert nomads, there was the written Arabic and Judaeo-Christian religion of traders and townsmen.

Often, too, there was conflict. Long-distance trade cut through ties of kinship and tribal allegiances. The desert raid was booty to the tribesman, but robbery to the trader. The tribal blood feud offered protection to local kin, but none to a trader in a distant town.

In places like Mecca and Medina, where nomads and peasants bartered, tribesmen and traders squabbled, and the traditions of desert and town collided, men and women discussed how the world worked – or rather, how they felt it should work. When they did this, they viewed matters in a religious frame. For, in the early medieval world, to consider such things was to reflect on God's purpose.

Amid this ferment, and experiencing it as inner mental anguish, was a young man of a minor Meccan merchant family. He had visions and believed that God – Allah in Arabic – spoke directly to him. He persuaded a small group of followers that this was true, and some of them began to write down the words he reported Allah as saying to him. His name was Muhammad and his reports of Allah's words became the Koran.

Islam retained many of the Judaeo-Christian myths and traditions. Abraham and Moses are prophets for Jews, Christians, and Muslims alike. Also common to all three religions is their universalism. Islam cut through both tribal codes and class differences. In place of the many competing gods of rival tribes, there was now one supreme deity. Where clan loyalty and the blood feud had reigned, there were now universal rules of conduct. Instead of abuse of the oppressed – women, slaves, the poor, the marginal – being a matter of indifference, compassion, charity, and protection became moral imperatives. The Muslims formed a community (*umma*) based on formal equality, universal rights, and a single code of laws. Islam was an attempt to create order in a fractured world.

Little wonder that Muhammad encountered fierce opposition. His mission began around AD 620, but he was driven out of Mecca in AD 622 and forced to find refuge in Medina. There, he built the nucleus of what was to become a mass movement. To his growing politico-religious cadre of eager young men and women, he joined traders seeking commercial advantage, tribal leaders bent on plunder, and townsmen and peasants longing for peace and civil order. Returning to Mecca with an army in AD 630, he was victorious, and the Muslims took control of western-central Arabia.

When Muhammad died in AD 632, his movement might have disintegrated, torn apart by the traditional raiding and feuding of the desert tribes. But it did not, for the first two caliphs (successors), Abu Bakr and Umar, chose to direct the violent energy of Arabia against external targets: the Persian and Byzantine (Eastern Roman) Empires.

When the Arab-Islamic armies struck, the old empires shattered. The great cities of antiquity fell like dominoes – Damascus in Syria in AD 636, Ctesiphon in Iraq in AD 637, Cairo in Egypt in AD 639, and Alexandria in Egypt in AD 642. Within ten years of his death, the followers of Muhammad had created a huge Middle Eastern empire.

Just as the Huns and Goths had done in Europe two centuries before, the Arabs had found the old empires, for all their pomp and pageantry, to be hollow. Persia and Byzantium had engaged in massive, and ultimately inconclusive, wars for centuries. The most recent, between AD 613 and 628, had left both exhausted, their treasuries depleted, manpower decimated, and populations made resentful by taxation, conscription, and forced requisitions.

The empires had fortifications, armoured warriors, and sophisticated weaponry. The Arabs had the desert and the camel. The Arabian Desert projects northwards, a tongue of sand and gravel, between Syria in the west and Iraq in the east. In these wastes, the camel is supreme, and armies mounted on camels can move like ships at sea. From the desert, suddenly, anywhere, the Arabs would emerge. When they did, lightly equipped and highly mobile, they would destroy the ponderous armies of tight-packed foot and heavy horse deployed against them in a dust cloud of swirling manoeuvres.

The sullen peasants of Syria and Iraq cared nothing for the defeat of their masters. Often they welcomed the Arabs as liberators. Many of the old landlords left. Taxes were lower. Judaism, Christianity, and Persian Zoroastrianism were tolerated; and many soon converted to Islam. Arab rule usually meant a marginally better life.

The Arab conquests continued. Their armies swept along the North African coast, taking Libya, Tunisia, Algeria, and Morocco, before finally crossing the Mediterranean and invading Spain, which was completely overrun by AD 711. Other armies pushed east; Kabul in Afghanistan fell to Islam as early as AD 664.

It had been one of the most extensive, sudden, and transformative campaigns of military conquest in history. But in transforming the world, the conquerors had also transformed themselves; and both processes were highly contradictory and contested. The people of the desert – nomads, traders, and raiders – first exploded across the Middle East and North Africa, and then, having inherited the riches of antiquity, imploded into acrimony, murder, and civil war.

5

The Medieval World
c. AD 650–1500

Genghis Khan (1162–1227), warlord and ruler of
the largest land empire in history. Contemporary
Chinese ink portrait.

Like the empires of antiquity, the empires of the medieval
period – in Asia, Africa, and America – acted as blocks on
human social development.

Modern capitalism was created in Europe. It first emerged in the fifteenth century, but its origins went back far further in time. Understanding why this was so will require a full chapter in itself. But before we get to it, we must pose another question: why did capitalism *not* develop at this time in other parts of the world?

In this chapter, we review events in the Middle East, Central Asia, India, China, sub-Saharan Africa, and the Americas in the millennium from about AD 500 to 1500. Despite great cultural achievements, all the civilisations in these regions ran into insuperable barriers to their economic and social development.

Like the Bronze and Iron Age empires of antiquity, the non-European empires of the Middle Ages remained under the control of powerful ruling classes able to monopolise control of surplus and channel it into unproductive expenditure. Technology was harnessed to war, not work, and human creativity was blunted, if not suppressed. Because of this, when they encountered the dynamic forces of expanding mercantile capitalism from about AD 1500 onwards, Asian, African, and American societies would succumb to the 'guns, germs, and steel' of the Europeans.

The Abbasid Revolution

The Arab conquests eventually gave Arab rulers and their warrior retinues control of territories that extended from the Atlantic to Afghanistan. They inherited the wealth of Byzantine Syria, Sassanid Iraq, and Visigothic Spain. Such accumulations of power and wealth made a social order based on desert tribes and the caravan trade unsustainable.

The Islamic Empire remained united immediately after Muhammad's death under the leadership of the first caliph, Abu Bakr, but the second caliph, Umar, was murdered in AD 644, the third, Uthman, in AD 656, and the fourth, Ali, in AD 661.

The crisis of AD 658–61 marked a crucial turning-point. 'Ali was overthrown after a full-scale civil war, and not only was he murdered, but so too, some 19 years later, was his son Husayn. The victor in the dynastic struggle was Mu'awiya, who founded the Damascus-based Umayyad dynasty in the year of 'Ali's murder.

These apparently obscure events are important. 'Ali was the son-in-law of the Prophet. Mu'awiya was a cousin of the murdered caliph 'Uthman, a onetime intimate of Muhammad. The Islamic politico-religious elite was tearing itself apart. The rift has never been healed. There is a direct line from 'Uthman and Mu'awiya to today's Sunni Muslims, and from 'Ali and Husayn to today's Shi'ites. The Umayyads wanted to enjoy the fruits of empire. The followers of 'Ali and Husayn wanted to preserve the purity of early Islam. It was, in part, a class split, and the Sunni/Shi'ite division still has something of this character even today.

For a century, the Umayyads retained power, held the empire together, and exploited the wealth and skills of the old civilisations. The Arab world enjoyed rich irrigation agriculture, sophisticated urban crafts, a dynamic banking system, and a strong tradition of scholarship, literature, and art. The Western world, by contrast, was living in the 'Dark Ages'.

Two contradictions undermined the Umayyad Empire and eventually brought it down. First, the geography of the Arab world contained several natural economic units, in which separate ruling classes with interests of their own rapidly developed. Distance limited the effectiveness of Umayyad rule. How could armies in Damascus expect to control Baghdad, Cairo, Tunis, and Fez?

Second, the Umayyads represented the Arab warrior aristocracy which had carried out the original Islamic conquests and then settled in the ancient cities of Syria. This elite built palaces and spent lavishly on architecture and luxury goods. They were supported by the Arab rank and file, who were settled in garrison towns, exempt from taxation, and supported by pensions paid for out of booty and tribute. The Umayyad ruling class was small and parasitic, and it rested on a narrow base of military freeloaders.

The economy, though, was booming. War between the old empires had devastated farms, disrupted trade, and drained away taxes and manpower. The *Pax Islamica* meant that agriculture and trade again flourished, ancient towns hollowed out by decay were transformed into commercial powerhouses, and the merchant and artisan classes grew in number, prosperity, and assertiveness. Here were the social roots of a new revolution.

Many converted to Islam and this created a fiscal problem for the Umayyad state, since Muslims were exempt from taxation. The state's solution was to create a new category of second-class Muslims: new converts were designated *mawali* and excluded from Arab privilege.

A barrier to social advancement within Arab-Islamic society was being constructed.

By the middle of the eighth century AD, the Arabs were a small military aristocracy living off the tribute paid by a growing mass of urban-based Muslim merchants and artisans. The latter provided a ready audience for Islamic dissidents like the Shi'ites, the yet more radical Kharijites, and various messianic *mahdis* (guided ones). None of the dissident movements was strong enough to break the power of the Umayyad state. What was decisive was an opportunist split in the Arab ruling class itself.

Abu'l-'Abbas, a descendant of Muhammad's family, built an underground network of supporters in Iraq, placed himself at the head of the various dissident groups, and then launched an insurrection to overthrow the ruling dynasty. The Umayyads were defeated and a new Abbasid dynasty was founded in AD 750, with its capital in Baghdad. Power passed to a broader-based and more inclusive urban elite of officials, merchants, and Islamic scholars and clerics. Arab ethnicity and warrior status lost much of their significance. Agriculture, trade, and towns continued to develop.

Even so, the two contradictions of Early Islamic empire were soon reasserted, now on a higher level. The towns were the centres of Islamic life, but they were largely self-sufficient and independent, the urban elites preoccupied with agriculture, trade, craft-production, religious observance, and the maintenance of order. Their concerns were parochial.

The Abbasid caliphs, on the other hand, were threatened by secession on the fringes of their empire, coups by disaffected elite factions, and revolt from below by religious sectarians or sections of the exploited rural masses. The Early Islamic state was therefore compelled to operate over and above society, becoming little more than a mechanism for accumulating the military resources necessary to perpetuate the ruling dynasty. A wide gap separated the mass of Middle Eastern society from the Early Islamic state that ruled them.

The Umayyads had already removed themselves from civil society by building palaces and consuming luxuries. The Abbasids took this much further. To free themselves from subordination to the Baghdad urban elite, they built a magnificent new palace-city on the River Tigris at Samarra. This first palace, built in AD 836–42, was far bigger than any of the palaces of medieval Europe. Yet two more palaces on the same scale were built in the next 40 years.

The Abbasid state was further de-anchored when it replaced the old Arab tribal host with a new army of mercenaries, mainly Turks from Central Asia, who were quartered at Samarra.

The court and the army were sustained by taxes, especially those levied on non-Muslims. The tribes and towns of Islamic society, meanwhile, developed strong local identities and ideologies. Though Islam created a single, overarching allegiance throughout the Arab-ruled world, no strong ties of any kind bound state and society. This explains the instability of the Abbasid state.

During the ninth and tenth centuries, the unity of the Islamic Empire disintegrated: the Abbasid caliph soon faced a rival Fatimid dynasty in Cairo, an Umayyad one at Córdoba in Spain, and numerous independent and semi-independent minor rulers elsewhere. Conflicts between and within these polities increased the cost of state power, drained national treasuries, and further weakened the Early Islamic rulers. During the eleventh century, the Abbasid caliphate effectively collapsed. The caliph's Seljuk Turkish mercenaries, reinforced by drafts from Central Asia and legitimised by their conversion to Islam, seized power for themselves.

It was a measure of the state's lack of social roots that it could be usurped by its own mercenaries. Among the population at large, worn down by taxes to pay for palaces, soldiers, and dynastic warfare, there was little enthusiasm for any of the ruling regimes. The region, moreover, remained a mosaic of minorities, so that political tension easily turned into resistance based on ethnic and religious difference.

By the end of the eleventh century the Middle East was a divided region of weak and unpopular regimes. For this it would pay a terrible price, when, in November 1095, Pope Urban II, speaking at Clermont in France, issued a call to the Western feudal elite to 'hasten to carry aid to your brethren in the East'. The Crusades were about to begin.

The Byzantine Empire, the Seljuk Turks, and the Ottoman Turks

The Byzantine Empire has been described as a 'living fossil'. When the Western Roman Empire collapsed during the fifth century AD, the Eastern Roman Empire survived and was destined to last another millennium. Why such radically different historical fates?

The defence of the West had required the deployment of two-thirds of the Late Roman Army. But the East had generated two-thirds of the tax revenues. When the Roman Empire split in half (in AD 395) – under mounting military pressure on the frontiers – the West collapsed because it lacked the resources to sustain its army. The East, on the other hand, was not only richer, but was also more secure, its frontiers along most of their extent protected by sea, mountain, or desert. Geography allowed a 'living fossil' to endure.

More than that: it provided the launch-pad for an abortive programme of revanchist Roman imperialism. Under the Emperor Justinian (AD 527–65), the Byzantine general Belisarius waged major wars against the Vandals in Africa and the Goths in Italy, re-establishing 'Roman' control over large swathes of territory.

But the effort put unsustainable strain on the empire, especially given the chronic insecurity of the eastern frontier, where the Byzantine and Persian Empires engaged in a series of huge, exhausting, and inconclusive wars. So for most of their subsequent history, the Byzantines remained on the defensive.

The Byzantine Empire was a conservative, tributary, military state. The emperors imposed taxes and labour services on the peasantry to sustain the imperial administration, to fund the Church, to maintain the army and the fleet, and to wage war on the frontiers. The ruling class was formed of palace bureaucrats, church patriarchs, army officers, and feudal landowners. The dominant ideology was a desiccated form of dogmatic, ritualised Christianity, all incense, icons, and chants. The Byzantine world was intellectually sterile – almost wholly devoid of imagination, creativity, or innovation. It owed its endurance to its geographical coherence and its inheritance of an advanced Graeco-Roman cultural tradition, above all, in relation to military affairs. Byzantine society may have been stagnant, but its total subordination to the state made possible the maintenance of a large, professional, high-tech army.

Byzantine territory was divided into military districts (*themas*) controlled by generals (*strategoi*). Each district was responsible for recruiting, equipping, and supplying an army corps of about 10,000 men, comprising heavy cavalry known as 'cataphracts' (who wore full chainmail armour and carried lance, bow, and sword), heavy infantry (with round shield, long spear, and sword), and light infantry (usually archers equipped with composite bows). These disciplined regular units were often supplemented – especially in later Byzantine history – by household troops, feudal levies, irregular auxiliaries, and foreign mercenaries. Equipment and weaponry, of the regulars at least, was technically sophisticated and of the highest quality. Tactics were a matter of close-quarters shock action, where superior weapons, armour, and discipline were expected to be decisive. This was a Graeco-Roman – or 'Western' – way of war.

What eventually defeated the Byzantine Empire was its encounter with an alternative, 'Eastern' way of war – one rooted in the anthropology of the Arabian deserts and the Central Asian steppes. The collapse of Byzantine civilisation was one of history's *longues durées* – a process rather than an event, one extending over eight centuries, beginning in the AD 630s, not complete until 1453, and reflecting fundamental differences of economy, society, and culture. The process is marked by four signal events, four dramatic turning-points – in AD 636, 1071, 1204, and 1453 – each a decisive military defeat resulting in a permanent haemorrhaging of territory and/or degrading of geopolitical power.

First, in AD 636, at the Battle of Yarmuk, the Byzantine Empire was defeated by an Arab-Islamic army and in consequence lost control of Syria. Damascus became the first capital of a new Umayyad Empire that would eventually extend from Spain to India. A process of deep-rooted cultural change in the region we know as 'the Middle East' now began. Most people, over time, converted to Islam and came to think of themselves as Arabs. Towns centred on medina and mosque – and dominated by merchants and the *ulema* ('learned ones': Islamic preachers and teachers) – became the basic building-blocks of an enduring social order that would survive successive waves of foreign invasion.

In 1071, at the Battle of Manzikert, the Byzantine Empire suffered its second catastrophe, this time at the hands of the Seljuk Turks. Like the Huns and the Mongols, the Turks were nomadic pastoralists of the Eurasian steppes, with a military system based on swarms of light horse-archers. Some had adopted the Islamic faith, having come into contact with Muslims either in border areas or during mercenary service. From the late tenth century onwards, and for the century or so following, successive waves of Turkic invaders swept across the civilisations to the south, attacking first north-west India, then Iran in the 1040s, Iraq in the 1050s, and finally Armenia and Anatolia in the 1060s.

The Abbasid Caliphate based on Baghdad had long since fractured into numerous separate polities, and the Islamic successor regimes were incapable of mounting effective resistance (though Islamic society proved resilient enough under new Turkish overlords). Then, at Manzikert in Armenia, Alp Arslan, the Seljuk Sultan of Baghdad, at the head of a horde of horse-archers, crushed a far larger army of Byzantine regulars and Western feudal mercenaries commanded by the Emperor Romanus IV Diogenes. The effects were transformative: the Byzantine Empire lost control of Armenia and much of Anatolia; the conversion of the region to Islam began; and the apparent resurgence of the Islamic cause helped trigger the Crusades.

A Byzantine enclave based on Constantinople and in control of western Anatolia and the Balkans survived, in part because it was propped up by the Crusaders, in part because the Seljuk Empire, like its predecessors, splintered into a mosaic of petty states ruled by rival warlords.

The Crusades dominated the history of the region in the twelfth and thirteenth centuries, but they were a mixed blessing for the empire. A third great military disaster was visited upon it by fellow Christians when the army and fleet of the Fourth Crusade attacked and captured Constantinople in 1204. Large parts of the city were destroyed, vast amounts of plunder seized, and the population, it is said, was reduced from 500,000 in 1203 to 35,000 in 1261.

It was therefore a much reduced and weakened Byzantine Empire that confronted a new Turkish-Islamic threat a century later. In the years around 1300, a Turkic warlord called Osman emerged as a rising hegemon among the Turks of north-western Anatolia. The dynasty he founded – that of the Ottomans – was destined to complete the destruction of the empire over the next century and a half.

The fracturing of the Seljuk Empire and the decay of Byzantine power had created an unstable frontier society of petty states and rival chieftains amid a shifting population of nomads, traders, dervishes, and freebooters. A victorious warlord could attract a growing following by offering protection and reward to his retinue. By some process of primitive politico-military accumulation – lost to historical record – Osman emerged from the mash of mini-potentates to unite a critical mass of Turkic warriors under his leadership.

By the middle of the fourteenth century, Osman's successors – the Ottoman Sultans – controlled the whole of north-western Anatolia. A hundred years later, they controlled much of both Anatolia and the Balkan Peninsula. Under Mehmet the Conqueror (1451–81), Ottoman armies then overran the rest of the Balkans, Central Anatolia, and even the Crimea and the northern Black Sea region. Mehmet's supreme achievement was to inflict the third and final of the three blows that broke Byzantine power. On 29 May 1453, after a 53-day siege by land and sea, the Ottomans captured the Byzantine capital, ending the 800-year long struggle between Graeco-Roman Christianity and Arab-Turkic Islam, and terminating a civilisation that had, in some sense, endured for 2,000 years.

The Mongol Empire

Around 1190, far removed from any of the great centres of world civilisation, a Mongolian chieftain called Temuchin launched a politico-military campaign to unite the steppe nomads of eastern Eurasia in a single centralised polity. By 1206, such was his achievement that he was hailed by the Mongolian tribes as 'Supreme Ruler': Genghis Khan.

Five years later, having by agreement or coercion united all the kindred peoples of the eastern steppe into a new Mongolian super-state, he emerged from his yurt – a tent of felt blankets over a wooden frame – to announce to that he had communed with the gods and been assured of 'the Mandate of Heaven'. It was the beginning of a campaign of conquest that would shake the foundations of Asian and European civilisation.

The storm broke first against the Chin Empire. In the First Chin War (1211–15), Mongol armies raided deep into China in a campaign of slaughter, rape, burning, and plunder that was to be repeated many times across the breadth of Eurasia over the next half century. The Chin Emperor was forced to recognise the supremacy of the Mongol Khan – but the invaders then withdrew to the north with their plunder.

Then they struck west, against the Turco-Persian empire of Khwarazm Shah, in a series of campaigns (1218–24) that saw the destruction of great Silk Road cities like Bukhara, Samarkand, Utrar, Merv, Nishapur, Balkh, and Herat – many of which remain heaps of ruins to this day. Hundreds of thousands perished in genocidal massacres. Amid the devastation and carnage, Genghis Khan proclaimed himself 'the Hammer of God'.

Further campaigns followed, under Genghis and his successors. In later wars against China, the Mongols at first aimed to exterminate the peasantry to create new grasslands for their herds. Only later, as a new imperial administration formed, with a capital at Karakorum and a bureaucracy which included Chinese and Persian officials, did the Mongol elite relent as they evolved into a tribute-based ruling class.

The empire was also extended westwards: the Kharazmian Empire was overrun, Russia subjugated, and, between 1237 and 1242, Mongol armies were at large in Europe, campaigning in Poland, Hungary, and the Balkans. Commentators in Christian Europe, as the continent's feudal chivalry went down to defeat in twin battles in April 1241, predicted 'the end of the world'.

But the Mongol armies, thousands of miles from home, suddenly vanished back into the vastness of the steppes – killing, enslaving, destroying as they went. The Great Khan was dead and the court at Karakorum was embroiled in a contested succession struggle. The forward impetus of Mongol conquest was momentarily arrested.

When it resumed, the force was less, the resistance greater, and in 1260 came a decisive victory over the Mongol horde, in the Middle East, at the hands of the Mamluks, at the Battle of Ayn Jalut (1260).

The surge from the steppes had finally exhausted itself. The territories conquered were so vast, the riches accumulated so great, that the energy for further conquest, especially in the face of hardening opposition, drained away. But, under Kubilai Khan (1260–94) – the fifth Great Khan – the Mongols were left ruling over four great Eurasian khanates.

Kubilai himself ruled China – 'the Khanate of the Great Khan' – as the first Emperor of a new Yuan Dynasty. Other Mongols ruled: the Golden Horde in the west, which extended as far as Moscow and Kiev; the Chaghadai Khanate in the heart of Central Asia, whence, 250 years later, would come the Mughal conquerors of India; and the Il-Khanate, centred on Persia and Iraq, but at its peak also in control of Anatolia, the Caucasus, and much of south-western Central Asia.

But these were new dynasties of foreign overlords ruling essentially unchanged social orders – whether in China, Central Asia, the Middle East, or India. The Mongol surge had flowed across the world in a stunning spectacle of whirlwind conquest, only to shrink back leaving nothing but a swathe of devastation. And Mongol rule, when, in the later decades, it was consolidated, was merely the imposition of another caste of militarists extracting surplus in the form of tribute and forced labour from the same underlying system of peasant-based production.

Why was the Mongol impact so spectacular and at the same time so superficial?

Mongolia is a vast plateau subject to dramatic extremes of climate, with temperatures often above 40°C in summer and sometimes falling below –40°C in winter. The soil is thin, loose, and gravelly, and frozen hard for much of the winter. This means the steppe is poor agricultural land, but produces a luxuriant growth of summer grass and a more restricted growth of winter grass, sufficient to maintain herds of sheep, goats, cattle, and horses.

The traditional lifeway of the Mongolian steppe was therefore that of transhumant pastoralism, with a diet of meat, milk, and cheese, and a material culture based on leather and wool. The people were divided into families, clans, and tribes, ruled by chieftains, each community in control of – and sometimes in conflict over – areas of both summer and winter pasture.

The military system was based on the horse, the stirrup, the lasso, the sword, and the composite bow. Mongol raiding parties – and armies – were essentially hordes of light horse-archers. The 'Eastern way of war' – based on movement, on skirmishing and evasion, on ambush and surprise, on harassment and shooting rather than close-quarters collision – was the natural way of the Mongol warrior.

Genghis Khan's achievement was to acquire military mass through political centralisation, and to create effective command, control, and coordination of the mass by replacing the old tribal system of military organisation with an artificial system based on regular units, high levels of training, ruthless discipline, and promotion on merit. He and his successors would later augment this further by integrating Chinese and Persian technique – especially in weapon technology and siege warfare – into the Mongol military system.

The Mongol state was therefore a hybrid formation. But it still rested on the unreconstructed barbarism of the nomadic tribes of the steppes. The effect, therefore, was to turn predatory raiding into a global catastrophe. Transformed into a world-conquering force, but far more primitive than the people of the villages, towns, and cities against which their blitzkriegs were unleashed, the Mongols were incapable of offering anything except violent devastation and social regression.

The Chin census in northern China showed a population of about 50 million people in 1195. When the new Mongol rulers carried out their own census 40 years later – after waging two major wars against the Chin – they counted only nine million.

Again and again, entire communities – the men, women, and children of captured settlements – were executed. Or the Mongols might spare artisans and clerks, having some use for them, but kill all the peasants.

Only in later decades, as the Mongol polity evolved into a traditional tributary state on the Chinese or Turkic-Persian model, was value to be attached to the lives of the common people. But this, of course, did not represent a Mongol achievement: it was merely the cultural assimilation of the Mongol elite by a superior civilisation – a transformation of Mongol chieftains into Chinese or Turkic-Persian courtiers. In the Golden Horde, the Chaghadai Khanate, and the Il-Khanate, the change was symbolised by conversion to Islam, the religion of existing Middle Eastern elites.

As one Chinese official adopted into Mongol service explained: 'Although the empire had been conquered on horseback, it would not be ruled on horseback.' To create sustainable polities – to remain in control of the more advanced societies they had come to dominate – it was necessary for the Mongols to cease to be Mongols.

Hindus, Buddhists, and the Gupta Empire

More than half a millennium separated the fall of India's Mauryan Empire in the late third century BC and the rise of the Gupta Empire in the early fourth century AD. Economic and social change in the interim altered the foundations of imperialism.

Agriculture prospered: there were more crop varieties, the systematic use of irrigation, and highly organised and regulated village communities. The village was a key administrative unit. It included the homes of the villagers, their plots, irrigation works (mainly water storage-tanks or wells), cattle enclosures, waste lands, the village common, woods around the village, streams passing through village lands, the village temple and its lands, the cremation ground, and, of course, the cultivated fields themselves, both 'wet' (irrigated) and 'dry'. Local affairs were managed by a village council, a village court, and occasional village assemblies.

Trade also expanded. Indian merchants were integrated into a global market, with links to Arabia, Western Asia, and the Mediterranean in one direction, and China and South-East Asia in the other. Textiles, metals, precious stones, spices, salt, and exotic animals were among the commodities exchanged. There was work for potters, weavers, metalworkers, architects, engineers, bricklayers, and dealers in every imaginable tradable commodity, from corn to ivory. Coins were minted in large quantities. Banking and money-lending became common practice. Ports and towns flourished. Just as village communities were highly organised, so too were merchants and artisans. Guilds, corporations, and cooperatives set rules of work, regulated the quality and prices of goods produced, and provided for the welfare and security of their members.

The growth of commerce both facilitated the spread of Buddhism and provided a mass audience for its apostles. Hinduism, the religion of the elite – the rulers, landowners, priests, and soldiers associated with the dynasties – upheld an essentially static, traditional order based on caste and state. It was the religion of a class-ridden and militaristic society divided into rival polities. Commerce, by contrast, cut across social boundaries, dissolved social distinctions, and created new social realities. Its imperatives contradicted those of caste and state. The spirit of commerce found its ideological expression in Buddhism.

The Buddha ('Enlightened One') was a Hindu warrior-prince called Siddhartha Gautama (c. 563–483 BC) who had broken with his caste, undergone a profound religious experience, and spent the rest of his life preaching a new philosophy. The essence of his teaching was that true happiness and contentment arises when one accepts the natural and social orders, recognises that everything is in a state of flux, and achieves a spiritual peace of mind above the froth of everyday life.

Buddhism's radicalism lay in its universalism and its relative marginalisation of such features of the status quo as property, rank, and status. It enjoined a way of life that was purposeful, morally upright, and equally open to all. As with all great religions, the original message of Buddhism was later corrupted by contact with intractable social realities. Yet it would retain its appeal, not just to merchants, artisans, and townspeople, but to many among the class victims of ancient and medieval India's mainly Hindu elite.

The villages, urban guilds, and Hindu and Buddhist temples gave Indian civil society a form and substance it had lacked under the Mauryans. This new socio-economic order of what is sometimes called the Classical Period (c. AD 300–700) shaped and limited the Gupta Empire erected on it.

The empire was constructed by three successive warrior-kings, Chandra Gupta I (c. AD 320–35), Samudra Gupta (c. AD 335–75), and Chandra Gupta II (c. AD 375–415). Like the Mauryan Empire, it originated in the rich Ganges Valley, with its capital at Patna, from where it spread first across the plains of northern India, then to the Deccan of central India, and finally to southern India.

The Gupta polity was parasitic. The state infrastructure was a hybrid of landholding and tribute payment. Many officials were paid in land: they did administrative or military service in return for their estates, which were often held tax-free. Peasant villages, on the other hand, paid a land tax of between a tenth and a sixth of their produce. This surplus supported the Gupta state's militarism. From the point of view of the peasants, of course, it was waste expenditure.

On the other hand, the strength of civil society meant that state surplus accumulation was limited. Local princes and chieftains enjoyed considerable autonomy under Gupta rule. State officials functioned as feudal estate-owners. The peasants had their village councils and assemblies, the merchants and artisans their urban guilds and temples. Gupta centralisation, therefore, was incomplete. The empire's administrative infrastructure was shallow, the arteries of state accumulation clogged. Consequently, the carapace of Gupta militarism shattered easily under pressure.

The Gupta dynasty held its vast domain for only a century. Then, relatively quickly during the sixth century AD, the empire dissolved. The second attempt to unite India under an imperial dynasty had proved as fragile and short-lived as the first. The catalyst of collapse was an incursion of steppe nomads – the Huns – entering north-western India down the traditional invasion route from Central Asia, through the Hindu Kush, into the Indus Valley. The fact that the Gupta Empire fragmented so easily exposed its lack of substance.

India again broke up into separate polities. For a millennium, it remained a shifting mosaic of rival powers, permanently at logger-heads, often at war. Throughout this period, there was little connection between the rival dynastic states and the world of village, production, and commerce. The states floated above society, parasitic on it, creaming off surplus, yet otherwise detached. Military compe-tition forced the states to accumulate and made them oppressive. But none could accumulate enough to achieve sufficient military power to defeat their enemies and establish a new empire. The resistance of landowners, merchants, and villagers was too great.

On the other hand, the weight of military infrastructures bore down on civil society. Trade declined and the pace of progress slowed. There was a 'feudalisation' of society. The caste system hardened. Elite culture became mystical and scholastic. Villages became inward-looking and conservative. The cyclical theories of time, which the major Indian religions shared, expressed an historical reality. The separation between state and society, and the contradictory demands of each, trapped the Indian subcontinent in an economic impasse.

Chinese History's Revolving Door

The construction of the Qin Empire, the first in Chinese history, had been a revolutionary act. The Bronze Age Shang Dynasty (1523–1027 BC) had ruled only in the Yellow River region of north-west China. The Iron Age Zhou elite (1027–221 BC) had never ruled an effectively centralised empire. During the Warring States Period (403–221 BC), any semblance of unity had been lost as nine or ten separate states competed for power. It was therefore the achievement of the King of Qin, Shi Huangdi, one of history's greatest and most brutal conquerors, to impose real national unity on the Chinese for the first time. The dynasty he founded did not long survive his death in 210 BC; but the empire, under one dynasty or another, was repeatedly reconstructed. In India, empire was exceptional and division into rival polities the norm. In China, after 221 BC, the opposite was true. Why was this?

India and China were both mixed feudal-tributary systems in which the elite was supported in part by landholding and in part by state salaries paid for out of tax revenues. But the balance was different in each case. In India, the imperial state was weak relative to local rulers, landowners, and merchants; consequently, it collapsed easily under pressure. The Mauryan (c. 321–180 BC), Gupta (c. AD 320–550), and Mughal (1526–1707) Empires were imperial interludes separated by long periods of 'warring states'. In Chinese history, it is the succession of imperial dynasties that dominates the sequence: Han (206 BC–AD 220), Sui (AD 581–618), Tang (AD 618–907), Song (AD 960–1126), Yuan or Mongol (1279–1368), Ming (1368–1644), and Manchu (1644–1912). In the two millennia before 1800, India was united for only a quarter of the time, China for three-quarters: a decisive difference.

In China, the central imperial state was a much more ruthless, powerful, and successful exploiter. This had three consequences. First, more secure, it was less militaristic. Second, with a large share of the available surplus and only modest military needs, it could invest in public works to raise productivity and increase the tax base further. Third, with its power unchecked by other social forces, it tended to become over-exploitative.

China is blessed with many navigable rivers. These were linked by massive canals to create a network of waterways 80,000 km long. This opened China up to both internal and overseas trade, giving merchants easy access to a vast market. This in turn stimulated agricultural and industrial production. Shipbuilding flourished, boosted by a host of technical innovations. The Chinese produced ships large enough to carry 1,000 people. Iron production in the eleventh century was greater than that of Britain in the eighteenth. China possessed gunpowder 240 years before the Europeans, printed books 500 years before, and manufactured porcelain 700 years before.

Medieval China spawned mega-cities. The Song Dynasty capital of Kaifeng enclosed an area 12 times the size of contemporary Paris. The city of Hangzhou housed at least a million and a half and perhaps as many as four million people at a time when the population of London was well below 100,000.

Towns could be huge, but they did not evolve into independent power-centres, and remained dominated by central state officials. The Tang Dynasty capital of Chang'an was the economic and cultural centre of the empire at the time. It was a great trading city of a million people. But it was overshadowed by its imperial palace and government offices, and its hundred or so walled residential wards, laid out in a grid of rectangular blocks, were locked at night.

Merchants as a class did not seek power. They aspired to personal advancement by educating their sons and entering the exclusive class of mandarins, the literate state officials who formed a highly privileged bureaucratic elite. Mandarins in turn aspired to ownership of country estates. The social ideal of the Chinese ruling class was the gentry official, not the merchant bourgeois. This is a measure of the central imperial state's dominance over civil society.

The ideological supremacy of Legalism and Confucianism also testifies to the power of the state. Legalism argued that the smooth functioning of the state was the basis of the general good and that state officials were therefore its embodiment. For many, this was too crude. What guarantee was there that administrators would not be corrupt and incompetent? The Chinese philosopher Confucius (c. 551–479 BC) supplied one answer. The son of a nobleman who became a leading official and philosopher of the state of Lu in the Warring States Period, Confucius taught respect for tradition and the social order, but stressed the importance of honesty, conscientiousness, and self-control.

Nevertheless, as elsewhere, the contradictions and oppression of an imperial society gave rise to more radical philosophies. Taoism advocated withdrawal from a world tainted by the excesses of greed, violence, and luxury. Harmony and contentment depended on keeping the opposing forces of yin and yang in balance. Buddhism was also influential and eventually made more converts in China than in India. To subordinate social classes it seemed to offer richer spiritual succour than the barren ideologies of self-satisfied state officials. For China was far from enjoying the harmony idealised by the mandarins. The life of peasants was one of endless drudgery in the grain fields of northern China or the rice paddies of the Central Plain. State officials and local landlords took up to half the produce. The margin of safety was almost nil. A bad harvest meant millions starved.

The Great Wall, the thousands of kilometres of canals, the imperial palaces, the huge walled cities – all depended on exploiting the peasantry. Since they were unorganised, peasants' voices went unheard, and bitterness accumulated in the depths of the Chinese countryside. Chinese history is punctuated by a succession of massive peasant rebellions. The Qin, Han, Tang, Yuan, Ming, and Manchu were all brought down by popular revolt.

Revolts were frequent, though most were unsuccessful. When a dynasty actually fell to revolt, it did so as part of a wider crisis, sometimes involving foreign invaders, always active opposition by groups of officials, landowners, or merchants. But it was peasant revolt that typically provided the main destructive force.

Destructive; but not constructive. The peasants, driven to desperation by poverty and bullying, could form a militia to overthrow the tax-collectors. But they would then disperse to their villages. As a class, scattered across the length and breadth of the countryside, dedicated to family and farm, largely ignorant of, and isolated from, the wider world, they could not create an alternative state in their own image. Thus the limit of peasant ambition was to replace a 'bad' emperor with a 'good' one. And in the absence of an urban class – a bourgeoisie, intelligentsia, or proletariat – able to provide revolutionary leadership, peasant revolt could go no further.

Political revolution did not lead to social transformation, merely to the replacement of one dynasty by another. For two millennia Chinese history was a revolving door. This did not change until contact with another world subjected it to a series of shocks sufficient to bring down the entire imperial system. But that did not happen until the twentieth century.

Africa: Cattle-Herders, Ironmasters, and Trading States

Eurasia is a gigantic east–west thoroughfare extending over 9,600 km. For thousands of years, people and ideas have moved along this thoroughfare and its many branches. Because Eurasia is aligned east–west, routeways are formed by its uniform climatic zones. In particular, the Eurasian steppes run almost unbroken from the Carpathian Mountains in Central Europe to the Pacific Ocean. Along this great corridor came the Aryans, the Huns, the Turks, and the Mongols. Down its byways spilled Greeks, Celts, Goths, and Slavs.

Traders, invaders, and settlers carried ideas along Eurasia's many routeways. When they did, because of uniform climate zones, what worked in one place also worked in others. All the great domesticates of the Agricultural Revolution – barley, wheat, and rice; cattle, sheep, goat, pigs, and chickens – were transferable.

Africa was different. Africa runs north–south for 6,500 km. As it does so, it passes across great barriers and through several climatic zones: from north to south, coastal plain, desert, savannah, tropical forest, savannah, desert, and coastal plain again.

The desert and the forest are barriers to movement and not amenable to farmers. There is also disease, especially that borne by the tsetse fly, which feeds on the blood of humans and animals. And, for all its variety and exoticism, African fauna does not include a disease-resistant traction animal strong enough to pull a plough. Geography determined that Africa would develop differently from Eurasia. Constraints were greater, opportunities fewer. Africans were as capable of great art, architecture, and engineering as Romans, Arabs, and Chinese; but physical barriers prevented them establishing great imperial civilisations.

The advance of farming was slow and patchy. Sub-Saharan Africa had no equivalent of the Nile Valley or Mesopotamia, the Indus or the Ganges, the Yellow River or the Yangtze; no giant bread baskets able to sustain an empire. On the other hand, ancient rock carvings in the Sahara depict men herding cattle and driving two-wheeled chariots – introductions from the north. From about 1000 BC to AD 600 the trans-Saharan trade routes linked West Africa to the Mediterranean and began its transformation. Sub-Saharan Africa traded gold, iron, slaves, salt, and ivory, all in growing demand in the Mediterranean. Back down the trade routes came knowledge of ironworking and cattle husbandry.

In developing West Africa, the Niger was a vital line of communication for the movement of trade goods and ideas. Running from west to east, it describes a vast curve through the whole region, flowing through savannah and forest to the coast, while its many large tributaries spread the influence of river-borne culture deep into the West African hinterland.

Iron, cattle, and the trade along the Niger were the basis of the Nok culture of Nigeria (*c.* 500 BC–AD 200). Ironworking began there as early as *c.* 450 BC, and African smiths were soon pioneering new techniques and forms. At the same time, African potters were demonstrating exceptional skill in the fashioning of life-size terracotta heads.

Mediterranean civilisation continued to act as an indirect catalyst of West African development, and as the demand for high-value commodities grew, larger surpluses could be accumulated. These created the basis, first, for trading towns, and later, for trading states.

Jenne-Jeno, a major trading town on an island in the Niger between AD 400 and 800, was surrounded by a 2 km-long wall made of cylindrical blocks. The interior was filled with round and rectangular mud-brick houses. Jenne-Jeno was part of the Kingdom of Ghana, a trading state which controlled the Niger Delta and, at its height, extended across 800 km of West Africa. The Arabs called it 'the Land of Gold'.

Elsewhere other regions of Africa had created their own civilisations. The Kushites or Merowites controlled much of the Upper Nile (modern Sudan) between *c.* 900 BC and AD 325, maintaining their independence against Egyptian, Hellenistic, and Roman threats.

The Kushites were finally overthrown by the Ethiopians. The small Red Sea trading state of Axum had grown from *c.* AD 50 into the Horn of Africa's major regional power. Later, though contained by the Arabs, the Ethiopian state would survive as an Early Christian enclave in an otherwise Muslim region, notable for its spectacular rock-hewn churches.

But West Africa was the continent's cultural powerhouse. It was from here that iron and cattle were traded across the continent. The agents of transmission were Bantu-speaking migrants. Their folk movements reached into East Africa and the Lakes during the half millennium after 500 BC, then deep into southern Africa during the subsequent half-millennium.

Ancient and medieval Africa was an extreme example of what has been called 'combined and uneven development'. Hunter-gatherers, cattle pastoralists, and slash-and-burn cultivators coexisted, for Africa's geography prevented the dominance of any one way of life. Furthermore, under the influence of foreign trade, Africa made the leap straight from the Stone Age to the Iron Age: there was no inter-mediate Bronze Age.

Between the eighth and twelfth centuries AD, Arab influence spread. Arabs traded with West Africa both north–south across the Sahara and east–west across the savannah belt. Towns like Timbuktu grew rich on Arab trade. The Arabs also established a string of trading settlements such as Kilwa along the coast of East Africa.

Again, Africa changed in response to foreign impact, and again, in responding revealed the creativity and dynamism of its own people. Between AD 1200 and 1750 a succession of trading states rose and fell in West Africa – Mali, Hausa, Benin, Kanem-Borno, Songhai, Akan/Ashanti, and others – while in Central-East Africa, the stimulus provided by coastal trade produced the civilisation of Great Zimbabwe.

The Benin civilisation of the Niger Delta produced bronzework of the highest standard, its famous bronze heads reminiscent of the Nok's terracotta sculpture; they are recognised today as among the greatest masterpieces of medieval art. Great Zimbabwe is renowned for its architecture. The Great Enclosure was the largest building in sub-Saharan Africa at the time, comprising a wall some 250 m long, 5 m thick, and 10 m high.

The wealth of the rulers of Great Zimbabwe was based on cattle and the trade in gold, iron, copper, and tin. The pattern was the same as in Benin and other West African states. Geographical constraints limited the surpluses that could be accrued from agriculture. All of Africa's many urban revolutions depended on trade.

From 1000 BC until the arrival of the Europeans in the fifteenth century AD, the main lines of African social development were contingent on the activities of others. Geography condemned Africa to dependent status.

New World Empires: Maya, Aztec, and Inca

Hominins first evolved in Africa up to 7 million years ago, modern humans about 350,000 years ago. But they may not have reached the Americas until as recently as 15,000 years ago.

Africa is the oldest continent, America the youngest. Yet the civilisations of sub-Saharan Africa and the Americas share key characteristics that set them apart from those of Eurasia. Both were constrained in similar ways by geographical barriers.

The Americas run north–south for almost 16,000 km through all the climatic zones. Because of this, what works in one part of the Americas often does not work in others. Different ecosystems require different subsistence strategies, so the value of cultural exchange between climatic zones is less than its value within a climatic zone.

The Americas were well endowed with plant staples – maize, potatoes, squash, beans, and manioc – but not with animal domesticates. Eurasia was home to the wild progenitors of cattle, sheep, goats, pigs, hens, oxen, horses, mules, donkeys, and camels. These provided meat, milk, wool, leather, traction, and transport. The Americas, by contrast, had only the llama, the turkey, and the guinea-pig.

In one key respect, Africa and the Americas were different. Africa is not cut off from Eurasia, and African civilisation developed under the influence of Egyptian, Roman, and Arab traders. Crucially, Africa received cattle and iron from Eurasia, and its own production of metals and other commodities was substantially a response to external demand. The Americas received no such cultural endowment. They were cut off from the global exchange of knowledge and techniques that is responsible for most advances in labour productivity. Consequently, the Americans had no wheel, no iron, and no plough.

These constraints limited the development of civilisation in North America. When the Europeans arrived, most North Americans were either Upper Palaeolithic hunter-gatherers or Early Neolithic hoe-cultivators. The proto-urban civilisations of the Pueblo farmers of the South-West (AD 700–1350) and the temple-mound builders of the Middle Mississippi (AD 700–1450) had already disappeared.

In Central and South America, on the other hand, the Europeans encountered extant civilisations that were both fully urbanised and representative of much older traditions – the Olmecs, Maya, Toltecs, and Aztecs in Mexico (1200 BC–AD 1521) and the Chavin, Nazca, Moche, Chimú, and Inca in Peru (900 BC–AD 1532).

The fact that American civilisation developed entirely independently of Eurasia is the ultimate proof of the common biological identity of humanity: all 'races' are equally capable of cultural creativity. On the other hand, American civilisation faced severe limitations. Its technology was Stone Age. Gold, silver, and copper were used only for ornaments. Its agricultural method was Early

Neolithic, and because productivity was low and the surplus small, American civilisation tended to be brutal. Successful accumulation often required extreme exploitation and violence.

The Mayan civilisation of southern Mexico and Guatemala lasted from *c.* 300 BC to AD 900. It was divided into rival city-states under hereditary dynasties of kings who identified themselves with deities. The Mayans built monumental ceremonial centres consisting of plazas surrounded by stone-built pyramids crowned with palaces, temples, and altars. A true urban revolution occurred in the Classic Maya period (*c.* AD 300–800), when ceremonial centres like Tikal swelled into jungle cities of up to 50,000 people.

Architecture, sculpture, and painting were developed. Obsidian and jade were worked into objects of quality. Writing, astronomical observation, and calendrical calculation were advanced. But it was the religion and ideology of the ruling class – not the needs of farmers – that underlay these cultural achievements. Art and science were at the service of militaristic god-kings and a theocracy. Wars were fought in part to obtain captives to sacrifice to Mayan gods. Art depicts victims being tortured in the presence of Mayan lords. Despite intensive agriculture, including the cultivation on raised fields of maize, beans, squash, chilli peppers, and root crops, Mayan technique was primitive. Without ploughs or animal fertiliser, soil exhaustion must have been a constant problem.

Against the odds, an Early Neolithic economy had given rise to an urban revolution and a network of royal city-states. But the Mayan kings and priests were parasitic, creaming off precious surplus and wasting it on war, pyramid building, and the religious mysticism that legitimised their existence. Like other ancient and medieval civilisations, the Mayan eventually collapsed under its own weight, the cost of the elite and the state bearing down ever more heavily on the economic base of the system.

Waves of barbarian invaders from the north entered the geopolitical space left by Mayan decline. The Toltecs eventually established dominance in central Mexico from *c.* AD 950 to 1170. This was followed by another period of fragmentation and warfare. The Aztec civilisation which emerged from this chaos bore the preceding period's hallmarks. It appears to have been an exceptionally brutal consequence of the contradiction between primitive technique and imperial ambition (though we must be cautious, for the Spanish writers who supply much of our information were deeply hostile to native civilisation).

The Aztecs founded their capital and ceremonial centre at Tenochtitlán in 1345. Between 1428 and 1519 they built an extensive empire. The Aztec state was a centralised autocracy, with a warrior and high-priestly ruling class and a large professional army. There appears to have been no attempt to assimilate subject-peoples or develop productive technique. Tribute – gold, cotton, turquoise, feathers, incense, and vast quantities of food – were sent to Tenochtitlán. Huge numbers of war captives were also taken there to be sacrificed at the Great Temple, their hearts torn out as an offering to the Aztec sun-god, their bodies then tipped down the steps.

The Aztec Empire was a crude military imperialism. Its brutality and futility expressed in an extreme form the limitations of an urban revolution based on Early Neolithic technique. The rate of exploitation, and the terrorism necessary to maintain it, was proportional to the inadequacy of the available surplus. The violence of the Aztec state and the poverty of its subject-people were two aspects of a single contradiction.

The Inca Empire of Peru began to expand in 1197, two centuries before the Aztec Empire of central Mexico. But it achieved its greatest extent at the same time – in 1493–1525 – and shared some of the Aztec Empire's essential characteristics. The Inca state was a centralised military autocracy, with a large professional army, and an administrative bureaucracy which attempted to control the daily life of every subject. At the heart of the empire were great monumental complexes, such as the capital at Cuzco, the fortress guarding it at Sacsahuaman, and the ceremonial centre at Machu Picchu.

The Incas controlled an area some 3,200 km long and 515 km wide comprising a mix of coastal plain, high mountains, and dense forests. They constructed a network of roads totalling an estimated 40,000 km, incorporating numerous tunnels, bridges, and causeways, with official rest-houses at intervals of a day's journey.

Both the Aztec and Inca Empires were anomalies. In central Mexico and the Peruvian Andes, ancient empires, with their ruling elites, professional armies, and monumental complexes, were constructed on a Stone Age economic base. The prodigious waste expenditure of the ruling class required ruthless surplus extraction.

Imperial rule, therefore, depended on terror. Aztec and Inca rulers were hated by their subject-peoples. Rebellion was rife.

In consequence, when the Spanish arrived in the early sixteenth century, the Aztec and Inca imperial states shattered. This was not simply a function of the superior military technique of a more advanced social order: it was also because the common people either welcomed the defeat of their masters or even participated actively in the struggle to bring them down.

6
European Feudalism
c. AD 650–1500

English feudal knight. Memorial brass, c. 1400.

A world of competing military elites, medieval Europe was exceptionally dynamic, and a new class of farmers, artisans, and traders – 'the middling sort' – soon emerged to challenge the rule of feudal lords.

Having summarised developments in the rest of the world over a millennium, this chapter turns exclusively to Europe in the same period. Why? Because capitalism and industrial society have their origins in medieval Europe. This great transformation – matched in scale and significance only by the Agricultural Revolution – was pioneered on the north-western fringe of the Eurasian landmass.

That this was so was the result of complex interactions between geography, politics, and society over several centuries. It depended on the economic connection between Europeans and the sea; on the social relationships between lords, vassals, and peasants; on the role of merchants, towns, and trade; on the endless wars waged by feudal magnates; on the eternal fragmentation of Europe into a patchwork of warring states; and on the class struggles mounted by ordinary men and women to improve their lot.

Understanding these interactions and the series of conjunctures that gave rise to capitalism has been one of the central preoccupations of Marxist historiography for almost two centuries. We must give the problem the attention it deserves.

Excursus 2: The Cycles and Arrows of Time

In Chapter 2, we discussed 'how history works'. It may be useful to pause to review some more of the general lessons of the narrative so far.

History is formed of cycles and arrows. History's cycles reflect Nature, a cycle of life, growth, death, and new life. The production cycles of farmers and the reproduction cycles of families are examples. History's arrows, on the other hand, are the linear progressions of innovation, evolution, and sometimes revolution by which the social world is periodically transformed.

History consists of both. Nature, society, and humankind must at all times reproduce themselves; the only alternative is extinction. Much of what we do is unavoidably repetitive and predictable. But history never repeats itself exactly. Each historical conjuncture is unique. (By conjuncture – or state of affairs – I mean a specific moment in historical time and geographical space in which related economic, social, and political events take place.) What accounts for the uniqueness of each conjuncture is the combination of continuity – history's cycle – and change – history's arrow. But there are critical differences of degree from one conjuncture to another. When history's cycle is dominant, change is quantitative and limited. When the arrow is dominant, it is qualitative and transforming.

Let us recall the three engines of history: the accumulation of knowledge, technique, and productivity; the struggle between rival ruling classes for control of surplus; and the struggle between classes over the size and distribution of surplus. It is the interaction of these three engines that drives the historical process.

Iron tools transformed ancient agriculture, bringing new land into cultivation, increasing the productivity of labour, and massively enlarging the social surplus. Technology was the prime mover. Human labour, after all, has its own dynamic. No worker chooses a blunt tool when there is a sharp one to hand.

The rise of the Roman Empire, on the other hand, though based on iron technology, was powered by military struggle between rival ruling classes and rival factions within the Roman elite. Here, struggle at the top for control of surplus was the prime mover.

The flowering of Classical Greek civilisation in the fifth century BC – another Iron Age culture – is an instance where the struggle *between* classes was decisive. It was the hoplite revolution of the sixth century BC that created city-state democracies and the context for naturalistic art, classical architecture, drama, and the academic disciplines of natural science, philosophy, and history.

The engines always operate in specific natural and social frameworks. Geography both provides opportunities and imposes constraints, and the tradition of social institutions, practices, and customs inherited from the past constitutes the context for further historical development.

Here is an example. The geography of Eurasia spread people, resources, tools, and ideas much more effectively than did that of Africa. But the strength of the centralised state prevented the development of an independent urban bourgeoisie in medieval China at the eastern limit of this landmass; whereas the weakness of the feudal states of Europe allowed one to develop at its western edge. This is a key part of the explanation as to why capitalism first arose in Europe.

Sometimes the interaction of history's three engines produces only a repeating cycle; sometimes it produces gradual change; and sometimes revolutionary crisis and radical social transformation. Among the Arabs, Turks, Mongols, Indians, Chinese, Africans, and Americans, history's cycle was dominant through the long centuries from antiquity to modernity. There was change, but it was slow. Change was quantitative rather than qualitative.

The lives of peasant-farmers, who made up the overwhelming bulk of the population in ancient and medieval times, were dominated by history's cycle. Even when they rebelled, as they sometimes did if exploitation intensified, they merely installed new leaders and then went back to their farms.

The lives of merchants were more changeable. Some were lucky and became rich. Some simply kept going. Others failed and went bankrupt. But their individual fates did not affect how society as a whole worked. Merchants oiled the wheels of the production process; they did not power it. They occupied the interstices of society, not its commanding heights.

The lives of rulers were more changeable still, with the rise and fall of dynasties, empires, and civilisations. But this made little difference to the lives of those they ruled. The identities of the rulers – personifications of the competitive logic of military imperialism – were a secondary matter. One king was much the same as another.

Only in one part of the world did a unique combination of circumstances and forces arise that was sufficiently powerful to generate a dynamic of change capable of producing radical social transformation. It had happened once before: the first great transformation was the Agricultural Revolution, which occurred in different parts of the world between about 7500 BC and as late as the twentieth century AD. All ancient and medieval civilisations were essentially the result of this revolution. The great majority of the population worked on the land and the great bulk of the social surplus took the form of agricultural produce. But in the last 250 years, the social world has been transformed again, with the development of industrial capitalism. This second transformation has created the social world we inhabit today. Because it began in Europe, and from there spread to the rest of the world, we must from this point onwards focus disproportionate attention on events in this relatively small part of the globe.

Excursus 3: The Peculiarity of Europe

At first, the predominance of Europe in world history since *c.* 1500 can seem surprising. Europe is but an outgrowth of Asia, and the great civilisations of both Bronze Age and Iron Age arose elsewhere – in Egypt, Iraq, Persia, India, and China. Even Greek and Roman civilisation were centred on the Mediterranean rather than Europe as such. By comparison, prehistoric and ancient Europe appears peripheral and backward.

Yet Europe has a unique geography. The relationship between Europe and the sea is more intimate than that of any other continent. Europe is a small continent formed of fingers and fists of land that project into the seas surrounding it on three sides – the Baltic, North Sea, Atlantic, Mediterranean, and Black Sea. There is no great expanse of continental interior. No European is ever far from the sea. Europeans cluster, as Socrates once said of the Greeks, 'like frogs around a pond'.

Europe's deeply indented coastline is 37,000 km long – equivalent to the circumference of the earth – and the interior is penetrated by numerous long, highly navigable rivers. The Volga, Dnieper, Vistula, Oder, Elbe, Rhine, Seine, Loire, Garonne, Ebro, Po, Danube: these and others have been Europe's major thoroughfares for thousands of years.

Though great mountain ranges extend across much of the continent, there are ways round. The Middle European Corridor runs from the steppes of south Russia, through the Danube's Iron Gates, across the Hungarian Plain, and on into Western Europe. The North European Plain is an open expanse extending from Moscow to Paris. Both have been routes of mass movement across Europe from the Neolithic to the Nazis.

North to south movement is harder, but the rivers make it possible, as do the numerous mountain passes. None of the ranges constitutes an impenetrable barrier. In any case, north–south movement matters less than movement from east to west: Eurasia is aligned east–west, and that is generally the way in which people, goods, and ideas have moved.

European topography harbours a greater variety of eco-zones than that of any other area of comparable size. The Gulf Stream, originating in the tropics and sweeping around the western, northern, and eastern fringes of the Atlantic, moderates the European climate and shapes a series of distinct zones. There is the frozen tundra of the far north; the cold forests of the taiga belt of northern Russia and Scandinavia; the wide temperate zone of deciduous woodland in Western Europe; the open steppes of Central and Eastern Europe, and the warm Mediterranean littoral between the mountains and the sea in the far south. This has had a decisive impact on the development of economy, society, and culture. To grasp its significance, we must distinguish between a single event, a conjuncture (or state of affairs), and what some historians call the *longue durée* (long duration).

The Battle of Naseby in 1645 was a single event. The English Revolution of 1640–60 was a conjuncture. But the rise of a 'middling sort' of minor gentry, yeoman farmers, and prosperous urban artisans and traders – the people who made the revolution – was a *longue durée* spanning three to four centuries.

Particularly in the context of the *longue durée*, geography matters. It does not drive history – history is driven by the decisions and actions of people – but it helps create the context within which history takes place. Geography both imposes constraints and provides opportunities. Because humans are part of nature, geography determines what is possible.

Because of its geography, Europe is pre-eminently a continent of communication, conflict, and interaction. People, goods, and ideas are able to move rapidly. The weak, the sluggish, the conservative are vulnerable. Europe's openness places a premium on dynamism and innovation.

In a world of roads, railways, and airlines, we struggle to grasp the centrality of water transport before the Industrial Revolution. An ox will consume the equivalent of its own load in a month of haulage work. In the same period, the crew of a river barge or a seagoing merchantman will travel much further and consume only a tiny fraction of their cargo. It is no accident that the most advanced parts of early modern Europe – and of the world – were also the most watery. The world's first bourgeois revolution took place in a country of islands, estuaries, reclaimed land, and drainage dykes: the Netherlands. Its second took place in one surrounded by the sea: Britain.

Only once in its history has even half of Europe been united in a stable imperial polity. The Roman Empire of the first to the fifth century AD included the whole of Europe west of the Rhine and south of the Danube. Other comparable imperial projects – those of Charlemagne, Philip II, Louis XIV, Napoleon, and Hitler – proved abortive. Europe is a continent of warring states. Europe's would-be imperial hegemons have been frustrated by geography. The continent's easy east–west communications, its seaways and inland waterways, and its diversity of eco-zones and ethnicities have combined to prevent the construction of mega-polities.

Empires, especially long-lived ones, are inherently conservative. The petty polities of medieval and early modern Europe, on the other hand, could not afford to be. Europe was a continent of conflict and, therefore, a continent of change. On the Nile, Euphrates, Ganges, and Yangtze, history's cycle predominated throughout medieval history. But on the Rhine, it was history's arrow.

The first great transformation in the history of *Homo sapiens* – the Early Neolithic or Agricultural Revolution – was pioneered in the Middle East and Central Asia in the eighth millennium BC. The second – the Industrial Revolution – was forged in Europe between the fourteenth and eighteenth centuries AD. We must now seek out the roots of that transformation in the European feudal system that preceded it.

The Rise of Western Feudalism

The end of the Roman Empire was neither uniform nor sudden – it was a complex process rather than a single event. First, the empire split in two. Then, between AD 395 and 476, the western half disinte-grated and was replaced by a patchwork of Germanic kingdoms. The eastern half, the Byzantine Empire, survived more or less intact for almost 250 years and, in an increasingly truncated form, for a further 750 years after that.

The Byzantine Empire was an attempt to fossilise the social order of Late Antiquity. A decaying form of ancient military imperialism, it was highly exploitative and deeply conservative. Despite this, it endured for more than a millennium after AD 395, whereas its western counterpart, with a similar social structure, lasted less than a century. The reason was that Byzantium, with far shorter fronts to defend, produced two-thirds of the former Roman Empire's tax revenues. Western Europe, by contrast, became a politically fragmented region of warring states. This was the geopolitical context for the rise of feudalism.

A digression is in order here. The rulers of complex class societies in ancient and medieval times had essentially three ways of mustering military forces. They could levy tribute on their subject populations and use the proceeds to hire soldiers. They could impose a mixture of tribute and labour service, with free men required to do militia service when called upon. Or they could grant land in return for military service.

The former was usually found in a strong centralised state; it was an ideal to which kings and emperors might aspire, since it meant they were not dependent on men who had rights as well as obligations. The second option usually implied a less dominant state and the existence of a strong free peasantry, while the third usually involved the existence of a powerful order of feudal landowners. In practice, many hybrid forms existed, and medieval European armies, for instance, could easily be a mixture of professional household troops, locally raised militia, and feudal retinues. But the balance could be critical in determining the coherence and stability of the polity.

Between the fifth and ninth centuries AD, most Western European states were essentially tributary in character. The state collected taxes and imposed military service. But these same states acquired some feudal characteristics as rulers sought to control territory more effec-tively by parcelling it out to their kinsmen and retainers in return for military service. This feudal element became more important over time. This was partly because the states were small, unstable, and relatively weak. It was also because heavily armoured cavalry increasingly dominated the battlefield.

The ninth and tenth centuries were a period of particular turmoil. Kings were deposed and civil wars raged. Urban life virtually ceased to exist. Long-distance trade declined. Vikings, Magyars, and Arabs mounted deep and devastating raids. In response to this crisis, without the dead weight of strong imperial elites and infrastructures, the way was open to forge a radically new social, political, and military order.

To crush domestic rebels, defend borders against raiders, and fend off the armies of rival kings, early medieval rulers made a virtue of necessity and turned embryonic feudalism into a fully-fledged system. They thereby created immensely strong bodies of armed men by rooting the state in private landlordism.

At first, when control of estates was still dependent on royal favour, the position of medieval rulers was greatly strengthened. Over time, however, as estates became hereditary assets, the balance of power shifted in favour of the king's landholding vassals.

The Duchy of Normandy, a state created by tenth-century Viking settlers, was an extreme example. Initially, power was highly centralised. The ruler was the legal owner of all land, and his appointees held all the great estates. These men were his vassals, his tenants-in-chief, liable to be ejected if they earned their master's disfavour.

Under them, land was further subdivided into fiefs, each able to support a knight, each sufficient to free a man from the need to labour, allowing him to devote himself fully to war and training for war, and to provide him with the horses, chainmail armour, and weaponry of a heavy cavalryman. Here was the core of the Norman state: several thousand armoured horsemen, organised in lordly retinues, bound by ties of personal loyalty and dependence, and rooted in control of landed estates.

The armoured knight was the tank of the eleventh-century battlefield. A frontal charge by several hundred knights, in close formation and several ranks deep, was virtually unstoppable on open ground. Heavy horse – the armed wing of the feudal landowning class – was as central to early medieval warfare as heavy foot – the phalanx of citizen-soldiers – had been to the classical civilisation of the Greeks and Romans.

By linking landholding and military service, feudalism forged a tight bond between the state and the ruling class. It also ensured that the agrarian base of the system was carefully tended, since maintaining rank depended in part on the good management of estates. But there were dangers. The system was inherently unstable. State power was directly related to the number of fiefs and knights controlled by the ruler, exacerbating the struggle between rival polities for territory. Moreover, to avoid fiefs being subdivided and becoming unable to support a knight, primogeniture prevailed, whereby the eldest son inherited the entire estate. Younger sons therefore had to fight for their place in the world. Denied an inheritance and threatened with loss of rank, they survived through mercenary service or by winning a fiefdom. This was true of knights, nobles, and princes – the younger sons of all ranks of the feudal aristocracy could maintain caste only through military force.

There were plenty of opportunities. Civil and foreign wars were frequent. Competition for territory ensured that feudal ruling classes were internally divided and rival feudal polities always at loggerheads. Younger sons, in the quest for booty, pay, and land, were the cutting edge of these conflicts.

Feudalism was therefore unstable, dynamic, and expansionist. During the mid-eleventh century, for example, the Normans conquered much of northern France, the whole of England, and virtually the whole of southern Italy and Sicily.

Feudal violence was contradictory. It was essential to the survival of the feudal states: the warrior host defended the homeland, conquered new territory, and maintained internal order. But the violence had a dynamic of its own and the potential to blow the feudal order apart.

Pressure valves were needed to vent the system's surplus violence. This was the bloody logic that led to the Crusades. The 200-year history of the Crusades represents the most extreme expression of the futile surplus violence inherent in Western feudalism.

Crusade and Jihad

When Pope Urban II launched the First Crusade at the Council of Clermont on 27 November 1095, he is recorded as saying:

> Let those ... who are accustomed to wantonly wage private war against the faithful march upon the infidels ... Let those who have long been robbers now be soldiers of Christ. Let those who once

fought against brothers and relatives now rightfully fight against the barbarians. Let those who have been hirelings for a few pieces of silver now attain an eternal reward...

The Church, with estates across Western Europe, was a vast feudal corporation. It competed for power and wealth with secular feudal princes. Anything that enhanced the Church's prestige, such as the wave of religious zeal and activity unleashed in 1095, was an advantage. And, like other feudal potentates, the bishops were keen to maintain peace at home by exporting violence overseas.

The response exceeded all expectations. Thousands answered the call. A great feudal army entered Syria in 1097, captured Antioch in 1098, took Jerusalem in 1099. Wherever they went, the Crusaders committed atrocities. Men, women, and children were slaughtered in the streets of captured cities. Prisoners were routinely decapitated. Mosques, synagogues, and 'heretic' churches were ransacked. Carts were loaded with plunder.

Four Crusader states were formed. The tactical dominance of feudal heavy cavalry on the battlefield made this possible. But the Crusaders remained a tiny military elite: just 500 knights defended the Principality of Antioch. To survive, therefore, they needed to invest in military power. This required intensive surplus accumulation. The result was extreme exploitation of the Arab peasantry, routine plunder of trade caravans, and a hostile relationship with neighbouring Islamic states.

The Crusaders had broken into the Middle East with great ease because it had become divided into rival states ruled by unpopular, palace-based autocrats propped up by mercenaries and largely divorced from civil society. Many of these Islamic rulers sought an accommodation with the Crusaders.

But no lasting peace was possible. Two contradictions were at work. First, the weakness and insecurity of the feudal settler-states made them annexationist – they needed more land to support more knights – and this was a direct threat to the Islamic rulers. Second, within the Crusader states, the imperative of military accumulation required onerous taxation, rents, and labour service. Consequently, the Crusaders were hated by their Muslim subjects and there was little prospect of raising reliable native forces to fight in their defence.

The 'shock and awe' of the First Crusade broke Muslim resistance for a generation. But the Crusader threat to the rulers of the Islamic states triggered a process of political centralisation. Northern Syria and northern Iraq were united in 1128. Then the nearby Crusader-ruled County of Edessa was recaptured and annexed in 1144. The Second Crusade of 1146–8, organised in response to the Islamic resurgence, was a disastrous failure, shattering the myth of Crusader invincibility. Damascus and southern Syria were added to the new Islamic state, and the Crusader Principality of Antioch reduced to a small coastal enclave. Finally, in 1183, Egypt was fused with Syria under the leadership of Saladin, an event that gave the Muslim resistance critical mass. Saladin answered the feudal Crusade with a call for popular *jihad*, and now Muslim forces went onto the offensive.

On 4 July 1187, at the Battle of Hattin, Saladin, at the head of 30,000 men, destroyed the entire army of the Crusader Kingdom of Jerusalem. The capture of the city of Jerusalem itself followed soon after. Despite further expeditions, the Crusaders never recovered. Though it took a century to complete the process, their castles were reduced one by one, their territory gradually stripped away.

The Crusader states contributed nothing to the Middle East. Their rulers were simply brutal exploiters who ruled by force and fear. They lasted as long as they did only because of the fragmentation and decadence of the Islamic ruling classes. Their violent incursion had, however, been the catalyst for an Islamic revival, with new unities and identities forged in the struggle.

The Crusades had also revealed the limits of Western feudalism. Knights and castles were expensive. Super-exploitation was therefore necessary to sustain them. Despite the cost, the violence of the warrior caste constituted a permanent threat to the property and security of the common people. The bitterness this created could be contained by fear of feudal violence, but it could not be eradicated. Feudalism was incapable of giving rise to a stable social order based on consent.

At home, these contradictions contributed to the rise of new social forces within the old order. Kings were elevating themselves above the feudal host. The central state was reining in over-mighty subjects. Gentry and yeomen (as the English called them) were rallying to the cause of royal order against baronial anarchy.

New social forces ushered in new ways of war. Common men armed with pikes, bows, and guns started challenging the battlefield supremacy of feudal chivalry.

Lord, Burgher, and Peasant in Medieval Europe

The medieval world can appear conservative, stagnant, and unenlightened. Ever since the end of antiquity, European elites have tended to model themselves on the 'glory that was Greece' and the 'grandeur that was Rome'. What followed has been depicted as an age of ignorance, poverty, and violence.

The opposite is true: the Roman imperial ruling class was a barrier to innovation, and the medieval world, in Europe at least, was far more dynamic than the ancient. The reason is simple enough. As the stock of knowledge, skill, and resources accumulates, humanity's capacity for further social development increases. The more advanced the know-how and equipment, the easier further improvements in the productivity of labour become. The pace of progress therefore tends to accelerate.

Technology, however, can determine only what is possible; it cannot guarantee that the potential will be realised. That depends on the other two engines of history: the struggle for control of surplus within the ruling class, and the struggle over the distribution of surplus between the classes.

Feudalism was a system of competitive military accumulation. Warfare – the most extreme form of competition – is never conservative. Those who do not adopt the latest technology and tactics are defeated. Military technique was therefore an especially dynamic sector of the medieval social order. Plate armour superseded chainmail. Firearms replaced bows. Timber castles were rebuilt in stone. Small feudal retinues gave way to large professional armies. To adapt was to survive.

But the new methods of war were more expensive, and demand for better arms, armour, and fortifications triggered economic growth and social change. So did the demand for the increasingly elaborate trappings of lordly power – grand houses, tapestries and wall hangings, fine furniture, fashionable clothing, jewellery and ornaments, tableware, quality wines, and much else. This, too, received impetus from the relentless competitive struggle for wealth and position among the magnates.

Feudal competition therefore created work for artisans and markets for traders. These congregated in the towns, where they organised themselves into guilds, and girded the perimeters of the settlements with walls, allowing them to maintain their independence. Kings granted urban charters. Townsmen favoured a strong state that could maintain law and order. Monarch and burghers found themselves in alliance against feudal anarchy.

In the countryside, even more important changes were underway. Increased demand for armaments, luxuries, and pageantry could be satisfied only by purchases in the market: the lords needed money. Labour services were therefore commuted to cash payments, and serfdom evolved into a more impersonal, less burdensome commercial contract. This strengthened the village and the peasant entrepreneur.

Serfdom, in any case, had never been universal. In medieval England − a society about which we are especially well informed because of the Domesday Book and a wealth of land charters and manorial records − most of the peasantry had always retained substantial rights; even 'villans' were protected by manorial custom, and 'sokemen' and 'freemen' were formally free. In practice, though subject to various feudal payments, and in some cases labour service, most English peasants worked as independent farmers on land they rented, held by custom, or owned freehold.

After the Norman Conquest, the Anglo-Saxon village, with its grades of peasant, its collective organisation, and its centuries-old custom and practice, remained largely unchanged. At the level of the individual manor, Norman England was a compromise between feudal authority and village traditions.

In parts of Europe where the village was strong, as in England, peasants were able to exploit the imperatives of feudal competition to advance their own position. And it is in the micro-relationship between manor and village that we find the germ of the transition from feudalism to capitalism.

European agriculture had made a giant leap forward between the seventh and twelfth centuries. The heavy wheeled plough was the key to this. Drawn first by yoked oxen, and later, once suitable harness had been developed, by horses, the medieval plough could cut through the most intractable soil, turn it over in great clods, and thereby tap fresh stores of nutrients. Much new land, previously unworkable, could be brought into cultivation. Old land, kept in good heart by crop rotation, fallow years, and manure, could be endlessly revitalised by plough-churned stubble and dung. Historians estimate that grain yields doubled.

Many other innovations contributed to increasing labour productivity. Watermills, with complex cranks and flywheels, mass-processed grain and powered blacksmiths' forges. Rivers were canalised to accommodate barges, and rudders replaced steering oars on seagoing ships. Wheelbarrows eased rural labour, and eyeglasses extended the working lives of clerks, copyists, and scholars.

The social surplus steadily increased. Europe in the thirteenth century had a rising population and increasing prosperity. On the land, beneath the level of the feudal elite – and largely beyond the gaze of history – minor gentry and better-off peasants were driving a process of economic advance.

The feudal lords had an interest in raising revenues from landholdings, but also an interest in waste expenditure on a colossal scale – building cathedrals and castles, paying and equipping soldiers, and competing in displays of pageantry, luxury, and grand living. The dynamic of feudalism – competitive politico-military accumulation – was in contradiction to economic improvement, which required investment of surplus in land clearance, drainage, enclosure, agricultural equipment, and so on.

Recent research has revealed that the improvers tended to be the middle section of medieval rural society. Their aim was to create more efficient and productive farms geared to the market. They paid close attention to the business of farm management, husbanding resources, investing with care, seeking to increase economic profit and their own social standing.

Put simply, between c. 1350 and 1500 many of the minor gentry and better-off peasants in the most economically advanced parts of Europe became capitalist farmers. And it was this 'middling sort' that powered the explosive social struggles that erupted across Europe in the late fourteenth and early fifteenth centuries.

The Class Struggle in Medieval Europe

Let us sum up what has been argued so far. Western feudalism, apparently so dominant in the eleventh century, was undermined by five dynamic processes.

First, the productivity of the medieval economy meant an accelerating rate of increase in both labour productivity and aggregate output. One consequence was rapid technological advance in the means of destruction. Military expenditures escalated.

Second, the fragmented political landscape and the intense competition for land, revenue, and manpower between rival feudal magnates compelled the ruling class to seek cash to hire soldiers, purchase equipment, and build fortifications. Feudal obligations were therefore commuted to cash payments.

Third, the resilience and resistance of the peasant village imposed limits on feudal landlordism in many parts of Europe. The peasants formed a collective powerful enough to defend customary rights and sometimes to make substantial gains.

Fourth, the growth of the market created opportunities for the economic and social development of the middle sections of society. At the top were feudal magnates wasting resources on war, display, and luxury. At the bottom were poor and middle peasants eking out a living as subsistence farmers. Between them were those who came to be called 'the middling sort'. These minor gentry, rich peasants, and prosperous urban artisans and traders formed the most economically enterprising sections of medieval society. As markets expanded and social relations were increasingly commercialised, the middling sort emerged as the petty-capitalists at the forefront of social change.

Fifth, feudalism was undermined by the rise of the centralised monarchical state. In some parts of Europe, kings failed to assert their power and warring regional barons remained politically dominant. In others, the state, despite occasional setbacks, grew steadily stronger.

England provides a clear example of the latter process. Over time, medieval English kings relied less on their feudal retinue and more on buying the services of professional soldiers or trained militia. The English royal state marginalised hostile regional barons and minimised the risk of feudal anarchy by forming a political alliance with loyalist magnates and the middling sort. This alliance explains England's astonishing battlefield supremacy in the fourteenth century. At Crécy, Poitiers, and Agincourt, heavily outnumbered English armies of dismounted men-at-arms and longbowmen (the latter recruited from the English and Welsh yeomanry, the rich-peasant class) destroyed French armies composed largely of feudal knights.

The forces of change were propelled by the great crisis of the fourteenth century. Feudal waste expenditure continued to rise in contradiction to the demands of population growth and general prosperity. Society faced a choice between war and grandeur on the one hand, and investment in estates, industries, and trade on the other. By the middle of the fourteenth century, the medieval European economy was seriously out of kilter. Many faced poverty and starvation. When, in 1348, the continent was struck by the Black Death, up to a third of the population perished. Depopulation and impoverishment threatened the incomes of lords and the very survival of the peasants. The crisis spawned bitter struggles.

In 1358, peasant revolts erupted across northern France, and in Paris, Etienne Marcel led 3,000 urban artisans to the royal palace and forced the Dauphin (the heir to the throne) to put on the colours of revolt. In 1381, the English peasants, led by Wat Tyler, entered London, forged an alliance with sections of the urban population, and confronted the King and the Lord Mayor. 'When Adam delved and Eve span,' asked the radical ex-priest John Ball, 'who was then the gentleman?'

In the towns and villages of Flanders, too, and in the city-states of northern Italy, the common people rose up against the oppression of landlords, merchants, and bishops. In 1378, the Florentine *ciompi*, the ordinary artisans of the woollen trades, overthrew the mercantile elite, seized power, and held the city for two months.

In distant Bohemia, when the radical preacher Jan Hus was burnt at the stake as a heretic in 1415, the Czech population rose in revolt. Armed with hand-guns and formed in defensive wagon laagers, the Hussites resisted suppression by the forces of feudal Europe for 20 years. 'All shall live together as brothers,' declared the democratic-egalitarian Taborite wing of the Hussite movement; 'none shall be subject to another.' Fighting to win such freedom in the face of ruthless counter-revolutionary violence, the Taborites were uncompromising about their struggle: 'All lords, nobles, and knights shall be cut down and exterminated in the forests like outlaws.'

The anti-feudal revolutionary wave generated by the fourteenth-century crisis was eventually defeated everywhere. It had been a revolution of the middling sort. It was in some of the most economically advanced regions of Europe that it had achieved its greatest momentum – in northern France, Flanders, England, northern Italy, and Bohemia. It was a premature eruption of social forces not yet fully formed. Feudalism was still powerful enough to contain the revolution in its early heartlands. Petty-capitalism and the middling sort were not yet hegemonic.

Even in the rebel movements, radical visions of the world transformed jostled for attention with the primitive prejudices of the past. From the biological horror of the Black Death arose the political horror of the pogrom. Bishops and kings denounced the Jews for poisoning the wells, and anti-semitic mobs rampaged through the ghettoes.

But the old order could not be restored. Acute labour shortages in the wake of the Black Death tilted the balance of class forces sharply in favour of the peasantry across much of Europe. The rebellions were crushed, but the commercialisation of social relations continued to erode the feudal order from within.

The new social forces – minor gentry and rich peasants producing for the market, small traders and artisans in the towns, the entrepreneurs of new industries, the seafarers, boatmen, and dockers – were not yet strong enough to break through politically. But 'market feudalism' – as it has been called – meant rising demand for urban crafts, industrial enterprise, long-distance trade, and money-lenders. That in turn created demand for the agricultural output of market-oriented farmers.

Ever more goods and services were commodified. Social relations were recast in the form of commercial contracts. Gold-lust dissolved the personal retinues of the feudal order. The economic advance of the middling sort continued. A spectre of revolution stalked late medieval Europe.

New Monarchs and New Worlds

In 1491, Charles VIII, King of France, married Anne, the heiress of the Duchy of Brittany, and thereby completed the unification of the country. His successors, in particular Francis I (1515–47), went on to build a strong, centralised, absolute monarchy. Nobles were forbidden to raise armies, the Paris *Parlement* was stripped of its political authority, and the Church was subordinated to the Crown. The royal state employed 12,000 officials to carry out its orders. Both secular and clerical aristocracy became courtiers dependent on royal favour.

In 1489, the marriage of Queen Isabella of Castile to King Ferdinand of Aragon prepared the way for the unification of Spain. Here, too, a royal absolutism was constructed. Nobles, towns, and the *cortes* (parliaments) became subordinate to royal agents. The Holy Inquisition was turned into a ruthless instrument of state terror. In time, with the unification of Germany and Spain under Charles V (1519–56), and in the face of the challenge of the Protestant Reformation, the Inquisition would become a pan-European system of repression.

In England, the Wars of the Roses (1455–85) proved to be the last civil war of the feudal period. The Tudor monarchs who ruled from 1485 turned barons into courtiers, nationalised church property, ruled in alliance with Parliament, and laid the foundations of English naval power. Mass national consciousness developed under the Tudors. People increasingly thought of themselves as English rather than as members of either a county community or a feudal retinue. Shakespeare's plays often echo the new mood. Henry V and his soldiers were 'a band of brothers' made equals by patriotic blood sacrifice.

Military competition between the new monarchs gave urgency to the nascent nationalism of their respective states. Between 1494 and 1559 Europe was convulsed by conflict between the Valois, who ruled France, and the Habsburgs, who ruled Spain and the Holy Roman Empire (essentially Germany and Central Europe). Northern Italy was the principal battleground. These were wars between mass armies of cannon, cavalry, musketeers, and pikemen – the result of what some scholars have called 'the military revolution' – wars which only large states could afford.

Regional magnates and small states succumbed. Backward states had to adapt to survive under the imperative of military competition. The more backward the economy, the more brutal the absolutism. The Muscovite Tsar Ivan the Terrible (1533–84) employed foreign mercenaries to build his empire and crush internal opposition from the traditional *boyar* aristocracy. The backwardness of the Russian economy meant that the absolutist state had no real base of social support. Civil society was simply cowed from above by sadistic terror.

The new monarchies spanned a period of transition. Feudalism was fast decaying, but the emergent bourgeoisie of market-oriented farmers, merchants, and industrialists was not yet strong enough to take power and remodel society in its own image. Neither one thing nor the other, early sixteenth-century society was fluid and unstable. State absolutism was the result. Usually with strong support from the middling sort, the state was powerful enough to suppress feudal anarchy. But having transformed over-mighty subjects into compliant courtiers, it resisted the more radical demands of parliamentary assemblies and popular rebels.

The new monarchies balanced between weakened and increasingly dependent feudalism and embryonic capitalism. That is why the Italian Wars were multifaceted, with feudal, dynastic, national, and, finally, politico-religious dimensions. They were the wars of a period of transition.

Through the dynamic of competition, the new model – unified states, centralised government, royal armies, the crushing of internal dissent, the waging of national-dynastic wars – imposed itself in one form or another on the whole of Europe. Nor was the impact of the new monarchies confined to Europe. The economic forces erupting across the continent were simultaneously engulfing the world in a wave of colonial violence. Europe was changing rapidly from the late fifteenth century onwards. The rest of the world was not. In Asia, Africa, and the Americas, empires rose and fell, but the socio-economic order remained essentially the same.

After the defeat of the Mongols in 1368, China was relatively unthreatened. The security of the Ming Dynasty (1368–1644) rested on the extreme conservatism of the Confucian bureaucrats who ruled it. India was more turbulent. Between 1526 and 1529, Babar the Tiger, a Muslim invader from the north-west equipped with cannon, conquered most of the subcontinent and established the Mughal Empire. But this did not alter the basic character of Indian society. Life and labour continued much as before in India's hundred thousand villages. The same was true of Safavid Persia and Ottoman Turkey. There were conquests, changes of dynasty, and new political and religious allegiances at the top of society, but the fabric of everyday life was barely touched. The dynastic states, some relatively stable, others less so, which floated above each of Asia's geopolitical units – Turkey, Persia, Central Asia, India, China, Japan – remained essentially rootless and parasitic.

Africa and the Americas were no different. The empires of the Songhai in West Africa, the Aztecs in Mexico, and the Inca in Peru were predatory systems of robbery with violence. There was no organic relationship between state superstructure and socio-economic base. The former simply siphoned surplus from the latter and consumed it in wars, monuments, and luxuries. Such states were like panes of glass liable to shatter at the impact of a small stone.

The new monarchies of sixteenth-century Europe, by contrast, were firmly rooted in their respective societies, and European gold-lust and gunpowder were poised to transform the world.

The Portuguese were the pioneers of European colonialism. Portugal is a mountainous country on the western fringe of Europe with a long Atlantic coastline and good natural harbours. The Portuguese were therefore pre-eminent among European seafarers. Crucial to the European 'voyages of discovery' was the development of large, sophisticated sailing vessels. One early innovation was the sternpost rudder. A more gradual and complex process was improving the rigging. By the late fifteenth century, the medieval cog – square-rigged with a single mast and sail – had evolved into a larger vessel with up to three masts and mixed sails, enabling it to sail closer to the wind and to use wind power more economically. Relatively fast and safe, oceangoing voyages became possible for the first time.

Between 1492 and 1504, Christopher Columbus led four expeditions to what came to be called the New World. Though Portuguese, he was funded by the King and Queen of Spain, so the colonies he established on Cuba and Haiti were Spanish possessions.

Between 1497 and 1499, Vasco da Gama sailed round Africa from Lisbon to Calicut. Within 20 years, the Portuguese had a trading empire extending along 20,000 km of coastline from Cape Bogador on the Atlantic coast of North Africa to the Moluccas Islands in the Pacific, with outposts in West Africa, Persia, and India.

Between 1519 and 1522, Ferdinand Magellan circumnavigated the globe and revealed the basic shape and location of its major continents. This Portuguese navigator thereby drew the map for the Spanish *conquistadores* who subjugated much of Central and South America in the early sixteenth century.

Columbus had found very little gold in the West Indies. He had tried to make the new colonies profitable by turning the natives into slaves and serfs. Instead, the combination of colonial barbarism and foreign diseases reduced the population of Haiti from over a million to just 200 in the space of 50 years.

The gold-lust was undiminished. So, in 1519, a force of 660 men, 18 horses, and ten cannon set out from Spain's Cuban colony under Hernan Cortés bound for the mainland. Within two years, they had conquered the Aztec Empire of Central America. In 1532–5, with just 106 infantry and 62 cavalry, Francisco Pizarro replicated Cortés' achievement by destroying the Inca Empire of Peru.

These were victories of steel, gunpowder, and horses over Stone Age technology. Equally important, however, were divisions among the Aztec and Inca rulers and the alienation of their subject-peoples. Because of the murderous brutality of the Aztec imperial elite, more native Americans fought on the side of the Spanish than of the Aztecs at the decisive Battle of Tenochtitlán.

Spain was one of the least developed parts of Europe. The Spanish monarchs were engaged in dynastic wars against geopolitical rivals and religious wars against the Protestant Reformation. They needed gold to pay soldiers. Consequently, the exploitation of 'New Spain' was ruthless. Natives not killed by guns, disease, or famine were often worked to death in the mines and on the estates of their new colonial masters. The Laws of Burgos of 1512–13 decreed that Indian men were to work for Spaniards for nine months of the year, that their wives and children would be enslaved and their property confiscated if they refused, and that tithes must be paid to the Catholic Church.

The population of the Lima area in Peru collapsed from 25,000 to just 2,000. The population of Mexico fell from ten million to three million. The mining town of Potosi in today's Bolivia, on the other hand, was swelled to 150,000 by forced labour. 'I moved across a good portion of the country,' wrote a Spanish noble to the King in 1535, 'and saw terrible destruction.'

The transformation of the world by European colonialism had begun. The Portuguese and Spanish overseas empires founded at the beginning of the sixteenth century were soon followed by Dutch, English, and French empires. At the very dawn of European capitalism, the system was already extending bloody hands across three continents.

But why did relatively backward, feudal, absolutist, Church-dominated Spain – the Spain of the Holy Inquisition – lead the way? The Spanish kings needed New World gold and silver to fund their geopolitical ambitions in Europe, and an accident of geography had given them privileged access to Portugal's maritime tradition. Europe was to pay a high price for this.

A new wave of revolution began in 1521. Revolts by townsmen, peasants, and lesser gentry engulfed Germany throughout the 1520s and into the early 1530s. Religious civil war soon raged across the country. A generation later, this spread to France. Above all, in 1566, full-blooded revolution broke out in the Low Countries. War would continue there between Protestant Dutch and Catholic Spanish until 1609.

It was bullion from the Americas that underpinned the power of Imperial Spain and sustained its armies for two generations in its attempt to drown the world's first bourgeois revolution in blood.

7
The First Wave of Bourgeois Revolutions
1517–1660

A German revolutionary peasant of 1525 bearing a banner inscribed 'Freedom'. Contemporary woodcut.

The religious Reformation that began in 1517 triggered a century and a half of social and political struggles that transformed the world.

By the beginning of the sixteenth century the new forces growing inside medieval European society had achieved critical mass. Yet that did not guarantee the triumph of mercantile capitalism. Powerful vested interests, rooted in long-standing social and political structures, might have caused it to be stillborn. Revolutionary action was necessary to clear away history's clutter of decayed social classes and antiquated ideologies. Only in this way could the old order be overturned and space made for the explosion of trade and accumulation that the productive capacity of humanity had now made possible.

This, in the first phase of world capitalism, during the fifteenth, sixteenth, and seventeenth centuries, was the inner meaning of the Renaissance, the Reformation, the Dutch Revolution, and, of greatest significance, the English Revolution of 1637–60. These events made mercantile capitalism the dominant economic form across large tracts of north-western Europe. The consequences during the eighteenth century would be slavery, colonialism, and global wars.

The Renaissance

History has a tendency to play leapfrog. When a surge of progressive change in one part of the world hits a barrier, new social forces may then push forwards on another front.

In fifteenth-century Europe, a mighty storm was brewing. Between 1517 and 1660, it would rage over the continent without let-up, until the power of the old feudal elite had been broken beyond recovery across a great swathe of it.

The coming storm was heralded by the lightning flashes of the Renaissance. But the great victories in the struggle to unleash the human spirit – to put matters in terms that would have been understood by men like Michelangelo and Leonardo – were destined to be won not in the main centres of this cultural revolution, not in cities like Florence and Rome, but in Amsterdam, Hamburg, and London.

The profoundly progressive character of the Renaissance in fifteenth-century Italy is beyond question. The entire feudal order found itself under a critical spotlight. Though the anti-feudal popular revolts of the late fourteenth and early fifteenth century – in France, England, Flanders, Florence, Bohemia, and elsewhere – had gone down to defeat, the new social forces that had given rise to them continued to gain strength.

Commerce, money-making, a capitalist approach to managing a farm, running a mine, or shipping cargo, were dissolving feudal social relations. The profit motive was undermining personal bonds based on patronage, fealty, and service.

The old ideas could not explain these new realities. The ancient dogmas of the Church, encrypted in the Latin of scholars and monks, seemed increasingly irrelevant. Through enterprise and invention, through skill and hard work, through their own solid efforts, people were remaking the world.

A 'humanist' movement in scholarship and the arts expressed a renewal of confidence in humanity's capacity for improvement. The priest-ridden pessimism and fatalism of the medieval Church – that pumping-station of obfuscation – was suddenly confronted by a human intelligence insisting upon achievement, enterprise, and a brash individualism.

This rebirth in scholarship and the arts – this literal 'renaissance' – developed in the hothouse atmosphere of booming fifteenth- and sixteenth-century Italian towns. To the pedantic scholasticism of medieval theologians was counterposed the learning of the ancients embodied in Greek and Latin texts. To the one-dimensional religious icons of the past were counterposed naturalistic representations of human figures bursting with vitality and creativity.

This was the culture of a rising urban bourgeoisie. As one character in a dialogue written by Italian humanist Leon Battista Alberti (1404–72) put it, 'A man cannot set his hand to more liberal work than making money, for what we sell is our labour: the goods are merely transferred.' Greed is good: accumulation is virtuous: wealth is the reward of effort and the true measure of the New Renaissance Man – not birth and blue blood.

Florence was the original forging-house of the new culture. Its late medieval wealth was based on banking and trade. The *nouveaux riches* advertised their elevation by becoming patrons of the arts. They funded a new architecture based on geometry and symmetry that produced buildings notable for their clarity, elegance, and economy – in contrast to the gloomy monumentality of the Gothic. They supported painters who used techniques like perspective and *chiaroscuro* to depict the world as it appeared in real life – in contrast to the medieval obsession with symbolising the divine.

The Renaissance was epitomised by four great Italian masters. Donato Bramante (1444–1514) was not merely an architect of genius, but one who gave expression in stonework to the ideals of order, utility, and a civilisation based on human action not holy worship. Leonardo da Vinci (1452–1519) was not just an artist and inventor, but an explorer, a pioneer, a trailblazer of human endeavour who has been described as 'the most relentlessly curious man in history'. Raphael (1483–1520) was not only a master artist, but a supreme synthesiser of the Classical and the Christian traditions, his giant frescoes in the papal apartments of the Vatican harmonising the lore of the ancients with the teachings of the Church.

Above all, there was Michelangelo (1475–1564), the great exponent in stone and paint of the struggle of the human spirit to free itself from its shackles, to soar heavenwards, to achieve its apotheosis in an unleashing of creative potential. In Michelangelo's work, the beauty, nobility, and power of humanity seem to acquire explosive force.

Men like Bramante, Leonardo, Raphael, and Michelangelo formed the vanguard of a European cultural revolution at the dawn of the modern age. They foreshadowed in art and thought the transition from feudalism to capitalism. But the political framework of fifteenth- and sixteenth-century Italy stifled the potential of the Renaissance. Instead, art was diverted into the glorification of established forms of power and wealth.

Italy at the time was divided into a plethora of rival states, courts, and cities. Each separate polity was itself divided by the feuding of its leading families. The fractured ruling class of the Italian Renaissance was therefore engaged in successive rounds of internally directed politico-military competition. The age of Michelangelo was also the age of the *condottieri* – bands of mercenary soldiers who could always find work selling their services to Italy's petty princes in their endless local wars.

The new urban bourgeoisie of bankers and merchants was trapped by the logic of this process. Most made their money in the service of existing feudal potentates, and the most successful aspired to become feudal potentates themselves. The Medicis of Florence were originally bankers. But they became the effective rulers of their native city in the later fifteenth century – losing the family fortune in the process – and went on to produce four popes and two queens of France.

For families like the Medici, wealth was not an end in itself: it was a mechanism for political elevation within an *existing* framework of power. Rather than overturn the feudal order, the merchant-bankers of the Italian Renaissance turned themselves into feudal princes. Instead of promoting social transformation, they sought personal transformation into 'gentlemen'. They did not read revolutionary tracts; they read Baldassare Castiglione's *The Courtier*, the Renaissance manual of good manners for the up-and-coming.

In any case, the commercial capitalism of the Italian city-states lacked what might be termed 'economic depth'. It was based on money-lending and trade. It fitted into an essentially feudal structure where demand was rising and goods were increasingly commodified. Italian capitalists were funding the palaces of princes and the wars of the *condottieri*; less often were they improving estates, sinking mines, or developing new techniques. Italian capital was invested in making money, not things; in the waste of politico-military competition, not in new methods of production.

This had other implications. It meant that the social base of the Italian Renaissance was very narrow. It had little impact on the everyday experience of the common people; their world of life and labour was little affected. It was the business of a small urban elite, and remained essentially a matter of the mind, of aesthetics and reflection, without practical application – a fact symbolised by the continuing use of Latin, instead of contemporary languages, making Renaissance discourse a form of scholasticism no more accessible than that of medieval monks.

The degeneration was already apparent in High Renaissance Rome, where Pope Julius II (1503–13) commissioned Bramante to design a new St Peters, Michelangelo to paint the Sistine Chapel, and Raphael to decorate the Vatican apartments. Here was the dazzling brilliance of the Renaissance in the service of ignorance and superstition. Here was human genius corrupted by wealth and power.

Elsewhere, however, a different kind of Renaissance was gathering momentum, one that appealed not so much to the gilded elite as to 'the middling sort' – farmers, traders, and artisans. This 'popular' Renaissance would prove more relentless in its questioning of the old order, in its spreading of doubt, in its undermining of authority and received wisdom. It would create geniuses of its own, and they would give voice to it in the languages of the common people – among them, Cervantes (1547–1616) in Spanish, Rabelais (1494–1553) in French, and Shakespeare (1564–1616) in English.

This Renaissance, moreover, would take on a truly revolutionary form, powered from below by new forces capable of breaking free of the old feudal order, to achieve not merely a revolution in the arts, but a revolution in social life itself. This was the inner meaning of the Reformation.

The Reformation

Before the eighteenth century, religious belief was almost universal, and theology provided the language in which men and women discussed their relationships not only with God, but also with each other. When they conformed, they did so because it was 'God's will'. When they rebelled, that was also 'God's will'. And when they moved from conformity to rebellion, it was not because God had changed his mind; it was because the world had changed. Theology provided the vocabulary of political discourse.

The Catholic Church had dominated Western Europe for a thousand years. Challenges to the authority of its prelates and dogmas had always been crushed. A succession of so-called heretics and infidels had been broken on the rack and burnt at the stake. Only undercurrents of resistance remained. There were secret networks of religious radicals like the Waldensians in European cities, the Hussites in Bohemia, and the Lollards in England. Each had once been a mass popular movement. But none had come close to doing what the Reformation was to do after 1521 – tear apart Church and state. What now made this possible was the maturity of the new social forces that had been growing inside late medieval Europe.

The crisis began at the ideological level. The Church was rotten with corruption. The papacy had become a prize fought over by rival Italian aristocratic families. Cardinals and bishops enriched themselves by holding multiple appointments. 'Indulgences' (for-giveness for sins) were sold like commodities. Many monks lived in luxury. Priests were often ignorant and lazy.

The Church owned vast tracts of land, and abbots and bishops were immensely rich. But this was also true of kings and secular nobles. What made the ecclesiastical section of the feudal ruling class especially vulnerable was the hypocrisy implicit in the corruption of the Church – the contradiction between wealth and mission.

When in 1517 a minor German cleric and scholar called Martin Luther (1483–1546) posted his *Ninety-Five Theses* on the door of Wittenberg Cathedral, his attack on the sale of indulgences and other abuses gained widespread support. This gave him the confidence to persist. When the Pope threatened him with excommunication in 1520, he burned the 'Bull of Antichrist' in Wittenberg town square. And when the Holy Roman Emperor summoned him to appear before the Diet of Worms (the parliament of the local state) in 1521 and threatened to burn him as a heretic, he refused to retract.

What made Luther's message revolutionary was his rejection of priestly authority. Protestants – as they came to be called – were encouraged to read and interpret the Bible for themselves. According to Luther, salvation depended not on church attendance, obedience to the priest, or charitable donations, but on a personal relationship with God. That explains why a printing press could be found at the centre of every religious storm. Medieval books were written in Latin, copied by hand in monasteries, and then stored in ecclesiastical libraries to be read only by a cloistered few. Books contained ideas, and ideas could be subversive; they were not for general use.

The Canterbury Tales by Geoffrey Chaucer (c. 1343–1400) was a case in point. Written in English in the late fourteenth century, its unflattering portrayal of friars, priests, and church officials had attracted a readership among religious radicals. It was later published by William Caxton (c. 1420–92), the pioneer of English printing, putting copies into the hands of a yet wider reading (and listening) public.

That was bad enough. More subversive still was the English-language Bible, popularised by John Wycliffe (c. 1320–84), the leader of the Lollards, whose doctrines anticipated the Reformation. Possession of an unlicensed copy incurred the death penalty: God's word was not to be heard in a language the common people could understand. The first English edition had to be printed in Germany and then smuggled into England in 1526. Its author, the English Protestant William Tyndale (c. 1492–1536), was later executed for heresy. The Reformation was a battle of ideas in which vernacular translations and printed copies of the Bible were primary weapons.

The second phase of the Reformation was led by John Calvin (1509–64), a Frenchman who settled in Geneva in Switzerland and imposed a theocratic dictatorship on the city. He carried the rupture with the Catholic Church to its logical conclusion, rejecting the entire hierarchy of bishops, and advocating in its place self-governing congregations ruled by elders – in effect, a church run by the local middle class.

The essence of the Reformation, therefore, was a break with the main ideological prop of feudalism – the Catholic Church – and a (controlled) explosion of free enquiry and debate.

Protestantism was, above all, the religion of the middling sort, the people who, across the most developed parts of Europe, were pioneers in capitalist farming and the growth of commerce and industry.

The German towns were immediately thrown into turmoil by Luther's message. The town guilds – resentful of feudal dues, church tithes, and the social dominance of mercantile elites – rallied to the new religion. Many towns embraced Lutheranism in the initial wave of enthusiasm (1521–2). Eventually, two-thirds of the German towns were to follow them.

The impoverished knights of southern Germany also launched a revolt (1522–3). They, however, were defeated by the ruling princes. The Reformation was already meeting resistance from above.

The far more serious revolt of the German peasants in 1524–5 was also defeated. Coming from the lowest stratum of society, it represented a challenge to the entire feudal order. The 'Twelve Points' of the Memmingen Charter – effectively the manifesto of the revolt – demanded an end to feudal dues, encroachments on common land, arbitrary justice, and serfdom. As the radical Protestant leader Thomas Müntzer put it, 'Our sovereigns and rulers are at the bottom of all usury, thievery, and robbery ... They oppress the poor husbandmen and craftsmen.'

But Luther and other mainstream Protestant leaders denounced revolt and preached obedience to social elites. 'Better the death of all peasants,' declared Luther, 'than of princes and magistrates.' He wrote a tract entitled *Against the Murdering, Thieving Hordes of the Peasants* in which he encouraged feudal lords to kill peasant rebels 'just as one must kill a mad dog'.

Many German princes were rallying to the Reformation. Luther himself had been rescued and given refuge by the Elector of Saxony in 1521. The popular Reformation from below was countered by an aristocratic Reformation from above.

The princes had several reasons for supporting the Reformation. It was very powerful and many felt it better to try to 'ride the tiger' than to confront it head on. Aristocratic leadership might stem the tide of more radical developments. But the Reformation was also useful in furthering noble ambition. Protestantism became a mechanism for throwing off the authority of secular and ecclesiastical overlords, mobilising support against aristocratic rivals, and taking over church property.

The German princes became Lutherans because they were hostile to both the Pope and the Holy Roman Emperor – but they employed fierce reactionary violence against more radical Protestants who appeared to threaten their wealth and power. And when this happened, the Lutheran leaders backed them.

Something similar happened in France. Many nobles became Protestant as part of a bitter struggle between rival families. The Calvinist leaders backed this Reformation from above. The result, in both Germany and France, was that the struggle between Catholics and Protestants devolved into a war of religion between opposing alliances of magnates.

But Protestantism lost momentum once it ceased to be an expression of popular, anti-feudal revolt and became little more than the badge of allegiance of an aristocratic faction. Southern Germany was recovered for the Emperor and the Church. The French Protestants remained a permanent minority in a mainly Catholic country ruled by an absolute monarch.

The defeat of the German Anabaptists symbolised this sharp break between the popular and aristocratic Reformations. For nearly two years (1534–5) Münster was controlled by Anabaptist radicals led by Jan van Leyden, a young Dutch tailor's apprentice. The Catholic and Lutheran elite was ejected, an egalitarian commune was established, and the Anabaptists prepared for the Day of Judgement. It never came. Instead, the local prince-bishop starved the city into submission, then tortured the captured Anabaptist leaders to death.

The disjuncture between conservative and radical reformers destroyed the revolutionary potential of the Reformation in both Germany and France and gave the gathering forces of feudal-absolutist reaction an opening.

The Ottoman Empire

The great rupture between Catholic and Protestant played out in the shadow of Islam. The Catholic lords of what came to be called 'the Counter-Reformation' found themselves fighting a war on two fronts – against 'heretics' in the north and 'infidels' in the east.

The Seljuk Turkish Empire of the eleventh and twelfth centuries had seen a superstructure of grandees, warriors, and slaves laid across the solid foundation of Arab-Islamic society. It had been a tributary system designed to support a Turkic military host. Lacking a strong political centre and without firm social roots, it broke up easily under the impact of the Crusades. The Turks became, for a while, simply one among a number of peoples – Arabs, Persians, Armenians, Kurds, Jews, others – in the Middle East.

The Ottoman Turkish Empire of the fourteenth and fifteenth centuries was a more substantial structure. Ottoman imperialism gathered momentum slowly and then exploded under the leadership of three great conquering sultans – Mehmet II (1451–81), 'the Conqueror'; Selim I (1512–20), 'the Grim'; and Sulayman I (1520–66), 'the Magnificent' or 'the Lawmaker'.

Mehmet liquidated the remnants of the Byzantine Empire with his capture of Constantinople in 1453 and had conquered most of Anatolia and the Balkans by the time of his death. Selim defeated the Safavids (of Persia) and the Mamluks (of Egypt), and added Syria, Egypt, and western Arabia, including the holy cities of Mecca and Medina, to the Ottoman Empire.

Sulayman defeated the Hungarians at the Battle of Mohacs in 1526, overran their country, and used it as a launch-pad for an attack on Vienna, which faced a month-long siege in 1529. His armies also conquered Iraq and Libya, captured the great naval base and fortress on the island of Rhodes, drove the Venetians out of the eastern Mediterranean, and underwrote the semi-official piracy of the Barbary Corsairs along the North African coast.

The imperial surge under Mehmet, Selim, and Sulayman turned the Ottoman Empire into perhaps the most powerful state in the world, its territory extending from the Danube to the Tigris, from the Crimea to the Maghreb. Christian Europe lived in permanent fear that the Ottoman tide would eventually sweep over them.

What powered Ottoman imperialism in the early sixteenth century, and what brought it to a halt in 1566?

Engaged in a relatively slow process of politico-military accumulation during the fourteenth century, the Ottomans acquired the critical mass in the fifteenth century that enabled them to overpower their weaker neighbours.

Control over the wealth of Syria, Egypt, and later Iraq represented a second qualitative shift, giving them access to the rich agricultural territory, prosperous towns, and lucrative trade-lines of the Middle East. Enhanced revenues enabled them to increase the size of their large, modern, professional army. The capture of Rhodes and the defeat of the Venetians also gave them naval supremacy in the eastern Mediterranean.

The Ottoman state was a highly centralised autocracy, ruled by a sultan with absolute powers, managed by a bureaucratic state apparatus, and defended by an army of household regulars and state feudalists.

Many officials and soldiers were slaves, recruited by a youth levy on the Christian communities of the empire; relatively few were Turks or Arabs. The state was therefore a curious 'de-nationalised' hybrid, with Ottoman, Islamic, and Byzantine elements. It was neither a national state nor a true dynastic one. Though the sons of sultans tended to succeed, they were chosen from the numerous offspring of the slave-concubines of the harem; and their unfortunate brothers were commonly strangled in the seclusion of the palace as a guarantee of political stability.

The army (along with the fleet) was the essence of the state. It was a high-tech army based on the modern firepower of massed cannon and thousands of hand-gunners. At its core were the janissaries, the elite slave musketeers of the sultan. They, along with the artillery, the arms factories, and the military transport corps, were paid for out of state revenues.

These household troops were supplemented by the spahis, a form of state-feudal provincial cavalry, required to do military service in return for land grants from the sultan.

The whole military-bureaucratic complex was sustained by taxes on non-Muslims (a poll tax), on livestock, and on agricultural produce, supplemented by revenues from internal customs duties and taxes on trade and industry. State funds were also expended on monumental art and architecture, court ceremonial and luxury, and the perquisites of the ruling bureaucratic caste.

This waste expenditure was symbolised by the imperial capital – so admired by tourists today – which filled up with superfluous prestige buildings. Constantinople became a city of palaces, mosques, and waterfront villas. In 1550, it was one of the two largest cities in the world; London was only a tenth of the size. But it was a city in which surpluses were consumed in waste expenditure, not a city that was creating wealth on its own account and spearheading social change.

The Empire was a polyglot of ethnicities and religions: Turkish Muslims, Arab Muslims, and Albanian and Bosnian Muslims; Serbian, Bulgarian, and Greek Orthodox; Armenians, Druses, Maronites, Copts; and the Jews. These diverse communities were enrolled in 'millets' under the authority of traditional leaders and subject to separate law codes. There was no attempt to override the complex socio-cultural mosaic ruled by the Ottoman sultans; no attempt to weld the pieces into some sort of union on the basis of shared administration, culture, and identity. The millet system was the antithesis of a modern nation-state: it was a fossilisation of fragments inherited from the medieval past.

A central contradiction was at work, therefore, eroding the foundations of Ottoman power, even as it ascended to its zenith. The Empire was an embedded economy and a state-regulated society. It was a place where economic and social development was arrested in the interests of a military-bureaucratic complex. Instead of surpluses being invested in the improvement of estates and the growth of industry, they were appropriated by the state to sustain Ottoman imperialism.

This, in the long run, was bound to undermine the empire's military vigour. Without investment in technology, skills, and new means of production, the Ottoman Empire was liable to be overtaken by great-power rivals where the state was less mighty, less overwhelming, less liable to squeeze the life out of its socio-economic base.

On 7 October 1571, an allied Christian fleet of 230 vessels clashed with an Ottoman fleet of 270 vessels near Lepanto on the coast of Greece: a titanic collision of naval power to contest control of the Mediterranean seaways. The battle turned into a massed head-on mêlée, the fleets locked together, the ships held by grappling irons and boarding planks, the action a 'land battle at sea' fought out hand-to-hand.

It ended after many hours in an overwhelming Christian victory – one of the most decisive in world history, for it broke the back of the Ottoman naval offensive against the West.

The Christian ships carried a heavier weight of cannon, and their marines wore armour and carried muskets. The Ottomans used slave rowers and relied on ramming and archery. The outcome turned on this difference. A new technology of naval warfare had triumphed over the old. The West – powered by innovation and industry – was already pulling ahead of the East.

The Ottoman surge was spent by the time of Lepanto. After the death of Sulayman the Magnificent, very little further territory was added to the empire.

For a century or so, the power of West and East was in equilibrium: the Ottoman Empire did not advance, but neither did it yet retreat. But when a second attempt on Vienna failed in 1683, as the first had done in 1529, the consequences were different. Christian Europe counterattacked, and by 1699 the Holy Roman Empire had recovered Hungary. The long process of Ottoman decline had begun.

The Spanish Empire

The sixteenth century was 'the Spanish Century'. For most of history, Spain has been relatively marginal to world politics. This is easily explained. As historian John Elliott wrote:

> A dry, barren, impoverished land: 10 per cent of its soil bare rock; 35 per cent poor and unproductive; 45 per cent moderately fertile; 10 per cent rich. A peninsula separated from the continent of Europe by the mountain barrier of the Pyrenees – isolate and remote. A country divided within itself, broken by a high central tableland that stretches from the Pyrenees to the southern coast. No natural centre, no easy routes. Fragmented, disparate, a complex of different races, languages, and civilisations – this was, and is, Spain.

Only once did Spain escape the iron cage of its geography: only briefly did it hold centre-stage as a global hegemon. Yet that heady moment, between 1492 and 1588, when Spain was a world superpower, was an earth-shaker. One consequence is that Spanish is today the world's second most widely-spoken native language (after Mandarin and ahead of English).

The Spanish supremacy was in part an accident of dynastic intrigue. When Ferdinand of Aragon married Isabella of Castile in 1469, the prospect arose that the two major kingdoms of the Iberian Peninsula would be united. Between Isabella's succession to the crown of Castile in 1474 and that of Ferdinand to the crown of Aragon in 1479, civil war raged, but resistance to the Union of the Crowns was defeated amid much carnage.

By 1492, with equal ruthlessness, Ferdinand and Isabella had liquidated the Moorish enclave of Granada in the south – bringing to a final conclusion the 800-year *Reconquista*, the struggle of Christian and Muslim for control of Iberia.

The unified state bore the imprint of both its violent birth and its inherited social structures. Ferdinand and Isabella used their victory to impose a ruthless absolutism on Castile, the core of the new Spain, where at least two-thirds of the population lived. Castile was a land of great estates, many of them converted to sheep-farming, and here royal absolutism was firmly established.

The *cortes* – the local parliaments – lost their powers and became mere rubberstamps of royal authority. Grandees who had wrested land from the Crown in former times were compelled to hand it back. The towns lost much of their former independence, and the urban-based *comunero* revolt of 1520–1 was crushed. The Moors and the Jews were expelled. Converts – known as *moriscos* – faced persecution.

The Inquisition was established as an instrument of state terror. The Church was empowered to pursue, interrogate, torture, and execute all manner of dissidents and non-conformists – branded 'heretics' in the religious discourse of the age. A pall of reaction and repression settled over much of Spain.

Charles V succeeded to the Spanish throne in 1516. Three years later, he inherited the title to the Habsburg territories in Austria, and was then elected Holy Roman Emperor, making him the ruler of the whole of Central Europe. Since he also controlled the Low Countries and most of Italy, he was effectively in control of half the continent.

Europe is a continent of warring states. Throughout its modern history, it has periodically exploded into war as one power or another has threatened to overturn what statesmen used to call 'the balance of power' and establish a pan-European hegemony. Charles V (1516–56) was the first modern European ruler to aspire to such power. The main battleground was Italy.

The Italian Wars raged from 1494 to 1559. They usually pitted the two main European powers against each other – Valois France against Habsburg Spain and the Holy Roman Empire – with secondary powers forming a series of shifting alliances around these main protagonists.

Inter-state warfare was becoming a technically more sophisticated and large-scale operation. Vast quantities of treasure were consumed in these struggles, such that the cost of eventual Habsburg victory in Italy far outweighed any benefit.

Philip II (1556–96) succeeded to the Spanish throne (though not to that of the Empire). The most powerful Catholic ruler in Europe during the second half of the sixteenth century, he was involved in a struggle on three fronts: against the advance of the Ottoman Turks in the eastern Mediterranean; against the Valois kings of France and the rulers of other great powers; and against the Protestant Reformation sweeping through northern Europe.

Vast quantities of gold and silver were now flowing across the Atlantic from Spain's New World colonies. Every year, two convoys of galleons would arrive in Spain, and one fifth of all the treasure landed would go straight into the royal coffers. This was used to finance a huge professional army. New World gold funded Old World power.

The Spanish Army had been transformed in the first part of the sixteenth century into the most formidable military force of its age. It was the Spanish who pioneered new methods of infantry fighting and a 'military revolution'. The Spanish *tercios* became the military elite of Renaissance Europe.

Numbering 3,000 men – the equivalent of a modern brigade – the *tercio* was divided evenly between musketeers and pikemen, the former deployed in depth on the flanks to maximise fire on a rolling basis, the latter forming a central bloc, perhaps ten or more ranks deep, to resist opposing phalanxes when it came to 'push of pike'. The *tercios* were Spain's answer to the massed heavy cavalry fielded by the French, the Germans, and the Italians. Supported by modern artillery, they were – like Rome's legions and Hitler's panzers in other ages – the terror of Europe.

Even so, Philip II's Spain found itself overextended – above all in what turned into an intractable conflict in the Low Countries between Catholic empire and Protestant revolution. The vast resources of Spain allowed the struggle there to be endlessly renewed – from 1566 to 1648 (though after 1609 with reduced intensity) – but the excellent defensive ground of Holland and the dogged resistance of the Protestant rebels kept the *tercios* bogged down.

The defeat of the Spanish Armada was a critical turning-point. English support for the Dutch rebels from 1585 onwards helped prevent a Spanish victory. Elizabeth I's execution of Mary Queen of Scots, the ousted Catholic ruler of the northern kingdom, confirmed England's position as a bulwark of Protestantism. Philip II's response was the largest amphibious expedition since the Crusades: 130 ships, 55,000 men, and 2,500 cannon, to deliver a killer blow to the Protestant cause in the north. The Spanish Armada's destruction by storm, fire, and cannonade in the English Channel marked the limits of Spanish power – and heralded its rapid decline.

Philip II, a humourless bureaucrat, a religious bigot, and a military despot, became the very embodiment of the Catholic Counter-Reformation in the second half of the sixteenth century. But his attempt to uphold Spanish imperial power by simultaneously keeping Valois France in check, holding back the Ottoman tide in the east, and crushing the Protestant Reformation in the north drained the lifeblood from his homeland.

Spanish absolutism had never succeeded in unifying the Iberian Peninsula. The three provinces of Aragon (Aragon, Catalonia, and Valencia), with more entrenched local powers, had retained many of their historic privileges. The main burden of empire always fell on Castile. That burden was crippling.

Royal revenues had risen from less than a million *reales* in 1474 to 26 million in 1504. By the mid-sixteenth century, 80 per cent of these revenues were being spent on the military. The field army increased in size from 30,000 in the 1520s, to 60,000 in the 1530s, and 150,000 by mid-century. Without New World bullion – which accounted for about a quarter of royal revenues – this would have been unsustainable.

As it was, the inflow of gold and silver was double-edged: it staved off bankruptcy for a while, but only by undermining the very basis of the Spanish economy. It did this in two ways.

First, the growing colonial market encouraged a shift to cash crops – mainly textiles, oil, and wine – in the mother country. But this boom lasted only until New World producers entered the market, at which point Spanish trans-Atlantic exports were priced out. By the 1570s, Spanish agriculture was severely depressed, and Spain had become a major grain-importing country.

Second, New World bullion stoked Old World inflation, to the extent that Castilian wool became prohibitively expensive on the European market, where English and Dutch traders became increasingly dominant, while domestic industries stagnated as a bloated, bullion-rich elite soaked up foreign imports.

Though treasure shipments reached record levels at the end of the sixteenth century – and Philip II's revenues had quadrupled by the end of his reign – it was not enough. Not only was Spanish absolutism bankrupt by the mid-1590s, the economy was prostrate, with the countryside impoverished and depopulated, the industrial base withered.

Discontent triggered revolts, but they were still-born. Spain's weak civil society – hollowed out by a century of Habsburg absolutism – was unable to mount an effective challenge to the parasitic elite of courtiers and grandees who were to dominate Spain for the next three centuries. The lesser nobility – the *hidalgos* – refused to work through pride of caste and slowly decayed into destitution. The common people, black-clad and miserable, lived on in relentless rural squalor.

Further decline followed the crisis of the 1640s, when Spain was defeated by France in the closing campaigns of the Thirty Years War, triggering foreign invasion and secessionist revolt against a background of bankruptcy, pestilence, and impoverishment.

But the rule of the Spanish Habsburgs and the Inquisition endured. Spain remained in the grip of law, monarchy, and the faith – repression, absolutism, and superstition.

The Spanish Century was over. The Spanish imperial counter-revolution in Europe had been defeated; and its fountainhead, drained of energy, sank into stagnation. Spain turned in on itself once again, and recovered its age-old form as a 'dry, barren, impoverished land ... isolate and remote'.

Spain had been broken by the unsustainable cost of Habsburg imperial ambition and European inter-state warfare. The vast continental weight of the Habsburg dynastic domain had flattened its Castilian geopolitical core.

Europe's centre of gravity then shifted from a semi-feudal absolutism that had rested on too narrow and rickety a foundation, to a more thoroughgoing absolutism with both firmer socio-political base and tighter political centralisation: Bourbon France.

The Counter-Reformation

'He who half makes a revolution merely digs his own grave' – so said the French revolutionary Louis de Saint-Just. The socialist historian R. H. Tawney made the same point slightly differently when he wrote that you cannot skin a tiger claw by claw. That was the danger inherent in the defeat of the popular Reformation.

Just as the bourgeois revolution had begun as an ideological movement of religious reform, so the counter-revolutionary response involved a dogmatic reassertion of Catholic orthodoxy: the Counter-Reformation.

The Council of Trent, meeting between 1545 and 1563, issued a series of decrees with two main aims: to weed out corruption in the Church and to reassert Catholic dogma.

Absenteeism, the holding of multiple posts, and the buying and selling of ecclesiastical positions were banned. New training seminaries were established. Thus were the quality and attentiveness of the priests and bishops who formed Catholicism's ideological front-line to be improved. At the same time, the Council was uncompromising in its reassertion of the medieval doctrines that distinguished Catholicism from Protestantism: the veneration of saints; salvation through good works; observation of the Seven Sacraments; the real presence of Christ in the holy Eucharist (a wafer of bread); and the 'infallibility' (ecclesiastical dictatorship) of the Pope.

The Council of Trent shored up the Church's defences. Two other features of the Counter-Reformation involved going onto the offensive.

In 1540, Pope Paul III gave his approval to the Society of Jesus, a religious order founded by Ignatius Loyola, a Spanish soldier turned ascetic, mystic, and theologian. Carefully selected, highly trained, and tightly disciplined, the Jesuits became the 'special forces' operatives of the Counter-Reformation. As well as being active in the Catholic heartlands and as missionaries in the Americas and the Indies, they formed an underground network of subversion in the Protestant-ruled states of Northern Europe.

The second offensive arm was the Inquisition. This sinister organisation had first taken shape during the Church's Albigensian Crusade against the heretic Cathars of southern France in the early thirteenth century. But it had survived only in Spain, first as an arm of the feudal struggle against the Moors (Spanish Muslims), then as a prop of the new absolutist monarchy. It was only with the unification of Spain, Austria, and Germany under Charles V (1519–56), and with the decision of the Pope in 1542 to re-establish the institution in Italy, that the Inquisition was transformed into a pan-European agency of repression.

Run by six cardinals in Rome, the Holy Office of the Inquisition became a permanent counter-revolutionary tribunal from which there was no appeal. Inquisitors could enter any Catholic country with the power to arrest and torture heretics, confiscate their property, and hand over the condemned for execution. The Inquisition also enforced the Index, a regularly updated list of books which should be burnt. Where the writ of the Inquisition ran, it threatened art, science, and freedom of thought and enquiry. The humanist culture of the Renaissance was transformed into a celebration of traditional authority. Art and architecture were fossilised in the Baroque's glorification of power, wealth, and mysticism. Scientists might be burnt at the stake along with their books. To think out loud could be dangerous in Counter-Reformation Europe.

The contrast between cultural potential and political reaction – between Renaissance and Counter-Reformation – was at its starkest in Italy. The city-states there had emerged as early as the twelfth century as major independent centres of commerce and power within the wider feudal world. In the fifteenth and sixteenth centuries they played host to many of the greatest artistic, architectural, and scientific achievements of the Renaissance. Yet the embryonic mercantile capitalism within each of these states was suffocated at birth. The new socio-economic forces failed to break through traditional politico-military structures. Commercial wealth remained under the control of old elites. In due course, the Renaissance was subordinated to the service of the Counter-Reformation.

Two factors proved decisive. First, the economies of the city-states were bound by a framework of feudal guilds and regulated markets. This framework was dominated by powerful mercantile oligarchies, in many cases by single families. Merchants and bankers thus evolved into urban-based potentates who used their control of city government and the guilds to shore up their own position and provide launch-pads for wider political ambitions. Second, because Italy remained divided into a plethora of rival polities, warfare between feudal factions was endemic and the territory was exposed to foreign intervention, becoming a battleground of the great powers. The struggle between Guelphs, who supported the Papacy, and Ghibellines, who supported the Holy Roman Emperor, continued throughout most of the medieval period. Similarly, between 1494 and 1559, northern Italy became the principal arena in the long military confrontation between France and the Emperor.

So Italy remained in thrall to merchant-princes, mercenary captains (*condottieri*), and foreign armies. Protestantism made few converts, and those few were soon crushed by the Counter-Reformation crusade emanating from Rome.

Spain, on the other hand, was a unified national state. Here, the Counter-Reformation triumphed as an instrument of royal despotism. Philip II (1556–98) was the archetypal Catholic ruler – gloomy, ponderous, bureaucratic, bigoted, life-hating. He asserted the divine right of kings. Everyone addressed him on bended knee. The *Cortes* was deprived of power, the nobility reduced to a caste of sycophants. Local powers were curtailed, authority centralised. The King himself presided over the horrific *autos-da-fé* (acts of faith) – the Inquisition's rituals of public execution – by which Spanish Protestantism was destroyed in the space of just ten years. The Moors were subject to extreme oppression: they were forbidden to speak Arabic, wear native dress, or follow traditional marriage and funerary customs. When they rebelled in 1568, order was restored by wholesale extermination.

France was different. Spanish feudalism had achieved a higher degree of centralisation during the Middle Ages because of the internal struggle against the Moors. The French monarchy had always been weaker. Parts of France were also more economically developed than Spain. The Protestant Reformation had therefore been able to make greater inroads, becoming established over about a third of France. Some 2,500 churches held synods (councils). As elsewhere, the French Reformation had been pushed from below by the middling sort; but sections of the French nobility had converted and placed themselves at the head of the Protestant community (the Huguenots) in order to advance their dynastic interests.

In 1562, soldiers in the pay of Francis, Duke of Guise, carried out a massacre of Protestants. Louis, Prince of Condé, a leading Protestant noble, immediately called his supporters and co-religionists to arms. For almost 40 years, France was wracked by religious wars between rival aristocratic factions. Then, in August 1572, these Wars of Religion took the extreme form of pogroms. The St Bartholomew's Day Massacre in Paris was followed by a series of similar massacres in other major French towns. The Inquisition had destroyed the weak popular Reformation in Spain. Catholic death-squads performed the same role in France.

The war continued, however. The massacres made it more bitter, but also strengthened aristocratic control, as ordinary people sought the protection of local nobles. The radical potential of the Reformation was further distorted by the logic of aristocratic faction and religious warfare.

The war finally ended in compromise. The Protestant leader Henry of Navarre succeeded to the French throne, becoming King Henry IV (1589–1610), but in order to reunite the fractured state, he renounced his faith and proclaimed his reconversion to Catholicism (1593). Once the last centres of resistance had been reduced, he issued the Edict of Nantes (1598), which granted freedom of conscience and worship to the Huguenots.

The wars had inflicted huge economic damage, and the degeneration of the Reformation into aristocratic factionalism had halted its advance. These consequences of the Wars of Religion would determine the course of French history for the next 200 years. A powerful absolute monarchy would emerge during the seventeenth century. Aristocratic castles, the regional power bases of the great feudal landowners, would be destroyed by royal cannon, and the nobility reduced to mere courtiers. A state-feudal regime would freeze social relations, retard economic development, and impose a massive military burden on French society. The triumph of the absolutist state over civil society would be symbolised by the revocation of the Edict of Nantes in 1685, which turned the Huguenots into a persecuted minority. The final result of the defeat of the popular Reformation would be the accumulation of contradictions that produced the Great French Revolution of 1789.

The Counter-Reformation was triumphant in Spain and Italy, and made major advances in Germany and France. But the Reformation survived in Northern Europe – and that is why this region now became the powerhouse of world history.

The Dutch Revolution

In the sixteenth century, three million people lived in the Low Countries – the same as in the whole of England and Wales. Of these, about half lived in towns. Bruges, Ghent, Brussels, Antwerp, Utrecht, Leiden, Haarlem, Amsterdam, and other Flemish and Dutch towns were among the foremost trading centres of Renaissance Europe. At least 25 of these towns had populations of more than 10,000. The region was dominated by its waterways – rivers, estuaries, canals, and dykes. Several great river systems – the Rhine, Meuse/Maas, and Scheldt – rise in the European hinterland, then flow through the Low Countries into a maze of estuaries, islands, and mudflats on the North Sea coast.

As the feudal order was transformed by money and the market, the geography of the Low Countries made it one of most economically dynamic parts of Europe. Flemish and Dutch society became dominated by merchants and artisans. Culture and civic organisation flourished. Powerful guilds dominated urban life. The defence of traditional liberties and privileges was robust.

The Reformation swept across the Low Countries like an electric storm. Here, above all other places in Europe, feudal overlords and church corruption were not tolerated. But the Low Countries were ruled by Imperial Spain, and taxes on Flemish and Dutch mercantile wealth were being increased to fund the 150,000-strong Spanish Army and support the dynastic ambitions of a distant Catholic Habsburg King.

The Flemish and Dutch nobility who ruled the Low Countries found themselves squeezed between the demands of the imperial state and resistance from Calvinist and Anabaptist urban populations. In 1564 they forced the dismissal of the Spanish viceroy Cardinal Granvelle. But this failed to appease rising opposition.

An attempted crackdown on heresy by the Catholic authorities two years later met unprecedented resistance. Mass open-air meetings of armed Protestants were held across the Low Countries. One Ghent patrician and chronicler marvelled that four or five sermons were sufficient to reverse beliefs that people had held for 30 or 40 years.

In August and September of that year, revolutionary crowds overturned the old order in town after town. Catholic churches were attacked in an 'iconoclastic fury'. Conservative municipal oligarchies collapsed. Ruling princes were forced to grant freedom of worship to Lutherans and Calvinists. Anabaptists simply took it for themselves. A section of the Dutch nobility led by William of Orange placed itself at the head of the revolutionary movement. The majority either withdrew into passivity or supported the counter-revolutionary violence now unleashed by the King of Spain.

Determined to hold together his far-flung empire by driving back the forces of religious reformation and political revolution that threatened it, Philip II turned the Low Countries into Europe's principal battleground. For more than 40 years, with wildly fluctuating fortunes, the Dutch Revolution took the form of a protracted popular war of national defence. Tens of thousands of Spanish troops were deployed and vast amounts of treasure consumed. Full-scale terror was unleashed by foreign soldiers and the Inquisition. During several days of 'Spanish Fury' in Antwerp after the capture of the city in November 1576, 1,000 houses were destroyed and 8,000 people killed. Military terror defeated the Flemish movement and restored Spanish rule in Belgium. The Dutch Revolution proved far more intractable.

The approaches to Holland from the south contract into a relatively narrow corridor dissected by a succession of major rivers. The land generally is low-lying, boggy, and criss-crossed by countless drainage dykes. The rivers and dykes provide natural defence lines. The effect was compounded by the density of settlement in Holland. There were many walled towns, and even villages could be turned into strongholds by improvising ramparts, barricades, and block-houses. The result was what military theorists call 'complex terrain' – a contested landscape where movement and supply are difficult and invading armies get bogged down amid natural obstacles, concealed positions, and defended strongpoints. The invaders' difficulties were compounded by the growing professionalism of the urban militia who formed the core of the Dutch forces, by the operations of a powerful fleet of 'Sea Beggars' (a confederacy of Dutch Calvinist nobles), and by the increasing numbers of foreign volunteers rallying to the aid of their co-religionists.

Members of Calvinist and Anabaptist congregations functioned like the activists of a revolutionary party. The war radicalised the revolution. The United Provinces (as Holland came to be known) soon had the highest proportion of Anabaptists in Europe – up to half the population in some districts. Anabaptists were advocates of political democracy and social equality.

At the same time, Calvinist churches in Germany, France, England, and Scotland – boosted by Dutch exiles – functioned as a sort of revolutionary 'international', raising support for the resistance. The foreign contingents fighting in Holland were the most tangible result – effectively a Protestant 'international brigade', for the Dutch Revolution had become the front-line in the struggle against the Counter-Reformation.

When a third Spanish offensive brought the Dutch to the brink of defeat in 1584, Elizabeth I of England declared war. The safety of the English Protestant state would have been compromised by a victorious Spanish Empire in secure control of the Channel coast. It was in England's interest to keep the Dutch fighting. What is more, the policy was popular with the Protestant middling sort, who formed the bedrock of the Tudor dynasty.

English intervention spurred Philip to his greatest effort: the Spanish Armada of 1588. The defeat of his fleet by a combination of bad weather and the English navy was the turning-point. The Spanish Empire was overextended. It was supporting its Catholic Habsburg cousins in Germany, safeguarding its interests in Italy, fighting the Ottomans in the Mediterranean, intervening in the French Wars of Religion, and defending its vast territories in the Americas and the treasure fleets plying the Atlantic trade-routes. Again and again, Spanish troops mutinied and ran riot on the Dutch front because they had not been paid. Again and again, despite herculean efforts by the imperial power, the Dutch resisted, the Spanish fell back exhausted, and the revolution renewed itself. The Spanish finally gave up in 1609. The United Provinces of Holland became the world's first bourgeois state.

Even Marxist historians sometimes miss the significance of the Dutch Revolution of 1566–1609. The Revolution was long, complex, and dominated by war. It comprised three distinct surges of politico-military resistance – in 1565-8, 1569–76, and 1576–81. Each was followed by a Spanish counter-offensive. The last was repulsed with English support, and after that the Revolution proceeded as a conventional military struggle.

The aristocratic leadership of the House of Orange, increasingly dominant in the later phases, distorted but did not alter the revolutionary character of the war. The mercantile bourgeoisie was victorious. The urban petty-bourgeoisie of small traders, artisans, and labourers had made victory possible. The Calvinist and Anabaptist churches had provided the essential revolutionary leadership.

In contrast to regions where the Counter-Reformation triumphed, the seventeenth century was a Golden Age for the Dutch. Their trade, navy, and overseas empire became pre-eminent. Their towns boasted grand buildings and their art was the finest in Europe.

But Holland was very small. This, in the long run, proved an insuperable constraint on the new state's economic growth and political power. If there was to be a decisive breakthrough to a new world economic order, the bourgeois revolution would have to win victories on a larger stage. This it was to do in the course of the seventeenth century.

The Thirty Years War

By 1609 Imperial Spain had been defeated in its effort to crush the Dutch Revolution, and Holland was able to flourish as a Protestant bourgeois state. But the end of the Dutch War freed the Catholic Habsburg rulers of Spain for action elsewhere.

The Holy Roman Empire was ruled by another branch of the Habsburgs. The Emperor's power base was Austria, where the family estates were concentrated, but his authority extended across Germany, Silesia, Bohemia, Moravia, Hungary, and parts of northern Italy. The Empire was a dynastic super-state encompassing most of Central Europe. But it was deeply divided. In Germany and Bohemia especially, the Reformation was dominant. The authority of the Emperor had been cast off by local princes and the wealth of the Church appropriated by new secular landowners.

In the early seventeenth century, the Habsburgs of Spain and Austria launched a feudal absolutist counter-revolution against the German Reformation. The unintended results of the conflict – the Thirty Years War (1618–48) – transformed Continental Europe more radically than any subsequent event until the French Revolution (1789–1815).

The crisis broke in Bohemia (today the Czech Republic). The independence and wealth of the Czech nobility was threatened by the centralising and Catholicising policy of Vienna. The nobles responded by throwing three imperial officials out of a castle window ('the defenestration of Prague'); they landed in a dung-heap. The following year, 1619, the nobles refused to recognise the new Catholic Habsburg Emperor Ferdinand II, instead granting the crown of the Kingdom of Bohemia to one of the leading Protestant princes of Germany, Frederick V, the Elector Palatine – in feudal-dynastic terms, a declaration of independence from both Empire and Church.

Bohemia was one of the most economically advanced parts of Europe. Though still dominated by feudal magnates, society was in transition as markets and money recast relations between lords, merchants, and peasants. It was in Bohemia that the proto-Protestant Hussite 'heresy' had flourished in the early fifteenth century. Protestantism and a tradition of religious toleration reflected the changing character of Bohemian society.

But at the Battle of the White Mountain near Prague in 1620, the Catholic League defeated Frederick. Imperial government was restored, Czech liberties were abolished, the Bohemian crown was declared hereditary in the Habsburg family, and the Counter-Reformation was unleashed in all its fury. The Bohemian nobility could have attempted to build resistance by turning the conflict into a popular war like the Hussite Revolt two centuries earlier. Class interest prevented this – they had no wish to resurrect the spectre of social revolution. Instead, they appealed, unsuccessfully, to other Protestant princes for support.

The North German Protestant Union had no forces to spare. The Emperor and the Catholic League were on the offensive, and the war quickly spread, drawing in Holland, Denmark, Sweden, and eventually France. The other powers intervened to prevent a Catholic victory and the domination of Europe by the Habsburgs. A religious war therefore turned into a geopolitical conflict. The transformative potential of the Reformation was deflected by princely leadership and transformed into a conventional military struggle between rival states.

Each time the Catholic League seemed poised for victory in Germany, a new defender would appear – the Elector Palatine, the Dutch Republic, King Christian of Denmark, King Gustavus Adolphus of Sweden, and finally Cardinal Richelieu, the chief minister of King Louis XIII of France. Because of this, the war was protracted; and it devastated Germany. What had been one of the most advanced economies in Europe was wrecked by insecurity, depopulation, disruption to trade, the destruction of property, and the plundering of armies. The population may have been reduced by half between 1618 and 1648.

The Habsburgs were fought to a standstill, their attempt to create a pan-European absolutism defeated. Germany was left a mosaic of petty states, often at war with one another, separated by customs barriers, divided by religion.

Where the Catholic League triumphed outright, there was unbridled reaction. The screws of feudal exploitation tightened on the Bohemian peasantry, many of whom ended up handing over half their produce to the landlords, draining the countryside of the surpluses needed to improve farms and raise productivity. The towns were depopulated. The Czech language went into decline.

The nations of Central Europe were either fragmented or agglomerated without regard to linguistic, ethnic, or cultural boundaries. Only in 1871 was Germany finally unified. Not before 1918 would the subject-peoples of the Habsburg Empire break free. This was the price paid for the 'deflected' Reformation – its transformation from popular revolution into aristocratic factionalism.

No less momentous was the impact of the war on Spain and France. Habsburg Spain, funded by its European and New World empires, had been the most formidable military power of the sixteenth century. But geopolitical pre-eminence had masked socio-economic stagnation. The feudal landowning class still dominated the Iberian peninsula. Trade and towns remained underdeveloped. Science and culture wilted under the dual pressure of Habsburg absolutism and the Holy Inquisition.

The sixteenth and seventeenth centuries were an age of transition. Mercantile capitalism and bourgeois revolution were elevating some polities and allowing them to pull ahead of others in socio-economic development. Imperial Spain's continent-spanning political ambition rested upon an unreformed feudal-absolutist base. This made the effort unsustainable in a world where the balance of power was shifting so decisively against the *ancien régime*. During the Thirty Years War, the law of gravity asserted itself. After a century-long struggle to crush the Reformation in Northern Europe, the drain on its resources between 1618 and 1648 caused Imperial Spain's military power finally to collapse. When it did so, geopolitical hegemony on the Continent passed to France.

With the late sixteenth-century Wars of Religion settled by compromise, during the 1620s and 1630s the French monarchy became a powerful absolutism under the political leadership of Cardinal Richelieu. The Huguenots lost their strongholds and ceased to be a state within the state. The nobles were brought to heel: castles were demolished, duelling outlawed, and plots crushed. The nobles became courtiers, the local *parlements* lost effective power, and royal *intendants* (administrators) and travelling commissioners ruled in their place.

Loyalists were rewarded with offices and privileges, and the French aristocracy evolved into a caste of pampered state function-aries and dependants. A combination of the feudal exactions of local nobles and state taxation to support the monarchy's war machine condemned the peasantry to grinding poverty, the pervasive hopeless-ness of village life punctuated only by occasional doomed uprisings.

Between 1635 and 1648 absolutist France intervened in the Thirty Years War to prevent a Habsburg victory. The result was French supremacy in Europe. The French Bourbons would dominate the continent for more than a century, such were the national resources at the command of the monarchy.

But in that time, Britain would prove to be France's most enduring and increasingly effective rival; and in the long run, Britain would triumph, both in the struggle for empire and in the effort to build a modern economy.

To understand why, we now turn to events in Britain during the seventeenth century. For there the outcome of the struggle between Reformation and Counter-Reformation, between bourgeois revolution and absolutism, was very different from that in France, Spain, and Germany. There, in a medium-sized island on the north-western edge of Europe, the revolutionary promise of the Reformation was most fully realised.

The Causes of the English Revolution

In Central Europe in the first half of the seventeenth century, counter-revolution ended in what Marx called 'the common ruin of the contending classes'. The Habsburg Catholic juggernaut was halted only after 30 years of war. The effort broke the power of feudal-absolutist Spain, but also wrecked the advanced economy of Germany.

In England, on the other hand, attempted counter-revolution led to the downfall of feudal absolutism, the execution of the King, and the establishment of a bourgeois republic. This very different outcome was a consequence of the resolute action of tens of thousands of revolutionaries at a succession of key turning-points during the 1640s. But the mass movement in which they were embedded had its roots in the English Reformation a century before.

During the 1530s, Reformation from above had brought about a break with the Papacy, royal control of the English Church, and the Dissolution of the Monasteries (the nationalisation of monastic estates). In explaining these events, most historians focus on the dynastic needs of the Tudor regime. It is true that Henry VIII (1509–47) wanted a divorce so that he could remarry and sire a legitimate male heir. But two other factors were of equal importance.

First, the Tudor regime rested partly on the support of the middling sort of small farmers, traders, and artisans. These were the pioneers of England's relatively advanced economy, and many were early and enthusiastic converts to the new religion. Central to the dynamism of the English economy at the time – and therefore to the prosperity of commercial farmers, merchants, and ship owners – was the wool trade.

Thomas Cromwell (1485–1540), Henry VIII's chief minister from 1532 to 1540, was from this class and a staunch Protestant. Anne

Boleyn, whose marriage to Henry was engineered by Cromwell, was also a Protestant. Henry himself was a religious conservative, but during the reign of his son, Edward VI (1547–53), the English Church was radically reformed.

Second, nationalised monastic land was rapidly sold off or given away. It was the biggest transfer of landownership since the Norman Conquest. It enlarged and enriched the English gentry and thereby created a strong base of support in the landowning class for both the Tudor dynasty and the Protestant religion.

The English Reformation from above was therefore a process of religious, political, and social change with deep roots. That is why the attempted Catholic restoration during the reign of Henry's daughter Mary (1553–8) was doomed. It is also why the Protestant regime of Elizabeth I (1558–1603) was popular and resilient. The defeat of the Spanish Armada in 1588 was only the most notable measure of the regime's strength.

But the old order had not suffered a decisive defeat. Regional magnates, especially in the north and west, often retained considerable power. Leading aristocrats used their position at court to secure honorific titles, appointments to high office, grants of land, business contracts, and monopoly rights. Feudal competition, once a matter of military force, now depended on court intrigue.

The Reformation of the 1530s had left the central contradiction in English society unresolved. Indeed, by strengthening the new economy, it caused it to deepen over subsequent decades. The old aristocracy became increasingly dependent on court patronage and sought to buttress its privileges. Meanwhile, the lesser gentry, the yeomanry (rich peasants), industrialists, and burghers (townsmen) developed their farms and businesses.

The population of England more than doubled between 1500 and 1650, by which time one in 12 people were living in towns, and hundreds of thousands were employed in rural industries. The rural gentry and burghers represented in Parliament became increasingly resentful of barriers to enterprise. Royal taxation, customs duties, and trade monopolies seemed designed to enrich idle courtiers.

The first two Stuart kings, James I (1603–25) and Charles I (1625–49), the successors of the Tudors, clashed repeatedly with their Parliaments. A turning-point in relations between 'Court and Country' was reached in 1629, when Charles dissolved Parliament and ruled without it. The 'Eleven Years Tyranny' (1629–40) was an attempt to establish Continental-style absolutism in England. The experience triggered all the class anxieties of England's gentry and burghers. Arbitrary taxation, requisitioning, and billeting threatened their property. Political centralisation undermined the traditional authority of local elites. Alignment with Catholic powers abroad conflicted with city trading interests. Catholic influence at Court cast a long shadow over the security of titles to confiscated church lands. An Irish Catholic army formed by Charles' chief minister, the Earl of Strafford, had the appearance of a coercive force, capable of being deployed to impose royal absolutism on England.

The crisis broke in 1637. The issue was religion. Archbishop Laud's High Church Anglicanism was a conservative brand of Protestantism barely distinguishable to many from Catholicism. Religious conformity had become synonymous with political obedience. The main line of division was between Calvinists on the one hand – 'Puritans' as they were known in England – and High Church Anglicans and Catholics on the other.

In Lowland Scotland, nobles, burghers, and Calvinist ministers had united to carry out their own Reformation long before. Charles, King of Scotland as well as England, was attempting to assert his authority on both sides of the border. Laud's attempt to impose the Anglican Book of Common Prayer on Scotland provoked a riot. When the Dean of St Giles in Edinburgh began to read from the new prayer book on 23 July 1637, Jenny Geddes, a market trader, threw her stool at him, shouting, 'Dare you say the Mass in my ear?' The service broke up in chaos, and shortly afterwards a huge crowd of Calvinist Scots assembled at the foot of Edinburgh Castle to sign a Solemn League and Covenant to defend their religion. Jenny Geddes sparked the English Revolution. (Scotland was heavily involved throughout, and 'British Revolution' would be the more appropriate term, but 'English Revolution' is too firmly embedded in the literature.)

The King attempted to suppress the Scottish Covenanters by force. But the mutinous militia of the northern English counties were no match for the Scots and the 'First Bishops' War' petered out inconclusively in 1639. The following year a much larger English army was recruited, but the Covenanters crossed the border and swept their enemies away with artillery fire. The Scots – with covert encouragement from the English Puritans with whom they were in contact – occupied the three most northerly English counties pending payment of the £400,000 indemnity they were due under the terms of the Treaty of Ripon signed at the end of the 'Second Bishops' War'.

To pay the bill and see the back of the Scots, Charles was left with no choice but to summon Parliament. The extraordinary tax-raising measures of his Eleven Years Tyranny were legally dubious, increasingly contested, and hopelessly insufficient to pay the indemnity. The proto-absolutist Stuart state had collapsed. Its rupture with the propertied classes of Scotland and England had left it insolvent in the face of revolt.

But the Long Parliament which assembled in November 1640 was in no mood to grant the funds to create a royal army or pay off the Scots. Its aim was nothing less than a dismantling of the entire apparatus of embryonic absolutism. And this, it turned out, could not be achieved without civil war.

Revolution and Civil War

Royal absolutism threatened the powers, privileges, and property of local elites. A victory for the Court would have been a victory for arbitrary authority, state monopolies, and countless restrictions on freedom of trade. Laud's High Church Anglicanism was the ideological spearhead of this political project and its target was the radical Protestantism of the opposition 'Country' party. That is why Laud's attempt to impose the mass on Scotland had provoked revolution.

The same issues now agitated the London Parliament's resistance to the King's request for new taxes to pay the Scots. Parliament demanded 'redress of grievances' before the granting of funds. This included the abolition of arbitrary taxation; the dismantling of the royal courts of justice; an end to the King's power to dissolve Parliament without its consent; the removal of the bishops from the House of Lords; and the prosecution for treason of the Earl of Strafford.

The members of the Long Parliament were conservative property-owners. They acted in a revolutionary way for two reasons. First, they regarded absolutism as a direct threat to their property. Second, they were variously buoyed, cajoled, and pressured by extra-parliamentary mass mobilisations of London's middling sort, the urban poor, and working women.

During the December Days (27–30 December 1641), huge crowds converged on Whitehall and Westminster after the King appointed a court loyalist as Lieutenant of the Tower of London. This new appointment, to the most important military post in the capital, implied that Charles was preparing an internal coup to suppress Parliament and cow London.

In the face of demonstrations, the appointment was overturned. But it was not enough. The cry went up, 'No bishops! No bishops!' The bishops were the most reactionary members of Parliament. Many were physically prevented from taking their seats, and at least one was thrown into the river.

Royalists attacked the crowd with swords. The crowd fought back with bricks, tiles, and cobblestones. As word of the fighting spread, London as a whole mobilised and Parliament was put under siege by 10,000 armed apprentices. The London Trained Bands – the city militia – refused to disperse them.

On 30 December, the House of Commons impeached 12 leading bishops and the House of Lords dispatched them to prison. Church bells pealed across the City and bonfires blazed in the streets. The revolution had been driven forward by mass action from below.

Less than a week later, the King attempted to launch his coup. On 4 January 1642 he entered the House of Commons with an armed guard of 100 officers, intent on arresting five leading oppositionists. Forewarned, the five members had fled to the City. Gates were shut, portcullises lowered, and chains put across streets. For several days, thousands stood ready, armed with halberds, swords, staves, whatever came to hand. Women brought stools and tubs from their homes to build barricades and boiled water 'to throw on the cavaliers'.

But the cavaliers did not come. London, it was clear, had passed to the side of the revolution. It was not to be recovered with the forces to hand. On 10 January the King fled. The following day the five members returned to Westminster through cheering crowds.

Charles now set up a rival capital at Oxford and was soon raising an army. Revolution was transformed into civil war. The urban insurrection in the capital was followed by hundreds of local struggles between Royalists and Parliamentarians for control of arsenals, strategic points, and militia units across the country.

Because Parliament represented the economically advanced sections of society, it controlled not only London but also the Home Counties, the South-East, East Anglia, and most ports and walled towns elsewhere. It therefore had the financial, manpower, and strategic resources to wage an effective war. But that was not enough. One problem was amateurism and parochialism. Local wars were fought across the country, but only a fraction of the men involved were willing to be amalgamated into large field armies with national strategic reach. Many refused to leave their own counties.

A second problem was the conservatism of Parliamentarian leadership. One third of the Lords and two-thirds of the Commons had remained loyal to Parliament in 1642. But the majority were Presbyterian property-owners who feared that the war might unleash 'the many-headed hydra' of social revolution. (Presbyterian was the term used for Calvinist Protestants in England and Scotland.) Only a minority favoured all-out war by whatever means necessary. Most of these were minor gentry. Because they wanted more decentralisation and democracy in church government than the Presbyterians, they were known as 'Independents'.

As a politico-religious tendency, the Independents merged on their left with the increasingly important Sectaries, radical Protestant groups who gave expression to the democratic and 'levelling' aspirations of many ordinary Parliamentarian supporters. The Independents became dominant among army officers. The army was the concentrated expression of revolutionary force. Here, the contradiction between conservatism and military necessity was an immediate life-and-death matter. Here, too, the pressure from below – from an armed rank and file – was most keenly felt.

Oliver Cromwell, a middle-aged squire who was MP for Cambridge and a Parliamentarian cavalry commander, emerged as a leading Independent among the officers, a protector of Sectaries in the ranks, and the foremost advocate of all-out revolutionary war. To his own regiment of 'Ironsides', he recruited 'men of a spirit', for, Cromwell believed, 'he who prays best will fight best'.

A few honest men are better than numbers … If you choose godly, honest men to be captains of horse, honest men will follow them … I had rather have a plain russet-coated captain that knows what he fights for, and loves what he knows, than that which you call a gentleman and is nothing more.

The aim was clear. Presbyterian lords and generals sought a compromise peace between the propertied classes ranged on either side. Cromwell, on the other hand, declared, 'If the King chanced to be in a body of the enemy I was to charge, I would as soon discharge my pistol upon him as at any other private person.'

On 15 February 1645 the conservative opposition in Parliament was defeated and the Self-Denying Ordinance passed into law. At a stroke, all members of both Houses of Parliament were debarred from holding military commands. The existing army structure – rooted in conservatism, parochialism, and vested interests – was swept away. In its place arose the New Model Army.

The New Model was a revolutionary army of the middling sort. Though many recruits were newly pressed men, they were grouped around a revolutionary spine of veterans and radicals. The tone was set by the sermons of preachers like Hugh Peters, by the broadsheets and pamphlets circulating among the soldiers, and by the role of political and religious enthusiasts in debate.

At Naseby, on 14 June 1645, the New Model Army defeated and destroyed the main Royalist field army. The King was never able to raise another. The Army never gave him the chance. Within a year, all Royalist military resistance had been suppressed.

The revolution had triumphed. But what sort of revolution was it? What vision of a new society was to guide its future work?

The Army, the Levellers, and the Commonwealth

The Presbyterian gentry who formed the majority in Parliament had always regarded the New Model Army as a regrettable necessity. Their immediate priorities in 1646 were to disband it, reach a settlement with the King, crush politico-religious dissent, and thereby end the revolutionary process. As big property-owners, they feared radicals more than Royalists.

The soldiers faced either deployment to fight a dismal colonial war in Ireland or immediate demobilisation without a pension or other provision. Their pay, moreover, was months in arrears. These economic grievances meshed with hopes for greater democracy.

Each regiment elected two 'agitators' to voice its demands and coordinate political action with other regiments. The Army activists also formed close links with the Levellers, a radical democratic party with a strong base in London and other towns. The most prominent Leveller leader was a former soldier called John Lilburne.

Army leaders like Cromwell were torn. As property-owning gentry themselves, their social instincts were conservative and their inclinations towards reaching an accommodation with the King if possible. But they were also successful revolutionaries determined to defend the gains they had won on the battlefield, and, as Army officers, were subject to direct pressure from the radicals among the rank and file in a way that MPs were not.

The political conflicts of 1646–9 therefore involved four distinct forces. The Royalists wanted to reverse the outcome of the Civil War. The Presbyterians wanted a settlement with the King to create a conservative regime of big property-owners. The Independents – the Army leaders and a small minority in Parliament – vacillated between compromise and revolutionary action. The Levellers – backed by the London crowd and much of the Army rank and file – were pushing for thoroughgoing democratic change.

By October 1647 the Levellers were strong enough to force a public debate ('the Putney Debates') with the Army leaders. 'I think that the poorest he that is in England has a life to live as the greatest he', explained the radical officer Colonel Thomas Rainsborough. 'The poorest man in England is not bound in a strict sense to that government that he hath not a voice to put himself under.'

'No one', replied Henry Ireton, speaking for the generals, 'has a right to ... a share ... in determining of the affairs of the kingdom ... that has not a permanent fixed interest in the kingdom ... that is, the person in whom all land lies, and those in the corporations in whom all trading lies.'

What was England to become? A radical democracy of small property-owners, or a conservative constitutional monarchy dominated by big landowners and merchants?

The matter was unresolved when the King escaped from captivity and launched a second civil war. The Royalists were now joined by Presbyterians in Scotland, Wales, and many parts of England, reacting against the radicalism unleashed by the revolution. But the

New Model Army crushed all its enemies in a whirlwind campaign in the summer of 1648.

In the face of attempted counter-revolution, and under continuing pressure from below, Cromwell and the Independents now swung over to revolutionary action. In December 1648 the Army carried out a second revolution. Colonel Pride deployed a unit of cavalry to exclude leading conservatives from the House of Commons. The Presbyterian-dominated Long Parliament was transformed into an Independent-dominated 'Rump'. The King was then tried, condemned, and publicly executed in Whitehall on 30 January 1649 as a traitor to the English people.

Having crushed the Right with the support of the Left, the Army leaders – whose position amounted to a precarious wobble between the two – now moved against the Levellers. 'I tell you, sir,' proclaimed Cromwell at a meeting of the ruling Council of State, 'you have no other way to deal with these men but to break them or they will break you.'

The Leveller leaders in London were arrested and imprisoned in the Tower, a mutiny of rank-and-file soldiers was crushed, and four of its leaders were shot in the churchyard at Burford in Oxfordshire.

The repression of spring 1649 broke the back of the mass movement which had powered the English Revolution ever since Jenny Geddes threw her stool at the Dean of St Giles in July 1637. The action of the middling sort had been decisive at several national crises of the Revolution and in hundreds of local struggles between Royalists and Parliamentarians across Britain. Again and again, either as urban crowds or New Model soldiers, the common people had acted collectively to drive the struggle forward. The defeat of the popular movement was therefore a turning-point – the point at which the Revolution's forward momentum was frozen by military dictatorship from above.

The Army leaders' rule after 1649 rested on a narrow social base of minor landowners, merchants, and officers. The majority of big property-owners were hostile. The majority of small property-owners lapsed into passivity and obscurity after the defeat of their party. The Army even fell out with the purged Rump Parliament. But new elections failed to produce a tractable assembly. So the military dicta-torship was formalised: in 1653 Cromwell became Lord Protector of the Commonwealth; and in 1654 England was divided into military districts ruled by major-generals.

The new system became increasingly unpopular and unstable, especially after Cromwell's death in 1658. The Army was unable to broaden its social base because the propertied classes were resentful of military rule and suspicious of the radicals it harboured.

When General George Monck, a relatively conservative army commander in Scotland, launched a coup in early 1660, resistance melted away. He entered London and invited Charles I's elder son to assume the throne as Charles II. The Restoration was, in effect, a coup of the New Model Army against itself. What made it possible was the hollowing out of the revolutionary movement of which the Army was the supreme expression.

Bourgeois revolution is a highly contradictory process. The bourgeoisie is a property-owning minority. It can overthrow the state by revolutionary action only if it succeeds in mobilising wider social forces. But these forces have interests of their own and revolution is an empowering process, such that expectations and demands rapidly exceed what bourgeois revolutionary leadership is willing to concede. The problem is then that the democratic and 'levelling' aspirations inherent in mass popular mobilisation trigger deep-rooted fears among big property-owners. This often causes would-be bourgeois revolutions to abort. This had been the case in Germany in the 1520s and again in the 1620s: on both occasions, conservative Protestant grandees had recoiled when confronted by radical Protestant movements of the common people.

The size and character of the mass movement are decisive. Revolutions are punctuated by successive crises. At each crisis, revolutionary and counter-revolutionary forces engage in a direct clash. Whether the revolution goes forward or retreats depends on the outcome. At some point, however, even the most radical bourgeois, if they are to preserve their property, must halt the momentum of the mass movement from below which has swept them to power.

8
Absolutist Europe and Capitalist Globalisation
1660–1775

African slave wearing pronged iron collar.
Early nineteenth-century print.

The world was transformed in the eighteenth century by capitalist globalisation. Soaring demand for primary commodities meant soaring demand for slaves.

The great epoch of bourgeois revolution that opened with the German Reformation in 1517 and closed with the English Restoration in 1660 had diverse outcomes. Only in two places did the commercial bourgeoisie become the dominant class: Holland and Britain. Elsewhere, an essentially feudal order survived, but one substantially reconfigured by the long crisis through which the old regime had passed. Most of Europe came to be ruled by absolutist state-feudal monarchies.

Yet the century between 1660 and 1775, when the opening shots of the American Revolution announced a second epoch of bourgeois revolution, was not a period of conservative reaction. On the contrary, the pace of global change accelerated, even in the framework of the absolute monarchies. The class struggle eased, but history's other two motors – cumulative technical advance and competition between rival elites – intensified.

In large part this was due to the effect of the bourgeois revolution in north-western Europe in boosting global capital accumulation. Absolute rulers, to maintain their power, became dependent upon the enterprise, technology, and productivity of the capitalist system developing inside their respective polities.

Absolutist France

'New monarchies' had first emerged in the later fifteenth century. The archetype of sixteenth-century absolutism had been Habsburg Spain, but the state had rested on too narrow a social base, had been too constrained by local privileges, and had relied too heavily on imported bullion. The burden of three great military struggles – of Christian Europe against the Ottoman Empire, of the Counter-Reformation against the Protestants, and of Habsburg imperialism against France – had brought Spanish absolutism to collapse by the first half of the seventeenth century.

Almost the entire burden of the Spanish Empire had fallen on a Castilian population of about five million. France, on the other hand, had a population of 20 million. And whereas Spanish absolutism had been compromised by the relative autonomy of Aragon, Catalonia, and Valencia, France had become a more unitary polity in the course of the Hundred Years War (1337–1453). During the long struggle against a succession of freebooting English expeditionary forces, the

French nobility had rallied around the monarchy. It had required national taxation and elements of a national army to win the war. Here was the kernel of French absolutism.

Even so, France was vast, its communications primitive, its administrative structures rudimentary, the territorial power of its feudal lords deeply entrenched. It therefore remained, from the mid-fifteenth to the mid-seventeenth century, highly fractured and ever liable to burst apart.

The Italian Wars (1494–1559) provided an effective outlet for surplus feudal violence, and enhanced the power of the monarchy as a mechanism for centralising military power in what was becoming 'a continent of warring states'. But the monarchy was not yet strong enough to endure the consequences of defeat in Italy, and when the conflict ended, France fell apart in the Wars of Religion (1562–98), as aristocratic factionalism and secessionism fused with a range of religious and social conflicts.

The civil wars ended as the nobility reunited around Henry of Navarre, who became King Henry IV (1589–1610), mainly in fear that the chaos at the top would create an opening for revolt from below. The rapprochement was symbolised by, on the one hand, the new King's conversion from Protestantism to Catholicism ('Paris is well worth a mass') and, on the other, by the 1598 Edict of Nantes, which granted toleration to the Huguenots (as French Protestants were known).

The restored French monarchy entered a new period of consolidation under a succession of great administrators – Sully, Richelieu, and Mazarin. The sale of offices was institutionalised, creating a court-based *noblesse de robe* (based on state service) in contrast to the traditional *noblesse d'épée* (based on feudal landownership). The French aristocracy was increasingly incorporated into the royal state by sinecures, pensions, and titles. A secondary effect was the partial incorporation of the nascent French bourgeoisie, much of whose capital came to be invested in offices, tax-farming, and state loans.

At the same time, a new centralised administrative structure based on *intendants* – regional commissioners responsible for justice, police, and finance – was imposed on the country. This ran parallel with the existing jurisdictions of noble *officiers* and local *parlements*, and its purpose was to circumvent the resistance of the latter to royal authority.

That authority was enforced, when necessary, by a fast-growing royal army paid for out of fast-rising taxes. Revenue from the *taille*, the general land-tax on all commoners, trebled between 1610 and 1644. Peasant revolt and urban riots were brutally suppressed. Royal cannon were used to smash the military resistance of Huguenot lords to the centralising state.

But France's see-saw between absolutist centralisation and feudal anarchy was not yet wholly stilled. At the end of the Thirty Years War, the tensions exploded into another round of civil war. The Fronde (1648–53) was a confused criss-cross of conflicts in which the monarchy faced opposition from regional nobles, local *parlements*, the Huguenots, the urban bourgeoisie in major towns, and the peasantry in many areas of France.

But the new state-feudal elite assembled around the absolutist court was too numerous, the new administrative infrastructure too firm, the resistance too decentralised in form and disunited in purpose, for the Fronde to succeed. And this time, the triumph of the monarchy would be complete. When the young king, Louis XIV (1643–1715), entered upon his personal rule following the death of Mazarin in 1661, his ascendancy was truly absolute.

The French aristocracy was transformed from a class of regional magnates into an elite of perfumed courtiers, state officials, and army officers. Their power, property, and privilege – including, crucially, their control over inherited feudal estates – was now upheld, not by private retinues, but by royal troops. Around 2 per cent of the population henceforward enjoyed exclusive access to virtually all top posts, and was able to appropriate about 25 per cent of the national income.

Mercantilism guided the economic policy of the state. Royal subventions were used to promote colonial expansion, trading companies, and new industries. The aim was to augment the wealth of the kingdom and raise more in tax revenue. The ultimate purpose was increased military expenditure to expand the size of the army – ten-fold during the reign of Louis XIV, reaching almost a third of a million men in the early eighteenth century.

Absolutist France was a dictatorship, an arsenal, and a military camp. The whole of French society was regulated and dragooned for war. Opposition – often desperate resistance to conscription and taxation that devastated great swathes of the countryside – was smashed by a permanent nationwide police force, backed, when necessary, by the army.

Louis XIV – the 'Sun King', the greatest European ruler of his age – fought three major wars in his effort to establish continental hegemony: the Dutch War (1672–8), the Nine Years War (1688–97), and the War of the Spanish Succession (1701–14). Each time, he was fought to a standstill by a hostile alliance able to block French advance and exhaust French resources. Each war ended in a wave of hunger, depopulation, and resentment at home.

France nonetheless remained the dominant power in Europe throughout the eighteenth century. It remained internally united and able to fight a further series of major wars in Europe, India, and North America. But the cost of these wars – the cost of politico-military competition with both continental and colonial rivals – was prohibitive for a state-feudal system based on aristocratic privilege.

This expressed itself in the form of a growing crisis of state debt. The collapse of the absolutist state in 1789 would be a direct consequence of its essentially state-feudal character. The stability of the monarchy had been achieved by converting the aristocracy into a parasitic class of courtiers, officials, and officers who paid no tax. The entire burden of French absolutism thus fell on the 'Third Estate', the commoners, mainly the peasants. Defence of aristocratic privilege would eventually trigger the terminal crisis of the *ancien régime*.

Absolutism has sometimes been interpreted as a transitional stage between medieval feudalism and modern capitalism. This is misleading. The absolutist regimes were state-feudal formations in which the power, property, and privilege of an aristocratic ruling class were defended by a centralised royal autocracy. The politico-military competition of feudal magnates in the medieval period became the inter-state competition of rival dynastic hegemons in the early modern period. In both cases, the main burden of war was carried by the peasantry. In both cases, the development of economy and society on a progressive basis was retarded by massive levels of waste expenditure on armaments and palaces.

What is true, however, is that Western absolutism – of which Louis XIV's France was the supreme example – rested upon a relative development of monetised exchange, commercial relations, urban life, and personal freedom. To some degree, at certain points, embryonic absolutism had been able to rally support from the subordinate classes against feudal anarchy. Those forces that had made the bourgeois revolution in Holland and Britain sometimes supported the absolutist state in places where they were too weak to take power themselves. They then continued to develop in the womb of the old society. France experienced a commercial and colonial boom during the eighteenth century, and the bourgeoisie increased in size, resources, and confidence.

In Eastern Europe, however, the dynamic of politico-military competition on a continental scale produced a substantially different kind of absolutism – one capable of imposing nothing less than a 'second serfdom' on the long-suffering peasants of Austria, Prussia, Poland, and Russia.

Eastern Despotism

Absolutism was a more advanced state form than medieval monarchy. Royal dictatorship centralised power and concentrated force. It was therefore better able to strike down both internal opponents and external rivals. The supremacy of France under Louis XIV was the clearest demonstration of this. It required a succession of pan-European alliances to contain Bourbon expansionism in the late seventeenth and early eighteenth centuries.

French society nonetheless retained a somewhat hybrid character. The bourgeois revolution had not broken through, but serfdom had been abolished, the towns were expanding, and mercantile capitalism was developing. Western absolutism involved an aristocratic accommodation to these new social realities. The nobility rallied to the monarchy because it upheld traditional privilege in an unstable world.

Something rather different happened in the East. Politico-military competition undermined medieval monarchy and feudal aristocracy here too. The same imperative to centralise and concentrate power, so as to create a military machine powerful enough to defend state territory, was at work. But the result – because of the relative backwardness of Eastern European society – was more ruthless and reactionary.

Not all succeeded. The Kingdom of Poland's failure to create an absolutism due to its domination by a fractious class of feudal militarists – the *szlachta* – would lead to its eventual destruction as an independent state, its territory divided between Austria, Prussia, and

Russia in the three partitions of 1772, 1793, and 1795. The Poles would remain a divided and colonised people until the state was reconstituted on a new basis in 1918.

The three predators were all more or less successful absolutisms. Central to the evolution of each was the impact of Swedish expansionism. A succession of 'Northern Wars' centred on the Baltic between the mid-sixteenth and early eighteenth century, including a decisive intervention by Gustavus Adolphus in the Thirty Years War, saw Swedish armies rampaging across Central Europe and at different times entering five capital cities (Moscow, Warsaw, Berlin, Dresden, and Prague). The shock effect on Austria, Prussia, and Russia was catalytic.

Austrian absolutism was, in fact, a response to multiple military threats. During the sixteenth and seventeenth centuries, the Habsburg monarchy was embroiled in struggles with the Ottoman Turks to the south-east, with Valois and (later) Bourbon France in the west, and with the German Reformation in the north, the latter culminating in two shattering defeats at the hands of the Swedes at Breitenfeld (1631) and Lützen (1632) during the Thirty Years War.

Nonetheless, Austrian absolutism was compromised by the heterogeneous character of the Habsburg domains and the historically rooted traditions of its many ethnic groups. This would limit royal power in the eighteenth century, and preclude the creation of a nation-state in the nineteenth, making the Habsburg Empire a somewhat anachronistic and ramshackle structure throughout the modern epoch. It eventually comprised about 50 million people, of whom only 12 million were Teutons, the others being 10 million Magyars (Hungarians), 6.6 million Czechs, 5 million Poles, 4 million Ukrainians, 3.2 million Croats, 2.9 million Rumanians, 2 million Slovaks, 2 million Serbs, 1.3 million Slovenes, and 0.7 million Italians. It proved impossible to fuse this amalgam of subject nationalities into a cohesive polity.

Prussia represented the opposite: instead of an old dynastic state ruling a patchwork of inherited provinces, it was a new national-military state. The core of that state was the traditional landowning aristocracy of Prussia: the *junkers*.

By origin a class of Teutonic crusader knights who had settled on conquered Slav land in the eastern part of the North German Plain, the *junkers'* social evolution since had been shaped by three factors.

First, because the land they farmed was of marginal fertility, being formed largely of sand, gravel, clay, and bog, the returns on their estates were poor; Marx dubbed them 'cabbage-*junkers*'. Second, their territory was wide open to attack. Germany occupies a central position in Europe, yet lacks clear natural frontiers, especially in the East, where the North German Plain merges into the great open spaces of Poland and European Russia. Third, Germany was politically divided. Until the early nineteenth century, it was a mosaic of some 300 separate feudal states – kingdoms, dukedoms, bishoprics, city-states – and, in consequence, Germany was a military cockpit of the great powers. During the Thirty Years War, fought almost entirely on German soil, largely by foreign armies, the population is estimated to have been cut by about a third.

The Prussian absolutist state built in the seventeenth and eighteenth centuries was a function of these three factors. Bearing down on the towns and the peasants, Frederick William, the 'Great Elector' of Brandenburg-Prussia (1640–88), forged a strong alliance with the embattled *junker* nobility, exempting them from tax, tightening their control over their estates, and transforming them into a service class of army officers. State revenues tripled during the reign, until they were double those of France (a much richer country), and the army swelled from 4,000 men to 30,000. Under King Frederick William I (1713–40), 'the Soldier King', the army grew further, to 80,000 men, an expansion made possible by new territorial acquisitions, an enlarged population, and increased royal revenues.

Under Frederick the Great (1740–86), Prussian militarism experienced a qualitative shift: having emerged as the most complete form of absolutism in Europe, it now attempted to establish a pan-German hegemony. In 1740 Frederick seized Silesia, increasing the population of Prussia by 50 per cent at one blow, and triggering the War of the Austrian Succession (1740–8). His success in defeating a series of Austrian counter-offensives and holding onto the new province confirmed the shift in the balance of power in Germany from (Austrian) Habsburg to (Prussian) Hohenzollern.

During the Seven Years War (1756–63), Russia, Austria, France, Sweden, and Saxony combined to attack Prussia from all sides. That Prussia endured is testimony to the success of its dynasty of ruthless royal autocrats in turning it into the Sparta of Europe. Five-sixths of state spending was devoted to war. Mass conscription raised an army of 150,000. Peasant-conscripts were trained by relentless drill and savage discipline to perform complex precision manoeuvres and deliver concentrated close-range fire. The *junkers* had become an elite officer-caste, defined by landownership and state service, and deeply loyal to the military monarchy on which the security of their property, privilege, and power depended.

If Prussian absolutism had the character of a modern barracks, Russian absolutism had that of a medieval prison. The Tsarist autocracy had been forged between the fifteenth and seventeenth centuries. The princes of Moscow – medieval proto-tsars – had grown powerful through craven submission to their Mongol-Tartar overlords of the Golden Horde, developing, in Marx's words, 'the characters of the Tartar's hangman, sycophant, and slave-in-chief'. The break-up of the Golden Horde then left this former client-state the dominant power in Russia, with a ruler formed in the Mongol-Tartar mould of autocracy, repression, and barbarism.

For the next two centuries, the Muscovite princes struggled to consolidate their supremacy against rival princes, city-states, boyar-nobles, and free peasants, their final victory symbolised by the establishment of the Romanov dynasty in 1613. The centralised Tsarist state that emerged was the product of three factors: the internal battles of its formation; the threat posed by powerful foreign states on its borders; and, not least, the primitive agricultural system on which it rested.

Old Russia comprised a vast territory with undeveloped communications. The continental climate – cold in winter, hot in summer – was harsh. Vast tracts of the country – the frozen tundra and the taiga forest of the north – were uncultivated wilderness. Much that was cultivated was poor: the belt in which Moscow stands, where the taiga grades into mixed forest, is a region of sand and clay, bogs and marshes, with acidic soils low in humus. Further south again, as the woodland opens into vast expanses of steppe-land, lies the black-earth region, where the soil is better, but agriculture is hampered by unreliable rainfall, a short growing season, and, in the past, primitive technique.

Because land was plentiful but poor, Russian agriculture had developed extensively: peasant pioneers from the old regions had gone into the wilderness to hack out new farms in successive waves of colonisation. Russian villages were poor but largely self-sufficient;

trade and towns were therefore little developed. The result was a civil society that was scattered, fragmented, unorganised. The extreme centralisation of the Tsarist state was the alter-ego of Russian society's atomisation: an accurate reflection of the absence of other sources of power within the polity.

Like a brutal rider driving an overburdened mule, the state followed its own independent historical path with little regard for the inert mass of degraded humanity on which it rested. Under the pressure of military competition with rival powers, the Tsarist state became an end in itself. In the mid-fifteenth century, when it was breaking free of the Golden Horde, Muscovy was a landlocked state about the size of Germany. By 1600 it had expanded to the size of Europe. By 1650, having absorbed Siberia, it was three times the size. In these two centuries the tsars of Russia gained territory equivalent to a country the size of Holland *every year*.

The poverty of Russian agriculture and the backwardness of its infrastructure meant that only a regime of exceptional ruthlessness could accumulate the surpluses needed to sustain such relentless imperialism. These two characteristics – backwardness and militarism – meant that Tsarist Russia was essentially an engine of war powered by peasant labour and peasant blood. Under Peter the Great (1682–1725), military expenditures consumed more than four-fifths of state revenue, the army swelled to a third of a million, and the state was at war every year bar one. In his eighteenth- and early nineteenth-century heyday, the Tsar was a military autocrat who employed 100,000 landowners and 50,000 bureaucrats to tax, conscript, and police a hundred million peasants. Abroad, as the Tsar's benighted peasant-conscripts shot down the revolutionaries of 1848, Russian absolutism was the gendarme of Europe; at home, it was the land of the goon, the priest, and the informer.

The imperatives of politico-military competition gave rise to a distinctive East European absolutism between the sixteenth and eighteenth centuries. The relative backwardness of the peasantry and the towns allowed the Eastern monarchies to forge a close alliance with the nobility, to impose a 'second serfdom', and to prioritise the interests of the central state over those of civil society. The Austrian, Prussian, and Russian autocracies were war-machines erected on a base of aristocratic privilege and peasant misery.

The siphoning of surplus by the state meant the economic stagnation of society. In the long run, these regimes would be unsustainable – for elsewhere, in north-west Europe, a radically different social order, one with world-transforming potential, had already taken root.

Holland, Britain, and Mercantile Capitalism

In only one part of Europe – its north-western fringe – had the bourgeois revolution broken through the defences of the old order and cleared the ground for the construction of a new social order. In Holland and Britain, the outcome of the great struggles of the sixteenth and seventeenth centuries was decisive enough to unleash the full socio-economic power of mercantile capitalism.

Traditional feudalism – like that in Western Europe at the time of the Crusades – had siphoned surplus into waste expenditure on knights, castles, and lordly display. State feudalism – Philip II's Spain, Louis XIV's France, the Great Elector's Prussia, Peter the Great's Russia – wasted it on royal armies, frontier fortifications, and state pageantry.

The Dutch victory over Spain in 1566–1609 and Parliament's victory over the English King in 1637–60 made a new world possible, one dominated by the market, the profit motive, and a class of gentry and merchants eager to accumulate capital. The economic dominance of capital, and the social dominance of the bourgeoisie, were framed by distinctive political institutions quite different from those in the absolute monarchies of continental Europe.

Holland was ruled by a States-General comprising representatives of the Seven United Provinces that formed the Dutch Republic. In some periods, there was also a Stadtholder (Steward), an elective office invariably held by a member of the House of Orange, so that the United Provinces might be described as a 'constitutional semi-monarchy'.

Britain remained a formal monarchy, but one that was most definitely 'constitutional' – as opposed to absolutist – where the King's authority was limited, and every major decision depended upon the will of a Parliament elected by the property-owning classes as a whole, with the traditional aristocracy represented in the House of Lords, the untitled gentry, bankers, and merchants in the House of Commons.

Though there were tensions – between (full-blooded) Republicans and (conservative) Orangists in Holland, and between (liberal) Whigs and (pro-monarchy) Tories in Britain – these were squabbles about taxation, spending, court influence, and the distribution of offices, not fundamental divisions. The Dutch and British ruling classes of the eighteenth century were cohesive enough to unite in defence of order against any renewed threat of revolt from below. In any case, whatever differences may have remained between traditional aristocracy and merchant capitalists, the rapid expansion of the new economy provided opportunities for all which tended to blur social differences at the top. Landowners grew rich digging coal on their estates or investing in colonial plantations. Bankers bought land and turned themselves into country gentry. Old title and new money merged in an increasingly uniform elite dedicated to capital accumulation.

This was not yet industrial capitalism. The era of mercantile capitalism did not really come to an end until 1800. Throughout this period, most wealth was still produced by pre-capitalist classes, with merchant capitalists accumulating profit by acting as middlemen, whether in national markets, overseas trade, or through the putting-out system, where they organised and marketed the output of independent artisans.

But a tremendous expansionism was imparted to the global economy. Capitalism has been history's most dynamic economic and social system, one which grows and morphs, engulfing the most distant corners of the globe, sucking in ever more human material, trampling underfoot all that stands in its way. The reason is simple enough: unlike earlier forms of class society, where surpluses were invested in politico-military competition (which, in economic terms, is waste), the surpluses generated by capital accumulation were invested in new rounds of economic development. Competing for markets, the farmers, merchants, and artisans of the new capitalist economy were obliged to invest their resources in estate improvement, bigger ships, and new technology if they were to keep ahead. In the cut-throat world of commerce and commodities, the pressure was relentless to expand sales, increase turnover, and raise profit –

or risk ruin. As Marx once put it, 'Accumulate, accumulate! This is Moses and the Prophets!'

So, under the imperative of competitive capital accumulation, the Dutch and the British were soon leading a global transformation. This is how Marx described the dynamic character of mercantile capitalism – a system of 'globalisation' – in *The Communist Manifesto*:

> The discovery of America, the rounding of the Cape, opened up fresh ground for the rising bourgeoisie. The East Indian and Chinese markets, the colonisation of America, trade with the colonies, the increase in means of exchange and in commodities generally, gave to commerce, to navigation, to industry, an impulse never before known, and thereby, to the revolutionary element in the tottering feudal society, a rapid development...
>
> The need of a constantly expanding market for its products chases the bourgeoisie over the whole surface of the globe. It must nestle everywhere, settle everywhere, establish conditions everywhere...

The Golden Age of the Dutch lasted from the late sixteenth into the early eighteenth century. Land was reclaimed and new farming methods introduced. The Zaanstreek zone north of Amsterdam boasted 128 industrial windmills. A Dutch explorer discovered Tasmania and New Zealand, and Dutch traders planted a post at Cape Town, evicted the Portuguese from Ceylon, and established a major colony in Indonesia (known as 'Batavia'). The profits of the Dutch East India Company made Amsterdam the financial capital of the world. Dutch towns filled with municipal monuments and grand houses, and prosperous Dutch burghers funded scientific experiments and commissioned works of art.

Such was the pace of development that commercial rivalry led to three naval wars between the Dutch and the British between 1652 and 1674. The first was triggered by restrictions on Dutch ships entering British ports, a measure designed to shift the carrying trade to British vessels. The second was mainly the result of British seizure of the Dutch colony of New Amsterdam on Manhattan (soon to become New York). The third was fought in an attempt by the British to subjugate the Dutch Republic altogether.

Soon, however, a common interest in resisting Louis XIV's France brought the two bourgeois states into alliance. Had the Anglo-Dutch conflict continued, Holland would have lost. The home-base was too small to sustain a long-term challenge to Britain. Size matters, both in economics and in politics. Only large economies can generate the resources for world-scale capital accumulation. Only large polities have the resources to sustain world-scale armies and navies. Holland was too small to rule the world.

The Dutch lost most of their footholds in the Americas during the seventeenth century – to the British in the north, to the Portuguese in the south – but they continued to prosper throughout the eighteenth century on the wealth of the Indies. In a booming mercantile economy dominated by only a handful of major maritime powers, there was space for all. Nonetheless, leadership in capitalist globalisation now passed to the British.

British history is shaped by the fact that it is a large island, rich in resources, on the edge of a dynamic continent. The seas around Britain are both a defensive moat and a commercial highway. The seventeenth-century revolution had unlocked the economic potential inherent in Britain's geography. It made possible a development of maritime trade, naval power, and overseas empire sufficient to launch Britain on the path to global superpower status.

The annual value of British foreign trade rose from about £10 million in 1700, to about £20 million in 1760, and about £40 million in 1790. Rising trade meant rising demand for both agricultural and industrial output. Coal production, for example, grew from 500,000 tons in 1650 to 15 million in 1800. The pace of industrial growth as a whole accelerated, from 0.7 per cent a year in 1710–60 to 2 per cent a year in 1780–1800. People were pulled from the countryside into booming urban areas: the proportion of the population living in towns increased from 9 per cent in 1650 to 20 per cent in 1800.

The boom in trade, agriculture, and industry underpinned the emergence of a modern banking system able to recycle savings into loans and feed the growing appetite for capital. This was symbolised by the founding of the Bank of England and the National Debt in 1694. The British government henceforward funded itself by borrowing from the rich. What made the system of credit sound was, of course, the growth of the economy as a whole, the confidence of investors in the solvency of the state, and the legislative control over the executive exercised by the propertied classes through Parliament.

The British state was thereby enabled to expand its military establishment in line with rising global commitments. Military expenditures increased from £50 million during the Nine Years War (1688–97), to £160 million during the Seven Years War (1756–63), and £1,660 million during the French Revolutionary and Napoleonic Wars (1793–1815).

Only towards the end of this period did an industrial take-off occur. During the late seventeenth and throughout the eighteenth century, virtually all industrial production continued to take the form of craftwork by artisans in small workshops. Mechanisation and factory production were still embryonic as late as 1800. The key figure in the development of capitalism remained the trader not the manufacturer, the middleman not the producer. The big profits were made by the bankers and merchants who controlled global flows of cargo, not by the masters of mines and mills. Capital accumulation was achieved through the control of distribution and exchange rather than production.

Globalisation is not new: capitalism has always been a world system. The first phase of that system – the mercantile capitalism of 1450 to 1800 – found its highest expression in the triangular trade. This saw the greatest accumulations of capital during the eighteenth century, and was, for those who controlled it, a source of stupendous riches. It supplied much of the surplus that would fuel the Industrial Revolution. But it was, at the same time, the supreme symbol of the barbarism of the capitalist system in its mercantile phase: for it was based on human slavery.

Colonies, Slavery, and Racism

Between the late seventeenth and early nineteenth century, millions of African men, women, and children were transported to the Americas to work on European-owned plantations.

Slave-traders on the West African coast paid local chieftains for deliveries of captives, thus fostering tribal wars, mass displacement, and the breakup of traditional societies. The captives were first imprisoned and then packed onto slave transports for 'the middle passage'. Chained to the lower decks, they had to perform all bodily functions where they lay. Excrement and urine covered the boards, the air became foul, and many sickened and died. Olaudah Equiano – a freed slave who became an abolition activist – was one who survived the middle passage and later recorded his experiences:

> ... the air soon became unfit for respiration, from a variety of loathsome smells, and brought on a sickness among the slaves, of which many died, thus falling victims to the improvident avarice, as I may call it, of their purchasers. This wretched situation was again aggravated by the galling of the chains, now become insupportable ... The shrieks of the women, and the groans of the dying, rendered the whole a scene of horror almost inconceivable.

Most who survived the middle passage were sold into plantation service in the West Indies or elsewhere in the Americas, where food, drink, clothing, and shelter were minimal, hard labour was imposed to the limit of human endurance, and subjugation was maintained by the shackle and the lash. Equiano recalled the overseers as 'for the most part persons of the worst character ... who cut and mangle the slaves in a shocking manner ... and altogether treat them in every respect like brutes'.

In the sixteenth century, the precious metals of the Aztecs and Incas had been the richest of imperial prizes. In the eighteenth century, it was the sugar plantations of the West Indies. In both cases, there had been a problem: shortage of labour. The native population of the Americas had been virtually exterminated by the guns and diseases of the first European settlers. But the settlers themselves – including indentured servants imported in their thousands as labourers – were annihilated by epidemics. What was needed was a new labour force resistant to malaria, yellow fever, and other tropical diseases. The solution was to import slaves from West Africa.

To supply Europe with sugar, coffee, and tobacco – and to make the men who supplied it very rich – around 12 million Africans were enslaved and transported over a period of about 150 years, and of these, around 1.5 million died on the voyage. It was more profitable to pack them in slave ships and accept these losses than to accommodate them in conditions that enabled more to survive. Life was no better for the survivors in the West Indies. Underfed, overworked, and disciplined by the lash, the death rate on the plantations was extremely high.

Compared with these 12 million African migrants, only around two million Europeans migrated to the New World in this period. Yet the white population was roughly twice that of the black in 1820. The Europeans had survived and reproduced. The Africans had simply died.

The annihilation of the native peoples of the New World was one of the greatest crimes against humanity in history. The slave trade was another. Both crimes were compounded by the racism deployed to justify them.

Racism of one sort or another exists in all class societies. There are four reasons for this.

First, ruling classes compete for control over surplus and they need to mobilise ordinary people in pursuit of these struggles. During the Crusades, for example, Muslims were demonised as infidels to justify wars of genocide, plunder, and conquest in the Middle East.

Second, class society pits ordinary people against each other in a struggle to survive. The ruling class exploits this to foster divisions that make it less likely that people will unite against their exploiters. The Roman aristocracy, for instance, allowed certain privileges to the citizen poor and enrolled them in networks of patronage; the latter were at the same time encouraged to despise foreigners and slaves as 'barbarians'.

Third, imperialism – the use of military force to seize the territory, resources, and manpower of other people – is easier to justify if the victims are portrayed as culturally or racially inferior. Imperialism can then be represented as a 'civilising' mission.

Finally, there is the impact of slavery. This is essentially the violent seizure of human beings, their absolute subordination to a master class, and the exploitation of their labour in an extreme form. It almost invariably arises in the context of conquest, and, since denial of her or his humanity is more or less implicit in the condition of the human chattel, it is invariably legitimised in racist terms. Colonialism, slavery, and racism thus form a tight nexus.

Rapid European colonial expansion and equally rapid growth in the slave trade during the eighteenth century combined to reconfigure racist ideology and magnify its historical significance. The new racism was developed in the context of the triangular trade. Ships carried trade goods to West Africa and were exchanged for black slaves. Local chiefs waged wars of enslavement to supply the market and gain access to imported prestige goods. The slaves were transported across the Atlantic and sold to plantation-owners in the slave markets. The ships returned to Europe with cargoes of sugar, coffee, tobacco, and later cotton.

It is impossible to exaggerate the economic value of the triangular trade. In eighteenth-century France, for example, seaports like Nantes, Bordeaux, and Marseilles, and industrial centres like Orleans, Lyons, and Paris, became the boom towns of an 'Atlantic economy' based on slavery. French ships transported hundreds of thousands of slaves from West Africa to the West Indies. Other ships carried flour, salted meats, wines, cloth, and machinery from France. They returned home with cargoes of sugar, coffee, cocoa, wood, indigo, and hides. Estimates of the number of Frenchmen whose livelihoods depended upon this trade vary between two and six million.

The British mercantile bourgeoisie was equally dependent on the triangular trade. Bristol became England's second city on the profits of slavery and sugar. One measure of the city's booming maritime economy was the increase in customs duties from £10,000 in 1634 to £334,000 in 1785. As one contemporary annalist recorded:

> There is not a brick in the city but what is cemented with the blood of a slave. Sumptuous mansions, luxurious living, liveried menials were the produce of the wealth made from the sufferings and groans of the slaves bought and sold by Bristol merchants...

Profit spawned racism. The slave's condition – on which such stupendous wealth had come to depend – was rationalised by racism. Africans were described as stupid, lazy, violent, and promiscuous; and such stereotypes, in keeping with the fashion of the age, were often given a pseudo-scientific gloss. The eighteenth-century historian Edward Long argued that Africans were 'a different species of the same genus', closer to orangutans than humans. The Enlightenment philosopher David Hume explained:

> I am apt to suspect the negroes ... to be naturally inferior to the whites ... There never was a civilised nation of any other complexion than white, or even any individual eminent in either

action or speculation. No ingenious manufacturers among them, no arts, no sciences.

Racism justified colonies and slavery on the grounds that the native people were inferior. At worst, they were seen as sub-humans fit only for heavy labour. At best, they were benighted and backward, in need of help to become civilised and Christian.

Capitalism has always been highly contradictory. On the one hand, its economic dynamism has dramatically increased our capacity to provide the goods and services people need. On the other, control of the world's wealth by a minority has condemned the mass of humanity to exploitation, oppression, and violence. The contradiction was expressed in the eighteenth century in the contrast between the wealth of the merchant-capitalist class of European port cities and the misery of the Atlantic passage and the West Indian plantations. As Marx put it, 'capital comes dripping from head to toe, from every pore, with blood and dirt'.

Nor was this the only human cost of the bourgeoisie's rise to global dominance. European rulers were ruthless in their pursuit of the dazzlingly rich prizes to be won in the colonies. Other rulers, sensing the balance of power tipping against them, felt compelled to contest domination of the world by their rivals. In consequence, Europe erupted repeatedly into war, and, increasingly, Europe's wars went global.

A Continent of Warring States: A World of Competing Empires

The Europeans had begun the exploration and colonisation of the world in the late fifteenth century. By the late eighteenth century, they had become the dominant force in global politics. Mercantile capitalism was bringing about a transformation of human society destined to be as all-encompassing as the Agricultural Revolution. As Marx put it in the late 1840s:

The bourgeoisie has, through its exploitation of the world market, given a cosmopolitan character to production and consumption in every country ... it has drawn from under the feet of industry the ground on which it stood ... The bourgeoisie, by the rapid improvement of all instruments of production, by the immensely facilitated means of communication, draws all, even the most barbarian, nations into civilisation ... It compels all nations, on pain of extinction, to adopt the bourgeois mode of production; it compels them to introduce what it calls 'civilisation' into their midst, that is, to become bourgeois themselves. In one word, it creates a world after its own image.

But the new system of economy developed within an old system of states. Mercantile capitalism coexisted with absolute monarchies. Two dynamics were at work: that of capital accumulation by rival groups of bankers, merchants, and industrialists; and that of politico-military accumulation by rival dynasties. Europeans clashed repeatedly throughout the eighteenth century in wars that were both struggles for mercantile advantage overseas and wars for territory and power on the continent.

The central spine of these wars was the conflict between bourgeois Britain and absolutist France. The English Revolution had been one of the most decisive events in world history because it had made Britain the springboard for the new, global, mercantile-capitalist economy. Once launched, it was unstoppable.

But the dominant European power at the end of the seventeenth century was not Britain but France. The latter's population was three times greater than Britain's, and the output of the French economy was correspondingly larger. Because of Britain's dynamic capitalist economy, however, its population and output grew more rapidly than those of France during the eighteenth century. France, moreover, as a continental power, had to maintain a large army to defend its land frontiers. Britain, by contrast, was a maritime power and an island fortress, so the policy of its rulers was to keep the army small and the navy strong.

The British state was also financially robust. Though the merchants and landowners who dominated Parliament favoured low-cost government and avoidance of continental warfare, Britain's growing capitalist economy meant that resources were available to support the military when vital interests were at stake. The Bank of England, for example, which quickly attracted funds after it was set up in 1694, was able to provide the loan finance for the expansion of the Royal Navy. Booming trade and modern banking conferred major advantages on Britain.

The conflict between Britain and France was the dominant global fracture-line between 1688 and 1815. At the beginning, it overlapped with the struggle against the English Revolution; at the end, with that against the French Revolution.

Let us recall here that Europe's geography has made it a continent of warring states. Its easy east–west communications and its seaways and navigable waterways facilitate movement. At the same time, its many peninsulas and distinct eco-zones have fostered a diversity of ethnicities and 'nations'. Since the fall of the Western Roman Empire, no continent-spanning imperial project has succeeded in Europe. Would-be imperial masters have invariably confronted too powerful a coalition of hostile forces.

From the sixteenth century onwards, traditional British policy was to prevent any single power from dominating Europe and, in particular, gaining control of the Channel ports and threatening the security of the island fortress. This was achieved by a combination of alliances, subsidies, and expeditionary forces. Throughout the eighteenth century, the British took a leading role in building a succession of alliances against France, provided subsidies to the rulers of minor German states to pay for military contingents, and regularly dispatched small armies of 'Redcoats' to fight alongside European allies.

At first, the British appeared weak. The destruction of the popular revolutionary movement between 1649 and 1660 had made possible a resurgence of Royalism after the Restoration, and this was exploited by the French monarchy. Charles II (1660–85), though nominally a Protestant, was broadly pro-Catholic and pro-French; he even formed an alliance with Louis XIV in an abortive attempt to smash the (Protestant) Dutch Republic.

He was succeeded by his brother James II in 1685. James was Catholic, pro-French, and committed to absolute monarchy. Supported by French subsidies, he was able to build up an Irish Catholic army as a potential instrument of Royalist counter-revolution. Initially, he had the backing of England's men of property. When Charles's illegitimate son, the staunchly Protestant Duke of Monmouth, landed in the West Country to claim the throne in 1685, Parliament and the army backed James. They feared a revival of the popular revolutionary movement of 1641–9, and the 'Good Old Cause' went down to defeat at the Battle of Sedgemoor.

But Royalism was a serious threat to the property, power, and religion of Protestant landowners and merchants. Once James's intentions became clear, and with the danger of popular revolution reduced after Sedgemoor, leading Parliamentary and army leaders planned a coup. The Glorious Revolution of 1688 was a reassertion of the victory of 1645 and the compromise of 1660. William of Orange, the ruler of Holland, and his wife Mary Stuart, James II's elder daughter, were invited to accept the thrones of England, Ireland, and Scotland. The army mutinied in William's interest, and James fled to France.

The Jacobites, as they became known, remained a threat until 1746. With French backing, they launched a series of attempts to overturn the Protestant succession to the throne of the 'three kingdoms' of England, Ireland, and Scotland, notably in 1689–91, 1715, and 1745–6. The Jacobite revolts were part of a wider global conflict between Britain and France. These two states fought six major wars against each other between 1688 and 1815. They were formally at war for a full half of this entire period.

This struggle for supremacy between Britain and France was a predominant issue in all of the following conflicts: the Nine Years War (1688–97), the War of the Spanish Succession (1701–14), the War of the Austrian Succession (1740–8), the Seven Years War (1756–63), the American Revolutionary War (in which the French were involved against the British from 1778 to 1783), and the French Revolutionary and Napoleonic Wars (during which the British and the French were almost continually at war from 1793 to 1815). The conflict was global. It was centred in Europe, but there were major struggles on land and sea in India, the West Indies, North America, and elsewhere.

Britain had three major advantages from the outset. First, a new army and a new way of war had been forged during the English Revolution. Under the absolute monarchy, the French Army fought slow, cautious, heavily defensive 'wars of position'. By contrast, in the tradition of the New Model Army of 1645–60, British military doctrine stressed mobility, firepower, and aggression.

Second, Britain's economic wealth and robust financial infrastructure enabled it to subsidise the military contributions of its continental allies. A recurring feature of the wars of this period, for example, was a powerful axis linking maritime-bourgeois

Britain and continental-absolutist Prussia. British victories over France in America and India were paid for in the blood of Prussian peasant-conscripts on the battlefields of Germany.

Third, the British could devote far greater resources than could the French to naval operations and colonial campaigns. The British were protected by the English Channel. The French had to prioritise the defence of their extensive land frontiers. The British way of war evolved to include the projection of small, professional, high-tech expeditionary forces; whereas the French were compelled to maintain mass conscript armies to fight continental wars.

These advantages, combined with the fact that Britain's population and output were growing faster than those of France, meant that French power was contained in Europe and French colonies overseas lost.

Britain's century of geopolitical triumph was bracketed by two decisive battles. The Duke of Marlborough's victory at the Battle of Blenheim in 1704 ended the continental hegemony of Louis XIV's France. The Duke of Wellington's victory at the Battle of Waterloo in 1815 ended that of Napoleon's France. Britain then remained the dominant global superpower for most of the nineteenth century. It did not fight a major war in Europe between 1815 and 1914. This dominance was made possible by its geopolitical victory over France and its pioneering of the Industrial Revolution. Both achievements were rooted in the revolutionary transformation of British society in the mid-seventeenth century.

Britain's ascendancy contributed substantially to a second wave of bourgeois revolution. The absolutist and state-feudal monarchies of Europe were incapable of matching the achievements of Britain's dynamic capitalist economy. The French fell ever further behind, and the growing pressure of geopolitical competition was a major factor in the explosion of 1789.

Before that, however, the Americans had performed a spectacular dress rehearsal. A new age of revolution opened in 1775 with a blaze of musket fire at Lexington and Bunker Hill in far-off Massachusetts.

9
The Second Wave of Bourgeois Revolutions
1775–1815

An armed French revolutionary of c. 1793.
Contemporary painted figurine.

The French Revolution, like all great revolutions, was driven forwards by mass action from below.

The English Reformation created a strong centralised state and a new aristocracy of courtiers and estate-owners. The English Revolution then created a constitutional monarchy which vested governmental authority in the property-owning classes. These two developments reconfigured the British ruling class into an elite dominated by bankers, merchants, and commercial farmers. The effect was to unleash the full potential of British mercantile capitalism.

The transformation of the world that had begun around 1450 could then accelerate rapidly. As British armies and fleets created a vast colonial empire in India, North America, and the West Indies, wealth flowed back to Britain and turned it into both an economic powerhouse and a geopolitical superpower.

One outcome was that military competition with Britain wrecked the finances and the political credibility of France's absolute monarchy. At the same time, the development of capitalism and a prosperous merchant and professional bourgeoisie within France created social forces with the potential to overthrow the monarchy and remodel society. The result – the French Revolution – shook the world. Nothing afterwards was ever quite the same.

This chapter presents a detailed analysis of this key event in modern world history. We begin, however, with the Enlightenment, the revolution in ideas leading up to 1789, and with the American Revolution, the great colonial revolt which provided the French with a model of ideas in action.

The Enlightenment

Eighteenth-century Europe was divided into three. One part – much of southern and eastern Europe – was trapped in a feudal-absolutist past, where royal autocrats ruled traditional societies of landlords and priest-ridden peasants which had barely changed since the Middle Ages.

The second – north-west Europe – was being transformed by a dynamic, fast-growing capitalist economy based on commercial farming, maritime trade, new industries, and modern banking. London's growth is a measure of this change: its population, which had stood at just over 100,000 in 1560, grew to 350,000 in 1640, 630,000 in 1715, and 1.4 million in 1815.

The third part was formed by an intermediate group. Here, feudal-absolutist survivals were interlaced with burgeoning commercial capitalism. France was the supreme example. It had a growing merchant navy, an expanding colonial empire in India and the Americas, and an increasingly wealthy and assertive urban bourgeoisie. But France also had a royal autocracy, a powerful Catholic Church, a parasitic class of state-subsidised courtiers, an equally parasitic class of ancient titled landowners, a peasantry weighed down by feudal dues and tithes, and an internal trading system hampered by tolls, duties, and petty regulations.

The growth of French capitalism meant that the contradictions could not be contained indefinitely. What brought them more rapidly to crisis point was the state's struggle for global supremacy with Britain. The population of Paris trebled between the mid-sixteenth century and the early nineteenth: this was a measure of the French economy's expansion. But in the same period London's population grew 12-fold. Whereas Paris had been twice the size of London in the mid-sixteenth century, it was only half the size in the early nineteenth: this was a measure of the greater dynamism of the British economy.

The cutting-edge of the problem was military competition between the two nation-states. During the Seven Years War (1756–63), France lost its empire in India and the Americas to the British. Military defeat was the external expression of a growing crisis in French society. A revolution in ideas was its internal expression. Long before its overthrow in the Revolution of 1789–94, France's feudal-absolutist *ancien régime* had been intellectually deconstructed.

The inability of the *ancien régime* to maintain its ideological defences exposed its reactionary character. A new wave of Enlightenment thinking so completely swept away the accumulated ideological detritus of the past that even despots and dukes embraced 'rational' and 'scientific' ways of viewing the world with the enthusiasm of new converts.

The price of seventeenth-century counter-revolution – which corresponded more or less with the Counter-Reformation in Austria, Italy, Spain, and (to a degree) France – was that Holland, England, and Scotland had become the focal points of intellectual, scientific, and artistic advance by the end of that century. The received wisdom of holy texts was discarded in favour of observation, experiment, and reasoning. Isaac Newton, for example, now had the freedom to solve the problems in physics that had puzzled Copernicus, Kepler, and Galileo in earlier attempts to explain how the universe worked.

But the new realm claimed by 'Reason' extended far beyond the natural sciences. The Dutch and English Revolutions had rejected the divine right of kings in favour of the rights and privileges of elected representatives. But if the political order was not ordained by God, if humans created their own political order, what form should it take?

The Putney Debates of 1647 had revealed the dangers: in the absence of divine authority, people were liable to disagree about how power should be exercised. At Putney, those of a 'higher station' had taken the view that none should have a say in the management of public affairs who had no 'permanent fixed interest'. Others, speaking for 'the lower sort', had argued that no one had an obligation to obey 'that government that he hath not had a voice to put himself under'. Little wonder that revolutionary England produced political philosophers like Thomas Hobbes and John Locke.

In the event, the debate subsided with the settlements of 1660 and 1688. England's fractured elite struck a deal and closed ranks against the lower orders. During the eighteenth century, as Whigs and Tories, the two main parties in Parliament, they may have continued squabbling over the spoils of office – becoming to the satirists of the day 'Old Corruption' – but to the rest of society they presented a united front. By the end of the century, some 200 crimes against property carried the death sentence in England.

Unreformed French society, on the other hand, found no such resolution of urgent political questions. It was here, therefore, that the Enlightenment blossomed. Its greatest achievement was the *Encyclopédie* (1751–72), a 35-volume compendium of human knowledge and thought to which hundreds of leading intellectuals contributed and which sold some 25,000 copies.

What gave the Enlightenment its subversive, politically corrosive character – irrespective of the relatively conservative intentions of many of its exponents – was its critique of institutions and practices that appeared irrational in the light of contemporary thinking. And what contemporary commentators considered irrational tended to be that which was not in the interests of the class of mercantile and professional bourgeois to which they belonged.

Commerce and market-based relationships were breaking down networks of patronage, privilege, and influence. Monetary exchange was replacing entitlement based on inherited rank and estate. What seemed irrational to the new thinkers, therefore, was the Church and its theology, the divine right claimed by kings, and the political supremacy of a decaying class of titled place-seekers.

What of private property itself? Was this rational? Some thought not. Here is Jean-Jacques Rousseau:

> The first man who, having fenced in a piece of land, said 'this is mine', and found people naïve enough to believe him, that man was the true founder of civil society. From how many crimes, wars, and murders, from how many horrors and misfortunes might not anyone have saved mankind, by pulling up the stakes, or filling up the ditch, and crying to his fellows: 'Beware of listening to this impostor; you are undone if you once forget that the fruits of the earth belong to us all, and the earth itself to nobody.'

The Enlightenment was a multidimensional intellectual movement, but its essence was radical critique, and anything and everything in human affairs that could not give an adequate account of itself in the court of free enquiry was open to challenge. And this, in the context of late eighteenth-century Europe, riddled as it was with contradictions, filled with hallowed institutions that seemed to many monuments to superstition, was an ideological powder-keg – especially so when the spirit of Reason reached 'the lower sort'. Then thrones might totter.

'A French bastard landing with an armed *banditti* and establishing himself king of England against the consent of the nation,' announced one of the Enlightenment's most radical pamphleteers in reference to William the Conqueror, 'is in plain terms a very paltry rascally original.' He continued: 'Monarchy and succession have laid … the world in blood and ashes … Freedom hath been hunted around the globe. Asia and Africa have long expelled her. Europe regards her like a stranger, and England hath given her warning to depart.'

This was January 1776. The voice was Tom Paine's. His pamphlet, *Common Sense*, had turned the pompous language of *salon* intellectuals into the everyday talk of alehouse 'mechanics' (artisans). It sold a record-breaking 150,000 copies immediately, and half a million within a year. Little wonder. Hundreds of thousands of ordinary men and women were embracing radical ideas and engaging in a struggle to remodel the world.

Nine months before the publication of *Common Sense* in the New England city of Philadelphia, militiamen in neighbouring Massachusetts had opened fire on British Redcoats at Lexington and sparked the American Revolution.

The American Revolution

In 1764, Americans living in the 13 colonies along the eastern seaboard of North America thought of themselves as British subjects of George III. By 1788, by their own decisions and actions, they had made themselves free citizens of a new republic forged in revolution and war.

Many other things also changed. The 13 colonies became an independent federal state. King and Parliament had been swept away, and in their place were a President, Senate, and House of Representatives.

Some men of wealth – loyalists who had backed the King – lost their fortunes. Others, who might once have run their affairs in the manner of feudal barons, found that their tenants were no longer deferential. Women – some at least – had become more forthright. They read newspapers, established schools to educate their daughters, conducted themselves with a 'reverence of self', and asked their 'patriot' husbands, 'Why should I not have liberty?'

For some black people, too, things were very different. The states of Massachusetts and Vermont had abolished slavery altogether. Others would soon follow. The few thousand free blacks along the Chesapeake River in 1776 would number 60,000 by 1810.

The change was not as great as it might have been; far less, in fact, than many had hoped. For the American Revolution (1775–83) was not just a struggle for national independence between the American colonies and the British Empire. It was also a struggle between different sorts and conditions of Americans, a struggle to determine what sort of republic they were fighting for.

The problems began at the end of the Seven Years War (1756–63). The British had beaten the French and taken over their empire in India and Canada. In this the Americans had played their part, colonial militias fighting alongside Redcoat regulars to secure the western frontier of the colonies. Victory ended the French threat; and with it, American dependence on British military support. It also left the British government saddled with war debt, and in need of tax increases to pay it off.

British taxes on American trade were triple-pronged. They were intended to: avoid levying higher taxes on British landowners; protect British commerce against foreign competition; and help pay off British debts. In a nutshell, the Sugar Act (1764), the Stamp Act (1765), the Townshend taxes (1767), and the Tea Act (1773) were designed to siphon off American wealth in the interests of the British ruling class. Had the Americans continued to pay, economic stagnation and underdevelopment would have been the consequence. That was the danger countered by the famous slogan 'No taxation without representation'. Threatened with taxes not in their interests, Americans demanded the right to decide.

Between 1764 and 1775, British efforts were frustrated by direct action. Though there were only three million Americans spread across the 13 colonies, and only one in 20 lived in a town, they came together in a mass movement of resistance that made British taxes unenforceable.

The movement was built by meetings, parades, the burning of effigies, and the erection of liberty poles. Crowds confronted customs men and soldiers. Would-be collaborators were intimidated. Official events were disrupted. In some cases property was destroyed.

Boycotts were enforced by a militant urban crowd of artisans ('mechanics'), small traders, local farmers, and dissident intellectuals. Leading activists organised themselves as 'Sons of Liberty'. There were branches in at least 15 towns, and they were knitted together in an inter-colony 'correspondence' union.

The pattern was for resistance to flare up, sometimes leading to bloody clashes, and for the British then to back down. But in 1773, after an entire cargo of East India Company tea was dumped in the sea by 100 activists disguised as Native Americans – the 'Boston Tea Party' – the British decided that a crackdown was in order. General Gage was sent out as Governor of Massachusetts, troops were dispatched to enforce his authority, and new laws (the 'Intolerable Acts') were passed, decreeing that American activists could be transported to Britain for trial.

A Continental Congress attended by representatives of all 13 colonies agreed to continue the tea boycott. Local committees were authorised to enforce this decision and colonial militias were mobilised to back the civil power. The Continental Congress was dominated by big landowners and merchants. So too, at first, were most local committees. But 'the revolution of the elite' soon gave way to 'the revolution of the middle classes'.

Revolution requires mass action to support radical demands. Men of property have much to fear. Many are tied into the existing economic system and profit from it. All fear that the common people, once roused against political authority, may be prompted to ask deeper questions about the social order as a whole. The strategy for many men of property was to keep pace with the movement in order to channel its energies. For the New York landowner and lawyer Robert Livingston, it was a matter of 'swimming with a stream it is impossible to stem' and of yielding 'to the torrent' in order to 'direct its course'.

Pushed into revolution by mass action from below, Congress had, in effect, sanctioned the construction of a new state apparatus. Every town now faced a choice between recognising the authority of the councillors, judges, customs men, and militia officers of the King, or that of the boycott committees empowered by Congress. Revolution turns on such choices. 'Dual power' – two rival authorities laying claim to political allegiance – forces everyone to make a choice, since they cannot give their allegiance to both at once.

The first shots were fired at Lexington on 19 April 1775. British Redcoats killed eight American militiamen and wounded ten more while on their way to seize rebel arms stored at Concord. When the Redcoats arrived there, they found the arms had been removed. As they fell back to Boston, they were harassed by swarms of militiamen and were then besieged in the city itself. The war had begun.

The colonial militias were soon supplemented by a Continental Army. Funded by Congress and commanded by its appointee, George Washington, it became the military expression of the embryonic United States. The militiamen defended their localities, but the Continentals waged a national war.

The British won most of the battles – the major exceptions were Saratoga in 1777 and Yorktown in 1781 – but they lost the war. There were three main reasons for this. First, geography favoured the revolutionaries, for the American colonies comprised vast tracts of wilderness, which imposed a heavy logistical burden on the British and provided ideal terrain for embedded guerrilla resistance.

Second, the Americans enjoyed strong and growing French support. At first this took the form of supplies of arms, but later involved full-scale military intervention on both land and sea. The British were left struggling to keep operations going at the end of a long and vulnerable maritime supply-line.

Third, the revolutionaries organised themselves politically and militarily to wage all-out war. The core of the resistance was supplied by the mechanics, small traders, and backcountry farmers who came to dominate the local committees and militias. The British controlled only the territory their soldiers occupied. The rebels, however often they were beaten, could always retreat, recuperate, and return to fight again.

The common people were empowered by their role in the struggle. They fought for what they considered to be ancient, inherited 'rights' and 'liberties'. They fought for a 'moral economy' in which each had a role that commanded respect and each worked more for the community than for personal gain. And they fought for a voice in public affairs – for a radical democracy where the poor voted as well as the rich.

In the event, the heady ideals of 1776 were diluted by the final settlement of 1788. The Declaration of Independence of 1776 had asserted that all men are created equal, that they have inalienable rights, and that among these are life, liberty, and the pursuit of happiness. But the Constitution of 1788 enshrined not radical democracy and moral economy, but the rule of property, free markets, and a gilded elite of landowners, merchants, and bankers. So America's bourgeois revolution, in this sense and in others, was left unfinished. Above all, slavery remained in place, and in the decades to come it would expand into an immensely profitable economic system. Less than a century after the Revolution, more than 620,000 Americans would die in a yet greater conflict, the Civil War, to establish the proposition proclaimed in 1776 that 'all men are created equal'.

The Revolution had therefore set the benchmark against which future generations of Americans – men and women, white and black, rich and poor – would measure their standing. Not only that: in its own time, it proved to be the curtain-raiser on a new epoch of world revolution. For, in the year following ratification of the US Constitution, the people of Paris stormed the Bastille, defeated a military coup, and unleashed the French Revolution.

The Storming of the Bastille

The Bastille was an ancient fortress and state prison in eastern Paris. A symbol of absolute monarchy, it loomed menacingly over streets inhabited by the city's working population of artisans, small traders, and general labourers. Like the monarchy, it seemed an immovable presence.

On 14 July 1789, the people of Paris, who had been seizing arms wherever they could find them for two days, massed outside the Bastille and demanded its surrender. The defenders opened fire. During three hours of fighting, 83 people were killed. But the determination of the assault broke the defenders' morale and the gates were opened.

The Bastille had been stormed to thwart a military coup by the French King against his own people. The insurrection broke the back of the absolute monarchy and transformed the self-declared National Assembly into the effective government of France. The National Assembly immediately abolished 'feudalism', passed a 'declaration of the rights of man', and created a new 'National Guard'. Towns across France followed the example of the capital and created new revolutionary authorities.

When the news reached the countryside, it inspired an elemental rising of the peasantry – 'the Great Fear'. Hundreds of thousands marched on the *chateaux* of their landlords and burnt the title deeds to feudal dues. In scores of local towns, the poor demonstrated against food shortages, price rises, and unemployment.

The world had been turned upside down. An absolute monarchy unchallenged for 140 years had been overthrown in three days of urban insurrection. The French Revolution had begun.

For the next 25 years, counter-revolutionary forces at home and abroad would attempt to destroy the achievement of 1789. Again and again, the Revolution would have to mobilise mass popular forces in its own defence. As early as October 1789, a royalist plot was being hatched. Its epicentre was the court of Louis XVI and Marie Antoinette at the Palace of Versailles outside Paris. So 20,000 market-women marched to Versailles, their menfolk trailing behind them, broke into the palace, and forced the King to return to Paris, where he and his followers would be under popular surveillance. The victory of the market-women consolidated the constitutional monarchy and ended the first phase of the French Revolution. Let us therefore pause to take stock.

Between 1688 and 1783, Britain and France had fought five long wars, lasting in total 42 years. The locations of these conflicts had ranged from the forests of North America to the plains of India, though they had usually been centred in Europe. Because the British economy was growing faster than the French, and because the French usually had to fight the British at sea and their European allies on land, the French had lost their empire and ruined their economy. Even the cost of occasional victories had been too high: the French state had been bankrupted by its role in the American Revolutionary War. In its aftermath, the absolute monarchy was forced to attempt a reform of the tax system.

These basic facts must be placed in a wider context. Capitalism is a dynamic economic system whose competitive edge threatens traditional societies and states. Britain grew much faster than France during the eighteenth century because of the forces unleashed by the English Revolution. The French economy certainly grew – at an estimated 1.9 per cent a year throughout the eighteenth century. Textile output increased 250 per cent, iron 350 per cent, and coal 750 per cent. By 1789 a fifth of the French population worked in industry or handicrafts. But this was not enough to keep up with Britain, so that the absolute monarchy failed the test of war, and by the 1780s France's imperial crisis had become a financial one too. Louis XVI was forced to attempt to modernise the state under the pressure of military competition from a more powerful economy.

War taxation was already a massive burden on the working population, but the nobility and the clergy paid no tax at all. The key to reform was to make them pay their share. But when the King appointed a 'reforming' ministry to rationalise the tax system, the *parlements* – aristocrat-controlled supreme courts in Paris and the provinces – rejected its proposals. Many leading aristocrats even called for mass demonstrations against the government. The central demand was that an Estates-General should be called to resolve the crisis.

The Estates-General of 1789 was the first to be convened since 1614. It was formed of three chambers representing the three 'estates': nobility, clergy, and commons. The election campaign for the commons (the Third Estate) reached into every small town and village, drawing the masses into political action and releasing a torrent of grievances and demands. The Third Estate represented the overwhelming majority of the people, but it was dominated by the professional middle classes, especially lawyers, mainly because they had the necessary political skills.

The Estates-General met from April to June 1789 at Versailles. The result was a political stand-off. The King's ministers demanded tax reform. The delegates demanded redress of grievances. The Third Estate refused to recognise the superiority of the nobility and the clergy.

When the Third Estate proclaimed itself a National Assembly and invited the nobility and clergy to join it, the King locked them out of their hall. The delegates then convened in a nearby tennis court and swore an oath not to disperse until a constitution was granted. In response, the King sacked his leading reformist minister and summoned 20,000 troops to Paris.

The capital was already a ferment of political clubs and meetings, the streets awash with news-sheets, pamphlets, and street-corner orators. Some 400 of the middle-class 'electors' who had taken part in the selection of delegates to the Estates-General met in the City Hall and formed themselves into a council or *commune*. But it was the intervention of the Paris crowd – predominantly artisans, petty-traders, and general labourers – that brought down the absolute monarchy. The crowd fraternised with the soldiers and won them over. The King did not dare send more soldiers into the city. The Bastille was successfully stormed. The peasant revolution, following the example of Paris and other large towns, was then decisive. France was a predominantly agricultural country and most soldiers were peasants. When the villages attacked the *chateaux*, there was no chance that the soldiers would fight for the landlords.

The Third Estate had been joined by a minority of aristocrats and clergy to form the National Assembly. The relatively conservative majority favoured a constitutional monarchy that would halt the Revolution and safeguard property and privilege. It was led by the

Marquis de Lafayette, a general who had served in the American Revolutionary War.

At first, during the Revolution's honeymoon period, the more radical revolutionaries were marginalised. But their strength was growing amid the continuing ferment of propaganda and agitation. Some 250 newspapers were launched in the last six months of 1789 alone. Soon to emerge as the most popular was the former doctor Jean-Paul Marat's *L'Ami du Peuple* ('The Friend of the People').

Numerous radical clubs provided opportunities to debate the way forward. The most famous were the Jacobins, dominated by the lawyer Maximilien de Robespierre, and the Cordeliers, dominated by another lawyer, George Jacques Danton.

In June 1791, the King attempted to flee to join the counter-revolutionary armies massing across the border. He was captured and brought back to Paris. But when, in the following month, ordinary Parisians queued up to sign a republican petition in the Field of Mars, Lafayette's National Guard opened fire and killed 50 of them.

In the same place, exactly a year before, people had gathered on the anniversary of the storming of the Bastille in a carnival-like Festival of Federation. Now a river of blood separated conservative constitutional monarchists like Lafayette and radical republicans like Marat, Robespierre, and Danton. The Revolution was entering a new phase.

The Jacobin Dictatorship

In the summer of 1792, the constitutional monarchy created by the urban insurrection three years earlier collapsed. On 10 August, tens of thousands of *sans-culottes* and *fédérés* surrounded and attacked the Tuileries, the King's Paris residence.

The *sans-culottes* ('those without breeches') were the trousered working people of Paris. They were organised in 48 *sections*. These were local assemblies which functioned as electoral wards for the city council or *commune*. The *sections* had become organs of participatory democracy for the artisans, small traders, and general labourers of Paris. The *fédérés* ('federals') were volunteer soldiers from the provinces on their way to the front, for war had been declared earlier that year. They represented the cream of the revolutionary activists from the rest of France.

The National Guard, instead of defending the King, joined the insurrection. But the Swiss Guard (foreign mercenaries) stayed loyal, and some 600 royalists and 370 revolutionaries were killed in the fighting. The palace was overrun and the King arrested.

The insurrection of 10 August 1792 was as decisive as that of 14 July 1789. The constitution agreed in 1791, with voting rights tied to property-ownership, was overturned. The Legislative Assembly elected on this restricted franchise, the successor to the National Assembly of 1789, was dissolved, and a National Convention was elected on the basis of adult male suffrage to frame a new constitution. The Convention, when it met, was dominated by republicans, who abolished the monarchy and declared a republic. The King was then tried and executed in January 1793.

Three insoluble contradictions destroyed the constitutional monarchy of 1789–92. First, the majority of the nobility and clergy remained deeply hostile to the Revolution and were intent on reversing it. The royal court became a centre of intrigue. *Emigré* armies were forming. The counter-revolution was a real and present danger.

Second, popular expectations, encouraged by the events of 1789, had been disappointed. Hopes of political empowerment and social reform had been dashed. Instead, there were food shortages, inflation, and unemployment. The result was rioting in Paris and elsewhere.

Third, in a desperate attempt to paper over growing splits within the regime, an unholy alliance of political forces had agreed to declare war against the Revolution's foreign enemies. The King and his supporters hoped the counter-revolution would prevail. Lafayette and the constitutional monarchists hoped to lead a crusade that would unite the nation. The Girondins – moderate republicans – hoped to be swept to power on a wave of national enthusiasm.

All were disappointed. The war backfired. Conservative generals defected to the enemy. The French suffered serious defeats. The enemy commander declared that he would impose 'exemplary vengeance' and 'hand over the city of Paris to soldiers and punish the rebels as they deserved'.

These tensions culminated in the insurrection of 10 August. The wave of popular enthusiasm that made it possible then flowed into the new volunteer army being formed. 'Audacity, audacity, and still more audacity', proclaimed Danton, a newly elected member of the

National Convention, and now a leading member of the revolution-ary government.

On 20 September 1792, at Valmy in north-eastern France, the French Revolutionary army halted the advance of the invaders. It was on the following day that the Convention abolished the monarchy.

But the new Girondin government was now as eager to halt the Revolution as its predecessor had been. The central contradiction of the bourgeois revolution reasserted itself. Once in power, the moderate republicans prioritised the defence of property against the popular movement. 'Your property is threatened', declared one of the Girondin leaders. A 'hydra of anarchy' is at large, proclaimed another. Unless 'recurrent insurrections' were stopped, warned a third, 'Paris would be destroyed'.

But the counter-revolutionary threat had not been expunged. On the contrary, by spring 1793 Britain had joined the war against France, there were royalist risings in the western Vendée region, foreign armies were again advancing on Paris from the north-east, and the Girondin general Dumouriez had deserted to the enemy.

On 26 May 1793, Robespierre called on the people to revolt again. On 29 May, the Paris *sections* met and elected a new *commune*. On 31 May and 2 June, mass demonstrations surrounded the Convention and compelled it to arrest 29 Girondin leaders. From then on, the purged assembly was dominated by the Jacobins.

The Committee of Public Safety – a body of 12 men elected by the Convention – now became the effective government. The Committee reported to the Convention once a week and was subject to re-election once a month. Three prominent Jacobins – Robe-spierre, Louis de Saint-Just, and Georges Couthon – became its guiding figures. The Committee established a total-war economy, with mass conscription, nationalised war industries, and progres-sive taxation. Forced loans were imposed on the rich. The estates of *émigrés* and the Church were confiscated, divided into small plots, and distributed to the peasantry. Price controls were imposed and speculation became a capital crime.

A policy of 'terror' was employed to deter counter-revolution. The guillotine, erected in the Place de la Concorde in central Paris, became a symbol of revolutionary justice. Jacobin authorities, in the capital and elsewhere, executed several thousand between September 1793 and July 1794.

Why was this necessary? The Terror was a product of two factors. First, the threat from the counter-revolution was extreme and ever-present. In the towns and villages they captured, counter-revolutionaries carried out wholesale massacres of Republicans; they almost certainly killed far more than the Jacobins. Had they been victorious, they would have drowned the revolution in blood. The death penalty was necessary to discourage counter-revolutionary activism.

The second factor is peculiar to the highly contradictory character of the Jacobin regime. The regime wobbled on a narrow and unstable base, because the Jacobins did not so much represent a specific class as a specific historical moment when opposing class forces were finely balanced. Most of the bourgeoisie – former royalists, constitutional monarchists, and moderate republicans – had now gone over to the counter-revolution. Only the most radical minority supported the Jacobin dictatorship. Its leaders were mainly professional men of modest means. Their rule rested largely on the support of the *sans-culotte* popular movement.

The revolutionary emergency demanded radical measures which most of the property-owning classes feared and resented. This strengthened the counter-revolution. At the same time, the Committee of Public Safety was an elected body of the Convention, and the Jacobin leaders remained strong defenders of private property as the basis of society. This put a strain on the government's relationship with its most radical supporters.

In the politico-military emergency of the Republic's Year II (1793–4), with the survival of the revolutionary regime at stake, the guillotine became the arbiter of these contradictions. As well as outright counter-revolutionaries, the Terror 'devoured its own children', striking down revolutionaries hostile to the dictatorship. In March 1794, the left-wing 'Hébertists' were executed. The following month, it was the turn of the right-wing 'Indulgents'. In this way, the centrist Committee of Public Safety sought to maintain its increasingly precarious political balance.

The effect was to paralyse resistance for a few months, but only by shrinking further the regime's mass base. The social-democratic promise of the regime was disappointed and the popular movement declined. 'The Revolution has frozen over', declared Saint-Just.

Meanwhile, on the frontiers, the remodelled French Revolution-ary armies had driven back the invaders. The emergency that had given rise to the Jacobin dictatorship was coming to an end. Those sections of the bourgeoisie that had supported it out of necessity now drew back. The Convention was turning against the Committee. The Revolution was about to go into reverse. The crisis broke in July 1794.

From Thermidor to Napoleon

Gratitude is not a political attitude. With internal revolt suppressed and the French Army occupying Brussels, the revolutionary bour-geoisie turned on its Jacobin saviours. Sensing that power was slipping away, Robespierre called for another mass purge. But on 27 July 1794, his enemies in the Convention howled him down and then issued an arrest warrant against him and his political allies.

The Jacobins retreated to the City Hall and called for a revolu-tionary *journée* (insurrection). But support was patchy. The regime had attacked its own supporters, executing left activists, lifting a ban on food speculation, and imposing wage cuts. Only 16 of the 48 Paris *sections* sent armed men to City Hall. These dispersed after several hours standing around without leadership. The Jacobin leaders were then arrested, tried, and executed. Robespierre, Saint-Just, Couthon, and 18 others were guillotined on 28 July. Another 71 Jacobins followed the next day.

Some left-wingers had participated in the coup of Thermidor (the name of the month when it occurred according to the revolutionary calendar). This was a mistake. Their mass base had crumbled, so that the destruction of Robespierre's centrist dictatorship shifted power decisively to the right, not the left. Thermidor was a reactionary coup.

The streets filled with gangs of rich young thugs (*jeunesse dorée*: gilded youth). A mob shut down the Jacobin Club. A property qual-ification for voting was introduced. A 'white terror' raged. Desperate risings of the *sans-culottes* were crushed in April and May 1795 (the revolts of Germinal and Prairial). The balance tipped further to the right and resurgent royalists attempted a coup in October 1795 (the revolt of Vendémiaire). This was crushed by a young artillery officer called Napoleon Bonaparte with 'a whiff of grapeshot'. But its occurrence revealed the instability of the Thermidorian regime.

Thermidor had not been a counter-revolution. It had been a bourgeois reaction against radical democracy *within* the Revolution. But by demoralising and demobilising the mass movement, the bourgeoisie had made royalist counter-revolution more likely. The Thermidorians therefore concentrated power in the hands of a five-man Directory – a strong-arm executive that would deal equally firmly with popular uprisings and royalist counter-revolution.

But the Directory was unable to secure an electoral mandate, so in 1797 it was transformed into an effective dictatorship dependent on the support of the army. This anomaly was resolved in November 1799, at the coup of Brumaire, when Napoleon, the Republic's most illustrious general, seized power. The new First Consul had himself crowned Emperor in 1804.

The coup of Brumaire ended the French Revolution, but it did not reverse it; on the contrary, it preserved and defended its essential gains. Napoleon, like Cromwell, was 'the Soldier of the Revolution', not its nemesis. Feudal dues had gone for good and the peasants kept their land. The economy remained free of internal customs. A national system of administration had been established, there was equality under the law, and the Church had been separated from the state. Even in 1815, when the monarchy was restored by foreign bayonets, the *ancien régime* could not be reconstructed.

The armies of the Directory, the Consulate, and the Empire, moreover, carried the revolutionary tradition abroad, abolishing serfdom, nationalising church land, and removing internal customs. And some of these changes – in parts of Germany, Austria, Italy, and elsewhere – proved irreversible. Not only that. The example of the Revolution was infectious. Intellectuals and activists across Europe were inspired by its ideals and victories. Some welcomed the armies of Napoleon. Others mounted their own copycat revolutions.

This was a glorious mental dawn. All thinking beings shared in the jubilation of this epoch. Emotions of a lofty character stirred men's minds ... a spiritual enthusiasm thrilled through the world.

That is how the German philosopher Georg Hegel (1770–1831) recalled the impact of the French Revolution. His sentiments were echoed by intellectuals across Europe. 'Bliss was it in that dawn to be alive,' proclaimed the English poet William Wordsworth, 'but to be young was very heaven!' The fiery symphonies of Beethoven were inspired by the French Revolution, and Mozart's chorus cries 'Long Live Liberty!' in *Don Giovanni*. Tom Paine's defence of the Revolution, *The Rights of Man*, sold 100,000 copies, thousands of British workers demonstrated in support of French victories, and the Royal Navy was paralysed by a mutiny of common sailors in 1797.

Among those moved to action by the French Revolution was a young Protestant lawyer called Wolfe Tone, who founded a radical organisation, the United Irishmen, to fight for independence from British rule. The movement began in Belfast among the Protestant middle class and then spread to many of the Catholic peasants across the rest of the country. But a premature rising in 1798, prior to the arrival of French troops, was crushed, and some 30,000 were killed in the reprisals that followed (a number, incidentally, that dwarfs those executed in the French revolutionary terror of 1793–4).

Comparable radical movements, all inspired by the French example, convulsed much of Europe and the wider world. But the downturn in the Revolution after its Jacobin heyday – its retreat from the ideals of 'liberty, equality, and fraternity' and the ebbing away of the mass popular movement that had driven it forwards between 1789 and 1794 – undermined its potential for unleashing fresh eruptions from below. This, in the long run, would bring the worldwide revolutionary movement to an end.

In February 1794, for example, the Jacobins had passed a decree abolishing slavery, whereas in 1801 Napoleon dispatched an army to Haiti to restore it. The contrast encapsulates the contradictory character of the bourgeois revolution: the empowerment of the masses necessary to drive the revolution forwards is a threat to a social order based on private property. The contradiction was writ large in Napoleon's empire and eventually ensured its defeat.

The French Revolution created a new military system based on mass mobilisation, popular enthusiasm, and promotion from the ranks. Mobility, aggression, and mass were used to overwhelm the ponderous armies of *ancien régime* Europe. At the Battle of Austerlitz in 1805, the combined armies of Austria and Russia were destroyed in a victory that made Napoleon master of Central Europe.

But Napoleon's huge armies were forced to live off the land through which they marched, and they milked the territories they conquered to provide the substance of war. The French posed as liberators, but were experienced as oppressors. Robespierre had predicted that few would welcome 'armed missionaries'; bitter experience proved him right.

By overturning the balance of power in Europe, Napoleon made implacable enemies of the continent's ruling classes. By imposing taxation, conscription, and requisitioning, he also made enemies of the common people.

A French invasion of Spain in 1808 turned into an intractable war against British regulars and Spanish guerrillas which drained away French military strength over the following six years. The 1812 invasion of Russia turned into a disaster when the Battle of Borodino and Napoleon's capture of Moscow failed to end the war and he was forced into a long winter retreat in which most of his army perished.

The Battle of Leipzig in 1813, against a combined Russian, Austrian, and Prussian army, reversed the result of Austerlitz. The following year, France itself was invaded and Napoleon forced to abdicate. His 'Hundred Days' comeback in 1815 ended in defeat at Waterloo and a second, this time permanent, exile.

The secret of Napoleon's success was that he was 'the Soldier of the Revolution'. He was himself an exemplar of the bourgeois revolution, a self-made man from a relatively humble background, a career professional who rose to the top through ability – though also a supreme opportunist motivated by personal ambition.

His genius personified the tremendous military dynamism unleashed by the Revolution – of citizens serving a nation-state rather than subjects obedient to a despot; of peasants fighting in defence of their land, led by officers risen from the ranks, instead of conscripted serfs commanded by titled estate-owners. This, in a sense, was the inner meaning of Austerlitz.

The extraordinary resilience of Napoleonic France was testimony to the power of the French Revolution. But the disintegration of Napoleon's empire, and the eventual overthrow of the Bonapartist regime, is testimony to the limitations of a bourgeois revolution based on property and nation. The peasants of occupied Europe turned on the rapacious French soldiery imposed upon them and backed a counter-revolutionary crusade under the leadership of their masters. This was the meaning of Borodino, Leipzig, and Waterloo.

But the defeat of Napoleon could not reverse 1789. Though the restored regimes were reactionary and repressive – regimes of 'throne and altar' – their conservative form obscured dynamic content. The French Revolution had cleared away the clutter of ages and unleashed the energy of a new capitalist economic order. The genie could not be put back in the bottle.

Toussaint L'Ouverture and the Haitian Slave Revolution

'The National Convention declares slavery abolished in all the colonies. In consequence it declares that all men, without distinction of colour, domiciled in the colonies, are French citizens and enjoy all the rights assured under the Constitution.'

This decree was passed by acclamation on 4 February 1794. It had not been proposed by the Jacobin Committee of Public Safety, the effective government of Revolutionary France. It had been a spontaneous response to the appearance before the National Convention in Paris of three delegates from the Caribbean island of Haiti. The three – a white colonist, a mixed-race mulatto, and a black freedman – had arrived to demand the abolition of slavery.

This demand was met by rapturous applause and granted without debate. 'Representatives of the French people,' declared Georges Danton, 'until now we have decreed liberty as egoists for ourselves. But today we proclaim universal liberty....'

The French Revolution had reached its radical climax. What had driven it there was an armed insurrection of 500,000 black slaves on the far side of the Atlantic. This insurrection had blasted a hole through the global edifice of mercantile capitalism.

Between 1760 and 1790 the annual output of sugar from the British and French colonies in the Caribbean doubled to almost 300,000 tons. Demand from the fashionable coffee-house culture of eighteenth-century London and Paris seemed insatiable. The Atlantic economy – a tight nexus of empire, slavery, and profit – was growing exponentially. The plantation-owners of Jamaica and Haiti, and the merchant capitalists of Bristol, Liverpool, Bordeaux, and Nantes, were the new super-rich of their age.

Two-thirds of the 12 million African slaves shipped across the Atlantic ended up on the sugar plantations. A typical plantation employed hundreds of slaves. They worked 16, even 18 hour days, in all weathers, through most of the year. Rations were a bare minimum; slaves were expected to supplement these with the produce of small garden-plots. Medical care was effectively non-existent. Discipline was maintained by brutalised overseers armed with whips and guns. Premature death through overwork and neglect was the norm. The iron logic of competitive capital accumulation ensured that this was so: it was cheaper to buy replacement slaves than to expend resources on slave welfare.

The largest and most profitable colony was French-controlled St Domingue – the western part of Haiti (the eastern part, San Domingo, was controlled by Spain). The free population of about 60,000 was organised as an armed force to defend slavery. But it was internally divided. A majority had some interest in slave exploitation, but the degree of interest varied. St Domingue involved, in the words of historian Robin Blackburn, 'a colonial and mercantile system, an aristocratic political order, a racial caste hierarchy, and a highly unequal distribution of private property within both the white and free coloured population'.

News of the revolution in Paris triggered splits in St Domingue's dominant bloc. This fracturing in the apparatus of colonial power created an opening for revolt from below.

It began on the night of 21 August 1791. 'Listen to the voice of Liberty which speaks in the hearts of all', cried the slave conspirators. Tens of thousands did so. The revolt spread rapidly across St Domingue's northern plain, engulfing hundreds of plantations. It spawned numerous armed rebel bands, and these soon became deeply rooted features of an increasingly complex, multi-sided conflict raging across the island.

At first, however, the black rebels did not wage a war of slave emancipation. Most black generals were not abolitionists; they aimed at little more than freedom for themselves and their followers, and better conditions for the mass of slaves.

Two factors transformed the conflict. One was the war against Revolutionary France and the desperate need of its Jacobin leaders for allies. The other was the radical leadership of the black general Toussaint L'Ouverture.

Under attack from royalists, the Spanish, and the British, the new Jacobin governor of St Domingue issued a decree abolishing slavery on 29 August 1793. It was published in Creole, the language of slaves, to ensure that it would be understood in the slave cabins. The result was 'a fire-cracker chain of slave revolts' (Blackburn).

Most black generals had been fighting alongside France's enemies. But the royalists, the Spanish, and the British were all pro-slavery. In May 1794, therefore, Toussaint L'Ouverture broke with his allies and joined the French Republicans. His new allegiance was confirmed when news reached Haiti of the National Convention's emancipation decree. Toussaint had become, as West Indian historian C. L. R. James describes him, a 'Black Jacobin'. He was now waging all-out war for the abolition of slavery.

At critical historical turning-points, revolutionary leadership can be decisive. Revolutionary leadership is neither purely utopian, nor purely pragmatic, but involves a dialectical meshing of the two. It requires a vision of an alternative future which transcends immediate circumstances yet reflects possibilities incubating inside them. It means looking forwards to a new world while remaining anchored in the old. This was the role assumed by Toussaint L'Ouverture and his army in 1794.

Toussaint became the leader of a swelling insurrection of the entire black population of Haiti. His army – disciplined, mobile, combat effective – became the spine of the slave revolution. Around it swirled myriad local resistance groups. Haiti soon became ungovernable for slave-lords and colonialists.

By 1798 the British, attempting a full-scale conquest of the colony, had been defeated. Their failure had cost them 20,000 men. (Their total losses in the Caribbean theatre – battling slave revolts and French expeditionary forces – reached 60,000.) The slaves had liberated Haiti.

Napoleon Bonaparte, the ruler of France from 1799, was determined to restore the French empire in the Americas. He dispatched a new army in 1802 with orders to crush the Black Jacobins. Toussaint was arrested, dispatched to France, and died of neglect in prison the following year.

But his movement did not die. The black and mulatto generals turned on the French, declared their independence, and launched a new war of liberation. They unleashed the rage of the oppressed and it consumed their enemies.

'But what men these blacks are!' recalled one of them later.

How they fight and how they die! One has to make war against them to know their reckless courage in braving danger when they can no longer have recourse to stratagem. I have seen a solid column, torn by grape-shot from four pieces of cannon, advance without making a retrograde step. The more they fell, the greater seemed to be the courage of the rest.

Napoleon sent 35,000 troops to Haiti. Of these, almost 30,000 perished on the battlefield or from disease. By the end of 1803 the Black Jacobins had won their independence for a second time.

They had defeated the two greatest colonial powers in the world. On 1 January 1804 they proclaimed the Republic of Haiti – an independent black-ruled state created by slave revolution. It would stand as a beacon lighting the road to eventual emancipation across the Americas.

Simon Bolivar and the Spanish-American Revolutions

Haiti was not the only part of the Americas transformed by the impact of the French Revolution. Between 1808 and 1826 most of the Spanish Empire in the New World fell to a rolling wave of revolutions headed by Spanish-speaking colonists.

The trigger was a French invasion of Spain. Napoleon overthrew the Spanish King and installed his own brother in his place. The Iberian peninsula was then engulfed by a six-year war that paralysed the Spanish imperial authorities.

'Do you wish to know what our future was?' asked South American revolutionary leader Simon Bolivar. 'We were mere consumers, confined to the cultivation of indigo, grain, coffee, sugar, cacao, and cotton; raising cattle on the empty plains; hunting wild game in the wilderness; mining in the earth to produce gold for the insatiable greed of Spain.'

South America's colonial dependency had intensified in the late eighteenth century. The policy of *comercio libre* had swept away restrictions on trade and opened colonial markets to Spanish monopolists. The colonies had been flooded with imports and colonial merchants ruined. Returns from America to Spain had soared.

Bullion and tax revenues from its colonies were used to underwrite Spain's great-power ambitions in Europe. Peruvian gold, Mexican silver, and the profits from Orinoco coffee plantations and Rio de la Plata cattle-ranches paid for Spanish armies.

It made little difference whether conservatives or liberals were in power in Madrid: both were intractable imperialists. After 1808, however, they were imperialists without teeth. The small Spanish colonial administration in South America soon found itself beleaguered and without support from home.

At the beginning of the nineteenth century, there were about 17 million people in Spanish America. Only 150,000 or so were *peninsulares* – immigrants from Spain. A further three million were *criollos* (creoles) – American-born descendants of Spanish settlers. The creoles' relationship with Spain in 1808 was very similar to that of North American colonists with Britain in 1776.

Government posts were usually reserved for Spanish officials. Commercial opportunity was restricted by Spanish monopolies. Racial caste privilege was a routine feature of everyday life.

In 1806 and 1807, creole militia units defeated two British attacks on Buenos Aires. From this kernel evolved a creole revolutionary challenge to Spanish rule once news arrived of the Napoleonic coup in Madrid. In May 1810 the local creole militia seized power in Buenos Aires.

The revolutionary movement quickly spread across much of South and Central America. By 1814, when the French were finally evicted from Spain, most of the empire's New World colonies had been lost. The main exception was Peru, the greatest bastion of royalist reaction in South America, where creole revolution had been crushed.

In 1815 the restored Spanish monarchy dispatched the largest army it had ever sent to the New World. It waged a war of counter-revolutionary terror. The creole patriot movement in Venezuela was shattered by executions and confiscations. By 1816 the revolution seemed to be on the brink of defeat.

But this was not the first major setback. Many of the initial risings of 1810 had been defeated. The movement had learned lessons from this, and later recovered and counterattacked. In the south, José de San Martin had transcended the parochialism of local militias and built a centralised revolutionary army – the Army of the Andes – capable of operating across the continent. In the north, Simon Bolivar had also grasped the need for organisation and leadership. And whereas San Martin was relatively conservative, Bolivar was a determined revolutionary.

'Only the majority is sovereign', he proclaimed. 'He who takes the place of the people is a tyrant and his power is usurpation.' Analysing recent defeats, he concluded that 'our own disunity, not Spanish arms, returned us to slavery'. Unity, centralisation, and all-out war – 'a terrible power' – was needed to defeat the royalists.

There could be no compromise, no temporising, with such a ruthless enemy. 'Our tolerance is now exhausted, and as our oppressors force us into a mortal war, they shall disappear from America and our land will be purged of the monsters that infest it. Our hatred will be implacable. The war will be to the death.'

Bolivar held the revolutionary movement together through the dark night of Venezuela's counter-revolution. He imposed centralised authority and rebuilt the army. Then, in 1819, in a spectacular campaign involving epic marches across the Andes, he led the revolution to victory in Colombia, Ecuador, and Venezuela. Royalist Peru finally succumbed in 1824.

But the struggle had been harder, longer, and more costly than it need have been. And the final victory was shallow. Bolivar went into exile shortly before his death in 1830 a disillusioned man.

His more radical aspirations for land reform to end the poverty of the peasants and for a 'United States' of South America to rival that of the North were stillborn. 'I am ashamed to admit it,' he said, 'but independence is the only benefit we have gained, at the cost of everything else.'

The expanse of South America and the disproportion between geographical space and politico-military reach; the sparse and scattered Spanish-American population; the economic and social differences between regions; the countless petty clashes of rival vested interests; all these militated against a coherent, united, continent-wide movement.

The result was a plethora of factions: Spaniards against creoles, royalists against patriots, conservatives against liberals, centralists against regionalists, monopolists against free-traders. Sometimes these conflicts resolved themselves into a straight split between revolutionaries and reactionaries. Just as often, the complexities and cross-currents stymied effective action.

Instead of fusing into a single United States, South America fragmented into a mosaic of separate nations: Argentina, Uruguay, Paraguay, Chile, Bolivia, Peru, Ecuador, Colombia, and Venezuela.

Worse still was the hamstringing of Latin America's bourgeois revolution by the weakness of its popular movements. More than 80 per cent of the people were not of Spanish descent at all. Most were native Indians. Many were black slaves. Others were of mixed race (*mestizos, pardos,* or *zambos*).

These were Latin America's beasts of burden. Many worked as peons (agricultural labourers) or *gauchos* (ranch-hands) on creole estates. Some were miners. Others eked out a living as dirt farmers on marginal land or as petty-traders in the larger settlements.

Countless contemporary commentators reported on Spanish America's grotesque social inequalities and the hopeless misery of the masses. The Bishop of Michoacan in Mexico identified only two social groups, 'those who have nothing and those who have everything ... There are no gradations or mean: they are all either rich or poor....'

Creole *hacienda*-owners lived in fear of the poor. Because of this, most creoles were royalist where the royalists were strong, and patriot where the patriots were strong; what mattered was armed power to keep the poor in their place, whoever wielded it.

Bolivar, the greatest of the creole revolutionaries, straddled and personified this contradiction. On the one hand, he condemned his peers, who 'speak of liberty and constitutions', yet 'prefer to regard the lower classes as their perpetual serfs'. But Bolivar's idealism was belied by his sense that South America was a volcano of racialised social contradictions that could 'only be kept in order and prosperity by absolute power'. Unwilling to lead an elemental revolt of the masses that might have transformed Latin America, he became the unwitting midwife of a stillborn social revolution the limitations of which he then lamented.

The Spanish-American Revolutions created independent states ruled by creole aristocrats. But as British bankers, merchants, and shippers replaced Spanish, a form of semi-colonial dependency persisted, and Latin America remained an underdeveloped continent of primary-export producers.

The conservative owners of big estates (*haciendas*) remained in full possession of their land. The *hacienda* became society's centre of gravity. Regional oligarchies assumed control of the newly independent states. Politics became an oscillation between conservative and liberal factions of the same ruling class. The Church – rich, powerful, omnipresent – remained a dominant influence. Armies swelled into corrupt vested interests with a taste for military coups.

For the great majority, life did not change at all. Relentless toil continued to be rewarded by poverty, hunger, and disease. Latin America's tragedy was that Spanish imperial rule was so hollowed out that it was never necessary to mobilise the masses to bring it down. Political revolution at the top was possible without social revolution from below.

But without the momentum of popular revolt, two decades of coups, decrees, and battles left Latin America's economic backwardness, social inequality, and cultural torpor unaltered. It remained one of the most conservative places on earth throughout the nineteenth century. As Mexican *campesinos* (peasants) said of the post-revolutionary order, 'New rider, same mule'.

10

The Rise of Industrial Capitalism
c. 1750–1850

Welsh iron-workers, 1865.

The Industrial Revolution, pioneered in Britain, created the industrial working class – a class 'with nothing to lose but its chains'.

The second wave of bourgeois revolutions accelerated the spread of mercantile capitalism across Europe and the wider world. Coincident with it was the start of a radical transformation of capitalism in its homeland: the Industrial Revolution.

Mercantile capitalism had seen frenetic increases in the exchange of commodities, the circulation of money, and the accumulation of capital, but these had not transformed production. The demand for goods expanded exponentially during the eighteenth century, but the way they were produced barely changed at all: the economy was still dominated by farms worked by people rather than machines, and by small workshops operated by independent artisans.

Between 1750 and 1800, a new production system – the factory – was pioneered in Britain. Between 1800 and 1850, this system began to transform the global economy as radically as anything had done since the Agricultural Revolution. As it did so, it created a new social class – the industrial proletariat – that soon revealed an unprecedented capacity for collective organisation and resistance.

Two young Rhineland intellectuals, Karl Marx and Frederick Engels, combined their understanding of these new social realities with the theoretical traditions represented by German philosophy, French socialism, and British economics. The synthesis – Marxism – was not just an explanation of the world: it was nothing less than a guide to world revolution and the emancipation of humanity from all forms of exploitation, violence, and oppression.

The Industrial Revolution

In 1814, the year before Waterloo, a German visitor wrote of a city where he had seen 'hundreds of factories ... which tower up to five and six storeys in height. Huge chimneys at the side of these buildings belch forth black coal vapours, and this tells us that powerful steam-engines are used.' He was describing Manchester, the first industrial city in the world.

Between 1773 and 1801 the city's population had trebled from 23,000 to 70,000. By 1799 it boasted 33 textile mills; by 1816 it had 86. Half a century later, the population would be 300,000 and most of the city's eventual total of 172 mills would already have been built. So dominant was the city's output of cotton textiles that, when they were sold on the other side of the world, they were known simply as 'Manchester goods'.

Three converging rivers provided water power and transport links. A network of canals, docks, and warehouses facilitated the first phase of Manchester's industrial revolution. Then came steam power and railways to underwrite the second phase of development. The first steam-powered mill was in operation as early as 1789, and a rail link with Liverpool was completed in 1830.

The speed of innovation and the massive increases in the goods produced were without precedent. Manchester represented an economic revolution – a revolution that would transform human experience more thoroughly than anything since the Agricultural Revolution almost 10,000 years earlier.

Why now, and why here? In the seventeenth century, the English Revolution had ended the rule of a would-be absolute monarch and the lords and bishops who supported him, replacing it with a constitutional monarchy controlled by a parliamentary assembly dominated by gentry and merchants.

England's bourgeois revolution made possible a rapid expansion of commercial farming, overseas trade, and empire-building. Wealth poured into the great port cities of London, Bristol, and Liverpool.

Of particular importance was the triangular trade: commodities were exported to West Africa and traded for slaves; these were transported across the Atlantic to work on sugar, coffee, tobacco, and cotton plantations in the Americas; and the produce of the plantations was shipped back to Britain and Europe for sale. In 1750 Bristol was England's second city, with a population of 45,000. It was filled with dockyards, warehouses, and terraces of prosperous townhouses owned by the merchant bourgeoisie. Bristol had grown fat on slavery.

The accumulation of commercial capital did not simply enrich the landowners, merchants, and bankers of Britain's new ruling class. It also fostered communities of scientists and engineers whose inventiveness began to open up new possibilities for yet further enrichment. The Ancient Greeks had worked out the principle of the steam-engine, but had never built one; the idea was simply a curiosity. Ingenuity was not enough. A process of competitive capital accumulation was necessary to transform a clever idea into a productive device that could be manufactured and used. This is what happened in eighteenth-century Britain. A steady drip-drip of quantitative change – increasing commercial wealth – eventually tipped into a new dynamic of industrial growth driven by innovation and investment.

As early as 1698, the English inventor-entrepreneur Thomas Savery had built and patented a simple steam-engine. More efficient engines quickly followed. Thomas Newcomen's, invented in about 1710, was used to operate beam-pumps in the coalmines. When James Watt developed an even more efficient engine in 1763–75, cutting its coal consumption by 75 per cent, far more extensive industrial use became economical. Watt worked with Birmingham metal-goods manufacturer Matthew Boulton to develop, patent, and sell a succession of engines.

Around the same time, Richard Arkwright, a pioneer in the use of water power in the textile industry, was making the first experimental use of steam power in Manchester. Arkwright had invented the spinning frame and carding engine. His pioneering combination in textile mills of power, machinery, and semi-skilled labour was the origin of the factory system.

In the past, Manchester's cotton magnates had grown rich on the putting-out system, with spinners and weavers working in their own homes, many in the small towns and villages of the surrounding countryside. Mid-eighteenth-century Manchester was a city of merchant townhouses and workshop dwellings. The latter were three-storey buildings in which the upper floor was designed as an individual workshop. A single wide window maximised light so that a skilled worker could operate a handloom or spinning jenny.

The factory system, by contrast, offered huge economies of scale. Mass production based on mechanical power, labour-saving machinery, and a cheap workforce of semi-skilled operatives, including many women and children, made huge increases in labour productivity and output possible.

Competitive pressure drove down the wages of handloom weavers and squeezed the profits of cotton merchants still relying on the putting-out system. The workers were eventually forced into the mills. The merchants invested in steam-engines and spinning frames.

Manchester changed from being a city of workshop dwellings, canals, and waterfronts into one of back-to-back tenements, textile mills, and railways. As it did, life for many of its rapidly increasing population became ever more oppressive.

This darker side of the Industrial Revolution had a profound impact on a 22-year-old German who had migrated to Britain to work in the family firm, which owned a textile mill in Manchester. Observing the city in 1844, he concluded that '350,000 working people of Manchester and its environs live, almost all of them, in wretched, damp, filthy cottages. The streets which surround them are usually in the most miserable and filthy condition, laid out without the slightest reference to ventilation, with reference solely to the profit secured by the contractor.'

The young man's father had sent him to Manchester partly in the hope it would rid him of his radical leanings. It had the opposite effect. Frederick Engels, soon to become the lifelong friend of Karl Marx, was converted to revolutionary socialism. Not only that. In the new industrial proletariat Engels described so well in his seminal study *The Condition of the Working Class in England*, he detected something more than mere wretchedness. The workers, massed together in factories and slums, were already a political force.

Engels arrived when England was being convulsed by the first great mass movement of the industrial proletariat. Hundreds of thousands were rallying to the Chartists. The potent mix of poverty and resistance that Engels found in Manchester would feed into his and Marx's understanding of history, human conflict, and the mechanics of social transformation. The result would be Marxism: the theory and practice of international working-class revolution.

The Chartists and the Origins of the Labour Movement

The French Revolution had been driven forward by a popular movement of working people. It had inspired hopes of far-reaching democratic and social reform. But after the coup of Thermidor, the popular radicals had gone down to defeat.

Their movement had been a class alliance riddled with contradictions. The Jacobin leaders had represented a small radical minority of the bourgeoisie. Most revolutionary activists had not been true bourgeois at all, but members of the urban middle class of lawyers and other professionals or the urban petty-bourgeoisie of artisans and small traders.

Wage-labourers, on the other hand, had not comprised a clearly defined social class with its own political identity. Almost all had been employed in small workplaces. Many had aspired to become small property-owners on their own account. Most had followed the lead of the petty-bourgeoisie with whom they lived and worked. The *sans-culottes* who formed the revolutionary crowds were therefore a mix of small property-owners and wage-labourers.

The peasantry had had a similar character. Poor peasants and rural wage-labourers had followed the lead of better-off peasants in the struggle against 'feudalism'. The revolutionary village had been united against landlords and tax-collectors. What had then made the armies of the French Revolution and Napoleon so powerful was the fact that they were formed of peasant-soldiers defending the gains of the village over the *chateau*. The soldiers had fought to prevent the return of the aristocrats.

But there had been limits to the gains. The French Revolution's promise had remained unfulfilled because it had always remained a bourgeois revolution committed to the defence of private property; and neither social equality nor genuine democracy is compatible with private property.

The popular movement had been knocked back by those who ruled France after Thermidor, but it had not been destroyed. The Revolution had radicalised an entire generation, and thousands of activists were inspired by its ideals long after 1794.

The lessons of defeat were eagerly debated. The conclusions drawn were often wrong. 'Gracchus' Babeuf and his Conspiracy of Equals sought to overthrow the Directory in a political coup in 1796. But an activist plot is no substitute for a mass movement. Terrorists cannot bring down the state. Babeuf was arrested, tried, and executed in 1797.

But his revolutionary ideas survived. 'Nature has given to every man the right to an enjoyment of an equal share in all property', he had declared. Here in a nutshell was the issue that would divide petty-bourgeois radicals from working-class socialists.

Ideas without a movement are powerless. A movement without ideas is directionless. The essence of what radical historian Eric Hobsbawm has called 'the dual revolution' – the combination of the French Revolution and the Industrial Revolution – is that it represents a fusion of ideas and movement such that all-encompassing social transformation becomes possible. The Chartists were the first full expression of that fusion.

The French Revolution had had a powerful impact in Britain. Tom Paine's defence of its principles, *The Rights of Man*, sold 100,000 copies. Radical networks with Jacobin politics like the London Corresponding Society enjoyed mushroom growth. Mutinies paralysed the Royal Navy in 1797. Ireland erupted in revolution in 1798.

Repression crushed the resistance. But, as Edward Thompson explains in *The Making of the English Working Class*, the agitation of the 1790s created a radical tradition which meshed with a rising wave of class struggle in the early nineteenth century as the Industrial Revolution created a new social class: a proletariat of wage-labourers concentrated in factories and cities.

'Monopoly and hideous accumulation of capital in a few hands', wrote the radical leader John Thelwall in 1796,

> carry in their own enormity the seeds of cure ... Whatever presses men together ... is favourable to the diffusion of knowledge, and ultimately promotive of human liberty. Hence, every large workshop and manufactory is a sort of political society, which no act of Parliament can silence and no magistrate disperse.

Unlike the property-owning or property-aspiring *sans-culottes* of the French Revolution, the proletariat of the Industrial Revolution could emancipate itself only through *collective* ownership. Steam-engines, coalmines, canal barges, and textile mills could not be subdivided. If the workers overthrew their bosses, they would have to run the workplaces as cooperatives. The proletariat was therefore a collective class in every sense. The workers' struggle tended towards the abolition of private property – tended, that is, towards creating the preconditions for the social equality and political democracy that the French Revolution had failed to deliver.

The early struggles of the British proletariat took many forms. There were Luddite campaigns of machine-breaking to prevent deskilling, wage cuts, and unemployment. There were mass demonstrations to demand political reform, like that at St Peter's Field in Manchester ('the Battle of Peterloo') in 1819, which was attacked by mounted militia with sabres. There were waves of strikes and unionisation, notably in the mid to late 1820s, and again in the mid-1830s.

The Grand National Consolidated Trades Union recruited half a million members in 1834. And when six Dorset farm labourers ('the Tolpuddle Martyrs') were deported for joining a union that year, 100,000 attended a solidarity demonstration at Kings Cross.

This rising tide of struggle peaked in the Chartist agitation of 1838–48. The movement grew out of a double failure. First, the 1832 Reform Bill had given the vote to most of the middle class, but had left the working class still disenfranchised. The cross-class alliance which had campaigned for reform broke up amid acrimony. Second, the revolutionary trade unionism of the Grand National Consolidated had collapsed when a wave of strikes was smashed and the organisation wrecked by internal rows. Neither alliance with the liberal middle class nor the call for a general strike had advanced the cause of the working class. But the turbulence of the 1830s was evidence of a broad radical mood.

In 1838 the newly formed London Working Men's Association published a 'People's Charter' of six demands: equal electoral districts; abolition of the property qualification for MPs; universal manhood suffrage; annual parliaments; vote by ballot; and payment of MPs. The Charter was endorsed by gigantic open-air meetings: 200,000 attended in Glasgow, 80,000 in Newcastle, 250,000 in Leeds, 300,000 in Manchester. A new mass movement was born.

A petition in support of the Charter collected 1,280,000 signatures, and a Chartist Convention assembled in London in 1839. But Parliament rejected the Charter and ordered suppression of the movement. Mass arrests followed. Police sent from London turned the Bull Ring in Birmingham into a battlefield. An armed demonstration of Chartist miners in Newport was ambushed and gunned down by soldiers.

Nevertheless, the Chartist movement soon recovered and was able to present a new petition in 1842, this time with 3,315,000 signatures. This, too, was rejected. A wave of strikes against wage cuts then turned into a political mass strike in defence of the Charter. But again, repression broke the movement.

It rose for a third time in 1848, but it was weaker now. Only 1,975,000 signatures had been collected against a hoped-for five million, and a planned mass demonstration on Kennington Green was smaller than anticipated. Many, no doubt, were deterred by the threat of state violence implicit in the ranks of police, auxiliaries, troops, and even artillery deployed against the demonstrators. But the real problem was a failure of political will: the Chartist leaders were not prepared to mount a direct challenge to the government.

There is no question that Chartism suffered from structural weaknesses. The movement's highpoints coincided with economic downturns. Demonstrations diminished as employment and wages rose. And after 1848, the British economy entered a long boom.

The working class was still embryonic in the 1840s. The majority of people continued to live in the countryside, and many of those in towns were workshop masters or self-employed craftsman rather than factory workers. This was the basis of a regional division within Chartism between a more petty-bourgeois movement in London and a more proletarian one in the new industrial districts of the North.

But political weaknesses were more important. Some leaders were relatively conservative advocates of 'moral force'. Others favoured 'physical force' – demonstrations, strikes, even insurrection – but were often inconsistent and indecisive. This was really a split between reformists who wanted to work within the existing political framework and revolutionaries – some more consistent than others – who believed that the state had to be overthrown.

Nonetheless, for all its faults and failings, Chartism represents the explosive entry of a new and revolutionary class onto history's stage. Capitalism had created what Marx called 'its own gravediggers'.

The 1848 Revolutions

Despite the best efforts of Europe's great powers, the defeat of Napoleon in 1813–15 could not restore the *ancien régime*. The 'dual revolution' – the French bourgeois revolution and Britain's industrial revolution – represented an irreversible transformation of human society on a global scale.

There were two insuperable barriers to full-scale reaction – a return, that is, to a world in which kings, bishops, and titled landowners held exclusive sway. First was the strength of the new property-owning classes: merchants growing rich on commerce and colonial trade; capitalist farmers who had bought up church land; peasants who had rid themselves of feudal burdens. Second was the pressure on nation-states to increase tax revenues, improve the infrastructure, develop modern industries, and support a growing population.

This pressure took the form of military competition. Strong armies depended on financial, industrial, and human resources.

The regimes of 'throne and altar' imposed on Europe in 1815 were wholly reactionary in form, but less so in content. Germany, for example, had been divided into 300 states in 1789. Napoleon created a Confederation of the Rhine in 1806 in which serfdom was abolished, freedom of commerce established, and a uniform law code introduced. Under the terms of the Congress of Vienna in 1815, the great powers may have handed the Rhineland to Prussia, but the liberal reforms remained, and the number of independent German states overall had been reduced to 39.

So political development in Germany was not reversed; it was simply stalled for 30 years. Meanwhile, economic development continued, and the contradiction between an absolutist police state run by Prussian *junkers* (titled aristocrats) and the wealth and self-confidence of the Rhineland bourgeoisie widened.

Similar tensions could be found across much of Europe. The storm finally broke in 1848. As so often in modern European history, it was the Gallic cock that proclaimed the new dawn. Paris had harboured an unbroken revolutionary tradition stretching back to 1789. This tradition had last been exercised in July 1830, when Charles X, the Bourbon King installed in 1815, had been overthrown in a four-day urban insurrection prompted by his absolutist pretensions. He had been replaced by Louis Philippe, from the Orléanist branch of the royal family, who had promised to rule as a constitutional monarch.

The 1830 Revolution had shifted power from the old landowning aristocracy to the financial bourgeoisie. The July Monarchy was a bankers' monarchy – only the richest 1 per cent had the vote.

In February 1848, republican protests by students and the middle class were attacked by the police. This was the signal for a mass rising of the urban poor of eastern Paris. The *sans-culottes* marched again and brought down a King.

The French Revolution of 1848 was echoed by successful insurrections in Berlin, Budapest, Milan, Palermo, Prague, Rome, Venice, and scores of other cities across Europe. The only major European states not affected by this 'Springtime of the Peoples' were Britain and Russia.

Everywhere, the *ancien régime* crumbled. Absolute monarchs withdrew their troops, granted liberal constitutions, and allowed new parliamentary assemblies to be installed in government buildings.

The dynamic of the 1848 Revolutions was similar to that of 1789. The police and troops of the *ancien régime* were driven off the streets by mass mobilisations of artisans, small traders, and labourers. What activated the masses were demands for social reform triggered by widespread distress. Europe had been in the grip of an acute economic crisis since 1845, and millions were unemployed and impoverished. But power passed mainly into the hands of bourgeois liberals. Whether republicans or constitutional monarchists, they looked in two directions, fearful of both absolutist reaction and popular radicalism. The result was hesitation and paralysis – fatal in a revolution.

The counter-revolution struck back. In June the new republican government in Paris announced the closure of the national workshops that had been set up in the capital in February to alleviate unemployment. The unemployed were told to return to their villages or join the army. The working people of Paris rose up again. But 40,000 insurgents found themselves confronted by 30,000 soldiers and some 100,000 militia. Over the four terrible days of 23–6 June, General Cavaignac's forces fought their way, barricade by barricade, into the eastern suburbs and crushed the resistance.

The June Days acted as a clarion call to counter-revolution across Europe. Everywhere in the second half of 1848 and well into 1849, the armies of absolutism attacked the radical revolution, while liberal politicians – like the lawyers and landowners who formed Germany's Frankfurt Parliament – made speeches and passed resolutions.

Why were the 1848 Revolutions defeated? The liberals of 1848 were but pale reflections of their predecessors in the English and French Revolutions. Whereas Cromwell and Robespierre had been prepared to push their revolutions forward to a decisive victory over royal absolutism, the bourgeois leaders of 1848 proved spineless.

In the first wave of bourgeois revolutions – Holland in 1566, England in 1642, America in 1775, and France in 1789 – the driving force had been mass action by the petty-bourgeoisie. This had been necessary not only to defeat the *ancien régime*, but also to overcome the conservatism of bourgeois leaders. The petty-bourgeoisie dominated both the urban and rural masses, and in every case townsmen and soldiers had been able to pull large numbers of peasants into action behind them. And because of its petty-bourgeois character, even in its most revolutionary moments, the movement had not threatened the principle of private property. The ideal, at its most radical, had been a democracy of small property-owners.

A crucial difference between 1789 and 1848 was the role of the peasantry. In 1789 the peasants were paying feudal dues, so the revolution spread to the countryside. In 1848 feudalism had already been abolished, so the villages remained quiet. This meant that red Paris could be isolated and smashed. The peasant-soldiers first shot down the revolutionaries, then, as we shall see, voted for Louis Bonaparte.

The liberal bourgeoisie – which in 1789 had been propelled forwards by the sheer momentum of the mass movement – was exposed by 1848 as an inherently conservative class of property-owners more afraid of revolution from below than of dictatorship from above.

Though Marx and Engels argued that the bourgeoisie had been spooked by 'the spectre of communism', this perspective seems to be based on a misunderstanding of the dynamics of the 1789 Revolution. In 1848 the proletariat (except in Britain) was relatively small, unorganised, and lacking in political consciousness. And the revolutions of that year played out too rapidly for this nascent proletariat to grow into an effective protagonist able to influence the course of events. The simple truth is that the bourgeoisie, as a minority property-owning class, never willingly leads a revolution from below; it has to be pushed.

In France, the February insurrection had destroyed the monarchy, but the June counter-revolution had then destroyed the popular movement. In the aftermath, in December 1848, a presidential election awarded a landslide victory to Louis Bonaparte, nephew of Napoleon. Two years later, in December 1851, Louis Bonaparte assumed dictatorial power in a military coup. The following year, he declared a Second Empire and proclaimed himself Napoleon III.

Something similar happened in other parts of Europe. The counter-revolutionary countryside was used to crush the revolution-ary cities. But just as 1815 could not turn the clock back to 1789, nor could the June Days erase the impact of the February Days in 1848. Serfdom was abolished in Prussia and Austria. Limited con-stitutions were established across much of Europe. Movements for unification gained traction in Germany and Italy. The stirrings of nationalism could not henceforward be stilled in the polyglot empire of the Austrian Habsburgs.

Other fracture-lines had opened. From Ireland to Poland to Macedonia, nationalism and social discontent were coalescing into a potent brew. And through the long economic boom of 1848–73, a new force would arise, a force with the potential to make the next 'springtime of the peoples' a truly earth-shaking event.

Excursus 4: What is Marxism?

Marxism is sometimes represented as a compound of German philosophy, French socialism, and British economics. That is correct, but incomplete. It treats Marxism as a purely theoretical matter, divorced from practice, and that is to miss its very essence.

The basic ideas of Marxism were formulated by Karl Marx (1818–83) and Frederick Engels (1820–95) in 1843–7. Their joint work represented a revolution in thought comparable with the achievements in science of Isaac Newton, Charles Darwin, Sigmund Freud, and Albert Einstein. They created a radically different paradigm for understanding the whole of human society.

But precisely because the subject of their intellectual revolution *was* human society, their laboratory had to be the social world in which they were living. Marxism was possible only because Marx and Engels were active revolutionaries embedded in the mass struggles of their epoch. In particular, they tested and refined their ideas in the political furnace of the 1848 Revolutions. Marx worked as the editor of *Rheinische Zeitung*, a revolutionary paper in Cologne. Engels defended the Rhineland Palatinate against Prussian invasion, serving as a soldier in a revolutionary army. Both were forced into exile by the Revolution's defeat in 1849.

Marx and Engels took contemporary ideas about philosophy, society, and economics and transformed them on the basis of their direct experience of concrete reality. It is in this sense that it is correct to describe Marxism as 'materialist' (the contrast is with 'idealism' – theories not based on experience and never successfully tested in practice).

Both men were trained in German philosophy. This was dominated at the time by the ideas of Georg Hegel (1770–1831), whose dialectic became central to Marxism. It was based on two concepts: that 'all things are contradictory in themselves'; and that 'contradiction is at the root of all movement and life, and it is only insofar as it contains a contradiction that anything moves and has impulse and activity'.

Hegel's dialectic was idealist. He was thinking mainly about changes in human thought. In particular, he thought of history as the unfolding of what he called Absolute Spirit, a grand idea changing the world through the contradiction between itself and a reality that failed to match up to it. Marx 'turned Hegel on his head' by transforming the idealist dialectic into a materialist dialectic. His point was very simple: the contradictions that matter exist in the real world not in people's heads, and it is therefore the clash of actual social forces that drives history. The role of thought is to understand these forces so that human intervention can be better directed and more effective.

Getting to grips with the real world meant studying the new capitalist economy emerging within it. British economists had led the way. The strongest influence on Marx and Engels in this respect was David Ricardo (1772–1823). Ricardo had made two radical discoveries about the nature of capitalism. First, that 'the value of a commodity depends on the relative quantity of labour that is necessary for its production'. In other words, human labour – not capital – is the source of all wealth. Second, he realised that 'there can be no rise in the value of labour without a fall in profits'. In other words, labour's gain was capital's loss, and vice versa. Wages and profits were inversely related.

The implication was that conflict over the distribution of income – class struggle – was inherent in capitalism. Ricardo had thereby revealed the system to be highly contradictory and potentially explosive. Because of this, his work represented the highpoint of mainstream classical economics. His successors retreated from the revolutionary implications of their own discipline, and bourgeois economics slowly degenerated into the ideological window-dressing of greed and free-market chaos that it has become today.

Marx, on the other hand, continued to pursue the scientific insights of Ricardo's economics. His crowning achievement was the publication of the first volume of *Capital* in 1867. (The second and third volumes were edited from his papers after his death and published in 1885 and 1894 respectively.) These texts remain the essential starting-point for any serious analysis of the modern world economy.

The third intellectual influence on Marx and Engels was French socialism. Born of the Great French Revolution and fostered by its failed promise of human liberation, French socialism had split into reformist-utopian and revolutionary-communist wings. The utopians – like the Comte de Saint-Simon, Charles Fourier, and, in Britain, Robert Owen – believed that rational argument, good example, and gradual reform would be sufficient to bring about social transformation. The communists – represented by Gracchus Babeuf and Auguste Blanqui – had no such illusions, insisting that armed insurrection was necessary to overthrow the exploiting classes. Their mistake was to assume that direct action by a secretive underground movement would be enough to trigger a general uprising of the masses.

Marx and Engels shared the French socialists' hatred of exploitation and poverty. Like the utopians, they could imagine a much better world and, like the communists, they had no doubt that revolutionary action was necessary to achieve it. But they had profound disagreements with both. The utopians they condemned for their naïve belief that the rich would voluntarily surrender their wealth and power. The communists they attacked for imagining that the state, with its army, police, and prisons, could be brought down by a conspiratorial coup. Only a popular revolution that mobilised millions could smash the state, dispossess the property-owning classes, and construct a new order based on democracy, equality, and cooperation.

The Great French Revolution had been sufficient in scale, but had simply created a new kind of exploitative society. What had been missing was a revolutionary class with *universal* interests. The revolutionary bourgeoisie had wanted power for itself. The *sans-culottes* and the peasants had been small property-owners. Even the poorest had aspired to own a workshop or farm. But the new industrial working class of Manchester was quite different. Not only was it a class of property-less wage-labourers; concentrated in textile mills and a fast-growing metropolis, it was a class whose circumstances obliged it to think of human liberation in terms of *collective* solutions. And the Chartist movement in England had shown that the working class was indeed potentially revolutionary.

The lessons of 1789, the experience of 1848, and Engels' study of the Manchester working class all pointed in the same direction – towards a solution to the riddle of history.

The riddle was this. The steady rise in the productivity of human labour throughout history meant increasing capacity to abolish want. Yet a minority continued to enjoy grotesque wealth while millions lived in poverty. The riddle came down to a question of agency: who might so reorder the world that human labour served human need?

The answer was the working class. This was partly because it was an exploited class, one with no vested interest in the system, with 'nothing to lose but its chains'. But this had been true of the slaves of ancient Rome and the serfs of medieval Europe. A second factor was decisive. The workers could not emancipate themselves through *individual* appropriation of private property. They were part of a vast and growing global division of labour, such that only *collective* control of the means of production, distribution, and exchange could provide a credible alternative to capitalism. The industrial working class was, therefore, the first class in history with a *general interest in the emancipation of humanity as a whole*. Its entry onto the historical stage made Marxism possible. Recognising the proletariat's revolutionary potential was Marx and Engels' most important intellectual achievement. Marxism's living heart is, therefore, the class struggle of working people against capitalism.

Excursus 5: What is Capitalism?

To grasp the scale of the social transformation represented by capitalism, it is useful to remind ourselves of the impact of the only other comparable economic revolution in human history: the Agricultural Revolution. This had ended an earlier existence based on hunting and gathering in the wilderness. It created a world of farmers in which people produced their own food, and farming made possible huge increases in productivity and output.

This in turn enabled the accumulation of surpluses capable of supporting non-productive social classes. These surpluses were used to maintain armies and engage in politico-military competition. Despite many great changes there was, in this respect, an essential similarity between, say, Sumerian civilisation around 2500 BC, the Roman Empire of the second century AD, and Louis XIV's France in 1700. In each case, the ruling classes appropriated the surpluses of agricultural producers in one form or another and used them to fund wars, monuments, and luxury living.

Because militarism and grandeur were competitive, the system was dynamic. It was also highly wasteful. War chariots and temples, armoured knights and castles, cannon and palaces drained wealth from the productive economy. Surpluses were not, for the most part, invested in technical innovation and improvement. Consequently, in pre-industrial society, increases in the productivity of human labour came slowly.

The contrast with industrial capitalism could not be starker. Marx describes it in a famous passage in *The Communist Manifesto*:

> The bourgeoisie cannot exist without constantly revolutionising the instruments of production, and thereby the relations of production, and with them the whole relations of society. Conservation of the old modes of production in unaltered form was ... the first condition of existence for all earlier industrial classes. Constant revolutionising of production, uninterrupted disturbance of all social conditions, everlasting uncertainty and agitation distinguish the bourgeois epoch from all earlier ones. All fixed, fast-frozen relations, with their train of ancient and venerable prejudices and

opinions, are swept away, all new-formed ones become antiquated before they can ossify. All that is solid melts into air …

The world's population reached an estimated 200 million about 2,500 years ago. It did not reach one billion until about 200 years ago. Since then, it has risen to seven billion. That means population growth has been 18 times faster since the Industrial Revolution.

The Roman Empire is estimated to have manufactured about 85,000 tonnes of iron a year. By 1900 the five main producing countries were turning out this tonnage *every day*. Today the top five produce the same tonnage *every hour*.

How are we to explain this transformation? The answer is given in Volume I of *Capital*. Marx begins with the commodity – the basic building-block of a capitalist economy – and explains that it has both 'use-value' and 'exchange-value'. The use-value of a commodity is based on the need it satisfies, so that the use-value of a banana is inherent in its nutritional content. The exchange-value of a commodity is based on what it has in common with all other commodities, which is the labour required to produce it for the market, and this value is represented by its price. There is at once a potential disconnect: a contradiction-in-the-making between the use-value and exchange-value of a commodity. Bananas may be needed and available, but unaffordable to the hungry.

Use-value was dominant in pre-capitalist exchange. The merchant was simply an intermediary between the producer selling a surplus and the consumer with a need. A yeoman farmer might sell his surplus grain in order to buy a new plough. A rich lord might buy the grain to feed his household retainers. The merchant made a profit, but his social role was simply that of an economic intermediary between other social classes.

Exchange-value is dominant under capitalism. Merchants buy only in order to sell at a profit: their principle is exchange for its own sake. When the principle of the merchant becomes the general principle of society, the transition to capitalism has been achieved.

The commercial capitalism of seventeenth-century Holland and eighteenth-century England was that of merchants accumulating capital through trade. But accumulations of merchant capital could then fund investment in the canals, machines, and factories of the Industrial Revolution. And industrialisation in turn made possible yet greater capital accumulation.

By 1800 capitalism was engaged in a self-feeding process of exponential growth. What powered it was competition: not the politico-military competition of ancient city-states and medieval kingdoms, but the economic competition of rival capitalists.

The spinning jenny meant that one worker could produce as much yarn as eight working alone. The power loom enabled one operator to do the work of six handloom weavers. Capitalists who did not invest in new technology were quickly priced out of the market by low-cost competitors using labour-saving machinery. They discovered the iron law of the market: the pressure of economic competition compelled each and every one to cut costs, increase output, and reduce prices. The measure of success was profit. The most successful capitalists captured a larger share of the market and made bigger profits. These profits were then reinvested in the business to enhance competitiveness even further.

Capitalism is, then, a system of competitive capital accumulation. It is the result of the dynamic fusion of three elements: the merchant principle of buying in order to sell at a profit; the transformation of labour productivity made possible by industrial innovation; and the division of the economy into competing units of capital.

The raw material of this process is, of course, labour-power. This now becomes a commodity in its own right, and one with the unique characteristic that it is routinely purchased at a market price *below* its true value to the consumer. The difference between the two – between the wages paid by capitalists and the value of the goods they obtain in return – is the source of profit.

It was Marx who first explained this. His contribution to Ricardo's 'labour theory of value' was to grasp that workers' wages were payment not for their *labour* – the work actually done – but for their *labour-power* – their ability to work. The difference was the inner secret of the system: if the former were the case, workers would receive the full value of all they produced and there would be no profit; in the latter case, they could be paid a market rate for their hire and then be required to carry out work of greater value.

The point is this. Under capitalism, labour produces the wealth represented by *both* wages *and* profit. Therefore, wages cannot represent the full value of the labour expended in the production process. What the capitalist buys in return for wages is the worker's capacity to labour at a certain level of skill for a fixed period of time. What he expects to gain is value added in production in excess of the value paid in wages. The difference between the two is 'surplus value' or profit.

Workers under capitalism are therefore both alienated and exploited. Their alienation derives from their lack of control over the labour process, their exploitation from the fact that they do not enjoy the full value of their labour. Endemic class conflict is the consequence. Capitalists and workers are locked in an endless struggle over process and reward at the point of production.

Capitalism is contradictory in other senses. Economic competition is blind and anarchic. Surges of investment lead to overproduction, unsold goods, and waves of bankruptcy. Boom turns to bust. Bubbles burst and become black holes of bad debt. Wealth is wasted, and wealth-creation collapses.

Capitalism has transformed the productivity of human labour and created such an abundance of material wealth that a solution to humanity's many problems has become a practical possibility. Yet that promise is negated by the system. On the one hand, competition and free-market anarchy mean a highly contradictory economy subject to crashes, slumps, and mass impoverishment. On the other, the alienation and exploitation of the workplace mean that most people's lives are ruined by toil, poverty, and stress.

The Making of the Working Class

In pre-capitalist societies, the labouring classes often enjoyed a large measure of control over the means of production. Medieval peasants, sometimes as individual owners, sometimes as members of a village collective, had direct access to the fields, pastures, woodlands, and plough teams on which their livelihoods depended. Medieval artisans plied their trades in urban workshops, using their own tools and as members of self-governing guilds.

Early capitalism emerged from the upper levels of this medieval social substrate. Rich peasants became agricultural entrepreneurs. The most successful master craftsmen became big traders. Both capitalism and the bourgeois revolution were driven forward by those called in seventeenth-century England 'the middling sort'. Rising output and expanding markets thereafter increased opportunities to get rich. Those able to invest in estate improvement or new workshops gained a competitive advantage. The gap between the richest merchants and farmers and the poorest labourers widened.

As capital accumulation accelerated, especially from the late seventeenth century, it first took the form of merchant capitalism and the putting-out system. Artisans continued to work in their own homes or premises, but they now produced to order for a merchant capitalist rather than on their own account.

The factory system changed all that. From the late eighteenth century onwards, industrialisation allowed capital accumulation to accelerate. As it did so, the middling sort fragmented into a minority of masters and a majority of wage-workers. The latter, fusing with the mass of general labourers, constituted a new social class: the proletariat (Marx and Engels chose to employ the Latin term for the urban poor of Ancient Rome).

This process of class formation – proletarianisation – was a violent one. Peasants clung tenaciously to their land. Artisans cherished the freedom and dignity of independent craftwork. To create a proletariat, it was necessary to separate the producers from the means of production. The history of capitalism is, therefore, a history of eviction, dispossession, and impoverishment.

The ruin of the English peasantry began in the Middle Ages, intensified during the sixteenth and seventeenth centuries, and culminated in the eighteenth and nineteenth centuries. The principal mechanism was enclosure.

Medieval agriculture was based on open fields. Two or three large fields were divided into strips, each allocated to a peasant family, but the strips were unfenced since much agricultural work was done collectively. Each family also enjoyed various common rights, such as use of woodland for gathering fuel and hunting, and of the commons for grazing.

Enclosure gave one or more big farmers the right to fence off land and treat it as private property. Enclosure therefore meant the dispossession of the peasantry. For this reason, over several centuries, enclosure was the focus of a bitter class war in the English countryside.

An anonymous contemporary verse says it all:

> They hang the man, and flog the woman,
> That steals the goose from off the common;
> But let the greater villain loose,
> That steals the common from the goose.

The land-grabbers were usually backed by the state. During the late eighteenth and early nineteenth centuries, enclosure was driven by a series of parliamentary Enclosure Acts. Parliament at this time was an assembly of property-owners.

At the same time, Scottish Highland lairds were evicting tenants from their estates in a wave of clearances designed to create profitable sheep-pasture. Between 1814 and 1820, the Duchess of Sutherland employed British soldiers to evict 15,000 peasants, burn down their villages, and repopulate 800,000 acres of clan land with 130,000 sheep.

The resistance of others was broken by poverty. The power loom eventually threw 800,000 handloom weavers out of work. This did not happen all at once. Growing competition from factory production caused a steady downward spiral of piecework rates.

The handloom weavers did not go quietly. They waged a desperate rearguard action, forming a secret movement led by the mythical 'General Ned Ludd' and engaging in machine-smashing attacks on factories. The Luddites were defeated by state repression. A mass show trial at York in 1812 resulted in executions and deportations. The handloom weavers were eventually ground down by starvation and driven into the fast-growing industrial cities in search of work.

The proletarianisation of the Irish was even more violent. Ireland was a British colony in which an Irish Catholic peasantry was dominated by a class of Anglo-Irish Protestant landlords. The Irish fought with tremendous resilience, but again and again their revolts were suppressed by superior military power and murderous repression.

Between 1845 and 1852, the staple crop of the Irish peasantry, the potato, was devastated by blight. While the landlords continued to export food for profit, famine killed one million and drove another million to emigrate, reducing the total population by around 25 per cent.

The proletariat of Manchester, Glasgow, and a dozen other northern industrial cities was created by the English Enclosures, the Highland Clearances, the Irish Famine, and the impoverishment of the handloom weavers and other craft workers. It was created by starvation.

So what Marx called 'the primitive accumulation of capital' necessarily involved the more or less forcible expropriation of peasants and artisans from control over the means of production. Only then could they be induced to labour for capital. 'The history of this', Marx explained, 'is written in the annals of mankind in letters of blood and fire.'

The dynamism of global capitalism over the last 250 years has meant that ever more communities of peasants and artisans have been dispossessed, impoverished, and turned into wage-labourers. The process can be seen today in China, India, and Brazil. But that dynamism continues to affect existing working classes. Old industries decline and new ones arise. There are as many call-centre workers in Glasgow today as there were engineering workers a century ago.

As the character and composition of the working class change, as it is repeatedly reconfigured by competitive capital accumulation, so must the process of building class identity, solidarity, and organisation be renewed. The Russian Marxist Leon Trotsky contrasted the terms 'class in itself' and 'class for itself'. By the first he meant the simple reality of class as a social relationship and an economic process, irrespective of whether or not workers were aware of their condition. By the latter he meant the development of class consciousness, union organisation, and active resistance.

The former is an objective fact, the latter the result of subjective decision. Workers may remain ignorant, fragmented, and passive – history's victims. Or they may seek to understand their condition, unite with their fellows, and engage in a struggle to change the world – becoming history's agents.

On this distinction, between 'class in itself' and 'class for itself', turns the future of humanity.

11
The Age of Blood and Iron
1848–1873

Private Louis Troutman, Company F, 108th Regiment,
US Colored Infantry, January–May 1865.

The bourgeois revolution 'from above': Troutman was one of
approximately 200,000 black men, mainly former slaves, who
fought in the Union Army during the American Civil War.

After the defeat of Chartism in England and the 1848 Revolutions across Europe, capitalism entered a long boom. It lasted until 1873, when the system crashed and was pitched into an equally long depression. The boom was spearheaded by railway construction, which mechanised the transport of goods and people, generated a mass market for the coal, iron, engineering, and construction industries, and created a highly visible symbol of the new 'age of capital'.

Booming capitalism destabilised the social and geopolitical order, however, providing the context for a third wave of bourgeois revolution, though one managed in large degree from above rather than driven by mass action from below. The Italian *Risorgimento*, the American Civil War, Japan's Meiji Restoration, and German Unification are all best understood as bourgeois revolutions from above.

But the period opened and ended with dramatic events that, in their different ways, heralded the great struggles of the twentieth century: China's Taiping Rebellion of 1850–64 and the Indian Mutiny of 1857–9 were anti-imperialist revolts in what would later be called the Third World; and the Paris Commune of 1871 was the first example of proletarian revolution in history.

The Indian Mutiny

The Agricultural Revolution and the Industrial Revolution stand alone in history as all-encompassing transformations of human experience. But there is an important difference between them.

The Agricultural Revolution spread slowly over thousands of years, and the traditional agrarian communities it generated were deeply conservative, changing only imperceptibly over centuries. The Industrial Revolution, by comparison, was a socio-economic maelstrom, involving, as Marx put it, the 'constant revolutionising of production' and 'uninterrupted disturbance of all social conditions'. Even before the Industrial Revolution, when European capitalism was still embryonic inside the old feudal-absolutist order, capitalism was reaching out across the globe, its explorers, seafarers, merchants, and slave-traders probing foreign continents in search of plunder and profit.

After 1750 the process of capital accumulation soared and the system's drive towards 'globalisation' intensified. Capitalism required primary products to feed growing industries, markets for manufactured goods, and new investment outlets for surplus capital. Empire became a necessity. And capitalism afforded Europeans the edge they needed to acquire it.

Technology and organisation made it possible for small groups of European soldiers to subjugate indigenous polities in America, Africa, and Asia. The states they faced were often corrupt, oppressive, and riddled with division and discontent. Armies of tens of thousands sometimes fled when confronted by hundreds or even just a few dozen European soldiers.

India was one of the richest prizes. Several European states established trading posts on the coast during the seventeenth century. By the middle of the following century, colonial rivalry between the British and the French had escalated into a series of small-scale wars in Bengal and Madras.

In 1757, Robert Clive, an officer in the service of the British East India Company, took Calcutta and defeated the army of the Nawab of Bengal at the Battle of Plassey. The Nawab was nominally the viceroy of the Mughal Emperor in Delhi. In practice, he was an independent ruler, one of several across India who were often at war with each other. The Europeans were able to subjugate India province by province.

A huge social gulf separated the opulence of the Nawab's court from the poverty of the villages. The Bengali peasantry regarded their rulers as oppressors. They had no incentive to fight for them. And because the court was essentially parasitic, without real roots in Bengali society, it was plagued with faction and intrigue.

It was not superior firepower that enabled Clive's army of 3,000 to defeat the Nawab's army of 50,000. In fact, the Bengalis had many more muskets and cannon than the East India Company. The key to victory was treachery among the Nawab's senior commanders, most of whose men took no part in the fighting, and the effectiveness of a new way of war based on mobility, firepower, and aggression.

Feudal armies fought as amalgams of individual warriors. Bourgeois armies fought as highly drilled blocks of men. The firearms of the age were slow to load, of limited range, and wildly inaccurate. The ideal was to deliver massed volleys at a distance of 50 metres or less. This could shred an opposing formation and break the enemy line at a decisive point. Clive's army fought only a small part of the Nawab's army at Plassey, but it still faced three or four times its own number at the point of decision. Bengal was therefore conquered by a combination of feudal division and bourgeois method. The same was true of European conquests throughout Asia, America, and Africa.

Plassey was a turning-point. The French were eclipsed and many native rulers sought an accommodation with the rising power of the East India Company. The Marathas in central India were conquered by 1823, Sind (south-west Pakistan) in 1843, the Sikhs of the Punjab (northern Pakistan and north-west India) in 1849, and Oudh (north-central India) in 1856. By the middle of the nineteenth century, the British controlled 200 million people with an army of just 250,000, 80 per cent of whom were sepoys under British officers. The Company ruled in alliance with puppet nawabs (viceroys) and maharajahs (princes). These native rulers lived in luxury and maintained a public façade of regal pomp, but it was Company officials who held real power.

Zamindars (landlords) and big merchants also thrived under Company rule, sharing with its officials the profits of intensified exploitation of the peasantry. Poverty in the countryside deepened. In 1769, 12 years after Plassey, crop failures led to famines, epidemics, and an estimated ten million deaths.

Imperialism caused economic regression. The clearest example is provided by the textile industry. As the industrialisation of British textile production took off, the captive Indian market was flooded with cheap imports. Native textile merchants and handicraft workers were ruined. The proportion of Indians dependent on agriculture rose from 50 per cent to 75 per cent during the nineteenth century. India under British rule was 'de-developed'.

In 1857 north-central India exploded. Hindu, Muslim, and Sikh sepoys mutinied when ordered to violate religious taboos by using cartridges greased with the fat of 'unclean' animals. The mutineers took the British by surprise, seized control of a large swathe of northern India, put isolated garrisons at Cawnpore and Lucknow under siege, and installed a new Mughal emperor in the ancient capital of Delhi.

The British campaign of re-conquest was hard fought and exceptionally savage. Troops were dispatched from Britain, and sepoys from Madras and Bombay in southern India were deployed against the rebels in the north. Captured Mutineers were tied across the muzzles of loaded cannon and executed by being blasted into fragments.

The Indian Mutiny (1857–9) was the subcontinent's first war of independence, an anti-imperialist struggle in which Indians of different ethnic and religious backgrounds fought side by side – the antithesis of the divide and rule fostered by the British. But the Mutineers fought with one foot in the past. The only alternative they could conceive to British rule was a return to the feudal past. There was no challenge to the property and power of traditional rulers, and therefore no promise of social emancipation that might have mobilised the majority of the peasantry.

Nonetheless, the threat to British rule was real enough, and it inspired wholesale remodelling of imperial administration in the aftermath of the Mutiny. Queen Victoria was declared Empress of India and a new Government of India was established. Relations with native Indian rulers were strengthened, a new Indian middle class of clerks, administrators, and lawyers developed, and village Brahmins and headmen became tax- and rent-collectors. The rule of law replaced the arbitrary authority of Company officials. Exploitation and impoverishment were now framed by a tightly controlled bureaucracy and a reformed Anglo-Indian army. A hierarchy of privilege and a deliberate fostering of ethnic, religious, and caste divisions were the mechanisms by which India's imperial rulers fragmented native resistance to the Raj.

Indians paid for their subjugation: 25 per cent of tax revenues were spent on the army, as against barely 1 per cent each for health, education, and agriculture. Famines killed one million in the 1860s, 3.5 million in the 1870s, and ten million in the 1890s – what the radical American historian Mike Davis has called the 'late Victorian holocausts' that 'made the Third World'.

The frequently repeated claim that India benefitted economically from the Raj is a lie. Agriculture was impoverished, native industries destroyed, and wealth siphoned away by foreign capital. This reality would, in time, produce a renewed struggle for Indian independence.

China's Taiping Rebellion

The Taiping Rebellion of 1850–64 is estimated to have cost the lives of between 20 and 30 million people, making it the bloodiest conflict in history before the Second World War. It was both a medieval peasant revolt against intolerable conditions and a modern nationalist revolt against colonial oppression. Like the Indian Mutiny, China's Taiping Rebellion was an elemental eruption from the social depths of a violated Asia that looked back to the past as it faced the future.

European merchants had coveted the wealth of China ever since the travels of Marco Polo in the thirteenth century. But China was conservative and self-sufficient. It did not need anything the Europeans had to offer. The British East India Company solved this problem in the early nineteenth century by turning large areas of India over to the cultivation of a commodity that creates its own demand: opium. By 1810 the Company was selling 350 tons of opium a year to the Chinese. When the imperial government attempted to stop the trade, the British went to war. The two Opium Wars of 1839–42 and 1856–60 were fought by the British Empire on behalf of corporate drug barons.

Chinese history had been a 'revolving door' in which imperial dynasties were occasionally displaced by revolt and conquest, but the essential structures of state and society were preserved. The last turn of the door had taken place in 1644 when the disintegrating Ming dynasty had been overthrown by the Manchus. By origin barbarian invaders from Manchuria in the north-east, the Manchu emperors had quickly accommodated to the dominant mandarin culture of the Chinese state. The mandarins were the highly trained, well-paid, and ultra-conservative bureaucrats who controlled the civil service. They ruled China in alliance with local landlords and city merchants.

By the middle of the nineteenth century, corruption and oppression had again reached crisis point, with the peasantry set to explode. This time, however, the revolving door was jammed by the intervention of European imperialism.

The two Opium Wars exposed the chronic military backwardness of the insular Chinese state. In the first war, the British used a flotilla of warships and an expeditionary force of soldiers and marines to seize Guangzhou, Shanghai, and other Chinese ports. They then moved up the Yangtze River and threatened Nanjing, forcing the imperial government to sue for peace. The Treaty of Nanjing required China to hand over Hong Kong, open four ports, including Guangzhou and Shanghai, to British trade, and pay a large war indemnity.

But this was not enough. Official Chinese resistance to further British demands led to a second war only 15 years later. This time, France, Russia, and the United States joined the rape. The war culminated in the capture of the Taku Forts at Tianjin and an advance inland to Beijing by 18,000 British and French troops. The imperial capital was captured and the summer palaces of the Emperor were looted and burnt.

One result of the Opium Wars was a vast increase in the highly profitable drugs trade. By the end of the nineteenth century, Chinese consumption of opium had increased 100-fold and a quarter of all adult males were addicted. Another result was European control of Chinese ports and trade. A string of foreign enclaves or mini-colonies ('concessions') was established on the coast. European officials had control of Chinese customs and European residents enjoyed 'extra-territorial rights' (immunity from Chinese jurisdiction). European missionaries were at liberty to seek converts wherever they could.

The Opium Wars and the foreign concessions exposed the decay of the ruling Manchu dynasty and the ancient imperial state. This in turn helped trigger the peasant revolt that had long been brewing in the villages of rural China. Ground down by debt, hunger, and lack of land, preyed upon by gentry, money-lenders, tax-collectors, and corrupt government officials, China's rural masses were primed for revolt.

The movement began among peasants, labourers, and impoverished dissident intellectuals in southern China in 1850. Its leader was a schoolteacher and Christian mystic called Hong Xiuchuan. Hong claimed that his divine mission was to destroy devils and establish a 'Heavenly Kingdom of Great Peace'. The Heavenly Kingdom would be characterised by equal division of land, communal ownership of goods, and the abolition of social distinctions, including the oppression of women. The Taiping rebels anticipated the revolutionary socialism of the twentieth century, but they framed their message of social liberation in the language of messianic Christianity.

Within three years, now two million strong, the movement was powerful enough to capture the former imperial capital at Nanjing and establish a Heavenly Kingdom that encompassed 40 per cent of China. For a decade, China was divided in two, with a conservative Manchu-ruled north, and a radical Taiping-ruled south.

But the extreme poverty of nineteenth-century China undermined the egalitarian idealism of the early years. Scarcity meant that only a few could live well, and the leaders of the revolt exploited their positions to ensure that they and their cronies were those few. In this, the Taiping Rebellion was true to type: previous peasant revolts had quickly given rise to new imperial dynasties only a little less oppressive than the old. The economic preconditions for true social emancipation did not exist in traditional China. Though a new ruler pushed for a more realistic programme of Western-style modernisation in the final years of the Taiping state, it came too late to gain traction. The Western powers had decided to intervene in support of the Manchu regime and the established order.

A reorganised army, funded by Chinese merchants, equipped with European weapons, and commanded successively by an American and a British officer (the latter, Charles George Gordon, destined to become a famous Victorian hero, first 'Chinese Gordon', later 'Gordon of Khartoum') eventually crushed the revolt.

The success of the 'Ever Victorious Army' (as it was known) had a profound effect on Chinese history. The Taiping Rebellion had mobilised all the progressive forces inside China – the peasants, the radical sects, the dissident intellectuals, the reform-minded officials. It had represented the possibility of a reinvigorated imperial state committed to reform and modernisation in response to the threat posed by imperialism. Its defeat blocked this avenue. Instead, the dynasty limped on, a political relic propped up by imperialism, for the Manchus and the Westerners needed each other as mutual support against the Chinese masses.

Foreign imperialist armies had occupied Beijing in 1860. They would do so again 40 years later. On 14 August 1900, an international invasion force of 19,000 men captured the Chinese imperial capital. British, French, German, Russian, Italian, Japanese, and American troops all took part in a military operation whose purpose was to suppress a nationalist revolt against colonialism. The revolt was led by members of a secret organisation called the Society of the Righteous Harmonious Fists, popularly known as 'Boxers'. It enjoyed the tacit support of the beleaguered imperial government of the Manchu Dowager Empress Zi Xi. Boxer rebels and Imperial troops fought side by side against the invaders.

Despite this, when the Boxer Rebellion was defeated, the Manchu dynasty was allowed to survive, tolerated by Western powers who still considered it indispensable to colonial penetration of China. The problem was that the Chinese were not only numerous – the population was perhaps 350 million in the mid-nineteenth century – but also linguistically, culturally, and historically a single people. Any attempt to conquer China would quickly have stretched the military power of the invader to breaking-point. Any attempt would have been doomed to eventual defeat. This was, in fact, to be the fate of the Japanese occupation of 1931–45. The Japanese succeeded in holding the coastal regions, but were never able to dominate China's vast hinterland, and the relentless military struggle required the permanent deployment of hundreds of thousands of troops.

The combination of Manchu rule and the foreign concessions effectively choked off independent Chinese development during the nineteenth and early twentieth centuries. While Europe, America, and Japan progressed, China regressed. But the inability of any of the foreign powers to dominate China politically, even as they despoiled its people economically, was a contradiction destined to give rise to a protracted sequence of revolutionary upheavals of mounting intensity. In a sense, the Taiping Rebellion was the first phase of the century-long Chinese Revolution that would culminate in 1949.

The Italian Risorgimento

When nationalist volunteers landed in Sicily in 1860 intent on over-throwing the corrupt absolute monarchy that ruled the island and uniting it with the rest of Italy, the local peasants assumed that the slogan *Viva Italia!* referred to the insurgents' queen. Italy, in the sense of a modern, unified, bourgeois nation-state, was an act of creation *de novo*.

The peninsula had been politically unsettled since experiencing an incomplete bourgeois revolution in 1796–1814. This had been a revolution from above in which the main agent of change had been Napoleon's army of conquest. The French overthrew the old regimes and installed republican governments led by Italian liberals. Later, as the French Republic mutated into the Napoleonic Empire, they replaced these with dynastic regimes ruled by members of the Bonaparte family. Feudalism was abolished and careers opened to the middle classes. But a combination of foreign rule and lack of land reform limited the appeal of the new regimes.

Absolutist governments were restored in 1814, but they could not return society to its former condition, and they faced opposition from the new social forces unleashed by the French Revolution. Italian politics was therefore dominated throughout the nineteenth century by the unfinished business of its spluttering bourgeois revolution.

Four issues were paramount. First, Italy was divided into several separate states, and economic development was hampered by the lack of a single national market under unified state authority.

Second, partly because of national division and consequent weakness, Italy continued to be dominated by foreign powers – in the first half of the nineteenth century, by Habsburg Austria.

Third, the bourgeoisie was almost entirely excluded from power by regimes based on absolute monarchies, the Catholic Church, and aristocratic landowners. The demand for liberal constitutional reform was a demand for bourgeois political empowerment.

Fourth, unlike in France, there had been no peasant revolution in Italy. The formal abolition of feudalism had not led to large-scale land redistribution. Italy remained a traditional society of landowners and peasants in which the mass of the people were desperately impoverished – physically, intellectually, culturally.

Because of these tensions, Italy experienced four revolutions in 40 years – in 1820, 1831, 1848, and 1860. The first three were defeated. The last achieved national unity and independence; it did not resolve the social question.

The *Risorgimento* (Rebirth) that gave rise to the modern Italian state was played out between 1859 and 1870. It was made possible by a combination of Piedmontese ambition, Franco-Austrian rivalry, and revolutionary insurrection in southern Italy – a bourgeois revolution very much from above *and* below.

The Kingdom of Piedmont and Sardinia, under its semi-constitutional monarch Victor Emmanuel and its liberal Prime Minister Count Camillo Cavour, had emerged as a dynamic centre of economic development. On this basis, in their own interest, the Piedmontese ruling class laid claim to a wider political leadership of the Italian national cause.

The Piedmontese formed an alliance with France and defeated the Austrians in northern Italy in 1859. This tilted the entire balance of power across the region. The Austrian-backed absolutist rulers of the minor Italian states toppled like dominoes. New liberal governments in Lombardy, Parma, Modena, Emilia, Romagna, and Tuscany then voted to fuse with Piedmont.

In May the following year, the veteran revolutionary Giuseppe Garibaldi landed in Sicily at the head of 1,000 red-shirted volunteers. His aim was to foment revolt against the absolutist regime which ruled Naples and Sicily. Four days after coming ashore at Marsala on the west coast, on 15 May 1860, his miniature army won the decisive military victory of the *Risorgimento*.

Aware that the Sicilian peasantry was watching, the veteran guerrilla fighter resolved on a frontal attack against superior numbers of better armed soldiers defending a hilltop, trusting to the morale and élan of his nationalist volunteers. As news spread that the Redshirts had stormed the hill and the hated Neapolitan soldiery had fled, revolution erupted across the island. Before the year was out, the Kingdom of the Two Sicilies (as it was known) had ceased to exist, and the whole of southern Italy became part of the new unified state.

In 1866, Piedmont's alliance with Prussia in the Austro-Prussian War secured Venice and Venetia. In 1870, Napoleon III's defeat at Sedan removed the Pope's main protector, and Italian troops entered the Papal States and annexed them to the Kingdom of Italy.

But there was still no social revolution. As early as August 1860, in an effort to win over southern landlords, some of Garibaldi's men had fired on peasant rebels. Soon there was full-scale war across much of the south as the peasants attempted to bring an end to their poverty by seizing uncultivated land and the landlords drove them back by recruiting the private armies that would soon evolve into the Mafia.

State-backed Mafia terror would keep the peasantry in poverty for another hundred years. In the late nineteenth century, three-quarters of the income of Italian peasant households was spent on food, but many still went hungry. Two million suffered from malaria every year. Most Italian villagers remained illiterate and lived in priest-ridden ignorance.

But national unification precipitated an industrial revolution. Between 1861 and 1870 the length of railway track almost trebled. Between 1896 and 1913 industry grew at 5 per cent a year, the fastest rate in Europe at the time. Milan, Turin, Genoa, and other north-western cities became major industrial centres. The booming north sucked in labour from Italy's impoverished rural hinterland. Thus were starving peasants turned into industrial workers – a process of proletarianisation that would explode in waves of fierce class struggle in the years before, during, and after the First World War.

The American Civil War

When the guns opened fire on Fort Sumter on 12 April 1861, most Americans thought the war would be over before the summer was out. President Lincoln called for 75,000 militiamen to serve for 90 days. That, he reckoned, would be enough. By the time the war ended four years later, 620,000 Americans were dead – more than in all the other wars in US history combined. What pushed the cost so high were the issues at stake.

The Civil War was the pivotal event in US history – a second revolutionary war to complete the work of the first and determine which of two incompatible social systems would dominate the North American continent. Eleven Southern states had seceded from the Union when Lincoln – a 'black' Republican – was elected President. The Southern leaders were clear about the reason: 'The undying opposition to slavery in the United States means war upon it', explained Confederate President Jefferson Davis. Confederate Vice-President Alexander Stephens defined the new nation's *raison d'être* as follows: 'Its foundations are laid, its cornerstone rests upon the great truth that the negro is not equal to the white man; that slavery, subordination to the superior race, is his natural and moral condition.' Slavery was the issue on which men fought and died through four bloody years of ferociously contested civil war.

There were military reasons for the war's intensity and duration – the vastness of the country, the dense wilderness across so much of it, the primitive communications, the killing-power of modern weaponry, and the ability of mass-production industry to equip and supply huge armies. But the main reason was that it was a revolutionary war to decide what sort of society the United States was going to be.

The 1860 election had been one of the most polarised in US history. The Republican programme expressed the aspirations of the fast-growing capitalist economy of the North and the fast-expanding pioneer communities of the West. Central planks were higher tariffs to protect American industry, free land for new settlers, and government subsidies for railway construction.

The slogan was 'Free soil, free speech, free labour, free men'. 'The free labour system', explained Lincoln, 'opens the way for all – gives hope to all, and energy, and progress, and improvement of condition to all.' This was the rhetoric of a young, confident, forward-looking bourgeoisie – and, if need be, a revolutionary one.

The South was a conservative agricultural society largely dependent on export earnings from a single commodity: cotton. The South, like the North, was booming. As the textile industry expanded in New England, Britain, France, and elsewhere, the demand for cotton soared, along with its price. In 1800 cotton exports had been worth $5 million and represented 7 per cent of total US exports; by 1860 the value was $191 million and the share 57 per cent. While mill owners, mine bosses, and rail operators grew rich in the North, the traditional planter aristocracy grew rich in the South.

The differences were many. Tariffs meant protection for Northern industry, but higher prices for Southern consumers. Westward expansion was fed mainly by Northern pioneers, threatening the balance of power between free and slave states within the Union. Rail subsidies enriched Northern capitalists, not Southern planters.

Two economic systems, two social orders, two types of ruling class with different needs and rival demands were strapped together in a single polity. Whose interests should the state represent?

One issue became the prism that concentrated the growing antagonism and turned it into a mighty conflagration: human slavery.

The wealth of the Southern plantations depended on the labour of four million black slaves. The Republican Party contained a radical wing that was abolitionist. But it was Lincoln, a relative moderate, who said, 'A house divided against itself cannot stand. I believe this government cannot endure, permanently half slave, half free.'

Lincoln won only 40 per cent of the national popular vote in the 1860 presidential election, but he carried almost every county in the Upper North, and won a clear majority of 54 per cent across the North as a whole. Throughout the South, by contrast, his vote was minimal, largely restricted to Unionist enclaves like West Virginia and East Tennessee. Northern abolitionists had no doubt about the significance of what had happened: 'The great revolution has actually taken place', wrote Charles Francis Adams. 'The country has once and for all thrown off the domination of the slaveholders.'

The resulting struggle was long and bloody because it was a revolutionary war fought between rival systems and opposing political ideologies; no compromise, no negotiated settlement, no happy halfway house was open to Americans as they embarked on their violent feud in the spring of 1861. The stakes were irreducibly high for both sides: for the North, the survival of the Union, a unified national economy, and policy geared to industrial growth; for the Southern elite, the defence of slavery, the foundation stone of their social order.

The intensity and duration of the struggle radicalised it. For the first 18 months, abolition was not a Union war aim. But under the cautious leadership of a pro-slavery general, there was stalemate, and war-weariness and defeatism infected the North. Lincoln was forced to re-energise the struggle by proclaiming the emancipation of the slaves.

There was a good practical reason: slave labour freed white men for service in the Confederate Army, whereas escaped slaves could be recruited as Union soldiers. But the political reason was the greater: a war against slavery would make the struggle for the Union morally unimpeachable, wrecking any chance of European backing for the South and enlisting the passion of abolitionists and the slaves themselves in the nation's 'fiery trial'. Lincoln concluded that 'we must free the slaves or be ourselves subdued'. Implicit in the Emancipation Proclamation issued in September 1862 was a redefinition of US democracy. 'As I would not be a slave,' said Lincoln, 'so I would not be a master. This expresses my idea of democracy.'

Many of the men and women who won the Civil War for the Union were inspired by Lincoln's vision of 'a new birth of freedom'. Among them was Joshua Chamberlain, a New England college professor, committed abolitionist, and friend of German revolutionary exiles in contact with Marx and Engels in London. Chamberlain would enter the history books as the colonel commanding the 20th Maine in its epic defence of Little Round Top on the second day of Gettysburg.

Then there was Colonel Robert Gould Shaw, a young Boston abolitionist, serving in the 54th Massachusetts. On 18 July 1863, the regiment attempted to storm the formidable defences of Fort

Wagner at the entrance to Charleston harbour in South Carolina. The attack was driven forward with consummate courage, but was defeated. Shaw was shot down on top of the enemy rampart. Here was the abolitionist revolution incarnate, for the battle was fought deep inside Confederate territory and Shaw's regiment was formed of black soldiers, many of them former slaves. By the end of the war, 200,000 black men would have served in the Union Army.

In 1864 the war entered its third phase. Union armies now waged total war to crush the South. 'War on the *chateaux*, peace to the cottages', Danton had proclaimed in the French Revolution. Now, at the climax of America's second revolution, General Sherman's army marched through the heartland of the Confederacy, burning mansions, freeing slaves.

The war ended in April 1865. The next decade was dominated by 'Reconstruction'. Much of the South was kept under military occupation. Northern get-rich-quick entrepreneurs – known as 'carpetbaggers' – moved in. Freed slaves got the vote and used it to elect black judges, state politicians, even congressmen.

But once the power of the Southern planter aristocracy was broken and the dominance of Northern capital secured, the Union Army withdrew and state governments were re-colonised by the old elite. Southern blacks were disenfranchised, segregated, and terrorised by the racist thugs of the Ku Klux Klan. They worked henceforward as menial labourers or impoverished sharecroppers. Slavery was replaced by a form of racial apartheid across the South. It would last for almost a century.

So the American Civil War, like all bourgeois revolutions, gave rise to both huge advances and bitter disappointments. It made possible the massive geographical and industrial expansion of the United States that would turn it into a global superpower; but it left the lives of most Americans blighted by exploitation, poverty, and racism.

Japan's Meiji Restoration

The year 1848 was a watershed in world history. Prior to this, the bourgeoisie had led popular revolutions to dismantle the state, overthrow the old ruling class, and remodel society on capitalist lines. This had been the essence of the Dutch, English, American, and

French Revolutions. After 1848 the bourgeoisie never again played this role. Why was this?

The Industrial Revolution meant that Europe was already being transformed into a capitalist economy and a society of factory-owners and workers. With the exception of Britain, the transformation was still at an early stage, but it was sufficiently advanced to disable the old mechanism of political change. The radical mass of the sixteenth, seventeenth, and eighteenth century petty-bourgeoisie was being transformed into a minority class of comfortable property-owners and a majority class of urban and rural wage-workers.

Private property had been sacrosanct in earlier radical movements dominated by a petty-bourgeoisie of farmers, traders, and workshop masters. It was increasingly in question as the new radical movements of the nineteenth century drew growing numbers of wage-workers – 'with nothing to lose but their chains' – into action. Revolution became more risky for any kind of property-owner.

On the other hand, competitive pressure from states already developing as capitalist economies – especially Britain – made established regimes more willing to grant the reforms demanded by capitalists, liberals, and nationalists. Great-power status was a matter of armies, guns, and battleships. These in turn depended on modern industry and infrastructure. Reform and modernisation became geopolitical imperatives. Such was the transformative power of capitalist globalisation.

Bitter struggles were often still necessary. Northern Italy had been united under the leadership of Piedmont following a war between France and Austria in 1859. But southern Italy had only been joined to the north as a result of mass insurrection triggered by the arrival of a small revolutionary army in Sicily in 1860.

During the American Civil War, the capitalists of the Northern states had been forced to mobilise two million men, one in ten of them former slaves, to crush the armed resistance of the Southern planter aristocracy. Lincoln had been a revolutionary leader – uncompromising in the face of rebellion, willing to radicalise the struggle by freeing the slaves, and determined to wage an all-out war to the finish. But the process had been managed from above using the existing state apparatus.

A yet more extreme example of bourgeois revolution from above is provided by the Meiji Restoration in Japan in 1868, an event that would shape the entire history of the Far East until 1945.

In the fifteenth and sixteenth centuries, Japan had been torn apart by feudal civil wars. Like the warlords of medieval Europe, the Japanese lords (*daimyo*) had employed armed retinues of professional warriors (*samurai*) to engage in a series of internal power struggles. At the beginning of the seventeenth century, the Tokugawa clan succeeded in defeating and subjugating all its rivals. The head of the clan became the shogun, the effective ruler of the country, with the Emperor relegated to ceremonial duties. A new capital was established at Edo (present-day Tokyo).

The Tokugawa shoguns were like the absolute monarchs of eighteenth-century Europe. The families of the *daimyo* were kept at court as hostages. Guns and foreign books were banned, and foreign trade restricted to a single port. Catholic converts were persecuted. Japan became a closed society under a political dictatorship suspicious of new ideas.

But the end of feudal anarchy allowed agriculture and trade to recover. Farmers, artisans, and merchants prospered, and the economy became increasingly monetised. Towns grew, and with them an urban culture of poetry, novels, and plays. The ban on foreign goods and foreign influence was less and less stringently enforced. The old classes declined. The long peace made many *samurai* redundant, forcing them to become farmers or traders. Those who remained *samurai* were a parasitic class, their way of life increasingly anachronistic.

These economic and social changes meant that by the middle of the nineteenth century the political edifice of the Tokugawa shogunate was fragile. The catalyst of its collapse was the arrival of US Commodore Perry's naval squadron in Edo Bay in 1853. Perry's mission was to secure trading concessions for American capitalism. The result was an 'unequal treaty' which involved opening Japan to foreign imports but facing restrictions on Japanese exports. It also meant the granting of commercial privileges and 'extraterritoriality' (immunity from Japanese jurisdiction) to foreign residents. Britain, France, Russia, and Holland all demanded and were granted concessions like those of the US.

The Tokugawa shogunate had revealed its politico-military weakness: it was unable to defend Japanese interests against foreign imperialists. Between 1867 and 1869, an alliance of great lords, with *samurai* support, forced the overthrow of the Tokugawa shogun and the 'restoration' of the power of the Emperor (whose name at the time was Meiji).

The Meiji Restoration was led by some of the most conservative forces in Japanese society. The slogans were traditionalist, there was no appeal for mass support, and the merchants, artisans, and peasants played only minor roles in events. But in an age of breechloaders and ironclads, traditional *samurai* were doomed. The Restorationists' manifesto stated that they wanted 'a uniform rule throughout the empire', so that 'the country will be able to rank equally with the other nations of the world'. In other words, they needed a modern nation-state and developed capitalist industry.

Change thereafter was rapid. Old class distinctions and privileges were swept away. A new parliamentary system was established. Railways and factories were built. Military conscription was introduced. The army was remodelled on German lines, the navy on British ones.

Japan's transformation was contested by both conservative and progressive forces. Revolts by discontented *ronin* – rootless *samurai* who hankered after the feudal past – had to be crushed by the new conscript army. The peasants – four-fifths of the population – were also losers. Modernisation was paid for by a heavy tax on land and low levels of consumption. There were scores of local agrarian revolts in the Meiji era. Japanese peasants continued to live in poverty until after the Second World War.

Modern Japan was shaped by this combination of geopolitical competition, internal resistance to modernisation and capital accumulation, and a warrior culture inherited from the past and now sublimated into new military institutions. It evolved under these pressures into a repressive state controlled by a militarist elite and devoted to national-imperial expansion.

In 1894 the Japanese participated in the imperial dismemberment of China. Ten years later they defeated the Russians in a struggle for control of Korea and Manchuria. Ten years after that they entered the First World War and mopped up German possessions in China. In the half-century after the Meiji Restoration, Japan's rulers recast themselves as a class of modern warlord-imperialists: *samurai* with battleships.

The Unification of Germany

In the middle of the nineteenth century, Germany was still divided into 39 separate states. Political unification to create a single national market was the central question on which the future of German capitalism turned.

The attempt to resolve 'the national question' by revolution from below had failed in 1848. The Frankfurt Parliament had attempted to unify Germany and impose a liberal constitution by making speeches and passing resolutions. It had been dissolved by the armies of the German states in the counter-revolution of 1849.

Prussia, with its absolute monarchy, *junker* aristocracy, and militarist culture, had become 'the Sparta of Europe' in the eighteenth century. This had enabled it to survive as a modern national-dynastic state, despite its unenviable geographical location, devoid of natural frontiers, wide open to attack, especially in the east.

The *junker* officers of the Prussian Army had shown themselves to be the black heart of the German counter-revolution which had crushed the 'Forty-Eighters'. They seemed the very antithesis of the national-liberal cause. But the world was changing in ways that the *junkers* could not control. The Industrial Revolution was transforming the economic, social, and military geography of Europe. The first railways were constructed in the mid-1830s, and by 1850 some 23,500 km of track had been laid. The military significance of the new technology was obvious: railways could move troops from one theatre of war to another in a fraction of the time taken to march. The *junkers* may not have needed parliaments, but they certainly needed railways.

In 1815, as part of the reordering of Europe after the defeat of Napoleon, Prussia had been granted the Rhineland – the region that was fast becoming Germany's industrial powerhouse. Though the Rhineland revolutionaries – including Marx and Engels – had been defeated in 1849, the *junker* state's military power was increasingly dependent on the region's mines, steelworks, and engineering plants.

One lesson of 1848 was that the new social classes of the industrial era – the bourgeoisie, the proletariat, and the middle class of professionals, managers, and civil servants – could not for long be accommodated inside a divided Germany ruled by a hotchpotch of semi-feudal potentates. The question was whether national-economic unification could be engineered from above as an alternative to popular revolution from below.

When the *junker* aristocrat Otto von Bismarck was appointed Prime Minister of Prussia in 1862, the historic mission he set himself was to save his class by placing the dynamic forces of nascent German capitalism at the service of the Prussian military monarchy. Instead of the bourgeois revolution bursting out of its medieval shell, Prussia would be reconstructed as 'a feudal turret on a capitalist base' (as Trotsky later put it). Instead of the great questions of the day being settled by 'speeches and the resolutions of majorities', they would be resolved by 'blood and iron' (Bismarck's words). Instead of the French model – armed insurrection, burning mansions, the shadow of the guillotine – there would be the Prussian: revolution from above by the conscripts and cannon of a royal army.

Bismarck's programme was accomplished in three lightning wars. The 1864 war against Denmark over the status of two disputed border provinces, Schleswig and Holstein, placed the King of Prussia at the head of the German national movement. The 1866 war against Austria – the prospective alternative hegemonic power – destroyed Habsburg influence in Germany and created a new Prussian-dominated North German Confederation. And the 1870–1 war against France – a traditional enemy – brought the smaller German states, more or less willingly, into a new Prussian-dominated empire.

In effect, during those seven years, Prussia conquered Germany. The new order was inaugurated by an act of calculated political theatre. The King of Prussia was proclaimed Emperor of Germany at a grand ceremony in the Palace of Versailles on 18 January 1871. The *junker* King, in the captured capital of the enemy, wrapped himself in the flag of modern German nationalism.

The politico-military triumph of 1871 was followed by 40 years of rapid industrialisation. Between 1870 and 1914, German coal production increased from 34 million to 277 million tons, pig-iron production from 1.3 million to 14.7 million, and steel production from 0.3 million to 14 million. The Krupp complex of steelworks and arms factories at Essen in the Ruhr became the biggest industrial enterprise in Europe, employing 16,000 workers in 1873, 45,000 in 1900, and 70,000 in 1912.

Industrial expansion was made possible by bank credit, state contracts, and protective tariffs. The total deposits held by large German banks increased by 40 per cent in the five years between 1907–8 and 1912–13. Banks lent the money for industrial investment and became major holders of industrial stock.

State expenditure on railways and armaments underpinned the industrial boom. The biggest state enterprise – the Prussian State Railway Administration – was the same size as the biggest private corporation – the Deutsche Bank. Government spending on the army and the navy increased ten-fold between 1870 and 1914.

In 1879 Germany introduced the first of a series of new tariffs – essentially taxes on imports designed to raise the price of foreign goods on the home market and thereby protect domestic industries. By 1914 Germany was charging an average of 13 per cent on foreign imports.

Britain, the dominant global economy in the middle of the nineteenth century, was overtaken by Germany in the early twentieth. German coal production almost equalled that of Britain by 1914, while pig-iron production was a third higher, and steel production twice as much. The advance of German capitalism in the new chemical and electrical industries was even more pronounced. By 1914 German firms dominated global production of synthetic dyes and were selling nearly half the world's electrical goods.

Germany's bourgeois revolution from above – carried out by an absolute monarch, aristocratic officers, and peasant conscripts – had unleashed breakneck industrial transformation. The effect was to destabilise both German society and the European state system.

Prussian *junkers* and Rhineland capitalists formed an uneasy political alliance based on mutual interdependence. The fast-growing German working class, on the other hand, constituted a mortal threat to the entire social order. At the same time, German capitalism's increasing need for raw materials, new markets, and investment outlets brought it into conflict with other European powers – above all, with Britain, the dominant global imperial power. Within a quarter of a century of the Franco-Prussian War, these two conflicts – the class struggle at home and the imperialist struggle abroad – were propelling the new Germany towards a cataclysmic crisis.

The Paris Commune

The unification of Germany was not the only outcome of the Franco-Prussian War. There were two more. First, it brought down the ramshackle dictatorship of Louis-Napoleon Bonaparte – Napoleon III as he styled himself from 1852. Second, it produced the first proletarian revolution in history and showed the world what a workers' state might look like. The Paris Commune lasted just two months, but its defenders, as Marx put it, had 'stormed the heavens' and provided 'a new point of departure of worldwide significance'.

Louis-Napoleon – 'Napoleon the Little' as Marx called him to distinguish him from his uncle – was lifted to power by the Gallic tradition of lopsided revolution, whereby Paris would always take the lead, but the rest of France would often fail to follow. The forward march of 1848 had been halted as early as June when the revolutionary vanguard, the working people of eastern Paris, were isolated and gunned down by General Cavaignac's soldiers. In the presidential election that December, Louis-Napoleon came from nowhere to win a landslide victory, taking 75 per cent of the popular vote across France. The secret of his success was hollowness: being nothing to anyone, he could be all things to everyone. Louis-Napoleon was the 'strong man' with an illustrious name who seemed to promise order, justice, and prosperity.

He ruled as President for three years, and then, in December 1852, declared himself Emperor, continuing in power until his defeat at Sedan in September 1870.

The rule of Napoleon III was a political paradox. It represented a bureaucratic fossilisation of revolutionary instability. A façade of dictatorial power obscured a precarious balancing act. After the June Days of 1848, the active political forces of France, still centred on the capital, were evenly divided between a reactionary bloc of monarchists, clericals, and other conservatives, and a progressive bloc of republicans, liberals, and democrats. The presidential election of December 1848 had flattened these divisions under a massive weight of peasant votes. Louis-Napoleon was elected by the passive majority. Thereafter, the Parisian factions were held in check by the bureaucratic apparatus of the Third Empire regime.

The role of the Bonapartist state, in Marx's view, was 'to impose an armistice on the class struggle', 'to break the parliamentary power of the appropriating classes', and thus 'to secure the old order a respite of life'. But if the state becomes semi-detached from civil society, if the political elite avoid scrutiny and accountability, then corruption can spread through the bureaucratic apparatus. While speculators and entrepreneurs close to the Emperor enriched themselves on government contracts, other capitalists became resentful of their exclusion from the charmed circle. At the same time, military adventures in Italy and Mexico, designed in part to inflate the national and dynastic claims of the regime, backfired. And though the economy grew – industrial output doubled under Louis-Napoleon – poverty stalked the suburbs of Paris and other big cities, and the dictator's police and informers were widely hated.

Bismarck had no difficulty provoking Napoleon III into war in June 1870. With its grip on power slipping, the regime could not risk losing face when the Prussian Chancellor contrived a diplomatic affront designed to insult the French Emperor. The war exposed the decadence of the regime: its army crashed to defeat; the Emperor was captured and deposed; and a new bourgeois-republican government took power in Paris.

After Prussia's decisive victory, Bismarck demanded punitive reparations: France was to hand over the eastern border provinces of Alsace and Lorraine and pay a huge war indemnity. The republican government refused and, for five months, Paris was besieged by the Prussian army. This was the democratic phase of the war. The national army had been defeated and its place was now taken by a Parisian militia. A newly formed National Guard soon numbered a third of a million. The struggle was transformed from a war between nation-states into a war of revolutionary defence.

A spectre of popular revolution now haunted the French ruling class. Two attempts by more radical forces to overthrow the republican government were defeated, but its leaders sensed their power draining away. 'Paris armed', wrote Marx, 'was the revolution armed.' The choice, it seemed, was between the Prussians and the Revolution. The bourgeois republicans opted to surrender the city to the national enemy.

They agreed to an armistice with the Prussians in late January 1871. They then organised an immediate general election. As in 1848, the purpose was to mobilise a passive rural electorate against the revolutionary capital. The result was that 400 of the 675 deputies returned were monarchists. Auguste Thiers, a veteran conservative politician, was appointed to head a new government.

On 18 March he sent in troops to begin disarming the Parisian National Guard. The troops refused to fire on the crowd that gathered to oppose them. That afternoon, having lost control, Thiers and his government fled the capital. Power passed first to the Central Committee of the National Guard. Ten days later, it was transferred to a newly elected Commune representing the revolutionary people of Paris.

The Commune was one of the most democratic assemblies in history. Elected by universal male suffrage in every locality, the members were subject to immediate recall by their electors if they deviated from their mandates, had personal responsibility for carrying out collective decisions, and were paid no more than the average wage of a skilled worker. The Commune revealed one of history's secrets: the necessary form that a workers' state must take.

Here was a new sort of power. Not a repressive state raised above society, controlled by the ruling class, and formed of armed bodies of police and soldiers for the suppression of protest; but a state embedded within society itself, where both elected bodies and armed militia were expressions of mass participatory democracy.

'The Commune constitution', wrote Marx after its suppression,

> would have restored to the social body all the forces hitherto absorbed by the state parasite feeding upon, and clogging up, the free movement of society ... It was essentially a working-class government, the product of the struggle of the producing against the appropriating class, the political form at last discovered under which to work out the political emancipation of labour.

The Commune was not perfect. It did not enfranchise women, though their role in the struggle was paramount from start to finish. Women had led the first demonstration of the revolution on 18 March. And the revolutionary activist Louise Michel's defiant words in court after the defeat of the Commune can be taken as its swansong: 'I will not defend myself. I will not be defended. I belong entirely to the social revolution. If you let me live, I shall not cease to cry vengeance.' Nor were the programme and strategy of the Commune sufficiently bold. Instead of going onto the offensive politically and militarily to carry the Revolution beyond Paris, the Commune allowed the counter-revolution time to recover and assemble its forces.

On 21 May, Thiers' troops broke into the city. For the next week, they fought block by block to recapture it. The fall of the eastern bastions of revolutionary Paris on 28 May was followed by an orgy of killing. Almost 2,000 were shot in the first two days. Many were summarily executed after street 'trials' lasting just 30 seconds, simply because they were poor. Eventually, between 20,000 and 30,000 were killed and a further 40,000 held in prison hulks awaiting trial.

The Paris Commune opened a new chapter in world history. The struggle between capitalist violence and proletarian revolution, between barbarism and socialism, dates from 1871.

12
Imperialism and War
1873–1918

'The Rhodes Colossus – Striding from Cape Town to
Cairo', *Punch*, 10 December 1892. Cecil Rhodes was
a millionaire mine-owner and imperialist.

The Age of Empire saw a scramble for colonies, mounting
international tension, and rising arms expenditure that
eventually exploded into world war.

Between 1800 and 1875, a new kind of industrial capitalism based on mass-production factories dominated world economic development. Competition between capitalists and nation-states in this period began to power a process of exponential growth and globalisation that transformed economies, social structures, and political systems.

Yet nothing ever ran smoothly. Capitalist development was unplanned and contradictory, and as the system expanded, the scale and impact of its periodic crises increased. The global capitalist market, though a creation of human labour, became a monstrous mechanism with a life of its own, apparently beyond human control, yet dominating all human activity. The system proved to be neither self-regulating – as the fantasies of classical economics would have it – nor amenable to human regulation; the logic of competitive capital accumulation imposed itself as an iron law on politicians, bankers, and industrialists. Each great crisis of the system therefore resolved itself into a simple choice between the logic of capital and the needs of humanity; between cut-throat competition and feeding the hungry; between imperialist war and international solidarity.

In this chapter, we analyse the way in which a deeply patholog-ical system gave rise to imperialism, arms spending, and world war between 1875 and 1918; and the degree to which mass movements of resistance were able to challenge the system during this period and pose a revolutionary alternative.

The Long Depression, 1873–96

Between 1848 and 1873 the European economy experienced an economic boom without precedent. Exports of British cotton goods increased in the single decade 1850–60 by the same amount as over the entire preceding three decades. Exports of Belgian iron doubled between 1851 and 1857. Overall, world trade, having barely doubled between 1800 and 1840, increased by more than 250 per cent between 1850 and 1870. Europe had just 23,335 km of rail track in 1850, but 102,000 km by 1870. The tonnage carried in British steamships rose sixteen-fold between 1850 and 1880; that of the rest of the world more than four-fold.

All the indices pointed upwards. After the trade depression and revolutionary ferment of the 1840s, a new epoch of confidence, growth, and endless opportunity seemed to have dawned. Eric

Hobsbawm dubbed 1848–75 'the Age of Capital'. The crash, when it came, was correspondingly shocking. In May 1873, the Vienna Stock Market collapsed, resulting in a series of bank failures as the money supply contracted. The panic quickly spread. In Germany, it was the collapse of the railway empire of Bethel Henry Strousberg that burst the speculative bubble. Over the next four years, shares in German companies lost 60 per cent of their value.

In September 1873, Jay Cooke and Company, a leading American bank with major investments in the railways, also went bankrupt. The failure triggered a panic that brought down 98 banks, 89 rail companies, and 18,000 other businesses. By 1876, one in seven Americans was out of work.

What had happened? The question can be answered at two levels. The immediate issue was that the booming economies of Europe and America were awash with surplus capital, which had then flowed into speculative investments, creating inflated asset values. Politics had played a part in this.

Bismarck's victory in the Franco-Prussian War, the creation of a united German state, and reparations payments from France had stoked a get-rich-quick speculative boom in Germany. The Union victory in the American Civil War and the government-backed capitalism of the Reconstruction era of 1865–77 had had a comparable impact in the United States. In both Europe and the US, political unification and a railway boom contributed to market frenzy.

But there were deeper factors at work, factors that would turn the financial crash into a protracted slump. Capitalism is unplanned. During a boom, capitalists rush to invest in profitable enterprises, but if too many enter the same industry, the result is excess capacity and a wave of bankruptcies when goods and services cannot be sold.

What further destabilises the boom is the limited purchasing power of the working class. Because capitalists aim to minimise wages and maximise profits, workers lack the income to buy all the goods and services their labour produces. Over-production and under-consumption are twin features of every capitalist crisis. Bubbles and crashes in financial markets always occur in the context of a deeper dysfunction of the wider economic system.

Profits and prices plunged after 1873. In a world of many small and medium-sized firms, intensified competition in contracting markets led to drastic cuts in prices and profit margins. The Long Depression of 1873–96 was characterised by deflation rather than inflation. Comparing the years 1850–73 with 1873–90, growth rates fell sharply – from 4.3 per cent a year to 2.9 per cent in Germany, from 6.2 per cent to 4.7 per cent in the US, and from 3.0 per cent to 1.7 per cent in Britain. This meant that the Long Depression, unlike the Great Depression of the 1930s, was relatively slow and shallow. Many firms prospered and many workers enjoyed rising living standards, partly because wages did not fall in line with prices. New industries, such as chemicals and electrics, grew apace. New centres of capital accumulation pulled ahead of old 'workshops of the world'. But agricultural prices remained depressed for a generation and mass unemployment became endemic. World capitalism settled into what the liberal economist John Maynard Keynes would later call 'an underemployment equilibrium'. The system, it turned out, did not always boom. The market was not self-correcting. The 'hidden hand' was as likely to deliver permanent slump as permanent boom.

Engels, surveying the scene in 1886, concluded that the world was 'in the slough of despond of a permanent and chronic depression'. The measure of it was the plight of the unemployed:

> each succeeding winter brings up afresh the great question, 'what to do with the unemployed'; but while the number of the unemployed keeps swelling from year to year, there is nobody to answer that question; and we can almost calculate the moment when the unemployed, losing patience, will take their own fate into their own hands.

How did the bourgeoisie respond to this first great crisis of their system? We can identify three trends. First, there was rapid concentration and centralisation of capital. Small and medium firms went to the wall, markets became dominated by giant corporations, and these organised themselves into trusts or cartels as a way of managing competition to protect prices and profits. The industrial giants relied heavily on government contracts and bank loans, creating a tight nexus between the state, finance capital, and industrial capital. 'Classical capitalism' was giving way to what contemporary Marxist commentators called 'monopoly capitalism', 'state capitalism', or 'finance capitalism' – but it was, in fact, all three at once. The process became most advanced in Germany and the US, the two countries that now pulled ahead of Britain to become the world's leading economic superpowers.

A key feature of the new capitalism was protectionism. Britain alone remained committed to free trade. The average tariff charged on foreign imports by 1914 was 13 per cent in Germany, 18 per cent in Austria-Hungary, 20 per cent in France, 38 per cent in Russia, and 30 per cent in the US (down from a staggering peak of 57 per cent in 1897).

The second trend was colonialism. In pursuit of cheap raw materials, captive markets, and new investment outlets, the great powers turned much of the 'underdeveloped' world into a geopolitical battleground. Colonial rivalries erupted in the Far East, Central Asia, the Middle East, Africa, and the Balkans. In 1876 only 10 per cent of Africa was under European rule. By 1900 more than 90 per cent had been colonised.

Railways were again at the centre of events. With the market glutted in Europe, new railways were constructed across the globe. The 'Berlin to Baghdad' railway, designed to link Germany, Austria-Hungary, the Balkans, and the Ottoman Empire, is a famous example. It was a direct challenge to British and French interests in the increasingly important Middle East.

Protectionism and colonialism were competitive. This accounts for the third consequence of the Long Depression: rising tension between the great powers and increasing arms expenditure. This itself had an economic impact and became part of a reconfigured nexus of power inside the major capitalist states: governments, generals, and arms manufacturers became linked in an early version of what a later age would call 'the military-industrial complex'. British military expenditure, for example, which had remained stable in the 1870s and 1880s, rose dramatically from £32 million in 1887 to £77 million by 1914. Britain's rulers were responding to a European-wide arms race, and in particular to the challenge of a growing German navy. German naval spending rose from 90 million marks in the mid-1890s to 400 million in 1914. To keep ahead of the German fleet, which was expanded from seven battleships to 29, the British fleet was increased from 29 battleships in 1899 to 49 in 1914.

The Long Depression was ended, like the Great Depression, by military expenditure. State arms contracts turned firms like

Armstrong-Whitworth in Britain into giant corporations. The company came to dominate Tyneside, where it eventually employed 40 per cent of all engineering workers. The multiplier effect was huge. Some 1,500 small firms worked as direct subcontractors of Armstrong-Whitworth, while uncounted thousands more supplied the goods and services required by a growing industrial city of 200,000 people.

The Long Depression created a new form of imperial capitalism – and thereby started the countdown to the First World War.

The Scramble for Africa

On 2 September 1898, a British army of 20,000 men confronted a Sudanese army of 50,000 at Omdurman, near Khartoum, at the heart of one of the few remaining independent states in Africa.

Sudan was a merciless country which ranged from scorching desert to disease-infested rainforest. This was the view of the Sudanese themselves: 'When Allah created the Sudan,' they would say, 'he laughed.' Life was hard in such an unforgiving land. Yet the British had come to take it from the people who lived there.

Formed of some 600 tribes, speaking 100 languages, and pursuing perhaps a dozen distinct ways of life, the Sudanese had only recently been welded into a single polity. What caused this to happen in the late nineteenth century, in an exceptionally violent way, was the impact of imperialism.

The Turco-Egyptian conquest of the Sudan had begun in the 1820s and was still in progress 60 years later. The occupation was exploitative and oppressive. Tax collection in the villages was a paramilitary operation, carried out with the assistance of the *kourbash* (a rhinoceros-hide whip). Officials were routinely corrupt, so that bribes and pay-offs were piled on top of taxes. To the harshness and poverty of the landscape, therefore, was added the bitter experience of bullying foreign overlords. But this, between 1881 and 1884, had produced a powerful wave of resistance which swept the foreigners out of Sudan and forged an independent Islamic state.

The resistance took an Islamic form because only religion offered a framework of leadership, activists, organisation, and ideology capable of overriding Sudan's diversity and fragmentation. And because it was forged in a struggle against imperialism, the state was not only Islamic, but also authoritarian and militarised.

Coincidentally, in 1882, the Egyptians had made their own revolution against a British-backed puppet regime in Cairo. But this had been crushed and the British had replaced the Turks as effective rulers of Egypt. Immediate British efforts to reconquer the Sudan had failed, however, leaving the new Islamic state in full control of its territory after 1885. These first efforts at re-conquest had, in fact, been half-hearted: Sudan was an impoverished wilderness, difficult to control, hardly worth having, and the British government had lacked the will to fight for it.

Much changed over the following decade. Until 1876 most of Africa had been an unknown 'dark continent' as far as Europeans were concerned. Their influence was limited largely to trading stations on or close to the coast, many dating from the seventeenth century, reflecting the predominantly mercantile character of European capitalism at the time. The rest of Africa remained a patchwork of polities at many different stages of development. Egypt had been governed for much of the nineteenth century by modernising nationalist regimes. The rest of North Africa was ruled by traditional Islamic potentates owing some sort of allegiance to the Ottoman Empire. Abyssinia (Ethiopia) was a landlocked highland kingdom with an ancient Christian culture. The Ashanti of West Africa and the Zulus of South Africa were militaristic tribal kingdoms. Much of the rest of sub-Saharan Africa was similar to the Sudan: a mosaic of smaller tribal entities. A major exception was South Africa, where the British ruled the Natal and Cape Colony, while the Boers (or Afrikaners) – white farmer-settlers of Dutch origin – controlled the Transvaal and the Orange Free State in the interior.

This African political geography was completely transformed in the generation after 1876 by British, French, Portuguese, Spanish, German, Belgian, and Italian imperialism. During the mid-nineteenth century, the spread of industrial capitalism across much of Europe had created a fast-growing demand for primary products, new markets, and outlets for the investment of surplus capital. The financial crash in 1873 and the global slump that followed had then intensified competition among European capitalists. In consequence, between 1876 and 1914, virtually the whole of Africa was carved into colonies by the European powers, a land grab known, both at the time and since, as 'the Scramble for Africa'.

Africa supplied gold, diamonds, copper, tin, rubber, cotton, palm oil, coffee, cocoa, tea, and much else to the growing industries and cities of Europe. The continent's inhabitants, including increasing numbers of white settlers, provided markets for European manufactures. Colonial infrastructure projects, such as railway construction, made European industrialists and bond-holders rich.

Because of this, and also because geopolitical tension between the great powers was rising, the carve-up of Africa was competitive and contested. This gave it a dynamic independent of the economic value of particular territories. The great powers seized colonies to pre-empt one another. They used them as barriers to block each other's expansion and as platforms for the projection of military power into one another's 'spheres of influence'. They also wanted them as bargaining chips in imperial horse-trading.

The French, who controlled virtually the whole of the Maghreb (Morocco, Algeria, and Tunisia) and West Africa, dreamed of an empire extending across the continent from the Atlantic to the Indian Ocean. The British, by contrast, talked of an empire extending north–south, 'from Cairo to the Cape', linking existing possessions in Egypt, East Africa, and South Africa. But the Germans grabbed Tanzania and got in the way of both.

The cost to the people of Africa was immense. Resistance was crushed by artillery, machine-guns, and massacre. Land was taken at gunpoint to create white-owned estates. Native farmers and herders were forced to become wage-labourers by a combination of dispossession, taxation, press-gangs, and straightforward thuggery.

Sir Frederick Lugard, British High Commissioner for the Protectorate of Northern Nigeria, insisted on 'annihilation' in response to a peasant revolt in 1906. Around 2,000 African villagers armed with hoes and hatchets were mowed down by soldiers using magazine-rifles. Prisoners were decapitated and their heads impaled on spikes. The rebel village was razed to the ground.

The German commander General Lothar von Trotha was, like Lugard, an explicit advocate of 'annihilation' as a way of dealing with bothersome Africans. Tens of thousands of Herero and Nama people died of starvation and thirst when the Germans drove them into the Namibian desert between 1904 and 1907.

In the Belgian Congo, millions died, possibly as many as half the population, due to war, starvation, and disease between 1885 and 1908, as the entire territory was transformed into a vast forced-labour camp. Native workers who failed to meet rubber or ivory collection quotas had their hands cut off.

It was the intensification of the Scramble for Africa between 1885 and 1895 that brought the British back to the Sudan. The example of an independent African-ruled state was regrettable enough. But it was the possibility of French intervention in Britain's backyard that made the matter urgent.

General Herbert Kitchener spent two years advancing down the Nile, building a railway to keep his army supplied as he went. His men were equipped with modern rifles, machine-guns, and artillery. Most of the Sudanese were armed with spears and swords. The Battle of Omdurman was a massacre. Kitchener's army suffered 429 casualties, while the Sudanese lost 10,000 killed, 13,000 wounded, and 5,000 taken prisoner. The British left the Sudanese wounded to die where they lay on the battlefield – or, in some cases, bayoneted them.

Meanwhile, a small French military expedition had arrived at Fashoda on the upper reaches of the Nile in southern Sudan. Kitchener moved upriver to confront them and Britain threatened war if they did not withdraw. The French backed down.

The 'Fashoda Incident' was an expression of the growing imperial tension between the great powers – not just in Africa, but in the Far East, Central Asia, the Middle East, the Balkans, Central Europe, and the North Sea. Capitalism had spawned not only a predatory colonialism of mines, plantations, and machine-guns. It was propelling humanity towards its first modern industrialised world war.

Excursus 6: What is Imperialism?

Between January and June 1916, the exiled leader of the Russian Bolshevik Party, Vladimir Ilyich Lenin, wrote a popular pamphlet entitled *Imperialism, the Highest Stage of Capitalism*. Written for an audience of working-class activists, its purpose was to explain the character of contemporary capitalism and the imperialist war which had begun in 1914.

Lenin made no claim to originality. His aim was to summarise and popularise the work of leading theoreticians of the global system, among them the British Liberal John Hobson in *Imperialism* (1902), the Austrian Marxist Rudolf Hilferding in *Finance Capital* (1910), the Polish-German Marxist Rosa Luxemburg in *The Accumulation of Capital* (1913), and the Russian Marxist Nikolai Bukharin in *Imperialism and World Economy* (1915).

These studies were attempts to understand what Eric Hobsbawm has since defined as 'the Age of Empire' (1875–1914). They amounted to a radical updating of Marx's theory of capitalism. Faced first with the ominous militarisation of Europe, then with its consummation in the First World War, these thinkers developed new theories to explain the extraordinary violence of the system.

The rapid pace of economic growth and the colossal scale of industrial investment had, they concluded, transformed the character of capitalism. In Marx's day, the system had been dominated by small and medium-sized firms competing mainly within national and colonial markets. But as Marx himself had observed in *Capital*, the trend was towards 'concentration and centralisation of capital'.

Capital accumulation is competitive, and because larger corporations can achieve greater economies of scale, they tend to drive smaller rivals out of business. Production becomes concentrated in large factories, with ownership centralised in large corporations. Crisis accelerates these processes: by intensifying competitive pressure, it bankrupts weaker firms and allows the stronger to buy up assets at reduced prices and expand market share. Developing centres of capital accumulation enjoy a particular advantage because they can adopt the latest technologies when they set up new industries.

The Long Depression had this effect. Much of late nineteenth-century capitalism came to be dominated by a few giant firms within each sector. At the same time, economic power shifted from Britain, with its long-established industries, to Germany and the US, whose output had overtaken Britain's by the turn of the century.

Lenin provided a succinct definition of imperialism in terms of five characteristics:

1. The concentration of production and capital has developed to such a stage that it has created monopolies which play a decisive role in economic life.
2. The merging of bank capital with industrial capital, and the creation, on the basis of this 'finance capital', of a financial oligarchy.
3. The export of capital, as distinguished from the export of commodities, acquires exceptional importance.
4. The formation of international monopolist capitalist associations which share the world among themselves.

5. The territorial division of the whole world among the biggest capitalist powers is completed.

Just as Marx had done in his analysis of capitalism in the mid-nineteenth century, Lenin and his contemporaries identified the key trends by focusing on the most advanced parts of the system. Their analysis mapped the path for global capitalism as a whole; but it was Germany and the US that showed the way.

The sheer size of the corporate giants of the early twentieth century was decisive: they were big enough to control the national economy and influence the state. Major firms in each sector formed cartels or trusts, dividing the market between them, and fixing output, prices, and profits.

Just two firms, Siemens and AEG, controlled virtually the whole of the German electrical industry. Two groups, each of three firms, controlled the chemicals industry. One study estimated that some 12,000 leading German firms were organised into 385 cartels by 1905. 'Cartels become one of the foundations of the whole of economic life', observed Lenin. 'Competition becomes transformed into monopoly.'

Because access to credit was a precondition of large-scale investment, finance capital rose in tandem with monopoly capital. The total deposits held by large German banks increased by 40 per cent in the five years between 1907–8 and 1912–13. And finance capital, like industrial capital, was increasingly centralised. By the end of 1913, the nine biggest Berlin banks, together with their affiliates, controlled about 83 per cent of all German bank capital. The biggest of all, the Deutsche Bank, alone controlled 23 per cent.

Industry and banks had become interdependent. 'A steadily increasing proportion of capital in industry', wrote Hilferding, 'ceases to belong to the industrialists who employ it. They obtain the use of it only through the medium of the banks, which, in relation to them, represent the owners of the capital. On the other hand, the bank is forced to sink an increasing share of its funds in industry.' Thus, by means of various forms of credit – extending loans and purchasing stocks and bonds – the banks became the owners and organisers of industry. 'Finance capital', concluded Hilferding, 'is capital controlled by banks and employed by industrialists.'

The power of the industrial cartels and banking syndicates transformed the role of the state. Only in Britain – and only prior to the First World War – did the state play almost no direct role in capital accumulation. In Germany, by contrast, the only corporate body whose capitalisation could match that of the private Deutsche Bank was the publicly owned Prussian State Railway Administration.

Railway investment – itself a strategic necessity – combined with arms expenditure to make the state the single biggest customer for the output of heavy industry. German government spending on the army and navy increased ten-fold between 1870 and 1914. State arms contracts were almost entirely responsible for the four-fold expansion of the Krupp works at Essen in the 40 years before the First World War. As well as direct investment and state contracts, the government also provided protection against foreign competition by imposing tariffs on foreign imports – a 'beggar thy neighbour' policy initiated by Germany in 1879 and followed by all the great powers except Britain.

By the early twentieth century, the development of world capitalism had become highly contradictory. On the one hand, there was globalisation: rapid economic growth, the dominance of giant firms, a restless search for new markets, and ever-expanding international trade. On the other, there was economic nationalism, as industrial cartels, banking syndicates, and military states fused into opposing national-capitalist blocs.

It was Germany, the most dynamic of these blocs, that experienced the contradiction in its most acute form. As the mass of German capital seeking markets continued to expand, it pushed beyond the limits of the existing national territory. But it then ran into barriers: protective tariffs, closed colonial markets, and competition from foreign capitalists. Here was the deepest root of the First World War. Finance capitalism – the growth of giant monopolies and the fusing of industrial, bank, and state capital – had created a dangerous world of competing nationalisms.

'When competition has finally reached its highest stage,' explained Bukharin,

> when it has become competition between state capitalist trusts, then the use of state power, and the possibilities connected with it, begin to play a very large part ... The more strained the situation in the world sphere of struggle – and our epoch is characterised by the greatest intensity of competition between 'national' groups of finance capital – the oftener an appeal is made to the mailed fist of state power.

The 1905 Revolution: Russia's Great Dress Rehearsal

On 9 January 1905 a huge demonstration of perhaps 200,000 converged on the Winter Palace of the Russian Tsar in St Petersburg. Led by a priest, the workers came wearing their Sunday best, with their families in tow, singing hymns, and carrying portraits of the Tsar. They had come to petition their 'Little Father' for redress of grievances.

A black throng standing in the snow in front of the palace. Suddenly, a charge of Cossacks, hacking at men, women, and children. Then, rolling volleys from Guardsmen as terrified people flee through the surrounding streets. Probably more than a thousand died: Bloody Sunday. The following day, 125,000 St Petersburg workers went on strike in protest at the massacre. The Russian Revolution of 1905 had begun.

From that moment it ebbed and flowed, a gigantic movement of mass strikes and demonstrations, of peasant insurrections and military mutinies. The revolution climaxed that autumn, following catastrophic defeats in the Far East, where the Tsarist state was fighting an imperialist war against Japan for control of Korea and Manchuria. For 50 days, from mid-October to early December, the capital was virtually ruled by the St Petersburg Soviet of Workers' Deputies, a democratic mass assembly representing some 200,000 workers. The police state was hammered by a mass strike in St Petersburg in October, another in November, and then armed insurrection in Moscow in early December.

But the movement could not break through, and the workers eventually fell back exhausted. The regime counterattacked: 3,500 people were killed in anti-semitic pogroms organised by the secret police and carried out by state-backed paramilitaries known as Black Hundreds; the St Petersburg Soviet was suppressed and its leaders arrested; the working-class suburbs of Moscow were shelled and prisoners shot in cold blood.

Thereafter, much diminished and widely scattered, little groups of revolutionary exiles debated what had gone wrong. The one who grasped it best – the inner dynamic of Russia's revolutionary turbulence – was the man who more than any other embodied its living spirit: the 25-year-old Jewish intellectual Leon Trotsky, the effective leader of the short-lived St Petersburg Soviet.

Trotsky's 'theory of permanent revolution' – subsequently proved correct by the events of 1917 – solved the century-old riddle of Russian history: what form must the revolution take in order to be victorious?

Throughout the nineteenth century, Russia's radical intellectuals had fought Tsarism, the dictatorship of a medieval autocrat, almost entirely alone, endlessly discussing their predicament, forever seeking, yet failing to find, a way to reach the masses. The intellectuals set themselves up as 'the Voice of the People' – yet their voice remained a disembodied echo.

The vision of most revolutionaries – the Narodniks – was of a peasant revolution to overthrow the Tsar, the landlords, and the priests, and of a post-revolutionary utopia based on villages, free farms, and local production. Some Narodniks 'went to the people', travelling into the countryside and agitating in the villages for revolution. Others believed in 'the propaganda of the deed', hoping to jump-start the revolution with acts of terrorism like high-profile assassinations. The Narodniks, in short, attempted to bring down Tsarism with a proclamation and a bomb. All they achieved was a police state that destroyed them. The peasant masses they wished to rouse remained in political slumber.

Peasant life was shaped by agricultural routine and social isolation. The limit of a peasant's ambition was to free his land of burdens and become a prosperous independent farmer. The Russian peasants were, as Marx had once described those of France, 'a sack of potatoes': not a collective *per se*, but a mass of individuals bound together as a class by the actuality or hope of petty-proprietorship.

Peasant revolt was a necessary condition of successful revolution. Without it, the army, formed overwhelmingly of peasant conscripts, would remain loyal and shoot down the revolutionaries. But it was not a sufficient condition, for the peasants, an amalgam of dispersed petty-proprietors, could not create their own revolutionary movement and party. They had to be led from the outside – from the towns. But which urban class would provide leadership? The intellectuals lacked social weight. It had to be the bourgeoisie or the proletariat.

Almost all Social Democrats (as socialists were known in Russia at the time) believed that Russia's backwardness meant that only a bourgeois revolution was possible. They rejected as utopian fantasy the Narodnik idea that the existing peasant village could simply be transformed into an agricultural commune. The Mensheviks (the 'minority', since they had been such when the Russian Social Democrats split at a conference in London in 1903) argued that the liberal bourgeoisie would spearhead the struggle and that it was therefore the job of Social Democrats to support them, while avoiding any 'excesses' or 'extremism' that might fracture the class alliance. The Bolsheviks (the 'majority') insisted that the Russian bourgeoisie was too small and weak, too dependent on Tsarism and foreign capital, and, as a class of big property-owners, too terrified by the prospect of revolutionary upheaval to provide the necessary leadership. Consequently, the revolution, albeit necessarily 'bourgeois' in its immediate historical outcome, would have to be led by the proletariat in alliance with the peasantry.

Lenin, the leader of the Bolsheviks, was proved right about the timidity of the bourgeoisie. In 1905, at the first crack of rifle fire, the liberals had run for cover. The workers had been left to fight alone.

But Trotsky saw deeper into the events of 1905: only the proletariat had the potential to lead the revolution; only mass strikes and insurrectionary demonstrations in the cities could detonate peasant revolt; and only then would the army mutiny and the state disintegrate. But then, to complete and consolidate the victory of democracy – to prevent the forces of reaction regrouping to crush the revolution – the proletariat would have to establish a workers' state.

And any such state, being class based, could not be other than an organ of proletarian interests – supporting workers' control of the factories, peasant seizures of land, and the dispossession of the rich. Anything less, argued Trotsky, would compromise the victory, leaving property and power in the hands of class enemies, and the workers and peasants on whom the revolution depended demoralised.

Thus, against Lenin's formulation of 'the democratic dictatorship of the proletariat and the peasantry' to carry through a 'bourgeois revolution', Trotsky counterposed 'the dictatorship of the proletariat' and a 'permanent revolution' in which the democratisation of Russia would unleash a struggle for world socialist revolution.

Trotsky's was an extraordinary vision. Russia was the most backward of the major European states. Towns were few and communications poor over the vast expanses of the Russian landmass. Most of the 150 million people were peasants, and most of these were impoverished by poor soils, harsh climate, and primitive techniques. Around 25 million were wage-labourers and their families, but most of these lived in the villages. The true urban proletariat comprised about 3.5 million workers employed in factories and mines. Only about two million of these were employed in plants large enough to qualify for government inspection.

But this small proletariat was highly concentrated and strategically located at the heart of Tsarist economic and political power. Rapid, state-sponsored industrialisation had forged this class in the space of a generation. In an age of railways, howitzers, and machine-guns, Russia needed coalmines, steelworks, and engineering plants to produce them if it was to remain a great power. This geopolitical imperative had triggered state action to create modern industry.

Government investment, funded by high taxes and foreign loans, and sheltered by protective tariffs, had sustained a record-breaking annual growth rate of 8 per cent a year. And the new industries were of the most advanced kind. Giant enterprises of 1,000 or more employed only 18 per cent of workers in the United States but no less than 41 per cent in Russia. Two-thirds of the Russian proletariat, moreover, were concentrated in just three regions: St Petersburg, Moscow, and the Ukraine.

Tsarism had created its own gravediggers. In 1905 the workers had failed to bury the beast; 1917 would be different.

The Ottoman Empire and the 1908 'Young Turk' Revolution

Revolutions are infectious. Russia's 1905 revolution was no exception. It set off a wave of revolutions, notably in Persia (1906), Turkey (1908), Mexico (1910), and China (1911). That in Turkey began a process that would transform the Middle East over the next two decades.

In 1908 the region was dominated by the Ottoman Empire, which ruled Turkey, Syria, Iraq, and western Arabia. This was the traditional empire founded by a Turkish-speaking warlord in the fourteenth century and built into a Eurasian colossus by great campaigns of conquest in the late fifteenth and early sixteenth century, when Ottoman armies had surged across the Balkans and into Central Europe as far as the gates of Vienna; across the East to the Caspian and the Persian Gulf; down both sides of the Red Sea, which became an Ottoman lake; and along almost the whole extent of North Africa, with Egypt, Libya, Tunisia, and Algeria all becoming Ottoman provinces.

The empire was ruled by an absolutist sultan and an apparatus of soldiers and officials. Ottoman civil society – landlords and peasants in the countryside, merchants and artisans in the towns – was divided for administrative purposes into separate ethno-religious 'millets' controlled by conservative community leaders. The main domestic preoccupations of the Ottoman state were maintaining internal order and collecting taxes. Civil society existed for the benefit of the imperial state. Economics served politics. The free development of economic and social forces was blocked by military-bureaucratic, feudal, and tribal elites determined to defend traditional power and privilege. Because of this, during the eighteenth century, geopolitical power had shifted from a stagnant Ottoman Empire to more dynamic European rivals.

As the central power waned, the inherent weakness of the empire – its lack of both geographical and national coherence – was exposed. In the early nineteenth century, Egypt became effectively independent under local satraps, and Greece won its freedom through armed insurrection. The Ottoman Empire became 'the Sick Man of Europe'. But despite the mounting threat of fragmentation, the Ottoman ruling class resisted reform and modernisation. Successive attempts to engineer a 'bourgeois revolution from above' ran into the buffers.

What saved the Ottomans during the nineteenth century was the rivalry of the great powers and a flow of foreign loans and investments. Britain and France supported the Turks in the Crimean War (1853–6) as a bulwark against Russian southward expansion. Thereafter British and French bankers made loans to fund railways and armaments. Late nineteenth-century modernisation therefore turned the Ottoman Empire into a semi-colonial dependency. The regime of Sultan Abdulhamid II (1876–1909) spent 60 per cent of state revenue on the army and administration and 30 per cent on interest payments to foreign bankers.

In 1905–7, inspired by the Russian example, the Armenian subject-people of eastern Turkey rose in revolt against new taxes and military conscription. The Ottoman regime was unable to suppress the revolt. The taxes were cancelled and an amnesty granted. But before this had happened, the revolt had spread to other parts of the empire.

An underground opposition network, the Committee of Union and Progress (CUP), had formed among junior army officers serving in the Balkans. The heart of this 'Young Turk' movement was Ottoman-ruled Salonika (now Thessaloniki in Greece). The CUP was a party of middle-class nationalists angered by the weakness and corruption of the Abdulhamid regime. It was committed to a liberal constitution and the reform and modernisation necessary to achieve great-power status.

On 3 July 1908 a maverick army major took unilateral action by issuing a revolutionary manifesto. Bounced into action, on 23 July the CUP leader Enver Pasha proclaimed that the Ottoman constitution – which had been granted in December 1876 only to be annulled three months later – was restored. The revolt immediately became general across the Ottoman armies in the Balkans. The day after Enver's proclamation, Sultan Abdulhamid announced parliamentary elections. With its army in revolt, the dictatorship had capitulated.

Was this a military coup or a popular revolution? It was both. The revolution was led by army officers. The military discipline of the regime's army had operated in reverse: the rank and file did not mutiny; they simply obeyed their officers' orders to act against the government. But the rank and file were deeply discontented because of unpaid wages and endemic corruption. And the revolution sparked a wave of strikes, with 111 recorded between August and December 1908, resulting in average wage increases of 15 per cent. The revolution also spread across the countryside, where it had begun as a peasant revolt against taxation and conscription. The Armenians had started it, but Turks and Arabs soon joined in.

So this was a popular revolution led by middle-class army officers. Why did the Young Turk Revolution take this distinctive form?

Industry was underdeveloped and dependent on foreign capital. Therefore, both the bourgeoisie and the proletariat were exceptionally weak. Outside the large towns, Ottoman society was geographically dispersed, socially fragmented, and culturally diverse. The state-service middle class, centred on army officers, was the only social group with the cohesion, organisation, and vision to lead a revolution. The Ottoman Empire was a military state, so the Ottoman Revolution acquired military leadership. A traditional empire in decline, threatened by the forces of modernity, thus conjured a distinctive form of bourgeois revolution: a hybrid of the French (from below) and the Prussian (from above).

The dictatorship had collapsed, but the dictator remained in office. The CUP stood at the head of a revolution, but was excluded from state power. Between July 1908 and April 1909, the Ottoman Empire was governed by an unstable dual power, with the palace and the barracks involved in an extended tussle over political authority.

In mid-April 1909 the crisis broke. Islamist conservatives, with the tacit support of the Sultan, mounted mass demonstrations against the new reform government in Istanbul, and paramilitaries loyal to the regime massacred 17,000 Armenians in the Adana district. The CUP now moved to crush what was, in effect, an attempted counter-revolution. On 22 April troops from the Balkans entered Istanbul and restored the constitution. A week later they occupied the Yildiz Palace and forced Abdulhamid to resign.

This second revolution put effective state power in the hands of the CUP leadership. But the accumulated contradictions of the Ottoman Empire proved insoluble for the new regime. The years 1909–14 were to be a period of continuing political crisis.

The revolution had unleashed powerful forces. The proletarian and peasant uprising in Turkey itself had to be contained if the CUP was to construct a modern capitalist nation-state. And the national aspirations of the subject-peoples of the wider empire – Serbs, Greeks, Bulgars, Armenians, Arabs – had to be suppressed.

The revolution was to be transformed by war. Turkey was embroiled in a succession of wars between 1911 and 1923 whose effect was to destroy the old Ottoman Empire and create a new Turkish Republic. The Ottomans lost control of Libya in 1912 and Macedonia in 1913. The embattled CUP leaders became increasingly authoritarian and heavily dependent on foreign loans and expertise to build railways and modernise the armed forces. In January 1913 the constitutional government was overthrown in a military coup and replaced by a dictatorship of three top CUP leaders. Growing dependence on German capital and German military advisers led, in early August 1914, to a secret military alliance with Berlin.

The CUP leaders were now proclaiming pan-Turkish national-ism. This was a threat both to subject-peoples inside the empire, about half of whom were not Turks, and to Russia's interests in Central Asia, where many Turks lived under Tsarist rule. Intensified oppression of national minorities became linked with warmongering in the Caucasus and the transformation of the Ottoman Empire into an outpost of German imperialism.

The Young Turk Revolution of 1908–9 was carried out by a middle-class leadership with bourgeois-nationalist aims. The popular revolution of workers, peasants, soldiers, and national minorities was suppressed. For this, the people of the former Ottoman Empire would pay a terrible price as their leaders led them into the inferno of a modern industrialised world war.

Emiliano Zapata and the Mexican Revolution

The distance from Mexico City to Cuernavaca, the state capital of Morelos, is less than 40 miles. But to make the journey in 1914 was to pass from one social universe to another. Mexico City was controlled by a liberal bourgeoisie of landowners, businessmen, and politicians. Cuernavaca was controlled by the Zapatistas.

All the men in Cuernavaca were wearing the white pyjamas, sombreros, and sandals of Mexico's working people. They all looked alike. It was impossible to tell who were *jefes* (chiefs) and who followers. Everyone spoke the plain language of the *pueblo* (village). Virtually all were of pure-blooded Indian descent. Few could read or write.

The town, in short, was controlled by revolutionary *campesinos* (peasant-farmers). The rich had fled. The leader of the *campesinos* was a small farmer turned guerrilla commander called Emiliano Zapata.

Zapata personified the revolution of the Mexican *campesinos*. He never entirely transcended the naivety and parochialism of the *pueblo*. He hated the city and distrusted men in suits and shoes. 'They're all a bunch of bastards', he said of the self-serving politicians of Mexico's governing elite. So he shunned Mexico City, national politics, and attempts to suborn him with offers of high office.

Personally incorruptible, he remained loyal through a decade of revolution to the cause of the *campesinos*. In return, the poor of southern Mexico idolised him. When an old woman in an isolated village was asked what she thought of him, she answered, 'us poor mountain Indians go along hanging on tight to the tail of chief Zapata's horse'.

The touchstone of Zapata's politics and the agrarian revolution he led was the Plan of Ayala. Clause 6 demanded the restoration of the fields, timber, and water which had been taken from the *pueblos* by the rich, Clause 7 that one-third of all large estates be seized and redistributed to the landless, and Clause 8 that the entire property of counter-revolutionaries be nationalised and two-thirds of the proceeds be used to pay war pensions and indemnities to the poor.

The Plan of Ayala was a response to betrayal – the betrayal of the revolutionary hope which had persuaded poor men to join an armed struggle against the dictatorship of Porfirio Diaz in 1910.

When the Revolution began, Mexico was dominated by a landowning elite of Spanish colonial descent. Politics was a matter of self-serving cliques, and elections were decided by backroom deals and ballot rigging. Whatever happened, the owners of the *haciendas* (big estates) continued to rule.

This did not mean nothing changed in Mexico; it simply meant change always benefitted the same people. Things were in fact changing. Global demand for Mexico's primary exports was rising, especially from the mid-1890s, and *hacienda*-owners were cashing in, expanding their estates, digging irrigation works, and installing new milling machines.

Standing in the way of profit was the *pueblo*. But the *hacienda*-owners had money, and the state was corrupt. They could easily get their way by hiring their own gangsters and by bribing local police and magistrates. The villagers would go to town to defend their ancient claims, and the courts would spew them back as garbage.

This was the Mexico of the Diaz dictatorship. But the regime – that of a self-interested faction grouped around an ageing autocrat – was too exclusive and unbending. When Francisco Madero, a liberal politician, challenged the Diaz dictatorship in 1910, he garnered widespread middle-class support. More importantly, when Diaz resisted, the villages exploded.

Once in power, however, Madero asked the guerrillas to disarm. He then reneged on his promises of land reform. When the *campesinos* protested, the countryside was flooded with armed police and federal soldiers. The class war in the Mexican countryside quickly resumed.

The central contradiction in Mexican society was that between *hacienda* and *pueblo*, between Spanish landowner and Indian peasant, between the few who were rich and the many who were not. The difference between conservative supporters of Diaz and liberal supporters of Madero was secondary.

Conservatives generally in Latin America backed dictators, were close to the army and the Church, and drew their support mainly from more traditional sections of the ruling class like the older landowning families. Liberals favoured parliamentary government, wanted greater independence from foreign influence (especially that of the US), and drew support from business interests and the middle class.

But conservatives and liberals had far more in common than divided them: they were two wings of a single property-owning elite of Spanish descent. That is why the liberals turned on the *campesinos* as soon as they had got rid of Diaz.

The principal *jefe* in the north was the former social bandit Pancho Villa. A social bandit is an outlaw who preys on the rich and enjoys the support of the common people from whom he has sprung. In periods of crisis, social banditry can swell into an agrarian revolutionary movement, transforming a figure like Pancho Villa into a national leader.

But Villa was politically unsophisticated and somewhat opportunist. Though he never broke with the *campesinos* of northern Mexico, neither did he provide clear and consistent revolutionary leadership.

Zapata quickly became the principal *jefe* in the south. A small farmer himself, he was more firmly rooted in the *pueblos* than Villa, and his politics were a more faithful reflection of the aspirations of the rural poor for land, water, and security.

The resistance of Villa, Zapata, and other popular chiefs paralysed the state apparatus across much of rural Mexico, leaving its police and troops holed up in the major towns, with the surrounding countryside in rebel hands.

History then repeated itself on a higher level. Madero was murdered by one of his own generals, Victoriano Huerta, but another liberal politician, Venustiano Carranza, quickly formed a 'Constitutionalist' army to renew the alliance with the peasantry and resume the struggle against dictatorship.

The peasant armies of Villa and Zapata entered Mexico City in 1914. But instead of taking state power, they handed control back to the liberal bourgeoisie.

Zapata's embodiment of the agrarian-social revolution of the Mexican *pueblos* was too absolute: it included the perennial parochialism of the peasantry. He hated the rich and the liberals. He grew wise from long experience of lies and betrayals. The Plan of Ayala exudes bitterness. It denounces Madero for his attempt 'with the brute force of bayonets to shut up and to drown in blood the *pueblos* that ask, solicit, or demand from him the fulfilment of the promises of the revolution'.

Yet, in November 1914, at the moment of his greatest power, Zapata handed state authority to Caranza's Constitutionalists, the liberal successors of Madero. Zapata was content to retire to Morelos and act as guardian of its local agrarian revolution.

Unable to imagine, let alone work to achieve, a democratic state of workers and peasants, Zapata allowed the space he and his followers had prised open at the top of Mexican society to be reoccupied by the class enemies of the *pueblo*. Sooner or later, when preparations were complete and the moment judged right, these enemies would counterattack to eradicate the dangerous example of Zapatismo: revolution from below by the common people of the countryside.

It took them six years. They campaigned in the north in alliance with US troops from across the border, and they soon had Villa on the run. Though guerrilla resistance continued, the northern revolutionary movement never really recovered. Villa was eventually murdered in July 1923.

The resistance in the south was more entrenched. But by the end, such was the devastation and depopulation that the Zapatista revolution was reduced to little more than dwindling guerrilla bands.

Even then, the old 'band of brothers' of southern revolutionary chiefs formed in 1910 held together. Some accepted amnesty, but none turned on their former comrades still in the field. And the common people, spurning rewards and threats, continued to give support to the fugitive rebels.

Zapata himself was tricked, walked into a trap, and was gunned down in April 1919. 'Zapata having disappeared, Zapatismo has died', proclaimed the government commander in Morelos. 'Zapata was simply a gangster.'

It was not quite so simple. The Zapatista chiefs formed an alliance with Alvaro Obregon and again entered Mexico City as part of a victorious army in 1920. Carranza was overthrown and assassinated.

This time, determined to retain power, the liberals left the *pueblos* of Morelos alone. It was enough that Zapata was dead and Mexico as a whole had been made safe for capitalism.

To win, a revolution must advance, drawing ever more of the masses into the struggle, seizing state power when this becomes possible, then using this as a lever to extend the gains of the revolution and spread it internationally. To stop, on the other hand, let alone to retreat, is to allow one's class enemies the opportunity to regroup, gather strength, and prepare a counterattack.

The extraordinary resilience of the Zapatistas through ten years of revolution resulted in lasting gains for the people of the *pueblos*. But their parochialism – their belief that it was enough to make revolution in their own villages – doomed their wider vision of a world transformed.

1914: Descent into Barbarism

On 28 June 1914, Gavrilo Princip, a Serbian nationalist student, assassinated Archduke Franz Ferdinand, the heir to the Austro-Hungarian throne, during a state visit to Sarajevo in Bosnia. Five weeks later, Austria, Russia, Germany, France, and Britain were all at war. Fifteen million would die during the four years of industrialised carnage that followed. What had happened?

Great events have multiple causes. More precisely, immediate events trigger a series of contradictions which are related to one another rather like a set of Russian dolls – the military encompassed by the diplomatic, the diplomatic by the geopolitical, the geopolitical by the economic. That is why historian A. J. P. Taylor could claim that world war broke out in July–August 1914 because of the railway timetables. He was referring to the fact that the belligerent powers believed that the war would be fast and short, such that the speed with which armies could be mobilised and deployed by rail would determine the outcome; therefore, once one country started to mobilise, the others had to follow suit.

But this was only the most immediate – and least important – register in which the crisis played out. A common mistake among mainstream historians when dealing with complex events is to get stuck in one register. The quip about railway timetables reflects the fact that big wars can be triggered by small things. But big wars always have big causes. The 'cock-up theory of history' explains relatively little. The First World War was an imperialist war decades in the making. Let us drill down to the underlying causes.

Though tension was high in Europe, the assassination at Sarajevo did not at first cause general alarm: it appeared to be an internal Austro-Hungarian matter. Austria-Hungary was a ramshackle dynastic empire in the heart of Europe ruled by the German-speaking Habsburgs. The Austrian and Hungarian ruling classes ran the empire in tandem, the ageing Habsburg autocrat Franz Josef serving as both Emperor of Austria and King of Hungary (an arrangement known as 'the Dual Monarchy'). But almost half the population was neither Austrian nor Hungarian, instead belonging to one or another of nine minority national groups.

The Habsburg regime was threatened by the militancy of a growing working class and by mounting nationalist agitation among its subject-peoples. It responded with an uneasy mix of repression and reform. By 1914 constitutional government had broken down and hawks like top general Conrad von Hötzendorf had taken control. 'Only an aggressive policy ... can save this state from destruction', he argued. The opposition was to be cowed and the authority of the state reasserted by decisive military action.

The chosen target was Serbia, an independent Balkan state that acted as a beacon of resistance for Serbians living under Austrian rule. Hötzendorf pressed for war against Serbia – 'this viper' – 25 times in the highest councils of state between 1906 and 1914. The assassination at Sarajevo was the Habsburg hawks' supreme opportunity.

On 23 July the Austrian government sent an ultimatum to Serbia, accusing the Serbs of complicity in Franz Ferdinand's assassination and threatening war if they did not cooperate fully in its investigation and the suppression of anti-Austrian agitation on their territory. Dissatisfied with the Serbian response, on 28 July the Austrians ordered mobilisation for war and opened fire on Belgrade (on the opposite side of the Danube). These were the first shots of the First World War.

Serbia was an ally of Russia. The Russians and Austrians were geopolitical rivals in the Balkans. Russia was also on the brink of revolution. Barricades had gone up in the Vyborg district of St

Petersburg and the workers were fighting street battles with Tsarist troops.

On 30 July the Tsar ordered his army to mobilise. The hawks were in control in St Petersburg just as they were in Vienna. Hard-line ministers and generals argued that war was necessary to defend Russian interests in the Balkans – and that it would engender an upsurge of nationalism and cauterise the revolutionary mood.

But Russian mobilisation constituted a mortal threat to Germany. National unification and rapid industrialisation had turned Germany into the greatest power in Europe. Nervous rivals had coalesced into a hostile alliance: the Triple Entente of Russia, France, and Britain. Germany had been left with only one major ally, Austria-Hungary, and therefore faced the daunting prospect of a war on two fronts against superior forces.

Germany's war plan was a carefully crafted response to this peril. The Schlieffen Plan (named after the Chief of Staff who devised it) envisaged a six-week lightning war to knock out France in the west before shifting the bulk of German forces east to face the 'Russian steamroller'. Timing was everything. When the Russians ordered mobilisation on 30 July, the clock of the Schlieffen Plan started ticking. Consequently, the German government declared war on Russia on 1 August and on France on 3 August.

The British hesitated only momentarily. They feared German domination of Europe and a direct threat to the security of the British Empire. The crisis now revealed its primary fault-line: the imperialist competition between Germany and Britain.

In the mid-nineteenth century, Britain, the original 'workshop of the world', had been the only industrial superpower, producing 50 per cent of the world's cotton, 60 per cent of its coal, and 70 per cent of its steel. By 1914 Britain's shares in these industries had fallen to 20 per cent for cotton, 20 per cent for coal, and just 10 per cent for steel. Both Germany and the US had overtaken Britain as industrial powers. Britain still had the largest empire. It peaked in the early twentieth century when Britain held authority over one-fifth of the world's landmass and a quarter of its people. But the industrial power needed to sustain global hegemony was waning.

At the same time, imperialist tensions were rising. National economies were increasingly dominated by a mere handful of giant monopoly firms in each sector. These firms were engaged in a relentless search for raw materials and new markets, bringing them into conflict with foreign rivals on a global scale. Traditional geo-political conflict between nation-states thus fused with economic competition between blocs of capital. The great powers engaged in an arms race powered by their imperialist rivalry.

On the eve of war, therefore, Europe was a continent of conscript armies of unprecedented size. Industrialised supplies of food, clothing, arms, equipment, and munitions meant that some six million men of Europe's active field armies would immediately march to war, with some 13 million reserves mustering to their rear.

Between 1906 and 1912 the Germans had pursued *Weltpolitik* (world policy). It was an assertion of rising German imperialism in opposition to the established empires of the British and the French. Its primary expression was a naval arms race with Britain. German *Weltpolitik* challenged two principles of British statesmanship: the need to maintain a balance of power on the Continent; and the need to prevent the Channel ports falling into the hands of a hostile power. Both principles were rooted in Britain's island position, commercial interests, and traditional maritime supremacy.

Britain and its shipping lanes were well protected by a large navy. A divided Europe left the British ruling class free to exploit its empire and profit from overseas trade. A Europe united under the hegemony of a single power, especially one in control of the Channel ports, was a threat. Herein lay the significance of the naval arms race. To maintain its lead over Germany, Britain had increased its fleet from 29 battleships in 1899 to 49 in 1914. It had also come out of 'splendid isolation' and formed an alliance with the French and the Russians.

This had imposed an unsustainable military burden on Germany. The French and Russian armies had been growing at the same time as the British fleet. Germany was a continental power with enemies on two sides. It had therefore been forced to abandon the naval arms race and focus its main effort on army expansion. Germany could not simultaneously defend itself in Europe and challenge Britain at sea.

By late 1912 Germany's leaders were convinced they were losing the European arms race and that the balance of forces was tipping against them. They came to favour a pre-emptive war sooner rather than later. The leader of the German Army, Helmuth von Moltke, argued that 'a war of nations' was unavoidable.

The First World War, then, was caused by military competition between opposing alliances of nation-states. And these nation-states represented the interests of rival blocs of imperialist capital.

The concentration and centralisation of capital – a long-term process which had accelerated rapidly after the mid-1870s – had created a world of global corporate rivals. The spread of industrialisation had also created major new centres of capitalist industry. Traditional conflicts between the great powers of Europe had thus been reconfigured and re-energised by competitive capital accumulation. These were the deeper contradictions reflected in the arms races, alliances, and war plans which marked the countdown to war. These were the underlying tensions triggered by the July–August crisis.

But industrialised imperialism had not only given rise to conflicts that plunged Europe into war. It had also created means of destruction on a scale that would make the war the most terrible in history. In 1914 capitalism tipped humanity into barbarism.

This had been anticipated by many on the Left. What none had been prepared for was the active connivance in the warmongering of the leaders of the various European socialist parties.

Reform or Revolution?

On 4 August 1914 the German Social Democratic Party (SPD), the largest socialist party in Europe, voted unanimously for war credits in the Reichstag (the German Parliament). The SPD thereby gave its support to an imperialist war in which 15 million would die. The decision stunned the European Left. It was 'the greatest tragedy of our lives' in the view of the Russian revolutionary Nikolai Bukharin. 'The capitulation of German Social Democracy', said Trotsky, 'shocked me even more than the declaration of war.' Lenin at first assumed that the newspaper in which he read the news was a forgery.

The German working-class movement was shattered. 'Everything seemed to collapse', wrote one young SPD activist, Toni Sender. She found herself on a freight train crowded with troops on the way to the front. Most were married men, grim-faced, with little enthusiasm for what was to come. Just days before, on 28 July, there had been 100,000 anti-war demonstrators on the streets of Berlin. Across Germany, during four days of mass protest in the final days of peace, there had been no fewer than 288 anti-war demonstrations involving up to three-quarters of a million people. This mass movement had been building since 1911. The SPD stood at its head. On 4 August the party vote killed the movement stone-dead and delivered the German working class into the hands of the *junker* officer caste and its war-machine.

On the evening of 4 August a handful of revolutionaries met in Rosa Luxemburg's Berlin flat. They issued an anti-imperialist statement and invited some 300 other leading socialists to sign. Clara Zetkin was the only one to cable immediate support. The German anti-war socialists had suddenly become a tiny minority.

The German pattern was replicated across Europe: socialist parties abandoned internationalism to support their own national governments in an imperialist world war. The Second International (a world federation of socialist parties) was exposed as a sham. Instead of upholding the internationalism implicit in proletarian solidarity, it disintegrated as soon as the war drums of national chauvinism were sounded.

Europe in 1914 was pregnant with two possibilities: socialist revolution or imperialist war. Had the leaders of European socialism, standing at the head of tens of millions of organised and militant workers, opted for the first, the carnage of the First World War might never have happened. What had gone wrong? Why had all the speeches and resolutions proclaiming international solidarity and opposition to war proved to be no more than hot air? Why, indeed, have socialist leaders, again and again over the last century, betrayed the interests of their working-class supporters and accommodated to the dictates of capitalism?

The explosive growth of European capitalism from the 1870s onwards had created an industrial proletariat of tens of millions by 1914. Mass strikes had welded this working class into a combative labour movement across much of Europe. This in turn had created a mass electoral base for parties like the SPD. By 1912, with a million members and 90 daily papers, the German SPD was the biggest working-class organisation in the world. It ran a women's section, a youth section, various trade unions and co-ops, and numerous sports clubs and cultural societies.

In that year the SPD made a dramatic electoral breakthrough, winning one in three votes and, with 110 seats, becoming the largest party in the Reichstag. But its transformation from a small outlawed minority to a mass electoral machine had also transformed the party's social and political character.

This was reflected in the rise of revisionism – or what would later be called reformism. Its leading advocate was Eduard Bernstein (1850–1932). He argued that capitalism was becoming less crisis-prone, prosperity was steadily increasing, and so, from now on, the condition of the working class could best be improved by gradual reform. Bernstein sought to redefine the SPD as a party of social-democratic reform as opposed to a party of social revolution.

Bernstein never dominated the SPD, but he pulled it sharply to the right. Karl Kautsky (1854–1938) was more representative of the majority. He was a centrist rather than a revisionist. He continued to believe that capitalism was exploitative and violent, and that socialism was rational and necessary. But he also took the view that the system was so riddled with contradictions that it would eventually collapse of its own accord, without the revolutionary action of the working class. Kautsky was therefore revolutionary in theory but reformist in practice. This enabled him to bridge the gap between the out-and-out reformism of Bernstein and the politics of revolutionary socialists like Rosa Luxemburg. All three tendencies, however, remained within the SPD rather than forming separate parties.

Reformism reflects both the limited consciousness of a class – the working class – and the actual material interests of a social group – the labour bureaucracy. Most workers under capitalism have 'mixed consciousness'. This arises from the interaction of three factors. First, because the system is based on exploitation, oppression, and violence, it engenders resentment and resistance in its victims. The class struggle is endemic to capitalism. On the other hand, the dominant ideas of society are those of the ruling class, and most workers accept at least some of these ideas for much of the time. What strengthens these ideas is a third factor: the fact that workers often lack the confidence to fight because the balance of class forces seems unfavourable.

Lenin distinguished between 'trade union consciousness' and 'revolutionary consciousness'. The former is the attitude of most workers most of the time; they do not like aspects of the system and will sometimes fight for specific reforms, but they are not committed to an all-out struggle to overthrow it. Reformism is the political form of trade union consciousness. It expresses the limited aspirations of workers for political change within the system. It does not reflect the interests of workers as a class. These lie in the overthrow of capitalism and its replacement by a system based on democracy, collective ownership, and human need.

Reformism does, however, reflect the interests of a distinct social layer within the working-class movement: trade union leaders, socialist politicians, and their respective bureaucracies of full-time officials, researchers, and spin-doctors.

The political role of the labour bureaucracy is to negotiate the terms of exploitation in the workplace or to secure social reforms in parliament. In performing this role, they work with representatives of the ruling class. Theirs is a mediating role between labour and capital. The social position of the labour bureaucracy is privileged compared with that of ordinary workers: union officials and politicians enjoy higher salaries, more rewarding jobs, and better working conditions. They inhabit a relatively comfortable and conservative milieu. The labour bureaucracy embodies the normal, everyday reformist consciousness of workers: the lowest common denominator of left politics.

This reformist consciousness includes nationalism. If the aim is to win reforms within the system, the bourgeois nation-state becomes the framework for political action rather than a target for revolutionary overthrow. The 'national interest' then imposes a limit on the reforms that are possible.

Until 1914 none of this was clear. Rosa Luxemburg was in the forefront of the struggle against revisionism. She played a central role in defending the revolutionary socialist tradition against the growing bureaucratic conservatism of the SPD leaders. Two pamphlets in particular – *Reform or Revolution* (1899) and *The Mass Strike* (1906) – are landmarks in the development of the Marxist tradition. But even Luxemburg did not anticipate the betrayal of 4 August 1914 – an event which blew the world socialist movement apart.

The First World War was ended by revolution, first in Russia in 1917, then in Germany in 1918. When this happened, 'socialist' ministers would be on opposite sides of the barricades from revolutionary workers. Having first led the workers into the carnage of the imperialist war, they then did their best to deliver them into the hands of fascist counter-revolution. Such is the historic role of reformism in moments of capitalist crisis.

The First World War

At the beginning of the First World War, lines of French infantry in blue coats and red trousers charged machine-guns and modern artillery. The French lost a quarter of their men in a single month.

Three years later, the face of war had changed forever. Battles lasted for months. They extended over dozens of square kilometres. The terrain was reduced to a wasteland of rubble, tree stumps, shell holes, barbed wire, and corpses. For most of the time no one could be seen. Troops remained in underground complexes of trenches and tunnels. When attacking, they crept forward in small groups making maximum use of cover.

Casualties were still horrendous. About a million men were killed or wounded in the Battle of Verdun (February–December 1916). Another million were killed or wounded in the Battle of the Somme (June–November 1916). In each case, only a few kilometres of ground were gained. Neither battle broke the impasse. The war continued as before. A million more were killed or wounded in the Battle of Passchendaele (July–November 1917). It rained incessantly, turning the battlefield into liquid mud. Thousands of wounded men drowned where they fell. Again, the front shifted by just a few kilometres, and the war ground on.

The First World War brought carnage, destruction, and waste without precedent. Industrial society's capacity to satisfy human need through mass production had turned into its opposite: industrialised slaughter. The war was an extreme expression of the competition between national-capitalist blocs. The whole industrial power of the rival blocs was harnessed to building, arming, and maintaining mass armies. The result was stalemate.

Mass conscription had created armies of millions. The Prussian army at Waterloo in 1815 had numbered 60,000; the Prussian army at Sedan in 1870, 200,000; but the German army on the Western Front in 1914 numbered 1.5 million. Mass production provided the guns, munitions, and supplies to keep such huge masses fighting. The British had 156 guns at Waterloo in 1815; they fired a few thousand rounds in total. At the Somme in 1916 they had 1,400 guns; they fired nearly two million shells in a few days.

Modern firepower created an impenetrable 'storm of steel' and an 'empty battlefield'. Men crawled from shell-hole to shell-hole, sheltered in the rubble of shelled buildings, or tunnelled into the ground. Stalemate and attrition shaped the entire conflict. Industrial output was decisive: the demand was always for more guns, more shells, more explosives. Millions of workers were mobilised in war industries. The home front became a target of bombing and blockade.

The trenches of the First World War have become symbols of the slaughter. But they did not cause it: in fact, they offered protection from the storm of steel on battlefields dominated by firepower.

Stalemate is only half the story. The dynamic of industrialised militarism also produced ever more lethal means of destruction. A technological arms race took off as rival scientists and engineers competed to increase their respective nations' killing power. In 1914 there were tens of thousands of cavalry; by 1918 there were thousands of tanks. In August 1914 the British had just 30 military aircraft on the entire Western Front; by August 1918 they were deploying 800 in a single battle.

So the character of the war necessarily changed. The war of movement in August and September 1914 was transformed into a war of trench stalemate by October and November. Attempts to break the deadlock by launching head-on attacks across no-man's-land during 1915 were bloodily repulsed. Politicians and generals concluded they needed more men and munitions. It was in the third phase of the war, during 1916 and 1917, that the murderous, months-long offensives at Verdun, the Somme, and Passchendaele were fought. They were the bitter fruit of conscription and mass production of *matériel* by fully mobilised, total-war economies.

Trench warfare prevailed on all fronts. The experience of the Western Front could be found on the Eastern Front, in the Balkans, and in the Middle East. Lines were often weaker and more easily broken on the extended fronts of the East. But poor lines of communications over vast distances slowed down victorious armies and allowed defeated ones to build new trench lines further back.

The impasse was eventually broken by a revolutionary combination of new infantry tactics based on 'fire and movement' and the support of massed tanks and airpower. But this did not bring an end to the slaughter. The new war of movement proved even more murderous than trench-war stalemate. The size of the butchers' bills was not determined by the nature of the fighting. It was determined by its scale. It was a product of industrial capitalism.

Two factors were decisive: first, the great powers were divided by imperial rivalry as their industries expanded and competed; and second, when the powers clashed, these same industries could mass produce the means of destruction. That is one reason the Second World War would be longer and bloodier than the First. It lasted six years and killed 60 million compared with the First's four years and 15 million. Global industrial capacity was that much greater 20 years later. It is certain that a world war today would be even more lethal.

Societies were torn apart by the slaughter and privation inherent in modern industrialised war. To maintain backing for the war, the ruling class demonised 'the enemy' and vilified 'traitors' and 'spies'. Sometimes this spilled over into genocidal racism. The Ottoman Turks murdered 1.5 million Armenians in an internal 'war on terror' during 1915. They killed with rifles, clubs, and neglect. A generation later, even genocide would be industrialised: the Nazis murdered six million Jews and six million others in purpose-built extermination factories.

The danger for the ruling class was that soldiers and workers would revolt against a murderous war of attrition. Instead of continuing a bosses' war for empire and profit, they might put class interests before national hatreds and make common cause with soldiers and workers in 'enemy' states.

The First World War was ended by just such a revolt from below. A wave of protest and revolution swept across Europe from 1917 onwards. First the Russian Revolution ended the war on the Eastern Front. Then the German Revolution ended the war on the Western Front. Afterwards, for several years, revolution threatened to go global. Popular revulsion against war came close to bringing down the ruling classes everywhere. Capitalism survived by a whisker. It is to this tidal wave of world revolution that we now turn.

13
The Revolutionary Wave
1917–1928

Russian revolutionary poster that reads 'Women workers, take up your rifles!', c. 1918.

The Bolshevik Revolution of 1917 was the catalyst of a wave of world revolution that ended the First World War and almost ended the capitalist system that had caused it.

The First World War was an imperialist war between rival national-capitalist blocs. The aim was a redistribution of global resources and power in the interests of one group of rulers at the expense of the other. The great majority of people were mere victims, with nothing to gain from victory and much to lose amid the carnage, destruction, and privation.

Because of this, and because of the agitation of a dedicated and steadily growing anti-war minority, a renewal of mass struggle, which had been abruptly halted by the outbreak of war in August 1914, gradually gathered pace. It eventually grew into the greatest wave of working-class revolution in history so far, one with the power first to stop the fighting on the Eastern Front, then the fighting on the Western Front, and finally to threaten the very survival of European capitalism.

The events of 1917–23, beginning with the outbreak of the Russian Revolution and ending with the defeat of the German Revolution, represent, for activists today, our single richest seam of historical experience. How was the movement built, what form did it take, and why did it fail?

1917: The February Revolution

In Vienna, Petrograd, Berlin, Paris, and London, the outbreak of war had brought cheering crowds of patriots onto the streets. Strikes ended, protests were called off, and the barricades came down in working-class suburbs. Trotsky wrote of 'the patriotic enthusiasm of the masses in Austria-Hungary', Arthur Ransome of how 'the moment welded the nation into one' in Russia, and Rosa Luxemburg of 'mad delirium' in Germany.

Not all were swept up. The crowds were predominantly middle class. The mood in the factories and the workers' districts was usually more subdued. But politics shifted sharply to the right, the leaders of the labour movement capitulated to chauvinism, and any anti-war voices that remained could at first get no hearing. Tens of millions eagerly backed the war and tens of millions more felt they had no choice but to support their own troops. Capitalism had not only plunged the world into barbarism; it had also driven humanity into a collective madness.

Almost everyone expected a short war on the model of the Franco-Prussian War of 1870. The Germans hoped to be in Paris in six weeks. French soldiers daubed *à Berlin* on the sides of their troop trains. British politicians announced that 'the war will be over by Christmas'. It was not to be. The war was protracted and of unprecedented ferocity, for the advanced industries of modern capitalism were capable of mass-producing the means of destruction on a scale previously unknown in history.

As the investment in slaughter increased, war aims expanded. German leaders planned to dominate the whole of Central Europe, to annex the industrial regions of Belgium and eastern France, and to create a sphere of influence extending to the Balkans, Turkey, and the Middle East. The British grabbed the German colonies in Africa and planned a carve-up of the Middle East with the French and the Russians. The French wanted to regain Alsace-Lorraine, which they had lost to Germany in 1871, and had designs on the industrial Rhineland. Military force had replaced economic competition as the primary mechanism of capital accumulation. The haemorrhage of blood and treasure was expected to return a profit.

The price paid by the soldiers, workers, and peasants of Europe was astronomical. Germany lost one in eight of its men of fighting age, France one in five. Millions more were permanently disabled. Entire towns were stripped of men when local regiments serving at the front were sent 'over the top'.

On the home front, there were wage cuts, rising prices, and food shortages as resources were diverted into war production. By 1917 German workers were getting on average only two-thirds of the calories they needed. Around 750,000 died of starvation before the war ended.

Society was turned upside down. Peasants who had never previously left their villages were sent to die on distant battlefields. Young workers were taken from urban slums and hurled into the maelstrom of modern industrialised war. Women who had been housewives replaced men in the munitions factories and joined trade unions.

Class tensions increased. Underfed soldiers living in waterlogged trenches under shell-fire grew resentful of staff officers lodged in country houses behind the lines. Workers were banned from striking as living standards fell, while bankers and bosses grew rich on the profits of war. By the winter of 1916–17, the mood in the trenches and on the home front across Europe was sullen. A perfect storm was brewing. But where would it break?

'We of the older generation may not live to see the decisive battles of the coming revolution', remarked Lenin to a group of young workers in Zurich in January 1917. Yet the backwardness of Russia made it one of Europe's weakest links. Russia's participation in the bloody struggle for world domination was beyond its capacities. It was doomed by vast distances, primitive agriculture, a sparse rail network, and an industrial base too small to sustain armies of millions in a war of munitions. 'In the first months', wrote Trotsky,

> the soldiers fell under shell-fire unthinkingly or thinking little; but from day to day, they gathered experience – bitter experience of the lower ranks who are ignorantly commanded. They measured the confusion of the generals by the number of purposeless manoeuvres on sole-less shoes, the number of dinners not eaten. From the bloody mash of people and things emerged a generalised word: 'the mess'.

Hunger and a sense of hopelessness gnawed at the peasant infantry in the trenches. Indiscipline and desertion became an epidemic. The line was held together by little more than flogging and shooting. Hunger stalked the workers' districts too. Still, on the morning of 23 February 1917, Tsar Nicholas II seemed as secure in power as ever. No one had the least inkling that a demonstration that day – International Women's Day – would detonate the Russian Revolution.

The revolutionary underground had intended marking the day with nothing more than meetings, speeches, and leaflets. There had been no call to strike or to demonstrate. It did not matter. Something had snapped. The masses would take no more. Women textile-workers came out on strike and marched through the streets chanting 'Down with high prices! Down with hunger! Bread for the workers!' As they passed other factories, they gesticulated, threw snowballs, and shouted for the workers inside to join them: 'Come out! Stop work!' The movement swelled into a spontaneous 'turn-out' strike as the energy of street protest pulled one group of workers after another into action.

The following day, half of Petrograd's 400,000 workers joined the movement, and now demands for cheap bread could be heard mingled with something far more ominous: 'Down with autocracy! Down with the war!'

On that day, and on those that followed, there were clashes with police, Cossacks, and finally regiments of soldiers. But not all were bloody. When Cossacks were ordered to charge 2,500 workers from the Erikson textile mill, they passed down a narrow corridor formed by their officers, and some smiled at the workers as they went. 'Of discipline', commented Trotsky, 'there remained but a thin transparent shell that threatened to break through any second.'

For five days, 23–27 February 1917, the Revolution hung in the balance as masses of workers confronted the armed forces of the state in the streets of the capital. 'There is no doubt', continued Trotsky, 'that the fate of every revolution at a certain point is decided by a break in the disposition of the army.' Whatever his own grievances and discontent, however great his tacit sympathy with the people he is ordered to shoot down, the soldier takes a terrible risk when he turns on his own officers. To find the confidence to mutiny, he must be assured that the mass before him has the strength and determination to win.

This matter was decided in a thousand encounters, big and small, on the streets of Petrograd during those five days. It was decided by a glance, a smile, a resonant slogan; by the appeal of a starving mother against the order of a brutal officer; by the press of common humanity in a crowded thoroughfare; by the micro-biology of revolution.

On the fourth day, a wave of mutinies swept through the barracks. Workers and soldiers merged on the streets and paraded together with guns and red flags. New regiments arriving from the front to restore order were carried along on the revolutionary tide. The generals had lost control of the army. They informed the Tsar there was no possibility of regaining it without his abdication. The medieval empire of the tsars had been destroyed in five days of proletarian revolution. Russia was a republic.

But what sort of republic? How would it be governed? Who would rule now? And would the people get the bread and peace they demanded? These questions remained to be answered. The Russian Revolution had only just begun.

Dual Power: The Mechanics of Revolution

It had been the greatest proletarian revolt in history. The battle had been fought and won entirely through the mass action of working people. The bourgeoisie and the middle class had played no part whatsoever. Yet power had passed not to the workers, but to the liberal-bourgeois politicians of the Kadet Party in the Tsarist Duma, a parliamentary body elected on a restricted franchise and with very limited powers. The Kadets were a party of liberal landlords, indus-trialists, and intellectuals. It seemed that the mountains in labour had given birth to a mouse. Trotsky called it 'the paradox of the February Revolution'. What had happened?

The masses were not yet organised as a political force capable of governing society. Nor did they have confidence in their ability to do so. And because, in politics, vacuums are always filled, the empty seats at Russia's top table were immediately occupied by an existing group of liberal-bourgeois 'opposition' politicians.

Many ordinary people still trusted the rhetoric and promises of these educated, experienced, smooth-talking politicians. They needed to learn through bitter experience that the Kadets were class enemies who represented the rich.

The confusion was compounded by the leaders of the parties of the Left. The Social Revolutionaries (SRs) were a party of radical intellectuals formed from a fusion of old Narodnik factions. They continued to focus on the peasantry and swelled into a mass movement on the basis of peasant votes during the Revolution. But they merely embodied in party form the conservatism of rich peasants, the wavering of middle peasants, and the passivity of poor peasants. This fractured and backward class base prevented the SRs from giving decisive revolutionary leadership. They soon split. The Right SRs backed the Provisional Government. The Left SRs became allies of the Bolsheviks.

The Mensheviks (reformist socialists) argued that the role of Russian Social Democrats was to support the liberal bourgeoisie's efforts to establish parliamentary democracy and civil liberties, not to make their own revolution. The Bolsheviks (revolutionary socialists) at first adopted a similar position. Even after breaking with the Mensheviks in 1903, they had continued to believe that the Russian Revolution would be a limited 'bourgeois revolution'. The logic of this position seemed to demand that they support the new Provisional Government in 1917.

On 3 April, Lenin, the leader of the Bolshevik Party, arrived at Petrograd's Finland Station. His return from exile was greeted by a crowd of several thousand workers and soldiers. He immediately contradicted his party's policy, calling for immediate peace, the downfall of the Provisional Government, and 'worldwide socialist revolution'.

The Bolshevik Party was an exceptionally democratic organisation – it was a ferment of internal debate throughout 1917 – and Lenin could not overturn its position with a single speech. He therefore had to wage a hard internal fight to change a policy strongly supported by more conservative leaders like Josef Stalin.

Three things proved decisive. First, Lenin embodied the mood of rank-and-file party activists, and they in turn were embedded in a mass working-class movement that was moving rapidly to the left in response to the deepening social and political crisis.

Second, because of the class forces it represented, the Provisional Government was unable to satisfy the popular demands that became encapsulated in the Bolshevik slogan 'Peace, Bread, and Land'. The government was determined to continue the war, could not solve the economic crisis, and would not give the land to the peasants.

Third, the masses were organised in a network of workers', soldiers', and peasants' councils ('soviets'). The soviets gave democratic expression to popular demands, organised mass protests to achieve them, and represented an embryonic alternative people's government.

The Bolsheviks would crystallise the potential inherent in the soviets with two slogans: 'Down with the Provisional Government' and 'All Power to the Soviets'. The implication was that the bourgeois state had to be overthrown and replaced by a new proletarian state.

The paradox of the February Revolution had created what Trotsky called 'dual power': the simultaneous existence within society of two alternative and competing centres of political authority. The Provisional Government, in control of the old state apparatus and representing the propertied classes, was one side of the dual power. The soviets, democratic assemblies of the revolutionary masses, formed the other.

The dual power was highly unstable, and therefore unsustainable. Either the Provisional Government would crush the soviets and re-establish the uncontested rule of private property, or the soviets would overthrow the Provisional Government and create a new social order.

Lenin's mission was to equip his party with this understanding and to prepare it for a second revolution. His position was strengthened in July when Trotsky and a small group of followers joined the Bolshevik Party; the two revolutionary leaders henceforward worked as close political allies.

Lenin's pamphlet *State and Revolution* was written in August 1917 as a major contribution to this rearming of the party. He insisted that the capitalist state was not a neutral force, but one committed to the defence of ruling-class interests. His polemic was a reassertion of the authentic Marxist tradition, for Marx, basing his ideas largely on the experience of the Paris Commune of 1871, had argued that the capitalist state had to be smashed and replaced by a new kind of state based on mass participatory democracy.

'The state is a product and a manifestation of the irreconcilability of class antagonisms', Lenin wrote. 'The state arises where, when, and insofar as class antagonisms objectively cannot be reconciled. And, conversely, the existence of the state proves that the class antagonisms are irreconcilable.' More simply, 'the state is an organ of class rule, an organ for the oppression of one class by another'. It consisted of 'bodies of armed men' for the suppression of popular resistance to the exploitation, oppression, and violence of the ruling class. Socialists, argued Lenin, seek the abolition of classes and therefore the abolition of the repressive state. But the state would only 'wither away' with the 'withering away' of class antagonisms. In the furnace of revolution, with the class struggle at white heat, the workers had to create their own state to protect and advance their interests.

This was what Lenin, following Marx, called 'the dictatorship of the proletariat'. The choice of phrase is poor. We think of dictatorship and democracy as polar opposites. But the idea is sound. The state *is* a repressive institution, regardless of which class controls it. But whereas a bourgeois state defends the property of the rich, a workers' state, in which elected delegates are accountable to mass assemblies and armed popular militias are under democratic control, defends the interests of the great majority – a task which sometimes involves 'authoritarian' methods.

The soviets played a growing role in the running of society in the course of 1917. More and more, ordinary workers, soldiers, and sailors in the revolutionary capital ignored the orders of the Provisional Government and obeyed only those issued by the soviets. Mass consciousness was moving sharply to the left under the impact of events and experience. Power was passing from the old state to the new democracy.

At some point, matters would go critical. The masses would look to the soviets for a final settlement of the revolutionary crisis, for the satisfaction of popular demands, for delivery on the revolution's promises.

Timing would be decisive. A premature insurrection would risk isolating the revolutionary vanguard and allowing the ruling class to destroy it. But to delay the insurrection could also prove fatal. If the revolutionaries failed to give a lead when the hopes of the broadest masses were at their peak, the people would soon relapse, resigned and apathetic, into the old routines of everyday life. The enthusiasm and energy that had fuelled the Revolution would then drain away and the ruling class would have the opportunity to rebuild the broken apparatus of power. Lenin's Bolshevik Party was being rearmed for a supreme test: the leadership and organisation of an armed proletarian insurrection for the seizure of state power.

February to October: The Rhythms of Revolution

The Russian Revolution passed through five major crises as the class struggle ebbed and flowed during 1917. Four of these crises – the February Days, the April Days, the Kornilov Coup in August, and the October Insurrection – involved successful mass action to drive the Revolution forward. They weakened the old order, strengthened popular organisation, increased the consciousness, confidence, and combativeness of the masses, and raised the platform from which the next advance would be made. One – the July Days – was a partial setback. It resulted in retreat, not advance, for the revolutionary movement. Even so, it brought down a prime minister and taught the masses valuable lessons.

The first crisis, the five-day insurrection that destroyed the monarchy, brought to power a Provisional Government dominated by bourgeois liberals, and spawned a fast-developing network of democratic popular assemblies or soviets.

The second crisis played out between 18 April and 5 May. It was triggered by the new Foreign Minister Miliukov's undertaking to continue the imperialist war in alliance with Britain and France. This provoked mass demonstrations on 20–21 April. Many soldiers marched with their arms. Many called for the overthrow of the Provisional Government. But it was too soon for a decisive battle. Lenin and the Bolsheviks reined the movement back. Nonetheless, the April Days produced a governmental crisis which saw the fall of Miliukov on 2 May and the creation of a coalition government which included Kerensky and five other 'socialist' ministers on 5 May.

The July Days crisis took the form of an abortive insurrection in Petrograd on 3–5 July. This represented a far more determined challenge to the Provisional Government than that of April. And it was followed by a wave of repression which drove the Bolshevik Party underground. The problem was the gap between Petrograd, where the mood in the factories and barracks was insurrectionary, and that in the rest of the country. The danger was that a revolution in Petrograd would be isolated and then drowned in blood like the Paris Commune. Iron discipline had been necessary. The Bolsheviks had marched with the masses, but mainly to argue against an immediate attempt to overthrow the government. Many workers denounced them as traitors. Many of their own members and close supporters were in despair. As the movement subsided, hundreds were arrested, the revolutionary press was shut down, and Lenin and other Bolshevik leaders were forced into hiding. In working-class districts the mood was sullen, and support for the party slumped.

But the July Days were not a decisive defeat. They brought about the fall of Prince Lvov, the Kadet Prime Minister, and his replacement by the 'socialist' Kerensky on 21 July. And the Bolsheviks had succeeded in leading a retreat and preventing the decapitation of the revolution. The Petrograd mass movement was temporarily cowed, but it had not been broken. The retreat was enough, however, to encourage an attempted Tsarist counter-revolution.

On 26 August General Kornilov demanded dictatorial powers in order to restore order both at home and in the army. Kerensky, on behalf of the Provisional Government, refused. Kornilov then marched on Petrograd. Lenin now argued that the Revolution was under threat and that all revolutionaries had to defend the soviets and the revolutionary capital (and therefore, indirectly, Kerensky's Provisional Government).

The Bolshevik intervention was decisive: it meant the entire revolutionary movement was mobilised against the coup. Kornilov's army simply melted away. The soldiers were not prepared to fight for a Tsarist general. 'The insurrection', wrote Trotsky, 'had rolled back, crumbled to pieces, been sucked up by the earth.' It had lasted four days (27–30 August).

The pendulum of revolution was now oscillating violently. The rising hopes of millions were approaching a critical condition. The gloom of July was dispelled by the elation of August. New recruits poured into the Bolshevik Party.

The Bolsheviks had entered the revolutionary year as a small mass party, counting around 2,000 members in Petrograd in early March. This had reached 16,000 by late April, and 36,000 by late July. By then, more than one in ten of Petrograd's industrial workers were party members. This meant growing influence over the working class as a whole. The Bolshevik vote in the capital increased from 20 per cent in May, to 33 per cent in August, and to 45 per cent in November. At the First Soviet Congress in early June, the Bolsheviks had 13 per cent of delegates. By the Second Congress, in late October, they had 53 per cent, and their allies, the Left Social Revolutionaries, had a further 21 per cent.

The swing to the Bolsheviks after the defeat of Kornilov coincided with a deepening of Russia's economic, social, and military crisis. The soldiers were refusing to fight, shooting their officers, and heading for home. The peasants were taking possession of the land. The national minorities were agitating for independence. Industry was grinding to a halt. The levers of state power had seized up. The soviets were increasingly in control of social life. The Provisional Government was effectively paralysed.

At some point between 12 and 14 September, Lenin, who was still in hiding, wrote a letter headed 'The Bolsheviks Must Assume State Power'. It was addressed to the Central Committee and the Petrograd and Moscow Committees of the Bolshevik Party. The Bolsheviks had secured a majority in both the Petrograd and Moscow soviets. This, Lenin argued, demonstrated that the revolutionary crisis had ripened. The swing to the left in mass consciousness was now sufficient to ensure that if the revolutionary vanguard acted, the masses would follow. The danger now was delay.

Yet delay there was. The Bolshevik leaders vacillated. Not until 10 October did the Central Committee approve a resolution proposed by Lenin – who had arrived for the meeting in disguise – for an immediate insurrection. Even so, there was further vacillation and then outright defiance when two dissident members of the Central Committee, Zinoviev and Kamenev, openly opposed Lenin's policy. On the very eve of the insurrection, 24 October, Lenin felt it necessary to write to the Central Committee that 'the situation is critical in the extreme ... it is now absolutely clear that to delay the uprising would be fatal ... history will not forgive revolutionaries for procrastinating when they could be victorious...'.

Why was the Bolshevik leadership so reluctant to act? Why did it almost fail the ultimate test? All parties, even the most revolutionary, give rise to their own organisational conservatism. Without caution and routine, no lasting organisation is possible. Wild adventurism is self-destructive. The Bolshevik Party, so painfully constructed over long years of struggle, so profoundly shaped by experience of underground work in a police state, was conservative as a matter of self-preservation. But then came the moment – and it would be brief – when the balance of forces finally tipped in favour of the revolutionaries. For most of the time, explained Tony Cliff in his biography of Lenin, the workers are weaker than their enemies:

> Any revolutionary party that did not control its impatience over the years in the light of this fact would condemn itself to adventurism and to its own destruction. But the moment comes – and this is the meaning of revolution – when the habit of considering the enemy as stronger becomes the main obstacle on the road to victory.

1917: The October Insurrection

Right-wing historians often describe the October Insurrection as a Bolshevik 'coup' made possible by the 'anarchy' into which Russia had fallen by autumn 1917. The misunderstanding is profound. Their basic error is to view history from above, not from below. What looks like anarchy to them was, in fact, the leaching away of state authority and the rise of new organs of popular power. What they describe as a coup was, in reality, an expression of the democratic will of millions of workers, soldiers, sailors, and peasants.

The Tsarist monarchy had commanded an army of millions, yet it was overthrown in the February Revolution. The Provisional Government had inherited that army of millions. Yet it too was swept away, by the October Insurrection. Historical events of this magnitude are not brought about by mere coups. The very success of the October Insurrection masks its true character. The revolution was so ripe, the social crisis so deep, the authority of the government so hollowed out, the masses so well prepared for decisive action, that a few tens of thousands were sufficient to execute the popular will.

The insurrection, like that of February, was the work of several days, beginning on 20 October and concluding on the night of 25/26 October. But unlike February, which had been an unplanned spontaneous eruption from below, with a chaotic mass movement under local leadership feeling its way to power organically, October was a centrally directed, military-style seizure of power by the Petrograd Soviet. It was directed by Leon Trotsky, a triumvirate of senior military organisers, and the wider 'Military Revolutionary Committee' – elected by, and accountable to, the Petrograd Soviet, the supreme expression of the popular will in the capital.

This being so, by the final day of the October Days insurrection, the whole energy of Russia's mighty conflagration became concentrated in the hands of perhaps 25,000 armed men and women – workers, soldiers, and sailors. These were the organised armed detachments of the people. There was little for anyone else to do. Most workers remained at home, most soldiers stayed in their barracks. They had debated, voted, and given their leaders and armed detachments a mandate. Now it was simply a matter of executing the formal transfer of power from one class to another. There was no looting or rioting. Theatres, cinemas, and shops remained open. Casualties were minimal, far fewer than in either the February or July Days.

The climax was an anti-climax. The Winter Palace, the seat of government, was held by a motley collection of Tsarist officers, Cossacks, war veterans, and a volunteer Women's Battalion. That was the sum total of the social forces prepared to fight for Kerensky.

Threatened from the River Neva by the guns of the battleship *Aurora* and unable to prevent armed workers and sailors infiltrating the palace's labyrinth of entrances and passageways, the defence crumbled amid frantic scuffles. It would all look far more impressive in Eisenstein's 1927 film of the event.

On the evening of 25 October, Trotsky reported to the Petrograd Soviet that 'the Provisional Government has ceased to exist'. Lenin emerged from hiding to announce 'a new era in the history of Russia'. 'We have the strength of a mass organisation which will triumph over everything and bring the proletariat to world revolution', he continued. 'In Russia, we must proceed at once to the construction of a proletarian socialist state. Long live the worldwide socialist revolution!'

The radicalism of the new government was without precedent. A decree on land transferred the property of the landlords to millions of peasants. A decree on industry gave the workers control of the factories. A decree on self-determination gave the oppressed nations of the Russian Empire the right to independence. The mansions of the rich were taken over to house the poor. Equal access to education and healthcare became the right of every citizen. Marriage and divorce laws were swept away, equality between the sexes became mandatory, and adultery, homosexuality, and abortion were decriminalised.

Nothing like this had ever happened before. Most previous revolutions, even in their most radical phases, had remained under bourgeois control. The major exception, the Paris Commune of 1871, had been restricted to one city and lasted only two months. Now, for the first time in history, the working class had taken power in a modern nation-state.

The preceding eight months of the Revolution had been the necessary preparation. The ebbs and flows of the struggle – the rhythms of the Revolution – had been an essential process of learning for the masses, of shedding illusions, of gaining confidence, and of moving to the left through the hard knocks of political experience. The dual power – the mechanics of the Revolution – had given organisational expression to the escalating confrontation of social forces, the Provisional Government becoming the rallying point for all the forces of reaction, the soviets embodying the growing consciousness and will of the masses. The Bolsheviks – the party of the Revolution – had provided the vital network of embedded rank-and-file activists able to give direction to the struggle at every level.

The relationship between the masses, the soviets, and the party was like that between the steam, the box, and the piston of an engine. It was the energy of the masses (the steam) that powered the revolution, but it was the soviets (the box) that concentrated that energy, and the party (the piston) that directed its force.

Nevertheless, the dizzy triumph of Red October was immediately threatened by economic collapse, peasant resistance, national disintegration, and military-imperial dismemberment.

Of Russia's 150 million people, only about 3.5 million were industrial workers. Most were peasants, and most of the 12 million soldiers mobilised during the war were conscripted from the villages. The class division between officers and men in the Tsarist army mirrored the class division between landlords and peasants in the countryside. The peasant-soldiers had supported the Revolution because they hated their officers, were sick of the war, and wanted the land. They supported the Bolsheviks because they gave them the land. But the cities were starving, and the collapse of industry meant that the workers had little to exchange with the peasants for food. The daily bread ration in Petrograd fell from 300 g in October 1917, to 150 g the following January, and then to just 50 g in February – a tenth of a loaf.

The crisis was compounded by German aggression. The Germans refused to make peace unless the Bolsheviks ceded large parts of the grain- and coal-rich Ukraine. The German ultimatum split the Bolshevik leadership. Some argued for 'revolutionary war' in defence of Russian territory. Lenin argued for acceptance of the ultimatum, since the Bolsheviks had no forces with which to fight. Trotsky argued for neither revolutionary war nor acceptance of the ultimatum, trusting instead to the imminent outbreak of revolution in Germany. The German Army invaded the Ukraine and met virtually no resistance. Lenin's position was then accepted. The Treaty of Brest-Litovsk handed large parts of the Ukraine to German imperialism. Food shortages intensified and the Revolution began to die slowly of starvation.

Soon there were other imperial predators to contend with: a Czech Legion on the Trans-Siberian Railway; British troops at Murmansk in the north and the Baku oilfields in the south; Japanese at Vladivostok on the Pacific coast. And these were encouraging and supplying counter-revolutionary 'White' armies. A ferocious civil war was beginning.

The Bolsheviks had always argued that socialism could be achieved only on a world scale. They had hesitated about socialist revolution in Russia precisely because they had assumed the country's economic backwardness precluded anything more than a bourgeois revolution to create a parliamentary democracy and facilitate capitalist development. Now they were trapped by economic contradictions that could not be solved on a national scale. Unless it could harness the industrial power of Europe, the proletarian revolution would either be smothered by the primeval poverty of the villages or drowned in blood by foreign and Tsarist armies.

'The final victory of socialism in a single country is ... impossible', Lenin told the Third Soviet Congress in January 1918. 'Our contingent of workers and peasants which is upholding Soviet power is one of the contingents of the great world army.' Two months later he put the matter more starkly: 'It is the absolute truth that without a German revolution, we are doomed.'

The revolution was in danger. Could it be rescued? Would it go global?

1918: How the War Ended

Revolution broke out in Russia early in 1917 because it was the weakest of the great powers. But it soon spread. By the third winter of the war, the pressure of industrialised warfare was imposing massive strain on the whole of European society.

The disasters of 1916 toppled governments and brought down generals. General Nivelle replaced General Joffre as head of the French Army and immediately launched a new offensive proclaiming, 'We have a formula ... victory is certain.' It was not. The French lost 120,000 men in five days. A month later Nivelle too was dismissed. By that time a wave of mutinies was sweeping across the French Army. The *poilus* – the French rank and file – had had enough.

The revolt started in late April 1917, spread during May, and peaked in June. Desertion became endemic, entire units refused to go back to the line, and demonstrations were held in which soldiers sang revolutionary songs. Around 40,000 men were directly involved and 68 divisions were affected. During one two-week period, the front-line was virtually denuded of French troops. The mutinies were suppressed, but only 49 of 554 death sentences were carried out, conditions in the trenches were improved, and the French Army remained on the defensive for the next year.

In October 1917, the Italian Army cracked. Between May 1915 and September 1917, General Cadorna had ordered no fewer than 11 offensives on the Isonzo River on Italy's north-eastern frontier. Each had failed. Italian casualties were a third of a million in the two 1917 offensives alone. When the Austrians and Germans counterattacked in late October, the Italian Army collapsed. The rout continued for 112 km. Twice as many men deserted as were lost on the battlefield. Tens of thousands discarded their rifles and streamed away from the front chanting, 'The war's over! We're going home! Up with Russia!' A new line was improvised deep inside north-eastern Italy. Cadorna was sacked, the soldiers' conditions were greatly improved, and no new offensive was attempted before the second half of 1918.

On the other side of no-man's-land – in Germany, Austria-Hungary, Bulgaria, and the Ottoman Empire – conditions were even worse. Total war meant murderous offensives and a 'war of munitions' at the battlefronts. It also meant an attempt to starve the enemy into submission – by a British naval blockade of German ports, and a German submarine offensive against British shipping.

Germany lost 1.8 million soldiers in the First World War, but almost half that number again died of starvation at home. Food production fell as the land was stripped of labour by the draft. War production took priority over consumption needs. German trade was crippled by the naval blockade. In the second half of the war, the diet of the average German worker averaged only two-thirds of the calories needed for long-term survival.

Around 200,000 German engineering workers struck against reductions in the bread ration in April 1917. Disaffection spread to the sailors of the High Seas Fleet at Kiel. Resentment at poor conditions, harsh discipline, and the privileges of the officer class boiled over when rations were cut. The sailors elected 'food committees' and demanded recognition from the authorities. But the movement was crushed. Two of the leaders were executed and others imprisoned with hard labour.

Then a fresh wave of strikes swept across Germany in January 1918, with 500,000 out in Berlin and a dozen other industrial centres. Embryonic workers' councils emerged to coordinate the action. Anti-war socialists played leading roles. Activists made direct comparison between events in Germany and the revolution in Russia. But the authorities cracked down hard, and again the movement subsided.

Germany's rulers had been given one last chance. The Russian Revolution and the Treaty of Brest-Litovsk had ended the war on the Eastern Front. It was now possible to reinforce the Western Front and go onto the offensive against the British and the French. But the United States had entered the war and was in the process of transporting hundreds of thousands of troops across the Atlantic. Germany's opportunity would be brief.

In spring 1918 General Ludendorff launched five separate offensives. The Allied line almost broke. The British Commander-in-Chief, Douglas Haig, issued an order stating, 'With our backs to the wall and believing in the justice of our cause, each one of us must fight to the end.' The line held, and when the offensives ended in July, the Germans had lost half a million men. The Allies had lost more, but American troops were arriving at the rate of 300,000 a month.

The Allies could now go onto the offensive, and they began to make massive gains. The fighting on the Western Front reached unparalleled ferocity. The Germans suffered a succession of defeats and lost large swathes of the territory they had conquered in 1914.

The First World War had the character of a gigantic siege of the Central Powers. By autumn 1918, there was heavy and mounting pressure on all fronts. Between September and November, all four of the Central Powers collapsed.

The Ottoman Turkish line in Palestine was broken at the Battle of Megiddo on 19–21 September. Three entire armies broke and fled northwards. The rout continued to the modern Turkish–Syrian border. Arab nationalist guerrillas had played a central role in the victory, liberating the Arabic-speaking territories east of the Jordan. The war in the Middle East was ended by the Armistice of Mudros on 30 October.

The Bulgarian line in Macedonia was broken by a combined army of British, French, Serbian, Greek, and Italian troops in a sustained two-week offensive in late September. Bulgaria was a small, underdeveloped country. It had lost a higher proportion of its military manpower during six years of war between 1912 and 1918 than any other belligerent state. Its agriculture had collapsed. Its infant industries had been yoked to the German war-machine. Bulgaria's leaders had led their people to national disaster. By the time an armistice was signed on the Salonika Front on 29 September, much of the army had disintegrated and a revolution had broken out at home.

The Austro-Hungarian line was broken by the Italians at the Battle of Vittorio Veneto (24 October–4 November). An armistice was signed on the day after the Italians captured the Adriatic port of Trieste. The military defeat destroyed the ramshackle Austro-Hungarian Empire. The army broke up into national fragments and liberal politicians seized power in dozens of cities – Czechs and Slovaks in Prague, Brno, and Bratislava; 'South Slavs' in Zagreb and Sarajevo; Poles in Cracow. The twin capitals of the Habsburg 'Dual Monarchy' – German-speaking Vienna and Magyar-speaking Budapest – were also swept up by the revolutionary tide. A coalition led by Social Democrats took power in Vienna, a liberal aristocrat in Budapest.

On 29 September, Hindenburg and Ludendorff, the leading German generals, informed the Kaiser that the war was lost. They demanded an armistice, a compromise peace, and a new government that would include Social Democrats, explaining that 'it is necessary to prevent an upheaval from below by a revolution from above'.

The Kaiser was too obdurate to comply and attempted to continue the war. The High Seas Fleet was ordered to sea in a last desperate do-or-die bid to defeat Britain's Royal Navy. Germany's sailors were to be a final sacrifice to the God of War.

On 29 October the sailors began to mutiny. This time, instead of simply sitting tight on their ships, they went onto the offensive, organising armed demonstrations to spread the revolt through the fleet and the docks. By 3 November the German naval base at Kiel was controlled by a revolutionary council. Kiel was the trigger. Huge demonstrations broke out across Germany. Within days, scores of German towns were controlled by councils of workers, soldiers, and sailors.

On 9 November the revolution reached Berlin. Hundreds of thousands were on the streets. The city was festooned with red flags and socialist banners. The anti-war revolutionary socialist Karl Liebknecht addressed the crowds from the balcony of the imperial palace and proclaimed a 'socialist republic' and 'world revolution'. The German Revolution had begun. Russia had had its February Days. Now Germany had its November Days. The film of 1917 was being re-run in the heart of Europe.

The First World War – the bloodiest carnage in human history up to that time – had been ended by the revolutionary action of millions of workers, soldiers, sailors, and peasants across Europe.

The German Revolution

Once it was clear they could not win the war, the Central Powers made a series of compromise peace offers. Each was rejected. The Entente powers – Britain, France, Italy, and the United States – wanted total victory and a free hand to carve up the world in their own interests. In these circumstances, the German, Austro-Hungarian, Ottoman, and Bulgarian leaders were determined to continue fighting.

The imperialist greed of the world's ruling classes would have condemned humanity to endless slaughter. What prevented this was revolution, first in Russia, then in Bulgaria, Austria-Hungary, and Germany. Nor did the contagion stop at the borders of the defeated Central Powers. It soon spread to Britain, France, and Italy. 'The whole of Europe is filled with the spirit of revolution', complained British Prime Minister David Lloyd George in a letter to his French counterpart in 1919. 'The whole existing order in its political, social, and economic aspects is questioned by the mass of the population from one end of Europe to the other.'

At the end of the war, the epicentre of the revolutionary storm moved from Petrograd to Berlin, from the edge of Europe to its heart. History would turn on the outcome of the German Revolution. Victory in Germany would have brought the richest industrial economy and the largest working class in Europe over to the side of socialist revolution, bringing immediate succour to the beleaguered Bolshevik regime in Russia, establishing workers' power from the North Sea to the Pacific, and, in all probability, ensuring that the revolution would go global.

Had this happened, the future course of human history would have been different. There would have been no Great Depression, no Nazism, no Stalinism, no Second World War, no Cold War. The stakes in 1918–23 could not have been higher.

Germany's November Days revolution had seen vast demonstrations, mass strikes and mutinies, and the rapid formation of a network of workers', soldiers', and sailors' councils. The Russian Revolution had shown that such a network represented a potential alternative state structure based on direct democracy. But, just as the Petrograd Soviet had done after the February Revolution, the German councils chose to hand over power to a traditional parliamentary-type government. A new administration formed of SPD (right-wing socialist) and USPD (left-wing socialist) ministers was endorsed by an assembly of 1,500 workers' and soldiers' delegates. This revealed both the strength of the councils – their backing was needed – and the weakness of their politics – they put their trust in professional career politicians.

The German socialists had split into three groups. The leaders of the SPD, the German Social Democratic Party, were pro-war and anti-revolution. Their main aim was to make Germany safe for capitalism by destroying the very movement that had swept them to power. The SPD leader Frederick Ebert became German premier in November. General Groener was soon on the phone. The High Command would recognise the new government provided it supported 'strict discipline and strict order' in the army and committed itself to the 'fight against Bolshevism'. Ebert and Groener became firm allies.

The leaders of the USPD, the Independent Social Democratic Party, were centrists. Their ranks included social-democratic revisionists like Eduard Bernstein, more radical parliamentary socialists like Karl Kautsky, and Marxist intellectuals like the economist Rudolf Hilferding. What united them was their combination, in varying proportions, of revolutionary rhetoric and reformist practice. In January 1919, SPD electoral support was five times that of the USPD (11.5 million as against 2.3 million votes). By June 1920, however, the two parties would be almost neck and neck. This is one measure of the dramatic shift to the left among German workers during Europe's two great years of revolution after the First World War.

The third group was the Spartakus League, or the KPD, the German Communist Party, as it became on 1 January 1919. A revolutionary socialist group led by Karl Liebknecht and Rosa Luxemburg, it was similar in character to the Russian Bolsheviks. In November

1918 the USPD probably had ten times as many members as the Spartakus League.

The SPD was the dominant party in government and its leaders were working hand-in-glove with the Army High Command. Because the soldiers were infected with 'the spirit of revolution', the Social Democrat Minister of the Interior, Gustav Noske, authorised the generals to create a new paramilitary force, the Free Corps (*Freikorps*).

The combination of military defeat, economic crisis, and social upheaval had torn the old world apart. Many Germans moved to the left. Others, including many junior officers, NCOs, elite soldiers, and military specialists, moved to the right. The *Freikorps* was recruited from these hard-right elements. It immediately gained a reputation for brutality, anti-semitism, extreme nationalism, and violent hostility to the workers' councils, the unions, and the Left. Many of its thugs would later join the Nazi Party.

Berlin was the capital of the revolution and the strongest base of the newly formed KPD. On 4 January the SPD-dominated government sacked Berlin's chief of police, the USPD member Emil Eichhorn, for refusing to take action against working-class protests. Hundreds of thousands of workers poured onto the streets, many of them armed. An Interim Revolutionary Committee was installed at police headquarters.

But the leadership was hesitant, local troops remained hostile, and support for the action outside Berlin was minimal. The Berlin activists had been goaded into action before the revolution had ripened. The revolutionary capital was isolated. Not only the *Freikorps* but many soldiers from outside Berlin were willing to participate in what turned out to be the bloody suppression of the Spartakus Rising. Liebknecht was knocked unconscious and shot. Luxemburg's skull was smashed with a rifle butt, she was then shot, and her body thrown into a canal. The German Revolution had been decapitated.

The KPD was a new party, its support outside Berlin was limited, it lacked the authority of a more established organisation, and many of its activists were inexperienced and prone to adventurism. In July 1917 the Bolsheviks had reined in the Petrograd proletariat to prevent a premature seizure of power in the capital. In January 1919 the Spartakists failed to do the same in Berlin and paid a terrible price.

Nonetheless, the setback was not necessarily fatal. The crisis continued to mature across Germany. Support switched from the SPD to the USPD and the KPD. The *Freikorps* faced increasingly effective resistance from armed workers and revolutionary soldiers. By March 1920 an estimated 20,000 had been killed in a series of regional civil wars.

At this point, the German ruling class launched a 'law and order' coup, sending troops into Berlin, overthrowing the SPD government, and appointing a conservative bureaucrat, Wolfgang Kapp, in its place.

Now it was the Right that had moved too soon. The head of the main union confederation called a general strike. Millions of workers not only walked out; they also formed new councils and took up arms. The Ruhr Red Army freed Germany's greatest industrial region of all right-wing troops. The Kapp Putsch collapsed in a few days and the SPD ministers returned to office. The coup had exposed the true nature of the ruling class, and German workers moved sharply to the left. Its defeat had also revealed the strength of the revolution, and confidence soared.

But the potential was not realised. The KPD drew back from preparing a proletarian insurrection. The Kapp Putsch did not, like the Kornilov Coup of August 1917, pave the way for socialist revolution. Too bold in January 1919, the KPD leaders had learnt their lesson too well, and now, in wholly different circumstances, proved far too timid.

The final act of the German Revolution played out in 1923. A fresh crisis for the tottering Weimar regime gave the German communists a third opportunity. French troops had occupied the Ruhr, the heartland of the German working class, hyper-inflation was destroying the currency, the savings of the middle class, and the purchasing power of working people, and a general strike against the government gained mass support. 'Workers' governments' were established in two states. These were supposed to be launch-pads for a national insurrection. The working class appeared ready. But the call never came: the leaders of the KPD again surrendered to their own timidity and doubt.

Timing is everything in the art of revolution. The summer of 1920 and the summer and autumn of 1923 were almost certainly moments when revolutionaries could have led the working class to victory in the heart of Europe. The price for their failure is incalculable.

Antonio Gramsci and Italy's 'Two Red Years'

Italy, like Germany, was on the brink of revolution in the summer of 1920, after the strains of imperialist war had prised open deep fractures in an unstable social order. During Italy's *Biennio Rosso* ('Two Red Years': 1919 and 1920) the country came close to resolving its tensions through socialist revolution. That this did not happen was to have dire consequences. The Left's failure became the Right's opportunity: Benito Mussolini's Fascists seized power in 1922.

The roots of the post-war crisis lay in the country's long, stuttering, never-quite-finished bourgeois revolution. Ever since the anti-feudal reforms of 1796–1814 imposed under French rule, and through the successive insurrections of 1820, 1831, 1848, and 1860, Italy had managed only half-baked modernisation. The country was a stark example of what Trotsky called 'combined and uneven development'. By May 1915, when it entered the First World War, it had an advanced capitalist industry and a modern working class in the northern cities of the 'industrial triangle' (Genoa, Milan, and Turin), but a rural south of desperately poor peasants dominated by landlords, priests, and the Mafia.

Before the war, the growing militancy and radicalism of the northern working class had begun to penetrate the rural hinterland and stir the villages into motion. This had been countered by harsh repression and a turn to nationalist rhetoric by a political elite notable mainly for its corruption. Imperialism, as elsewhere in Europe, was deployed to undercut the appeal of socialism. Italy embarked on colonial wars in Ethiopia in 1896 and Libya in 1911–12. It then entered the world war with the primary aim of securing territory in the Balkans at the expense of Austria-Hungary.

Despite recent economic development, Italy lacked the industrial base to underpin these imperial ambitions. As Bismarck once remarked, Italy had a large appetite but rotten teeth. The war imposed massive strains on Italian society and brought its deep-rooted social tensions to crisis point.

The majority of Italians were against the war from the outset and continued to oppose it for as long as it lasted. Unfortunately, the

Socialist Party, which included both reformists and revolutionaries, failed to give a clear anti-war lead. Its slogan was 'Neither support nor sabotage'. Lenin's had been 'Down with the imperialist war'.

Italy lost half a million dead in the war, and the misery of the trenches was matched by bread shortages and hunger on the home front. Mass strikes broke out in Turin factories in August 1917 and there were widespread desertions from the army in October and November.

The age-old poverty of the villages, the new exploitation of the factories, and the carnage and privation of the war combined to produce the Two Red Years.

Summer 1919 witnessed a three-day general strike in solidarity with the Russian Revolution. Spring 1920 saw Turin metalworkers on strike demanding recognition for their *camere del lavoro* (factory councils), which the leading revolutionary Antonio Gramsci saw as the Italian equivalent of Russia's soviets. The movement peaked in August 1920. Engineering workers in Milan occupied their factories in response to a lockout by the employers. An occupation movement then swept the industrial triangle. Some 400,000 metalworkers and 100,000 others took part. The occupied factories were treated like military bases: they were defended against the police and arms were stockpiled inside them. The Italian working class had had enough: the mood among workers was insurrectionary.

The government was paralysed. The Prime Minister, Giovanni Giolitti, admitted to the Senate that he had insufficient forces to suppress the movement. So he made some concessions and cut a deal with the union leaders. The Socialist Party was not prepared to challenge this decision. Reformists dominated the apparatus of both unions and party. Had a large, well-rooted revolutionary party led an insurrection in August 1920, it is likely that the Italian working class could have taken state power and pulled the mass of the peasants and the rural and urban poor into action behind it. The primary reason this did not happen was lack of revolutionary clarity, organisation, and direction.

Again, as with the German Revolution, the cost of proletarian defeat would be a sharp swing to the right; and in Italy's case, fascism followed almost immediately.

Antonio Gramsci, the greatest revolutionary of the *Biennio Rosso*, and one of the leading Marxist theoreticians of his day, was among those who would pay with his life. Imprisoned by Mussolini's Fascists in 1926, he died in 1937, his poor health finally destroyed by the conditions in which he was kept.

A comment about his contribution to Marxism is necessary, since his work has been subject to grotesque distortion – by Stalinists, 'Eurocommunists', and 'academic Marxists' – and a thoroughly bowdlerised version of 'Gramscian Marxism' has become widespread. This has been facilitated by the fact that his later work, the famous *Prison Notebooks*, is notable for its exceptional obscurity – a necessity forced upon him by fascist prison censorship.

In prison Gramsci developed important ideas about the complex, multi-layered character of 'civil society' in Western capitalism, and about the distinction in revolutionary strategy between 'wars of position' and 'wars of manoeuvre'. Though sometimes in need of refinement and qualification, these concepts represent significant contributions to Marxist theory.

What they do *not* represent – and what Gramsci never intended they should represent – is a rejection of his revolutionary theory and practice during the *Biennio Rosso*. Contrary to the claims of Stalinists, reformists, and seminar-room critics, there is no evidence in the *Prison Notebooks* that Gramsci had ceased to believe in the centrality of the working class, in spontaneity and the struggle from below, and in the need for rank-and-file organisation, mass participatory democracy, and armed insurrection to overthrow the state. That is why, at his trial in 1926, the fascist prosecutor had demanded his incarceration 'to stop this brain working for 20 years'.

World Revolution

Capitalism is a world system. Much recent talk about 'globalisation' imagines it to have assumed this form only recently. This was not Marx's view. For him, 'the establishment of modern industry and the world market' went hand in hand. Globalisation, in short, is as old as capitalism. It pre-dates the digital technology of the early twenty-first century, the radio communications of the twentieth, and the telegraph cables of the nineteenth. It pre-dates the slave trade in the eighteenth century and the first colonies in the seventeenth. It goes back to the very birth-pangs of the system in the trade networks of fifteenth- and sixteenth-century merchant capitalists.

Capitalism is not only global; it is also highly pervasive. Once it has a grip in one part of the world, it spreads rapidly. This is a function of the competitive character of a world divided into rival corporations and states. Those who fail to develop economically, but remain trapped in pre-industrial social systems, are doomed to defeat. The steel and guns of the *conquistadores* triumphed over the stone weapons of the Aztecs and the Inca. Europeans conquered India with flintlocks and fire discipline. Machine-guns and artillery crushed the Zulus and the Dervishes. This is the basic reason why bourgeois revolutions from below – in Holland, Britain, America, and France – were soon followed by bourgeois revolutions from above – in Italy, Germany, Japan, Turkey, and many other places. Because capitalism unleashes an industrial revolution, ruling classes elsewhere are forced to embrace change or fall behind in the geopolitical struggle. So the imperatives of economic and politico-military competition ensure that industrialisation, once in motion, leaps across the world. The globalisation of commerce becomes the globalisation of industry.

If capitalism is a world system, it follows that the working class is an international class. Workers are divided by nationalism, but this does not reflect their true interests. To take on the bosses, who operate globally, workers have to unite across national boundaries. To achieve social emancipation, they have to destroy the nation-state and create a mass participatory democracy. To defend their gains against counter-revolution by international capital, they have to spread their struggle across the world.

It is not possible to build 'socialism in one country'. Marx, Engels, Lenin, Trotsky, and many other leading Marxist thinkers have all stressed that proletarian revolution has to be worldwide or it will fail. A socialist 'siege economy' can only ever be a temporary measure. Eventually, either poverty and insecurity will force the revolution to turn in on itself and create new forms of exploitation and militarisation in order to survive, or the workers' state will succumb to hostile pressure – a combination of economic boycott, civil war, and foreign military aggression. This knowledge was fundamental to the thinking of the Bolshevik leaders after the October Insurrection. It was why they prioritised the creation of the Communist International (the Comintern or Third International) in 1919.

The Bolsheviks wanted to create a revolutionary international to replace the Second International of Social Democratic parties which had broken up as its respective constituents voted to back their own governments at the outbreak of the First World War. The new Comintern was to be the high command of world revolution. The first four congresses of the Comintern were genuinely revolutionary assemblies of growing size and importance. The First, in March 1919, comprised 51 delegates from 33 countries, the Fourth, in November–December 1922, had 408 delegates from 61 countries.

How realistic was the aim of world revolution?

Revolution is infectious. Because capitalism is a world system, its major crises are international. Similar conditions provoke similar responses, and news of revolution elsewhere can quickly shatter the thin veneer of conformity and obedience. The American Revolution inspired the French Revolution. The 1848 Revolutions spread across Europe. The Russian Revolution of 1917 triggered the most powerful wave of revolutions in human history. The convulsions were not restricted to Germany and Italy. They were felt across the whole of Europe and beyond.

At the end of 1918, the liberal-nationalist government in Hungary collapsed and was replaced by a radical 'Soviet' government of Communists and Social Democrats led by Béla Kun. In April 1919, a 'Soviet Republic' was established in Munich, and in the same month revolutionaries attempted to seize power in Vienna. A fleeting glimpse was offered of a possible alternative future: Budapest, Munich, and Vienna might have formed a revolutionary bloc at the heart of Europe.

It was not to be. In each case, the revolutionaries were not strong enough to prevent the reformists from derailing the revolution. One of the Bavarian revolutionary leaders, facing execution after the Soviet Republic's overthrow, summed up the experience of working with Social Democrat and Independent Socialist 'allies': 'The Social Democrats start, then run away and betray us. The Independents fall for the bait, join us, and then let us down. And we Communists are stood up against the wall. We Communists are all dead men on leave.' The point is simple. Revolution was possible. What frustrated it time and again was the trust workers placed in reformist leaders committed to the defence of capitalism and the state.

Nor was the revolutionary ferment restricted to defeated states like Austria-Hungary and Germany or weak ones like Russia and

Italy. Britain, France, and Spain were all swept by the revolutionary mood.

British troops mutinied because of delays in repatriating them from France, and they refused to go into action against Bolshevik forces when sent to Russia. Engineering strikes in Glasgow led to bitter clashes with the police and the deployment of troops in 1919. The formation of a 'triple alliance' of mining, transport, and rail unions terrified the government in early 1920.

Spain had its 'Three Bolshevik Years' (*Trienio Bolchevista*) of 1918–20, with bread riots, mass strikes, peasant land seizures, violent street clashes, and the proclamation of Bolshevik republics in the towns. 'Here, as everywhere else,' wrote the American novelist John Dos Passos, 'Russia has been the beacon fire.'

The contagion jumped continents. Australia, Canada, and the US experienced mass strikes as workers fought to build unions, raise wages, and improve conditions. It also passed from the major metropolitan countries to the colonial periphery. Irish Republicans waged guerrilla warfare to win independence. Egyptian crowds demanded an end to British rule. Strikes, demonstrations, and riots swept across India. Chinese students triggered a mass movement against colonialism.

Between 1918 and 1923 the future of humanity hung in the balance. Mainstream historians deny the potential and gloss the period with crude references to anarchy. They are more comfortable with the manoeuvres of generals and the routines of statesmen than with mass movements of ordinary people. They lack the historical imagination to envision a world transformed by revolution from below.

The First Chinese Revolution

Between 1911 and 1949 China was transformed by a protracted and complex process of war and revolution. The first phase of this process, accelerated by the impact of the First World War and the Russian Revolution, was ended by counter-revolution in 1927. The second phase, triggered by the Second World War, ended with the victory of the Chinese Communist Party and the establishment of the People's Republic of China in 1949. In the first phase, a proletarian insurrection on the Russian model was a possibility. Its defeat in 1927 was to shape the whole of the country's subsequent history.

China's revolutionary crisis was triggered by imperialism. During the nineteenth century, leading foreign powers had established a series of concessions (colonies and associated commercial privileges) on the Chinese coast. The concessions had been obtained by a combination of bribes, threats, and military action. Chinese nationalist resistance had been crushed, and the decaying Manchu dynasty in Beijing had been propped up by the foreign powers as a shield for the concessions.

But in October 1911, the Manchus, hopelessly discredited by their inability to defend national territory, were overthrown in a military revolt. A republic was proclaimed and the nationalist leader Sun Yatsen, newly returned from exile, was made President.

Sun Yatsen was soon displaced by army commander Yuan Shikai, who dissolved parliament and made himself dictator. The nationalist bourgeoisie was too weak to carry out its historic tasks – forming a stable government, unifying the country, and carrying out modernising reforms. So its place was taken by army officers. But they too lacked the means to overcome the conflicts tearing Chinese society apart.

Sun Yatsen and his Chinese National People's Party (Guomindang) established a new political base in the southern port city of Guangzhou. Most of China, however, was ruled by neither the Beijing dictator nor the Guangzhou liberal; most was under the sway of one or another of more than a thousand regional warlords.

The Chinese bourgeoisie was weak for three reasons. First, only one in five of China's 350 million people lived in towns of any size; it was an essentially agricultural country of landlords and peasants with few railways, bad roads, and little large-scale industry.

Second, the bourgeoisie was divided by its contradictory relationship with imperialism. Some Chinese capitalists wanted to build up native industries and resented the foreign concessions. Others had close economic ties with foreign capitalists.

Third, the bourgeoisie feared the masses. Even those who wanted to fight for national independence worried they might lose control of events to more radical forces. They remembered with foreboding the Taiping and Boxer Rebellions.

The weakness of both the Guangzhou bourgeoisie and the Beijing dictatorship left a political vacuum. This was filled by the warlords, regional military strongmen who built power bases by forming alliances with landlords, businessmen, army officers, and criminal gangs in the areas they controlled. The collapse of central state authority meant a breakdown of order and a threat to property. An unstable mosaic of petty bandit-states was the result. The overthrow of the Manchus therefore had the effect of making China more vulnerable to the depredations of foreign imperialism. The main threat was from Japan.

The Japanese had won effective control of Korea following the Sino-Japanese War of 1894–5, and then of Manchuria following the Russo-Japanese War of 1904–5. These two conflicts made Japan the dominant imperial power in China. During the First World War, Japan seized the German colonies in China and issued a list of 21 Demands which amounted to a claim to a Japanese protectorate over the entire country. By the end of the war, Japan, with the third biggest navy in the world, was a great power, and its appropriation of the German colonies was recognised by the other victorious powers at the 1919 Versailles peace conference.

In consequence, Chinese delegates refused to sign the Versailles Treaty, and when news of it reached Beijing, it triggered a new revolutionary upsurge. Student-led protests against imperialism unleashed a wave of action involving millions of ordinary Chinese, with mass meetings, demonstrations, boycotts of Japanese goods, and a general strike in Shanghai.

The '4 May Movement' of 1919 was far more powerful than that of 1911. War production had increased the size and confidence of the embryonic working class in major ports and production centres like Shanghai. The Russian Revolution had shown how the working class might lead a socialist revolution in a predominantly peasant country. A Marxist study circle had begun meeting at Beijing University in 1918, and the Chinese Communist Party (CCP) was founded in Shanghai in 1921. The following year, major strikes erupted across several cities, with Chinese workers pitted against company thugs, foreign police, and warlord armies. The new CCP now became a mass party.

The national and social struggles began to reinforce one another. National independence could not be achieved without mobilising the masses to defeat imperialism and warlordism; and the workers could not end their poverty without taking on foreign capitalists and police.

Between 1924 and 1927, the Guomindang and the Communists formed an alliance. The Russians set up a military academy at Whampoa to train Guomindang army officers, and Chinese Communists were encouraged to follow the political lead of Sun Yatsen's Nationalists.

When General Jiang Kaishek led the Guomindang into action in the Northern Expedition of 1926, workers' and peasants' risings were organised against local warlords as the Nationalist army approached. A rolling tide of national and social revolution swept across southern China.

Landlords, merchants, and money-lenders fled. Village cooperatives were set up. Urban workers took over their factories. Campaigns against foot binding, child prostitution, opium addiction, and other ancient oppressions took off. A new age of social liberation seemed to be dawning.

Shanghai was the Petrograd of the Chinese Revolution. In March 1927, as Jiang Kaishek approached the city, 600,000 workers joined a 12-day general strike. Armed union militias took control of the city. A government dominated by workers' leaders took power. When the Guomindang army arrived, the workers were told by their leaders to lay down their arms and welcome the Nationalist soldiers as liberators. No sooner had they done so than, in April 1927, Jiang Kaishek unleashed his army on the city in a counter-revolutionary pogrom. More than 50,000 were butchered, the unions broken, and activist networks liquidated. The working-class revolutionary movement in Shanghai was destroyed in a matter of days.

From Shanghai the counter-revolutionary terror spread to other cities and provinces. By the end of the summer, the Nationalists – now in alliance with landlords, capitalists, and foreign powers – had smashed the First Chinese Revolution. In doing so, they had wrecked any possibility of mobilising the mass forces required to win national independence.

The Guomindang was a bourgeois nationalist party. Its leaders and army officers came from the propertied classes. The proletarian and peasant revolution of 1926–7 was therefore seen as a greater threat than warlords and imperialists.

But why had the workers of Shanghai put down their weapons? Why had they surrendered power to the nationalist bourgeoisie? How could the Communist leadership of the working class have made such a catastrophic mistake?

Trotsky had argued vehemently against an alliance with the Guomindang. The Chinese workers had to maintain an independent organisation, he had insisted, including an armed revolutionary militia, and carry out a socialist revolution. But he was overruled. Lenin was dead, Trotsky had been marginalised, and Stalin was now the dominant political figure in Russia.

The Chinese Communists had been led to disaster by their foreign advisers because the Russian leadership, isolated and beleaguered, was turning into a bureaucratic dictatorship hostile to international working-class revolution.

Revolts Against Colonialism

The Chinese Revolution was the most important revolt in the colonial and semi-colonial countries in the aftermath of the First World War. But there were many others of similar kind.

Anti-colonial revolts during the nineteenth century had usually taken a traditional form. Leadership had been provided by tribal chieftains and dynastic potentates. Old weapons and antiquated tactics had been employed against modern firepower. The aim had been to restore the old order.

Anti-colonial revolts in the early twentieth century were different. Led by new resistance movements and spearheaded by the most advanced sections of colonial society, they were inspired by the Russian Revolution and the most radical ideas of the period. What made this possible was the transformation of traditional societies by imperialism. The rapid development of infrastructure and industry by foreign capital had created a new working class. Shanghai and Guangzhou, Bombay and Calcutta, Belfast and Dublin became modern industrial cities. The market penetrated distant villages and threw their economies into crisis. Indian textile weavers were ruined by imports of machine-made goods from Manchester. Collapsing commodity prices pitched Latin American peasants into destitution.

The war accelerated both industrialisation and impoverishment. New war industries sucked in workers from the countryside. Millions of Asians and Africans were mobilised as soldiers or labourers. But conscription, war taxes, and food shortages also meant misery in the slums and villages. Capitalism and war were tearing traditional societies apart, while creating new social forces – an educated middle class and an industrial working class – capable of creating modern movements of mass resistance.

Trotsky wrote of the 'combined and uneven development' that characterised world capitalism at the time. Advanced technology, large-scale industry, and modern cities coexisted with villages where illiterate peasants still relied on hand-drawn ploughs. University students attended communist study circles in cities inhabited by feudal warlords and their armed retainers. Pickets of striking workers were confronted by thugs brandishing medieval swords.

Because combined and uneven development took an extreme form in the colonies and semi-colonies of the periphery, class struggles were often explosive. Events in Ireland and India provide contrasting examples.

Ireland was Britain's oldest colony and had a long history of poverty, oppression, and resistance. During Easter 1916, 800 armed Republican rebels seized key public buildings in central Dublin, notably the General Post Office, and fought a pitched battle against the security forces. Belfast and Dublin had seen fierce class struggles immediately before the First World War, and Ireland had seemed on the brink of Home Rule in 1914. But the Easter Rising was premature. Popular support was limited and planned participation by the Irish Volunteers (essentially a pro-Home Rule militia) was cancelled at the last minute. The result was that the Republican vanguard was isolated and defeated.

But the subsequent execution of the captured leaders outraged Irish opinion and contributed to a sharp swing to the left, which gave Sinn Fein, the main Republican party, a landslide victory in the general election of late 1918. The Sinn Feiners refused to take their seats in the London Parliament and instead formed an Irish Dáil. An Irish Republican Army was organised by Michael Collins to mount a military campaign to destroy the British security apparatus.

The British waged a brutal colonial war against the Irish between 1919 and 1921. Outright victory proved impossible, but they did succeed in splitting the resistance by offering independence to Southern Ireland in return for recognition of British rule over Ulster in the North. The war of independence then degenerated into a civil war. The British backed conservative pro-partition 'Free Staters' like Michael Collins against rejectionist 'Republicans' like Eamon De Valera.

The Irish revolutionary socialist James Connolly, who had been executed for his participation in the Easter Rising, had predicted that partition would lead to 'a carnival of reaction on both sides of the border'. He was right. The mainly peasant South came to be dominated by a 'Green' political elite of Irish Catholic Republicans, the more industrialised North by an 'Orange' political elite of Anglo-Irish Protestant Loyalists. The border turned sectarian cracks into chasms, leaving the Irish working class deeply divided and thereby disempowered.

If Ireland was Britain's oldest colony, India was its biggest, with some 250 million inhabitants. Manpower, supplies, and finance had flowed to European and Middle Eastern battlefronts during the war. When the war ended, demonstrations, strikes, and food riots swept across the country.

On 16 April 1919, General Dyer ordered 50 riflemen to open fire on a crowd of about 20,000 demonstrators gathered inside a walled enclosure at Amritsar. They continued firing for ten minutes and killed up to 1,000 people. As news of the massacre spread, resistance rose to new heights. Millions of peasants, workers, and urban poor became involved in mass action. Hindus and Muslims fought side by side against bosses, landlords, and police. The Governor of Bombay later admitted that the movement 'gave us a scare' and 'came within an inch of succeeding'.

Its failure had nothing to do with the British. The action was called off by Mahatma Gandhi and the leaders of Congress, the main Indian nationalist party. Gandhi had turned 'non-violence' (*ahimsa*) into a principle. Despite the violence of the recent imperialist war, which he had supported, despite the violence of a foreign army of occupation prepared to use lethal force against protestors, Gandhi opposed the use of armed self-defence by the Indian national movement in its struggle for independence.

For Gandhi – a moderate nationalist in the guise of a mystic – *ahimsa* may have been a matter of principle. Its political significance, however, was that it limited the struggle to nationalist agitation for independence and prevented it evolving into a class struggle against exploitation – which would have threatened the interests of the Indian bourgeoisie represented by Congress. Under determined revolutionary leadership, the Indian national movement might have ended British rule in the early 1920s. Under vacillating liberal leadership, it allowed foreign rule to continue for another quarter of a century, and, when it ended, it would be immediately followed by communal violence, ethnic cleansing, and genocide of unprecedented ferocity.

Why did the colonial revolutions fail? Trotsky's theory of permanent revolution, first developed to explain the character of the Russian Revolution, provides an answer. The nationalist bourgeoisie vacillated because it was bound by strong ties to a social order based on private ownership of land and capital. Whenever mass movements of workers and peasants became powerful enough to threaten colonial rule, they also threatened the property and power of native landlords and capitalists. Class instincts then ensured that nationalist leaders either reined in the movement or joined the counter-revolution to crush it. The lesson was an old one: the emancipation of the masses would have to be undertaken by the masses themselves. Freedom would never be granted. It would have to be taken.

Stalinism: The Bitter Fruit of Revolutionary Defeat

By late 1923, almost everywhere in the world, the great revolutionary wave stirred into motion by the First World War was ebbing away. The German Revolution had been defeated, and the Weimar Republic, a liberal parliamentary regime, had achieved a measure of stability. The October Insurrection of 1917 had not ignited the world socialist revolution that the Bolsheviks had worked for. Lenin himself became a poignant symbol of the decay of revolutionary hope: increasingly incapacitated by a series of strokes, he died in 1924. The Russian Revolution was left isolated, surrounded by enemies, devastated by war, and impoverished by economic collapse. Struggling to survive in desperate conditions, the Bolshevik regime turned in on itself and degenerated into a hideous mockery of its former socialist ideals.

The great lie of twentieth-century political history is that this outcome was inevitable, that Stalinism was the direct result of the Bolshevik Revolution. The reality was very different. In the winter of 1927/8 the party-state bureaucracy that had emerged in Russia under Stalin's leadership carried out a counter-revolution. It had been accumulating power for a decade, and when it moved decisively in the late 1920s, it was able to destroy all remaining vestiges of working-class democracy. Meetings were packed, speakers shouted down, and oppositionists purged and deported by a party-state machine now dominated by officials who had joined the Communist Party since the Revolution. The United Opposition, led by Trotsky and Zinoviev, was broken up.

During the 1930s the bureaucracy consolidated its grip by liquidating virtually the whole of the old Bolshevik Party. Veterans of the October Insurrection were arrested, tortured, paraded in show trials, denounced as 'saboteurs' and 'wreckers', executed by Stalin's secret police, or incarcerated in Siberian gulags.

Of the nine members of Lenin's last Politburo (in 1923), only Stalin, Molotov, and Kollontai were still alive at the end of 1940. Of the others, Lenin had died of natural causes, Tomsky had committed suicide in fear of arrest, and Kamenev, Zinoviev, Bukharin, Rykov, and Trotsky had all been murdered.

How was this possible? Again and again, the Bolshevik leaders had insisted that backward Russia could not achieve socialism in isolation. 'The final victory of socialism in a single country is, of course, impossible', explained Lenin on 11 January 1918. 'Our contingent of workers and peasants which is upholding Soviet power is one of the contingents of the great world army.' What the Bolshevik leaders had not been able to predict was the form of the counter-revolution which eventually overwhelmed them. Three crushing material factors eventually destroyed the Russian Revolution: the social weight of the peasantry, the economic collapse caused by war, and the disintegration of the working class.

The alliance between workers and peasants had made the Revolution possible. The peasants outnumbered the workers ten to one. If the workers had not won over the peasants, they would have been shot down by peasant-soldiers loyal to the Tsar. Instead, the Bolsheviks had promised 'bread, peace, and land', and the peasants had supported the October Insurrection.

But the interests of the workers and peasants then diverged. The working class is a collective class because its labour is collective. Workers cannot divide the mines, factories, and railways into individual units. They have to run the economy as an integrated whole. The peasantry, on the other hand, is a class of individualists, because every peasant aspires to be a prosperous independent farmer. The peasants will support urban revolutionaries who allow them to seize the land. But further cooperation depends on the ability of the towns to produce goods they can trade with the villages. If they fail to do this, the peasants will not trade and the towns will starve. The Bolsheviks understood this. Their problem was that production had collapsed. The combination of world war, revolution, and civil war caused such massive disruption that industrial output fell to less than a fifth of its 1914 level.

Shortages of food, fuel, and other basic necessities meant that between late 1918 and late 1920 at least ten million Russians died of hunger, disease, and cold – more than twice the number lost in the world war. This drove the third factor. The working class physically disintegrated as millions abandoned the towns and returned to the villages where they had family. The urban population of Russia was reduced by more than half.

Even the workers who remained were not the same. The revolutionary government had to administer a vast territory, regenerate a broken economy, and fight a civil war against White armies backed by no fewer than 14 foreign expeditionary forces. The revolutionary proletariat of 1917 was therefore transformed into the Red Army of 1920. Then, as sections of the economy cranked up again, new workers were sucked in from the countryside. So the Russian working class of 1920 was not only much smaller than that of 1917; its composition was also very different.

By the end of the Civil War, the revolutionary working class had dissolved, the peasantry was in control of the land, and the landlord and capitalist classes had been vanquished. The only organised social force operating at national level was the party-state administration.

Had full democracy been restored, the country would have been torn apart by the contradiction between the interests of the international working class and the interests of the Russian peasantry. The Bolsheviks had no choice but to attempt to hold onto power in the hope that they would be rescued by world revolution. For a while, the revolutionary tradition itself could act as an historical force, even though now embodied in a revolutionary apparatus rather than a revolutionary class.

But the Bolsheviks could not defy gravity. Eventually, they would succumb to the hostile social forces all around them. Lenin could see it: 'Ours is not actually a workers' state,' he said as early as 1920, 'but a workers' and peasants' state ... But that is not all. Our party programme shows that ours is a workers' state with bureaucratic distortions.' Later, alarmed at the influence of former Tsarist officials and newly recruited careerists in the government apparatus, he posed the question: 'This mass of bureaucrats – who is leading whom?'

The New Economic Policy (NEP) of 1921–8 was an attempt to resolve the economic contradictions and win breathing space before the next global revolutionary upsurge. It allowed private production and a free market to develop alongside state enterprise. The effect was to foster the development of a class of entrepreneurs, the 'NEPmen', and a class of rich peasants, the *kulaks*. At the same time, the 'red industrialists' who ran state enterprises behaved increasingly like conventional capitalists in relation to their own workers. The imperatives of running a backward economy in an embattled state were transforming the political character of the ruling regime.

In the winter of 1927/8 Lenin's question 'who is leading whom?' received its definitive answer. Crushing both the Right (representing the NEPmen and the *kulaks*) and the Left (representing the Bolshevik tradition), Stalin's Centre emerged from the backrooms of the Communist Party as the political expression of a new bureaucratic ruling class.

14

The Great Depression and
the Rise of Fascism
1929–1939

Spanish revolutionary militia, 1936.

The Great Depression polarised European politics as
revolutionary workers battled to halt the advance of fascism.

The defeat of the Russian Revolution and the global movement it had inspired was followed by a brief period of relative stability. The capitalist system made a partial economic recovery, the post-war regimes settled into the dull routines of parliamentary politics, and the millions who had been stirred into action by the revolutionary mass movements of 1917–23 lapsed back into the alienation and apathy of everyday life. But the breathing-space was brief.

The modest economic boom of the mid to late 1920s was built on the shifting sands of financial speculation. The 'fundamentals' – industrial investment, rising labour productivity, increased manufacturing output – remained weak. When boom turned to bust in 1929, the system was plunged into an intractable crisis deeper than any previously known. So desperate were social conditions in what came to be called 'the Great Depression' that millions of ordinary people were once again drawn into mass struggles against the system.

But other forces were also in motion. The crisis broke the centre and led to polarisation to both left and right. The 1930s became dominated by an apocalyptic confrontation between socialist revolution and fascist reaction. The victory of the latter would lead directly to another world war, even longer, bloodier, and more barbaric than the first.

The Roaring Twenties

The post-war wave of struggle and radicalisation was short-lived in the United States. From 1920 the economy boomed and a new culture of individualism took hold. By 1928 output was double the level of 1914. Economists announced that capitalism's 'childhood diseases' were things of the past and that 'the economic condition of the world seems on the verge of a great forward movement'.

The American market was flooded with consumer goods that had previously been available only to a small minority. Ordinary homes were supplied with electric power. Middle-class families acquired telephones, radios, gramophones, vacuum cleaners, and refrigerators. Millions went to the cinema each week. Cars ceased to be a luxury and became mass-market commodities. The American Dream seemed to have become an everyday reality. 'Everybody ought to be rich', announced John J. Raskob, director of General Motors and chair of the Democratic Party's National Committee. Many ordinary Americans agreed.

Europe was slower to join the 'Roaring Twenties'. The economic impact of the war, the social dislocation, the great upsurge of revolution had all been far more powerful in Europe than in the States. But after 1923, Europeans also joined the 'Jazz Age'.

The Dawes Plan, which provided a flow of US loans, helped revive German capitalism and stabilise the Weimar Republic in the later 1920s. Britain embarked on a new industrial revolution, with high-tech industries like cars, aircraft, and consumer durables developing in the Midlands and the South-East, and new suburbs being built around old urban centres.

As in the United States, the re-stabilisation of capitalism prompted optimistic predictions of permanent prosperity and harmony. 'Our economy is sound,' proclaimed Germany's Social Democratic Chancellor Hermann Müller in 1928, 'our system of social welfare is sound, and you will see that the Communists as well as the Nazis will be absorbed by the traditional parties.' Germany's leading economists thought so too: 'There has been a clear tendency in European economic life for antagonistic tendencies to balance each other, to grow less, and finally to disappear.'

But the contradictions of capitalism had not been abolished. Equally significant – though less noted – were the clear limits to the economic recovery. State arms expenditure had sustained the world economy in the run-up to and during the First World War. It had been the pre-war arms race that had ended the Long Depression of 1873–96. Even in the late nineteenth century, the signs were there that the system had a fatal addiction to guns. But arms spending was cut to a fraction of wartime levels after 1918. The result was mass unemployment. The system thus proved incapable of an orderly resumption of civilian production. The market turned out not to be 'self-regulating'.

Growth remained patchy and modest throughout the 1920s. For every success, there was a failure. Unemployment never dropped below one million in Britain in the interwar years. Wage cuts in the pits provoked a six-month miners' strike and a nine-day general strike in 1926. War reparations brought the German economy to its knees in the early 1920s, and hyperinflation wiped out the value of savings in 1923.

The French economy was propped up by German war reparations, the US economy by war-loan repayments and a policy of 'easy money' (cheap credit through low interest rates). It was this that enabled the US economy to boom for a decade. But, even in the US, some capitalists were 'roaring' only because others were squealing.

A central contradiction of capitalism is that it imposes low wages in the workplace but requires high spending in the marketplace. In the long run, you cannot have both. When wages are squeezed to reduce costs and raise profits, workers cannot afford to buy the goods that their labour has produced. But if wages increase and profits are reduced, capitalists have no incentive to invest. The search for profit powers the system.

In America's Roaring Twenties, farm incomes were down and wages did not rise. Demand in the 'real economy' was therefore depressed. Industrial investment was in consequence too sluggish to absorb the surplus capital with which the system was awash. So it flowed into speculation. Specifically, it fed a self-sustaining speculative bubble on the Wall Street Stock Exchange.

F. Scott Fitzgerald's novel *The Great Gatsby* (1926) captures the vacuousness of the period. The futility of the lives of its characters – obscenely wealthy members of the American bourgeoisie – mirrors their absence of social function. The empty minds and endless round of self-indulgence reflect the bubble economy of financial parasitism.

Financial bubbles are as old as capitalism. There was a bubble of speculation in tulips in early seventeenth-century Holland ('Tulipmania') and a bubble of speculation in colonial investment in early eighteenth-century England (the 'South Sea Bubble'). The Long Depression of 1873–96 had begun with a financial crash following a speculative boom.

The way a bubble works is simple. If demand for a paper asset is high enough, its price will rise. If the price of an asset is rising, more investors will want to buy it, hoping to profit from further rises when they sell it on. If there is enough surplus capital, and if paper assets keep rising in price because of high demand, take-off becomes possible: assets continue to rise in value simply because more and more investors want to buy them – *irrespective* of the relationship between their price and the actual value of the goods or services represented.

Paper assets are essentially loans of money in return for titles to ownership. They can take the form of corporate shares, government bonds, insurance policies, currency holdings, bundles of mortgages, advance purchases of commodities, and many other things; the 'financial services industry' is very inventive. The 'normal' return on capital is a share in the profits of the real economy. A 'speculative' return arises when the link between the price of paper assets and the value of actual commodities has broken down. Price rises then become self-sustaining and sometimes go stratospheric in a frenzy of get-rich-quick buying and selling.

Global debt increased by about 50 per cent during the 1920s. This is one measure of the creation of fictitious capital. Whole new classes of holding companies and investment trusts emerged. These companies produced nothing. They simply traded in the stock of other companies. Often, the companies they invested in were other holding companies and investment trusts. Sometimes the layers of fictitious capital could be five, even ten deep.

Goldman Sachs Trading Corporation is an example. It was formed on 4 December 1928 and issued an initial $100 million of stock, 90 per cent of it sold direct to the general public. With this capital, it invested in the stock of other companies. In February 1929 Goldman Sachs merged with another investment trust. Assets were now valued at $235 million. In July the joint enterprise launched the Shenandoah Corporation. When it offered $102 million of stock for sale, the issue was oversubscribed sevenfold. No one wanted to miss out on this money-for-nothing miracle. The company duly obliged and issued yet more stock.

As the frenzy mounted, capital was sucked out of foreign loans, industrial investment, and infrastructure projects. Nothing was as profitable as speculation on Wall Street. Loose money and a weak economy gave rise to a massive imbalance between the price of paper assets and the value of real commodities.

The bubble was a trap. Some observers tried to sound a warning. 'Sooner or later a crash is coming,' declared Roger Babson to the Annual National Business Conference on 5 September 1929, 'and it may be terrific.' But prophets of doom were not welcome at the party. A lot of very rich people had staked a fortune on making themselves even richer. They wholeheartedly endorsed President Coolidge's optimistic State of the Union address the previous December: 'No

Congress of the United States ever assembled has met with a more pleasing prospect than that which appears at the present time ... there is tranquillity and contentment ... and the highest record of years of prosperity.'

When, a short while later, the Stock Market got the jitters, Secretary of the Treasury Andrew Mellon was quick to offer reassurance: 'There is no cause for worry. The high tide of prosperity will continue.' *The Wall Street Journal* was also keen to dispel investors' anxieties: 'price movements in the main body of stocks yesterday continued to display the characteristics of a major advance temporarily halted for technical readjustment'.

On 24 October 1929, the Wall Street Stock Market crashed. The financial collapse pitched the world into the Great Depression and triggered the sequence of events that led eventually to Stalingrad, Auschwitz, and Hiroshima. The first act in the greatest tragedy in human history had begun.

The Hungry Thirties

On 'Black Thursday' the Wall Street Stock Exchange fell by almost a third. Thousands of finance capitalists were wiped out. Millions of ordinary people lost their savings. Once started, the crash, like the bubble that preceded it, was self-sustaining. Just as rising prices had sucked speculative capital into the vortex, now collapsing prices generated a stampede to sell, to 'liquidate' capital, to withdraw from the market before prices fell further. When investors found themselves overexposed, moreover, debts were called in to pay other debts, fuelling the reverse frenzy of panic selling and falling prices. The whole complex of financial obligations was suddenly unravelling.

The value of shares in the Shenandoah Corporation had peaked at $36. They eventually went down to 50 cents. Goldman Sachs Trading Corporation stocks had hit $222.50. Two years later, you could buy them for a dollar or two.

The crash did not come from nowhere. Agriculture had been depressed since 1927, and industry was afflicted by a classic cyclical downturn due to over-expansion and under-consumption during the spring and summer of 1929. The agricultural and industrial crises triggered the financial crash. But the crash then fed back into the real economy, collapsing credit, choking off loans and investment, shrinking demand.

The concentration and centralisation of capital magnified the scale of the crisis. When a small or medium-sized firm is bankrupted, the overall impact is limited; many others remain open for business. When a major bank or industrial corporation is bankrupted, it pulls many others down with it, sending a deflationary wave across the wider economy. That is what happened now. By 1933, 9,000 American banks had failed, industrial production had almost halved, and one in three workers was unemployed. Nor was there so much as a glimmer of recovery. American capitalism appeared to be dead in the water.

A world system meant a world crisis. The Wall Street Crash triggered a global slump. The value of world trade collapsed to a third of its 1929 figure. Unemployment leapt from ten million worldwide to 40 million by 1932. In that year, one in three workers was unemployed in Germany, one in five in Britain.

What made the Great Depression so disastrous were the policies pursued by world leaders. Drastic cuts were not the immediate response to the crash. But when the global economy nosedived in 1931, politicians panicked. US President Hoover was obsessed with 'sound money' and a 'balanced budget'. He denounced programmes for large-scale spending, and was soon lecturing his successor-elect, Franklin D. Roosevelt, on the virtues of what would today be called 'deficit cutting'. His Treasury Secretary's remedy was to 'liquidate labour, liquidate stocks, liquidate the farmers'.

Democracy, moreover, was soon under attack as hard-right regimes drove through cuts in the face of mass resistance. Conservative German Chancellor Heinrich Brüning's response to the crash was to cut wages, cut salaries, cut prices, and raise taxes. He did this at a time when one in four German workers was unemployed. The effect was to push it up to one in three.

Brüning did not last long. The depth of the economic crisis and the polarisation of German society paralysed the political system. After Brüning's resignation, President Hindenburg appointed a rapid succession of Chancellors: von Papen, von Schleicher, then Adolf Hitler. None commanded a parliamentary majority. German Chancellors ruled by emergency decree. Democracy ceased to operate in Germany from 1930 onwards. After January 1933 its very possibility was destroyed by the Nazi dictatorship, installed in power by Hindenburg, acting on behalf of Germany's traditional rulers.

In Britain a minority Labour government elected in 1929 found itself under siege by finance capital. As unemployment soared, dole payments were to be cut to satisfy 'the vital need for securing budget equilibrium'. One Cabinet minister later recalled:

One of the memories that abides with me ... is that of 20 men and one woman, representing the government of the country, standing one black Sunday evening in the Downing Street garden awaiting a cable from New York as to whether the pound was to be saved or not, and whether the condition would be insisted upon that the unemployed [rate] would be cut [by] 10 per cent.

The condition was insisted on. The bankers wanted the impoverishment of the unemployed as a token of the Labour government's total submission. They also wanted unanimity: the whole Cabinet was to vote it through. Otherwise the government was to resign. 'So it is the financiers, British and American, who will settle the personnel and the policy of the British Government', wrote the leading Fabian Beatrice Webb in her diary. 'The dictatorship of the capitalist class with a vengeance!'

The Cabinet split. The government resigned. The former Labour Prime Minister Ramsay MacDonald became head of a reactionary, deficit-cutting 'National' Government.

Governments also devalued their currencies to make their exports cheaper, while imposing tariffs on imports to make them more expensive. But protectionism is a competitive process. When rival states did the same, the effect was an accelerating 'race to the bottom', with falling prices and shrinking markets leading to a catastrophic collapse in international trade.

Deflation and protectionism, on top of the economic downturn and the financial crash, destroyed any possibility of recovery. They locked the world into a decade of economic slump and mass impoverishment. They guaranteed what the Liberal economist and critic of state policy John Maynard Keynes called 'an underemployment equilibrium' – permanent mass unemployment.

The economics of the Great Depression were the economics of the madhouse. The purpose of any economic system should be to produce the goods and services people need to live full and happy lives. But that is not the purpose of capitalism.

Capitalism is a system of competitive capital accumulation driven by profit and the enrichment of the few. The drive for profit – as much as possible, as quick as possible, no matter how – had created the speculative bubble of the late 1920s. Now, in the crash, shoring up profits meant cutting wages, slashing services, and choking trade, thereby plunging the world into permanent slump.

Hundreds of millions of lives were torn apart. Farmers were ruined as markets disappeared and commodity prices collapsed. Workers lost their jobs and lived on hand-outs from soup kitchens. Those still in work lived in fear of the sack, and bosses went onto the offensive over wages, conditions, and workloads.

Across Europe, support for mainstream parties associated with austerity collapsed and politics became polarised between radical movements of the working class and fascist movements of the middle class. On the streets of Berlin, Vienna, Paris, Barcelona, and London, the forces of hope and despair, of revolution and counter-revolution, clashed repeatedly during the 1930s in a struggle for the heart and soul of Europe.

1933: The Nazi Seizure of Power

On 31 January 1933, Adolf Hitler, leader of the National Socialist German Workers (Nazi) Party, became German Chancellor. A month later, the Communist Party was banned, its newspapers shut down, and 10,000 of its members sent to concentration camps. Soon after, the leaders of the Social Democratic Party and of the German trade unions were also sent to concentration camps. In a matter of months, the Nazis had destroyed the most powerful labour movement in the world.

The unions and the socialist parties are the basis of democracy. Without mass working-class organisation, capital and the state rule unchallenged. Consequently, by the end of 1933, the conservative and liberal parties had also been destroyed. Germany had become a totalitarian police state.

The final cost of Nazism would be astronomical. Seven million Germans would die and 14 million be made homeless during the Second World War. Millions of men would be shot and millions of women raped as the Russian Army advanced across eastern Germany in 1944 and 1945. Across the globe, the war unleashed by the Nazis would kill 60 million. Between 1939 and 1945, the race myths of the tenth century would fuse with the technology of the twentieth to create the greatest disaster in human history. What had made this possible?

The Great Depression hit Germany harder than any other European state. The American bankers demanded repayment of the Dawes Plan loans which had boosted the economy in the mid-1920s. The bankers demanded massive cuts to balance the books. German governments obliged, cutting jobs, wages, and benefits. The economy nose-dived and a third of workers were unemployed. Farms and small businesses were ruined. Managers, professionals, and clerical workers found themselves out of work alongside miners and steelworkers.

Capitalist crisis shreds the social fabric and polarises politics. When people's anger is directed against bankers, politicians, and the system, they move to the left, towards class struggle and revolutionary change. When they turn against one another, they move to the right, towards the politics of hate. The Great Depression created a sharp polarity between socialist parties of revolutionary hope and fascist parties of counter-revolutionary despair.

Fascism was a new type of political movement first pioneered in Italy immediately after the First World War. The very word is Italian. Benito Mussolini – an unstable political adventurer who had broken with the Socialist Party because he supported the imperialist war – had begun recruiting a right-wing nationalist following during Italy's 'Two Red Years' in 1919 and 1920.

The Fascists were essentially a middle-class movement of army veterans, professionals, students, minor landowners, and petty proprietors. Paramilitary squads of Fascist Blackshirts (*squadristi*) carried out attacks on occupations, picket-lines, union offices, socialist printing presses, and individual activists. But their influence was limited when the workers' movement was on the offensive. Only with the defeat of the factory occupations in the summer of 1920 did the Fascists become a major force. The number of active squads increased from 190 in October 1920 to 2,300 in November 1921.

The failure of the Left made the Fascists attractive to many of the unemployed and to working-class youth in slums and villages lacking a socialist tradition. It also made them appear more plausible to their core middle-class supporters. But the Left was still a threat, and this ensured support for Mussolini from industrialists and liberal politicians. Henceforward the *squadristi* were funded by leading capitalists and given a free hand by the police. Fascist thugs were unleashed by the Italian ruling class to smash the retreating workers' movement.

By October 1922 Mussolini was strong enough to demand a place in government. A Fascist 'March on Rome' was unopposed and King Victor Emmanuel appointed Mussolini Prime Minister. Thereafter Blackshirts and police worked together to destroy the working-class movement and establish a totalitarian state.

Mussolini was widely admired in European ruling-class circles as a 'strongman' who had brought order out of chaos. Italy's Blackshirts provided a political model for others to follow. Among those who attempted to do so was Hitler, a failed artist, doss-house dropout, war veteran, and virulent anti-semite. But the infant Nazi Party's Beer Hall Putsch (an attempted right-wing coup in Munich in November 1923) was broken up by the police.

Hitler's party remained in the doldrums for six years. But its vote rocketed from 800,000 (3 per cent) in 1928 to six million (18 per cent) in 1930 and almost 14 million (37 per cent) in July 1932. Its paramilitary wing, the Brownshirts of the SA (*Sturmabteilung*), quadrupled from 100,000 at the end of 1930 to 400,000 by mid-1932.

The Nazi struggle for power was three-pronged. Mass rallies and parades created an impression of strength and determination in the face of the social crisis. The Brownshirts engaged in a relentless struggle on the streets to destroy working-class organisation. And Hitler lobbied big business and state leaders for funding, support, and a share in power.

The core of Nazi support, like that of the Italian Fascists, was the middle class. Hitler expressed the rage of the socially aspirant in a world that was falling apart and shattering their hopes. The petty proprietor, the junior executive, the small-town professional hated in equal measure the capitalists and politicians who had caused the crisis and the unions and left parties which represented the workers. Their powerlessness enraged them.

The concept of an 'international Jewish conspiracy' linking Moscow and Wall Street, communists and capitalists, the workers and the rich, was the supreme expression of the Nazis' irrational worldview. It became the hideous ideology of those described by

Trotsky as 'human dust' – a glue to bind together the otherwise atomised individuals who formed the fascist mass movement.

The Nazis also appropriated the German national cause. The Versailles Treaty had confiscated chunks of Germany's territory, restricted the size of its armed forces, and imposed massive reparations payments. The Weimar politicians had failed to challenge this architecture of national disempowerment. Hitler promised action.

By late 1932 powerful sections of the traditional German elite were prepared to back the Nazis in an attempt to solve the economic crisis in their own way. Hitler would tear up the Versailles Treaty, end crippling reparations payments, and rebuild German power in Europe. The Brownshirts would destroy the Left at home.

The Nazis would end the drift and unite the nation. They would make the world safe for German capital. That is why one leading Ruhr industrialist, Fritz Thyssen, became 'a keen Nazi supporter', why Chancellor von Papen said 'it would be a disaster if the Hitler movement collapsed or was crushed', and why President Hindenburg, a First World War field-marshal, invited Hitler, a First World War corporal, to form a government in January 1933 at the very moment when Nazi support was beginning to wane.

The fascist victory was not inevitable. In July 1932 the combined SPD (Social Democrat) and KPD (Communist) vote was a little over 13 million (36 per cent), almost as many as the Nazis (37 per cent). Both the SPD and KPD had their own armed self-defence forces. Nazi marches in working-class areas had frequently been attacked and broken up. As late as the afternoon and evening of 30 January 1933, mass demonstrations against Hitler had erupted spontaneously across Germany. Millions of workers understood the danger and were prepared to fight.

But the SPD leaders were supine in the face of both the Depression and the Nazis. They had argued for 'toleration' of austerity cuts and 'legality' in response to the Brownshirts' violence. As Hitler took power, their main paper proclaimed that the party stood 'foursquare on the grounds of the constitution and legality'.

The charge against the Communist leaders is equally serious. They should have appealed to the Social Democratic workers to form a united front against fascist violence and takeover. Instead, their strategy was one of sectarian stupidity and self-imposed isolation. They talked down the fascist danger, denounced the Social

Democrats as 'social-fascists', and refused to unite with them on the basis that they posed a greater threat to the working class than Hitler.

Why did the Communist leaders follow this line? The SPD had, of course, engineered the defeat of the German Revolution between 1918 and 1923. The KPD had been prone to 'ultra-leftism' ever since, being deeply hostile to reformist leaders and unwilling to form a united front with them in pursuit of common goals. But the KPD's sectarian instincts were reinforced by 'the line' dictated by Moscow.

The Comintern, the Moscow-based Communist International, was now under the control of Stalin and the new bureaucratic ruling class in Russia. Ultra-left sectarianism had become official Soviet policy as a cover for the counter-revolutionary character of the dramatic changes underway within Russia.

In 1923 the young German Communist Party had missed its chance to lead a socialist revolution. In 1933 the same Communist Party – now older, but no wiser, and much deformed by Stalinism – had failed to prevent a fascist coup. The historical importance of revolutionary leadership has never been clearer.

State Capitalism in Russia

First the Wall Street Crash plunged the world into the Great Depression and put 40 million out of work. Then the Nazis, the most barbaric political movement of modern times, seized power in Germany. No wonder millions of desperate activists looked for an alternative. No wonder they believed Stalin's claim to be the world's standard-bearer against capitalism and fascism. Mass unemployment and the menace of fascism made them uncritical. Why should they believe reports in the West of atrocities and injustices in the Soviet Union? Was it not inevitable that the capitalist press would denigrate the homeland of socialist revolution?

After all, the Soviet economy was booming, while the rest of the world was mired in depression. The success of Stalin's Five Year Plans seemed prodigious. Between 1927/8 and 1937, industrial output increased five-fold. Whereas the Soviet Union had accounted for just 4 percent of global industrial production in 1929, this had risen to 12 percent by 1939.

But this was not the triumph of socialism. On the contrary, all vestiges of workers' control of industry had been stamped out. In its place, a new model of state-capitalist development was being pioneered, where the ruling class was formed of government bureaucrats, the national economy was run like a single giant corporation, and all forms of dissent and resistance were treated as crimes against the state.

This transformation – from workers' democracy to a new form of class society – had resulted from the disintegration and defeat of the revolutionary mass movement.

Lenin had seen the danger: 'The party's proletarian policy', he had written, 'is determined at present not by its rank and file, but by the immense and undivided authority of tiny sections of what might be called the party's "old guard".' The party had been filled with the *arrivistes* of post-revolutionary times because party membership had become a passport to a paid post in government, army, or industry. As early as 1922, only one in 40 members had joined before the February Revolution.

Lenin had also identified Stalin as the potential leader of the emerging party-state bureaucracy. In a secret 'Testament' written shortly before his death, Lenin had warned leading party comrades that Stalin, the Secretary-General of the Party, had unlimited authority concentrated in his hands, that he was too boorish and bureaucratic to wield such power, and that they should consider 'removing Stalin from that post and appointing another man in his stead'. The Testament was suppressed, and, with civil society hollowed out by war and economic collapse, the party-state apparatus swelled to fill the vacuum. Stalin's position gave him control of this apparatus. By the mid-1920s, it was the dominant force in society.

The annihilation of opposition currents inside the party was easily accomplished by the police agents of the bureaucracy in 1928 – both the Right, led by Bukharin and representing the private capitalist interests which had developed under the New Economic Policy, and the Left, led by Trotsky and representing the revolutionary socialist tradition of the Bolsheviks.

Against Trotsky was the power of inertia in an exhausted, impoverished, peasant country. Without world revolution to reinforce them, backward war-torn Russia had simply consumed its native revolutionaries – until they were so few that they could be swept into the oblivion of the gulags.

Even so, the idealism and self-emancipation of the revolutionary years survived in popular memory and served to indict all that followed. For this reason, the remaining revolutionaries were hounded to their deaths during the 1930s. Only one in 14 of the Bolshevik Party's 1917 members still belonged to the Communist Party of the Soviet Union in 1939; virtually all the rest were dead.

The bureaucracy had acted in 1928 because it had the power to do so and because it was confronted by an acute crisis. The peasants were refusing to supply enough grain to the cities, while foreign governments were cutting diplomatic relations, banning trade links, and threatening war. The leadership's response was to seize the grain, drive down wages, and impose rapid industrialisation. 'To slacken the pace of industrialisation would mean to lag behind,' Stalin announced, 'and those who lag behind are beaten … We are 50 to 100 years behind the advanced countries. We must make good this lag in ten years or they will crush us.'

Russia had survived civil war and foreign invasion: the new regime had not been destroyed by military force. But the defeat of the world revolution had left Russia isolated and impoverished in a global economy dominated by capitalism. So the counter-revolution was achieved not by violent overthrow, but by the relentless external pressure of economic and military competition. The Soviet Union needed to export grain to pay for machine tools. It needed machine tools to build modern industries. And it needed modern industries to produce the guns, tanks, and planes with which to defend itself in a predatory global system of competing nation-states.

Private capital accumulation was too slow. What Bukharin in the 1920s had called 'socialism at a snail's pace' would have left it trailing behind and vulnerable to dismemberment by hostile powers. Only the state had the power to concentrate resources, impose a plan, override opposition, and drive through rapid forced industrialisation.

Stalin's policy reflected wider trends in the world economy. Under the impact of the Great Depression, there was a global shift towards state-managed capitalism, with more public spending and government intervention in the economy to compensate for the failure of private capital to invest. The Soviet system represented the extreme end of a spectrum. Stalin's aim was mass production to build state power. Soviet rulers thus became the personification of state-capitalist accumulation.

But they also used their power to reward themselves handsomely, even as they plundered the peasantry, cut wages, increased work pressure, and filled the gulags with slave-labourers. By 1937, plant directors were paid 2,000 roubles a month, skilled workers 200–300 roubles, and workers on the minimum wage 110–15 roubles. Pay differentials in the army were even more extreme: during the Second World War, colonels were paid 2,400 roubles a month, private soldiers 10 roubles. The pay of plant directors and army colonels was modest, however, compared with that of top members of the state bourgeoisie, who could earn up to 25,000 roubles a month – more than 200 times the minimum wage.

So the bureaucracy evolved into a privileged class with a clear material interest in remaining loyal to Stalin and the state-capitalist system. It proved utterly ruthless in imposing forced industrialisation on society at a colossal cost in human suffering. Consumption was sacrificed to investment in heavy industry. The proportion of investment devoted to plant, machinery, and raw materials, as opposed to consumer goods, rose from 33 per cent in 1927/8, to 53 per cent by 1932, and 69 per cent by 1950. The result was shortages and queues – though less than there might have been, because at the same time wages were cut by an estimated 50 per cent over six years.

Grain was expropriated from the peasantry to feed the growing urban population and to pay for imports of foreign machinery. Because of this, when the price collapsed on world markets in 1929, at least three million peasants starved to death.

It was still not enough. The state decreed the 'collectivisation [state control] of agriculture'. Millions of peasants – denounced as *kulaks* (rich peasants producing for the market) – were dispossessed and transported. Many died. Others became slave-labourers in the gulags.

The Siberian gulags expanded into a vast slave empire run by Stalin's security apparatus. The 30,000 prisoners of 1928 had become two million by 1931, five million by 1935, and probably more than ten million by the end of the decade. A million or more were simply murdered by the police, the annual death toll rising from 20,000 in 1930 to a peak of 350,000 in 1937.

State terror on this scale reflected the backwardness of the economy, the pace of state-capitalist accumulation, and the levels of exploitation necessary to achieve it. The working class, the peasantry, and the national minorities had to be pulverised into submission.

The damage was not confined to the Soviet Union. The revolutionary content of Marxism was abandoned, but its verbal formulas were retained and redeployed to justify the policies of the bureaucracy. The Comintern became a vehicle for imposing the ideology and policies of the Soviet state on foreign communist parties.

In 1927, having abandoned world revolution in favour of 'socialism in one country', Stalin tried to break out of his country's isolation by seeking respectable allies abroad. So the Chinese Communist Party was instructed to subordinate itself to the Nationalist general Jiang Kaishek and to order the Shanghai working class to lay down its arms. The result was a counter-revolutionary massacre.

The following year the policy switched abruptly to sectarianism and adventurism. In the Comintern's disastrous 'Third Period', Stalin proclaimed a new revolutionary advance – Communists were to break all ties with Social Democrats and prepare for an imminent seizure of power. This mirrored and helped justify the policy at home. The attack on the *kulaks* was presented as an attack on private capitalism (which was true) and as a major advance towards socialism (which was not). At home, the ultra-left turn of the Third Period provided a smokescreen for bureaucratic power and forced industrialisation. Abroad, it fostered disastrous sectarianism, above all in Germany, where a divided labour movement allowed Hitler to take power in 1933.

But the Nazis threatened a resurgence of aggressive German imperialism, and Stalin began casting around for European allies. The Comintern duly lurched from ultra-left madness to 'popular frontism': Communists were now to form alliances with the liberal bourgeoisie, reining back the working class to placate potential allies of the Russian state. Thus, instead of promoting world revolution, the Stalinist Comintern had, by the mid-1930s, become actively counter-revolutionary. This was to produce another catastrophic disaster to set alongside those of 1927 and 1933.

June 1936: The French General Strike and Factory Occupations

The Nazi seizure of power sent shockwaves across Europe. Hitler offered a solution to the economic crisis based on dictatorship at home and imperialism abroad. His was a model other ruling classes might follow.

The destruction of labour organisation by state repression and fascist terror allowed capitalists to ratchet up the rate of exploitation in the workplaces. It also eliminated any possibility of a socialist alternative. 'The historic function of fascism', explained Trotsky, 'is to smash the working class, to destroy its organisations, and to stifle political liberties when the capitalists find themselves unable to govern and dominate with the help of democratic machinery.'

The first successful attempt to replicate the pattern was in Austria. The revolutionary wave after the First World War had created a powerful Social Democratic Party with 600,000 members, 40 per cent of the popular vote, and its own paramilitary defence force. The Austrian ruling class wanted to crush this movement.

Federal Chancellor Engelbert Dollfuss carried out an internal coup in March 1933, dispensing with parliament, imposing rule by decree, and cracking down on working-class organisation. The Social Democratic leaders advised their supporters to do nothing. They preferred to support the pro-Catholic fascist Dollfuss against his pro-Nazi fascist rivals. On 12 February 1934, the Dollfuss regime launched a full-scale police attack on the Social Democrats. For four days the workers fought back, but were finally crushed. Eleven activists were hanged. The Austrian labour movement was driven underground.

At least the Austrian workers had resisted, unlike the German workers the year before. 'Better Vienna than Berlin' became a rallying cry on the European Left. It would be heard often in the mid-1930s.

Vienna was not the only capital city where fascists made a bid for power in February 1934. On 6 February a huge right-wing demonstration in Paris had demanded the resignation of a newly formed liberal government headed by Edouard Daladier. After a night of vicious fighting between demonstrators and police that left 15 dead, Daladier, fearing he could not maintain order, stepped down. The fascists seemed able to unmake a government by force.

But the CGT union federation called a general strike on 12 February. The Socialist Party (SFIO) and the Communist Party (PCF) organised mass demonstrations. As the separate SFIO and PCF demonstrations came together in Paris, there was an explosion of shouts and applause, with cries of 'Unity! Unity!' The PCF leaders had wanted to keep the two demonstrations apart. They were still peddling the Third Period madness that the Socialists were 'social-fascists'. But the working class had imposed unity on their sectarian leaders.

Stalin, isolated in Europe and threatened by Hitler, was now desperately seeking allies among the Western powers. So the Comintern flipped over to a policy of political alliances not just with Social Democrats but also with liberals. In France, this meant an electoral pact – a Popular Front – of Communists, Socialists, and Radicals (as the French liberals were known). The Popular Front won the general election of May 1936 and a new government was formed by Socialist leader Léon Blum.

The workers, inspired by the victory of 'their' parties, immediately went onto the offensive. From 26 May onwards, this movement swelled into a massive general strike involving two million workers. Over three-quarters of the strikes took the form of factory occupations. The British ambassador compared the situation to that of Russia in 1917.

The employers and the police were powerless. The ruling class looked to the Socialist premier for salvation. He duly called for 'public security' and convened a meeting of employers and union representatives to negotiate a settlement at the Matignon Hotel. With the employers on the back foot, the concessions were massive: wage increases of between 7 and 15 per cent; the working week cut from 48 to 40 hours with no loss of pay; two weeks' paid holiday; and agreement in principle to free collective bargaining.

All Popular Front parties recommended acceptance of the Matignon Agreement and an immediate return to work. This included the Communist Party, whose leader, Maurice Thorez, declared: 'So what next? … we must know how to end a strike when satisfaction has been obtained. We must even know how to accept a compromise when all demands have not yet been met.'

But the economic gains of the workers were bound to be whittled away as soon as the employers regained the initiative. This was especially so during a slump. Yet Thorez said nothing about creating a network of workers' councils to protect the gains and organise future action for more. He did not see the June movement as an opportunity to establish permanent organs of mass democracy. He led his supporters backwards instead of using the factory occupations as a platform for further advance.

The majority of workers may not have been willing to fight for more in June 1936. But their mood was shifting rapidly to the left. Communist Party membership leapt from 90,000 to 290,000 in the course of the year. It was fast becoming the dominant force within the Popular Front.

But the PCF leadership was fiercely loyal to Stalin. It adhered staunchly to the Popular Front. This meant doing nothing to upset liberal politicians. It also meant minimising political demands and discouraging strikes and demonstrations. Dissidents who questioned this approach were expelled. The effect was to subordinate the interests of the working class to those of the ruling class. 'The "People's Front"', wrote Trotsky,

> represents the coalition of the proletariat with the imperialist bourgeoisie ... The coalition extends both to the parliamentary and to the extra-parliamentary spheres. In both spheres, the Radical Party, preserving for itself complete freedom of action, savagely imposes restrictions upon the freedom of action of the proletariat.

As the working-class movement receded, the government moved to the right. Blum abandoned his policy of economic expansion and social reform in favour of deflation and rearmament. The Popular Front opted for guns instead of butter. This did not save him. A flight of capital created a financial crisis that forced Blum's resignation in June 1937. A second Popular Front government was a right-of-centre administration led by a Radical rather than a Socialist. A third government was formed in April 1938. This saw the return of Edouard Daladier, a right-wing Radical, as premier. In reality, it was not a Popular Front administration at all, since it included no Socialists but did include the parties of the Right.

On 12 November 1938, Paul Reynaud, Minister of Finance, declared: 'We are living in a capitalist system. The capitalist system, being what it is, its laws must be obeyed. These are the laws of profit, of individual risk, of a free market, of the incentive of competition.' The government then issued a series of decrees cutting wages, increasing the working week, and undermining terms and conditions of employment. Inflation had already wiped out the wage rises won in June 1936. The new attacks represented a full-scale counter-offensive against French workers.

The CGT called a general strike. But support was patchy, and the police attacked those who did take action with exceptional violence. The Renault workers at the giant Billancourt works outside Paris fought a 24-hour battle with 1,500 riot police. After their defeat, they were forced to march out of the factory giving the fascist salute and shouting '*Vive la police!*'

The defeat of the strike broke the great workers' movement spawned by the events of February 1934 and May–June 1936. Union membership collapsed from a peak of four million to one million. One in six CGT local branches folded. Thousands of workplace militants were victimised.

In 1934, Trotsky had written:

Whoever consoles himself with the phrase 'France is not Germany' is hopeless. In all countries, the same historical laws operate, the laws of capitalist decline ... The bourgeoisie is leading its society to complete bankruptcy. It is capable of providing the people with neither bread nor peace. This is precisely why it cannot any longer tolerate the democratic order.

The choice, Trotsky concluded, was socialist revolution or fascist barbarism.

The defeat, disintegration, and demoralisation of the French labour movement created the basis for France's military capitulation in 1940, the occupation of the north of the country by the Nazis, and the establishment in the south of the pro-fascist Vichy regime of Marshal Pétain. Trotsky's analysis was confirmed.

The Spanish Civil War

'It was the first time I had ever been in a town where the working class was in the saddle', wrote George Orwell of Barcelona in November 1936.

Practically every building had been seized by the workers and was draped with red flags ... Every shop and café had an inscription saying that it had been collectivised ... There were no private motor cars, they had all been commandeered, and all the trams and taxis and much of the other transport was painted red and black … In outward appearance, it was a town in which the wealthy classes had practically ceased to exist … Above all, there was a belief in the revolution and the future, a feeling of having suddenly emerged into an era of equality and freedom. Human beings were trying to behave as human beings and not as cogs in the capitalist machine.

Spain had become two armed camps. On 17–18 July, General Francisco Franco had staged a military coup in an attempt to wrest control from the democratically elected Popular Front government in Madrid. The coup was backed by army, Church, big landowners, and all the right-wing parties – Carlists, monarchists, and Falangists (fascists). It was generally successful in the more backward, rural parts of Spain. But on 19–20 July, armed workers had surrounded the barracks in Barcelona and Madrid and forced the soldiers to surrender. Their action triggered popular revolts across working-class Spain.

The Spanish working class had doubled in size between 1910 and 1930, and now made up about a quarter of the population. In July 1936 there were revolutionary risings in five main areas – the Basque country, with 70 per cent of Spain's iron, steel, and shipbuilding; the coalmining region of Asturias; Madrid, the capital; Andalucia, where 800,000 day-labourers worked on big estates; and Catalonia, where more than half the working class was concentrated.

Class tension had been high in Spain since the late nineteenth century. Industrialisation had produced a well-organised working class with a tradition of militant struggle. But it was politically divided. The General Union of Labour (UGT), dominant in Madrid, was led by the Socialist Party (PSOE). The National Confederation of Labour (CNT), dominant in Catalonia, was, by contrast, an anarcho-syndicalist organisation. Smaller left parties included the Spanish Communist Party (PCE), the Unified Socialist Party of Catalonia (PSUC), the Workers' Party of Marxist Unity (POUM), and the Iberian Anarchist Federation (FAI).

In 1931 a combined monarchy and dictatorship had been overthrown and replaced by an elected liberal-republican government. But the new government failed to carry out promised reforms and cracked down hard on land occupations and strikes. In October 1934 the government lost its parliamentary majority and gave way to a new conservative administration. When 20,000 Asturian coalminers rose in revolt, they were crushed in two weeks of fierce fighting; more than 3,000 were murdered after surrendering and 40,000 activists were jailed across Spain.

But in February 1936 a Popular Front of liberal, socialist, and separatist parties won the general election. The victory brought millions of workers and peasants into action – storming prisons to free jailed activists, taking strike action for both economic and political demands, and seizing land from the landowners. It was this movement that prompted the right-wing coup. And the coup's defeat across half of Spain had nothing to do with the Popular Front government. Official advice was 'to guarantee the normality of daily life, in order to set an example of serenity and of confidence in the means of military strength of the state'.

Since 'the means of military strength of the state' were carrying out a coup, the government's advice amounted to capitulation to Franco. Both the Socialist and Communist leaders, moreover, parroted this message: 'The moment is a difficult one, but by no means desperate. The government is certain that it has sufficient resources to overcome the criminal attempt.'

The workers ignored them. Revolution from below secured most of northern and eastern Spain, with workers' control of the factories, peasant land seizures, and the creation of popular militias. In the militias, officers were elected, rank carried no privileges, and tactics were debated. Much had to be improvised, as the Nationalists began the war with most of the weapons. But the Republicans had one potentially decisive advantage: the appeal of their revolutionary message to ordinary Nationalist soldiers conscripted to fight in the interests of officers, landlords, and priests.

'A civil war is waged ... not only with military but also with political weapons', explained Trotsky.

From a purely military point of view, the Spanish Revolution is much weaker than its enemy. Its strength lies in its ability to rouse great masses to action. It can even take away the army from its reactionary officers. To accomplish this, it is only necessary to advance seriously and courageously the programme of the socialist revolution. It is necessary to proclaim that from now on the land, factories, and shops will pass from the hands of the capitalists into the hands of the people ... The fascist army could not resist the influence of such a programme for 24 hours.

But it was not to be. The leaders of the CNT ceded power in Barcelona to the Liberals, and the leaders of the POUM would not break with the CNT and offer decisive, independent, revolutionary leadership.

Barcelona was the Petrograd of the Spanish Revolution. But it was Petrograd without soviets or Bolsheviks. There was no network of democratic councils able to give organised expression to the will of the masses, nor a revolutionary party committed to a decisive struggle for power and the creation of a workers' state. There was the steam of revolution, but no box or piston.

In Madrid the PCE grew increasingly powerful. This was partly because workers were attracted to its radical-sounding rhetoric and partly because Stalin was supplying military hardware. He who pays the piper calls the tune: communist guns meant communist influence. But the PCE was now playing an actively counter-revolutionary role. Its slogan 'First win the war, then win the revolution' gave workers false hope while justifying the disarming of the militias and the return of the factories to the capitalists and the land to the landlords. In homage to Moscow's 'popular front' line, the PCE used its control of Russian arms to help the Republican bourgeoisie create a conventional 'Popular Army' controlled from above that would defend private property.

By April 1937 Orwell could see the difference in Barcelona: 'The smart restaurants and hotels were full of rich people wolfing expensive meals, while for the working-class population food prices had jumped enormously without any corresponding rise in wages ... the queues for bread, olive oil, and other necessities were hundreds of yards long.'

The following month, the liberal bourgeoisie and their Stalinist allies felt strong enough to go onto the offensive. They used three lorry-loads of Assault Guards to evict the CNT from the Barcelona telephone exchange, one of the first buildings to be put under workers' control the previous July. In response, barricades went up across the city. Even at that point, had the CNT and POUM leaders acted with determination – organising an insurrection to seize state power in Catalonia, then issuing a general call for land seizures, workers' control, and colonial independence (25,000 of Franco's best troops were Moroccans) – they might still have won.

But they did not. They did the opposite. They called on their supporters to lay down their guns. After five days of fighting in which 500 had died, most of the barricades came down.

Savage repression followed. The city was flooded with 5,000 Assault Guards. The POUM was made illegal. Its leaders were arrested, tortured, and murdered. The CNT and POUM militias were forcibly incorporated into the Popular Army and put under regular military discipline. Dissidents were denounced as 'Trotsky-fascists'. Estates and factories were returned to their former owners.

The counter-revolution of May 1937 killed the revolution of July 1936. The Spanish Civil War was transformed from a revolutionary war between classes into a conventional war between rival factions of the same class, one liberal, the other fascist. The outcome was now determined by firepower, not politics. This meant victory for Franco, who was supported by Fascist Italy and Nazi Germany.

Barcelona fell to fascism in January 1939, Madrid in March, confirming the truth of Trotsky's epitaph for the Spanish Revolution: 'The demand not to transgress the bounds of bourgeois democracy signifies in practice not a defence of the democratic revolution but a repudiation of it.'

The Causes of the Second World War

By late 1939 the working-class movement lay defeated and broken across most of Europe. Stalinism and fascism were dominant. Dictatorship had triumphed over democracy; revolutionary hope had given way to counter-revolutionary despair.

Ten million were imprisoned in Stalin's gulags, 150,000 in Hitler's concentration camps. Franco's Nationalists had murdered 200,000 people in Spain. Union membership in France had fallen by three-quarters. Authoritarian governments, in varying degrees fascist, were now installed across Europe. They had been established in Turkey, Hungary, Italy, Poland, and Portugal during the 1920s, and in Yugoslavia, Germany, Austria, Bulgaria, the Baltic States, Greece, and Spain during the 1930s.

Totalitarianism was not, however, a uniform phenomenon. Stalinism and Nazism were equally brutal, but different in character and purpose. Russia's economic backwardness meant that rapid accumulation of capital to create infrastructure, heavy industry, and armaments was possible only with very high levels of exploitation. This was made possible by state terror to eradicate any possibility of resistance. Germany was not backward at all: it was at the time the greatest industrial power in Europe. But economic collapse had torn society apart, driven the middle class to despair, and resurrected the spectre of socialist revolution. Nazism was an extreme right-wing response to this crisis.

The Nazi regime had three basic characteristics. First, it was a mass movement of the middle classes and the most backward sections of the working class. What held this otherwise disparate 'human dust' together was the party and its mission – the destruction of internal enemies and the restoration of German might.

Second, Nazism was an instrument of counter-revolution. Before coming to power, its paramilitary army of 400,000 Brownshirts had been used to attack the unions, left-wing parties, and workers' protests. After January 1933 the Nazi paramilitaries fused with the German state and swelled into a monstrous police apparatus that liquidated all opposition.

Third, Nazism was an expression of German imperialism. Hitler's demands for *Lebensraum* ('living space') at the expense of Slavic *Untermenschen* ('sub-humans') echoed the traditional imperialist ambitions of German capitalism in Central and Eastern Europe.

During the First World War, German leaders had dreamed of a vast imperial domain stretching from the Baltic to the Bosphorus – *Mitteleuropa* ('Middle Europe') – and a further sphere of influence extending from there down to the Persian Gulf. Hitler revived and expanded these ambitions in the 1930s. He was a racist psychopath and a totalitarian dictator, but he was not hell-bent on a world war for global domination for its own sake. His foreign policy was a reflection of the long-term interests of German capitalism.

The tensions between the great powers had not been resolved in 1918; in many ways, they had intensified. The Treaty of Versailles had partly dismembered Germany, built up rival states on its borders, and imposed crippling reparations payments and arms limitations.

This did not end the conflict; it simply created the context for its next phase.

Underlying the rising tensions of the 1930s was the impact of the Great Depression. As trade collapsed, each state devalued its currency to make home-produced goods cheaper on world markets and imposed protective tariffs on foreign imports. The world became divided into autarkic (economically self-sufficient) blocs of rival capitalists.

State power was also used to stimulate growth through public investment. Russia, where all economic activity was state-controlled, was the most extreme example, but Germany also borrowed to invest in infrastructure – especially motorway construction – and rearmament.

Lucrative state contracts combined with wage cuts of around 25 per cent led to a huge expansion of German industrial investment. Unemployment fell from six million in 1933 to virtually none in 1939. But Germany's booming capitalist economy was at risk of being choked by lack of raw materials and closed markets. Further capital accumulation could not be accommodated within existing national boundaries. Germany needed the ironworks of Alsace-Lorraine which had been returned to France in 1919, the arms industries of Czechoslovakia, the coalmines of Poland, and the oilfields of Romania; perhaps even the grain-producing regions of Ukraine and the oilfields of the distant Caucasus or Middle East.

Hitler's challenge to the Versailles settlement ramped up as German economic and military strength increased. In March 1936 the demilitarised Rhineland, designed as a buffer zone protecting France's eastern frontier, was reoccupied by German troops. Between 1936 and 1939, Germany supplied guns, tanks, bombers, and 'volunteers' to the Nationalists in Spain, using the war there as a training ground for its fast-growing armed forces. In March 1938 Hitler annexed Austria to the German Reich. The *Anschluss* (union) was uncontested by the Austrian authorities and widely welcomed by Austrian Nazis. In October 1938 he annexed the mainly German-speaking Sudetenland of neighbouring Czechoslovakia, a seizure made possible by the Munich Agreement signed by Germany, Italy, Britain, and France on 30 September. Loss of the Sudetenland stripped Czechoslovakia of its mountain barrier and rendered it defenceless against further aggression. In March 1939 the rest of Czechoslovakia was duly absorbed into the growing Nazi empire.

By now, Europe was firmly divided into two blocs. Germany and Italy had formed an Axis in November 1936. Both were expansionist powers with ambitions that threatened the interests of Britain and France. The British government, however, was keen to avoid war, and the rulers of France could not challenge the Axis on their own. Appeasement became the official policy of the Western powers. That meant refusing to supply the Spanish Republic, acquiescing in Hitler's European annexations, and ignoring Italy's conquest of Ethiopia in north-east Africa.

The British ruling class was increasingly divided, but appeasement reflected the interests of the majority, at least until September 1939. Britain's rulers wanted to defend the substance of the 1919 carve-up. Minor European states were expendable in the wider game. They hoped to contain Hitler and preserve the balance of power. They were also sympathetic to fascism as a hammer with which to beat down the working class, and they saw Germany as a bulwark against Soviet Russia. World war, moreover, might end in another round of revolutionary turmoil. Appeasement, therefore, was not wilful stupidity: it reflected the interests of British capitalism at the time.

What made it unsustainable was the way in which the expansion of German capital continued to push against the limits of the European geopolitical system. The danger for British and French imperialism was that a tipping-point would be reached when German economic and military power became overwhelming.

Poland was judged to be that tipping-point. The result was frenetic, last-minute diplomacy. On 31 March 1939 Britain and France guaranteed military support to Poland in the event of invasion. But they continued to seek a diplomatic solution to German territorial demands and refused to enter into any sort of agreement with the Soviet Union.

Stalin, unable to secure an alliance with Britain and France, opted instead for a non-aggression pact with Hitler and an agreement to partition Poland between them (the Molotov–Ribbentrop Pact of 23 August 1939). Just over a week later, on 1 September 1939, the Germans attacked Poland from the west. The Russians followed, attacking from the east on 17 September. Within three weeks, Poland had been defeated and, despite pockets of resistance, ceased to exist as an independent nation-state. Although Britain and France had declared war on Germany on 3 September, they failed to provide any military assistance to Poland. Nonetheless, the Second World War had begun.

The defeat of the socialist revolution in the interwar period meant the victory of fascism. That victory meant that the crisis of the 1930s was resolved not by the overthrow of capitalism but by a new imperialist war. The cost of working-class defeat in interwar Europe was the bloodiest and most barbaric war in human history.

15
World War and Cold War
1939–1967

Hiroshima Atomic Bomb, 6 August 1945.

The barbarism of the Second World War was followed by the barbarism of the Cold War. The world continues to live in the shadow of the Bomb.

Between 1914 and 1945 a single geopolitical crisis played out in Europe. Though it was interrupted by the world revolution of 1917–23, and to some degree by the popular revolts of the mid to late 1930s, the defeat of these upsurges from below allowed the geopolitical crisis to determine the direction of global affairs.

The root of the crisis was competition between opposing national-capitalist blocs in the form of arms races, imperialist wars, and forcible re-divisions of the world. The primary axis of this competition, at least until 1941, was the struggle between British and German imperialism for European, and to some degree global, hegemony.

The crisis was substantially reconfigured by the entry of both the Soviet Union and the United States into the Second World War in 1941. By the winter of 1942/3 at the latest, it was clear that the Axis powers – Nazi Germany, Fascist Italy, and Imperial Japan – were heading for defeat. Equally clear was the relative decline of British (and European) imperialism and the emergence of two global superpowers, the USSR and the US, that were set to dominate the post-war world. The tension between the two led to a post-war division of Europe, a nuclear arms-race, and a global confrontation between opposing national-capitalist blocs that came to be called 'the Cold War'.

For the next two decades, world politics was shaped by three main factors: the nuclear-armed stand-off and global proxy wars of the two superpowers; a long economic boom based on arms spending and US economic and financial pre-eminence; and a wave of anti-colonial liberation struggles in the Third World.

The Second World War: Imperialism

The Second World War was the greatest tragedy in human history. It lasted six years, killed 60 million people, and tore apart the lives of hundreds of millions of others. Like the First World War, it transformed the productive and liberating potential of the modern economy into its opposite: an industrialised mechanism for killing and destruction. It revealed the alienation at the very heart of the capitalist system as the war turned the products of human labour into instruments of carnage on an unprecedented scale.

The waste of life and wealth was phenomenal. Between September 1939 and August 1945, an average of 27,000 people perished every day. By 1942 Russian factories were turning out 24,000 tanks and 22,000 aircraft a year. On the first day of the final assault on Berlin in April 1945, almost 9,000 Russian guns fired more than 1,200,000 shells. The bombardment was so intense that walls vibrated 60 km away.

What motivated this stupendous expenditure of blood and resources? Not, as the British, Russian, and American ruling classes claimed, a desire to defeat fascism and make the world safe for democracy. The motives of the Allied leaders were no nobler than those of the Axis. Let us consider the evidence.

Germany was attempting to restore its dominant position in Europe and secure access to the raw materials, labour reserves, factories, and markets necessary for the continued expansion of German capitalism. Italy entered the war when it appeared that Germany would be victorious. Still a second-rate power, Fascist Italy needed a strong ally, for it had ambitions to build an empire in North Africa and the Balkans, and to turn the Mediterranean into an Italian lake.

The Soviet Union's vast size, its wealth of resources, and its focus on basic industrialisation made it more inward-looking. Stalin's main preoccupation was national security. But to achieve it, he was prepared to attack Finland, annex the Baltic States, and divide Poland with Nazi Germany.

Such was the incompetence and brutality of the Stalinist regime that it was almost overwhelmed by the German invasion of June 1941. Mass purges had largely destroyed the officer corps of the Red Army. Millions of men were lost in the first months of the war. But Russia's vastness – in terms of territory, manpower, and resources – absorbed the shock and swallowed up the German Army. Then, fully mobilised, Russia turned the tide at the Battle of Stalingrad (August 1942–January 1943). Thereafter, as the Red Army advanced, Stalin's imperial ambition grew.

The 'Big Three' – Stalin, US President Roosevelt, and British Prime Minister Churchill – held a series of meetings in the last two years of the war to discuss the post-war settlement. At one of these meetings – in Moscow in October 1944 – Churchill wrote the following note and passed it to Stalin:

Rumania: Russia 90 per cent; the others 10 per cent
Greece: Britain (in accord with USA) 90 per cent;
    Russia 10 per cent
Yugoslavia: 50 per cent 50 per cent
Hungary: 50 per cent 50 per cent
Bulgaria: Russia 75 per cent; the others 25 per cent

Stalin looked at the note, changed the Russian proportion of Bulgaria to 90 per cent, ticked the top left corner with a blue pencil, then passed it back to Churchill. Thus was the fate of tens of millions decided by the latter-day conquerors of Europe.

The war in Europe was won on the Eastern Front. The Russians killed about 4.5 million German soldiers, the British and Americans about 500,000. The disparity was partly because Britain was much weaker and partly because both Britain and the US were simultaneously fighting a full-scale war against the Japanese in the Far East.

Churchill's main war aim was to defend the British Empire. He favoured war as soon as it became clear that Germany might become hegemonic in Europe. Britain's rulers always feared a threat to their maritime supremacy and trade from a hostile power in control of north-west Europe. This threat materialised when a new German *Blitzkrieg* ('lightning war') strategy based on armoured spearheads brought about the collapse of France in six weeks in May–June 1940. Britain itself was not invaded, but communications with the overseas empire were immediately imperilled. That is why, until late in the war, Churchill prioritised operations in the Mediterranean, the Middle East, and the Far East over the opening of a Second Front in north-west Europe. He wanted to defend Egypt, the Suez Canal, and India. 'I have not become the King's first minister', he declared, 'to oversee the dismemberment of the British Empire.'

This made the war harder, longer, and bloodier than it might have been. In 1942 the British had more troops policing India than fighting the Japanese. Nationalist demonstrations there were brutally suppressed with shootings, floggings, and gang-rapes of protestors; 30,000 oppositionists were incarcerated. A year later, three million died of hunger in Bengal because the British authorities failed to organise relief. Little wonder that some Indians chose to fight on the side of the Japanese in an 'Indian National Army'.

Britain was a declining industrial and imperial power. It was saved from Nazi occupation by the sea. That meant that it could become a platform for the projection of US military power from 1942 onwards. US bombers attacked Germany from British airfields; US troops invaded France from British ports.

Financially, economically, and militarily unable to sustain the world war on its own, Britain needed the US to become 'the arsenal of democracy', supplying food, fuel, and armaments on a Lend-Lease basis. But this had nothing to do with solidarity among 'democratic' ruling classes. The US had imperialist ambitions of its own. It hoped to emerge from the war as the dominant global power. This meant opening up the protected markets of the old European empires to American trade. Lend-Lease was designed to advance American interests at the expense of the British Empire. The terms required the British to liquidate virtually all their financial reserves and overseas holdings. The choice for the British ruling class was either to sue for peace and lose their empire or become an economic and military dependency of the US. They chose the latter. The 'special relationship' forged during the Second World War is still in place.

The British and the Americans were in fact fighting two imperialist wars, one in Europe and the Mediterranean against Germany and Italy, and another in the Far East against Japan.

Japan had emerged from the Sino-Japanese, Russo-Japanese, and First World Wars as a major imperialist power. Japan was industrialising fast, but lacked vital resources. Unions were weak, democracy had not taken root, and from 1927 onwards Japanese government policy was increasingly shaped by the Militarist wing of the ruling class. The Japanese Militarists wanted to replace the British, French, Dutch, and American empires in the Far East with an empire of their own. In 1931 they occupied Manchuria. In 1937 they launched a full-scale war against China. And in 1940 they announced their intention to create the 'Greater East Asia Co-Prosperity Sphere'.

War with Britain and the US started in December 1941 with simultaneous attacks on British-occupied Malaya and the US Pacific Fleet at Pearl Harbor. Within six months the Japanese had overrun virtually the whole of South-East Asia and the Western Pacific. The British maintained large forces both to hold down India and to defend its border against the Japanese. The US committed vast naval and marine resources to the defeat of the Japanese Empire. At the

Battle of Leyte Gulf in October 1944, the US fleet comprised 225 warships, 34 of them aircraft-carriers, and around 1,500 planes.

In a long war of attrition, the combined industrial power of the Soviet Union and the US was decisive. The contribution of other states to victory was secondary. Because of this, the war meant the end not only of the German, Italian, and Japanese Empires; it also meant the eclipse of the British and French Empires. The British fought their way into Germany driving American tanks and trucks. The French returned to Paris in the wake of the US Army. Berlin was captured by the Soviet Army advancing from the East.

The Second World War was an imperialist war to re-divide the world between competing blocs of capitalists. Dominant among the victors were the US and Soviet ruling classes. The imperialist world war had created a new bipolar division of the globe.

The Second World War: Barbarism

Nazi Germany, Stalinist Russia, and Militarist Japan had at least three things in common: a weak or non-existent labour movement, an authoritarian police state, and a way of waging war character-ised by primeval savagery. These three things were linked. A strong working class is the basis of democracy; an atomised working class is the precondition for dictatorship. The defeat of revolutionary movements in the 1930s meant the dominance of nationalism, racism, and militarism; it meant a descent into barbarism.

Anti-semitism provided Nazism with its ideological framework. The fantasy of an international Jewish conspiracy linking Wall Street and Moscow expressed the irrationality of an enraged middle class that was being ruined by the economic crisis and lived in fear of the working class. A wider anti-Slav racism echoed millennium-old race myths as a justification for new wars of empire: the *Untermenschen* ('sub-humans') of Eastern Europe – the Poles and Russians – were to be enslaved or ethnically cleansed to create *Lebensraum* ('living space') for an Aryan master-race modelled on the Teutonic knights of the Middle Ages. The dual logic of Nazi racism and German imperialism led to genocide as swathes of Poland and Russia were overrun. The genocide intensified as the tide of war turned against the invaders. The Jews in particular became scapegoats for defeat.

Around six million Poles were killed (16 per cent of the total population). Half were Jews, who were first forcibly moved into ghettos, then, from 1942, transported to purpose-built extermination camps. Auschwitz-Birkenau, the largest of these camps, was an industrial complex built with the sole purpose of killing as many people as possible as quickly as possible. Three million died at the camp, 2.5 million of them in its gas chambers, the others from starvation or disease.

In total, the Nazis murdered six million Jews and six million others during the genocide we know as the Holocaust. But millions more died as a result of starvation, neglect, and random shooting. The war on the Eastern Front cost the Russians 27 million lives (16 per cent of the total population). The majority of these were prisoners-of-war or civilians in the occupied zone.

Stalin's conduct of the war was almost as brutal. He did not order racial genocide or build death factories. But he did use his armies as instruments of conquest, he did employ millions of slave-labourers, and he did operate a police terror as ruthless as that of Hitler's Gestapo.

In 1918 the Bolsheviks had leafleted the German trenches calling on German soldiers to turn their guns on their officers and join the world revolution. In 1941 Stalin dubbed the war against Hitler 'the Great Patriotic War' and extolled the achievements of nineteenth-century Tsarist generals. When the Soviet Army entered German territory in 1944, it began a rampage of state-sanctioned and wholly indiscriminate murder, rape, and destruction. An estimated two million women were raped, many of them repeatedly. Such was the terror that 14 million civilians fled their homes and trekked westwards in the largest mass migration in history.

The Japanese occupation of China was just as murderous as the Nazi occupation of Poland or the Stalinist occupation of East Germany. At least 15 million Chinese were killed during the Second World War. These included young women used as slave prostitutes, prisoners subjected to medical experiments and weapons tests, and local people used as human livestock and eaten by Japanese soldiers cut off from their supply bases.

The barbarism was not restricted to totalitarian regimes. The 'democracies' were also imperialist powers committed to the subjugation of native populations – the British in India, the French in

Indochina, the Americans in the Philippines. The 'democracies' also committed terrible war crimes. The carpet-bombing of German cities by the British and US air forces often had no military purpose whatsoever. The bombing of Hamburg on 27 July 1943 created an uncontrollable firestorm. Houses exploded. People hiding in cellars suffocated or were roasted alive. Tarmac boiled and fleeing people stuck to it like flypaper. Hair burned, eyes melted, flesh was carbonised. Twice as many people, 40,000, died in one night as in the whole of the eight-month London Blitz. Virtually all of them were civilians.

Air Chief Marshal Arthur Harris, head of RAF Bomber Command, was an unashamed advocate of vengeance and terror bombing. His aim was to destroy every major city in Germany. His night-time raids, deploying as many as 1,000 planes, killed 600,000 German civilians, and destroyed 3.4 million homes across 64 cities.

But the most terrible fate was reserved for the cities of Hiroshima and Nagasaki in Japan. On 6 August 1945, the American B-29 bomber *Enola Gay* dropped an atomic bomb, nicknamed 'Little Boy', on the city of Hiroshima. The detonation killed at least 45,000 people on the first day, and a similar number from injury and sickness later, most of whom died slowly and in agony. Three days later, 'Fat Man' was dropped on Nagasaki, killing at least 30,000 on the first day and a similar number later.

Neither city had any military significance. The war was almost over. A demonstration that the weapon existed would probably have secured a Japanese surrender. But the US government wanted to display its newfound military power and assert the global dominance it afforded. It also wanted to test the effects of the weapon on a live target. The people of Hiroshima and Nagasaki were, in a sense, the first victims of what would become the Cold War.

The imperialist character of the Second World War trapped the peoples of the world in a war of industrialised attrition and genocide. The war would not have happened but for the defeat of the great revolutionary wave of 1917–23.

After the First World War, humanity had faced a stark alternative: a socialist revolution or unemployment, fascism, and war. The outcome was decided in large part by failures of revolutionary organisation and leadership. The price of those failures continued to be paid to the very end of the war and beyond, for the destruction of the working-class movement across most of Europe during the interwar period prevented an eruption of revolution similar to what had occurred in 1917. Instead, at the end of the war, the Nazis presided over an apocalyptic crescendo of violence.

While Hitler, hiding in his Berlin bunker, fantasised about non-existent armies, issued impossible orders to 'fight to the death', and raved against Jews, Bolsheviks, and traitors, his secret police conscripted teenagers and old men to fight Russian tanks and hanged batches of 'deserters' along the roadside. The Stalinist terror also peaked in 1944–5: an estimated three million returning prisoners-of-war were sent to the gulags accused of surrendering or collaborating; a further 135,000 soldiers were arrested for 'counter-revolutionary crimes'.

The post-war carve-up of the world after 1945 faced a less powerful challenge than that after 1918. This was in large part because of the peculiar nature and influence of Stalinism. At its core was a class of party-state bureaucrats whose politics were counter-revolutionary and national-capitalist. Yet it claimed the mantle of the Bolsheviks and the October Revolution, and this claim was accepted by most socialist activists, who continued to regard Stalin as the leader of a worldwide revolutionary movement, and Russia as a genuine socialist society. Such was the huge prestige of the Stalinist regime that Moscow's instructions to the world's communist parties were usually obeyed, and the effect, again and again, was to sabotage post-war revolutionary movements in line with the interests of the Russian bureaucracy.

The Second World War: Resistance

The Axis powers faced growing internal opposition to their brutal regimes during the Second World War. When the Japanese Militarists attacked China in 1937, they expected a rapid conquest before embarking on a wider war. Instead, their savagery provoked fierce and sustained resistance from both Nationalist and Communist movements, forcing them to keep some 650,000 troops in China until the end of the war. The Germans, despite the police terror they imposed on Occupied Europe, were also obliged to deploy huge armies to hold down subject populations. Even at the very end of the war, with Berlin itself under attack, Hitler still kept 400,000 troops in Norway.

Many occupied countries freed themselves. Yugoslavia was liberated not by Allied armies but by the Partisans, a communist-led mass movement headed by Josip Broz ('Tito'). The Partisans drove out the Germans, crushed their Croat Ustaše fascist allies, and marginalised the ineffective Chetnik royalist movement. The Partisans were a genuinely multi-ethnic mass movement. By the end of the war, almost a million Yugoslavs were actively involved. This gave Tito a strong independent base. During the subsequent Cold War, Yugoslavia was aligned with neither the West nor the East.

Poland also had a powerful resistance movement. At its height, the Polish Home Army numbered an estimated 400,000 members. As the Soviet Army approached Warsaw, Radio Moscow announced that 'the hour of action has already arrived' and called on the Poles to 'join the struggle against the Germans'. Around 50,000 Poles responded, including many communists and Jews, who now emerged from hiding. The centre of Warsaw was captured. The concentration camp built on the site of the Jewish ghetto was liberated. Weapons were seized, arms workshops improvised, and canteens and hospitals established.

But Stalin then halted the Soviet advance, allowing the Nazis to concentrate their forces to crush the uprising. It took two months. The city was first bombed and shelled into submission, then subjected to a punitive terror. Wounded fighters were burned alive in their beds with flamethrowers. Nurses were raped, flogged, and murdered. Polish children were shot down for fun. At least 30,000 were killed in the Old Town alone.

The Polish resistance was decapitated. The Nazis performed the execution, but the Stalinists had erected the scaffold. The Soviet Union was an imperialist power waging a war of conquest. It wanted no home-grown rivals to the puppet regimes it planned to impose. It was therefore actively counter-revolutionary.

Stalin's policy in the East was matched by that of the British and Americans in the West. But Stalin's role was again decisive. The Second World War found the British and French ruling classes deeply divided. They were torn between fear of socialist revolution and fear of German imperialism. Churchill had opposed appeasement because he believed the threat of revolution was receding and that of the Nazis increasing. His aim was to defend the British Empire and keep the world safe for big business and the rich.

The deal agreed by the Big Three at their wartime conferences was for the division of Europe into spheres of influence. Stalin was given a free hand in the East, Churchill and Roosevelt in the West. The latter faced three major challenges – in France, Italy, and Greece.

Following the military defeat of May–June 1940, the French ruling class had split irrevocably into a collaborationist wing which supported the Vichy regime of Marshal Pétain in southern France and an exiled nationalist wing based in Britain led by General Charles de Gaulle, which, with American assistance, was organising an army of Free French soldiers.

The Free French participated in Allied campaigns in North Africa and north-west Europe. But the communist-led underground resistance in France grew to be much more powerful. During the liberation of France in June–November 1944, workers took strike action and the resistance defeated local German units and set up liberation committees and people's courts.

But when the exiled French Communist Party leader Maurice Thorez returned from Moscow to Paris, he called on the working class to subordinate itself to the Gaullists, coining the slogan 'One state, one army, one police force'.

In Italy, Mussolini had been overthrown by the Grand Fascist Council in July 1943. Marshal Badoglio, a conservative general, had formed a new government and made peace with the Allies. But the Germans rushed troops to Italy and reinstated Mussolini as the head of a puppet fascist regime in the north. The Nazi occupation triggered a communist-led insurgency which swelled rapidly from 10,000 armed rural partisans in late 1943 to 100,000 or more by the end of the war.

Underground resistance groups also formed in the cities, and hundreds of thousands of workers eventually took strike action. The three northern industrial cities of Genoa, Milan, and Turin were liberated by armed insurrections in spring 1945. Communist Party membership grew from 5,000 to 400,000.

But when the Italian communist leader Palmiro Togliatti returned from exile in Russia, he announced that his party was joining Badoglio's government. The partisans should lay down their arms and the workers return to their benches.

In Greece the Nazis had faced a mounting guerrilla insurgency. Their evacuation at the end of 1944 had left the country under the virtual control of EAM-ELAS, the communist-dominated resistance movement. In France and Italy, local communist parties obeyed Stalin's orders and disarmed. In Greece they attempted to do the same. Explaining that it was 'everybody's primary national duty to ensure order', they urged their supporters to back the 'United National Government'. But Churchill was determined to use force to restore the monarchy and crush the Left: 'Do not hesitate to act as if you were in a conquered city where a local rebellion is in process', he cabled the local British commander. The result was a protracted, vicious, British-backed civil war to destroy EAM-ELAS, the resistance movement that had liberated Greece from the Nazis. Again, the action of the Western leaders was supported by Stalin, who told Churchill, 'I have every confidence in British policy in Greece.'

Large parts of Occupied Europe were liberated from the Nazis by local resistance organisations in the last two years of the war. As Nazi power crumbled, these organisations had evolved from small underground units into mass movements involving millions of people. Most were dominated by communists.

Yet the potential for a thoroughgoing revolutionary transformation of European society was smothered at birth. Old ruling classes, including former fascists and collaborators, were restored to power, both at home and in the colonies. In both East and West, the principal agent of this counter-revolution was Stalinism – in the East because of the power of the Soviet Army to crush all independent political forces; in the West because millions of workers looked for leadership to communist parties which took their orders from Moscow.

The Cold War

'The mushroom cloud which changed the world' was how military historian Max Hastings described the nuclear bombing of Hiroshima.

It caused injuries never seen before:

> the cavalry horse standing pink, stripped of its hide; people with clothing patterns imprinted upon their flesh; the line of schoolgirls with ribbons of skin dangling from their faces; doomed survivors,

hideously burned, without hope of effective medical relief; the host of charred and shrivelled corpses.

The bomb exploded with the power of 12,500 tons of TNT. The temperature at ground level reached 4,000°C. More than 90 per cent of the city's buildings were destroyed by blast or fire. About a quarter of its population were killed immediately. Another quarter began to die slowly from their injuries.

Despite the insanity and horror of such weapons, by 1952 the Americans were testing H-bombs 100 times more powerful than the A-bomb used at Hiroshima. The Russians were not far behind in the nuclear arms race, testing their first A-bomb in 1949, their first H-bomb in 1955.

Military expenditure soared to unprecedented peacetime levels, with the US spending 20 per cent of GDP on armaments, the Russians, with a smaller economy, as much as 40 per cent. By the late 1960s, the total mega-tonnage of destructive power deployed by the rival superpowers was around a million times that of the Hiroshima bomb. The rulers of the US and the Soviet Union had the capacity to destroy human civilisation several times over.

'Mutual Assured Destruction' (MAD) was the term applied to the balance of terror between the two imperialist blocs. Their respective nuclear arsenals acted as a deterrent to full-scale war. But suspicion and rivalry meant that war was never far away. It came closest during the Cuban Missile Crisis of October 1962. The Soviets were secretly installing nuclear missiles on Cuba, a Caribbean island within easy range of the US. The Americans demanded they be withdrawn and prepared for nuclear war.

The US put its intercontinental ballistic missiles, submarine-based missiles, and aerial bombers on alert. It also assembled an invasion force of 100,000 men. 'We all agreed,' recalled US Attorney-General Robert Kennedy, 'if the Russians were prepared to go to war over Cuba, they were prepared to go to nuclear war, and we might as well have the showdown then as six months later.' The Russians backed down. But for two weeks the world held its breath, the whole of humanity hovering on the brink of the ultimate insanity – global annihilation at the behest of a tiny group of nuclear-powered pharaohs.

MAD did, in the event, avert all-out war between the superpowers. But it did not prevent countless proxy wars on the peripheries of the rival empires. The first erupted within five years of the Second World War.

Korea had been divided at the 38th Parallel into Soviet and US occupation zones in 1945. As the Cold War intensified, the division became permanent, with two separate states formed in 1948. A subsequent three-year war (1950–3) to reunify the country drew in the great powers, the Soviet-backed Chinese on the side of the North, the US and its allies on that of the South. Two million Koreans and two million Chinese and Western soldiers were killed. Half the Southern population lost their homes. Both North and South were left economically prostrate. Yet the war ended in stalemate along the original border, without any formal peace agreement, and the conflict has remained fossilised ever since, the front-line defined by barbed wire, watch-towers, and ritualised military confrontation. The war was utterly futile.

What lay behind this sustained military confrontation?

The Second World War had created a world divided between two superpowers. Each had ended the war in effective control of a global 'sphere of influence' within which it was economically dominant. These two spheres were, to an exceptional degree, independent of one another. They formed largely self-contained imperialist blocs.

Stalin had at first imposed governments on Eastern Europe that included Nationalists, Liberals, and Social Democrats as well as Communists. But as Soviet control hardened, non-communists were forced out of office. So too were local communists who proved too independent-minded. By 1948 pro-Soviet Stalinist dictatorships had been established across Eastern Europe. Major industries were nationalised and government planning introduced. The state-capitalist model of economic development pioneered in Russia was now rolled out across Eastern Europe. But this took place within an imperialist framework. The economies of East Germany, Poland, Czechoslovakia, Hungary, Romania, and Bulgaria were subordinated to that of the Soviet Union.

'The traditional imperialist countries', explained Tony Cliff in his seminal study *State Capitalism in Russia*, exploited their colonies in three ways: by buying the products of their colonies for low prices; by selling them the products of the 'mother' countries for high prices; and by establishing enterprises owned by the capitalists of the 'mother' country and employing 'natives'. Russian state capitalism uses the same three methods to exploit its colonies.

The Soviet Union was still a relatively backward economy. Its rulers therefore aimed to create a closed imperial market. The United States, by contrast, had the most advanced economy in the world, produced about 50 percent of global manufactured goods and dominated world trade. Its rulers therefore wanted open markets. This meant breaking up the old colonial empires of the European powers and limiting the extent of the new Soviet empire.

The Marshall Plan (1948–52) was a primary mechanism for achieving this. European states were offered large US loans on generous terms to help rebuild their shattered economies. In return they had to promote free trade and marginalise the communists. The idea, as an American economist who worked on the plan later explained, was 'to strengthen the area still outside Stalin's grasp'.

'An iron curtain has descended on the [European] continent', said Churchill, addressing an American audience in March 1946. The phrase stuck. 'Iron Curtain' became the term to describe the world's main economic, political, and ideological fracture-line during the long 'Cold War' between 1945 and 1989.

In the East, dissidents were demonised as 'imperialist agents' and 'fascists' and consigned to the gulags. In the West, communists were blacklisted and told 'to go back to Russia'. Some British unions banned communists from holding office. US Senator Joe McCarthy's House Un-American Activities Committee engaged in a systematic witch-hunt of 'communist sympathisers'. Radicals of all stripes were sacked and prevented from working. Some were driven to suicide. Two, Julius and Ethel Rosenberg, were executed for allegedly passing atomic secrets to Russia.

Dissidents often made the mistake of identifying with imperialist forces on the opposite side of the divide. In the East, anti-Stalinists idealised Western capitalist democracy. In the West, communists continued to regard Russia as a 'socialist motherland'. The workers of the Eastern Bloc were exploited by state capitalism, those of the

West by corporate capitalism, yet people everywhere were confused by Cold War ideology and a false dichotomy between rival 'systems'.

Some activists, however, understood that neither Western 'democracy' nor Eastern 'communism' offered a real alternative for humanity. Some retained a far more radical vision of revolution, people power, and an egalitarian society geared to human need not profit and war. When mass struggles erupted against the exploitation, oppression, and violence of the rival Cold War systems, these activists, bearers of the age-old tradition of struggle from below, would reconnect with new mass forces.

The Great Boom

Capitalism is an irrational and dysfunctional system. Crisis is never far away. Boom and slump are its natural rhythms.

The Long Depression of the late nineteenth century was ended only by imperialism, rearmament, and world war. The system's sluggishness in the 1920s caused a bubble of speculation as capital flowed into banking instead of industry. When the bubble burst in 1929, the system was pitched into the Great Depression. Again, it required imperialism, rearmament, and world war to end the downturn. It is in this context that the Great Boom, which lasted from 1948 to 1973, is so remarkable.

Growth rates were phenomenal and unprecedented. Total US economic output was three times higher in 1970 than in 1940. German industrial output increased five-fold between 1948 and 1970, French output four-fold. Old industries expanded and new ones formed, with giant plants employing hundreds, thousands, even tens of thousands of workers. Car plants in particular, with assembly-line production for a growing mass market, symbolised a new consumer economy. The US eventually had 70 million workers employed in manufacturing.

Unemployment fell across the developed world, to 3 per cent in the US, 1.5 per cent in Britain, 1 per cent in Germany. New workers were sucked into the workplaces. Black Americans migrated from Southern estates to Northern factories. Italian peasants left impoverished farms in Sicily to work in Turin and Milan. Turks found work in Cologne car plants, Algerians in Parisian hotels, Punjabis in British textile factories. Such was the demand for labour that women, too, entered the workforce in unprecedented peacetime numbers. Only one in five married women in Britain was working in 1950. Thereafter, the proportion rose steadily, reaching two in five by 1970, three in five by 2000. Wages and living standards rose. Working-class families bought vacuum cleaners, washing machines, fridges, televisions, and second-hand cars.

'From the cradle to the grave' welfare states were constructed. Governments invested heavily in public-sector jobs, social housing, state hospitals, new schools, and increased benefits for the poor. Youth culture was born, because for the first time young people had sufficient independence, income, and freedom from work in their teenage years to cultivate their own forms of dress, music, and identity.

High growth rates, rapidly rising living standards, a business cycle whose occasional slowdowns were so slight as to be barely noticeable – these things made it appear to many that capitalism had solved its problems and could now deliver endless and increasing prosperity for all. The social-democratic politician Tony Crosland caught the mood in his much praised 1956 book *The Future of Socialism*:

> The full employment welfare state ... would have seemed like a paradise to many early socialist pioneers. Poverty and insecurity are in the process of disappearing. Living standards are rising rapidly; the fear of unemployment is steadily weakening; and the ordinary young worker has hopes that would never have entered his father's head ... We stand in Britain on the threshold of mass abundance.

Academics came forward to give the new era of 'mass abundance' an intellectual gloss. Sociologists spoke of the 'embourgeoisement' of the 'affluent worker' – comfortable, secure, contented, and therefore no longer interested in class politics, only in lifestyle. Others constructed models of society that stressed its cohesion and consensus, or they proclaimed 'the end of ideology' on the grounds that it had become irrelevant in an era of technocratic management and social engineering. Politicians established a broad consensus: most favoured state planning and public expenditure, while lauding reform, modernisation, and what British Labour Party leader Harold Wilson called 'the white heat of the technological revolution'.

The optimism of the age was a re-run of an old film. Previous booms – between 1848 and 1873, and again between 1896 and 1914 – had also been greeted with euphoric predictions of a new society of ever-increasing wealth. Crosland's revisionism echoed that of German social-democratic theorist Eduard Bernstein before the First World War.

But the contradictions of capitalism had not been abolished. The boom rested on unstable foundations and was in the long run unsustainable. It was, in fact, a product of three factors, all of them rooted in the Second World War: arms spending, state management, and working-class militancy.

Though it declined after 1945, arms expenditure remained exceptionally high because of the Cold War. State arms contracts provided a host of top corporations with guaranteed sales and profits. Once a contract was signed, investment in arms production, including research and development, was virtually risk-free. The multiplier effect meant that the boom in arms production stimulated the economy as a whole, as arms manufacturers bought raw materials, components, power, and various services from other capitalists, and as arms-industry workers spent their wages on a wide range of consumer goods. What is more, because arms production was waste expenditure, it leaked surplus wealth out of the system, reducing the tendency for capital accumulation to overheat the economy and put a squeeze on markets, prices, and profits, thereby precipitating a slump.

The second factor was the enhanced economic role of the state more generally. As well as buying arms, post-war states nationalised major industries, built infrastructure, expanded the government workforce, and redistributed income in the form of benefits, pensions, and the 'social wage' represented by hospitals, schools, and other public services. This, too, provided markets and profits for capitalists – for construction firms building social housing, for example, or pharmaceuticals companies supplying medicines to public hospitals, or factories building rolling stock for nationalised rail networks. Here again, the multiplier effect was at work.

This factor was closely linked with the third: the militancy of a working class radicalised by the Depression and the war.

The ruling class knew that the First World War had ended in a wave of revolution between 1917 and 1923. They knew that economic depression in the interwar period had stimulated renewed revolutionary upsurges, like those in France and Spain in 1936. They knew, too, that the European working class had emerged from the Second World War both embittered by memories of interwar dole queues and poverty, but also empowered by full employment in the war economies of 1939–45. The immediate post-war communist threat might have receded, but the Left's demands for planning and welfare had become universal in a European working class determined that there would be no return to the 1930s.

Quentin Hogg, a Conservative officer and MP, had put the case for reform in Britain's House of Commons in 1943: 'If you do not give the people social reform, they are going to give you social revolution.' Post-war Marshall Aid had similar motives: stopping the spread of communism by alleviating social distress. European capitalism survived after the Second World War thanks in part to US loans to fund investment, maintain full employment, and build welfare states.

The combined economic effect of the 'permanent arms economy' and the 'welfare state consensus' was a state-sponsored boom that enabled capitalism to grow at an unprecedented rate for a whole generation.

It could not last. It did not last. The contradictions of the system were temporarily submerged, but they had not been resolved, and by the late 1960s Western capitalism was, as we shall see, entering a new phase of crisis.

Maoist China

In the summer of 1949, the Chinese Communist Party (CCP), at the head of the People's Liberation Army (PLA), entered Beijing and took power. The Nationalist leader Jiang Kaishek had fled to Taiwan as his armies disintegrated at the end of a four-year civil war. Mao Zedong, the CCP leader, proclaimed a 'socialist revolution' and the foundation of a 'people's republic'. Many across the world accepted these claims, and Maoism would become the ideological inspiration for many activists in the 1960s and 1970s.

That the events of 1949 were a genuine revolution is beyond question. A million-strong peasant army had overthrown the old ruling classes, broken the power of Western imperialism, and created the basis for a new social order. Jiang Kaishek had represented landlords and capitalists. His army had been corrupt. Many of his soldiers had ruthlessly plundered the peasantry in areas they controlled. And the Nationalists had failed in the primary duty of any state: the defence of national territory against foreign enemies.

At the end of the Second World War, the Nationalists had appeared stronger than the Communists: they controlled more territory and their army was equipped and supplied by the US. But Nationalist authority was no more than a thin veneer. The Communists, on the other hand, were socially embedded in their Liberated Zones. The PLA was highly disciplined and did not plunder the peasantry. The CCP limited the rents charged by landlords. The Communists were powerful in fighting warlords, Nationalists, and Japanese alike.

Mao's appeal was that he was both an effective nationalist and a social reformer. The Communists attracted middle-class support for their fight against imperialism and peasant support because they protected the villages from predatory soldiers, landlords, and officials. The result was that hundreds of thousands of Nationalist troops simply deserted to the Communists during the civil war.

But this did not mean that 1949 was a socialist revolution. It did not even mean that it was a revolution from below. It did not involve a mass movement of workers democratically organised and acting for themselves to bring about their own emancipation. On the contrary, the CCP had virtually no urban working-class members at all. At the end of 1926, two-thirds of party members had been workers. But this had collapsed to 10 per cent in 1928, 2 per cent in 1930, and almost zero thereafter. By 1949 the CCP was a party of middle-class leaders and peasant followers.

How had this arisen? In 1927 the First Chinese Revolution had been drowned in blood when Jiang Kaishek's Nationalists butchered 50,000 Shanghai workers and destroyed the embryonic Chinese labour movement. Mao and a group of about 1,000 Communists survived only by retreating to a remote mountain area. They operated as a guerrilla army and slowly expanded their 'Chinese Soviet Republic'. But they then came under sustained Nationalist military attack.

Threatened with extinction, in October 1934 Mao's group set out on its famous Long March, taking them deep into China's rural interior. It was an epic of human endurance. Between 80,000 and 90,000 people set out, but most died en route, some left to set up new 'red bases' on the way, and only around 4,000 completed the year-long journey. By that time, Mao was the undisputed leader, and the CCP had ceased to be an urban working-class party. Re-established in one of the most backward parts of China, cut off from all the major cities, the CCP's character as a movement of middle-class leaders and peasant guerrillas became fossilised as a permanent change.

The CCP leaders were not self-serving politicians. They were revolutionaries who made huge sacrifices for a cause they believed in. But, in the absence of a revolutionary working-class movement able to hold them to account, they were not *socialist* revolutionaries. The CCP was dominated by its middle-class leaders and, while consent and enthusiasm were high, the peasant rank-and-file did not exercise democratic control over the party. As the PLA advanced on major cities, it issued a proclamation: 'It is hoped that workers and employees in all trades will continue to work and that business will operate as usual.' It also instructed government officials and police to remain at their posts. There was to be no urban revolution that might challenge their leadership.

China in 1949 was one of the poorest countries in the world. It was much more backward compared with the advanced industrial countries than Russia had been in 1928, when Stalin assumed full control. China was also threatened by imperialism. The US had backed the Nationalists. The Cold War had just begun. Mao's victory came as a huge shock to America's leaders. Then the Korean War broke out just a year after the PLA entered Beijing.

To safeguard their national independence, China's leaders had to industrialise and militarise as quickly as possible. Starting from a low economic base, this meant high levels of exploitation to generate the surpluses needed. Private capitalism was too weak to accomplish this and foreign capitalism was hostile. Only state capitalism could provide a mechanism for rapid economic development in the new China. This meant the transformation of the CCP leadership from nationalist revolutionaries into a bureaucratic ruling class. During the 1950s, about 25 per cent of national output was invested in heavy industry and armaments; whereas living standards barely increased at all.

To build well means to build on solid foundations. China's backwardness made this a very slow process. Its leaders wanted a shortcut to industrial and military power. They lacked technology and infrastructure, but they had labour in abundance. Perhaps they could substitute the latter for the former. This was the genesis of the disastrous 'Great Leap Forward' (1958–61). Grossly inflated targets were set for agriculture and industry. Land was forcibly collectivised and up to 25,000 peasants at a time were grouped in 'people's communes' – essentially state-run agribusinesses. 'Backyard steel furnaces' were set up. Mass campaigns were launched to increase working hours and tighten workplace discipline.

But factory managers lied about output and caused chaos. Maintenance was neglected and machinery broke down. The backyard furnaces simply wasted raw material. Workers were exhausted by long shifts. Peasant productivity slumped.

By 1961 famine again stalked northern China, desperate peasants were fleeing their villages, and armed rebellions had broken out in at least two provinces. It is estimated that the Great Leap Forward set China back a decade. Mao was marginalised within the Chinese leadership for his role in promoting the policy.

In 1966 he attempted a comeback by launching the Cultural Revolution. This involved mobilising popular forces – especially young Chinese enrolled as Red Guards – to attack Mao's enemies in the bureaucracy. Local officials and intellectuals were denounced as 'capitalist roaders' and 'counter-revolutionaries' and tried for their 'crimes' in kangaroo courts. The personality cult around Mao became fanatical. His *Little Red Book* was brandished like holy text.

When dictators attack one another in public, they risk unleashing forces they cannot control. Within a year, China was in turmoil. The educational system had effectively shut down. Many towns were divided between armed factions supporting rival officials. Workers took strike action. The party-state apparatus was increasingly paralysed.

The PLA was brought in to suppress the growing disorder. Old officials returned to their posts. Millions – around 10 per cent of the urban population – were deported to the countryside. Sometimes the repression was lethal. In the southern province of Guangxi, an estimated 100,000 were killed and most of the town of Wuzhou was destroyed.

Even so, the CCP could not re-establish full control until 1971. By then, Mao's health was failing. When he finally died in 1976, a power struggle erupted inside the leadership. The hard-line Maoists – led by 'the Gang of Four' – found themselves unpopular, isolated, and rapidly outmanoeuvred. They were purged and control passed into the hands of modernisers led by Deng Xiaoping.

In 1978 the modernisers launched an ambitious programme to transform the Chinese economy. It had two main features: opening up China to foreign investment and technology; and reducing state control of the economy in favour of market forces. Chinese backwardness had hamstrung Maoist state capitalism. The great experiment in capital accumulation through propaganda, willpower, and 'socialist labour' had failed. China's rulers now turned to neoliberalism.

End of Empire?

The Second World War had been an imperialist war. The victorious powers had fought to keep their empires, and they had every intention of holding on to them when the war ended. In some cases this meant restoring colonial authority they had lost. The Japanese had driven the British out of Malaya, the French out of Vietnam, and the Dutch out of Indonesia. All returned.

But much had changed. Not only were the European powers overshadowed by the two superpowers in what had become a bipolar world; they had also become financially dependent on US loans to rebuild their shattered economies. This was especially true of Britain, which had been fully engaged in the world war throughout its six years and had become heavily reliant on US financial and military aid from 1941 onwards.

At the same time, nationalist resistance to British rule in the colonies was growing. This reflected the increasing wealth of the native bourgeoisie and middle class, the growing size of the urban working class, the strengthening of political and trade union organisation, the radical mood that had developed during the war, and ever more frequent examples of successful anti-colonial struggles.

British rule in India had been shaken by three previous waves of nationalist agitation – in the early 1920s, early 1930s, and early 1940s. The 'Quit India' campaign of 1942 had been especially potent, challenging Britain's right to declare war on behalf of 325 million Indians. Exceptional violence was deployed to suppress the movement, but the events left some of Britain's rulers under no illusions. The British Viceroy, Field-Marshal Archibald Wavell, told

Churchill in 1943 that 'the repressive force necessary to hold India after the war would exceed Britain's means'.

Post-war imperial overstretch evoked three kinds of response: repression, divide and rule, and support for client rulers. Repression triggered several full-scale colonial wars. The French fought a long war against the Vietnamese (1946–54) at a cost of half a million lives, and another long war against the Algerians (1954–62) at a cost of a million lives. The British fought colonial wars in Malaya (1948–60), Kenya (1952–6), Cyprus (1955–9), and Aden (1963–7). These 'dirty wars' involved massacres, concentration camps, and the widespread use of torture.

Colonial wars fought a long way from home against embedded nationalist guerrillas imposed a huge burden on declining imperial powers. This was most clear in the case of Portugal, a small European state with an old empire in Africa. The strain of fighting simultaneous wars in Guinea-Bissau (1956–74), Angola (1961–74), and Mozambique (1964–74) was a direct cause of the Portuguese Revolution of 1974–5, which was led by disaffected army officers.

The last in this sequence of post-war conflicts was the war against the racist regime in Rhodesia (today's Zimbabwe) between 1964 and 1979. In this case, the 'mother country' refused to back the white settlers. The Conservative Prime Minister Harold Macmillan had summed up the view of Britain's rulers on a visit to South Africa in 1960 when he said: 'The wind of change is blowing through this continent. Whether we like it or not, this growth of national consciousness is a political fact.' Other, more subtle ways of protecting imperial interests were needed – such as those successfully deployed in the 'decolonisation' of India in 1947.

The principal expression of Indian nationalism had for long been the Indian National Congress founded in 1885. Its most radical elements favoured Hindu–Muslim–Sikh unity, a single state spanning the subcontinent, thoroughgoing land reform, and support for workers' rights. The potential was shown in February 1946 when the Indian crews on 78 British ships and 20 shore stations mutinied. The mutineers were supported by students and workers. Hindus and Muslims marched side by side.

But more right-wing elements hostile to class struggles that threatened the interests of Indian landowners and capitalists were dominant inside the nationalist movement. Congress was a bourgeois-nationalist party, not a revolutionary one. Mahatma Gandhi, on the right wing of Congress, opposed the mutiny, and even the more left-leaning Jawaharlal Nehru busied himself trying to contain it. This left a weakness in the nationalist movement that could be exploited by Hindu chauvinists, Muslim separatists, and the British imperial authorities. Class struggle tends to unite the exploited against their exploiters. Absence of class struggle can have the opposite effect, leaving people divided and susceptible to the politics of communal hatred.

The British actively encouraged Mohammed Ali Jinnah's Muslim League – which favoured a separate Muslim state – as a counterweight to Congress. The effect was to unleash a torrent of communal violence in which poor Hindus and Muslims turned on each other.

Hindu, Muslim, and Sikh populations were intermixed, especially in the Punjab region in the north-west of the subcontinent. Once the Congress and Muslim League leaders had agreed to partition – with British connivance – right-wing thugs moved into action on both sides of the new border to ethnically cleanse 'their' territory. Between 250,000 and a million people died in communal massacres as India and Pakistan become independent in 1947. The divisions created by partition remain unresolved. India and Pakistan are still at loggerheads over the status of Kashmir, and chauvinism and communalism continue to poison the politics of the region.

The British had divided their opponents, marginalised Congress radicals, and ensured that the new regimes in Delhi and Karachi were sympathetic to foreign capital. Similar methods were employed elsewhere to manage the transition to native rule.

In Malaya, the British waged a counterinsurgency war against a communist-led guerrilla movement. The guerrillas were mainly ethnic Chinese. The British exploited this by playing on Malay distrust of the Chinese minority, while promising eventual independence to moderate Malay politicians.

In Kenya, the British first defeated the Mau Mau Revolt in 1956, then, some years later, released from detention the principal nationalist leader, the relatively moderate Jomo Kenyatta, in order to negotiate an orderly transition to independence with him in 1963.

Something similar happened in Cyprus. The British were unable to defeat the EOKA nationalist guerrilla movement on the island. Instead, they arranged a ceasefire and negotiated a transfer of power to Archbishop Makarios, a more conservative nationalist leader than General Grivas, who had commanded the guerrillas.

Formal empire – direct colonial rule – ended in a series of conflicts, some very bloody, some less so, between the late 1940s and the late 1970s. But this did not mean the end of imperialism. Foreign interests had often been well protected in the transition. A high degree of economic dependency shackled many of the newly independent states. Few would find it easy to develop their way out of poverty in a world dominated by giant corporations and military superpowers.

More radical nationalist regimes would sometimes try to break the shackles. When they did, they would once again find the economic and military power of imperialism ranged against them. The trappings of global power had changed. But the framework remained essentially the same.

Oil, Zionism, and Western Imperialism

One area of the world has assumed particular significance for the great powers since 1945: the Middle East. The reason is that it holds about 70 per cent of the world's known oil reserves.

Oil is the global economy's most important commodity. It is fuel, heat, and light. Without it, capitalism would grind to a halt. Oil is also immensely profitable. Five of the world's top ten corporations are oil companies.

Post-1945 US economic growth fast outstripped domestic oil production. In the 1950s the US imported only 10 per cent of its oil. By the late 1980s this had risen to more than half. At the same time, newly industrialising countries like China and India have been putting growing pressure on oil supplies. With annual growth rates of around 8 per cent, China's share of global output has risen from about 5 per cent in 1978 to about 20 per cent today.

Oil is a vital commodity, demand for it is rising, but it is a finite resource. That is the principal reason why the Middle East has become a battleground.

In the late nineteenth century, the British took control of Egypt and the Suez Canal, mainly to secure their communications with India and Australia. Shortly before the First World War, they acquired a second, equally pressing reason for influence in the Middle East:

Britain's Royal Navy was converting its fleet from coal to oil power. Control of the oilfields of southern Iran became a strategic priority.

The modern Middle East was created by the First World War. Half a million British soldiers were deployed to drive the Ottoman Turks out of Iraq and Syria in 1918. The Middle East was then partitioned into colonies by the British and their French allies in line with a secret wartime agreement.

But the British had also entered into two other wartime agreements: they had promised independence to the Hashemite leaders of an Arab native rebellion against Turkish rule; and they had proffered support for Zionist settlement in Palestine to create a national home for the Jewish people. The first of these promises was broken. The second was kept.

Zionism was a right-wing nationalist movement founded in the late nineteenth century and supported by a minority of European Jews in the years before the First World War. Most politically active Jews in this period were on the left. Judaism is a religious persuasion, not a race, nor even a nationality. The vast majority of European Jews were descendants of converts to Judaism in the Middle Ages. Their only real 'homeland' was Europe. But the Zionists claimed that anti-semitism was inevitable, the Jews were a separate 'nation', and Jewish people from different parts of the world should therefore settle in a single place and live together. Where this should be was secondary. One suggestion was Madagascar.

Most Jews regarded the scheme as fantasy. They had jobs, homes, and businesses where they lived. They were integrated into local communities. Anti-semitism was a real threat, but the most practical response seemed to be to fight it in alliance with socialist and trade union allies, not to daydream about escape to an idealised 'homeland'.

What gave Zionism traction was imperialism. The Zionist leaders understood this. They lobbied hard for high-level backing from, among others, the German Kaiser, the Russian Tsar, and the Ottoman Sultan. But it was the British who delivered. They wanted the Zionists to encourage Jews to volunteer for military service during the war, and they could see the advantage in a pro-British Zionist enclave in post-war Palestine. 'We could develop the country,' one Zionist leader had written in 1914, 'bring back civilisation, and form a very effective guard for the Suez Canal.'

The problem was that Palestine was already occupied. And of its 700,000 people in 1918, only 60,000 were Jews. The rest were Arabs, most of them tenant-farmers. Yet by 1947, when the British surrendered their 'mandate' to rule Palestine, Jewish numbers had increased more than ten-fold to 650,000, Arab numbers less than three-fold to 2,000,000. The difference is explained by the large-scale Jewish immigration permitted under British rule.

The Zionists were well funded by European and American benefactors. So they were able to buy land by offering attractive prices to absentee Arab landlords. They then moved in to evict Arab farmers whose families had worked the land for centuries. The Zionist land grab, and British repression of Arab protests, triggered the Palestinian Revolt of 1936–9. Zionist militia units fought alongside 20,000 British troops to crush it. About 5,000 Palestinians were killed.

The British then tried to limit the rate of Jewish immigration to ease tensions. This brought them into armed conflict during the 1940s with the increasingly confident Zionist militias. The defeat of the Palestinians meant that the Zionist movement the British had nurtured now had a life of its own.

What gave Zionism massive further impetus was the Holocaust. The discovery that six million Jews had been murdered in a systematic extermination programme stunned the world. It seemed to substantiate Zionist claims that anti-semitism was so pervasive that the only solution was a separate Jewish homeland. It left many feeling that the world community was morally obliged to support Zionist demands.

In 1947, with British withdrawal imminent, the United Nations brokered an international peace plan. Palestine was to be partitioned, with 55 per cent of it allocated to the Zionists – who represented only 30 per cent of the population, the vast majority of them immigrant settlers. The Arabs rejected the plan. Huge anti-imperialist demonstrations erupted in Arab capitals. The Palestinians organised for self-defence and hoped for wider Arab backing. But the Zionists were now too numerous, too well organised, and too heavily armed to be stopped. They went onto the offensive and seized 80 per cent of historic Palestine.

Terror was an essential instrument of their conquest. After the Irgun group massacred 250 Palestinians in Deir Yassin, truck-loads of Zionist militia drove around chanting 'Deir Yassin! Deir Yassin!' as a warning to others. At least 700,000 Palestinians fled in 1948.

The Arab monarchs committed their small, ramshackle armies to war. They were quickly defeated, but settled for a land grab of their own, the rump of Palestinian territory being divided between Egypt and Jordan.

The State of Israel was proclaimed in 1948. It has since fought wars against its neighbours in 1956, 1967, 1973, and 1982. It captured the Golan Heights from Syria, the West Bank from Jordan, and the Gaza Strip and the Sinai Desert from Egypt in 1967. Another 350,000 Palestinians joined a second exodus in that year. Much of the additional territory acquired in 1967 has been retained. Israel continues to annex land, build settlements, and encourage Jewish immigration. It also engages in exceptionally high levels of internal repression against Palestinians. This peaked during the First Intifada (1987–93), the Second Intifada (2000–5), and the Gaza War (2008–9).

Israel is inherently militarised and expansionist because it is a colonial settler state founded on dispossession. It can never live at peace with its neighbours because it has taken their land. Insecurity imposes permanent pressure to increase territory and manpower.

Israel is also an outpost of imperialism. It regularly receives up to 25 per cent of total US foreign military aid. The Zionist state is the paid watchdog of Western imperialism in the Middle East.

Zionism and US imperialism are permanent sources of oppression, violence, and instability in the Middle East. Only an Arab revolution from below with the power to recast the whole geopolitical structure of the region offers hope of lasting peace. The road to Jerusalem runs through Cairo.

1956: Hungary and Suez

1956 was a year of war, revolution, and disillusionment – a year after which nothing could ever be quite the same again.

The 1948 war and the creation of Israel had been a catastrophic defeat for Arab nationalism. The effect was felt across the Middle East as corrupt, reactionary, puppet kings came under intense pressure from below. The junior officers of Arab armies provided the most effective expression of this popular discontent. They had been in the forefront of military failure in 1948. They had good reason to favour reform and modernisation. And because of their professional role, they were organised as a national force.

Amid rising mass protests, on 23 July 1952 the Free Officers Movement staged a military coup in Egypt and ended the rule of King Farouk. The most important figure in the Movement was Colonel Gamal Abdul Nasser.

Nasser became a dictator, but his programme of land reform, state-capitalist development, and strident attacks on Zionism and Western imperialism made him popular at home and a beacon of Arab nationalism across the Middle East. Three years after taking power, Nasser nationalised the Suez Canal. In November 1956 the British and the French responded by invading Egypt in alliance with Israel.

The invasion was a political disaster for the imperial powers. It provoked a storm of rage in the Arab world and mass protests at home. A demonstration called by the Labour Party and Trades Union Congress was the biggest in London since the Second World War and culminated in clashes between protestors and police outside 10 Downing Street. The US took advantage of the hostile reaction to pull the plug on the operation by threatening to cut off the funding on which the British economy depended. Its aim was to displace Britain as the major imperial power in the oil-rich Middle East. The Suez Crisis thus destroyed any illusions about the British Empire: it was clearly in terminal decline; it could no longer play a role in the world independent of the US. Nasser's standing in the Arab world, on the other hand, soared to new heights.

Even more dramatic events were unfolding at the same time on the other side of the Iron Curtain. Stalin had died in 1953. His dictatorship had claimed many victims at the highest levels; now the Russian ruling class took the opportunity to rein in the apparatus of terror. Stalin's police chief Beria was executed.

A struggle for power inside the bureaucracy erupted onto the public stage in February 1956 when the new Soviet leader, Nikita Khrushchev, denounced Stalin at the 20th Party Congress. Stalin, he said, had murdered thousands, deported millions, and proved cowardly and incompetent in the crisis of the German invasion of June 1941. The shockwave was immense. The Stalinist propaganda machine had silenced the slightest whisper of dissent for a quarter of a century. Suddenly, everything was in question. Perhaps all was not well in the 'socialist motherland' after all. Perhaps some of the criticisms were not just 'capitalist lies'.

Discontent had been growing inside the Soviet Empire since 1953. In June of that year, building workers on a giant construction site in East Berlin had walked out when told they would have to work longer hours for the same pay. When they marched through the city, tens of thousands joined them. The following day, the whole of East Germany was in the grip of a general strike. In some towns, demonstrators ransacked party offices, attacked police stations, and broke open the prisons.

In July revolt also broke out at the giant slave-labour camp at Vorkuta in the far north of Russia itself. Within five days, 50 pits had stopped work and 250,000 miners were on strike. Both risings were crushed by the army. But the need for reform was clear, and within two years, 90 per cent of the millions held in the gulags had been released. Khrushchev's speech at the 20th Congress had a context.

The reopening of debate and the first tentative moves towards reform are always danger points for dictatorial regimes. Suppressed longing for change can suddenly swell into a torrent.

In Poland, memories were still fresh of the long Nazi occupation and of the high hopes of freedom and prosperity engendered by the end of the war. The death and subsequent denunciation of the Soviet dictator had rekindled these hopes. In June 1956, like the workers of East Berlin three years earlier, the workers of Poznań stopped work, marched through the city, and were soon battling the police, releasing prisoners, and seizing arms. The insurrection was contained, but rather than crush the movement outright, a section of the bureaucracy that favoured limited reform manoeuvred for power. Wladyslaw Gomulka, an independent-minded communist leader jailed under Stalin, was released from prison and formed a new regime.

The Russians threatened to invade, but were persuaded to back off. Gomulka addressed a mass rally of 250,000 enthusiastic supporters. What had begun as a working-class revolt had been turned into a bureaucratic coup. The Polish Spring in October – as it was called – merely gave power to the reformist wing of Poland's state-capitalist ruling class.

Events in Hungary played out very differently. Poznań and the Polish Spring were the detonators of a great working-class revolution in the heart of Europe. On 22 October 1956, students at the Budapest Polytechnic Institute drew up a 14-point manifesto calling for democracy, free speech, the release of prisoners, the withdrawal of Russian troops, and an end to compulsory state levies on peasant farm produce. The following day, the students marched to present their demands. As they did so, they were joined by tens of thousands of workers. In the evening, as they converged on the radio station, they were fired on by the secret police.

Workers armed themselves with guns from sports clubs. Soldiers handed their weapons to demonstrators. Across the city, and then across the country, power was seized by popular committees and armed militias.

Peter Fryer, covering events for the British Communist Party paper *The Daily Worker*, reported that the new democratic bodies were like

> the workers', peasants', and soldiers' councils which were thrown up in Russia in the 1905 Revolution and in February 1917 ... They were at once organs of insurrection – the coming together of delegates elected in the factories and universities, mines and army units – and organs of popular self-government which the armed people trusted.

A section of the Hungarian ruling class, led by Imre Nagy, attempted to regain control in the same way as Gomulka had done in Poland – by riding the tiger of popular revolt. But the movement was too powerful. Events had moved beyond a government reshuffle.

On 4 November Russian tanks rolled into Budapest. The city was turned into a war zone as working-class suburbs were reduced to rubble and thousands of Hungarians died fighting the invaders from street to street. The Greater Budapest Central Workers' Council, playing the role of the Petrogràd Soviet in 1905 and 1917, ordered a general strike which paralysed the city for a fortnight.

That November, Budapest was under dual power. The Workers' Council organised essential supplies, distributed bread, maintained health services, and manufactured weapons. The authority of the newly installed regime of János Kádár, by contrast, was based on Russian tanks.

But the workers could not win against 3,000 tanks and 200,000 troops – not without the revolution spreading to other parts of Eastern Europe. The strike was defeated, the Workers' Council suppressed, and 350 oppositionists, including Nagy, were executed. Even so, the collaborationist Kádár regime remained fragile. As it struggled to regain control, it was forced to raise wages by 22 percent and promise 'democratic elections … in all existing administrative bodies'.

The events of 1956 had cracked the Stalinist monolith. The real Marxist tradition of revolution from below and workers' self-emancipation had been reborn on the streets of Budapest. Tens of thousands of left activists across the world were forced to reconsider their political allegiance.

In East Germany, 68 per cent of those purged from the Communist Party for their part in the 1953 uprising had been members before 1933. The old revolutionaries had fought with their class. The suited apparatchiks of the new ruling class had remained at their posts.

Peter Fryer's reports from Budapest were spiked. He resigned from *The Daily Worker* and was then expelled from the Communist Party. He was not alone. In the immediate aftermath of the Hungarian Revolution, the British Communist Party lost 7,000 of its members, a fifth of the total, including many leading intellectuals and trade unionists.

As Stalinism crumbled, a New Left began to form. And as activists re-crystallised into new groupings, they were drawn to a number of competing 'anti-Stalinist' political traditions. Many of these, like Stalinism, were delusionary. Maoism was one. Another was taking shape in a remote mountain range on a distant Caribbean island. It was to produce an inspirational and iconic figure who seemed to personify revolutionary idealism in a world scarred by exploitation and injustice: his name was Che Guevara.

Che Guevara and the Cuban Revolution

In December 1956, a group of 82 revolutionaries landed on the Cuban coast with the intention of overthrowing the corrupt, brutal, US-backed dictatorship of Fulgencio Batista. They called themselves the 26 July Movement in honour of a failed attack on the Moncada army barracks in 1953. The principal leader of the expedition was

Fidel Castro. Among the other leaders were Fidel's brother, Raul, and an Argentinian doctor, Ernesto ('Che') Guevara.

Only 12 of them survived long enough to launch a guerrilla war in the remote Sierra Maestra mountains. Despite this, the group held together and attracted fresh recruits. By the summer of 1958, they had 200 members. Six months later, in January 1959, they entered Havana, the Cuban capital, as victors in the revolutionary war.

It was a stunning achievement. At the moment of victory, there were still only 800 guerrillas, yet they had defeated Batista's armed forces and taken control of a Caribbean island of seven million people.

The US regarded Central America and the Caribbean as its 'backyard'. Nominally independent states were run by US client regimes formed of assorted generals, landowners, industrialists, and gangsters. The system, designed to protect American business interests in the region, was policed by the US intelligence agencies. When a mildly reformist regime had taken power in Guatemala in 1954, for instance, it had been overthrown in a CIA-organised coup.

As it happened, however, Batista had become so unpopular that the US had decided to dump him at the last minute, believing they could cut a deal with Castro. And why not? The Russian Revolution had been carried out by workers. The Chinese Revolution had been carried out by peasants. The Cuban Revolution had been carried out by neither: it was a movement of middle-class intellectuals.

Castro had issued a series of statements indicating support for liberal reforms but little more. As late as May 1959 he declared: 'We are not opposed to private investment ... We believe in the usefulness, in the experience, and in the enthusiasm of private investors ... Companies with international investments will have the same guarantees and the same rights as national firms.'

The revolutionaries were naïve. What had made victory possible was the support of Cuba's peasants and rural labourers. These were US capital's beasts of burden. Their lives could not be improved without confronting the interests of big business.

The contradictions of Cuba's economic underdevelopment confronted Castro with a simple choice: he could either end up running a client regime like Batista's, or he could carry out land reform and use the wealth of the island to fund schools, hospitals, and welfare.

Castro moved cautiously at first, but he faced fierce retaliation against any perceived threat to US interests. An increasingly tense stand-off culminated in wholesale nationalisation of American businesses on the island, the development of strong commercial links with Russia, and a belated declaration that Cuba's revolution had been 'socialist'. The CIA then backed an armed attack on the island by rich Cuban exiles in April 1961. Just as ordinary Cubans had abandoned Batista to his fate, now they rallied in defence of the Castro regime. The Bay of Pigs invasion was a fiasco. The Cuban Missile Crisis in October the following year, when Castro's Soviet ally (temporarily) installed nuclear weapons on the island and almost triggered nuclear war, sealed the rift between the US and Cuba.

The urban workers had played no part in the revolution and exercised no power after it. The rural labourers had cheered the revolution from the side-lines, but hardly any had become guerrillas. The revolution was almost entirely the work of middle-class idealists and a small number of peasant-farmers they succeeded in recruiting along the way. The Cuban Revolution was not, therefore, an example of 'the self-emancipation of the working class'. And in consequence, Cuban 'socialism' was the impoverished state capitalism and economic dependency of a Caribbean sugar island subject to a US boycott. The reforms were real, but they were bestowed from above and straitjacketed by poverty.

Che Guevara nonetheless generalised the Cuban experience into a theory of revolutionary guerrilla warfare that could be applied worldwide. He identified three key lessons:

1. Popular guerrilla armies can defeat regular government forces.
2. The countryside, not the town, is the natural terrain of struggle in the underdeveloped world.
3. The revolutionaries do not need to wait until conditions have ripened; they can themselves create the revolution by forming a guerrilla group and acting as the catalyst.

Small, mobile, hard-hitting bands of dedicated revolutionaries, Che argued, could provide insurrectionary *focos* (bases), kick-starting revolutionary guerrilla wars and toppling US-backed dictators across Africa, Asia, and the Americas.

Che was as good as his word. He could have remained a comfortable, popular, high-ranking official in Cuba. But he was soon disillusioned with the Soviet-style economics and diplomacy embraced by the Cuban leadership. He remained at heart what he had always been: a brave, idealistic, and dedicated revolutionary fighter. So he disappeared from public view and travelled secretly, first to the Congo in 1965, then to Bolivia in 1966, in an attempt to make a reality of his *foco* theory of revolution.

But the theory turned out to be false. Revolution could not be replicated by mere acts of willpower and dynamism. History could not be forced by voluntarism. Subjective factors – leadership, organisation, ideas – were decisive in revolutionary situations. But the objective conditions had to be right. Whether or not revolution was possible also depended on the balance of class forces, the coherence of the state, and the consciousness and confidence of the masses.

And there had to be a proper relationship between the two: revolutionary organisation had to be embedded in society, in its class struggles and mass movements, so that the revolutionaries were sensitive to the popular mood and could match demands and calls to action to what was possible.

In Cuba, all social forces had been weak: the social elites, the Batista regime, the middle class, the labour movement, the peasantry, rural labourers. Corruption and exploitation were endemic. Life was bitter, but alienation and lethargy were pervasive. Entering this hollowed-out society, the guerrillas were the grit in the void.

Things were different elsewhere. Che was defeated in the Congo by the corruption and factionalism of rival warlords, and by his own poor health. But he faced far worse in Bolivia. His guerrilla force of about 50 men, inserted into a remote mountain region, found itself isolated amid the indifference and fear of the local population. The guerrillas stumbled from disaster to disaster, and then, in early October 1967, the remaining handful was surrounded and overwhelmed by 1,800 Bolivian soldiers.

Che was captured and summarily executed. Nevertheless, he became an icon of revolutionary resistance because of his heroism and idealism in a world soured by suffering. His has since become perhaps the most famous face on the planet. But to change the world in the way he hoped for, we must learn from his mistakes.

16
The World on Fire
1968–1975

Revolutionary demonstration of workers and soldiers,
Lisbon, Portugal, 25 April 1974.

Mass popular revolt brought the world closer to international revolution
between 1968 and 1975 than at any time since the Russian Revolution.

The period from the Second World War to the late 1960s had been one of relative political consensus across much of the developed world. Colonial wars continued to rage in parts of the Third World, but dissidence in the Eastern Bloc and demonstrations and strikes in the West seemed to have little impact beyond the minorities involved. Then, in 1968, the whole world exploded in a new wave of mass protest.

In the framework of the Great Boom – with record levels of economic growth, rapidly rising living-standards, and the birth of a new 'consumer society' – major social changes had been underway. The growth of the workforce involved women going out to work in larger numbers, people moving from country areas to the cities, and others migrating from the underdeveloped world to the major metropolitan centres. Workers became more confident, better organised, more militant. Old oppressions were less tolerable. The moral strictures and social conformity of the 1950s seemed irksome.

Struggles for Civil Rights in the early 1960s and against the Vietnam War in the late 1960s saw huge numbers of young Americans radicalised and drawn into political activity. They turned out to be the vanguard of a global youth revolt, often centred on university campuses, that was soon sweeping the Western world, infecting the Eastern Bloc, and resonating in the Global South.

When youth and student struggles fused with workers' resistance to attacks on jobs, wages, and conditions as the post-war boom slowed down in the late 1960s and then juddered to a halt in 1973, the capitalist world was shaken by mass struggles from below which, at their peak, turned into revolutionary offensives. The lessons of this period – of 'the fire last time' – are so rich in implications for the present that we must pay them special attention.

Excursus 7: What is Oppression?

Exploitation can be defined as the extraction of surplus wealth from the working population by a ruling class. It involves both an economic process – the appropriation and accumulation of surplus – and a social relationship – between a powerful minority and a subordinate majority in which the former expropriates the fruits of the latter's labour. Class arises from such processes and relationships.

What about oppression? The words 'exploitation' and 'oppression' are sometimes used casually, even interchangeably, without defined meaning. They should not be: imprecise terminology reflects theoretical confusion and leads to political muddle. We need to understand the world if we are to organise to change it.

Oppression is systematic discrimination against a distinct social group on the basis of gender, race, religion, nationality, tribe, sexual orientation, disability, age, or any other real or imagined common characteristic. In an institutional form, it involves unequal access to social opportunities – jobs, careers, homes, education, healthcare, welfare benefits, and so on – when the enforcers are usually employers, officials, and police. But it also takes the form of prejudice, abuse, and violence from ordinary people influenced by the ideas of right-wing politicians, the media, religious bigots, fascist groups, and others.

Exploitation and oppression are conceptually quite distinct. All workers in capitalist society are exploited, irrespective of whether or not they belong to an oppressed group. Some capitalists, on the other hand, may belong to an oppressed group, even though they are exploiters. The intersection of exploitation and oppression can therefore be sociologically complex. But this broad generalisation holds: the more oppressed a social group, the more likely it is to experience extreme forms of exploitation. And common identity as an oppressed group can make it easier to bind people together and build collective organisation. The dual experience of oppression and exploitation can then be explosive.

But why does oppression arise at all? Many modern societies adhere to an official ideology that proclaims equal rights. Many have laws making discrimination illegal. Yet oppression persists. Why is this?

Just as the rate of exploitation varies – largely according to the degree to which workers organise and fight back – so too does the intensity of oppression. Past victories over sexism and racism may be enshrined in anti-discrimination laws and reflected in changing social attitudes and practices. The gains are real, but they remain in danger of being rolled back, and they are rarely absolute. That is because oppression is hard-wired into the matrix of capitalist society as surely as exploitation is hard-wired into the workings of the capitalist economy. Here is why.

Capitalism is a process of accumulation that siphons the wealth created by society as a whole to a minority at the top. It is based upon the expropriation of the many by the few. Its operations are chaotic, unplanned, indifferent to social need, devoid of social purpose. It creates a dystopian world of grotesque greed based on alienated labour and mass impoverishment.

This would be unsustainable if the common people understood their condition and united to overthrow the rich. The great radical poet Percy Bysshe Shelley captured it beautifully in *The Mask of Anarchy* (1819), written after the Peterloo Massacre, in which mounted yeomanry attacked a pro-democracy demonstration in Manchester, killing 15 people.

> Rise, like lions after slumber
> In unvanquishable number!
> Shake your chains to earth like dew
> Which in sleep had fallen on you;
> Ye are many – they are few!

What is the essential lesson here? It is that the stability of any class society – that is, any society based upon the exploitation of the many by the few – requires that the masses be divided against themselves, lest they unite against their rulers. Sexism, racism, and other forms of oppression have an essential social function: to obscure the *primary* fracture-line in society – that between rich and poor – by interposing various *secondary* differences and gradations, so as to prevent the formation of a united popular movement from below against the system as a whole.

These differences and gradations are real enough, but their effect is to lock down the overarching system of exploitation. Take the example of Northern Ireland during the Troubles. The Catholic minority was the victim of institutionalised discrimination. The Protestant majority – the rich, the middle class, and the workers – were united in their support of this set-up. Discrimination meant that, if you were Protestant, you were more likely to have a job, a council house, and decent local services. But the effect of the sectarian division of the working class was to cripple its ability to fight for general social improvement, so that Northern Irish workers – Catholic *and* Protestant – were the poorest in the United Kingdom. Eamonn McCann, a leading activist in the Civil Rights Movement, put it succinctly:

> The fact that, from the Protestant worker's point of view, the privilege is pretty small, matters not at all. When tuppence-halfpenny is looking down on tuppence, the halfpenny difference can assume an importance out of all proportion to its actual size.

This is not to imply that social division is the result of a deliberate conspiracy on the part of the ruling class. History is a messy process of muddling through. What actually happens is that existing fractures – historically determined differences between the social groups living within the territory of any particular state – are reconfigured

according to circumstances by a range of social institutions and ideological mechanisms embedded in the status quo. Old form thereby
acquires new content.

This becomes clear as soon as we consider the diverse character of
intra-communal strife in the modern world – and the speed and ease
with which the targets of vilification and hatred can change. What is
constant is the system's need to disorient and disorganise the masses:
what varies is the specific form this takes at any moment.

The racism of the Turkish state, for example, has taken three
main forms over the last century – anti-Armenian, anti-Greek, and
anti-Kurdish – with the focus changing with circumstances. The
main division in the modern Middle East is not racial, but religious.
Sunni-Islamic fascists target Shias, Sufis, Christians, and other
religious minorities. In India, too, religion has traditionally provided
the main fracture-line, with political elites fostering Hindu–Muslim
'communal' pogroms. British racism was mainly anti-Irish in the
nineteenth century, mainly anti-semitic in the early twentieth century,
mainly anti-black and anti-Asian in the late twentieth century, and
is now mainly anti-migrant (especially anti-East European) and
anti-Muslim.

Often enough, the targets are multiple. Fascism – in both its
Western and Islamic forms – tends to target a range of ethnic and
religious minorities, and, at the same time, to direct misogynistic
attacks on women and homophobic attacks on LGBT people.

There are three main responses to oppression. First, people may
simply be cowed into submission and resign themselves to discrimination and prejudice. Second, people may seek acceptance
and advancement within the existing set-up on an individual basis,
realising that they will face obstacles on the way, but nonetheless
seeking conventional 'middle class' success in the sense allowed and
defined by the system. Or third, people may fight back. This typically
involves a proud assertion of identity, the creation of an affirmative
subculture, and the building of collective organisations of resistance.

Struggles against oppression can degenerate into 'identity politics'
and/or 'separatism'. Both are dead-ends. Both represent nothing more
than an inversion of the dominant ideology of division – black against
white, women against men, LGBT against straight, Muslim against
Christian, Kurd against Turk. Throughout history, the oppressed have
won their greatest victories by rejecting the divisive categories of the
system, asserting the common humanity of all, inviting the solidarity
of other groups, and engaging in mass united struggle from below.

The great popular struggles of the 1960s and 1970s bear witness to
this. To these – to a world on fire – we now turn.

Civil Rights and Black Power

It really got going in December 1955, in Montgomery, Alabama, on the day Rosa Parks decided she had had enough. A white man wanted her seat. The rest were occupied. She refused to move. The driver stopped the bus, the police were called, and Rosa Parks was arrested.

> People always say that I didn't give up my seat because I was tired, but that isn't true. I was not tired physically, or no more tired than I usually was at the end of a working day. I was not old, although some people have an image of me as being old then. I was 42. No, the only tired I was, was tired of giving in.

She was not the only one. On the day of her trial – 5 December – black activists called for a boycott of the Montgomery buses. The boycott was rock-solid: 40,000 African-Americans refused to use the buses, some walking 20 miles in the rain to get to work that day.

Such was the success of the protest that the call went out for an indefinite boycott until the bus service was desegregated. It lasted a year. Then the Supreme Court ruled that segregation on buses was 'unconstitutional'. By that time, similar struggles had taken off in other big cities of the American South, and the leader of the Montgomery boycott had become a national figure and leading spokesman for the emergent Civil Rights movement. He was a 26-year-old black preacher called Martin Luther King.

It was an old fight renewed. The struggle of African-Americans for racial justice runs like a black thread through the history of the United States. The abolition of slavery at the end of the Civil War in 1865 had failed to end black oppression. Northern attempts at 'radical reconstruction' were foiled by Southern reaction. The Ku Klux Klan emerged as a mass counter-revolutionary movement with up to half a million members based on white-supremacism and anti-black racism. One Northern army officer reported that murders of blacks had become 'so common as to render it impossible to keep an accurate record of them'.

The effects of this reign of terror would be felt for a century. The 'Jim Crow' laws disenfranchised black voters, segregated public services and spaces on racial lines, and impoverished the black population of the Southern states by restricting them to low-paid menial labour and sharecropping tenancies that were little better than slavery.

Labourers and tenants living in isolated rural communities were easily intimidated. As late as 1910, 90 per cent of the Southern blacks still worked on the land. But hundreds of thousands emigrated to the cities, both North and South, in the decades following, and by 1960 an estimated three-quarters of African-Americans belonged to the urban working-class. This did not end the racism: but it made it far easier to organise against it.

Other things, too, were changing. Hundreds of thousands of black soldiers had served in the Second World War. Cold War propaganda heralded the United States as the standard-bearer of 'the free world'. The economy was booming, labour was in demand, wages were rising, and pundits spoke of 'the consumer society'. The contradiction between Jim Crow oppression and American ideals of 'life, liberty, and the pursuit of happiness' was becoming ever more stark.

The first moves towards Civil Rights had been slow, legalistic, and almost entirely ineffective efforts by the middle-class National Association for the Advancement of Colored People (NAACP). Then, in June 1953, the black people of Baton Rouge in Louisiana, meeting in 3,000-strong nightly assemblies, had organised the first bus boycott. This was the example later followed in Montgomery – and then in Tallahassee, Florida, in Birmingham, Alabama, and in other Southern cities. These struggles were led by a new organisation based on the ministers and congregations of the black churches: the Southern Christian Leadership Conference (SCLC). By the late 1950s, the Civil Rights struggle in the Southern states had become a national crisis.

A second wave of struggle opened in February 1960, when four black students sat down at the whites-only lunch counter in the Woolworths store in Greensboro, North Carolina. Hundreds of fellow students joined them over the next few days. Their example was followed by some 50,000 students in 70 Southern cities within two months. The student movement was backed by the SCLC, but it was led by its own organisations, the Northern-based Congress of Racial Equality (CORE) and the Southern-based Student Nonviolent Coordinating Committee (SNCC).

The movement continued to grow. In the early 1960s, the South was aflame with protests, boycotts, strikes, direct action, 'freedom rides', and voter-registration drives. It has been estimated that during 1963, in the 11 Southern states – the former Confederate states of Civil War days – there were 930 protests in 115 cities resulting in 20,000 arrests. The TV news was now carrying images into family living-rooms of a country that most Americans did not recognise – images of violent attacks on black protestors by police armed with guns, batons, dogs, and tear-gas, backed by snarling mobs of white racists. In that year, too, King's SCLC organised a March on Washington, attended by 250,000, where he delivered one of the most famous speeches in US history. It was broadcast live by American TV stations. It merits an extended quote:

I have a dream that one day this nation will rise up and live out the true meaning of its creed: 'We hold these truths to be self-evident: that all men are created equal.'

I have a dream that one day, on the red hills of Georgia, the sons of former slaves and the sons of former slave-owners will be able to sit down together at the table of brotherhood.

I have a dream that one day, even the state of Mississippi, a state sweltering with the heat of injustice, sweltering with the heat of oppression, will be transformed into an oasis of freedom and justice.

I have a dream that my four little children will one day live in a nation where they will not be judged by the colour of their skin but by the content of their character.

I have a dream today.

By the mid-1960s, the struggle sparked by Rosa Parks on an urban bus-ride had become a national uprising of the oppressed. The Federal state was now racing to catch up in an effort to contain the movement. Congress finally passed the Civil Rights Act in 1964, making discrimination and segregation illegal throughout the United States.

This was not enough. The movement hit a new peak the following year, when a series of voter-registration marches from Selma to Montgomery in Alabama culminated, in March 1965, in violent clashes that were broadcast across America. The Federal government was forced to pass the Voting Rights Act.

By this time, the black struggle had spread into the Northern ghettos, where black workers faced systematic job discrimination and routine police harassment. On average, white workers earned almost twice as much as black workers, and were only half as likely to be unemployed. Black youth, often jobless and hanging around on the streets, were involved in endless run-ins with racist cops. Many looked not to middle-class moderates like King, but to more radical leaders like Malcolm X.

An urban street-hustler who had become a Black Muslim while serving a prison term, Malcolm X's political ideas were in flux when he was assassinated in February 1965. His last formal speech indicates the direction of his ideas and the nature of his influence:

We are living in an era of revolution, and the revolt of the American negro is part of the rebellion against oppression and colonialism which has characterised this era ... It is incorrect to classify the revolt of the negro as simply a racial conflict of black against white, or as a purely American problem. Rather, we are today seeing a global rebellion of the oppressed against the oppressor, the exploited against the exploiter.

In the urban ghettos, clashes between black youth and the police ever more frequently escalated into full-scale riots. Then, in August 1965, the Watts district of Los Angeles exploded. The insurrection covered a 50-square mile area, lasted six whole days, and led to the deaths of 34 people, the arrest of 4,200 more, and damage to 600 buildings estimated at $100 million. Around 65,000 people are believed to have participated, with 15 per cent of the population actively involved, and up to 50 per cent actually on the streets. The 34 deaths were mainly of young black men shot down by the LA police and the National Guard.

Watts was only the first. Riots followed in 13 other places during 1966, and then, in July 1967, there were massive confrontations in Newark, New Jersey, on the edge of New York, and in Detroit, Michigan, home of the US motor industry, where, as one report described it, the protests turned the nation's fifth biggest city into a theatre of war. Whole streets lay ravaged by looting, whole blocks immolated in flames. Federal troops occupied American streets at bayonet point. Patton tanks – with machine-guns ablaze – and Huey helicopters patrolled a city of blackened brick chimneys poking out of gutted basements.

The ghetto uprisings fuelled the growth of a new, revolutionary, black-nationalist organisation: the Black Panther Party for Self-Defence. The violence of racist police and mobs against Civil Rights protestors had already radicalised some black activists, like Stokely Carmichael, who coined the term 'Black Power' to describe a new attitude of anger, assertiveness, and militancy. Huey Newton and Bobby Seale then gave this organisational form when they founded the Black Panthers in 1966. The aim was to provide political leadership to the black youth awakened by the urban uprisings and turn them into a revolutionary force. As Seale argued:

> The youth are a vast reservoir of revolutionary potential. The lumpenproletarian brothers on the block, and sisters, and everybody in the streets who are trying to make it, are part of the reservoir which one day will stream forth like a wild, rushing stream.

The decade-long struggle for Civil Rights had radicalised a generation of young activists, black and white, and shaken American society to its foundations. Then came the war – a long, intractable, murderous, immoral war against a poor peasant people on the other side of the world. A war that was tearing America in two. The war in Vietnam.

In the vanguard of what soon became the most powerful anti-war movement since 1917 were the young.

The Student Revolt

The young have always been at the forefront of radical change. Contemporary observers referred repeatedly, for example, to the hundreds of London apprentices armed with swords, staves, and cudgels present in the revolutionary crowds that assembled at Westminster during the opening clashes of the English Revolution in

December 1641. Many of the leaders of that revolution were also relatively young: John Lilburne was first arrested at the age of 23, had become a Civil War colonel by the time he was 30, and wrote *An Agreement of the People*, the Leveller manifesto, when he was 33.

But that does not mean that the English Revolution was a 'youth revolt'. The crowds, the armies, and the leadership cadre included many older people. The best estimate we have of the average age of the crowd that stormed the Bastille in July 1789 is 34, and the average age of the 12 Jacobin leaders who formed the Committee of Public Safety in 1793 was 38. The youth were often in the front-line on the barricades and the battlefields, but they fought as part of a broader plebeian mass.

Youth revolt *per se* is a modern phenomenon. It implies that youth have become somewhat separate from the rest of society and have formed a distinct group with its own identity, interests, and initiative. The youth of 1641 or 1789 were embedded in the mini-hierarchies of traditional families and workshops. When they rioted, they did so alongside their parents and employers; that is, as part of a class movement, not a youth revolt. What happened in the 1950s and 1960s seems to have been something new in history.

The combination of a booming world economy and strong trade-union organisation had ensured rising working-class living standards during the post-war period. Poverty and inequality remained, but most workers enjoyed improved housing, better education and health services, and sufficient income to buy a range of consumer durables like fridges, washing-machines, TVs, motorbikes, even cars.

The 'affluent' or 'consumer' society had a major impact on the experience of young people. They enjoyed an unprecedented measure of independence and income, and this allowed them to develop their own forms of sociability, culture, and consumption outside the framework of family and work. A 'youth culture' centred around modern music and dress, motorbikes and cars, bars and fast-food, dances and discos, emerged during the 1950s and 1960s. Parents, teachers, police, 'authority' in general, seemed at best out of sync, at worst a repressive presence to be avoided or outwitted.

Much of youth culture, though often subversive of traditional attitudes, was apolitical. But not all. The Beatniks of the 1950s, a counter-culture centred on the US West Coast and inspired by gurus like Jack Kerouac and Allen Ginsberg, not only 'dropped out' of mainstream society and adopted an alternative lifestyle based around music, sex, drugs, mysticism, and 'taking to the road' on bikes, but became critical of social conformity and consensus politics. The Hippies of the 1960s represented a development of this tradition, but were more widespread, more numerous, and more radical. The politics were flaky and naïve: 'flower power' and 'the power of love' were counter-posed to the hard realities of the military-industrial complex. Abbie Hoffman and Jerry Rubin founded a Youth International Party (dubbed 'Yippies') that was a wild mix of eccentricity, anarchism, and Hippie counter-culture. But a more serious kind of revolutionary politics developed within this broader milieu – especially among students.

On university campuses, during the 1960s, youth culture became a political concentrate. To understand why this happened, we need to step back and review the development of higher education in the post-war world. Let us take Britain as an example.

In 1926, at the time of the General Strike, there had been about 25,000 students in Britain. Virtually without exception, they were drawn from the elite, and most had been educated at private schools. Many students volunteered to work as scabs during the strike. As late as 1939, when the Second World War began, there were still only about 70,000 students in Britain. But after 1945, with rising demand for educated labour in a booming post-war economy, and with heavy state investment in universities, the number shot up, reaching 300,000 by 1964. Even in 1950, students had formed only 1.5 per cent of their age group; two decades later, the proportion had risen to 15 per cent. The pattern was similar across both the First (Western) and Second (Eastern) Worlds: all advanced industrial economies were compelled to expand higher education because they needed more scientists, engineers, doctors, and teachers.

The great majority of students still came from relatively privileged backgrounds: most were middle class. But this was less significant than other aspects of the student condition during the 1960s. Youth culture meant that many were at odds with the 'authority' of the older generation. Campus accommodation and facilities, reflecting the rapid expansion of higher education, were often crowded and substandard. University regulations – in particular in relation to political activity and sexual relationships – tended to be antiquated and pettifogging. Many courses were perceived to be dull, irrelevant, and old-fashioned. And the grind of the exam system seemed at odds with the ideal of a community of scholars engaged in collaborative work and academic debate in a crisis-ridden world.

Because the universities were hierarchical and conservative institutions – 'ivory towers' of detachment from the wider world – conflict with the student intakes of the 1960s was inevitable. The students brought the rebellious spirit of youth culture and an awareness of wider social and political issues onto the campuses. Here, moreover, they found themselves thrown together in close association, and, because they were young, relatively unformed, and socially mobile, they were free to explore, critique, and re-imagine the world. They became – like the black activists of the Civil Rights Movement – another kind of radical vanguard.

On 2 December 1964, more than a thousand students on the Berkeley campus of the University of California occupied Sproul Hall. They were protesting the threatened expulsion of activist Mario Savio. As they mounted the steps to enter the building, they carried the Stars and Stripes and listened to a young Joan Baez singing 'Blowin' in the Wind' through a megaphone.

The following morning, California cops armed with guns and clubs – having been ordered to 'kick their way through' the demonstrators – cleared Sproul Hall and arrested 800 students. As news spread across the campus, between 60 and 80 per cent of the 30,000-strong student body joined a protest strike.

This was the first in a decade-long chain reaction of student struggles on the campuses of the advanced capitalist world. Chris Harman, a participant in the 1967 LSE occupation, describes the scale of it:

The events at Berkeley were unprecedented in an advanced capitalist country. But in the decade that followed, similar student struggles would spread from campus to campus round the world, jumping like electrical sparks from terminal to terminal – to the Free University in West Berlin in June 1966, the London School of Economics in March 1967, to most major German universities in June 1967, to Turin, Trento, and the Catholic University of Milan in the autumn of 1967, and then to almost all the Italian universities in January-February 1968, to Warsaw and to the Nanterre outside Paris in March 1968, to one of the most prestigious US universities, Columbia in New York, and to virtually every German university in April, to the whole of higher education in France in May, then on to Leicester, Essex, Hull, Sussex, and Birmingham universities and Hornsey, Guildford, and Croydon schools of art in England, to Madrid and Santiago in fascist Spain, and back to Berkeley for a second time.

Civil Rights. The Student Revolt. These two streams of struggle were connected. Many white activists had been radicalised by Civil Rights, and the main organisation of campus radicals, Students for a Democratic Society (SDS), had played a major role in building solidarity with the black struggle. Many student struggles had erupted around the issue of racism.

But there was, of course, another issue. Between 1965 and 1968, US involvement in Vietnam had ramped up from 25,000 'advisors' to half a million combat troops. Young men were being conscripted *en masse* – though various 'exemptions' meant the burden fell disproportionately on working-class and black Americans. It was Vietnam that ensured that 1968 would see the beginning of the greatest eruption of revolt from below since the Russian Revolution.

The Vietnam War

Napalm is jellied gasoline designed to stick to the flesh and burn through to the bone. The American reporter Martha Gellhorn saw its effects on children when she visited a hospital in South Vietnam in 1966:

> Flesh melts right down their faces onto their chests and it sits there and grows there … These children can't turn their heads, they were so thick with flesh … And when gangrene sets in, they cut off their hands or fingers or their feet; the only thing they cannot cut off is their head.

During its wars in Indochina against the people of South Vietnam, North Vietnam, Laos, and Cambodia, the US dropped more than eight million tons of explosives. This was three times the total tonnage dropped by all belligerents during the whole of the Second World War.

At least two million people were killed in the Vietnam War. Some 58,000 of these were American soldiers. The rest were Vietnamese, half a million or so soldiers of one sort or another, but the majority civilians. Most of those who died were killed by aerial bombing. The reason was simple. The US was waging war against an entire population. So the easiest – and safest – way to kill the enemy was to bomb them from the air. This, in the circumstances, seemed the most efficient means of stopping 'the spread of communism'.

The military problem for the invaders was that the Vietcong (VC) – the South Vietnamese communist guerrillas – were rooted in the villages. They were the sons and daughters of villagers. They were the armed wing of the Vietnamese peasantry.

The US estimated that, had an election been held, the communists would have won 80 per cent of the vote. So there was no election. Instead, half a million US troops were deployed to prop up a corrupt dictatorship supported by landlords and profiteers. The enemy was everyone else. That is why, after his men had destroyed the Vietnamese village of Ben Tre, a US Army major could explain that 'it was necessary to destroy the village in order to save it'. Such is the logic of 'counterinsurgency' warfare.

Incredibly, the Vietnamese refused to give up. On the contrary, the worse the bombing and burning, the greater the bitterness and the stronger the flow of young Vietnamese to the resistance. The growing violence of US imperialism was like throwing petrol on a fire.

Vietnam was a poor country. The guerrillas fought with outdated weapons, home-made bombs, and jungle booby-traps. They spent much of their time hiding in underground tunnel complexes. But they were formidable opponents. For one thing, they were highly organised in the communist-led National Liberation Front. For another, they were an ethnically and culturally homogeneous people with a long history of resistance to foreign invaders. They had, in recent times, fought successfully against the Japanese and then the French.

At the end of the Second World War, after the defeat of the Japanese, Ho Chi Minh, the leader of the Vietminh nationalist resistance movement, had proclaimed the independence of Vietnam. But the French had been determined to re-establish colonial rule. The

Vietminh then fought the French for eight years. They eventually won a decisive victory at the Battle of Dien Bien Phu in 1954.

Afterwards, the Vietnamese leaders were persuaded by their Soviet and Chinese backers to accept partition of the country pending subsequent elections. This was a serious mistake. There was no historic basis for a division of Vietnam, any more than there had been for the division of Germany, Korea, or Palestine. Partition was Cold War politics.

A US-backed dictatorship was established in Saigon, which became the capital of South Vietnam. No Vietnamese had the opportunity to vote on this. The partition of the country between a nationalist regime in the North and a client regime in the South looked set to become permanent. The problem for the US was the former Vietminh fighters in the South. They formed an extensive underground network able to organise resistance to landlords, tax-collectors, and police. Soon, there was a low-level guerrilla insurgency in parts of the countryside.

President Kennedy escalated the conflict by increasing US military support for the Saigon dictatorship from 400 'advisers' in 1960 to 18,000 two years later. This seemed routine. US Attorney-General Robert Kennedy told a journalist at the time, 'We have 30 Vietnams.'

But Vietnam was different. It escalated rapidly into full-scale war. By the end of 1965, there were 200,000 US troops on the ground; by 1968, 500,000. And North Vietnam came under massive aerial bombardment from 1965 onwards.

So did neighbouring Cambodia after 1970. In just six months in 1973 the Americans dropped one and a half times the bomb tonnage on Cambodia that they had dropped on Japan in the Second World War. Several hundred thousand people were killed in the aerial terror. The Khmer Rouge (the Cambodian communists) were stopped. But they were filled with hatred for the collaborationist regime in Phnom Penh, which had sanctioned the bombing of its own people to root out popular resistance. When the war ended in 1975, the rage of the peasant army was channelled by its Stalinist leaders into political genocide, de-urbanisation, and the imposition of agricultural slave-labour. Millions perished in Pol Pot's 'killing fields'. But the seeds had been sown by B-52 bombers: the violence unleashed on an impoverished country had destroyed its economy, its social fabric, and, to a large degree, its political sanity.

By late 1967, US public opinion had begun to turn against the war. The administration of President Johnson responded by claiming it was on the brink of victory. General Westmoreland, the US commander-in-chief in Vietnam, claimed that the communists were 'unable to mount a major offensive'. He continued: 'I am absolutely certain that whereas in 1965 the enemy was winning, today he is certainly losing ... We have reached an important point when the end begins to come into view.'

In the early hours of 31 January 1968, the National Liberation Front launched the Tet Offensive. Across South Vietnam, Vietcong guerrilla units, supported by North Vietnamese soldiers, mounted coordinated attacks on about 100 targets, including most provincial capitals, major US military bases, and even the heavily defended US embassy in the centre of Saigon. A commando group of 19 men blasted its way into the embassy compound and held the main building for several hours.

American television viewers were stunned by the images broadcast that night. Just when the war was supposed to be almost over, fighting had erupted in every major town and city in South Vietnam. General Westmoreland demanded 200,000 more troops.

But three weeks later, President Johnson, the pro-war incumbent, announced that he would not be seeking a second term of office. The five-year-long rundown of the US military commitment to Vietnam had begun. It would culminate in the ending of the US occupation of South Vietnam (1973), the overthrow of the Saigon dictatorship (1975), and the reunification of the divided country under communist rule (1976).

An army of peasant guerrillas had defeated US imperialism in a full-scale war. They had not fought alone. During the struggle, the American people had become their allies. So too had millions of others across the globe. In 1968 the war had come home. The heartlands of world capitalism were ablaze with revolt.

1968

The Tet Offensive was the beginning of a year of revolt across the world. A wave of militant demonstrations, mass strikes, and urban riots swept across the major cities of the capitalist system. Many who lived through it felt it was a year of revolution like 1848 or 1919.

The mood everywhere was ripe with expectation and hope. A new post-war generation – the children of the Boom, raised in the shadow of the Bomb – had come of age and erupted onto history's stage.

Revolt against the whole system was a common thread in the events of 1968. So too was the central role of young people – students and workers. Protestors thought of themselves as part of a single movement. Action in one place inspired action in the next. But the events of 1968 were also diverse. The struggle erupted along social fracture-lines that were different from one country to another.

In Britain, Vietnam was the principal focus. In March, thousands marched on the US embassy in Grosvenor Square, arriving with arms linked, carrying Vietnamese resistance flags, and chanting 'Hey, Hey, LBJ, How many kids did you kill today?' There were violent clashes with police. In October, the Vietnam Solidarity Campaign called a second demonstration. With around 100,000 people, three or four times the size of the March protest, it was on a scale unprecedented for a political demonstration at the time. As well as contingents of thousands from the major universities, large numbers of workers also marched behind trade union banners.

In the US, too, the war was a central focus. It had started very small a few years before: a mere 600 anti-war protestors in New York in 1964, still only 20,000 in Washington in 1965. But the campuses were stirring, with a wave of 'teach-ins' that second year involving hundreds of thousands of students across the US. Two years later, the US anti-war protests had become a mass movement, with 75,000 marching in San Francisco, led by black nationalists, and 400,000 marching behind Martin Luther King, the Civil Rights leader, Stokely Carmichael, the Black Power leader, and Benjamin Spock, the internationally famous liberal childcare specialist, in New York.

The following year, the struggle against the war became the focus of ferocious state violence. Chicago's Mayor Daley unleashed the police and National Guard on a demonstration outside the Democratic Party Convention in August 1968, in full view of the world's TV cameras, and millions across the world watched in horror the graphic images of the way in which the capitalist state treated democratic dissent.

But it was in the black urban ghettos that the movement peaked. When Martin Luther King was assassinated in Memphis in April 1968, black America erupted in a storm of rage. There had been big anti-police riots before – in Harlem in 1964, Watts in 1965, and a dozen places in 1966 and 1967. But this time, in an unparalleled night of destruction, looting, and fighting, a hundred cities burned across America in the biggest outbreak of mass violence in the United States since the end of the Civil War. Around 50 people were killed, more than 2,500 injured, and 15,000 arrested.

A different kind of struggle unfolded in Czechoslovakia. A ferment of debate among intellectuals and students had broken down the Stalinist censorship as splits opened in the ruling bureaucracy. The students formed a free union. The workers voted out government appointees from the leadership of state-run unions. The media filled with debate.

The 'Prague Spring' was the fourth in a series of mass popular movements against the Stalinist dictatorships of Eastern Europe. It followed the East German Uprising of June 1953 and the Polish 'Spring in October', and the Hungarian Revolution of 1956. Czechoslovakia had one of the most advanced economies in Eastern Europe, but it was afflicted with growing sluggishness, and the reformists in the leadership, led by Alexander Dubcek, had at first encouraged the development of a democratic movement, seeking allies against the party old guard in their efforts to reform an ailing system. But the movement acquired a momentum of its own, and Dubcek was soon backtracking and warning of 'anarchy'.

Too late: the party reformers could not restore what the Kremlin called 'normality' – and in August 1968 Russian tanks rolled in to crush the 'Prague Spring'. The reformist leaders were arrested and deported. Protestors on the streets were overwhelmed by the sheer scale of the invasion, involving thousands of tanks and hundreds of thousands of soldiers. But it would take the Russians nine months to defeat the passive resistance they encountered.

Many other places in the developed world saw demonstrations, strikes, and occupations that year. From Derry to New York, West Berlin to Mexico City, Warsaw to Rome, there was mass protest. But it was in France, in May–June 1968, that the movement came closest to revolution.

As well as campaigning against the war, the French student movement had been protesting about conditions in the universities, the character of education, and the whole authoritarian system in France under the ten-year rule of President Charles de Gaulle.

Campus strikes, occupations, and demonstrations became commonplace events during 1967. In March 1968, the leadership was assumed by 'the 22 March Movement', whose most prominent leader was a French-German student at Nanterre called Daniel Cohn-Bendit. With the level of protest rising, the Gaullist state clamped down, sending police onto campuses to break up occupations and arrest student leaders. This exposed the essential authoritarianism of the regime and drew more students into the struggle. Democracy became the central issue.

In early May, the authorities went much further, announcing the shut-down of the University of Paris, the Sorbonne, sending in the police in full riot-gear to enforce the order. The violence of the police provoked mass resistance. On the 'Night of the Barricades' (10/11 May), students and young workers battled the riot police for several hours and eventually drove them from the Left Bank university district.

Workers elsewhere listened to live reports of the fighting on their radios or watched the events on television. They too hated de Gaulle's police. They too had faced them on the picket lines, where police had sometimes killed striking workers with impunity. The union leaders, under pressure from below, called a one-day general strike in support of the students. The response surpassed all expectations. On 13 May, hundreds of thousands of workers marched alongside tens of thousands of students. The chants were ominous: '*Adieu*, de Gaulle! Ten years is enough!' The following day young workers at the Sud Aviation plant in Nantes began an occupation. Their example was infectious. Within two weeks, France had ground to a halt, with an estimated ten million on strike and hundreds of thousands occupying their workplaces.

It was a re-run of 1936 on a larger scale. France was close to revolution. De Gaulle fled to consult the generals: would they deploy military force to defend the government if necessary? In the event, it ended as 1936 had done. The Communist Party, still with immense prestige among the working class, engineered a return to work on a promise of wage increases and a general election. It was reformist leaders – not reactionary generals – who ended the revolutionary strike and saved French capitalism.

The events of 1968, in France and across the world, were the tumultuous beginning of a political crisis that would continue until

1975. What had caused it? What had brought to an end the long sleep of the 1950s and early 1960s?

For the British feminist Sheila Rowbotham, 'Vietnam was my generation's Spain, and the suffering of the people became imprinted in our psyches.' Vietnam, with its monstrous use of military hardware against a peasant people, seemed to encapsulate all that was wrong with the world: imperialism, violence, injustice, poverty. But it was the catalyst rather than the cause of the crisis which shook world capitalism between 1968 and 1975.

The war had its biggest impact in the US. Americans came out on the streets because their own country was the aggressor and because young men were being conscripted to fight. But even here the war was linked to other issues. 'No Vietcong ever called me "nigger"', said world heavyweight boxing champion Muhammad Ali. The real enemy, of course, was at home.

What gave the movement its power was the social transformation wrought by the Great Boom. Black Americans would not take any more because too many had moved from the isolation and fear of labouring on farms to take up work in the big cities. It was the same worldwide. The Boom had sucked millions into the factories – from poor countries to rich, from rural areas to urban, from the home to the workplace. It had also created whole new industries, suburbs, and concentrations of people. Not least, it had transformed higher education from the preserve of a privileged few to an opportunity for a large proportion of the youth. There were 200,000 students in Paris in 1968, of whom around 30,000 joined the demonstrations that year.

As African-Americans, anti-war activists, and students showed that it was possible to fight, other oppressed groups, and working people as a whole, gained confidence. The black struggle and the youth revolt encouraged women, LGBT people, and eventually the working class as a whole to join the battle to change the world.

The Family, the Women's Liberation Movement, and the Gay Liberation Front

The family is one of the building-blocks of capitalist society. Though it has changed radically over time, especially in the developed world in the last half century or so, the family remains essential to the low-cost maintenance, reproduction, and socialisation of the labour force. It is central to each of the following social processes: satisfying the basic physical and emotional needs of workers; providing the money, time, and effort involved in rearing children; caring for the elderly and the disabled; and supporting students, the unemployed, and other family dependants.

All these processes could be collectivised. Some are to a limited extent. But the expense amounts to a tax on the system and therefore becomes a target for right-wing attacks on 'profligate spending', 'the nanny state', 'welfare dependency', and so on. Better, from a capitalist perspective, that the working-class family should carry the burden than that the state should spend on nurseries, care homes, social services, and adequate grants, benefits, and pensions.

Collective provision would have another consequence for the system: it would sharply reduce privatised consumption and therefore economic demand. The individual family household is an exceptionally high-cost unit, each requiring a full array of home, car, furnishings, gadgets, clothing, food, heating, light, and so on. The family-centred frenzy to consume is sustained by an anxious competitiveness among households fostered by a massive corporate sales-effort. Consumers are encouraged to shop for the products that will make them classy, affluent, fashionable, educated, and sexy; the message is that you are what you have. This all-pervasive social disease of alienated consumption is centred on the household. Capitalism needs the family as a mass market.

The family has other advantages for the system: it is a mechanism of social and ideological control. Its very existence means that society is broken down into the smallest of atoms – family households – and that social life is largely reduced to privatised consumption and personal ambition. It is difficult to exaggerate the significance of this. Every problem – earning a living, finding a home, paying the bills, getting into university, accessing medical care, and so on – becomes a problem of the individual and her family. Despite the fact that all of these problems are *socially* determined – employment opportunities, the affordability of housing, charges for utilities, the cost of education, the availability of health services – they are experienced as *private* matters. Thus the family hard-wires privatised ways of thinking about collective matters into our consciousness.

It is this, as much as anything, that makes the modern family an incubator of conformity and conservatism. Many families are still blighted by traditional patriarchal authority. But even in relatively liberal households – where parental roles are less gender-specific and parental authority less repressive – an irreducible core of top-down control and socialisation endures. Parents have power because they are providers and their children dependants. And they exercise that power in various ways, sometimes to satisfy their own psychological needs, sometimes in what they consider 'the best interests' of their children, which tends to mean encouraging or enforcing behaviour that conforms to the imperatives of the social order. Even the most liberal parents can hardly avoid being the prototype of the teacher, the office supervisor, and the police officer.

Finally, even in its modern form, the family is a mechanism of psychic repression – a barrier to full libidinal freedom. Libido is the basic instinctual drive, the life-force, of the human mind. Its inner essence is a striving for union, for emotive and sensual connection with others. Its most extreme expression is sexual union, but it powers all forms of human sociability, cooperation, and collective labour. It is society's psychic glue, the instinctual need that makes all humans social animals.

But capitalism violates what Marx called our 'species-being' – our basic nature and needs as humans. We inhabit a world of exploitation, oppression, and alienation: a world where we are denied control over our labour and the products of our labour; where our social experience is atomised, dragooned, and regulated; where human freedom is overshadowed by the inhuman power of capital and the state.

The corollary of this is psychic repression and infantile regression – repression of the instinctual drives of liberated libido; regression to the anal, narcissistic, self-centred forms of sexuality peculiar to earlier phases of child development.

The family – the monogamous, heterosexual, nuclear family idealised by right-wing commentators – is a prison-cage of libido. Freud described human sexuality as 'polymorphously perverse': the implication is that humans have the capacity to achieve sensual and emotional fulfilment in an almost infinite variety of ways. But libidinal freedom is liable to be subversive of a social order based on alienation and repression. So the social structures and sexual mores of capitalist society are designed to channel and corral libido. The traditional family becomes the social order's container for humanity's frustrated instinctual needs. This makes it both 'a haven in a heartless world' and also a pressure-cooker of patriarchy, narcissism, misogyny, homophobia, domestic abuse, and psychotic rage.

The oppression of women in the home and at work – carrying the main burden of domestic labour and childcare; facing discrimination, lower pay, and sexual harassment in the workplace – is rooted in the fact that the traditional 'bourgeois' family is one of the basic building-blocks of class society. Liberated women are a threat to the family. The oppression of LGBT people – abuse, discrimination, illegality, threats of violence, police harassment – is also rooted in the centrality of the family to a repressive social order. Liberated LGBT people represent a negation of the imprisoned libido of socially approved sexuality.

A new women's liberation movement burst into life during the 1960s. This reflected the rapid growth of female employment during the Great Boom, with millions of women entering the labour force as sales assistants, clerical workers, nurses, teachers, and so on. Women going out to work called into question traditional roles as housewives and mothers. Women earning their own money meant more independence and self-confidence. Women becoming a more active part of the working class meant women in a stronger position to challenge oppression. The wider context of mass revolt from below encouraged them to do this.

The new women's movement – 'second wave' feminism – took many forms, from local 'consciousness-raising' groups, to women's groups on campuses and in unions, to strikes against low pay, to national campaigns on issues like abortion rights. Landmark events in the early history of the movement in Britain, for example, included the 1968 strike against unequal pay by women sewing-machinists at Ford's Dagenham plant, and the 50,000-strong national demonstration in August 1970 calling for free abortion on demand, public provision for 24-hour childcare, and equal pay for equal work. There were major gains: the Equal Pay Act was passed in 1970, the Sex Discrimination Act in 1975.

The advent of the gay liberation movement was more sudden. It happened at the Stonewall Bar in New York's Greenwich Village on the evening of Friday 27 June 1969. The bar was a social centre for young, gay, working-class men. It was expensive, partly because it was Mafia-run, partly because of pay-offs to the police. That night it was raided by eight cops, who followed the usual routine of making arrests and bundling young men into the backs of police vans.

But something had changed. The crowd, instead of dispersing, turned on the police, who were driven into the bar and trapped there. The arrested men were released from the vans. The trapped cops called for help. This soon arrived in the form of the 'Tactical Police Force', the New York riot cops usually deployed only in Harlem's black ghetto and against anti-war protestors. This triggered a riot.

It continued for three nights, with fighting from dusk to dawn as windows were smashed, fire alarms set off, trash cans used as missiles, and police cars set alight. Each time, the cops were forced to retreat. Smaller-scale clashes continued through the summer.

This new mood of resistance gave birth to a new movement: the Gay Liberation Front was formed in August 1969. The name was chosen to echo that of Vietnam's National Liberation Front. Americans oppressed for their sexual orientation had joined the struggle for change alongside Vietnamese on the other side of the world fighting for national independence.

The world had been set alight by a firecracker sequence of revolts of the oppressed. The Women's Liberation Movement and the Gay Liberation Front both drew upon and fed into the global upsurge of 1968–75. But the oppressed, even had they united into a single movement, lacked the strategic power to overturn the system and transform the world. They could win reforms, but they could not make revolution.

But the oppressed were also workers. And when they infected the working class as a whole with their radicalism and militancy, when the mass of working people moved into action behind them, the survival of the entire global system of exploitation, oppression, and violence became the issue. Nowhere in this period was the issue posed more starkly than in Portugal in 1974–5.

The Portuguese Revolution

Portugal in 1974 was one of European capitalism's weakest links. It had been ruled by a brutal fascist dictatorship for almost half a century. Two giant conglomerates dominated the economy. Unions were banned, strikers were shot down, and everyone was terrorised by the secret police. The fascist Portuguese Legion had 100,000 members – one for every 85 people. The whole system ran on corruption, nepotism, and fear. This hideous relic of the 1930s was now ruled by Marcelo Caetano. As well as being ruthlessly repressive at home, the regime was embroiled in three major colonial wars in Africa.

Such was the pitiful weakness of Portuguese capitalism, and such the parasitic nature of the two giant monopolies at its core, that the dictatorship had attempted to resist Africa's 'wind of change' and hold onto its three colonial territories of Angola, Guinea-Bissau, and Mozambique. These provided cheap raw materials and captive markets for Portugal's uncompetitive industries. The Portuguese colonial set-up was notable for its barbarism, even by the dismal standards of European imperialism in Africa. It involved forced labour, compulsory cash-crop production, punishment beatings, censorship and curfews, and the doffing of caps to white overlords.

Nationalist guerrilla insurgencies launched in the Angolan, Guinean, and Mozambican bush in 1961 had quickly escalated into full-scale colonial wars. By 1974 there were 160,000 Portuguese troops in Africa, and the cost of sustaining them was consuming half the Portuguese budget. Fighting three intractable 'dirty wars' far from home, the soldiers had become deeply demoralised and disaffected.

Much of the corporate elite had come to the conclusion that the wars were unwinnable and that a negotiated settlement was essential to staunch the drain of resources needed for the modernisation of Portugal's antiquated infrastructure.

On the morning of 25 April 1974, the streets of Lisbon, the Portuguese capital, were filled with troops and tanks. Caetano was overthrown, and General Antonio de Spinola became the head of a new military junta. The Portuguese elite hoped to restrict events to this stage-managed transfer of power, designed to replace a pro-war dictatorship with a government willing to negotiate an end to the wars in Africa and oversee industrial modernisation. It did not work out that way.

The military action had been orchestrated by a conspiracy of left-wing army officers, the Armed Forces Movement (AFM), and on the streets the workers were soon fraternising with the soldiers, putting flowers down their rifle-barrels, riding on the backs of tanks, and working with them to root out the secret police. It became 'the Carnation Revolution'. Portugal had suddenly joined the global upsurge of popular revolt that had begun in 1968. What followed was 18 months of revolution in which the question of state power and class rule hung in the balance.

A week after the coup, on May Day, 100,000 workers marched through Lisbon under red banners. The demonstration revealed the power of the popular movement, and the workers immediately moved into action in the factories, intent on settling grievances they had harboured for decades. Their demands were both economic, for big pay rises, and political, for the rooting out of fascist managers and spies – a process known as *saneamento* or 'cleansing'. Some 200,000 workers in 158 workplaces took strike action in May. The giant Lisnave shipyard was occupied by its 8,000 workers.

Spinola belonged to the same political tradition as the fallen dictator. Around him the forces of reaction grouped themselves. The junta, with the backing of the corporations, called a demonstration of the 'silent majority' in September. The people were asked 'to wake up to defend themselves against extremist totalitarianisms'. Guns were distributed to the old fascist organisations. The generals aimed to 'restore order' under the cover of a right-wing demonstration.

Like Kornilov's coup in 1917, the Spinola coup was destroyed by mass working-class action. The rail workers and coach drivers refused to transport right-wing demonstrators into Lisbon. Road-blocks were set up to stop cars entering the capital. The Lisbon workers came onto the streets 40,000-strong to confront the fascists. They were joined by rank-and-file soldiers.

Spinola was forced to call off the demonstration. The following day he resigned. The popular victory of 28 September had the effect of deepening and spreading the revolutionary ferment in society.

A second attempted coup on 11 March 1975 was defeated in the same way and with similar consequences. Right-wing officers took control of a military airbase, and elite paratroopers surrounded the barracks of a leading left-wing unit on the outskirts of Lisbon. This was meant to trigger wider action. Instead, the working class moved to block the plotters at every point. A contemporary Portuguese press account gives an impression of the scale and character of the resistance:

Workers at Radio Renascensa ... broadcast the news. The Lisbon workers closed down the banks ... Shops and offices were shut after lunch and the phones went out of order as workers rushed to join demonstrations and man barricades. In Barreiro ... factory and fire sirens shrieked continuously as workers formed pickets round barricades to stop and search all vehicles. In Savacem ... workers formed a dense barricade across the main road, backed up with four bulldozers and tons of cement. A representative ... went to the barracks and asked that the workers be armed so that they could join in the fight. At Cartaxo, the barricade was built from lorries from the occupied brewery works ... but was quickly joined by hundreds of workers from other factories, armed with clubs, spades, or anything else to hand ... Huge demonstrations were jamming the streets of Lisbon, Oporto, and other towns.

But despite the power of the working-class movement, the revolution was at an impasse. It lacked a network of mass partici-patory assemblies – like the soviets of 1917 – capable of embodying working-class democracy and providing the embryo of a workers' state. And it lacked a large revolutionary-socialist party of rooted working-class activists capable of giving leadership to such a network. The vacuum was filled by three political forces of very different character.

The underground during the dictatorship had been dominated by the Communist Party, which had about 5,000 members at the beginning of the revolution. The party grew rapidly at first, but was hamstrung by its deeply ingrained Stalinism. It peddled a narrow vision of the revolution's potential, and it operated in a manipula-tive top-down way. It seemed devoid of any democratic instincts; it was a party of would-be bureaucrats intent on creating an East European-type dictatorship. It entered government at any early stage, and quickly earned a reputation for opportunism and strike-breaking.

More radical – certainly more in touch with popular moods – were the 400 or so officers of the Armed Forces Movement. The central weakness here was the minimal social weight of this group. They were a small minority even of the officer corps – which was 10,000 strong – and, as men of middle-class status trained to give orders, they preferred bureaucratic manoeuvring to popular democracy. In so far as he had a coherent vision, Otelo de Carvalho, the leading AFM figure, seems to have aspired to a role like that of Nasser in Egypt or Castro in Cuba (or later, Chavez in Venezuela) – that of a left-wing 'strongman' driving through reform from above.

What enabled the tiny AFM to play a major role was the equilibrium of forces in Portuguese society between April 1974 and November 1975. Neither the Right, centred on the ousted fascist elite, nor the Left, centred on the working-class movement, was able to break through. This equilibrium – and the temporary dominance of the AFM – could not, however, outlast the emergence of a strong centre based on liberal parliamentary democracy and social-democratic reformism.

Mario Soares's Socialist Party was a miniscule organisation of 200 members in April 1974. Soares, however, was a skilled opportunist who positioned his party to the left of the Communist Party (at least rhetorically). At elections for a Constituent Assembly on 25 April 1975, the Socialists won 38 per cent of the vote, as against 17 per cent for the Communist Party, and 34 per cent for the right-wing parties. Increasingly thereafter, Soares attacked the Communist Party from the left to build his party's support in the working class, while at the same time undermining the AFM's precarious grip on power by standing aside as the country's economic, social, and political crisis deepened.

Portuguese society remained highly polarised. Rank-and-file movements were developing among both workers and soldiers, and the Far Left was increasingly influential. On one occasion, 12,000 soldiers – a fifth of the army – led a demonstration of 85,000 workers through the streets of Lisbon. By the autumn of 1975, a split had opened between the left-wing officers of the AFM and the revolutionary soldiers of the newly formed SUV (Soldiers United Will Win). As one SUV leaflet addressed to workers explained:

In recent weeks, we have been fighting hard for better conditions in the barracks and against reaction … for better pay, for an end to arbitrary punishment, for the right to refuse reactionary orders, for the right to meet and discuss freely … Our fight is part of the great fight for popular power, for power to the workers. The gentlemen in gold-braid epaulettes do not want to lose their privileges. We rely on you to say 'No' to the military conspirators … The soldiers always, always on the side of the people.

The problem was that the soldiers were now ahead of the workers, most of whom were under the influence of either the Communist Party, which was aiming at a Stalinist dictatorship, or the Socialist Party, the limit of whose vision was Western-style parliamentary democracy.

The emergent rank-and-file movement was not given time to mature. With the national crisis worsening by the day, the Portuguese state acted to terminate the revolution. Otelo de Carvalho, the AFM leader, was sacked from his post as head of the Lisbon military region, and on 25 November 1975 government forces went into action to disarm the most left-wing military units. The coup was carried out quickly with minimal opposition.

On 25 April 1976, following the adoption of a new constitution and a general election based upon it, Mario Soares became Prime Minister of Portugal.

It had been a strange dénouement. The Communist Party had emerged from the underground with enormous prestige. But it had devoted itself to an alliance with radical army officers and a campaign to disable and disorient a mass working-class movement. It had then watched from the side-lines as right-wing officers suppressed its left-wing allies – a coup supported by all the mainstream parties, including the Socialist Party, which became the main beneficiary. The Portuguese Revolution – in the absence of mass participatory democracy and a mass revolutionary party to organise a popular seizure of power – simply fizzled out in the dull routines of the parliamentary game. The rule of capital, shaken for 18 months, was stabilised.

The Other 9/11: Revolution and Counter-Revolution in Chile

The mass movement in Chile was defeated in a far more brutal way. If the Portuguese Revolution was suffocated by a reformist politician, the Chilean Revolution was murdered by a military dictator.

'You can't make a revolution by playing marbles': that was the conclusion of a working-class activist at a factory in Chile in October 1972. 'When there's a problem, we workers have to take the front-line. We've learned more in these few days than in all the previous two years.'

The Chilean bourgeoisie had gone onto the offensive against the two-year-old Popular Unity (UP) government of Salvador Allende. In a long, thin country almost entirely dependent on road haulage for the movement of goods, the lorry owners had gone on strike.

They were the spearhead of a wider attempt to destabilise the left-wing government and defeat a rising popular movement of industrial workers, agricultural labourers, and the shanty-town poor. Shop-owners were also on strike and factory bosses were sabotaging production. Chile was threatened with economic paralysis.

Salvador Allende had been elected President in late 1970 at the head of a coalition of left parties dominated by the social-democratic and communist parties. The UP coalition had secured 36 per cent of the national vote following a wave of strikes, land occupations, and radicalisation during the 1960s.

Allende's aims were moderate. He wanted to resume a stalled land-reform programme, nationalise key industries, reflate a sluggish economy, increase wages, and reduce unemployment. He believed this could be done through parliament.

Eager to reassure the rich, big business, and the middle class, he expressed firm support for private property and the existing state. The police were used against popular protests and left-wing groups. He denounced 'divisive action whose effect is to undermine the homogeneity of the UP movement'.

This did nothing to conciliate the bourgeoisie. They feared the mass movement from below on whose support the government rested. Allende's moderation divided and discouraged his own supporters while giving confidence to his enemies. The lorry owners' strike of October 1972 was the result. It was a full-on attempt to bring down the government.

The outcome did not depend on Allende: it depended on the *cordones*. These were popular democratic organisations that linked together working people in factories and communities. The *cordones* were capable of acting independently of the government. They acted now to lead mass direct action to defeat the bosses' strike.

Transport was commandeered to move food and other essentials. Shops were re-opened and factories taken over by the workers. Distribution systems were set up in the shanty-towns, including collective kitchens for the children of the poor. Defence and vigilance committees were established to resist fascist violence. The *cordones* mushroomed into a nationwide network.

The events of October 1972 created a revolutionary crisis. The *cordones* were alliances of unionised workers, unorganised workers, agricultural labourers, and the urban poor. They embodied leadership from below unshackled by the conservatism of UP politicians. They gained a sense of their own power from the struggle against the lorry owners. They were the embryo of a true people's democracy.

The rise of the *cordones* raised the stakes. The response of the government was a shift *to the right*. Allende declared a national state of emergency and invited several generals to join his cabinet.

The lorry owners immediately called off their strike: the reconstituted government represented, for them at least, a major victory. The army proceeded to 'restore order' by taking action to demobilise the popular movement and return control of the factories to their former owners.

Increasingly, the UP government was less a protagonist and more a spectator in the escalating class confrontation between the Chilean bourgeoisie, represented by the army, and the popular movement, represented by the *cordones*. More and more the secret talk among top generals was of a military coup. In the *cordones*, on the other hand, there was a fatal lack of clear-sighted leadership.

Most of the Chilean Left was part of the UP coalition. Many activists were critical of Allende and the right-wing ministers in his cabinet. But none thought in terms of a complete break to create a new organisation. Their aim was to transform UP, a reformist coalition, into a revolutionary party.

Even those to the left of UP, like the Revolutionary Movement of the Left (MIR), were too confused to provide effective popular leadership. The MIR journal responded to Allende's invitation to the generals to join his cabinet by arguing that 'the armed forces have a patriotic and democratic role to play in ... supporting the workers in their struggle against exploitation'. Later, in July 1973, the same journal called for 'a joint dictatorship of the people and the armed forces'.

The entire Chilean Left was in a disastrous muddle about the nature of the state, the character of dual power, and the difference between reform and revolution.

The existing state, representing the rich and big business, was inherently hostile to the popular movement. On the other hand, the *cordones* had the potential to evolve into an alternative state based on mass participatory democracy. These two political forces constituted a form of 'dual power' between October 1972 and September 1973.

Dual power is unstable. That is why revolution cannot stand still. Either it advances to new victories or it ends in the defeat of the mass movement. By late 1972, the social and political polarisation in Chile was on such a scale that compromise had become impossible: there was no 'middle way' out of the crisis. At some point, *either* the army, acting on behalf of the bourgeoisie, would overthrow the reformist UP government and crush the popular movement, *or* the government would have to be pushed aside, the state overturned, and a revolutionary regime based on mass democracy established.

This – until it was too late – the Chilean Left failed to grasp. In consequence, the potential of the *cordones* went unrealised; they were never forged into a single, united, insurrectionary movement for the seizure of state power, the dispossession of the rich, and the socialist transformation of Chilean society.

A maverick coup attempt on 29 June 1973 evoked a similar response from Allende as that during the October crisis: he declared a state of emergency, brought a second raft of generals into his government, and called on the army to restore order.

July and August were months of escalating crisis. The economy was paralysed by a second lorry owners' strike, and parliament log-jammed by anti-Allende impeachment resolutions. But UP ministers reserved their venom for their own supporters, denouncing the Left while praising the 'patriotism and loyalty' of the armed forces.

Even now, events could have ended differently. In parliamentary elections in March the UP vote had increased to 44 per cent. The *cordones* had extended their influence. New sections of the working class had been drawn into battle. Popular resistance to military repression during the second state of emergency had been widespread and militant. Many workers had refused to hand the factories back to their former owners and instead demanded that the whole of industry be taken over.

But national coordination and revolutionary leadership were lacking as the crisis approached its climax. Increasingly the army was able to dismantle and disarm a fragmented mass movement, preparing the ground for the coup they were planning in collusion with Chilean landowners and bosses, US corporations, and the CIA.

At nine o'clock on the morning of 11 September 1973, the presidential palace in Santiago was surrounded by tanks. Allende committed suicide. Thousands of his supporters were rounded up and imprisoned in military bases or improvised camps, including the National Football Stadium. Many were later raped, tortured, and murdered. An estimated 30,000 in all were detained, and up to 5,000 killed in the years following the coup.

The Chilean revolutionary movement was thereby decapitated. The common people relapsed into resignation and passivity. And as the military dictatorship of Augusto Pinochet consolidated its power, the sinister gurus of 'monetarist' economics emerged from the shadows to test-run their schemes on the broken back of Chilean democracy.

The Rise and Fall of the Workers' Movement

The events in France in May 1968 were a concentrated expression of a general political crisis of world capitalism. Exceptionally militant student demonstrations triggered a general strike of ten million workers, which immediately posed the question of state power.

At the beginning of May, the authorities had closed Paris University and the police had violently attacked student demonstrators. By the end of the month, France was on the brink of working-class revolution. Events elsewhere sometimes followed a similar trajectory, but with differences, and usually at slower pace.

In West Germany, the universities continued to be centres of radicalism and militant protest through the early 1970s. But the working class, in what was the most successful of the post-war European economies, remained largely passive, leaving student activists isolated from wider German society and therefore prone to ultra-leftism and even, in extreme cases, terrorism. In the US too the workers played only a limited role. The movement was dominated throughout by students, black activists, and young radicals involved in a range of campaigns from anti-war protests to gay rights. This was partly because of the weakness of organised labour, but also because the war, the draft, and racism were such central issues. The biggest protests came in May 1970, when the National Guard opened fire and killed four student anti-war protestors and wounded nine others on the campus of Kent State University in Ohio. Colleges were occupied across the US in response to the atrocity.

Violent confrontations also took place in the North of Ireland, where the Catholic minority had faced systematic discrimination since the partition of the island in 1921. Repeatedly battered by sectarian police and right-wing mobs as they demonstrated for Civil Rights, the Catholic population of Derry rose in revolt in August 1969 and turned the Bogside district into a no-go area under popular control. This became the only part of Europe where what was, in effect, a successful working-class urban insurrection created a 'liberated zone' able to defy state control for a sustained period.

Elsewhere, too, the working class was moving to centre-stage. In Italy's 'hot autumn' of 1969, strikes peaked with a wave of factory occupations by rank-and-file metalworkers acting outside official union channels. The strikers demanded recognition of new democratic workplace structures, local negotiation of contracts, shorter working hours, and upgrading of insurance, pension, and social benefits to parity with white-collar workers.

In Britain, the government's pay controls and anti-union laws were broken by strike action and mass picketing in 1972. The Conservative administration was then defeated in a general election in 1974 when the miners went on strike in response to renewed attempts to hold down pay.

In Greece, where a military junta had seized power in a coup in 1967, 10,000 students occupied Athens Polytechnic in November 1973, demanded reform, and issued radio appeals for solidarity. By the evening of the first day, 100,000 were on the streets and a joint student-worker committee had been formed. The Greek Colonels – as the junta was known – sent in marine commandos and tanks and smashed the occupation with machine-gun fire. Scores of people were killed, hundreds wounded.

The junta was now doomed. It had murdered the children of the middle class and now had the whole population against it. Junior officers staged an internal coup and invited a conservative politician to form a constitutional government in July 1974.

South European dictators began to fall like dominoes – Portugal's Caetano in April 1974, the Greek Colonels in July 1974, and then the long-serving Spanish dictator Francisco Franco died in November 1975 and his handpicked successor regime, a restored monarchy staffed by fascists, was immediately engulfed by protests.

Spanish capitalism was rocked by a wave of mass strikes involving millions of workers across virtually every industry in the early months of 1976. Big business forced the regime to establish a parliamentary democracy as the only way to restore stability. In a replay of events in Portugal – where a revolutionary movement had been diverted into parliamentary reformism and had then simply soaked away – Spain's general election of June 1977 effectively terminated the period of mass struggle.

The global crisis of 1968–75 did not, in the end, result in successful socialist revolutions anywhere – not in France in 1968, or Chile in 1972, or Portugal in 1974, or Spain in 1976; and certainly not in the US, Britain, or Germany.

The crisis was resolved in one of two ways: by murderous repression or, more often, by carefully engineered demobilisation. In both cases, political confusion and error on the Left was usually vital in providing the ruling class with an opportunity to defeat the movement and restore the stability of the system.

Repression was the norm in Latin America. It was tried first in Mexico City on 2 October 1968. With the Olympic Games due to start in ten days, Mexico's authoritarian, single-party regime was determined that nothing should detract from the state-sponsored spectacle. It was also determined to destroy the protest movement among Mexican students before it could have a radicalising impact on wider society. A mass demonstration on that day was corralled in a major downtown square by 5,000 troops. Ordered to open fire, they killed at least 100. Hundreds more were wounded or arrested. The whole protest movement was broken in a single day of state terror.

Something similar happened in Argentina: a mass movement for change was diverted into constitutional channels; and a subsequent military coup in 1974 led to the murder or 'disappearance' of tens of thousands of left-wing activists.

Repression was always in the mix. Everywhere, demonstrators and strikers were attacked by the police and stitched up by the courts. Sometimes, they were killed outright. Thirteen Civil Rights demonstrators were murdered by British soldiers in Derry on 30 January 1972 – the event known since as 'Bloody Sunday'.

But wholesale repression was not usually an option. Bloody Sunday was a mistake. Its aim was to crush the protest movement, but it had the opposite effect: it turned it into an armed struggle as hundreds of young Catholics joined the Irish Republican Army (IRA). The Civil Rights Movement followed the same trajectory in the US, where state violence against black protest, culminating in the assassination of Martin Luther King, spawned a militant armed response in the form of the Black Panthers. The British Cabinet rejected using troops against striking miners in 1972 precisely because they feared the working-class response if pickets were killed. In the end, the survival of the system depended less on police and soldiers, more on reformist politicians and union officials.

France had provided the model. The communist-dominated CGT had led a return to work in early June 1968 on the basis of the Grenelle Agreement for limited economic concessions by the employers and the state. The political re-stabilisation of European capitalism generally followed this pattern. Trade union leaders and social-democratic or communist politicians used the power of the mass movement to exact some concessions, but then exercised their influence over the workers to demobilise the movement and destroy its power. In Italy, it was called the 'Historic Compromise' – which meant the Communist Party's willingness to govern in harmony with right-wing Christian Democrats; in Britain, the 'Social Contract' – union-policed wage cuts and strike bans in return for government promises of reform; in Spain, the 'Pact of Moncloa' – wage limits, public spending cuts, and union opposition to strikes that afforded liberal politicians just the breathing-space they needed after the fall of fascism.

However it was done – whether by bloodshed or bureaucratic manoeuvre – the defeat of the mass movements of 1968–75 was to have huge and unforeseen consequences. For the Great Boom had ended. Capitalism now faced an economic crisis as well as a political one. By the mid-1970s, as the crisis deepened, the ruling class was in a far better position to resolve it at the expense of the working class than it would have been had the mass movement still been on the offensive.

17
The New World Disorder
1975–2008

Luxury limo smashed, anti-Trump protest, 20 January 2017.

Photo by Mobilus In Mobili, Inauguration Protests, The Limo,
Washington, accessed on Commons Wikimedia.

The history of the future has begun. The system is taking us into the abyss.
We are threatened by poverty, fascism, war, and climate catastrophe. We
have a world to win.

As the great social movements against oppression, war, exploitation, and dictatorship receded during the late 1970s, the international ruling class went onto the offensive. The world economy had slumped into crisis in 1973. Growth slowed, profits fell, competition intensified. This made the strong union organisation, high wages, social benefits, and public services built up during the Great Boom increasingly problematic for the system; it made the radical demands of 1968–75 unaffordable in a capitalist framework.

The counterattack was launched by social-democratic governments in the mid-1970s and then pursued with much greater vigour by neoliberal ones in the 1980s, spearheaded by Margaret Thatcher's Tory government in Britain and Ronald Reagan's Republican administration in the United States. The neoliberal counter-revolution – for such it was – amounted to an attempt to redistribute wealth from labour to capital by overturning the post-war consensus and reversing the advances made by working people since 1945. The long-term effect, however, was to create an unstable, parasitic, slow-growth bubble economy based on financial speculation.

This took place in an increasingly unstable world. US imperialism suffered major global defeats in the 1970s – in Vietnam, Southern Africa, Central America, and the Middle East – and Reagan's neo-conservative foreign policy was an attempt to restore US power by ramping up arms expenditure, intensifying the Cold War, and waging murderous proxy wars.

The greatest success of this policy was to break the back of the Soviet economy – which struggled to match increased US arms expenditure – and to contribute to the political and social breakdown that led to the 1989 anti-Stalinist revolutions in Eastern Europe. But US power continued to slip, a function of relative economic decline, in what was becoming an increasingly multi-focal world. The 'War on Terror', launched in 2001 in a further attempt to shore up US global hegemony by armed force, spiralled out of control and spread mayhem across much of Central Asia, the Middle East, and North Africa.

Neoliberal economics and neoconservative imperialism have created a 'new world disorder'.

The Long Recession, 1973–92

The Great Boom came to an abrupt end in the autumn of 1973. Problems had emerged in parts of the world economy in the late

1960s, slowing the rate of growth, but the sudden lurch into global recession came as a shock. Crisis was supposed to be a thing of the past. Capitalism's defenders, from social democrats to right-wing conservatives, argued that the boom–slump cycle had been abolished and the system now guaranteed steady growth, full employment, and rising living standards. But in the downturn of 1974–6 unemployment doubled. Then, having failed to recover, it doubled again during a second downturn in 1980–2. High unemployment rates continued thereafter, and growth rates during the 1980s were only half what they had been during the 1960s.

The crisis was never as severe as it had been during the 1930s, but it was chronic – a sustained period of stagnation and slow growth, perhaps best described as 'the Long Recession'. The levers of state economic management that had operated during the Great Boom no longer worked. Government spending to offset downturns by injecting demand into the economy appeared to have little effect, except to stoke inflation.

Politicians responded by moving rapidly to the right. 'We used to think you could just spend your way out of recession by cutting taxes and boosting government borrowing', Prime Minister Callaghan told the British Labour Party Conference in September 1976. 'I tell you in all candour that that option no longer exists; and in so far as it ever did exist, it worked by injecting inflation into the economy. And each time that has happened, the average level of unemployment has risen.'

In fact, unemployment went up whatever governments did. The contradictions of capitalism – the irrationalities of an economic system based on competition and profit – were again defying the managerial powers of its political representatives. What had gone wrong?

The Great Boom – considered at the time to be the new norm – was actually an anomaly. The only comparable period of sustained growth was that from 1848 to 1873. Since the onset of the Long Depression in 1873, crisis of one sort or another had been the norm. Capitalism had become a highly pathological system sustained only by its addiction to arms spending, imperialism, and war.

What prevented a return to slump after 1945 was a variant of this addiction: unprecedented levels of peacetime government spending on arms, infrastructure, and public services. This had been driven by three factors: the requirements of post-war reconstruction; the pressure for social reform from a radicalised working class; and the militarisation of international relations during the Cold War. The Great Boom, in short, was engineered by state-capitalist economic intervention. This was obviously true in fully state-capitalist economies like Russia, but it was also true in ostensibly free-market economies like the US. At the height of the Second World War, government military expenditure had accounted for about 50 per cent of US economic output. Ten years later it was still around 15 per cent. The effect was to sustain and stabilise the boom.

But if capitalism had become an arms junkie, it was only a temporary fix. The Great Boom was undermined by three intractable problems. These became more acute as the global economy expanded during the 1950s and 1960s.

First, economies with high levels of arms expenditure were able to sustain the boom only by sacrificing their competitiveness. Arms expenditure is waste expenditure. Unlike expenditure on labour-saving machinery, it contributes nothing to raising the productivity of labour, cutting unit costs, and thereby boosting the competitiveness of industry. That is why the defeated countries in the Second World War, Germany and Japan, became powerhouses of post-war economic development. West Germany spent 3 or 4 per cent of GDP on arms, a substantially lower proportion than Britain, a much lower proportion than the US. Japan spent even less, just 1 per cent. Both economies, in consequence, were able to invest heavily in new technology and achieve exceptionally high levels of growth from the early 1950s onwards. West German and Japanese growth rates were roughly treble those of the US over the following two decades.

A gap therefore opened between sluggish, arms-based economies and dynamic, export-led ones. West Germany's share of the combined output of the advanced economies doubled and Japan's more than quadrupled during the Great Boom. The US share fell from more than two-thirds to less than half.

So the arms burden had to be reduced. The proportion of US output devoted to arms halved between the early 1950s and the mid-1970s. As Chris Harman put it: 'The dynamic of market competition was relentlessly undercutting the dynamic of military competition.' But the effect was to reduce the pump-priming and stabilising effects of arms expenditure on the global economy.

The second problem was less tractable. While the US and the Soviet Union were able to pursue a policy of détente to reduce their respective arms burden, getting the agreement of the domestic working class to the wage and welfare cuts also considered necessary proved harder.

Unemployment is an economic necessity under capitalism. What Marx called 'the reserve army of labour' reduces the price of labour-power by forcing workers to accept lower wages through fear of unemployment. But the Great Boom meant virtually full employment for an entire generation. Labour was in short supply, employers were competing for staff, fear of unemployment largely disappeared, and workers were able to build powerful workplace union organisation to demand a better deal.

Governments were also under pressure to provide affordable homes, new hospitals, better schools, and improved welfare provision. The 'social wage' increased in line with personal wages. In Britain, for example, the working-class share of national wealth increased from about half to about two-thirds of GDP during the Great Boom.

Rising wages and government spending created demand and helped sustain the boom. But they also meant that capitalists faced increased costs, reduced competitiveness, and a squeeze on profits. This was a particular problem where the labour movement was strong. British capitalists, for example, lost ground to West German and Japanese capitalists for this reason.

The third problem was a consequence of the continuing long-term tendency for capital to become more concentrated and centralised – that is, for the world economy to become increasingly dominated by ever-fewer giant corporations. The rise of the multinationals during the Great Boom meant the rise of an economic power largely beyond the control of governments and therefore outside the framework of state-managed capitalism. In Britain, while the top 100 firms accounted for 21 per cent of manufacturing output in 1949, their share had risen to 46 per cent by 1970. Cutting-edge enterprise in key industries like armaments, cars, pharmaceuticals, and electronics depended increasingly on globalised access to finance, technology, raw materials, production facilities, and markets.

The multinationals came to dwarf most national economies. Globalised operations enabled them to avoid regulation and taxes, get round capital controls, and secure subsidies and other concessions. To gain access to technology, investment, and markets, nation-states were forced to offer increasingly generous terms to private business. Competitive capital accumulation was breaking through the boundaries of national economies and making redundant the mechanisms of the previous phase of capitalist development.

By the mid-1970s, not only was the Great Boom over, but the state-managed capitalism that had made it possible was breaking down amid crisis and conflict. What emerged to replace it was a new form of globalised corporate 'neoliberal' capitalism.

Excursus 8: What is Neoliberalism?

Neoliberalism (previously called 'monetarism' and 'Thatcherism') is sometimes dismissed as little more than an ideological aberration. This is seriously mistaken. It is certainly true that the 'free-market' theory espoused by neoliberal academics, journalists, politicians, bankers, and entrepreneurs fails completely to explain how the capitalist economy actually works. Instead, it provides a pseudo-scientific justification for the greed, poverty, and chaos endemic to the system, and for the grotesque, unearned wealth of the political and business elite. In this sense, neoliberalism is simply the self-justifying ideology of the ruling class.

But until the 1970s, neoliberalism was confined to an obscure right-wing fringe. Free-market theorists like Friedrich Hayek and Milton Friedman were regarded as little more than cranks. The great majority of economists and policy-makers favoured a mixed economy, with high levels of state intervention and public spending.

What changed in the 1970s was that the mounting contradictions of state-managed capitalism precipitated a crisis which ended the Great Boom and tipped the world into the Long Recession. Neoliberalism is a response to that crisis. In essence, it is a class war of the global rich against everyone else. Its purpose is to destroy the gains made by working people since 1945, to increase the rate of exploitation and profit, and to redistribute wealth from labour to capital.

The initial impulse was intensified competition between capitalists during the Long Recession. Shrinking markets meant that bosses needed to reduce costs by sacking workers and driving down the wages of those they retained. Once begun, this became a global 'race to the bottom' and a permanent feature of a new economic order emerging from the crisis. The age of national economies, autarkic blocs, and state-managed capitalism was passing. A new age in which the global economy was dominated by international banks and multinational corporations outside the control of nation-states was dawning.

The rise of the financial and industrial mega-corporations of neoliberal capitalism can be charted in many ways. US foreign direct investment, for instance, rose from $11 billion in 1950 to $133 billion in 1976. The long-term borrowing of US corporations increased from 87 per cent of their share value in 1955 to 181 per cent in 1970.

To take another example, the foreign currency operations of West European banks increased from $25 billion in 1968 to $200 billion in 1974. The combined debt of the 74 less-developed countries soared from $39 billion in 1965 to $119 billion in 1974.

The steady drip-feed of these quantitative changes during the Great Boom reached a tipping-point in the 1970s. Global corporations had by then come to overshadow nation-states. Commenting on the Long Recession in 1984, Chris Harman put it like this:

> It is as if the film of the pre-war crisis is being re-run – but with a difference. The competing individual firms which borrowed from banks within a national economy have given way to state capitalisms and multinational firms borrowing from international banks within an international economy.

The effect was to impose relentless pressure on national ruling classes to increase the exploitation of 'their own' working class. High wages might deter new investment. So might taxes on business to pay for public services or welfare benefits. Similarly, laws designed to make workplaces safe, limit working hours, or guarantee maternity leave.

The ruling-class counter-offensive was first tested in Chile after the military coup of 1973. It was soon being championed by Margaret Thatcher, who had been elected leader of the British Conservative Party in 1975. She became Prime Minister in 1979 and went on to win two more general elections, remaining in office until 1990. She was a firm advocate of neoliberalism.

The previous Conservative government under Edward Heath had been broken by industrial action in 1972 and again in 1974. Thatcher was determined to mount a full-scale counterattack against the unions, the welfare state, and the working class. The miners were the most important target. They had spearheaded the struggle against Heath's administration.

A massive programme of pit closures provoked the miners into a desperate battle to save their livelihoods and communities. It turned into the longest mass strike in history – 150,000 men on strike for a year (1984–5). The miners faced paramilitary-style police violence, courtroom frame-ups, and a barrage of media lies. They were eventually starved back to work. The defeat of the miners broke the back of British trade unionism. In the early 1970s, the British working class had been one of the best organised and most militant in the world. Since 1985 union membership has halved, and over the last 25 years the British strike rate has been lower than at any time since the nineteenth century.

It is now clear that the miners' defeat had global significance: it was the single most important breakthrough in the international ruling class's attempt to smash working-class resistance to neoliberalism. Most immediately, it enabled Thatcher and her successors to roll out a programme of cuts and sell-offs.

Privatising nationalised industries and public services fragments large bargaining units of well-organised public-service workers and creates the conditions in which wages can be driven down as rival employers seek to undercut each other in the competition for franchises and contracts. That is the real purpose of marketisation and privatisation: they are mechanisms to weaken union organisation, ratchet up insecurity, drive down wages, and redistribute wealth from working people to the corporate rich.

Private capital replaces state capital as the main provider of public services. Instead of recycling tax revenues as a social wage in the form of housing, hospitals, schools, and welfare, the state pays corporate profiteers to become providers, and they remodel provision according to ability to pay. Unions are weakened, services rationed, costs cut. The main beneficiaries are the global mega-corporations of neoliberal capitalism.

The security firm G4S is an example. It is the product of a series of acquisitions and mergers. It now employs 650,000 people in 125 countries – 39 per cent of them in Asia, 19 per cent in Europe, 17 per cent in Africa, 9 per cent in North America, 8 per cent in Latin America, and 8 per cent in the Middle East. In Britain, it runs prisons, police services, and security at public events. It is one of the main beneficiaries of public-sector privatisation. Its revenue from British operations in 2011 was £1.59 billion. It paid only £67 million (1.5 per cent) in corporation tax.

The end of state-managed capitalism does not, therefore, mean the end of the state. Its roles in economic management, industrial investment, and welfare provision have been curtailed. But other roles have been enhanced.

The state has always been a huge market for capital. But business opportunities are increasing massively as public services are sold off. The British government is currently privatising the National Health Service, for example. The annual health budget is worth £125 billion. A handful of private companies will soon dominate healthcare in Britain.

The state – including inter-state bodies like the European Union and the International Monetary Fund – also continues to play a central role in economic crisis-management. Since 2008, it has functioned as a mechanism for shovelling trillions of dollars into bankrupt banks in order to prop up international finance capital.

Not least, the state's primary and original role as an armed force for use against the enemies of the ruling class at home and abroad – anti-capitalist demonstrators, striking workers, guerrilla insurgents, independent regional powers – has increased during the neoliberal era. Cuts, privatisation, and growing inequality have made society less cohesive and consensual. If you are building hospitals, you need nurses. If you are shutting them, you need police.

Globalisation, privatisation, and militarisation are the characteristic features of neoliberal capitalism. They have given us a new world order radically different from the state-managed capitalism of the Great Boom.

The Nicaraguan Revolution

In February 1990, Nicaragua's Sandinista government crashed to defeat in a general election. It secured only 41 per cent of the national vote compared with 55 per cent for its conservative opponents.

The UNO opposition alliance represented the middle class, big business, the Church, and the Contras. The Contras were a murderous militia funded, armed, and trained by the United States with the express purpose of destabilising Nicaragua.

The US had cut off all aid to Nicaragua and launched a proxy war against the country in 1982. The war had killed around 40,000 people, destroyed 15 per cent of Nicaragua's productive capacity, and forced the Sandinistas to devote more than 50 per cent of the national budget to defence.

The war had devastated the living standards of the Nicaraguan poor and the social programmes of the Sandinista regime. The real value of wages fell by a third between 1981 and 1984. By the end of the decade, unemployment was above 25 per cent. Schools and hospitals were being forced to close for lack of funds. The illiteracy rate, cut to 12 per cent in 1981, had soared again to 30 per cent. Infant mortality, having fallen for years, began to rise once more.

The people of Nicaragua understood the reasons for their poverty. They did not blame the Sandinistas. In the November 1984 general election, 67 per cent of them had voted for the government. But they could only take so much, and by 1990 the effects of the siege of their country by US imperialism and world capitalism – for that is what it was – broke their will and they voted to end the torment. In a sense, as Mike Gonzalez put it, 'the Contras were the iron fist, UNO the velvet glove'.

Why did the rulers of the world, especially the rulers of the US, hate Nicaragua so much? It was one of the smallest and poorest countries on earth. There were only three million Nicaraguans in all, and most of them were very poor indeed. Per capita GDP was around $750, and the country as a whole accounted for just 0.02 per cent of global production. Per capita GDP in the US at the time was around $18,000, and the US accounted for around 27 per cent of global production. Nicaragua constituted no conceivable economic or military threat to the United States.

The problem was political. In July 1979 the people of Nicaragua had destroyed a brutal military dictatorship and propelled to power the guerrilla fighters of the Sandinista National Liberation Front (FSLN). If this could be done in Nicaragua, maybe it could be done elsewhere in Central America – in Guatemala, El Salvador, Honduras, and Costa Rica. And if here, perhaps elsewhere in Latin America; indeed, perhaps yet further afield, since the long post-war boom was over, the world economy was again mired in slump, and workers and poor people were fighting back from Brazil to Poland to South Korea.

At first, still reeling from defeat in Vietnam, US leaders had experimented with a 'soft power' approach to global dominance, trumpeting a new commitment to democracy and human rights. It did not last. The election of Ronald Reagan to the White House in 1980 had seen a return to Cold War rhetoric, increased arms spending, and military aggression.

Nicaragua was a prime target. Here was a bright beacon of resistance in the US 'backyard'. So the aim was to destroy the Sandinista regime and suffocate at birth any possibility of a wider

Central American revolution. Local dictators were rearmed. Death-squads were dispatched to El Salvador. The CIA was granted an initial $19 million for covert operations against Nicaragua. And before long, US government agents would be secretly funding the Nicaraguan Contras from the proceeds of arms sales to Iran (*sic*: to the Islamic Republic of Iran).

The Sandinistas thus found themselves in the front-line of Reagan's attempt to reverse 'the Vietnam Syndrome' and reassert US power across the globe.

The US waged a dirty war against revolutionaries in Central America throughout the 1980s. The men they armed and trained were often sadistic terrorists. Because the resistance was rooted among the poor, virtually everyone was a target: crops were burned, villages destroyed, men murdered, and women raped.

The worst was often reserved for captured Sandinista fighters. One militiaman later reported: 'Rosa had her breasts cut off. Then they cut into her chest and took out her heart. The men had their arms broken, their testicles cut off. They were killed by slitting their throats and pulling the tongue out through the slit.'

Half a million people fled the Contra terror in the first four years of the war, reducing the productive capacity of the economy, and creating a refugee crisis in the cities.

The strategy was to destroy the Sandinista regime by a process of isolation, terror, and slow strangulation. The aim was to expunge the example of July 1979 – to show that revolution could not succeed.

Anastasio Somoza had been the third in a dynasty of Nicaraguan dictators who had first seized power in 1937. The Somoza family became Nicaragua's richest, accumulating wealth through land-holding, financial investments, and, latterly, the appropriation of international relief funds donated after a huge earthquake destroyed 75 per cent of Managua, the capital city, in 1972.

This crony-capitalism was underpinned by the dictator's direct control over the National Guard. Protest was met with brutal repression. For more than 40 years this worked. In particular, the guerrilla resistance of the FSLN in parts of the countryside was effectively contained. Only in September 1978 did things begin to change.

Mass uprisings in several towns were suppressed with the usual violence. But this time people were too enraged to stop, and the resistance was not cowed. The US, smelling change on the wind, cut off arms supplies to Somoza. The FSLN launched a new offensive. By early June, its leaders were confident enough to summon a general uprising.

The last few weeks were exceptionally bloody. Insurrections in the *barrios* (urban slums) were sometimes crushed. The regime sent planes and helicopters to bomb them from the air. The National Guard rampaged through them, killing, raping, and torturing without distinction. But each murderous assault swept young street-fighters out of the urban *barrios* into Sandinista training-camps in the bush.

On 19 July, Managua fell to the revolutionary forces. Four of Nicaragua's seven cities were in ruins. A desperately poor country was even poorer. The Sandinista inheritance was grim.

The FSLN took its name from Augusto Cesar Sandino, an anti-imperialist who had refused to compromise and lay down his arms after a liberal revolt in 1926, sustaining guerrilla resistance to Nicaragua's pro-US government until 1933. The choice of name reflected the Sandinistas' politics: they were anti-imperialists and radical reformists, not socialist revolutionaries. The Cuban Revolution had provided the primary model when the FSLN was founded in 1961. Rural guerrilla warfare had been their principal *modus operandi* ever since.

Nicaragua was not only impoverished and devastated. It remained what it had always been: a country of subsistence farmers and producers of agricultural exports like coffee.

The Sandinistas did their best to redistribute some wealth and provide a basic minimum for all. But there were strict limits to this process. They needed foreign aid, foreign loans, foreign investment, and foreign markets. They needed these things both to grow their economy and to defend their state. This involved making major concessions to capitalists, both at home and abroad.

Two-thirds of the economy remained in private hands. Dollar supermarkets sold imported goods to Nicaraguans with the wealth and hard currency to buy them. In nearby people's stores the shelves might be empty, often of such essentials as toothpaste and toilet paper, sometimes even of staples like rice and coffee.

The burden of building basic infrastructure and industry, and of maintaining a huge army, fell primarily on the workers, the peasants, and the poor. The regime's priorities were austerity, production, and defence. The Sandinista state had its own interests – national survival – and they were in contradiction with the material needs of the people.

The regime remained popular. Its mass base was huge: more than half a million Nicaraguans, 20 per cent of the population, were enrolled in one or another Sandinista organisation in 1982. But this was a top-down 'command' structure for transmitting the priorities of the Sandinista leadership to society – not a bottom-up democracy capable of formulating and advancing alternatives.

The Nicaraguan Revolution was trapped by poverty and war, and these constraints were warping it into a caricature of its noble aspirations. National independence in a world of giant corporations and imperial powers was proving a mirage.

The only way out would have been to have formed an alliance with workers, peasants, and poor people elsewhere, to have given full support to their struggles, and thus to have attempted to spread the revolution, perhaps first to Central America, then to the great centres of the Latin American working-class like Mexico City, Sao Paulo, Buenos Aires, and elsewhere.

The key lesson of Chile's Allende government is that the achievement of socialism depends on the overthrow of the capitalist state. The key lesson of the Nicaraguan Revolution is that it also depends on internationalism.

Capitalism is a global system. Therefore, you cannot build 'socialism in one country'. The economic power of global markets and the military power of imperialism will, sooner or later, destroy any islands of socialism that attempt to survive in isolation from the rest of the world.

Nicaragua was a victim of bad timing. By the time of the Sandinista Revolution, the tide of world politics had turned against the Left. This was to be demonstrated in another way by a very different revolution in that same year of 1979.

The Iranian Revolution

Iran – or Persia – straddles two worlds. It has a long history as a distinct civilisation and an imperial centre. The Achaemenids in the sixth century BC, the Sassanids in the fourth century AD, and the

Safavids in the sixteenth century AD were each among the greatest rulers in the world at their time.

Most of the people of Iran are of Persian descent and speak Farsi. Unlike the Arabs, who succumbed to Ottoman power in the sixteenth century, the Persians have always retained their independence.

Yet Iran is also part of the wider Middle East – not just on account of its location, being a great block of land across the region's eastern edge, but also because it became Muslim in the seventh century, and a major oil producer in the twentieth.

Between 1909 and 1951, however, Iran was little more than a client state of British imperialism. Its whole existence revolved around the operations of the Anglo-Persian Oil Company (now BP). The neo-colonial setup meant that the company took £750 million a year, Iran got £100 million, and the oil workers' wages covered only the bare necessities. Strikes were smashed by company police.

In 1951, Mohammad Mossadegh's National Front, supported by the Tudeh Party (the communists), took power in Iran and nationalised the oil industry. But the nationalist government called on the army to clear the streets of demonstrators and strikers who wanted radical reform. It thereby destroyed its own social base. The government was overthrown within days by an internal coup backed by the CIA and MI6.

The Shah, Mohammad Reza Pahlavi, proceeded to establish one of most brutal security apparatuses in the world. SAVAK, the secret police, swelled into an organisation of 5,000 full-time agents and an unknown number of paid part-time informers. The armed forces, funded by oil wealth, were re-equipped with ultra-modern American, British, and French kit. This apparatus was used to turn Iran into a one-party state ruled by a dictator dressed up as a king.

The Shah launched a 'White Revolution' designed to transform Iran into a modern industrial economy. This was a programme of state-driven capital accumulation. The Plan for 1973–8, for example, shows an investment breakdown of $46 billion of state capital, $23 billion of private Iranian capital, and $3 billion of foreign capital. The Iranian economy became a mix of oil, manufacturing, construction, and services. By the late 1970s, Iran had 2.5 million factory workers and three million service workers.

The regime, however, was in crisis. Global demand for oil had collapsed with the onset of the Long Recession in 1973. Social distress now reinforced political agitation for democracy and reform. From early summer 1977 onwards, strikes and demonstrations became frequent events. Students, intellectuals, and professionals took to the streets to attack censorship and despotism. Shanty-town dwellers marched against the bulldozing of their homes. Hundreds were shot down.

The exiled Shia religious leader Ayatollah Khomeini called on the clergy and the faithful to resist the repression. The movement henceforward involved diverse forces: the modern middle-class, the clergy and the petty-bourgeoisie of the bazaars, the industrial working class, and the urban poor. In February 1978, moreover, in the industrial city of Tabriz, demonstrators fought back against police violence for the first time; they went on to attack police stations, party headquarters, banks, luxury hotels, and porn cinemas.

The movement continued to build through 1978. By June the workers were raising political demands alongside economic ones, and by September massive strikes, now including the oil workers, were spilling over into street demonstrations millions strong. Management was losing control of the workplaces, the secret police were being hunted down, and strike committees, called *shoras*, were evolving into mass democratic assemblies akin to the soviets of 1917.

On 16 January 1979, after 18 months of violent struggle, the Shah fled the country. The streets filled with celebration as crowds of protestors embraced conscript soldiers. On 1 February the Ayatollah Khomeini returned from exile, and five days later he declared himself head of state, with Mehdi Bazargan as Prime Minister.

The old security apparatus was now powerless, with SAVAK effectively destroyed, and the Iranian Army paralysed by a split between the officer corps and the conscript soldiers who had joined the revolutionary crowds. The question of state power was therefore open. Two main forces were in play.

Khomeini, standing at the head of the clergy, the bazaaris, and a backward mass of the urban and rural poor, had seized the reins of power and proclaimed an 'Islamic Republic'. His aim was to halt the revolution, crush the popular movement, and drive through a reactionary social programme based on religious bigotry. Henceforward – given the paralysis of the forces of the *ancien régime*

– counter-revolution would take an Islamic form. But Khomeini's power was, as yet, far from secure.

He faced opposition from a powerful coalition of left-wing forces. First, the workers' movement and the *shoras* became a coordinated national force with the establishment of the Founding Council of the Iranian National Workers' Union on 1 March. Second, a militant unemployed workers' movement – representing one in three of the workforce – sprang up alongside it. Third, in response to the new theocracy's attacks on the rights of women, with decrees affecting jobs, divorce, and dress, several million Iranian women braved the violence of Islamist thugs to participate in a week of protests starting on International Women's Day (8 March). Fourth, large national and religious minorities (comprising a third of the population) – Azaris, Kurds, Arabs, Baluchis, Turkmen, Sunnis, Christians, and others – began organising to assert their rights in the framework provided by the revolution.

On 1 May, International Workers Day, the potential power of this coalition was displayed on the streets of Tehran, as 1.5 million people marched shouting the slogans of the Left in Farsi, Arabic, Kurdish, and Azeri: 'Death to imperialism', 'Nationalisation of all industries', 'Equal pay for men and women', 'Work for the unemployed', 'Long live real unions and real *shoras*'.

In the summer of 1979, then, Iran was in the grip of a dual power. Everything depended on clear revolutionary leadership. Of this, however, there was none.

The National Front was a loose coalition of liberal-secular and moderate-Islamist groups, the former drawing support from the modern middle-class, the latter from the petty-bourgeoisie of the bazaars. The Tudeh Party, to the left of the National Front, was an old-fashioned Stalinist party that sought alliances with 'progressive' bourgeois forces – instead of orienting on the *shoras*, the working class, and the popular movement on the streets. Two offshoots of the opposition, the Islamist Mojahedin and the leftist Fedayeen, had been pursuing a guerrilla struggle, but this had proved a dead-end in the context of an increasingly urban-capitalist society.

None of these forces was fit for revolutionary leadership. Lacking political clarity, the Left, such as it was, made a series of catastrophic mistakes. Sections of it failed to support the women's movement and the minority movements when they came under attack. The Tudeh

Party backed the regime in a rigged referendum on the proposed constitution of the Islamic Republic. Much of the Left was taken in by Khomeini's fake 'anti-imperialist' posturing. This came to a climax in November 1979, when the government mounted an elaborate stunt – the occupation of the American embassy by Islamist students – and virtually the whole of the Left lined up behind Khomeini.

This left the popular movement – under increasing attack from Islamists on the ground – confused and directionless. Many local bodies, including many *shoras*, came under Islamist control. Islamist societies, committees, and *shoras* became the enforcers of attacks on personal freedom, civil liberties, and women's rights that had been enshrined in the new constitution.

This constitution had created an inner and an outer state. The inner state was formed of the Shia hierarchy, the Islamic Revolutionary Guards, and the nationwide network of imams, mosques, and religious societies under their influence. The outer state was represented by the Prime Minister, the Iranian Parliament, and secular institutions like the army, the police, the courts, and the civil service.

Thus, though Khomeini's party, the Islamic Republic Party, failed to win a majority in the January 1980 general election, it made little difference. The Revolutionary Guards and the Islamist organisations continued their offensive against the workers' *shoras*, and in August the Iranian Parliament backed them with a law that stripped the *shoras* of authority. The rule of capital was restored in the factories.

What finally destroyed the retreating popular movement definitively was Iran's declaration of war on Iraq in September 1980. Under cover of the military crisis – which would last for eight years and cost a million dead – Revolutionary Guards closed down the universities, Islamist thugs roamed the streets attacking women not wearing the veil with clubs and acid, and Khomeini launched a cultural campaign to 'Islamicise' Iranian education.

Nothing remained of the revolution of the workers, the unemployed, the women, and the minorities. The popular movement had been smashed by counter-revolutionary violence. And a new form of reaction – political Islam – had emerged.

1989: The Fall of Stalinism

On the evening of 9 November 1989, the people of Berlin changed the world. A city divided by warmongering ruling classes since 1945 was reunited by a revolt of ordinary people. With news spreading like a firestorm across the city, hundreds of thousands converged on the Berlin Wall, supreme symbol of the Iron Curtain and the Cold War, and began to tear it down. Since its construction in 1961, an estimated 5,000 people had attempted to cross the Wall, and between 100 and 200 had been killed. Suddenly, in one of history's great moments of revolutionary insurrection, it was demolished.

The fall of the Berlin Wall was a signal event in a year of such events. But matters could have played out very differently. Beijing on 3–4 June had revealed the face of a possible alternative future. In a few days in April, pro-democracy protests in the capital's huge Tiananmen Square had swelled to 100,000 people. Within a month, the movement had spread across China, with protests in 400 cities. For a while, the authorities – a one-party dictatorship of ageing bureaucrats – were paralysed by indecision. But the movement kept growing, and fearing they would lose control altogether and be swept away, China's leaders launched a military coup against their own people.

The soldiers billeted in the city knew too much of what was really going on and many sympathised with the demonstrators. So the regime brought in soldiers from the provinces. They poisoned their minds with lies, then sent them into Tiananmen Square to gun down the unarmed demonstrators. Around 3,000 were killed. The mass movement was murdered.

The Chinese are still living with the consequences of this counter-revolutionary massacre. They have the worst of both worlds: the drudgery, poverty, and insecurity of free-market capitalism, and the authoritarianism of a Stalinist police state.

But 1989 turned out differently in Eastern Europe. The Long Recession of the 1970s had plunged the state-capitalist regimes into economic and political crisis, and the signs had been growing since that something had to give.

Poland had a long history of resistance to Stalinism. There had been major workers' revolts in 1956 and 1970. Dissident intellectuals and victimised working-class activists had maintained an underground opposition – the Workers' Defence Committee and the newspaper *Robotnik* ('Worker') – during the 1970s. When, in the summer of 1980, the regime attempted to impose price increases, the

Lenin Shipyard in Gdańsk was occupied in protest. This was one of the workplaces regularly leafleted by the underground opposition.

Strikes and occupations spread rapidly. The protests melded into a single mass movement at a conference attended by delegates representing 3,500 factories. The movement, *Solidarność* (Solidarity), was a hybrid of a trade union and a network of revolutionary workers' councils. It eventually had ten million members and was to last for 16 months.

But its leaders, paralysed by fear of Soviet military intervention, announced a 'self-limiting revolution': they would not attempt to seize state power and overthrow the old ruling class; they would try to cut a deal. For this they paid the inevitable price: in mid-December 1981, General Jaruzelski declared martial law, arrested the Solidarity leadership, and used troops to crush the workers' movement.

Nevertheless, Jaruzelski stopped short of full-blooded repression. So deep was the economic and political crisis that wholesale restoration of the old order was impossible. The coup was designed to win the time and space the ruling class needed to manage a process of reform rather than have it forced upon them.

The Eastern Bloc had achieved economic growth rates higher than those in Western Europe during the 1950s and 1960s. The Stalinist regimes had built autarkic economies in which state power had been used to direct investment into heavy industry and arms production. The second phase of industrialisation, however, required access to technology available only in global markets dominated by foreign multinationals. By the 1970s, autarky had run its course. An 'opening to the market' was necessary if the state-capitalist economies were not to fall behind. The imperatives of market competition were reinforced by those of military competition.

The Cold War had imposed massive strains on the Soviet Union. With an economy only half the size of the US's, the Soviet rulers had been compelled to maintain much higher relative levels of arms expenditure in order to keep pace. The strain had been eased by détente during the 1970s. But in 1980 US President Reagan launched what was, in effect, a second Cold War with his Strategic Defence Initiative. US arms spending rose from $295 billion in 1979 to $425 billion in 1986. New computer-guided cruise missiles were stationed in Europe, and a programme was initiated to put weapons into outer space (dubbed 'Star Wars' in the media). At the same time,

US military intervention was ramped up in Central America, the Caribbean, the Middle East, and Central Asia. The sluggish Soviet economy of the 1980s found the strain of a new arms race unsustainable. The clearest indication of waning military power was defeat in a colonial war in the Soviet backyard of Central Asia.

In December 1979 the Soviet Union had invaded Afghanistan to prop up a beleaguered, nominally communist client regime in Kabul. The invasion triggered a massive escalation in guerrilla resistance by Islamic *mujahideen* based in the countryside. The *mujahideen* were soon being armed by the CIA. Funding soared from $30 million in 1981 to $280 million in 1985. The combination of Islamic insurgency and US arms broke the Soviet occupation. Russian troop withdrawals began in spring 1988 and were completed a year later.

The end of the Afghan War coincided with the beginning of the terminal crisis of Stalinism in Russia and Eastern Europe. Mikhail Gorbachev had become Soviet leader in 1985. In 1987 and 1988 he launched a policy of *glasnost* ('openness') and *perestroika* ('restructuring'). His aim was managed reform from above in order to deal with an economic crisis that was now endangering the ruling bureaucracy's grip on power, both at home and abroad. He quickly lost control of events. Deep splits within the regime created openings for mass protest unseen since the 1920s. As the monolith cracked, the more adept bureaucrats reinvented themselves as 'reformers' and 'nationalists'.

Most adept of all was Boris Yeltsin, a political maverick who broke with both Gorbachev and the Soviet Communist Party, winning election as Deputy for Moscow in 1989, then President of Russia in 1991. By this time, the Soviet Union was breaking up into separate republics. With the imperial hegemon itself in crisis, the threat of external military intervention that had held the people of Eastern Europe in thrall was removed. The combination of economic crisis, faltering power, and talk of reform culminated in an explosion. The detonator, as so often, was a tiny device.

Late in June 1989 a pan-European picnic was held on the Austro-Hungarian frontier. A border crossing closed since 1948 was opened for the occasion to allow the passage of a small delegation. As news spread, thousands of East Germans headed for the crossing. The Hungarians made no attempt to stop them. First some hundreds went through, then thousands more, until eventually some 40,000

East Germans had 'escaped' to the West during six weeks in August and September.

By October the masses moving into action across Eastern Europe had become a flood tide. But now, with millions on the streets, they no longer sought 'escape'. On 4 November, when a million demonstrated in the heart of East Berlin, the chant 'We want out' had become 'We want to stay'. Flight had turned into revolution.

The old regimes toppled like dominoes. The Polish leaders had been deep in discussion with Solidarity since January. Now Hungary voted to transform itself into a parliamentary democracy on 7 October and to end the Stalinist system on the 23rd. Berlin was reunited on 9 November, and the Bulgarian dictator Todor Zhivkov was overthrown on the 10th. The Czechs brought their 'Velvet Revolution' to victory on 28 November. Only in Romania did the regime make a determined effort to fight it out. But the Securitate, the state's hated secret police apparatus, was overwhelmed, and the dictator, Nicolae Ceauşescu, was captured before he could escape. He and his wife were immediately tried and executed.

The revolutions of 1989 represent impressive victories for mass action. But they were limited in effect. The crowds in Moscow, Berlin, Budapest, Warsaw, Sofia, Prague, and Bucharest had wanted freedom and prosperity. What they got was rather less. State bureaucrats recycled themselves as parliamentary politicians. State-managed capitalism was reconfigured into neoliberal capitalism. The ideology of Stalinism was discarded and that of Western-style 'freedom' embraced – only to discover that it too, like its Cold War alter-ego, was a chimera.

What had gone wrong? Why had the revolutions developed no popular momentum? How had such powerful class struggles been deflected into the dreary routines of parliamentary politics?

With the key prop of Soviet imperial power kicked away and the state-capitalist regimes so hollowed out, limited pressure was sufficient to bring them down. Both Cold War ideology and the rapid advance of neoliberal globalisation implied that Western-style, free-market capitalism and parliamentary democracy must be the alternative to Eastern Bloc 'socialism' (as it had always been called). It was in the interests of the old ruling class both to manage the transition and to promote this alternative vision. In this way, most of them held on to their property, power, and privilege. The political revolutions of 1989 were successfully prevented from evolving into social revolutions.

Soweto, Mandela, and Apartheid

On 16 June 1976, black students poured onto the streets of the impoverished South African township of Soweto to protest the compulsory use of Afrikaans in local schools. Inspired by the ideas of the Black Consciousness Movement, and by the victories of black liberation movements in neighbouring Angola, Mozambique, and Zimbabwe, they were rejecting the language of their white rulers and asserting their identity as an oppressed people.

They were gunned down by the police. The first to be killed were aged 13 and 15. In all, there were 23 fatalities.

The effect was to turn a demonstration into an urban insurrection that spread across South Africa and raged for a year. The movement was finally broken by 700 officially recorded deaths, mass detentions, and the suppression of Black Consciousness, including the murder of its most prominent figure, Steve Biko, in police custody.

History appeared to be repeating itself. An earlier wave of black resistance in the 1950s, led by the African National Congress (ANC), had also been broken, when 69 protestors were killed by police at Sharpeville on 21 March 1960.

Many black activists then had responded by going underground and attempting to launch a guerrilla war. They included a young lawyer called Nelson Mandela. But the strategy was misconceived: the guerrillas of the ANC's armed wing, Umkhonto weSizwe (MK), were hopelessly outgunned by the South African state, and in July 1963 Mandela and the rest of the underground leadership were captured. They were subsequently tried and sentenced to life imprisonment. The resistance effectively collapsed.

South African apartheid – the word means 'separation' – had its roots in the British-controlled gold mines of the Rand region of the Transvaal in the late nineteenth century. Gold was the basis of the global monetary system. Following the discovery of rich reserves on the Rand, South Africa became the world's largest producer, with gold accounting for half the country's export earnings.

But there was a technical problem. The deposits were vast, but the gold content of the ore was low. This meant huge quantities of rock had to be cut and shifted – something that required heavy investment in technology and large supplies of cheap labour. The former was provided by the Rand-lords – essentially expatriate mining capitalists with connections to European finance. The latter resulted from the dispossession and displacement of the South African peasantry.

The disintegration of traditional African society was already well advanced. White settlers – mainly British and Afrikaner (the latter of Dutch origin and known as 'Boers') – had taken most of the best land, and the corralling of black farmers into marginal areas had resulted in overpopulation, overgrazing, and soil erosion. Further pressure was added by the imposition of taxes which had to be paid in money. Large numbers of impoverished Africans found themselves driven to wage-labour in the mines.

British mine-owners and Afrikaner big-farmers shared an interest in effective control over black labour. Despite the Great Trek (an Afrikaner attempt to escape British rule by moving to the interior between 1835 and 1846) and two Anglo-Boer Wars (in 1881 and 1899–1902), the two white races came together in the Union of South Africa in 1910. The Native Land Act of 1913 set aside less than 13 per cent of the country for Africans. A government commission gave away the purpose: 'It cannot but be an advantage to the natives to be induced without compulsion to become more industrious. Economic pressure and the struggle for existence will be felt by many of them at no very distant date.'

When Africans – responding to 'economic pressure and the struggle for existence' – entered 'white' areas to work, they did so as migrants, required to carry a pass, and subject to eviction to the reserves once their employment was terminated. The election of an Afrikaner Nationalist government in 1948 merely formalised and entrenched the South African state's commitment to what was henceforward called 'apartheid'.

The ANC, originally founded in 1912 as a moderate lobbying group of the small black middle class, was radicalised by an upsurge of industrial struggle in the 1940s and by the Afrikaner National-ist victory of 1948. In 1955 it enshrined a set of basic political and economic demands in its 'Freedom Charter'. By the late 1950s, inspired in part by the example of the Civil Rights Movement in the United States, the ANC was leading mass campaigns of direct action. This was the movement crushed by the Sharpeville Massacre.

The Soweto uprising of 1976–7 had a very different outcome. It took the state a year to achieve what proved to be only a temporary suppression of the movement. A rumble of resistance continued in the black townships and labour compounds. Two waves of strikes rolled across the metal industry of the eastern Rand in 1981–2. Revolts in the mines led to bloody clashes in which a hundred were killed and thousands deported.

Some bosses, desperate to stabilise labour relations, offered concessions, including union recognition. But the result was an explosion of strike action and union membership. Almost 400,000 black strike-days were 'lost' in 1984. Around 80,000 miners took strike action in the first three months of 1985. By the middle of that year, the National Union of Mineworkers was organising 200,000 of South Africa's 550,000 black miners.

The labour revolt was part of what had now become a second nationwide conflagration on an even greater scale than that of 1976–7. Though the organised working-class was central to the 1984–6 uprising, the townships were also aflame, with mass resistance to forced removals, rent rises, and the collaborationist councils created by the regime. The movement peaked at those moments when economic struggles fused with political demands, when industrial workers fought alongside township residents, as during a two-day strike on 5–6 November 1984, when about half a million participated.

South Africa's racialised capitalism had become unsustainable. What had changed the balance of forces was the huge expansion of the black working class. The regime divided people into four categories: whites (5 million); blacks (25 million); coloureds (3 million); and Asians (1 million). Of critical significance was the size of the white working class and its relatively privileged social position. White workers held most of the skilled and supervisory positions in industry, and they were paid on average five times as much as black workers; they tended to be deeply racist. The core of the army, police, and prison service was recruited from this hardened white-supremacist bloc.

The white security apparatus had been sufficient when most blacks were concentrated in rural reserves (known as 'bantustans'). But post-war industrialisation had transformed much of the black population into workers. By 1970 there were four million black workers in 'white' areas, of whom one-third were migrants, two-thirds settled. The number continued to rise thereafter by about a million every five years.

During the struggles of the 1970s, there had been little coordination between industrial and community action. This changed in the 1980s. The regime then faced a much stronger challenge because strong union organisation gave the resistance an unbreakable spine.

Apartheid had become incompatible with the political stability essential to successful capital accumulation. The bosses were turning against the regime. A reformist wing emerged inside the Nationalist Party. Having become State President in August 1989, F. W. de Klerk made the critical decision to unban the ANC and free Nelson Mandela in February 1990.

The jailed Mandela had become an iconic figure for the black resistance, the demands for his release increasingly shrill. Secret talks between the regime and the ANC leadership had established Mandela's willingness to negotiate an orderly end to white-minority rule.

The danger for the ruling class was that South African capitalism would succumb in a violent confrontation between the white state and an insurgent black proletariat. Was there a middle way between white-supremacism and black revolution?

Mandela and the ANC were essentially African nationalists committed to black-majority rule and a liberal parliamentary regime. They were not socialist revolutionaries. This created the basis for the agreement between de Klerk and Mandela which culminated in South Africa's first democratic elections in April 1994. The ANC won a landslide victory and Mandela was elected State President.

A political revolution had been managed from above so as to prevent social revolution from below. This was hailed as a triumph by mainstream opinion. The primary beneficiaries were a minority of black professionals and politicians now able to advance themselves in a new multiracial capitalism. The black working class continued to live in poverty.

On 16 August 2012, under orders from an ANC regime riddled with cronyism and corruption, police opened fire on striking miners with automatic weapons and shot down more than a hundred, killing 34. The ANC, the South African state, and international corporate capital now stood in united opposition to the black working class that had brought down apartheid.

9/11, the War on Terror, and the New Imperialism

On 11 September 2001, Al-Qaeda terrorists hijacked four American aircraft in order to carry out attacks on the Twin Towers of the World Trade Center in New York, the Pentagon in Arlington, Virginia, and the Capitol Building in Washington, DC. Three of these attacks were successful: the Pentagon sustained major damage, the Twin Towers were both struck and later collapsed, and about 3,000 people were killed.

9/11 was a gift to the US ruling class: it allowed them to rebrand their own aggression – which has since been a thousand times more deadly than Al-Qaeda's – as a 'War on Terror'. It helped them fabricate the 'threats' and 'enemies' they needed to justify new imperialist wars.

The War on Terror is the geopolitical correlate of neoliberal capitalism. Neoliberalism wrecks economies and destroys lives. It tears societies apart and leads to revolutions and wars. The great powers then intervene to safeguard the interests of global capital. The War on Terror provides the current framework for intervention, and also, since the end of the Cold War, the primary justification for maintaining high levels of arms expenditure.

As state-managed capitalism was dismantled in Eastern Europe, and an old elite of party bureaucrats morphed into a new elite of neoliberal oligarchs, entire economies collapsed. Ten years after 1989, the Russian economy had contracted by 40 per cent. East German unemployment rates hit 20 per cent and more. Yugoslav living standards halved in just two years.

The economic and social dislocation was not restricted to former communist regimes. The state-managed model was picked apart on every continent. From Egypt to India to Latin America, state enterprises were sold off, public services run down, welfare provision retrenched.

The World Bank and the International Monetary Fund (IMF), representing global finance capital, became the supreme arbiters of neoliberal virtue. Those who signed up to 'structural adjustment programmes' (a euphemism for neoliberal cuts) were rewarded with access to finance, technology, and investment. Those who did not were consigned to oblivion.

Of 76 countries subjected to 'structural adjustment' in the 1980s, almost all failed to return to the growth rates of previous decades. The effect was to leave 55 per cent of Africans and 45 per cent of Latin Americans living below the poverty line. The social tensions exploded in many ways. Yugoslavia can serve as a case study in neoliberal chaos.

As the heavily indebted Yugoslav state broke up, Western banks cut off access to further funding, and IMF-imposed 'structural adjustment' plunged the sundered fragments into a depression. Party bosses reinvented themselves as nationalist politicians and rekindled ancient identities. The region was then ripped apart by vicious civil wars marked by genocide and ethnic cleansing of a kind unknown in Europe since 1945. This proved a convenient testing-ground for a new kind of Western imperialism masquerading as 'humanitarian intervention' and 'peace-keeping'. NATO, the US-dominated Cold War military alliance, was now recast as the military guardian of a post-1989 'New World Order'.

Serbia was attacked by NATO bombers during the Bosnian War (1992–5) and again during the Kosovo War (1999). The aim of the Western powers was to manage the transition from state-managed to neoliberal capitalism and create a stable political order safe for foreign capital. Tony Blair proclaimed the new imperial doctrine in a speech to the Chicago Economic Club during the Kosovo War:

> We are all internationalists now ... We cannot refuse to partici-
> pate in global markets if we want to prosper ... We cannot turn
> our backs on conflicts and the violation of human rights within
> other countries if we want still to be secure. We are witnessing
> the beginnings of a new doctrine of international community
> ... Global financial markets, the global environment, and global
> security and disarmament issues: none of these can be solved
> without intense international co-operation.

Blair exuded the arrogance of imperialists throughout history. His 'we' meant the neoliberal bourgeoisie. His 'international community' meant the great powers. The major war he helped launch against Iraq in 2003 laid this bare. It represented the new imperialism's coming of age.

The principal threat to global peace today is the United States. This is because the US is in decline economically, yet remains dominant militarily. Control over oil – the single most important global commodity – is at the heart of US strategic calculations. That is why the Middle East, with about 70 per cent of all known reserves, remains a central focus.

The War on Terror is not a struggle between Islam and the West. It is a struggle on the part of imperialist capital for control of oil and other vital interests. But it derives its ideological character from political developments inside the Middle East since 1979. Islam is a religious persuasion that can take as many forms as Christianity, Hinduism, or Buddhism. It can express a wide range of class interests and political attitudes. 'Islamism' or 'political Islam' is not, therefore, a single, cohesive, organised force. The label encompasses traditions as diverse as the benighted tribal conservatives of Afghanistan's Taliban, the present ruling regime in Iran, Egypt's relatively liberal Muslim Brotherhood, and radical resistance organisations like Hezbollah in Lebanon and Hamas in the Palestinian territories. Indeed, Islamism's lack of political definition is part of its appeal. It seems able to offer a political home to anyone opposed to imperialism, Zionism, and dictatorship. It has the apparent capacity to unite the young professional, the unemployed graduate, the stallholder, the slum-dweller, and the village mullah in a single mass movement.

Islamism's appeal has been enhanced by the failure of other, secular traditions. The Arab nationalist regimes were defeated in the Arab–Israeli wars of 1956, 1967, and 1973. They later turned into brutal dictatorships, like that of Saddam Hussein in Iraq, Hosni Mubarak in Egypt, and Bashar Al-Assad in Syria. The old Arab communist parties, following the Stalinist line, led their supporters to repeated defeat by subordinating working-class movements to treacherous bourgeois-nationalist leaders. The Palestinian guerrillas – outnumbered and outgunned – struggled heroically but hopelessly against the might of the Zionist state.

The Iranian Revolution of 1979 seemed to represent a new way forward. A mass movement of millions had overthrown a vicious, heavily armed, US-backed dictator. The reality is that the Left was then smashed by a counter-revolutionary Islamist movement.

But this reality was obscured by the anti-imperialist rhetoric and posturing of the new regime; it had confused a large chunk of the Iranian Left during the Revolution, so it is hardly surprising that it has confused millions outside Iran ever since.

But the Islamic Republic of Iran, however reactionary the regime, is still a real threat to the United States. Iran itself is a local 'sub-imperialism', competing for Middle Eastern hegemony with Saudi Arabia, a primary US ally, and Iranian-sponsored Islamism is destabilising large parts of the region in ways that threaten US interests.

9/11 provided the US 'neocons' (neoconservatives: the hawkish advocates of the new imperialism) with their opportunity to go onto the offensive. US military power was to be projected across Central Asia and the Middle East to steal a march on imperial rivals, impose a *Pax Americana* on the region, and secure a military platform for the indefinite defence of US access to vital oil and gas reserves. The cost would be a million dead.

But the Afghan and Iraq Wars would spin out of control, conjuring intractable guerrilla insurgencies in the occupied countries, and a mass anti-war movement of unprecedented size at home. After 2008, moreover, this great resurgence of street protest in the heartlands of old capitalism would feed into a new movement against austerity as the world's banks crashed and the global economy was tipped into a the Great Stagnation.

Chavez, Venezuela, and the 'Bolivarian Revolution'

By late afternoon on 11 April 2002, the organisers of a right-wing coup, having occupied the Miraflores presidential palace in Caracas, capital of Venezuela, were congratulating themselves on their success. Some 200,000 people had marched on the palace earlier that day. Opposition leaders had then entered the palace and demanded the President's resignation. He had since been arrested and taken to a military prison.

The plotters now toasting victory with champagne included the head of the country's main business organisation, the owner of a TV station, the leader of a collaborationist union federation, and several oil executives.

Venezuela was a major oil producer, the fifth largest in the world. Though Venezuelan oil had been nationalised in 1976, the state oil company, the PDVSA, worked in close cooperation with foreign multinationals. The oil interest was a tight nexus binding together Venezuelan state bureaucrats, foreign business executives, and a privileged layer of union bosses and skilled workers.

The people in the oil nexus, especially those at the top, grew fantastically rich. Caracas was a more expensive city than Chicago. It had more Cadillacs per head of population. But only 2 per cent of Venezuelans were in the nexus, and the gap between rich and poor was getting wider.

The Venezuelan government of Carlos Andres Perez had adopted neoliberalism at the height of the fashion in 1989. It had had the same effect as everywhere else. The share of national income going to the richest tenth of the population had jumped from 22 per cent to 33 per cent by the late 1990s. Meantime, the number living below the poverty line had soared from 36 per cent to 66 per cent.

To keep it so was the reason the Venezuelan bourgeoisie had organised a coup in April 2002. But the champagne was premature. Something was happening in the streets outside. It was slow but unmistakable: the approaches to the palace were filling with people again, only this time not the smart middle-class demonstrators of the afternoon, but shabby people in baseball caps and T-shirts.

They were taking time to arrive. They had a way to come. They were from the shanty-towns perched on crumbling hill-sides overlooking the posh business and residential districts of central Caracas.

Soon the streets were solid with people. They refused to move. And the presidential guard, loyal to the ousted President, refused to try and make them.

Within 48 hours a military helicopter had brought President Hugo Chavez back to the Miraflores. The coup was over. It had been crushed by a mass movement of the urban poor.

The people of Venezuela had been in open conflict with their rulers since 1989. Protests against price increases had swept the country in February that year. The Perez government had put troops on the streets and up to 2,000 had been killed. The protests had been suppressed, but not the mood of resistance in the slums.

Three years later, a radical army officer, Hugo Chavez, led an attempted coup against the Perez government. The coup failed and Chavez was imprisoned.

Chavez had made a successful career for himself in the military, but he had never identified with the cronyism and corruption of most Venezuelan army officers. He had not been born into the Venezuelan elite; he was of lower-middle-class origin, and his features implied native American descent.

In the 1970s Chavez joined with a small group of likeminded officers in setting up the Bolivarian Revolutionary Movement (MRB2000). They took as their model the nationalism and idealism of Simon Bolivar.

Venezuela's crisis deepened while Chavez was in jail. Perez was impeached for fraud and corruption. The PDVSA signed away Venezuelan oil revenues to foreign corporations. The banks collapsed and required a massive state bailout. An IMF loan was negotiated, with the usual austerity conditions. Poverty and unemployment kept rising.

Bourgeois politics were bankrupt. But so were those of the official Left. Hollowed out by collaborationism, it was unable to offer a credible alternative. One faction ended up supporting the presidential candidature of a right-wing beauty queen.

So Chavez, at the head of a newly formed 'Fifth Republic Movement' (MVR), stood for President and secured 56 per cent of the vote in the election of 1998.

The Venezuelan bourgeoisie, centred on the oil nexus, was stunned. It thereafter made a series of attempts to recover political power, using its control over wealth and the mass media to poison public opinion against the Chavez government, and, when this failed, organising strikes and mass demonstrations in an effort to overthrow it by direct action.

The government survived virtually all challenges. It won 71 per cent in a constitutional referendum in 1999, and 59 per cent in a second presidential election in 2000. It then pressed ahead with radical reforms to the economy and the political system, prompting two right-wing general strikes, that of April 2002, culminating in the failed coup attempt, and another from December 2002 to February 2003, which was frustrated by mass working-class activity to keep the economy moving.

The Right then secured a referendum on the presidency in 2004, which Chavez won with 59 per cent of the vote. He was re-elected in 2006 with 63 per cent, and again in 2013, shortly before his death, with 54 per cent. His only major electoral setback was narrow defeat in 2007 in a constitutional referendum over increased presidential powers.

The bourgeoisie's hostility to the Chavez presidency, and its enduring popularity among Venezuela's working people, are easy to understand. Chavez preached what he called 'socialism of the twenty-first century'. He was the most prominent of a group of Latin American leaders seeking to make a breach in the neoliberal global order. He seemed to express the aspirations of mass movements of resistance across the continent. He embodied the idea of a radical alternative in which the needs of the many would take precedence over the greed of a few.

The social gains of Chavismo were real. Oil wealth was recycled to fund schools, hospitals, food networks, community groups, and agrarian reform. Mass grassroots activity flourished in the slums. Around one in 20 of the entire population was enrolled in some form of popular, pro-government organisation.

But the Chavista movement was top-down, not bottom-up. It was a stage army to be wheeled out when necessary to support the government and its initiatives, not a popular movement taking control of society from below, formulating and advancing its own demands, and, increasingly, challenging the bourgeoisie's control over the main levers of power.

After the coup of April 2002, most of the conspirators were not prosecuted. In the two days that Chavez spent in prison, the Venezuelan masses had become an independent revolutionary force. But instead of fostering the development of an alternative 'popular power' (*poder popular*), Chavez demobilised his supporters and returned to the 'command' methods of measured top-down reform combined with compromise and reconciliation with the bourgeoisie.

Chavez did not suffer the fate of Allende in Chile: a military coup by an unbroken state machine. Nor that of the Sandinistas in Nicaragua: slow strangulation under siege by world imperialism. But nor did Chavez inflict a decisive and irreversible defeat on the Venezuela bourgeoisie and the foreign-backed oil nexus.

Because of this, 50 per cent of Venezuelans continue to live in poverty, and 20 per cent or more are without work. And such gains as have been made might in the future be reversed. For, as Rosa Luxemburg explained a century ago, the struggle for reforms is a Labour of Sisyphus, in which that which has been won by a strong movement in one generation can as easily be lost in the next.

The radical reforms of Hugo Chavez should be seen as what they are: gains to be defended against a hostile class enemy, and a platform for further advance towards a revolutionary transformation of society.

18

Capitalism's Greatest Crisis?
The Early Twenty-first Century

The global economy is mired in a long-term crisis of stagnation-slump. Humanity is capable of producing unprecedented amounts of wealth. Around half of this wealth is appropriated by banks, corporations, states, and the super-rich. The bulk of this vast surplus – created by the labour of working people – is no longer invested productively: it is used to fund a deeply dysfunctional system based on debt and speculation.

This parasitic 'neoliberalism' is part of a wider crisis of world capitalism. Inequality and injustice are tearing apart the social fabric. The international order is breaking down. War has engulfed entire societies and displaced tens of millions. Fascists, racists, and misogynists are gaining ground. Democracy is being hollowed out and civil liberties eroded. Global warming threatens the planet and the whole of humanity with climate catastrophe.

Mainstream commentators notice the problems, but either belittle the significance or ignore the connections. The single greatest insight of Marx – which he derived from the philosopher Georg Hegel – is that society is a complex and contradictory whole, that everything is connected with everything else, and that the particular can be understood only in relation to the general.

This has been the underlying assumption throughout this 'radical history'. Now we must apply this approach to our own epoch. This will involve some backtracking and repetition, because we cannot understand the compound crisis of the world capitalist system in the early twenty-first century without reference to the *longue durée* that has brought us to this point.

The Rise of the Corporations

Growth is hard-wired into the way capitalism works. You cannot have growth-free capitalism. The system is divided into competing corporations. These corporations invest money in order to make more money (profit), and they do this under the pressure of competition from rivals. Once part of this, you cannot opt out. Any corporation that did so would soon become uncompetitive. Still using yesterday's technology, paying wages above the going rate, reducing prices to help the poor, cutting back on carbon emissions: all very virtuous, but commercial suicide when your rivals are doing the opposite.

You need profit to fund executive salaries and bonuses, pay share-holders, and, most important, finance the next round of investment. High profit is the measure of corporate success and the essential foundation for further expansion. Low profit is the road to ruin.

So the system is driven by competition and profit. That means it has to grow. What you invest in one year you must recoup with profit in the next. Capital, in other words, is not a thing, but an economic process and a set of social relationships arising from that process. Nothing is static; everything is fluid and changeable; never in a state of being, always in a state of becoming.

Marx defined capital as 'the self-expansion of value', or, translated into a formula, as $M - C - M+$, where M is the money originally invested, C are the commodities (raw materials, machines, labour-power, etc.) used in the production process, and $M+$ is the money recouped *with a profit* when the output is sold.

This is the basic circuit of industrial capital. It is the same whether you are a mill-owner in mid-nineteenth-century Manchester or a sweatshop boss in early twenty-first century Dhaka. The point is that it is all about motion and expansion. It is capital turning itself into more capital, without any overall plan, higher purpose, or final endpoint.

This process is contradictory and crisis-ridden. History has shown again and again that the market is blind and anarchic, with the system in a perpetual cycle of boom, bubble, and bust. When Marx was writing, the infant capitalist system had already passed through a succession of 'business cycles'. There were financial 'crashes' in 1825, 1837, 1847, 1857, and 1866 – that is, roughly one every ten years. Each time, a raft of businesses would go bankrupt, debts would go unpaid, demand would plummet, the system would come to a juddering halt, and thousands would be jettisoned into unemployment and poverty.

This was the result of competition and the absence of an overall plan. During the preceding boom, as growth picked up and markets expanded, capitalists had invested in new production facilities. Competitive pressure meant that everyone did this at the same time. This increased demand, strengthened the boom, and encouraged even more frenzied investment.

Then, suddenly, with so much new output coming onto the market at the same time, there was a glut. Prices fell. Goods went unsold. Suppliers could not be paid. Workers had to be laid off. A reverse chain-reaction of bankruptcies, unemployment, and collapsing demand now turned boom to bust.

Yet, in the early days of capitalism, the system managed to bounce back each time. What happened was this. The weaker firms, with higher costs and lower margins, would be the first to go bust. They were usually smaller: having less capital to invest in labour-saving technology and fewer opportunities to realise 'economies of scale', small firms tended to be less competitive.

When these firms went to the wall, their rivals benefitted from fire-sales of assets at knock-down prices and from the chance to grab a larger slice of the market. So the bigger firms tended to get bigger still. And the bigger they got, the more capital they had to invest in new technology to cut costs and expand output – giving them an ever greater advantage over the small fry in the next round of capital accumulation.

So 'free-market' capitalism was not just anarchic – a system of blind competition, of boom and bust. It was also highly predatory: the market was a pool of sharks trying to eat each other. The process was at an early stage, but Marx could see the long-term trend. He wrote of 'the concentration and centralisation of capital', where production becomes 'concentrated' in large factories, ownership 'centralised' in large corporations. This, clearly, was where things were headed. Competition guaranteed it. Competition favoured the strong, especially in a crash, when margins had to be cut and losses absorbed.

Small changes accumulate over time until they reach a tipping-point and give rise to a sudden sharp shift. The concentration and centralisation of capital has this character: it is a cumulative process that periodically gives rise to abrupt changes in the character of the system. We can identify five main phases in the long-term development of capitalism.

Under *mercantile capitalism* (c. 1450–1800), most wealth was produced by pre-capitalist classes, but merchant capitalists accumulated profit by acting as middlemen, whether in national markets, overseas trade, or through the putting-out system, where they organised and marketed the output of independent artisans.

Under *industrial capitalism* (c. 1800–75), new forms of factory-based production based on steam power and labour-saving machines developed, resulting in a mass of small and medium-sized firms competing in national and colonial markets.

Under *imperial capitalism* (c. 1875–1935), the most advanced sectors of the economy were dominated by giant monopoly firms organised in cartels, financed by banks, and expanding on the basis of state contracts, international sales, and the export of capital to overseas colonies and dependencies.

Under *state-managed capitalism* (c. 1935–75), the state took the initiative in economic affairs, in extreme cases (like Stalinist Russia) transforming itself into a single national-capitalist enterprise, in others (like Cold War America) acting as a major organiser, regulator, and funder of industrial development within the territory of the nation-state.

Each of these phases was characterised by a progressively greater degree of concentration and centralisation of capital. In the 1700s, for example, virtually all production took place on farms and in workshops; such factories as existed – like the arms factories established by some absolute monarchs – were quite atypical.

By the mid-nineteenth century, however, when Britain had become 'the workshop of the world', there were more than a hundred cotton mills in Manchester, the largest employing 2,000 people, most a good few hundred or so. By the time of the First World War on the other hand, the largest workplaces were emoploying tens of thousands – 75,000 at London's Woolwich Arsenal, 70,000 at Essen's Krupp complex, 40,000 at Petrograd's Putilov works.

Fast-forward to the middle of the twentieth century and we find that the United States was producing fully half the world's manufactured goods. The share in this output of the top 100 US corporations increased from 44 per cent in 1929 to 58 per cent in 1964. This was the norm in the developed world: the share in British output of the top 100 UK manufacturing firms, for instance, increased from 21 per cent in 1949 to 46 per cent in 1970.

The long-term process of concentration and centralisation of capital is decisive: it is this that determines the essential character of the system in each of its successive phases; this that underlies such seismic crises as the Long Depression of 1873–96, the Great Depression of 1929–39, and the Long Recession of 1973–92.

State-managed capitalism entered crisis in the 1970s, the growing size of the multinationals during the Great Boom having created an economic power largely beyond the control of national governments. Cutting-edge enterprise in key industries like armaments, cars, pharmaceuticals, and electronics depended increasingly on access to finance, technology, raw materials, production facilities, and markets on a global scale. The multinationals came to dwarf in size most national economies. Globalised operations enabled them to avoid regulation, dodge taxes, evade capital controls, and secure subsidies and other concessions. To gain access to the technology, capital, and markets controlled by the corporations, nation-states were forced to offer increasingly generous terms to private business.

Competitive capital accumulation was thus breaking through the boundaries of national economies and making redundant the mechanisms of the previous phase of capitalist development. By the mid-1970s, not only was the Great Boom over, but the state-managed 'Keynesian' capitalism that had made it possible was in retreat. What emerged to replace it was *neoliberal capitalism* (c. 1975–present) – a system of global financialised monopoly-capitalism – a system more parasitic, dysfunctional, crisis-ridden, and destructive of human welfare than ever before.

Permanent Stagnation

A few years back, the world's biggest corporation was Walmart stores. With annual revenues approaching half a trillion dollars, it was bigger than Greece; in fact, had it been a country, Walmart would have ranked 25th largest in the world, ahead of 157 smaller countries.

Among the other giants in the top 25 global corporations were oil majors like Exxon Mobil and Chevron, banks like Bank of America and JPMorgan Chase, motor manufacturers like Ford and GM, electronics firms like General Electric and IBM, and even the private health conglomerate UnitedHealth Group. All these had annual revenues above those of Iraq (about $80 billion).

We now have a system where a handful of giant firms dominate the global market in everything from supermarkets to oil to cars to computers to private health insurance. This is what, for more than a century, radicals have called 'monopoly capitalism'. This phrase captures its essential character: it does not mean one corporation runs everything; it means a handful do so, and because they are few, they can work together to manage the market.

Where there are lots of small and medium firms operating, the competition is pretty ruthless. Capitalists hate this: it means risk and the possibility of bankruptcy. They crave the certainties of a managed market with guaranteed sales and stable prices. This is what monopoly makes possible. It transforms the big firms from 'price-takers' into 'price-makers'.

This is how the American Marxist economists Paul Baran and Paul Sweezy, writing in the 1960s, described the process:

> This objective [avoiding uncertainty and risk] is achieved by the simple expedient of banning price-cutting as a legitimate weapon of economic warfare. Naturally this has not happened all at once or as a conscious decision. Like other powerful taboos, that against price-cutting has grown up gradually out of long and often bitter experience, and it derives its strength from the fact that it serves the interests of powerful forces in society. As long as it is accepted and observed, the dangerous uncertainties are removed from the rationalised pursuit of maximum profits.

The temptation to break ranks, cut prices, and grab increased market share is always there. But a price war is in no one's interest. In the nineteenth century, with lots of small and medium firms competing, it was unavoidable and prices often went down. Nowadays, they often go up, but rarely down – because monopoly means managed prices across an industry and increased profits for the corporations.

Corporate price-making is not the only thing setting monopoly capitalism apart from market capitalism. The corporations do not just make the price. They also make the 'want'.

Neoclassical economics gets this hopelessly wrong. It makes no distinction between 'needs' and 'wants', and pretends that what corporations are doing is simply responding to consumer 'demand'. There is no suggestion in the orthodox textbooks that the corporations actively create 'demand' through branding, packaging, advertising, redesigns, upgrades, and so on. No suggestion that they invest vast sums trying to seduce and bamboozle consumers into buying stuff they do not need. Yet the scale of what Baran and Sweezy called 'the sales effort' is hard to miss, hard to exaggerate. On one estimate, *one in six* American workers is employed in 'sales'.

Intrinsic to this is monumental waste. Stuff is designed to fall to bits so it has to be replaced ('built-in obsolescence'). Stuff is denigrated as out-of-date and out-of-fashion within a year, and consumers are bombarded with messages about the need to buy the latest stuff if they want to be cool, sexy, classy, sophisticated. Needs are not the same as wants. Needs are intrinsic to the human condition. Wants can be conjured and manipulated by corporate capital to stoke up consumption.

The ideology is 'free-market' competition; the reality is monopoly capitalism, managed markets, rip-off prices, artificial wants, and colossal waste. We are told that consumer choice shapes the market, that 'supply and demand' determines prices. The truth is that monopoly corporations create and control the market.

Now we come to the crunch. If prices keep going up, the corporations are making profit twice over, once by exploiting their own workers, second time by overcharging consumers. This means ever more profit in the hands of the corporations. At the same time, workers and consumers are getting squeezed, reducing overall demand, making it harder to find a market for everything produced.

This is one of the central contradictions of capitalism. Walmart pays rock-bottom wages to its two million workers, but wants high wages everywhere else so consumers have lots to spend in its stores. Every capitalist is the same. And the bigger the slice taken by profit overall, the less there is for wages overall, and the wider the gap between what is produced and what can be sold.

Some Marxists talk about 'over-accumulation' – too much capital swilling around. Others talk about 'under-consumption' – the total paid out in wages falling short of what is needed to consume the output. In fact, these are simply two sides of the same coin. And the problem gets much worse under monopoly capitalism because the corporations are raking in super-profits by managing the market.

That is one issue. Here is another. Reduced competition means reduced incentive to invest in new production. To build a factory with state-of-the-art robots to compete on a global scale is a massive, long-term, high-risk investment. Capitalists are risk-averse, especially the corporate bureaucracies that run today's global giants; and the managed markets of monopoly capitalism make it much easier to avoid risk.

So corporations today are more likely to invest in government bonds or company shares, buy up privatised state assets, put money into real estate, trade in debt, or speculate on rising asset values. Which does it choose: investment in production, that is, in the real economy, or investment in the money markets, in speculation?

We know the answer because we can see how the system as a whole is operating. There has been a massive shift during the neoliberal era from relatively risky long-term productive investment into relatively safe short-term financial speculation. That shift has been fast-geared by the exceptional mobility of money achieved by modern IT systems. Railways, steel mills, and supermarket chains represent expensive, fixed, immobile capital. They mean corporations tying up capital in long-term ventures they cannot exit without massive losses. Financial investments, on the other hand, are click-button fixes for capital in search of quick and easy profit.

So the ageing system is lumbered with massive problems. Managed markets mean super-profits and risk-avoidance. This intensifies the inherent tendency towards both 'over-accumulation' of capital and 'under-consumption' of workers/consumers.

The growth rate slumps. In the US, it was 5.9 per cent during the Second World War, 4.4 per cent during the Cold War, 3.1 per cent in the in the 1980s and 1990s, and has been around 2.6 per cent in the years since. This is a direct consequence of the concentration and centralisation of capital – the economic process analysed by Marx 150 years ago.

This has to be the starting-point for any serious analysis of the current economic crisis. First and foremost, it is a crisis of *monopoly capitalism* and its inherent long-term tendency towards *permanent stagnation*.

Permanent Debt

Neoliberalism was a response to the problem of low profits and sluggish growth as the global system stalled in the 1970s. It involved a frontal assault on unions, wages, and the welfare state. The aim was to redistribute wealth from labour to capital. Higher profit, argued Thatcher, Reagan, and their successors, would encourage enterprise, investment, and growth. But when neoliberal governments imposed programmes of cuts and sell-offs, the main beneficiaries were the global mega-corporations of neoliberal capitalism.

The concentration and centralisation of capital has now developed to a point that the dominant corporate form has burst its national shell and operates as a multinational (or 'de-nationalised') firm within a worldwide market. Finance, investment, and trade, in the past firmly anchored within individual nation-states, have become globalised. The direct economic role of the state has been reduced. Nationalised industries have been privatised. The ability of the state to regulate private capital has been undermined. The state has become less a manager of capital and more its client, bidding for corporate favour in competition with other states.

Globalisation is the underlying reason for the hollowing out of parliamentary government, the erosion of democratic choice, and the development of technocratic and managerial forms of politics – the core reason for 'the democratic deficit'. But while the economic management and welfare functions of the state have declined, its role as a market for capital and a conduit for the transfer of surplus from workers to capitalists has increased. Arms contracts, infrastructure projects, government borrowing, privatisation of public assets, and bank bailouts are among the obvious examples. All of these amount to transfers of public wealth to the private sector. The political elite are widely – and rightly – reviled because they are in the pocket of corporate capital.

But neoliberalism has aggravated two of the central contradictions of the capitalist system – the twin problems of 'over-accumulation' and 'under-consumption'.

These together can be imagined like a pair of scissors. During the Great Boom, the scissors narrowed, with high levels of productive investment matched by rising levels of personal consumption. In the neoliberal era, the scissors have opened. Social inequality, falling until the 1970s, has since increased dramatically. Surplus capital has accumulated at one pole, while consumer demand has fallen at the other. This has exacerbated an existing, more deep-rooted crisis of over-accumulation. Let us remind ourselves of what we said before about monopoly capitalism's long-term tendency to stagnation.

This, to repeat, is for three main reasons. First, because capitalists drive down wages in their own workplaces. Second, because monopoly corporations manage the market and jack up prices. Third, because big capital is risk-averse and wary of large-scale productive investment.

So the modern corporation is awash with surplus capital. Some of this gets invested in secondary activities like marketing. Reduced price competition need not mean reduced competition *per se* – it can, and does, mean a huge expansion of advertising, branding, packaging, redesign, and so on, in an effort to expand market share without the risks inherent in price competition.

But the sales effort does not absorb enough. So a lot gets redirected into mergers and acquisitions, asset stripping, privatisation, financial speculation, and so on. There is a vast expansion of the 'financial services industry' – and an explosion of diverse 'financial products' – because there is so much surplus capital looking for an easy, quick, and safe way to make profit.

This is *financialisation*. It is not just to do with banks. Industrial corporations are also heavily involved in all sorts of financial trading. The whole system has made a shift from production (of real goods and services) to speculation (in financial assets).

Financialisation is grounded in debt. Essentially what are being traded are claims on resources expressed in monetary form – bonds, shares, mortgages, derivatives, currencies, etc. Just as industrial capital is grounded in personal consumption of goods and services, financial capital is grounded in personal debt – the bulk of it, when you trace it to source, real-estate debt.

Financialisation works for the system in two ways: it sustains demand in the form of debt-funded expenditure; and it is an alternative source of profit because debt is a tradable commodity like any other, and it can therefore soak up the rising mass of surplus capital.

Financialisation has been central to the neoliberal counter-revolution. Governments have been promoting market deregulation, low interest rates, financial innovation, and rising corporate and household debt for a generation. The economy has been flooded with electronic loan-money. This process is self-feeding: if capital flows into speculation rather than production, asset prices rise faster than profits and wages in the real economy; this means yet more capital flows into property holdings instead of productive investment.

Which way investment goes depends upon – to use a technical term – the 'marginal efficiency of capital': that is, where you get the best return. Under neoliberal capitalism, nine times out of ten, it is safer, quicker, and more profitable to invest in finance.

Although Marx defined the dynamic of capitalism in his own day as 'the self-expansion of value', or $M - C - M+$, there is another way of making money. It is through 'the self-expansion of money', or $M - (M) - M+$, where M is the money originally invested, (M) is a monetary asset, and M+ is the original money recouped *with a profit* when the asset delivers a return (interest on debt) or is sold on at a higher price (due to rising asset value).

Note that nothing is being produced. This is not 'self-expansion of value', because there is no new value being created. From the point of view of society as a whole, it is pointless. The financial circuit of capital is simply a mechanism whereby the rich reroute wealth that has already been created – or claims on wealth yet to be created – from everyone else to themselves.

The financial circuit of capital – like the industrial circuit – is inherently expansionary. The money supply – the chain of debts expressed in the form of electronic numbers in bank computers – must endlessly increase: otherwise there can be no profit. So if industrial capitalism is the self-expansion of value, financialised capitalism is the self-expansion of debt/money. The system, once it is dependent on debt/money, must create ever more of it.

The scale of the debt economy is staggering. By the end of the last century, 95 per cent of all currency trading was speculative – that is, it was not to facilitate the exchange of real goods, but to make money on changing relative monetary values. Before the crash of 2008, at the peak of the bubble, the trade in derivatives – debt-based financial assets – was estimated to have had a global value of \$500 trillion, equal to ten times global GDP. The value of debt and speculation in Britain is estimated to run at around five times the value of the real economy. Across the EU, bank assets are estimated to be worth about 350 per cent of total European GDP.

Most of the money-market operations represented are funded by 'leveraged' finance. This means banks borrowing from banks in order to speculate – creating countless chains of electronic money ('fictitious capital') threaded across the global financial system in networks of impenetrable complexity.

At the base of this great edifice of debt are consumers. Workers in many parts of the developed world have become heavily indebted because of stagnant incomes, easy credit, and rising house prices. And workers buying on tick then become the foundation of a vast inverted pyramid of financial 'derivatives', unsecured debts, and inflated asset values. Average US household debt more than doubled between the late 1970s and 2006. US credit card debt alone in 2009 was estimated to be worth $850 billion. Total debt grew from about 1.5 times US national output in the early 1980s to nearly 3.5 in 2007. The financial sector's share of US profits increased from about 15 per cent in the early 1950s to almost 50 per cent in 2001.

Given a fall in wages relative to profits, consumer debt has helped maintain aggregate demand. Instead of paying for goods and services with wages already received, working people are paying for stuff by taking out loans secured against future earnings.

Capital cannot stand still – it is a *process* of accumulation. The rising surpluses swirling around inside the system have to be reinvested in order to grow further. Investing in debt offers easy, fast-flow, high-value returns.

Financial profit is also hard to detect. The real economy can be measured and taxed. Finance – wealth in the form of electronic numbers – can be secreted away in offshore tax-havens.

Debt is the very basis of modern capitalism. The system is a debt junkie with a habit it cannot kick without collapsing. The drug is the only thing sustaining its zombie-like existence. The lords of capital have become as parasitic, as devoid of social function, as the pharaohs.

Even in its own terms, the system is deeply dysfunctional. The permanent debt economy is a vast edifice of paper assets without real substance. It was this contradiction – between the inflated asset values of finance capital and the actual wealth of society – that underlay the global banking crash of 2008.

The 2008 Crash: From Bubble to Black Hole

'I have found a flaw. I don't know how significant or permanent it is. But I have been very distressed by that fact.' That is how a leading architect of neoliberal capitalism – Alan Greenspan, former Chairman of the Federal Reserve, the US central bank – described the onset of the global economic disaster of 2008.

Perhaps the most explosive of Greenspan's contributions to the biggest financial bubble ever seen was to destroy the Glass-Steagall Act of 1933, by which banks were prevented from speculating with their customers' savings. *Newsnight* economist Paul Mason put the consequences of this and the whole 'bonfire of regulations' more strongly than Greenspan: it had resulted in 'the greatest man-made economic catastrophe in human history'.

In September 2007, the so-called 'credit crunch' turned critical when the British building society Northern Rock went bust. Exactly a year later, the giant US investment bank Lehman Brothers announced astronomical losses of $3.9 billion and declared itself bankrupt. On 18 September, fearing a chain reaction of bank failures, Ben Bernanke, successor to Greenspan at the Federal Reserve, and Henry Paulson, US finance minister, announced that 'We are headed for the worst financial crisis in the nation's history. We're talking about a matter of days.'

To prevent this, world rulers ripped up their free-market textbooks and carried out a series of monster nationalisations and bailouts. Almost immediately, a global total of around $2 trillion of state funding was injected into the banks, two-thirds in direct spending, one-third in the form of guarantees. Since then, trillions more have been handed over. One estimate of US government spending on bailouts between 2008 and 2012 puts the total at $30 trillion.

The pumping of unprecedented amounts of state capital into private banks stabilised the global financial system. It covered immediate losses, and, more importantly, restored 'confidence' by demonstrating to finance capitalists that the state would not allow major banks to fail. Profits remained private, but losses were a public matter. The speculators would continue to sweep up the winning chips, but tax-payers would cover the bad bets.

But this has not solved the crisis; it has merely reconfigured it. The crash, unprecedented in scale, has shrunk the financial reserves of states, corporations, and households, and pitched the world economy into slump. The state funds shovelled into the banks have simply disappeared into a black hole of bad debt. Since 2008, moreover, the rich have been getting richer even faster than before. The casino economy is again in full swing. The next bubble is inflating fast and the world hovers on the brink of another crash.

Financial assets are essentially loans of money in return for titles to ownership. They can be corporate shares, government bonds, insurance policies, currency holdings, bundles of mortgages, advance purchases of commodities, and many other things. During the neoliberal era, many of these assets became absurdly overvalued. They became the expanding particles in a bubble of speculation.

The 'normal' return on capital is a share in the profits of the real economy. A 'speculative' return arises when the link between the price of paper assets and the value of actual commodities has broken down. Price rises become self-sustaining and stratospheric in a frenzy of 'get-rich-quick' buying and selling. This is unsustainable, and when the crash comes and prices collapse, the bubble of inflated values morphs into a black hole of bad debt.

At the height of the speculative frenzy in the early 2000s, any madcap scheme was good to go. Banks started giving mortgages to people who could not afford to repay them. The value of this 'subprime' lending rose 230 per cent between 2000 and 2007. It did not matter that the mortgagees were too poor to pay the money back. The houses they bought were expected to rise in price, so when the buyers defaulted, the bank could turf them out, sell the property, and pocket the profit.

But it was more complicated than that. Subprime loans were repackaged with better-quality loans, and these 'financial derivatives' were sold on. The idea of derivatives was to spread the risk. They were considered a clever invention of the 'financial services industry'. What they actually did was to infect the entire banking system with bad debt.

It was in the subprime mortgage market that the panic began. A slowdown in consumer demand and an easing of house prices suddenly made subprime loans look like bad debts. The subprime panic quickly turned into a contagion sweeping across global financial markets on fears about the degree to which the banking system as a whole was infected by 'toxic' derivatives. The entire world banking system was suddenly revealed as a vast edifice of speculation, inflated values, and paper assets.

Nothing has changed since 2008. The trillions of dollars of taxpayers' money funnelled into private banks have been used to cover bad debts and fund a new round of speculation. That is why the fortunes of the global super-rich have exploded over the last eight years. That is why all forms of debt – household, corporate, public – continue to accumulate to unsustainable levels. Public money, instead of being used to fund public investment in homes, hospitals, schools, transport, and a green transition, is wasted in propping up a broken system of private debt, speculation, and greed. Meantime, public services are degraded by draconian programmes of cuts and sell-offs, the value of workers' wages falls by 15 per cent, and the poor are driven into destitution by austerity unknown since the 1930s.

The madness of the post-2008 austerity regimes was demonstrated to anyone who cared to heed the lesson by the history of relations between the Troika (the European Union, the European Central Bank, and the International Monetary Fund) and the Syriza government of Greece during the first six months of 2015. Here was a supreme object lesson in the moral bankruptcy of the world's political and corporate elite in the neoliberal era.

The Syriza government had a democratic mandate to negotiate a rescheduling of the state's debt so that the Greek economy could recover and the resources to pay those debts be generated. The Troika refused, insisting upon levels of debt repayment everyone knew to be unsustainable, thereby ensuring that Greece remained trapped in an economic death-spiral. The Greek people were to be pushed deeper into poverty to prop up French and German banks and ring-fence the fortunes of the global super-rich. The whole process is described in chilling detail by Yanis Varoufakis, the Syriza Finance Minister throughout the 162-day crisis, in a book that the entire world should read: *Adults in the Room: My Battle With Europe's Deep Establishment* (2017).

The Troika was revealed as a gigantic financial engine for redistributing wealth from labour to capital, from welfare to profit, from working people and the poor to the banks and the rich. It was shown to be waging a class war on behalf of finance capital against the ordinary people of Europe.

The cuts are feeding the depression. Years of austerity budgets have deflated demand and increased unemployment across the continent. Financialisation, privatisation, and austerity are compulsory in EU states. Sanctions are imposed on states that fail to meet stringent targets for 'balancing budgets' and 'cutting debts'. Annual budget deficits are restricted to 0.5 per cent of GDP, and there must be annual 5 per cent cuts in any excess national debt above an agreed maximum of 60 per cent of GDP. In the context of a deepening slump, this is a recipe for massive deflation and economic prostration.

Austerity ruins lives and wrecks economies. As government spending falls, markets shrink, firms sell less, workers are laid off, and demand is deflated. A spiral of decline sets in. This is the mechanism that helped drive stagnation in the 1930s. Our rulers are the architects of a new great depression.

As the economy tanks under the hammer blows of austerity-driven deflation, the debt burden grows. This happens in three ways. First, more debts go bad as more firms and households go bankrupt. Second, new debts become necessary to roll over old debt, cover further losses, and bridge yawning deficits. Third, as the economy shrinks, the relative weight of the existing debt burden rises.

The fate of Greece proves this. At the end of 2009, Greece had a debt-to-GDP ratio of around 130 per cent. After nearly two years of bailouts and austerity, it had a debt-to-GDP ratio of about 190 per cent. Why had this happened? Because the Greek economy had suffered an austerity-induced collapse of around 20 per cent of GDP. 'No purpose was ever served', wrote Simon Jenkins in *The Guardian*, 'by locking Mr Dorrit in the Marshalsea Prison and thus stopping him from earning the means of repayment ... It makes no sense to drive an economy into recession where it stops people from working and thus paying more taxes.'

Greece is not alone. Ireland was hit hard by the onset of the financial crash in 2008. It was then hammered by a succession of austerity budgets, contracting by 8.5 per cent in 2009 and 14 per cent in 2010. Greece and Ireland, along with Portugal, Spain, and Italy, represent the extreme end of a spectrum. But Europe as a whole is sinking deeper into slump, with 10 per cent average unemployment across the continent, rising to 25 per cent in Greece and Spain. Millions more are condemned to low-paid, part-time, casual jobs because there is nothing else (massive levels of hidden under-employment are a particular feature of the current crisis). The future for Europe's young people is especially bleak: overall, one in four of those seeking work cannot find a job, rising to one in three in Ireland, Portugal, and Italy, and one in two in Greece and Spain. The cull of the 'Grim Reaper' is one measure of the social crisis: the suicide rate increased by 40 per cent in Greece in one year.

The banking crash was not a natural catastrophe: it was a human-made disaster caused by speculation and greed in a casino economy based on neoliberal ideology. The depression we have now entered is not a natural catastrophe: it is a direct consequence of government-imposed austerity. As one leading mainstream economist, former Bank of England Monetary Policy Committee member David Blanchflower, explained:

> Lesson one in a deep recession is you don't cut public spending until you are into the boom phase. Keynes taught us that. The consequence of cutting too soon is to drive the economy into a depression. That means rapidly rising unemployment, social disorder, rising poverty, falling living-standards, and even soup kitchens.

The problem for the capitalist class is that the Keynesian strategy is itself hazardous. State debt is a commodity that must be sold on financial markets like any other. If record government deficits are ratcheted up to fund public spending, the risk of default rises, loans become more expensive, and at some point 'confidence' will evaporate and state debt become unsaleable. State bankruptcy will then herald the very economic meltdown and social revolt that Blanchflower predicts under the austerity regime. Greece is the clearest embodiment of this dilemma.

The neoliberal elite is therefore trapped by the contradictions of the system on which its wealth depends. The only way out of a slump is to invest in new growth. But this cannot be done within the constraints imposed by private ownership of finance capital.

This is the heart of the matter. The wealth of the rich is inseparable from the dominance of the banks. As Larry Elliott, also writing in *The Guardian*, put it:

Seen in its simplest terms, the story of political economy over the last four decades is a class war between capital and labour, which capital has won hands-down. The battlefield is littered with evidence of labour's defeat: nugatory pay awards, precarious work, the collapse of collective bargaining, and cuts in public spending. And to the victors have gone the spoils: higher profits and dividends; lower personal tax rates; a higher share of national income.

To this class war – capitalism's inner social essence – we now turn.

The Rich and the Rest

We live in a class society ruled by the 1 per cent. The banks and the corporations are run by a small class of super-rich. These in turn are served by a layer of comfortable middle-class administrators, managers, and professionals. Everyone else, around 80 per cent, belongs to the working class.

A lot of nonsense is spoken about class. It is not in the interests of our rulers that we should understand it. They are content that people imagine it has something to do with your accent and whether you wear overalls at work. They rather welcome the petty snobbery of people who think themselves 'better' than others because they work in a high-rise office and can afford the latest electronic gadget.

But class is not a sociological identity parade. It is an economic process and a social relationship. The 80 per cent – factory workers, nurses, sales assistants, teachers, train drivers, call-centre workers, local government officers, electricians, lecturers, care workers, junior civil servants, hospital porters, computer programmers, fast-food workers, and so many more – all are part of one class. They all engage in collective labour to create wealth – an economic process. They are all exploited, both as workers and consumers, by the 1 per cent, who live off the surplus created by their labour – a social relationship.

Let us take three examples: housing, health, and higher education in modern Britain. In the 1970s, local authorities built almost half of all new homes, more than 40 per cent of the population was securely housed in cheap public accommodation, and maintenance was carried out by directly employed council staff. Today, local authorities build just 1.25 per cent of all new homes, the proportion of people living in public homes has fallen to 7 per cent, and almost all house-building, refurbishment, and maintenance has been contracted out to private firms. This massive programme of privatisation – of all aspects of housing provision – has led to a chronic shortage of affordable homes, crippling mortgages, skyrocketing rents, and a crisis of homelessness. It has also meant billions in profit to building firms, private landlords, and the banks.

Britain's National Health Service used to be regarded as one of the most cost-efficient, effective, and equal healthcare systems in the world. That is because it was a planned, coordinated, publicly run system based on the principle that healthcare should be freely available to all when and where needed. Corporate capital hankered after a share of the £125 billion a year health budget, and in the 1990s the political elite began the deliberate run-down and privatisation of the service. The 'outsourcing' to private contractors of everything from hospital building to routine treatments means rising costs, declining service, and failing care. All the gain – in the form of huge revenue streams from the public purse – is to private health conglomerates.

The British government used to pay the fees of all British university students. This began to change in the late 1990s, and most students in England now pay £9,250 a year, effectively the full cost of their education. The majority are forced to take out loans to cover both fees and maintenance. This debt is now interest-bearing and is set to be privatised. The effect is to create yet another revenue stream for private capital.

These are examples of the way in which the exploitation of working people has changed under the permanent debt economy. There has been a relative shift from exploitation 'at the point of production' (of workers in the workplaces) to exploitation 'at the point of consumption' (in the form of rents, rip-off prices, mortgage debt, public-service charges, student debt, card debt, Wonga debt, and so on). The reason these things are happening is very simple: it makes the rich richer. Financialised capitalism, backed by state power, is siphoning wealth from the productive 80 per cent to the parasitic 1 per cent. The life-blood of society is being leached away by the pointless vampire-like existence of the super-rich.

The rate of exploitation is rising on an international scale. Oxfam has shown that the richest eight people in the world – the occupants of a golf buggy – now control as much wealth as the poorest 50 per cent of humanity (3.5 billion people). The richest 1 per cent – the world's ruling class as a whole – control more wealth than the remaining 99 per cent.

Social inequality has increased sharply throughout the neoliberal era. In 1990, in Britain, the average chief executive earned 25 times the pay of the average worker. By 2008, this had risen to 150 times as much. During the same period, the number of people worth at least £5 million doubled, and the number of billionaires tripled.

Since the 2008 crash, across the world, the siphoning of wealth to the top has accelerated. In 2010, the richest 388 people owned the same as the poorest 50 per cent. Four years later, just 85 people had this much wealth. Two years after that, it was 62 people. Now it is down to those eight people in the golf buggy.

Most of the wealth of the mega-corporations and the super-rich is held in tax havens. Oxfam reckons the global rich have $7.6 trillion stashed out of reach of government taxation. Take the example of Africa, the world's poorest continent. The charity estimates that 30 per cent of Africa's financial wealth is held offshore. The annual tax loss is estimated at $14 billion – enough to save the lives of 4 million children if spent on healthcare, or to provide a teacher for every child on the continent if spent on schools.

These grotesque and growing inequalities reflect the rising rate of exploitation of workers and consumers across the global system. Surplus appropriation through exploitation at work ('the point of production') has increased massively. Workforces have been broken up and de-unionised by privatisation, outsourcing, and casualisation. Unemployment has eroded job security and allowed bosses to drive down wages, impose zero-hours contracts, and get away with unpaid internships. Bullying and stress are workplace norms.

The 'reserve army of labour' – the mass of unemployed, semi-employed, and casually (or 'precariously') employed – has expanded. In the metropolitan economies, this has been achieved by introducing market mechanisms, privatising public services, fragmenting large unionised workforces, and unpicking the welfare 'safety-nets' characteristic of state-managed capitalism. Globally, it has been achieved by the internationalisation of capital, the growth of new centres of capital accumulation, and the increased opportunities for capitalists to relocate production to low-wage economies. Playing off one group of workers against another in a global 'race to the bottom' has become central to the operation of the global system.

Increasing exploitation at work has been supplemented by an expansion of surplus appropriation at 'the point of consumption' (or 'reproduction'). Three primary mechanisms are at work: monopoly pricing, where large corporations price commodities above their real value; interest, where banks and other financial institutions make profit out of personal debt; and state taxation, where taxes paid by ordinary people are recycled as payments, grants, and bailouts to private business.

This exploitation at the point of consumption forms the base of that vast inverted pyramid of 'financialised' capital accumulation – the permanent debt economy – characterised by stagnation-slump, social decay, grotesque greed, and growing inequality.

This system cannot be reformed: financialisation, privatisation, corporate power, enrichment for the few, austerity for the many, these are in the DNA of neoliberal capitalism. To end the slump, it is necessary to cancel the debt, take over the banks, tax the rich, and invest for jobs, services, and a green transition. To do that, it is necessary to overthrow the rule of finance capital and put the economy under democratic control. As in the 1930s – when the choice was barbarism or socialism – politics will be decisive.

Nor are stagnation-slump and social decay the only problems of the crisis-ridden global order. Imperialism and militarism threaten us with world war.

Imperialism, War, and the Shadow of the Bomb

Since the War on Terror began in 2001, the great powers have expended $1.3 trillion on waging it. They have killed about a million people and displaced about five million. They have wrecked economies, destroyed societies, and created a swathe of instability from Central Asia to West Africa. Broken states and proxy wars now rage across the region. A record 33 million people have been forced to flee their homes.

The tectonic plates of global power are shifting. This is making the world more violent. In 1945 the US accounted for more than 50 per cent of total world output. This share has declined to barely 20 per cent today. On the other hand, the US still accounts for more than a third of global arms expenditure – three times that of China, eight times that of Russia, 40 times that of Iran, and 200 times that of Iraq. It is this contradictory pairing – relative economic decline and absolute military superiority – that explains US warmongering today. Military power is making up for lack of economic clout. Control over energy supplies and competition with China and Russia are the two main strategic priorities.

Energy supplies are finite. Capital accumulation is exponential. As new capitalist economies grow – China, India, Brazil, Indonesia, Mexico, Turkey, Iran, Nigeria – US military power is deployed to secure privileged control over energy-rich regions of the globe. Above all, everyone needs oil – it is fuel, light, and heat. This is the main reason the Middle East is a battleground: it has about 70 per cent of known oil reserves. To ensure effective control of these, consistent US policy has been to back pro-Western clients, make war on anti-Western regimes, and keep the Middle East divided.

The Iraq War was an oil war. Afghanistan was also an oil war. Afghanistan is one of the poorest countries on earth. But it is a military platform from which power can be projected in an energy-rich region – especially towards the Caspian Basin, with up to 30 billion barrels of oil and 30 per cent of the world's gas reserves.

Imperial violence is about political and economic dominance over rivals. In the case of the US, that means China and Russia. China is a new capitalist superpower with global reach. It is already consuming 7 per cent of the world's oil, 31 per cent of its coal, and 27 per cent of its steel. Desperate for resources to feed their fast-growing economy, China's leaders are moving into the Middle East, Africa, and South America, signing a succession of deals for loans (China is awash with surplus capital) in return for long-term access to supplies of oil, gas, and minerals. Russia, with a vast territory rich in natural resources, massive energy reserves, and the second biggest nuclear arsenal in the world, is the other major rival. Flashpoints are the Caspian Basin, the Middle East, and the Ukraine.

The US War on Terror is really a series of imperialist wars. Its aim is to protect the interests of the giant corporations that dominate the US economy. That means control over energy supplies, raw materials, production facilities, and mass markets. These interests can be threatened by rival superpowers (like China and Russia), regional powers (like Iran and Syria), popular movements (like Hamas in

Palestine), or terrorist insurgencies (like ISIS in Syria and Iraq). Military power is projected across the world to make it safe for US power and profit.

But it does not make it safe for the rest of us: it makes it more unstable and deadly. Because weapons proliferate and get more sophisticated, wars become ever more destructive. Capitalism makes possible industrialised 'total wars' of mass production and attrition. As it develops, the system's productive capacity rises, and so does its output of armaments.

The First World War lasted four years and killed 20 million people. The Second World War last six years and killed 60 million. Killing-power has increased further since then. The tonnage of munitions expended in war by the US per man-year of combat rose from one ton in the Second World War, to eight tons in the Korean War (1950–53), to 26 tons in the Vietnam War (1965–75). The US then dropped more munitions on Iraq during its six-week aerial bombing campaign in early 1991 than were dropped on Germany during the whole of the Second World War.

The international order is unravelling, global tensions are rising, the world is rearming, and war is tearing societies apart. Our rulers spend $1.7 trillion on armaments every year. This is a world gone mad. Every dollar of this is waste. Every dollar of this makes violence more likely.

A world war today would probably be the most cataclysmic event in human history. A nuclear missile exchange between major powers could kill tens of millions, even hundreds of millions, in a matter of days. This is the clear and present danger – global nuclear genocide – represented by the armed forces of the great powers in a world of competing corporations and states.

The Coming Climate Catastrophe

Our planet is slowly dying. It first became sick about 250 years ago at the start of the Industrial Revolution, when the world economy began to grow at an exponential rate. The sickness is now approaching a terminal crisis.

Global production increased more than 80 times between 1750 and 1980. Nowadays it tends to double every 25 years. Because of this, energy consumption has soared. World coal production has risen from 15 million tons in 1800 to 8,000 million tons today. World oil production was 150 million barrels in 1900 but is now around 30 billion barrels a year.

Exponential economic growth has meant exponential growth in population and cities. The world was home to about 750 million people in 1750, 1.25 billion in 1850, and 2.5 billion in 1950; now the total is 7 billion. Only 2.5 per cent of a much smaller global population lived in cities in 1800. Today the proportion is roughly half.

More output, more power, more people, more cities: the result has been massive strain on the earth's resources. It takes many forms. Forests are cut down, wetlands drained, and soil eroded. Water extraction turns farmland into desert. Habitats are destroyed and 75 species become extinct every day. Chemicals are dumped in oceans, lakes, and rivers. Toxins leak into groundwater. Fertilisers, herbicides, and pesticides contaminate food supplies. Landfills overflow with synthetic waste. Nuclear plants explode and fill air, land, and sea with carcinogenic particles.

But one ecological crisis predominates. In the last 200 years, the burning of coal, oil, and gas has increased the amount of carbon dioxide in the atmosphere from 280 ppm (parts per million) to 400 ppm. The rate of increase is accelerating. It passed 300 ppm around 1950, was above 350 ppm by 1990, and reached 390 ppm in 2012. The effect is to warm the earth, because the carbon dioxide layer in the atmosphere traps the sun's heat. Average global temperature has risen by 0.8°C since 1880, but 75 per cent of that increase has happened in the last 30 years. The ten warmest years in the last 134 years have all occurred since 1998. The Arctic Ice Cap is shrinking at a rate of 9 per cent per decade, and average sea-level is rising at a rate of 2 cm per decade.

Climate change is already happening. Floods temporarily covered 65 per cent of Bangladesh in 1998, destroying villages, farms, and infrastructure. Half the island of Bhola, home to 1.6 million people, had been permanently washed away by 2004. The worst bushfires in Australia's history ravaged the continent in 2011. Around 20 million people were displaced by the effects of climate change in 2008 alone, and 150,000 people a year are now dying from its effects as diseases spread faster at higher temperatures.

These things are happening with just 400 ppm of atmospheric carbon and 0.8°C of global warming. With 450 ppm of carbon in the atmosphere, the warming would probably reach 2°C on average. Scientists reckon this to be the maximum before we get sudden, irreversible, and highly destructive change. That is at 2°C of warming. On current trends, global temperatures could rise by five or six times the suggested target. Even the target level will probably result in hundreds of millions affected by displacement, thirst, hunger, and disease.

The complexity of the global system, its multiple variables and feedback mechanisms, means the tipping-points cannot be predicted with accuracy. The warming of frozen tundra, for example, could suddenly release huge quantities of carbon-rich methane into the atmosphere.

If abrupt change was triggered, billions could be affected. The West Antarctic Ice Sheet has begun to melt. It contains enough water to raise global sea-levels by 3 metres – enough, that is, to inundate parts of London, Mumbai, New York, and Tokyo. Research on past de-glaciations implies that ice sheets can suddenly go into reverse and disintegrate as rising and warming seas undercut them.

Six of the top ten corporations in the world are oil companies. Three more are car manufacturers. The top two corporations in Germany and Japan are car manufacturers. The top four in Russia are oil and gas producers. India's top five are all oil companies.

The 80–90 per cent carbon cuts necessary to save the planet imply head-on confrontation with corporate capital. We need trillions of pounds of investment in carbon capture and storage, renewable energy, public transport, energy-efficient homes, and building insulation. We need massive cuts in fossil-fuel consumption, road transport, and air travel. We need heavy taxes on the rich and the corporations to support the victims of climate change in the impoverished Global South. We need coordinated international action – democratically decided and rationally planned – to stop climate change.

None of that is going to happen so long as the 1 per cent rule the world. They had a chance at the UN-sponsored climate talks in Copenhagen in 2009. The previous Kyoto Protocol, agreed in 1997, contained a commitment to cut carbon dioxide emissions by 5.2 per cent by 2012. It bore no relation to the scale of the problem. But at least there were targets. The Copenhagen Accord went backwards. There were no longer agreed targets. Each country now sets its own targets.

Copenhagen was a victory for corporate power. The 'carbon corporations' – coal, oil, and gas producers, power companies, car manufacturers, airlines – are free to burn the planet in the interests of profit.

The lords of capital have turned the earth – its lands, it waters, its minerals – into their private property. They have transformed its bounty into commodities and profit. They spew waste and pollution.

At Copenhagen, the politicians gave them free rein to carry on. They did not waste any time. Since then, fossil-fuel production and carbon emissions have soared. And now they are fracking as well: tearing up the countryside and pumping toxic chemicals into the ground to extract shale gas. To burn. To release more carbon.

Some scientists say we have entered a new geological epoch in the history of the earth: the 'Anthropocene' – the epoch when humans destroy the planet's ecosystem.

Creeping Fascism

It was one of those moments when the world changed. Like the fall of the Berlin Wall in 1989, the bombing of the Twin Towers in 2001, the financial crash of 2008, the election of Donald Trump as US President in November 2016 sent shockwaves across the globe.

Commentators struggled for words. A billionaire tax-dodger, a ranting racist, a misogynist and self-confessed abuser of women, a bully who taunts the disabled and the bereaved, a serial liar, a man proud of his bigotry, his hatred, his contempt for most of humanity, this man had just been elected to the most powerful political position on the planet. Sixty-three million Americans had voted for a political psychopath.

Trump is part of a global phenomenon: the emergence of a class of authoritarian far-right rulers. Vladimir Putin heads a Russian-nationalist regime in Moscow, Xi Jinping a Chinese-nationalist regime in Beijing, Narendra Modi a Hindu-nationalist regime in Delhi, and Recep Tayyib Erdogan a Muslim-nationalist regime in

Istanbul. Across the world, democracy is being eroded, civil liberties are under attack, and human rights are being trampled.

Europe is host to what might be described as 'second wave' fascism. Far-right governments hold power in Poland and Hungary. The leader of Austria's far-right Freedom Party came within a whisker of becoming national president. The leader of France's far-right National Front secured 34 per cent of the popular vote in her most recent presidential bid. The far-right Freedom Party took 13 per cent of the vote in the Dutch general election in 2017, and the far-right Alternative for Germany did equally well in the German federal election that same year. And in Britain, an alliance of right-wing forces – UKIP and the Tory Right – won a narrow majority for Brexit (British exit from the EU) on a platform of nationalism and anti-migrant racism.

Far-right parties have become mass electoral formations holding second or third place in the polls in about half the countries of Europe. These parties have infected the entire mainstream political spectrum with racism. Traditional conservative, liberal, and social-democratic parties are responding to a haemorrhaging of votes by echoing the anti-migrant and Islamophobic rhetoric of the Far Right. This reinforces the racist discourse, strengthens its most extreme proponents, and further undermines the electoral stability of mainstream parties: a vicious spiral.

The term 'fascism' is sometimes used too loosely to describe any authoritarian behaviour. Far more worrying, however, is a tendency to define it too narrowly and deny that it applies to contemporary far-right movements – usually on the basis that they do not sufficiently resemble the German Nazis of the interwar period.

This is a very dangerous mistake. History repeats itself, but never exactly. In any case, the interwar experience shows that fascism can take many forms. It is a movement in the most literal sense of being a *process* – varying from place to place, changing over time, evolving through interaction with other forces in concrete historical circumstances. Fascism, like all socio-political movements, is defined by motion, and it must be analysed in terms of its inner content, not its episodic forms.

The extreme 'battering-ram' fascism of the interwar period – that of the Italian Fascists, the German Nazis, and the Spanish Falangists – was a reaction to a revolutionary working-class movement. It involved exceptional levels of paramilitary violence because it was necessary to smash the labour movement in physical struggle in order to clear the road to power.

The situation today is very different. The neoliberal counter-revolution unleashed in the late 1970s has weakened civil society in general and the labour movement in particular. The international ruling class broke through in the 1980s, inflicting a succession of massive defeats on the working class, and the four decades since have seen large-scale redistribution of wealth and power in favour of capital. We may now be witness to a second phase in that counter-revolution – a radical intensification of the atomisation, disempowerment, and depoliticisation of the working class.

Fascism does not need to batter its way to power today. Some far-right movements are already in government, either in their own right, or by colonising other parties, or by joining right-wing coalitions; and they are using their position to leverage their nationalist-racist programme. Even where they do not yet exercise governmental power, their presence is reconfiguring the political landscape, creating terrain that affords them maximum traction for future advance. The space for the development of more racist, more authoritarian, and more violent forms of fascism is steadily expanding.

Fascism can be defined as the active mobilisation of atomised 'human dust' (Trotsky's expression) around a right-wing cocktail of nationalism, racism, sexism, and authoritarianism. This cocktail is an irrational hotchpotch – a bundle of fables, prejudices, and icons. It represents regression to a pre-Enlightenment, anti-scientific, ultra-reactionary way of thinking. Yet, in pursuing its programme, the Far Right also seeks control over the most modern forms of coercive state power. Fascism is the myths of the eleventh century powered by the technology of the twenty-first.

Fascism is not a 'tool' designed for a specific historical task. It is not 'controlled' by capitalist puppet-masters. It is a concentrated expression of nationalism, racism, xenophobia, sexism, militarism, deference, religious bigotry, power-worship, and psychotic rage – what Marx called 'the shit of ages' – which wells up from the sewers of capitalist society in periods of crisis. This is the magnetic core which attracts a human dust of atomised, alienated, anomic people around it, the detritus of decaying social layers at the base of the system. Fascism turns this material into a counter-revolutionary mass movement to protect the capitalist order from the explosive potential inherent in society's accumulating discontents.

The capitulation of the liberal centre to the imperatives of financialised capital accumulation – even after the 2008 crash had revealed its bankruptcy and parasitism – provides the political context for the advance of the Far Right. The weakness of the Left – after four decades of neoliberal counter-revolution – means that there is minimal resistance (and therefore little need for fascist paramilitaries).

The appeal of the Far Right is obvious. On one side, banks are bailed out, corporate power expands, and the rich get richer. On the other, public services are privatised, housing becomes unaffordable, prices soar, wages stagnate, and the poor get screwed. Great pools of bitterness and dissent accumulate in the social depths. The conservatives, liberals, and fake 'socialists' of the mainstream parties who preside over this travesty look like tawdry racketeers – part of a corrupt political elite in the pocket of speculators and asset-strippers.

Consent drains away from the discredited centre, but discontent finds no leadership on the Left. Creeping fascism arises when the political system has been hollowed out, social distress is mounting, and the labour movement is unable to advance a socialist alternative. Instead, discontent is channelled into nationalism and bigotry, and anger is directed not against the system, but against its victims.

Paramilitary thugs have always been secondary components of fascist repression. The state apparatus has always been the primary instrument for the suppression of liberal democracy and labour organisation. This was true in every case of interwar fascism – in Italy in 1922, in Germany in 1933, in Spain in 1939. It remains true today. The real danger is not fascist paramilitaries, but far-right control of the police.

Interwar 'battering-ram' fascism was an explosion of violence directed at a revolutionary working-class movement. The 'creeping' fascism of the present is the implosion of a society already hollowed out. In early twenty-first-century Europe, fascism is a clear and present danger.

Conclusion: Making the Future

A baby cries with hunger on the East African savannah. Her mother's breasts are dry because she is starving. The cattle have died because the rains have failed. There is no food in the village. The rains have failed because the seas are warming, and the rain-bearing winds are weakening. The baby is crying because of climate change.

A world away, a Bengali father weeps for his lost daughters – crushed under a heap of concrete by the collapse of a factory in Dhaka, corporate sweatshop capital of Bangladesh. Every factory is built by the lowest tender. Hours are long, wages meagre, bullying routine. The walls of the eight-storey Rana Plaza were visibly cracking when the 5,000 workers were ordered in. The collapse killed 1,138 of them. Safe factories cost more. Safe factories mean lower profits – for Primark and half a dozen other fashion retailers on a high street near you.

Half a mile from the high street, a disabled man hangs himself. His benefits have been cut and he cannot feed his family. He dies in Burnley in Britain – the tenth richest country in the world. He is not alone: one million Britons are now using food banks. For the poorest are getting poorer. It is called 'reducing the deficit'.

The rich turned the banks into gambling casinos. Then the debts went bad and the banks almost collapsed. So they plundered the public purse to bail out the banks. But someone had to pay. They decided it should be the poor. It is called 'austerity'.

Another world away, a Yemeni mother weeps for her children – also crushed under a heap of concrete, this time brought down by a Saudi air-strike. British corporations supply the weapons. They call it 'the War on Terror'. A million or more are dead across Central Asia and the Middle East. Tens of millions are homeless. But the war goes on, and the arms dealers get richer.

In the Mediterranean, a rotting boat overloaded with people capsizes and sinks. A hundred drown before the rescue-launch arrives. All told, around a thousand die on the crossing every year.

A thousand among the millions on the move in a world ravaged by militarism and corporate power.

Those who make the journey are herded into concentration camps, imprisoned behind wire, bullied by uniformed thugs, taunted by racist politicians. They are the lepers of modern capitalism – the unwanted, the outcast, the 'unclean'. More than 400 attempt suicide after arriving in Germany alone. Twenty succeed.

Climate change, war, and poverty are tearing our world apart. These are not separate issues; they are not 'single issues'. They are connected. They are part of a system of rival states and corporations. The driver of the system is competition for profit.

Hard-wired into it is the enrichment of the few, the impoverishment of the many, and the destruction of the planet. Only profit matters. Human misery and environmental devastation are cost-free 'externalities'. Broken societies and blackened Nature are the system's waste products.

The system is now driving us into an abyss – more pollution, more war, more poverty. The planet is fast heating up. The international order is breaking down. The social fabric is being ripped apart by grotesque inequality.

The system cannot be reformed. The corporations have turned parliaments into puppet theatres. Millionaire politicians strut upon the stage, signifying nothing. Parliament has become an echo-chamber of corporate sound-bites.

The 1 per cent will not surrender their wealth and power. No elite in history has ever done this. They will not dismantle the system on which their wealth and power depends. Either we end the rule of the rich, the banks, and the corporations, or the crisis-racked system will drag us into barbarism and our planet to destruction.

The Wealth of the World

For the last 5,000 years, ever since the Agricultural Revolution first made possible substantial accumulations of surplus wealth, humanity has been engaged in an uneven and uncertain ascent towards the abolition of want. This has been driven by the three motors of history – technological progress, ruling-class competition, and the struggle between classes – and it has been uneven and uncertain because the working of these mechanisms, especially in combination, has been fraught.

Over the last 250 years, since the start of the Industrial Revolution, the pace of change has accelerated sharply. A dynamic system of competitive capital accumulation has created a global economy of incessant innovation. Humanity's ingenuity and industry have brought us to the brink of material abundance for all.

Yet the potential for emancipation from want inherent in the economy remains unrealised. Instead, there is exploitation and poverty, imperialism and war, famine and disease. We have created unprecedented resources of know-how and wealth – the fruits of five millennia of collective human labour – yet they are harnessed to the greed and violence of a tiny minority who do no productive work at all.

One aim of this book has been to explain why this should be. Another has been to show that it could have been different. Central to the argument has been the simple fact that human beings make their own history. They do not do it in circumstances of their own choosing. Their actions are framed by the economic, social, and political structures of their age. But, subject to these constraints – indeed, because of them – humans face a succession of choices. Sometimes, they choose not to act, but to acquiesce. Then they remain history's victims, in thrall to the decisions of others, their rulers, the self-appointed arbiters of human destiny. Other times, far too rarely perhaps, they choose to organise and fight. When enough make this choice, they become a mass movement and an historical force. And then the earth shakes.

We have arrived at a juncture when momentous choices must be made. Either we acquiesce to austerity and poverty, to grotesque and growing social injustice, and, quite possibly, to a descent into the darkness of fascism, war, and ecocide. Or we decide that this latest crisis of capitalism should be its last, and that we must overthrow the rule of bankers and warlords, and create a new society based on democracy, equality, sustainability, and production for need not profit.

This much is clear. Capitalism now faces a systemic and existential crisis. The crisis has economic, social, imperial, ecological, and political dimensions. A decade on from the 2008 crash, we appear to have entered a Great Stagnation which may prove to be the most intractable depression in history. The metropolitan heartlands of the system are afflicted with falling living standards, rising poverty, and decaying infrastructure and public services. Whole regions of the developing world have been turned into gigantic corporate sweatshops, and tens of millions have been displaced by war in a great swathe of mayhem that extends from Central Asia to West Africa.

Despite massive military investment, the declining global hegemon, the United States, has proved unable to impose its will on Afghanistan and Iraq, unable to re-stabilise the Middle East, unable to stall the advance of new imperial rivals like China. The response has been more armaments, militarisation, and violence.

Meantime, the countdown continues to runaway global warming and a climate catastrophe that could destroy industrial civilisation.

And from the sewers of the system, as in the 1930s, a monster of fascism is rising.

Human alienation has never been greater. On the one hand, collective labour has created productive forces with an unprecedented potential to abolish want. On the other, these same forces have been transformed into agencies of destruction inimical to our health, our well-being, even our very survival.

What is to be done?

Revolution in the Twenty-First Century?

The global elite cannot continue to rule in the old way. But the only viable alternative to poverty, war, and global warming is to dismantle the very system on which their wealth and power is based. This they cannot do. The ruling class can resolve the crisis only by a descent into barbarism. Their role as the lords of capital makes them, in the early twenty-first century, a parasitic social class without historic function.

Human progress has come to depend on the overthrow of the neoliberal ruling class, the taking of state power by working people, and the reorganisation of economic and social life under democratic control.

The lesson of twentieth-century history is that, to succeed, this must be done globally. The lesson of the last 40 years is that 'socialism in one country' is a more fantastical delusion than ever. But is world revolution really possible in the twenty-first century?

Revolutions are typically unanticipated, highly infectious, and immensely powerful mechanisms of change. The French Revolution of 1789 exploded when the people of Paris armed themselves and took to the streets to prevent a royal coup. Then, between 1789 and 1794, they intervened repeatedly in the political process to drive the Revolution forwards against the resistance of half-hearted moderates, counter-revolutionaries, and foreign armies of invasion.

The revolutionary movement subsided after 1815, but then erupted again, first in 1830 in France, then in 1848 with a wave of insurrections in Paris, Berlin, Vienna, Budapest, Rome, and other European cities. Though the revolutionaries were defeated, the impetus they gave to reform was unstoppable. Europe's rulers knew they had to manage change from above or risk further explosions from below. France became a republic, Italy was united, and Germany was forged into a modern nation-state.

In February 1917 the police dictatorship of the Russian Tsar was overthrown by working-class insurrection. In October 1917, under the leadership of the Bolsheviks and the Petrograd Soviet, the Russian working class seized power. The factories were run by workers' councils, the land was given to the peasants, and Russia withdrew from the First World War. For a few brief years, until the Revolution was destroyed by economic collapse, civil war, and foreign invasion, Russia was the most democratic country in the world.

The Bolshevik Revolution sparked a chain reaction of revolutions from Germany to China. The revolutions in Germany and Austria-Hungary ended the First World War. The revolutionary movement as a whole, between 1917 and 1923, came close to bringing down the entire world capitalist system.

That system has remained pregnant with revolution ever since. In 1936 revolution in Spain blocked a fascist-backed military coup. In 1956 revolution erupted in Hungary in response to a Soviet invasion. In 1968 ten million workers joined a general strike in France, hundreds of thousands occupied their factories, and students and young workers fought pitched battles with riot police in central Paris.

In 1979 revolution brought down a vicious, heavily armed, US-backed dictatorship in Iran. In 1989 a wave of revolutions across Eastern Europe brought down a succession of Stalinist dictators despite their networks of informers, secret police, and political prisons.

On 11 February 2011, after 18 days of mass demonstrations, the 30-year military dictatorship of Egyptian President Hosni Mubarak collapsed in the most spectacular victory of the Arab Spring.

Before all these revolutions, opponents had looked at the regimes they confronted and despaired at their military power, their monolithic police control of society, the apparent apathy of the masses. Each time, the arrogance of the ruling class had continued unchecked until the moment of insurrection. What Marx called 'the old mole' of history loves surprises.

In 1924 the Hungarian Marxist theoretician Georg Lukács, reflecting on the great epoch of war and revolution that had just passed, wrote of 'the actuality of the revolution'. It is worth recalling, in the context of our own age of crisis, what Lukács had in mind. Marxism, he explained,

> presupposes the universal actuality of the proletarian revolution. In this sense, as both the objective basis of the whole epoch and the key to understanding of it, the proletarian revolution constitutes the living core of Marxism ... The actuality of the revolution provides the key-note of a whole epoch ... The actuality of the revolution therefore implies the study of each individual daily problem ... as moments in the liberation of the proletariat ...

For Lukács, international working-class revolution was a vital and ever-present possibility against which all political action should be judged. It was not inevitable. It might never happen. It could be far off. The point, however, was that the old order contained within itself the ever-present possibility of revolution, and that this was the only conceivable solution to the ever-growing sum of human suffering.

The eventual defeat of the revolutionary wave of 1917–23 did not disprove the essential validity of Lukács's insight. On the contrary, it confirmed it, for the result was the barbarism of Stalingrad, Auschwitz, and Hiroshima.

Rebel Cities

Seattle in 1999, Washington in 2000, and Genoa in 2001 saw mass anti-globalisation protests erupt into violent clashes with the police. On 15 February 2003, there were coordinated anti-war demonstrations in 600 cities across the world, involving up to 25 million people in all, with three million marching in Rome, two million in London, one and a half million in Madrid.

Between 2011 and 2015, in Tunis, Cairo, Athens, Madrid, Santiago, Istanbul, and Rio, and in a dozen other major urban centres, hundreds of thousands battled state forces on the streets to protest authoritarian rule and austerity economics.

Cairo's Tahrir Square, Athens' Syntagma Square, Madrid's Puerto del Sol, Istanbul's Taksim Square became front-line battlegrounds in a struggle of people power against the neoliberal order. The battles for the squares repeatedly spread into surrounding streets, as protestors were temporarily pushed back and forced to seek refuge in buildings and behind barricades. When they did so, hundreds of thousands more, from alleyways and balconies, were seen to be cheering them on. And millions more watching on TV screens were lifted by the images of people fighting back.

The democracy of a new mass movement was challenging the arrogance and corruption of an entrenched neoliberal regime. And that regime was responding in the only way it knew how: with batons, water cannon, tear gas, and percussion bombs.

There are national variations, but a new pattern of mass struggle from below is apparent across the globe: control of our cities by corporate capital and authoritarian states is being contested by a radical vanguard of mainly young street protestors. The hollowing out of parliamentary democracy and the weakening of the unions and other popular organisations has destroyed the social order's pressure-gauges and safety-values. Instead, bitterness festers at the base of society, alienation with 'the system' grows, and then, when it bursts through, takes explosive form.

The modern city, with its heterogeneous, precarious, shifting working class, has become a primary arena of struggle. Social media have facilitated the creation of loose networks and rapid mobilisations of otherwise atomised individuals. Then, when they come together, the disparate radicals of the counter-culture discover that they are a mass movement. Capitalism seems to be facing a wave of urban uprisings in its metropolitan heartlands.

The city is a concentrate of social contradictions. It contains the gargantuan prestige monuments of the state, the steel-and-glass towers of the corporations, and the luxury residences of the elite. Yet in streets often only a short walk away are the terraces of rack-rented flats where young workers live, the high streets full of charity shops, pound shops, and boarded-up shops of an economy in slump, and the dirty hospitals, run-down schools, and rubbish-strewn streets of a public sector squeezed by austerity cuts. The widening gap between rich and poor, between corporate profit and public squalor, is a physical and social fracture-line drawn across shared urban space.

What is more, as union organisation weakens on the one hand, and as financialised forms of exploitation in consumption loom larger on the other, the urban working-class community as a whole (as opposed to its separate workplace sections) assumes greater social significance. Struggles against low pay and bullying managers centre on the workplace. Struggles over tax, rent, benefits, public services, and environmental protection necessarily centre on the community.

The workplace is inherently sectional. Strong workplace organisation strengthens sectionalism even as it provides a firmer platform for unity and solidarity across the class. The city works the other way round. Urban communities and crowds tend to be diverse. Big demonstrations bring together workers from different industries, the organised with the unorganised, the secure with the precarious, the employed with the unemployed, the students with the minorities. Quickly, easily, naturally, the urban crowd can unite the urban working-class as a whole in struggle on the streets.

On the streets, too, there is safety in the anonymity of the mass. It is not simply that the unorganised, the precarious, and the unemployed can fight on the streets. It is also that organised workers who face management intimidation in their workplaces can more easily give expression to their anger in street protest than in strike action.

The modern city has been created by the labour of workers. Yet control over public spaces is usurped by corporations and the state, and less and less of the city is free of enclosure, control, surveillance, and commodification. A recurring feature of the new urban uprisings is the collision between the democracy of the streets and the violence of the state.

The city is a product of human labour, a source of capitalist profit, and a centre of class power. As such, it is vulnerable. Just as strike action can shut down factories, offices, and entire industries, so too can street protest shut down infrastructure, workplaces, and entire cities. The street can close the factories. The urban mass, fully mobilised, can paralyse the city economy.

Whose Apocalypse?

A biblical myth sees the end of the world heralded by the appearance of the Four Horsemen of the Apocalypse, representing Conquest, Slaughter, Famine, and Death.

The prospect before humanity today can seem truly apocalyptic. Neoliberal capitalism has developed the productive forces of the global economy to an unprecedented degree. But these forces are not subject to democratic control and rational planning; they are propelled by the economic and military imperatives of competitive capital accumulation. In consequence, despite their potential to emancipate the whole of humanity from material need, they now threaten to do the opposite: destroy industrial civilisation itself.

The ignorance, cupidity, and irresponsibility of our rulers in the face of this crisis are rooted in the irrationality of the system. Climate catastrophe, economic slump, and imperialist war have their roots in the madness of the market: the blind economic and military competition which propels the nation-states and mega-corporations of neoliberal capitalism. The system is deeply pathological and destructive. It has brought us to what is perhaps the most serious crisis in human history.

Another biblical myth was sometimes counterposed to that of the Four Horseman. In this version of the Apocalypse, the culmination was a popular Jubilee. Tax-collectors and landlords would be swept away. Slaves and serfs would be set free. The land would be restored to the people who worked it. A new Golden Age of freedom and plenty would begin.

To turn Apocalypse into Jubilee in the early twenty-first century, five things are required:

1. We have to understand the necessity for total system change. Only by linking disparate campaigns, protests, and struggles in a general assault on the system that is at the root of humanity's problems can we hope to solve them.

2. We have to understand the necessity for internationalism. This means rejecting all forms of racism, nationalism, and 'socialism

in one country', and building global networks of solidarity and resistance capable of challenging the global power of the rich.

3. We have to understand the centrality of the working class – defined as the 80 per cent – to any serious strategy for system change. Only by mobilising the majority of ordinary working people can we find the power to confront and defeat corporate capital and the nation-states.

4. We have to build a network of mass social movements and popular participatory assemblies to organise, spread, and sustain the struggles of working people against the system.

5. We have to organise the revolutionaries into networks of activists able to lead and organise mass resistance from below, fanning popular anger into a wave of working-class struggle that eventually swells into a new, global revolutionary movement comparable with, but greater than, those of 1789, 1848, 1917, 1968, and 1989.

A different world has become an absolute historical necessity. Another world is possible. The revolution is, in this sense, an 'actuality'.

But it is not a certainty. It has to be fought for. Its achievement depends on what we all do.

The historical stakes have never been higher.

Timeline

Historical Period or Date*	Great Transitions/Global Events	Europe	Western Asia	Eastern Asia and Australasia	Africa	America
c. 7–6 million BP	First Hominin Transformation**				First hominins appear in Chad or Kenya	
c. 3–7 million BP					Australopithecus afarensis emerges in East Africa	
Lower Palaeolithic/ Old Stone Age c. 3.3 million–200,000 BP						
c. 3.3 million BP	Second Hominin Transformation				Hominins start making stone tools	
c. 2.5 million BP	Ice Age epoch begins				Genus Homo emerges (Homo habilis)	
c. 1.9–1.8 million BP				Homo erectus colonises South and East Asia	Homo ergaster emerges in East and South Africa	
c. 800,000 BP		Homo antecessor present in Britain				
c. 500,000 BP		Homo heidelbergensis present in Britain				
c. 350,000 BP	Third Hominin Transformation	Homo neanderthalensis adapts to the cold			Homo sapiens emerges in Morocco	
Middle and Upper Palaeolithic/Old Stone Age c. 200,000–10,000 BP	Hunting Revolution					

Historical Period or Date*	Great Transitions/ Global Events	Europe	Western Asia	Eastern Asia and Australasia	Africa	America
c. 85,000 BP			Homo sapiens crosses from Africa into Asia			
c. 50,000 BP				Homo sapiens colonises South Asia and Australasia		
c. 40,000 BP		Homo sapiens colonises Europe		Homo sapiens colonises North Asia		
c. 30,000 BP		Homo neanderthalensis becomes extinct				
c. 15,000 BP						Homo sapiens colonises America
Mesolithic/ Middle Stone Age c. 8000–3500 BC						
Neolithic/ New Stone Age c. 7500 BC–present	**Agricultural Revolution**					
c. 7000 BC		Neolithic pioneers arrive in Greece from Western Asia		First Neolithic farmers in parts of South and East Asia		
c. 6000 BC				First Neolithic farmers in Yellow River valley, northern China		
c. 5000 BC		Early Neolithic farming dominant across Europe				

Historical Period or Date*	Great Transitions/ Global Events	Europe	Western Asia	Eastern Asia and Australasia	Africa	America
Chalcolithic (Copper) Age c. 4500–3000 BC	Ecological crisis and transition from Early Neolithic hoe-based cultivation to Late Neolithic plough-based agriculture					
c. 4000 BC			Late Neolithic economy develops in parts of Western Asia	Farming spreads along Indus Valley, Pakistan		
c. 3800 BC		Early Neolithic farming reaches all parts of Europe				
c. 3700–3400 BC		Large tribal polities emerge in southern Britain and engage in warfare				
Bronze Age c. 3000–1200/700 BC	Urban Revolution: first class societies					
c. 3000–1500 BC			Sumerian civilisation in Iraq			
c. 3000–1000 BC			Successive Bronze Age citadels at Troy, north-western Turkey			
c. 2705–2250 BC					Old Kingdom civilisation in Egypt: pyramids constructed	
c. 2600–1900 BC				Indus Valley civilisation in Pakistan		

Historical Period or Date*	Great Transitions/ Global Events	Europe	Western Asia	Eastern Asia and Australasia	Africa	America
c. 2330–2190 BC			Empire of Sargon of Akkad in Iraq			
c. 2300–1900	Crisis of Early Bronze Age empires					
c. 1950–1450 BC		Minoan palace civilisation on Crete				
c. 1800–1027 BC				Shang civilisation in Yellow River Valley, northern China		
c. 1650–1200 BC			Hittite Empire in Turkey			
c. 1600–1150 BC		Mycenaean civilisation in Greece				
c. 1570–1085 BC					New Kingdom civilisation in Egypt	
1523–1027 BC				Shang Dynasty in northern China		
c. 1500 BC				Aryan invaders from Central Asia begin to settle in Pakistan and north-western India		
c. 1500–1335 BC			Mittanian Empire in northern Iraq			
c. 1323 BC					Egyptian Pharaoh Tutankhamun buried in Valley of Kings	

Historical Period or Date*	Great Transitions/ Global Events	Europe	Western Asia	Eastern Asia and Australasia	Africa	America
c. 1200–1050 BC	Crisis of Late Bronze Age empires		Mass production of iron begins in Western Asia			
Iron Age						
c. 1200/700–present	Ironworking revolution transforms productivity					
c. 1200 BC–AD 1521						Succession of civilisations – Olmecs, Maya, Toltecs, and Aztecs – in Mexico
c. 1190 BC			Trojan War			
1170 BC					Egyptian artisans organise first recorded strike	
1027–221 BC				Zhou civilisation in China		
c. 1000 BC					First trans-Saharan trade routes established	
c. 900 BC– AD 325					Kushite civilisation in Sudan	
c. 900 BC– AD 1532						Succession of civilisations – Chavín, Nazca, Moche, Chimú, and Inca – in Peru
c. 800 BC				Iron technology reaches India		

Historical Period or Date*	Great Transitions/ Global Events	Europe	Western Asia	Eastern Asia and Australasia	Africa	America
c. 750 BC		Homer's *Iliad* and *Odyssey* composed				
c. 650–625 BC		Foundation of Rome				
c. 563–483 BC				Life and teaching of Buddha in India		
c. 551–479 BC				Life and teaching of Confucius in China		
c. 550–331 BC			Achaemenid Empire in Persia			
537 BC			Jewish exiles 'return' from Babylon to Palestine			
510–506 BC		Athenian Democratic Revolution in Greece				
c. 500 BC–200 AD					Nok culture in Nigeria	
490–479 BC		Persian invasions of Greece defeated				
c. 450 BC					First ironworking in West Africa	
431–404 BC		Athens defeated in Peloponnesian War				
403–221 BC				'Warring States' period in China		
343–272 BC		Roman conquest of Italy				
338 BC		Macedonian conquest of Greece				

Historical Period or Date*	Great Transitions/ Global Events	Europe	Western Asia	Eastern Asia and Australasia	Africa	America
334–323 BC			Conquests of Alexander the Great			
321–185 BC				Mauryan Empire in India		
c. 300 BC– AD 900						Maya civilisation in southern Mexico and Guatemala
264–202 BC		Roman conquest of Western Mediterranean				
221–210 BC				King of Qin conquers China, becomes First Emperor, builds Great Wall, and is buried with Terracotta Army		
206 BC– AD 220				Han Dynasty in China		
200–63 BC			Roman conquest of Eastern Mediterranean			
167–142 BC			Maccabaean Revolt secures Jewish independence			
133–30 BC		Roman Revolution				
44 BC		Caesar assassinated				

Historical Period or Date*	Great Transitions/ Global Events	Europe	Western Asia	Eastern Asia and Australasia	Africa	America
c. AD 1–33			Life and teaching of Jesus in Palestine			
AD 9		Battle of Teutoburg Forest: Roman defeat signals limits of empire				
AD 50					Foundation of Red Sea port of Axum	
AD 66–73			First Jewish Revolt against Rome			
AD 115–117			Second Jewish Revolt against Rome			
AD 132–136			Third Jewish Revolt against Rome			
c. AD 300–700				'Classical Period' of Indian history		
c. AD 300–800						Urban Revolution of 'Classic Maya' period in southern Mexico and Guatemala
AD 312		Roman Emperor Constantine legalises Christianity				
c. AD 320–550				Gupta Empire in India		

Historical Period or Date*	Great Transitions/ Global Events	Europe	Western Asia	Eastern Asia and Australasia	Africa	America
AD 325					Kushites of Sudan overthrown by Axum/Ethiopia	
AD 378		Battle of Adrianople: Eastern Romans defeated by Visigoths				
AD 391		Roman Emperor Theodosius makes paganism illegal				
AD 395		Final separation of Eastern and Western Roman Empires				
c. AD 395–476	Disintegration of Western Roman Empire					
c. AD 400–800					Ghanaian trading town of Jenne-Jeno on River Niger	
AD 434–453		Reign of Attila as King of Huns				
AD 451		Battle of Chalons: Romans and Visigoths unite to defeat Huns				
c. AD 500				Huns invade north-western India		
c. AD 500–900	Tribute-based political systems dominant in Western Europe					
c. AD 570–632			Life and teaching of Muhammad in western Arabia			

Historical Period or Date*	Great Transitions/ Global Events	Europe	Western Asia	Eastern Asia and Australasia	Africa	America
AD 581–618				Sui Dynasty in China		
AD 618–907				Tang Dynasty in China		
AD 622			Muhammad flees from Mecca to Medina			
AD 630			Muhammad returns to Mecca			
AD 636			Battle of Yarmuk; Arabs conquer Syria			
AD 637			Arabs conquer Iraq			
AD 642					Arabs conquer Egypt	
c. AD 650	First use of heavy plough in Western Europe				Arab traders first become active on trans-Saharan routes	
AD 661			Umayyad Caliphate established in Damascus after civil war			
AD 664				Arabs conquer Afghanistan		
c. AD 700–1350						Pueblo farmers civilisation in south-west of North America

Historical Period or Date*	Great Transitions/ Global Events	Europe	Western Asia	Eastern Asia and Australasia	Africa	America
c. AD 700–1450						Temple-mound builders civilisation in Middle Mississippi of North America
AD 711		Arabs conquer Spain				
AD 750			Abbasid Caliphate established in Baghdad after civil war			
c. AD 850–1050		Viking, Magyar, and Arab raids on Western Europe				
c. AD 900–1100	**Feudalism established across much of Western Europe**					
AD 960–1126				Song Dynasty in China		
1027–1091		Norman conquest of southern Italy and Sicily				
1066–1071		Norman conquest of England				
1071			Battle of Manzikert: Seljuk Turks conquer eastern Turkey			
1095–1291			The Crusades			

Historical Period or Date*	Great Transitions/ Global Events	Europe	Western Asia	Eastern Asia and Australasia	Africa	America
1099			First Crusade culminates in capture of Jerusalem			
1100–1500					Great Zimbabwe civilisation in East-Central Africa	
1183			Syria and Egypt united under Saladin			
1187			Battle of Hattin: Saladin wins decisive victory over Crusaders			
1197–1525						Inca Empire in Peru
1204			Crusaders sack Byzantium (Istanbul)			
1206–1241				Reign of Genghis Khan		
1260			Battle of Ayn Jalut: Mamluks halt Mongol surge			
1279–1368				Yuan or Mongol Dynasty in China		

Historical Period or Date*	Great Transitions/ Global Events	Europe	Western Asia	Eastern Asia and Australasia	Africa	America
1348–1350		Black Death kills one in three across Europe				
c. 1350–1500	Development of proto-capitalist farming in most advanced parts of Western Europe					
1358–1436	Wave of anti-feudal revolts across much of Europe					
1358		Peasant and artisan revolt in northern France				
1368–1644				Ming Dynasty in China		
1378		Artisan revolt in Florence, northern Italy				
1381		Peasant and artisan revolt in southern England				
c. 1400–1550		The Renaissance				
1419–1436		Peasant revolt and Hussite Wars in Bohemia				
1428–1519						Aztec Empire in central Mexico
1440–1897					Benin civilisation in Nigeria	
c. 1450–1800	Mercantile capitalism					

Historical Period or Date*	Great Transitions/ Global Events	Europe	Western Asia	Eastern Asia and Australasia	Africa	America
1453			Ottoman Turks capture Constantinople (Istanbul)			
c. 1485–1685	Absolute monarchies established across much of Europe					
1492–1504						Voyages of Columbus to West Indies
1493–1525						Inca Empire in Peru at zenith
1494–1559		Italian Wars between French and Habsburgs				
1497–1499				Voyage of Vasco da Gama from Lisbon to Calicut via Cape of Good Hope		
1519–1521						Cortés destroys Aztec Empire and conquers Mexico
1519–1522						Voyage of Magellan around world via Cape Horn
1520–1566			Reign of Sulayman the Magnificent			

Historical Period or Date*	Great Transitions/ Global Events	Europe	Western Asia	Eastern Asia and Australasia	Africa	America
1521–1688	**First wave of bourgeois revolutions**					
1521–1525		**German Reformation**: mass struggles by burghers, knights, and peasants				
1526–1707				Mughal Empire in India		
1532–1535						Pizarro destroys Inca Empire and conquers Peru
1534–1535		Anabaptist commune at Munster, Germany				
1536–1541		Dissolution of monasteries in England				
1541–1564		Calvin makes Geneva main centre of Reformation teaching				
1545–1563		Council of Trent organises Europe-wide Counter-Reformation				
1562–1598		French Wars of Religion: Reformation frozen in France				
1566–1609		**Dutch Revolution**				
1571		Battle of Lepanto: Christians halt Ottoman surge				

Historical Period or Date*	Great Transitions/ Global Events	Europe	Western Asia	Eastern Asia and Australasia	Africa	America
1588		Defeat of Spanish Armada halts advance of Counter-Reformation				
1609		Romanov dynasty founded in Russia				
1618–1648		Thirty Years War: Reformation frozen in Germany				
1629–1640		Eleven Years Tyranny: abortive attempt to establish absolute monarchy in Britain				
1637–1660		English Revolution				
1644–1912				Manchu Dynasty in China		
c. 1650–1800		The Enlightenment				
1652–1674		Anglo-Dutch naval wars triggered by commercial rivalry				
1688		'Glorious Revolution' overthrows James II in England				
1688–1815		Succession of major wars between Britain and France for global supremacy				
1689–1746		Series of abortive Jacobite rebellions in Britain				

Historical Period or Date*	Great Transitions/ Global Events	Europe	Western Asia	Eastern Asia and Australasia	Africa	America
c. 1750–1850	**Industrial Revolution**	British working class created by combination of enclosures, clearances, famine, and starvation				
1751–1772		Publication of French *Encyclopédie*				
1756–1763		Seven Years War: establishment of British Empire in Canada and India				
1757–1856				British conquest of India		
1763–1775		British inventor Watt perfects efficient steam engine				
1770s		British entrepreneur Arkwright creates first factories				
1775–1848	**Second wave of bourgeois revolutions**					
1775–1783						**American Revolution**
1776						Publication of Paine's *Common Sense* American Declaration of Independence
1789–1794		**Great French Revolution**				

Historical Period or Date*	Great Transitions/ Global Events	Europe	Western Asia	Eastern Asia and Australasia	Africa	America
1791–1804						Slave revolution in Haiti
1792–1815		French Revolutionary and Napoleonic Wars				
1793–1794		Jacobin dictatorship of 'Year II' in France: high point of bourgeois revolution				
1798		Abortive rising of United Irishmen against British rule				
c. 1800–1875	**Industrial capitalism**					
1808–1814		French invasion of Spain defeated				
1810–1830						'Bolivarian' revolutions against Spanish rule in South America
1812		French invasion of Russia defeated				
1813–1815		Napoleon defeated at Leipzig in Germany and Waterloo in Belgium				
1815–1848		Europe ruled by regimes of 'throne and altar' imposed by Congress of Vienna				
1838–1848		Chartist campaigns in Britain: first working-class mass movement				

Historical Period or Date*	Great Transitions/Global Events	Europe	Western Asia	Eastern Asia and Australasia	Africa	America
1839–1842				First Opium War against China		
1848		Revolutions in France, Germany, Austria-Hungary, and Italy				
1848–1873	Long Boom/Age of Capital					
1849–1870		Bonapartist regime in France				
1850–1864				Taiping Rebellion in China		
1853–1856			Crimean War			
1856–1860				Second Opium War against China		
1857–1859				Indian Mutiny		
1859–1871	Third wave of bourgeois revolutions					
1859–1870		Italian Risorgimento				
1861–1865						American Civil War
1864–1871		Unification of Germany				
1867		Marx publishes Capital				
1867–1869				Meiji Restoration in Japan		
1871		Paris Commune: first working-class revolution				
1873–1896	Long Depression					
c. 1875–1935	Imperial capitalism					

Historical Period or Date*	Great Transitions/Global Events	Europe	Western Asia	Eastern Asia and Australasia	Africa	America
1876–1914					'Scramble for Africa'	
1881–1898					Sudanese Islamist struggle for independence	
1894–1895				Sino-Japanese War over Korea		
1899–1901				Boxer Rebellion in China		
c. 1900–1914		Anglo-German naval arms race				
1903		Split between reformist Mensheviks and revolutionary Bolsheviks among Russian socialists				
1904–1905				Russo-Japanese War over Manchuria		
1905–1906		1905 Revolution in Russia				
1908–1909			Young Turk Revolution in Ottoman Empire			
1910–1920						Mexican Revolution
1911–1923			Disintegration of Ottoman Empire and creation of Turkish Republic			

Historical Period or Date*	Great Transitions/Global Events	Europe	Western Asia	Eastern Asia and Australasia	Africa	America
1911–1927				First Chinese Revolution		
1911				Nationalist insurrection in China		
1912–1913		Balkan Wars				
1914–1918	**First World War**					
1916		Easter Rising in Ireland Publication of Lenin's *Imperialism*				
1917–1923	**Wave of socialist revolution**					
1917		**Russian Revolution** February Revolution in Russia April–June: French army mutinies August: publication of Lenin's *State and Revolution* **October Insurrection in Russia** October–November: Italian army collapses				
1918–1920		'Three Bolshevik Years' in Spain				
1918–1921		Russian Civil War				
1918–1923		**German Revolution**				

Historical Period or Date*	Great Transitions/ Global Events	Europe	Western Asia	Eastern Asia and Australasia	Africa	America
1918		January: strike wave in Germany September–November: military collapse of Central Powers leads to revolutions in Bulgaria, Austria-Hungary, and Germany				
1919–1922	**First four Congresses of Communist International**					
1919		January: 'Spartakus Rising' in Berlin March–August: Hungarian Soviet Republic April–May: Bavarian Soviet Republic Treaty of Versailles agreed		Amritsar Massacre leads to upsurge of resistance to British rule in India '4 May Movement' anti-imperialist insurrection in China		
1919–1921		Italy's 'Two Red Years' Irish War of Independence				
1920		March: 'Kapp Putsch' in Berlin August: wave of factory occupations in northern Italy				
1921–1928		Period of 'New Economic Policy' in Russia				
1922		Mussolini's Fascists seize power in Italy				
1922–1923		Irish Civil War				

Historical Period or Date*	Great Transitions/ Global Events	Europe	Western Asia	Eastern Asia and Australasia	Africa	America
1923		Hyper-inflation destroys value of savings in Germany Hitler's abortive 'Beer Hall Putsch'				
1926		General Strike in Britain				
1926–1927				Workers' and peasants' revolution in China crushed		
1927/1928		Stalinist counter-revolution in Russia First 'Five Year Plan' in Russia				
1929	Great Depression					Wall Street Crash
1929–1939						
1931–1945				Japanese war of conquest in China		
1933		Hitler's Nazi Party seizes power in Germany				
1934		Workers' anti-fascist revolt crushed in Vienna Workers' demonstration marginalises fascists in Paris Miners' revolt in Asturias in Spain				
1934–1935				'Long March' of Chinese Communists under Mao Zedong		
c. 1935–1975	State-managed capitalism					

Historical Period or Date*	Great Transitions/ Global Events	Europe	Western Asia	Eastern Asia and Australasia	Africa	America
1936		May–June: general strike and wave of factory occupations in France				
		July: revolution in response to military coup in Spain				
1937		Stalinist counter-revolution in Spain				
1937–1945				Japanese war of conquest in China		
1939–1945	Second World War					
1941–1945		War becomes global with entry of Russia, Japan, and US				
1944–1945		Communist resistance movements disarm themselves in West				
1945		US drops nuclear bombs on Japan				
1945–1989	Cold War					
1945–1948		Stalinist regimes imposed on Eastern Europe				
1946–1947				Indian struggle for independence: partition and communal violence		
1946–1949				Chinese Civil War ends in Communist victory		

Historical Period or Date*	Great Transitions/ Global Events	Europe	Western Asia	Eastern Asia and Australasia	Africa	America
1948			First Arab–Israeli War: creation of Israel			
1948–1952		US Marshall Plan provides loans to Europe				
1948–1954				Vietnamese War of Independence		
1948–1973	**Great Boom**					
1949		Russians carry out first nuclear bomb test				
1950–1953				Korean War		
1952					Free Officers coup in Egypt	
1954–1962					Algerian War of Independence	
1956		February: Khrushchev's speech October–November: Hungarian Revolution and Suez Crisis				
1956–1959						Cuban Revolution
1958–1961				Mao's 'Great Leap Forward' in China		
1960–1975				Vietnam War		
1961		Construction of Berlin Wall				
1962						Cuban Missiles Crisis

Historical Period or Date*	Great Transitions/ Global Events	Europe	Western Asia	Eastern Asia and Australasia	Africa	America
1966–1971				Mao's 'Cultural Revolution' in China		
1968–1975	**Global wave of mass struggle**					
1968		May–June: mass protests, general strike, and factory occupations in France August: Russian invasion of Czechoslovakia to suppress 'Prague Spring'		Tet Offensive in South Vietnam		April: wave of black ghetto riots August: Chicago police attack anti-war demonstration October: massacre of student protestors in Mexico City
1969		August: Battle of the Bogside in Derry, Ireland 'Hot Autumn' of strikes and occupations in Italy				
1973						Military coup overthrows Allende government in Chile
1973–1992	**Long Recession**					
1974		Portuguese Revolution				
1974–1975						Military coup in Argentina
c. 1975–present	**Neoliberal capitalism**					

Historical Period or Date*	Great Transitions/ Global Events	Europe	Western Asia	Eastern Asia and Australasia	Africa	America
1978				China turns to neoliberalism under Deng Xiaoping		
1979			**Iranian Revolution**			Nicaraguan Revolution
1979–1989				Soviet–Afghan War		
1979–1990		Thatcher government imposes neoliberalism in Britain				
1980–1981		Solidarność movement in Poland				
1980–1988			Iran–Iraq War			Reagan government imposes neoliberalism and 'Second Cold War' in US
1984–1985		**Defeat of British miners' strike**				
1987–1988		Gorbachev launches *glasnost* and *perestroika* reforms in Soviet Union				
1989		**1989 East European Revolutions**		Tiananmen Square Massacre of pro-democracy protestors in China		
1989–1991		Breakup of Soviet Union				

Historical Period or Date*	Great Transitions/ Global Events	Europe	Western Asia	Eastern Asia and Australasia	Africa	America
1992–1995		Bosnian War in former Yugoslavia				
1994					End of apartheid rule in South Africa	
1999–2013						Presidency of Hugo Chavez in Venezuela
2001						Terrorist attacks in US on Twin Towers and Pentagon
2001–present	'War on Terror'			US and British war against Afghanistan		
2003–2011			US and British war against Iraq			
2007	Global 'credit crunch'					
2008	**Global financial crash**					
2008–present	**Great Stagnation**					

* Dates are given as BP (before the present) before 10,000 and 1 BC, as BC (before Christ) between 8,000 and 1 BC, and AD (*anno domini*: in the Year of the Lord) between AD 1 and 1000; dates later than this are given simply as numerals. Some periods overlap, especially in prehistory, because similar developments occurred at different points in time in different parts of the world.

** Events and processes of exceptional importance are shown **in bold.**

NB The periods and events listed are based on references in the text; the timeline does not constitute a fully comprehensive chronology for human history.

Sources

These notes, and the bibliography that follows, are an alternative to footnotes. In a work of radical synthesis and theory, as any world history is bound to be, conventional academic footnotes make for a clumsy apparatus. What do you reference? Well-known facts, or only little known ones? All ideas, or just the more controversial ones? Every source consulted, or the main one? Far easier, and I hope more useful to the reader, is the method adopted here of providing bibliographical notes followed by an annotated list of sources. In the first, I discuss historiographical debates, their key sources, and my position in relation to them. In the second, sources are listed as in a conventional bibliography (the dates usually being those of the editions I have used), but with certain additional information. I have given the chapters to which the source is particularly relevant in parentheses, e.g. (1–3), employed a single asterisk (*) to indicate studies of particular value, both Marxist and non-Marxist, double asterisks (**) for those of exceptional significance, usually seminal works of Marxist historiography, and smiley faces (☺) for works notable for their elegance and accessibility.

Neither the notes nor the bibliography proper claim to be authoritative. Both are patchy. They reflect, as I explain in the Introduction, my training, experience, and reading. I know the historiography of some periods and places far better than others. The sources cited are simply those I know, have used, and can therefore recommend. Not the least importance of the bibliography is that it will alert specialists to gaps in my knowledge and allow them to assess the reliability of my judgements on the basis of what I appear to have read. In addition, the notes and the bibliography should direct the general reader to useful further reading.

Bibliographical Notes

Marxism has informed the work of several generations of historians. Much that follows owes a large debt to these forebears, and readers will find them acknowledged in the bibliography. That said, Marxists often disagree, and I certainly disagree with many of the interpretations of other Marxists, including some whose claim to the descriptor is questionable. Because of this, I am obliged to say something about where I stand on the Marxist spectrum.

Marx's own work can be read in different ways. How much of a constraint is social structure? To what degree are humans socialised and manipulated by the social order? Or, to turn the question around, how potent is human agency – the collective will and action of people in society – in changing the course of events? Is history largely determined by structure? Or is it contingent, open, and shaped by what we do?

Determinist approaches were largely dominant within Marxism from the late nineteenth to the mid-twentieth centuries. This suited the political agendas of both reformist politicians and Stalinist bureaucrats, neither of whom were keen to encourage the self-activity of the working class. The exceptions were revolutionaries like Lenin, Trotsky, Luxemburg, Gramsci, and Lukács. Those trying to make revolution always stressed the power of agency: for them, the consciousness, organisation, and activity of the working class were the very essence of Marxism.

Historiography did not catch up until after the Second World War. Then, a new generation of Marxist historians, mainly in Britain and France, many of them (initially at least) members of their respective communist parties, produced an unsurpassed body of empirical and theoretical work which amounted to a decisive rejection of determinist interpretations of Marxism. Their primary focus was the material circumstances, thought-worlds, and collective actions of ordinary men and women. Their aim was to write 'history from below', though not in the anodyne sense of mere description in which it is often used today, but in the dynamic sense of revealing the common people to be history's movers and shakers.

Edward Thompson's *The Making of the English Working Class* is a classic study of this type, one in which the embryonic proletariat ceases to be a submerged and invisible victim, and becomes instead a class of real men and women creating their own identity, culture, and history. In much the same way, Rodney Hilton analysed the medieval peasantry, Christopher Hill 'the middling sort' of the English Revolution, and Albert Soboul the

Parisian *sans-culottes* of the French Revolution. This, for me, represents the authentic Marxist tradition. It is certainly the spirit that infuses what is possibly the greatest work of Marxist history ever written: Leon Trotsky's *History of the Russian Revolution*. Trotsky, leader of the October Insurrection in 1917 and commander of the Red Army during the Civil War, was a supreme embodiment of the unity of theory and practice. This equipped him to write a masterpiece which analysed great events in which he himself had been a central protagonist. Trotsky's *Russian Revolution* is the book I would recommend above all others to those who wish to read more Marxist history.

Now down to detail. I must mention a few general volumes of which I have made extensive use. J. M. Roberts' *History of the World* (1976) is a heavyweight narrative, encyclopaedic in coverage, correspondingly useful, and relatively unencumbered, as far as I can tell, with theoretical baggage. Quite different, and for our purposes far more important, is Chris Harman's *People's History of the World* (1999). This is an outstanding work of Marxist historiography, representing a very high order of scholarship and interpretation. But it has a tendency towards a) economic, even technological, determinism, and b) teleology (the idea that events are trending towards a predetermined end-point); reading it, one has the feeling that we are passing through a succession of inevitable stages, each higher than the last, each advancing human progress. I think this is mistaken: I see history as open, contingent, and shaped by human agency; and while more determinist interpretations can sometimes be found in Marx, I believe the essence of his method implies the opposite. A study of particular value in getting a handle on this is John Rees's *Algebra of Revolution* (1998). A quite different kind of book, but one I cannot avoid mentioning because of its influence on me, is John Keegan's *History of Warfare* (1994), a work of profound originality and insight, and a monument to the fact that right-wing historians may occasionally write far better books than many 'academic' Marxists (a term, incidentally, which I consider to be self-contradictory).

Hominin evolution has been the subject of much outstanding work over the last 20 years, and some of the best modern summaries of current thinking are those by Chris Stringer and colleagues (1993, 1996, 2006). For later prehistory, there is a good collection of synthetic essays on the European evidence edited by Barry Cunliffe (1994), and two excellent studies written by Cunliffe himself, one on the Atlantic seaboard (2001), the other on Europe and the Mediterranean (2008). But the essential Marxist framework is still best provided by Vere Gordon Childe's *What Happened in History* (1942), a seminal work of archaeological narrative covering the whole of human social development from the first hominins to the fall of the Roman Empire, written by a brilliant scholar closely linked to the Communist Party Historians' Group. Childe should be read in conjunction with Engels' *Origins* (1884), which, despite relentless academic and polemical onslaught, remains another pivotal work for understanding prehistory, especially for its insights into the roots of the oppression of women.

Childe's sequence of socio-economic 'revolutions' in prehistory remains compelling, and his account of the origins of class society seems uncontroversial. However, though an important authority, Childe's Marxism was heavily infected by the kind of stages theory I refer to above in relation to Harman's work. The same is true of Geoffrey de Ste Croix, whose *Class Struggle in the Ancient Greek World* (1981), while essential, must be read critically. De Ste Croix makes a tendentious effort to redefine Late Roman serfs as slaves in order to salvage the concept – derived from Marx and Engels – of a 'slave mode of production'. This concept is hopelessly flawed, both empirically and theoretically, and has no analytical value; it is part of the interpretive apparatus criticised above as economically determinist and teleological.

There was really only one dominant mode of production in the 2,500 years between *c.* 1000 BC and AD 1500: village-based agriculture using iron-tool technology. In this long period, ruling classes and states were organised in many different ways and they appropriated surplus in many different forms. The difference between, for example, the bureaucratic ruling class of a centralised imperial state levying money-tribute (like the Roman Empire) and the feudal retinue of a Germanic warlord living off food-rent (like Anglo-Saxon England) is considerable. But in both cases the economic base consists of peasants working the land and handing over part of their surplus. It makes little difference whether they are slaves, serfs, tenants, or freeholders, and little again whether appropriation takes the form of tribute, rent, tithe, interest, wage-labour, or forced labour.

This being so, we need to turn our attention to what some Marxists, along with Fernand Braudel and the French *Annales* school (e.g. 1993), are inclined to discount as the 'froth' of history: events. The notion that wars and revolutions are somehow of secondary importance compared with technology, production, and trade flows is false; all these phenomena can be understood only as part of a single social order and historical process. The political 'superstructure' is not simply a reflection of the economic 'base'. There is no pyramid of significance which has celebrity culture at the top, the education system in the middle, and industrial technology at the bottom.

The key to historical analysis is to identify the essential dynamic of any social process. In pre-capitalist class societies this had very little to do with 'modes of production'. For all practical purposes, technique and productivity were static; the only question was how the surplus, more or less fixed in size, was distributed. The most effective way of increasing one's share was by military force. So the world was divided between rival ruling classes engaged in competitive accumulation of military resources. The dynamic of the Roman Empire, for example, can be defined as 'ancient military imperialism', or, more crudely, robbery with violence. Within the empire, a dual economy operated: peasant subsistence production continued as it had done for centuries, if not millennia; but a system of military supply and elite consumption was superimposed on this, involving heavy (and rising) appropriation of surplus by the ruling class.

The form of social relations of landowners and agricultural producers varied over time and space, but the essential character of the system was unaffected. My book on the Roman Empire (2008) is an attempt to order an historical narrative on the basis of the theory of 'ancient military imperialism' rather than that of the 'slave mode of production'. I think it demonstrates both the explanatory power of the former and the redundancy of the latter. I think, too, that the approach can be equally applied to other pre-capitalist class societies.

Feudalism has been the subject of intense and ongoing debate within Marxist historiography. My inclination is to sidestep much of this since, for reasons already explained, I reject the notion that feudalism was a new and higher mode of production. I therefore accept definitions of it which depend, not on the social relations of exploiter and exploited, but on the way the ruling class organised itself; definitions, that is, which largely ignore the socio-economic basis of the system. For this reason, I still consider Bloch (1965) of great value. On the other hand, I have no difficulty integrating Chris Wickham's important distinction between tax-based and land-based elites in the transition from antiquity to feudalism (2005).

For the second part of the story – the emergence of capitalism within the womb of feudal society – my main debts are to Maurice Dobb (1946), Rodney Hilton (1973, 1978, 1990), Robert Brenner (e.g. in Aston and Philpin, 1985), and Chris Dyer (2003, 2005). I reject the essential argument of Pirenne, Sweezy, Wallerstein, Hodges, and others that exchange, trade, and merchant profit have played primary roles in processes of economic transformation. Production is decisive. Therefore, any analysis of the transition from feudalism to capitalism has to focus on farms, workshops, and the social relations that frame their operation. The revolutionary essence of the Reformation is well represented by a little-read early work of Frederick Engels on the German Peasants' War (1850). The best book in English on the Dutch Revolution is still Geoffrey Parker's (1985). The literature on the English Revolution is vast, but much of the recent output is revisionist dross, so readers must go back to the solid Marxist scholarship of Christopher Hill (1961, 1972, 1975, 1986) and his pupil Brian Manning (1978, 1992, 1999, 2003); I consider Manning's *English Revolution and English People* to be a masterpiece of Marxist scholarship.

I should say that, in relation to the bourgeois revolutions, my inclination is to stress the effect of popular activity in driving the process forward. The distinction here is between the radicalism of the bourgeoisie's aspirations, or those of the most advanced sections of it at least, and its behaviour in a crisis, which tends to be fretful and timid because of its instinctive fear, as a property-owning class, of 'disorder' and 'anarchy'. Cromwell, Washington, Robespierre, and Lincoln were genuine revolutionaries. But their determination to change the world was not the same as surefootedness in setting about it. In each case, mass forces were necessary as much to propel the radical bourgeoisie forwards as to defeat the counter-revolution.

The brilliance of Manning's contribution was that he brought the essential role of the common people in the events of the 1640s into the daylight. The same can be said for Edward Countryman's *American Revolution* (1987), Albert Soboul's *Sans-culottes* (1980), and George Rudé's *Crowd in the French Revolution* (1967). What these and many other good Marxist studies of the period share is their determination to reveal, describe, and foreground the popular revolutionary movement, in contrast to the work of historians like Mathiez (1964) and Lefebvre (1962), where the revolutionary process is presented as being 'led by the bourgeoisie' in a much more mechanical and literal sense. Mention must also be made of C. L. R. James' superb account of the Haitian slave revolt, *The Black Jacobins* (1980), and of T. A. Jackson's *Ireland Her Own* (1991), a concise narrative of the Irish struggle against British rule over 800 years. I must also recommend Neil Davidson's recent study, *How Revolutionary Were the Bourgeois Revolutions?* (2017), which is packed with the kind of new commentary we have come to expect from him, and, with a broader compass, Perry Anderson's old classic, *Lineages of the Absolutist State* (1979), for its insights into the character of state-feudalism in this period.

To understand the development of industrial capitalism, the starting-point has to be Marx himself, especially the first volume of *Capital* (1867), which contains much historical analysis, and *The Communist Manifesto* (1848), for an efficient summary. The 'long nineteenth century' (1789–1914) has been brilliantly synthesised in Eric Hobsbawm's trilogy (1962, 1985, 1994a). His sequel on the twentieth century (1994b) is useful for reference but theoretically poor; Hobsbawm seems unable to apply a Marxist method to the events of his own lifetime. The character of the early working class and the origins of the labour movement are covered in two Marxist classics, Engels' *Condition of the Working Class* (1845) and Thompson's *Making of the English Working Class* (1980). For the impact on the wider world, Victor Kiernan's *European Empires from Conquest to Collapse* (1982) is unbeatable.

Marx and Engels' writings are also valuable for their analyses of major political events in the mid-nineteenth century; especially important are *The Class Struggles in France* (1895), *The Eighteenth Brumaire of Louis Bonaparte* (1869), and *The Civil War in France* (1871). For diplomatic history underwritten by a sound understanding of the social forces at work, I invariably find A. J. P. Taylor's many studies (1955, 1961, 1964a, 1971) very useful.

James McPherson's history of the American Civil War is seminal (1990). Donny Gluckstein's is a fine account of the Paris Commune (2006).

A raft of classic Marxist studies was published in the early twentieth century, notably those of Hilferding (1910), Lenin (1917a), and Bukharin (1917) on imperialism, Luxemburg on reformism and class struggle (1900, 1906), Lenin again on the nature of the state (1917b), and Trotsky on 'permanent revolution' (1906). Trotsky (1922 and 1932) is also the essential guide to the two Russian Revolutions of 1905 and 1917. Also of exceptional value on the Russian Revolution are Carr (1966), a solid scholarly study of the years 1917–23; Chamberlin (1965), an account of 1917 comparable in some ways with Trotsky's; and Reed (1977), a vivid eyewitness account by a radical journalist.

The Young Turk Revolution of 1908 is covered by Uzun (2004), the German Revolution of 1918–23 by Broué (2006) and Harman (1982), and the Chinese Revolution by Isaacs (1961). Two volumes of Trotsky's writings associated with the first five years of the Communist International (1973–4) are also of great value for this period. The degeneration of the Russian Revolution is best understood with reference to Trotsky (1936), supplemented by Cliff's landmark, four-volume biographies of Lenin (1975–9) and Trotsky (1989–93).

Cliff deserves further comment. He was, in my view, the greatest revolutionary thinker of the second half of the twentieth century, and the theories which he helped to develop of state capitalism (1955/1974), the permanent arms economy (see Kidron, 1970, and Harman, 1984), and deflected permanent revolution (1963) are the basis for any real understanding of the post-Second World War period.

Cliff – in opposition to both Stalinism and Orthodox Trotskyism – continued the authentic Marxist tradition of working-class struggle from below. He was building on the work of Trotsky in the 1920s and 1930s, valuable collections of which have been published covering events in China (1976), Germany (1971), France (1979), and Spain (1973). The wider literature on the Spanish Revolution is especially rich. Broué and Témime (1972) provide an excellent Marxist analysis, and Orwell's *Homage to Catalonia* (1938) is a classic eyewitness account of revolution in action.

The post-war world is well covered by a series of solid Marxist analyses: Birchall (1974 and 1986) and Harman (1988a) on reformism, Stalinism, and Cold War Europe; Cliff (see Gluckstein, 1957), Harris (1978), and Hore (1991) on China; Marshall (1989) on the Middle East; and Gonzalez (2004) on Che Guevara and Cuba. For the period 1968–75, Jonathan Neale (2001) is excellent on the Vietnam War, and Chris Harman on both the political turmoil (1988b) and the economic crisis (1984). Barker (1987) also has valuable essays on France, Chile, and Portugal, as well as covering the Iranian Revolution and Poland's Solidarity. There is also Marshall (1988) on Iran,

Barker and Weber (1982) on Solidarity, Callinicos on South Africa (1988), and Gonzalez (1990) on Nicaragua. Rees (2006) is essential on both the new imperialism and recent revolutions, including the anti-Stalinist revolutions in Eastern Europe in 1989.

The current economic crisis of neoliberal capitalism is the subject of much comment and debate. Clinging to a 1970s understanding of capitalism, much of the Left has failed to come to terms with financialisation. The essential theoretical background is provided by Baran and Sweezy (1966), while Harris (1983) provides a clear analysis of the new form of capitalism, and Bellamy Foster and Magdoff (2009), Elliott and Atkinson (2007), Harvey (2003 and 2005), Lapavitsas (2013), Mason (2009), Mellor (2010), and Varoufakis (2015) all offer detailed analyses of different aspects of financial-isation, the permanent debt economy, and the 2008 crash. Varoufakis (2017) provides an excellent insight into the politics of financialisation. El-Gingihy (2015) offers a case-study in privatisation. Monbiot (2007) and Bellamy Foster (2009) deal with the ecological crisis. Bellamy Foster (2017) and Faulkner and Dathi (2017) discuss creeping fascism. Harvey (2015) offers an overview of the world crisis as a whole, and Harvey (2013) explores the revolutionary potential of the modern city. Those keen to keep abreast of Marxist thinking about current affairs should consider reading the inde-pendent journals *Monthly Review* and *Transform*.

Many works can now be found online and readers should use the bibliog-raphy as an aid to searching.

Select Bibliography

Aldred, C., 1987, *The Egyptians*, London, Thames & Hudson (2).

Alexander, P., 1987, *Racism, Resistance, and Revolution*, London, Bookmarks (8, 16). ☺

Anderson, J. L., 1997, *Che Guevara: A revolutionary life*, London, Bantam (15).

Anderson, P., 1979, *Lineages of the Absolutist State*, London, Verso (6–9).**

Arthur, A., *The Tailor-King: The rise and fall of the Anabaptist kingdom of Münster*, New York, Thomas Dunne (7).

Aston, T. H. and Philpin, C. H. E. (eds.), 1985, *The Brenner Debate: Agrarian class structure and economic development in pre-industrial Europe*, Cambridge, Cambridge University Press (6).*

Baran, P. and Sweezy, P., 1968, *Monopoly Capital: An essay on the American economic and social order*, Harmondsworth, Penguin (18).**

Barker, C. and Weber, K., 1982, *Solidarnosc: From Gdansk to military repression*, London, International Socialism (17).* ☺

Barker, C. (ed.), 1987, *Revolutionary Rehearsals*, London, Bookmarks (16–17).* ☺

Barraclough, G., 1979, *The Times Atlas of World History*, London, Times Books (all).

Bellamy Foster, J., 2009, *The Ecological Revolution: Making peace with the planet*, New York, Monthly Review Press (18).*

Bellamy Foster, J., 2017, *Trump in the White House: Tragedy and farce* (18).*

Bellamy Foster, J. and Magdoff, F., 2009, *The Great Financial Crisis: Causes and consequences*, New York, Monthly Review Press (18).*

Birchall, I., 1974, *Workers Against the Monolith: The Communist Parties since 1943*, London, Pluto (15).*

Birchall, I., 1986, *Bailing out the System: Reformist socialism in Western Europe, 1944–1985*, London, Bookmarks (15).*

Blackburn, R., *The Overthrow of Colonial Slavery, 1776–1848*, London, Verso (8–9).*

Bloch, M., 1965, *Feudal Society*, London, Routledge (6).*

Brailsford, H., 1983, *The Levellers and the English Revolution*, Nottingham, Spokesman (7).*

Braudel, F., 1993, *A History of Civilisations*, London, Penguin (all).*

Broué, P., 2006, *The German Revolution, 1917–1923*, London, Merlin (13).*

Broué, P. and Témime, E., 1972, *The Revolution and the Civil War in Spain*, Cambridge, MA, MIT Press (14).*

Brunt, P. A., 1971, *Social Conflicts in the Roman Republic*, London, Chatto & Windus (3).

Bukharin, N., 1917, *Imperialism and World Economy*, www.marxists.org (12).**

Burn, A. R., 1978, *The Pelican History of Greece*, Harmondsworth, Penguin (3).*

Callinicos, A., 1988, *South Africa Between Reform and Revolution*, London, Bookmarks (17).* ☺

Carr, E. H., 1966, *The Bolshevik Revolution* (3 vols), Harmondsworth, Penguin (13).*

Chadwick, H., 1967, *The Early Church*, London, Penguin (4).

Chamberlin, W. H., 1965, *The Russian Revolution, 1917–1918: From the overthrow of the Czar to the assumption of power by the Bolsheviks*, New York, Grosset & Dunlap (13).*

Childe, V. G., 1936, *Man Makes Himself*, London, NCLC Publishing Society (1–2).* ☺

Childe, V. G., 1942, *What Happened in History*, Harmondsworth, Penguin (1–3).** ☺

Chomsky, N., 1999, *Fateful Triangle: The United States, Israel, and the Palestinians*, London, Pluto (15).

Clark, G. and Piggott, S., 1970, *Prehistoric Societies*, Harmondsworth, Penguin (1).

Clements, J., 2006, *The First Emperor of China*, Stroud, Sutton (3).

Cliff, T., 1955/1974, *State Capitalism in Russia*, www.marxists.org (13–17).**

Cliff, T., 1963, *Deflected Permanent Revolution*, www.marxists.org (15).**

Cliff, T., 1975–9, *Lenin* (4 vols.), www.marxists.org (12–13).*

Cliff, T, 1989–93, *Trotsky* (4 vols.), www.marxists.org (12–14).*

Cohn, N., 1970, *The Pursuit of the Millennium: Revolutionary millenarians and mystical anarchists of the Middle Ages*, London, Granada (6).*

Cole, G. D. H., 1932, *A Short History of the British Working Class Movement, 1789–1927*, London, Allen & Unwin (10–14).*

Cole, G. D. H. and Postgate, R., 1946, *The Common People, 1746–1946*, London, Methuen (10–14).

Countryman, E., 1987, *The American Revolution*, Harmondsworth, Penguin (9).** ☺

Crawford, M., 1992, *The Roman Republic*, London, Fontana (3).

Cunliffe, B. (ed.), 1994, *The Oxford Illustrated Prehistory of Europe*, Oxford, Oxford University Press (1–4).

Cunliffe, B., 2001, *Facing the Ocean: The Atlantic and its peoples, 8000 BC–AD 1500*, Oxford, Oxford University Press (1–6).

Cunliffe, B., 2008, *Europe Between the Oceans, 9000 BC–AD 1000*, London, Yale University Press (1–6).*

Darvill, T., 1987, *Prehistoric Britain*, London, Routledge (1).

Davidson, N., 2017, *How Revolutionary Were the Bourgeois Revolutions?*, Chicago, Haymarket (7–9, 11).*

De Ste Croix, G. E. M., 1981, *The Class Struggle in the Ancient Greek World*, London, Duckworth (3, 4).**

Diamond, J., 1999, *Guns, Germs, and Steel: The fates of human societies*, New York, Norton (5, 6).** ☺

Dobb, M., 1946, *Studies in the Development of Capitalism*, London, Routledge (6).*

Dyer, C., 2003, *Making a Living in the Middle Ages: The people of Britain, 850–1520*, London, Penguin (6).

Dyer, C., 2005, *An Age of Transition? Economy and society in England in the later Middle Ages*, Oxford, Oxford University Press (6).*

El-Gingihy, Y., 2015, *How to Dismantle the NHS in 10 Easy Steps*, Alresford, Zero (18). ☺

Elliott, J. H., 1970, *Imperial Spain, 1469–1716*, Harmondsworth, Penguin (6, 7).

Elliott, L. and Atkinson, D., 2007, *Fantasy Island: Waking up to the incredible economic, political, and social illusions of the Blair legacy*, London, Constable (18). ☺

Elton, G. R., 1955, *England under the Tudors*, London, Methuen (6, 7).

Elton, G. R., 1963, *Reformation Europe, 1517–1559*, New York, Harper & Row (6, 7).

Engels, F., 1845, *The Condition of the Working Class in England*, www.marxists.org (10).**

Engels, F., 1850, *The Peasant War in Germany*, www.marxists.org (7).*

Engels, F., 1884, *The Origin of the Family, Private Property, and the State*, www.marxists.org (1). **

Engels, F., 1892, *Socialism: Utopian and scientific*, www.marxists.org (all).**

Fagan, B. (ed.), 2009, *The Complete Ice Age: How climate change shaped the world*, London, Thames & Hudson (1). ☺

Faulkner, N., 2002, *Apocalypse: The great Jewish revolt against Rome, AD 66–73*, Stroud, Tempus (4).*

Faulkner, N., 2008, *Rome: Empire of the eagles*, Harlow, Pearson Education (3, 4).*

Faulkner, N., 2017, *A People's History of the Russian Revolution*, London, Pluto/Left Book Club (13).

Faulkner, N. (with Samir Dathi), 2017, *Creeping Fascism: Brexit, Trump, and the rise of the Far Right*, London, Public Reading Rooms (14, 17).*

Finkel, C., 2005, *Osman's Dream: The story of the Ottoman Empire, 1300–1923*, London, John Murray (7, 12).

Finley, M. I., 1956, *The World of Odysseus*, London, Chatto & Windus (2).

Finley, M. I., 1963, *The Ancient Greeks*, London, Chatto & Windus (3). ☺

Finley, M. I., 1985, *The Ancient Economy*, London, Hogarth Press (3).*

Fisk, R., 1991, *Pity the Nation: Lebanon at War*, Oxford, Oxford University Press (15, 17). ☺

Galbraith, J. K., 1975, *Money: Whence it came, where it went*, Harmondsworth, Penguin (8–15). ☺

Galbraith, J. K., 1975, *The Great Crash, 1929*, Harmondsworth, Penguin (14). ☺

Glatter, P. (ed.), 2005, *The Russian Revolution of 1905: Change through struggle*, London, Socialist Platform (12).

Gluckstein, Y., 1957, *Mao's China: Economic and political survey*, London, Allen & Unwin (15).*

Gluckstein, D., 2006, *The Paris Commune: A revolution in democracy*, London, Bookmarks (11).

Gonzalez, M., 1990, *Nicaragua: What went wrong?*, London, Bookmarks (17). ☺

Gonzalez, M., 2004, *Che Guevara and the Cuban Revolution*, London, Bookmarks (15).* ☺

Grant, M., 1973, *The Jews in the Roman World*, London, Weidenfeld & Nicolson (4).

Grant, M., 1984, *The History of Ancient Israel*, London, Weidenfeld & Nicolson (4).

Guillaume, A., 1956, *Islam*, London, Penguin (4).

Hale, J. R., 1971, *Renaissance Europe, 1480–1520*, London, Collins (6).

Halifax, N., 1988, *Out, Proud, and Fighting: Gay liberation and the struggle for socialism*, London, Socialist Workers Party (16). ☺

Hampson, N., 1968, *The Enlightenment*, Harmondsworth, Penguin (9).

Harman, C., 1982, *The Lost Revolution: Germany 1918 to 1923*, London, Bookmarks (13).*

Harman, C., 1983, *Gramsci versus Reformism*, London, Socialist Workers Party (13). ☺

Harman, C., 1984, *Explaining the Crisis: A Marxist reappraisal*, London, Bookmarks (15, 17–18).*

Harman, C., 1988a, *Class Struggles in Eastern Europe, 1945–83*, London, Bookmarks (15–16).* ☺

Harman, C., 1988b, *The Fire Last Time: 1968 and after*, London, Bookmarks (16).* ☺

Harman, C., 1999, *A People's History of the World*, London, Bookmarks (all).** ☺

Harris, N., 1978, *The Mandate of Heaven: Marx and Mao in modern China*, London, Quartet (15).*

Harris, N., 1983, *Of Bread and Guns: The world economy in crisis*, Harmondsworth, Penguin (17–18).* ☺

Harvey, D., 2003, *The New Imperialism*, Oxford, Oxford University Press (17).*

Harvey, D., 2005, *A Brief History of Neoliberalism*, Oxford, Oxford University Press (17).*

Harvey, D., 2013, *Rebel Cities: From the right to the city to the urban revolution*, London, Verso (18–Conclusion).*

Harvey, D., 2015, *Seventeen Contradictions and the End of Capitalism*, London, Profile (18).*

Hastings, M., 2011, *All Hell Let Loose: The world at war, 1939–1945*, London, Harper Press (15).* ☺

Haynes, M., 2002, *Russia: Class and power, 1917–2000*, London, Bookmarks (13–17).*

Hilferding, R., 1910, *Finance Capital: A study of the latest phase of capitalist development*, www.marxists.org (12).*

Hill, C., 1961, *The Century of Revolution, 1603–1714*, London, Nelson (7).

Hill, C., 1972, *God's Englishman: Oliver Cromwell and the English Revolution*, Harmondsworth, Penguin (7).* ☺

Hill, C., 1975, *The World Turned Upside Down: Radical ideas during the English Revolution*, Harmondsworth, Penguin (7).*

Hill, C., 1986, *Society and Puritanism in Pre-Revolutionary England*, Harmondsworth, Penguin (7).*

Hilton, R., 1973, *Bond Men Made Free: Medieval peasant movements and the English rising of 1381*, London, Maurice Temple Smith (6).*

Hilton, R., 1978, *The Transition from Feudalism to Capitalism*, London, Verso (6).*

Hilton, R., 1990, *Class Conflict and the Crisis of Feudalism: Essays in medieval social history*, London, Verso (6).*

Hobsbawm, E., 1962, *The Age of Revolution: Europe, 1789–1848*, London, Abacus (9–10).*

Hobsbawm, E., 1985, *The Age of Capital, 1848–1875*, London, Abacus (10–11).*

Hobsbawm, E., 1994a, *The Age of Empire, 1875–1914*, London, Abacus (11–12).*

Hobsbawm, E., 1994b, *The Age of Extremes: The short twentieth century, 1914–1991*, London, Michael Joseph (12–17).

Hodges, R., 2012, *Dark Age Economics: A new audit*, London, Bristol Classical Press (6).

Holland, T., 2005, *Persian Fire: The first world empire and the battle for the West*, London, Little, Brown (3). ☺

Holland, T., 2003, *Rubicon: The triumph and tragedy of the Roman Republic*, London, Little, Brown (3). ☺

Hore, C., 1991, *The Road to Tiananmen Square*, London, Bookmarks (15, 17).* ☺

Hourani, A., 1991, *A History of the Arab Peoples*, London, Faber and Faber (5).

Isaacs, H. R., 1961, *The Tragedy of the Chinese Revolution*, Stanford, CA, Stanford University Press (13).**

Jackson, T. A., 1991, *Ireland Her Own*, London, Lawrence & Wishart (9, 13).* ☺

James, C. L. R., 1980, *The Black Jacobins: Toussaint L'Ouverture and the San Domingo revolution*, London, Allison & Busby (9).* ☺

James, T. G. H., 2005, *Ancient Egypt*, London, British Museum Press (2).

Jones, A. H. M., 1966, *The Decline of the Ancient World*, London, Longmans (4).*

Kamen, H., 1971, *The Iron Century: Social change in Europe, 1550–1660*, London, Weidenfeld & Nicolson (7).*

Keegan, J., 1994, *A History of Warfare*, London, Pimlico (all).* ☺

Kidron, M., 1970, *Western Capitalism Since the War*, Harmondsworth, Penguin (15).* ☺

Kiernan, V. G., 1982, *European Empires From Conquest to Collapse, 1815–1960*, London, Fontana (10–12, 15).* ☺

Lane Fox, R., 1991, *The Unauthorised Version: Truth and fiction in the Bible*, London, Penguin (4).*

Lapavitsas, C., 2013, *Profiting Without Producing: How finance exploits us all*, London, Verso (18).*

Lapping, B., 1989, *End of Empire*, London, Paladin (15).

Leakey, R. E., 1981, *The Making of Mankind*, London, Book Club Associates (1). ☺

Lefebvre, G., 1962, *The French Revolution, Volume I, from its origins to 1793*, New York, Columbia University Press (8).*

Lefebvre, G., 1964, *The French Revolution, Volume II, from 1793 to 1799*, New York, Columbia University Press (9).*

Lenin, V. I., 1917a, *Imperialism: The highest stage of capitalism*, www.marxists.org (12).** ☺

Lenin, V. I., 1917b, *State and Revolution*, www.marxists.org (11–13).** ☺

Luxemburg, R., 1900, *Reform and Revolution*, www.marxists.org (12–13).**

Luxemburg, R., 1906, *The Mass Strike*, www.marxists.org (12–13).**

Lynch, J., 2006/2007, *Simón Bolívar: A life*, London, Yale University Press (9).

McPherson, J. M., 1990, *Battle Cry of Freedom: The American Civil War*, London, Penguin (11).*

Manning, B., 1978, *The English People and the English Revolution*, London, Peregrine (7).**

Manning, B., 1992, *1649: The crisis of the English Revolution*, London, Bookmarks (7).*

Manning, B., 1999, *The Far Left in the English Revolution*, London, Bookmarks (7).

Manning, B., 2003, *Revolution and Counter-Revolution in England, Ireland, and Scotland, 1658–1660*, London, Bookmarks (7).

Marshall, P., 1988, *Revolution and Counterrevolution in Iran*, London, Bookmarks (17).*☺

Marshall, P., 1989, *Intifada: Zionism, imperialism, and Palestinian resistance*, London, Bookmarks (15, 17).*☺

Marshall, R., 1994, *Storm From the East: From Genghis Khan to Khubilai Khan*, London, Penguin/BBC Books (5). ☺

Marx, K., 1848, *The Manifesto of the Communist Party*, www.marxists.org (10). **

Marx, K., 1859, *A Contribution to the Critique of Political Economy*, www.marxists.org (10).**

Marx, K., 1867, *Capital, Volume 1*, www.marxists.org (10).**

Marx, K., 1869, *The Eighteenth Brumaire of Louis Bonaparte*, www.marxists.org (10–11).*

Marx, K., 1871, *The Civil War in France*, www.marxists.org (11).**

Marx, K., 1895, *The Class Struggles in France*, www.marxists.org (10).*

Mason, P., 2009, *Meltdown: The end of the age of greed*, London, Verso (18). ☺

Mathiez, A., 1964, *The French Revolution*, New York, Grosset and Dunlap (9).*

Mellor, M., 2010, *The Future of Money: From financial crisis to public resource*, London, Pluto (18). ☺

Monbiot, G., 2007, *Heat: How we can stop the planet burning*, London, Penguin (18). ☺

Morton, A. L., 1938, *A People's History of England*, London, Gollanz (5–14). ☺

Neale, J., 2001, *The American War: Vietnam, 1960–1975*, London, Bookmarks (16).*☺

Orwell, G., 1938, *Homage to Catalonia*, London, Secker & Warburg (14).*☺

Pakenham, T., 1992, *The Scramble for Africa, 1876–1912*, London, Abacus (12). ☺

Parker, G., 1985, *The Dutch Revolt*, Harmondsworth, Penguin (7).*

Petty, C., Roberts, D., and Smith, S., 1987, *Women's Liberation and Socialism*, London, Bookmarks (16). ☺

Pirenne, H., 1939, *A History of Europe, from the invasions to the sixteenth century*, London, Allen & Unwin (6).*

Pitts, M. and Roberts, M., 1997, *Fairweather Eden: Life in Britain half a million years ago as revealed by the excavations at Boxgrove*, London, Century (1). ☺

Pocock, T., 1998, *Battle for Empire: The very first world war, 1756–63*, London, Michael O'Mara (8). ☺

Pryor, F., 2003, *Britain BC: Life in Britain and Ireland before the Romans*, London, HarperCollins (2). ☺

Reade, J., 1991, *Mesopotamia*, London, British Museum Press (2).

Reed, J., 1977, *Ten Days that Shook the World*, Harmondsworth, Penguin (13).* ☺

Rees, J., 1998, *The Algebra of Revolution: The dialectic and the classical Marxist tradition*, London, Routledge (all).*

Rees, J., 2006, *Imperialism and Resistance*, London, Routledge (17–18).* ☺

Rees, J., 2012, *Timelines: A political history of the modern world*, London, Routledge (17).* ☺

Reynolds, P. J., *Iron-Age Farm: The Butser Experiment*, London, British Museum Publications (2).

Roberts, A., 2009, *The Incredible Human Journey*, London, Bloomsbury (1). ☺

Roberts, J. M., 1976, *The Hutchinson History of the World*, London, Hutchinson (all).

Rodzinkski, W., 1991, *The Walled Kingdom: A history of China from 2000 BC to the present*, London, Fontana (3, 5).

Rostovtzeff, M., 1928, *A History of the Ancient World, Volume II, Rome*, Oxford, Clarendon (3).*

Rostovtzeff, M., 1930, *A History of the Ancient World, Volume I, The Orient and Greece*, Oxford, Clarendon (3).*

Roux, G., 1980, *Ancient Iraq*, London, Penguin (2).

Rudé, G., 1967, *The Crowd in the French Revolution*, Oxford, Oxford University Press (9).*

Scarre, C., 1988, *Past Worlds: The Times atlas of archaeology*, London, Times Books (1–5).

Skidelsky, R., 2004, *John Maynard Keynes, 1883–1946: Economist, philosopher, statesman*, London, Pan (14).*

Skidelsky, R., 2010, *Keynes: The return of the master*, London, Penguin (18).

Soboul, A., 1977, *A Short History of the French Revolution, 1789–1799*, London, University of California (9).* ☺

Soboul, A., 1980, *The Sans-culottes: The popular movement and revolutionary government, 1793–1794*, Princeton, NJ, Princeton University Press (9).*

Soboul, A., 1989, *The French Revolution, 1787–1799, from the storming of the Bastille to Napoleon*, London, Unwin Hyman (9).**

Stringer, C. and Gamble, C., 1993, *In Search of the Neanderthals*, London, Thames & Hudson (1).* ☺

Stringer, C. and McKie R., 1996, *African Exodus: The origins of modern humanity*, New York, Henry Holt (1).*

Stringer, C., 2006, *Homo Britannicus: The incredible story of human life in Britain*, London, Allen Lane (1).* ☺

Sweezy, P., 1968a, *The Theory of Capitalist Development*, New York, Monthly Review Press (18).*

Sweezy, P., 1968b, *Monopoly Capital: An essay on the American economic and social order*, Harmondsworth, Penguin (18).*

Taylor, A. J. P., 1955, *Bismarck: The man and the statesman*, London, Hamish Hamilton (11).

Taylor, A. J. P., 1961, *The Course of German History: A survey of the development of German history since 1815*, London, Methuen (11–14).

Taylor, A. J. P., 1964a, *The Habsburg Monarchy, 1809–1918: A history of the Austrian Empire and Austria-Hungary*, London, Peregrine (12).

Taylor, A. J. P., 1964b, *The Origins of the Second World War*, London, Penguin (14).*

Taylor, A. J. P., 1966, *The First World War*, London, Penguin (12). ☺

Taylor, A. J. P., 1971, *The Struggle for Mastery in Europe, 1848–1918*, Oxford, Oxford University Press (11–12).*

Terraine, J., 1967, *The Great War, 1914–18*, London, Arrow (12). ☺

Thapar, R., 1966, *A History of India, Volume 1*, Harmondsworth, Penguin (3, 5).

Thompson, E. A., 1948, *A History of Attila and the Huns*, Oxford, Clarendon (4).*

Thompson, E. P., 1980, *The Making of the English Working Class*, Harmondsworth, Penguin (10).**

Thomson, G., 1965, *Studies in Ancient Greek Society: The prehistoric Aegean*, New York, Citadel (1).*

Trotsky, L., 1906, *Results and Prospects*, www.marxists.org (12–13).**

Trotsky, L., 1922, *1905*, www.marxists.org (12).** ☺

Trotsky, L., 1932, *The History of the Russian Revolution*, www.marxists.org (13).** ☺

Trotsky, L., 1936, *The Revolution Betrayed: What is the Soviet Union and where is it going?*, www.marxists.org (13–14).*

Trotsky, L., 1971, *The Struggle against Fascism in Germany*, London, New Park (14).**

Trotsky, L., 1973, *The Spanish Revolution (1931–39)*, London, New Park (14).**

Trotsky, L., 1973–4, *The First Five Years of the Communist International* (2 vols.), London, New Park (13).**

Trotsky, L., 1976, *Leon Trotsky on China*, London, New Park (13).**

Trotsky, L., 1979, *Leon Trotsky on France*, London, New Park (14).**

Uzun, C., 2004, *Making the Turkish Revolution*, Istanbul, Antikapitalist (12).

Varoufakis, Y., 2015, *The Global Minotaur: America, Europe, and the future of the global economy*, London, Zed (18). ☺

Varoufakis, Y., 2017, *Adults in the Room: My battle with Europe's deep Establishment*, London, Bodley Head (18). ☺

Wedgwood, C. V., 1938, *The Thirty Years War*, London, Jonathan Cape (7).

Wells, C., 1992, *The Roman Empire*, London, Fontana (4).

Wheeler, R. E. M., 1966 *Civilisations of the Indus Valley and Beyond*, London, Thames & Hudson (2). ☺

Wheeler, R. E. M., 1968, *Flames over Persepolis*, London, Weidenfeld & Nicolson (3). ☺

Whitehead, P., 1985, *The Writing on the Wall: Britain in the Seventies*, London, Michael Joseph (16–17). ☺

Wickham, C., 2005, *Framing the Early Middle Ages: Europe and the Mediterranean, 400–800*, Oxford, Oxford University Press (4).*

Widgery, D., 1976, *The Left in Britain, 1956–1968*, Harmondsworth, Penguin (15–16).

Williams, E., 1964, *Capitalism and Slavery*, London, Andrew Deutsch (8).*

Womack, J., 1969/1972, *Zapata and the Mexican Revolution*, Harmondsworth, Penguin (12).

Wood, M., 1985, *In Search of the Trojan War*, London, Guild Publishing (2).* ☺

Young, H., 1990, *One of Us: A biography of Margaret Thatcher*, London, Pan (17). ☺

Ziegler, P., 1969, *The Black Death*, London, Collins (5).

Index

I have tried to make this index both comprehensive and useful, so I have included all substantive references to the subjects listed. A characteristic of this history, however, is that it seeks to make generalisations and to draw attention to underlying tendencies by linking events together. This makes separation of subject-matter awkward and poses particular difficulties when creating an index. I have done my best. Some subjects – like competition, revolution, nationalism, and strikes – are so generic that they defy any attempt at indexing. Hopefully, the combination of index, timeline, and sub-heads within chapters will enable readers to find what they seek.